March 4–5, 2014
Atlanta, Georgia, USA

I0038015

Association for Computing Machinery

Advancing Computing as a Science & Profession

L@S 2014

Proceedings of the First ACM Conference on
Learning @ Scale

Sponsored by:
ACM Ed Board

Supported by:
Google, Microsoft Research, and Oracle Academy

Association for Computing Machinery

Advancing Computing as a Science & Profession

The Association for Computing Machinery
2 Penn Plaza, Suite 701
New York, New York 10121-0701

Notice to Past Authors of ACM-Published Articles
ACM intends to create a complete electronic archive of all articles and/or other material previously published by ACM. If you have written a work that has been previously published by ACM in any journal or conference proceedings prior to 1978, or any SIG Newsletter at any time, and you do NOT want this work to appear in the ACM Digital Library, please inform permissions@acm.org, stating the title of the work, the author(s), and where and when published.

ISBN: 978-1-4503-2669-8 (Digital)

ISBN: 978-1-4503-3103-6 (Print)

Additional copies may be ordered prepaid from:

ACM Order Department
PO Box 30777
New York, NY 10087-0777, USA

Phone: 1-800-342-6626 (USA and Canada)
+1-212-626-0500 (Global)
Fax: +1-212-944-1318
E-mail: acmhelp@acm.org
Hours of Operation: 8:30 am – 4:30 pm ET

Printed in the USA

Chairs' Welcome Message

Welcome to the first annual meeting of the ACM Conference on Learning at Scale! This conference is intended to promote scientific exchange of interdisciplinary research at the intersection of the learning sciences and computer science. Inspired by the emergence of Massive Open Online Courses (MOOCs) and the accompanying huge shift in thinking about education, this conference was created by ACM as a new scholarly venue and focal point for the review and presentation of the highest quality research on how learning and teaching can change—and improve—when done at scale.

When we were asked to organize this conference, we were faced with the challenge of making many decisions about what kind of conference this would be, starting with its name. We decided on "Learning at Scale," which is intended to be broader than the term of the moment, MOOC, and to have a longer shelf life. We are pleased that the term has caught on, with a similarly-named journal special issue (ACM TOCHI) and workshop (ACM SIGCHI) already announced.

What would the scope of L@S be and how would it be different from other learning technology conferences? We decided that a broad array of topics, from usability studies and systems building to data mining and theories of learning, would be in scope as long as the work focused on what changed when the approach involved engaging very large numbers of students, either face to face or remotely. While there was overall agreement within the Program Committee about this definition, in a few cases they struggled in to determine whether a given paper was in scope. We hope that in future years the meaning will become increasingly well-defined.

Another top goal for this inaugural offering was quality. The entire program committee was dedicated to accepting only top-notch results for the full papers, and we hope you agree that the 14 full papers selected for presentation are of uniformly excellent quality and represent breadth and interdisciplinary collaboration among leading researchers in the various fields L@S brings together. (There were 38 full papers submitted, for an acceptance rate of 37%.) With very few exceptions, papers were reviewed by the PC members themselves.

The extensive work-in-progress/poster abstracts and demonstrations give a hint of the exciting work still to come in this vigorous new area. These were reviewed more liberally, with an acceptance rate of 76%: 37 posters and 5 demos.

The invited speakers and panels showcase the topical breadth of L@S: keynote speaker Prof. Chris Dede of Harvard on immersive, personal, ubiquitous learning; Dr. Ed Cutrell and Dr. Bill Thies of Microsoft Research India describing their experience with MOOCs in the developing world; Dr. Janet Kolodner of the National Science Foundation discussing the agency's programs relevant to research in learning at scale; and tutorials on learning through discussion (Carolyn Penstein Rosé, Carnegie Mellon University) and item response theory (Eliana Feasley, Jace Kohlmeier, and Jascha Sohl-Dickstein of Khan Academy).

We see L@S as a challenge and an opportunity to start building a truly interdisciplinary community of practice between researchers and practitioners, computer scientists and learning scientists. We are proud of the caliber and diversity of the members of our stellar program committee, which contains a balance of learning scientists and computer scientists. That said, we hope that a longer submission timeline for next year's conference, combined with this year's success establishing L@S as the premier venue for this interdisciplinary research, will lead to more contributed papers from learning scientists.

In particular, we see an opportunity in which MOOCs and other instruments of learning at scale become common artifacts around which learning scientists, computer scientists, educators, and instructors can collaborate. And because MOOCs rely on software-as-a-service for delivering materials, we can encapsulate research findings in the tools provided to thousands of instructors and millions of learners, increasing both the leverage of the research and the speed with which it can be put into practice. Our program includes a panel of experts who will discuss what software platforms for large online courses need from research, and vice versa.

We thank our dedicated Program Committee for stimulating the interest necessary to generate such a great set of submissions, for their thorough and thoughtful reviews, and for their ideas on invited speakers, panels, and many other aspects of the conference format, which represents the best conference practices from a variety of fields. We especially thank Mehran Sahami for organizing the Platforms panel. Thanks to the ACM Education Board for being our sponsor, to Google, Microsoft, and Oracle for being supporters, to SIGCSE for co-locating with the inaugural L@S, and to UC Berkeley for use of facilities. We also thank Donna Cappo of ACM and Dorothea Heck of DL Plan for effective, reliable, and efficient conference support, and John White, Executive Director of ACM, for spearheading this conference and putting the support and resources of ACM behind ensuring its success.

We hope you share our enthusiasm and optimism and that you will find Learning@Scale a worthy venue for laying the foundations for ongoing collaboration in this exciting space.

Armando Fox
Program Co-Chair
University of California, Berkeley, USA

Marti A. Hearst
Program Co-Chair
University of California, Berkeley, USA

Michelene T.H. Chi
Program Co-Chair
Arizona State University, USA

Table of Contents

L@S 2014 Organization ix

L@S 2014 Sponsor & Supporters x

Keynote Talk

- **New Wine in No Bottles: Immersive, Personalized Ubiquitous Learning** 1
  Christopher J. Dede *(Harvard University)*

Session: Student Skills and Behavior

- **Student Skill and Goal Achievement in the Mapping with Google MOOC** 3
  Julia Wilkowski, Amit Deutsch, Daniel M. Russell *(Google)*

- **Correlating Skill and Improvement in 2 MOOCs with a Student's Time on Tasks** 11
  John Champaign, Kimberly F. Colvin, Alwina Liu, Colin Fredericks, Daniel Seaton, David E. Pritchard
  (Massachusetts Institute of Technology)

- **Demographic Differences in How Students Navigate Through MOOCs** 21
  Philip J. Guo *(Massachusetts Institute of Technology & University of Rochester)*,
  Katharina Reinecke *(University of Michigan)*

Session: Course Materials

- **Understanding In-Video Dropouts and Interaction Peaks in Online Lecture Videos** 31
  Juho Kim *(Massachusetts Institute of Technology)*, Philip J. Guo *(University of Rochester)*,
  Daniel T. Seaton *(Massachusetts Institute of Technology)*, Piotr Mitros *(edX)*, Krzysztof Z. Gajos *(Harvard SEAS)*,
  Robert C. Miller *(Massachusetts Institute of Technology)*

- **How Video Production Affects Student Engagement:
  An Empirical Study of MOOC Videos** 41
  Philip J. Guo *(Massachusetts Institute of Technology & University of Rochester)*,
  Juho Kim *(Massachusetts Institute of Technology)*, Rob Rubin *(edX)*

- **Hint Systems May Negatively Impact Performance in Educational Games** 51
  Eleanor O'Rourke, Christy Ballweber, Zoran Popović *(University of Washington)*

Session: The Role of the Instructor

- **Teaching Recommender Systems at Large Scale: Evaluation and Lessons Learned
  from a Hybrid MOOC** 61
  Joseph A. Konstan, J.D. Walker *(University of Minnesota)*, D. Christopher Brooks *(EDUCAUSE)*,
  Keith Brown, Michael D. Ekstrand *(University of Minnesota)*

- **Do Professors Matter? Using an A/B Test to Evaluate the Impact of Instructor
  Involvement on MOOC Student Outcomes** 71
  Jonathan H. Tomkin *(University of Illinois at Urbana-Champaign)*, Donna Charlevoix *(UNAVCO)*

- **Monitoring MOOCs: Which Information Sources Do Instructors Value?** 79
  Kristin Stephens-Martinez, Marti A. Hearst, Armando Fox *(University of California, Berkeley)*

Session: Assessment

- **Divide and Correct: Using Clusters to Grade Short Answers at Scale** 89
  Michael Brooks *(University of Washington & Microsoft Research)*,
  Sumit Basu, Charles Jacobs, Lucy Vanderwende *(Microsoft Research)*

- **Scaling Short-Answer Grading by Combining Peer Assessment with Algorithmic Scoring**..99
  Chinmay Kulkarni, Richard Socher, Michael S. Bernstein *(Stanford University)*,
  Scott R. Klemmer *(University of California, San Diego)*

- **Self-evaluation in Advanced Power Searching and Mapping with Google MOOCs**...........109
  Julia Wilkowski, Daniel M. Russell, Amit Deutsch *(Google)*

Session: Forums and Chat Rooms

- **Superposter Behavior in MOOC Forums**...117
  Jonathan Huang *(Stanford University)*, Anirban Dasgupta *(Yahoo! Labs)*, Arpita Ghosh *(Cornell University)*,
  Jane Manning, Marc Sanders *(Stanford University)*

- **Chatrooms in MOOCs: All Talk and No Action**..127
  Derrick Coetzee, Armando Fox, Marti A. Hearst, Björn Hartmann *(University of California, Berkeley)*

Panel

- **Panel: Online Learning Platforms and Data Science**..137
  Mehran Sahami *(Stanford University)*, Jace Kohlmeier *(Khan Academy)*, Peter Norvig *(Google)*,
  Andreas Paepcke *(Stanford University)*, Amin Saberi *(NovoEd)*

Posters

- **ForumDash: Analyzing Online Discussion Forums**..139
  Jacquelin Speck, Eugene Gualtieri, Gaurav Naik, Thach Nguyen, Kevin Cheung, Larry Alexander, David Fenske
  (Drexel University)

- **OCTAL: Online Course Tool for Adaptive Learning**..141
  Daniel Armendariz, Zachary MacHardy, Daniel D. Garcia *(University of California, Berkeley)*

- **Reducing Non-Response Bias with Survey Reweighting: Applications for Online Learning Researchers**..143
  René F. Kizilcec *(Stanford University)*

- **Model Thinking: Demographics and Performance of MOOC Students Unable to Afford a Formal Education**...145
  Tawanna Dillahunt, Bingxin Chen, Stephanie Teasley *(University of Michigan)*

- **"Why did you enroll in this course?" Developing a Standardized Survey Question for Reasons to Enroll**..147
  Emily Schneider, René F. Kizilcec *(Stanford University)*

- **Improving Problem Solving Performance in Computer-Based Learning Environments Through Subgoal Labels**..149
  Lauren Margulieux, Richard Catrambone *(Georgia Institute of Technology)*

- **Initial Experiences with Small Group Discussions in MOOCs**.....................................151
  Seongtaek Lim, Derrick Coetzee, Björn Hartmann, Armando Fox, Marti A. Hearst
  (University of California, Berkeley)

- **Open System for Video Learning Analytics**...153
  Konstantinos Chorianopoulos *(Ionian University)*,
  Michail N. Giannakos, Nikos Chrisochoides *(Old Dominion University)*

- **Forming Beneficial Teams of Students in Massive Online Classes**.............................155
  Rakesh Agrawal *(Microsoft Research)*, Behzad Golshan, Evimaria Terzi *(Boston University)*

- **Uncovering Hidden Engagement Patterns for Predicting Learner Performance in MOOCs**...157
  Arti Ramesh, Dan Goldwasser, Bert Huang, Hal Daumé III *(University of Maryland, College Park)*,
  Lise Getoor *(University of California, Santa Cruz)*

- **A Multiplayer Online Game for Teaching Software Engineering Practices**.................159
  David Xiao, Robert C. Miller *(Massachusetts Institute of Technology)*

- **Talkabout: Small-group Discussions in Massive Global Classes** 161
  Julia Cambre, Chinmay Kulkarni, Michael S. Bernstein *(Stanford University)*,
  Scott R. Klemmer *(University of California, San Diego)*

- **Community TAs Scale High-Touch Learning, Provide Student-Staff Brokering, and Build Esprit de Corps** 163
  Kathryn Papadopoulos *(Citrix Customer Experience)*, Lalida Sritanyaratana *(Stanford University)*,
  Scott R. Klemmer *(University of California, San Diego)*

- **Adaptive and Social Mechanisms for Automated Improvement of eLearning Materials** .. 165
  Kevin Buffardi, Stephen H. Edwards *(Virginia Tech)*

- **Distance Learning, OER, and MOOCs: Some UK Experiences** 167
  Eileen Scanlon, Patrick McAndrew *(Open University)*, Tim O'Shea *(University of Edinburgh)*

- **Tracking Progress: Predictors of Students' Weekly Achievement During a Circuits and Electronics MOOC** 169
  Jennifer DeBoer, Lori Breslow *(Massachusetts Institute of Technology)*

- **Feature Engineering for Clustering Student Solutions** 171
  Elena L. Glassman, Rishabh Singh, Robert C. Miller *(Massachusetts Institute of Technology)*

- **Improving Online Class Forums by Seeding Discussions and Managing Section Size** ... 173
  Kelly Miller *(Harvard University)*, Sacha Zyto, David R. Karger *(Massachusetts Institute of Technology)*,
  Eric Mazur *(Harvard University)*

- **Student Explorer: A Tool for Supporting Academic Advising at Scale** 175
  Steven Lonn, Stephanie D. Teasley *(University of Michigan)*

- **Educational Programming Systems for Learning at Scale** 177
  Qianxiang Wang, Wenxin Li *(Peking University)*, Tao Xie *(University of Illinois at Urbana-Champaign)*

- **Online Learning versus Blended Learning: An Exploratory Study** 179
  Andrew Cross, B. Ashok, Srinath Bala, Edward Cutrell, Naren Datha, Rahul Kumar *(Microsoft Research India)*,
  Viraj Kumar *(PES University)*, Madhusudan Parthasarathy *(University of Illinois at Urbana Champaign)*,
  Siddharth Prakash, Sriram Rajamani, Satish Sangameswaran *(Microsoft Research India)*,
  Deepika Sharma, William Thies *(Microsoft Research India)*

- **Modeling Programming Knowledge for Mentoring at Scale** 181
  Anvisha H. Pai *(Massachusetts Institute of Technology)*,
  Philip J. Guo *(Massachusetts Institute of Technology & University of Rochester)*,
  Robert C. Miller *(Massachusetts Institute of Technology)*

- **Facilitating MOOCs Learning through Weekly Meet-up: A Case Study in Taiwan** 183
  Pin-Ju Chen, Yang-Hsueh Chen *(National University of Tainan)*

- **Java Tutor: Bootstrapping with Python to Learn Java** 185
  Casey O'Brien, Max Goldman, Robert C. Miller *(Massachusetts Institute of Technology)*

- **Corporate Learning at Scale: Lessons from a Large Online Course at Google** 187
  Arthur Asuncion, Jac de Haan, Mehryar Mohri, Kayur Patel, Afshin Rostamizadeh, Umar Syed, Lauren Wong
  (Google)

- **Teacher Usage Behaviors within an Online Open Educational Resource Repository** 189
  Jennifer Sabourin, Lucy Kosturko, Scott McQuiggan *(SAS Institute, Inc.)*

- **ACCE: Automatic Coding Composition Evaluator** 191
  Stephanie Rogers, Steven Tang, John Canny *(University of California, Berkeley)*

- **Due Dates in MOOCs: Does Stricter Mean Better?** 193
  Sergiy O. Nesterko *(Harvard University)*, Daniel Seaton *(Massachusetts Institute of Technology)*,
  Justin Reich, Joseph McIntyre, Qiuyi Han *(Harvard University)*,
  Isaac Chuang *(Massachusetts Institute of Technology)*, Andrew Ho *(Harvard University)*

- **Visual Analytics of MOOCs at Maryland** 195
  Zhengzheng Xu, Dan Goldwasser, Benjamin B. Bederson, Jimmy Lin *(University of Maryland)*

- **Social Factors that Contribute to Attrition in MOOCs** 197
  Carolyn Penstein Rosé, Ryan Carlson, Diyi Yang, Miaomiao Wen *(Carnegie Mellon University)*,
  Lauren Resnick, Pam Goldman, Jennifer Sherer *(University of Pittsburgh)*

- **Assigning Videos to Textbooks at Appropriate Granularity** 199
  Marios Kokkodis *(NYU Stern)*, Anitha Kannan, Krishnaram Kenthapadi *(Microsoft Research)*

- **A Behavioral Biometrics based Authentication Method for MOOC's that is Robust against Imitation Attempts** 201
  Markus Krause *(Leibniz University)*

- **What Does Enrollment in a MOOC Mean?** 203
  Eni Mustafaraj *(Wellesley College)*

- **Promoting Active Learning & Leveraging Dashboards for Curriculum Assessment in an OpenEdX Introductory CS Course for Middle School** 205
  Shuchi Grover, Roy Pea, Stephen Cooper *(Stanford University)*

- **Evaluating Educational Interventions at Scale** 207
  Rakesh Agrawal *(Microsoft Research)*, M. Hanif Jhaveri *(Stanford University)*, Krishnaram Kenthapadi *(Microsoft Research)*

- **DeepTutor: Towards Macro- and Micro-Adaptive Conversational Intelligent Tutoring at Scale** 209
  Vasile Rus, Dan Stefanescu, Nobal Niraula, Arthur C. Graesser *(The University of Memphis)*

- **The Challenges of Using a MOOC to Introduce "Absolute Beginners" to Programming on Specialized Hardware** 211
  Jennifer S. Kay *(Rowan University)*, Tom McKlin *(SageFox Consulting Group)*

Demonstrations

- **Runestone Interactive: Tools for Creating Interactive Course Materials** 213
  Brad Miller, David Ranum *(Luther College)*

- **Work-in-Progress: Program Grading and Feedback Generation with Web-CAT** 215
  Stephen H. Edwards *(Virginia Tech)*

- **L@S 2014 Demo: Best Practices for MOOC Video** 217
  Dan Garcia, Michael Ball, Aatash Parikh *(University of California, Berkeley)*

- **A System for Sending the Right Hint at the Right Time** 219
  Matthew Elkherj, Yoav Freund *(University of California, San Diego)*

- **Code Hunt: Gamifying Teaching and Learning of Computer Science at Scale** 221
  Nikolai Tillmann *(Microsoft Research)*, Jonathan de Halleux *(Microsoft Research)*, Tao Xie *(University of Illinois at Urbana-Champaign)*, Judith Bishop *(Microsoft Research)*

Author Index

Author Index 223

Learning @ Scale 2014 Organization

Program Chairs: Armando Fox, University of California, Berkeley, USA
Marti A. Hearst, University of California, Berkeley, USA
Michelene T. H. Chi, Arizona State University, USA

General Chair: Mehran Sahami, Stanford University, USA

Program Committee: Russell Almond, Florida State University, USA
Ryan Baker, Teachers College, Columbia University, USA
Tiffany Barnes, North Carolina State University, USA
Ben Bederson, University of Maryland, College Park, USA
Michelene Chi, Arizona State University, USA
Ed Chi, Google, USA
Ed Cutrell, Microsoft Research, India
Pierre Dillenbourg, EPFL, Switzerland
Gilles Dowek, INRIA, France
Doug Fisher, Vanderbilt University, USA
Armando Fox, University of California, Berkeley, USA
Ken Goldberg, University of California, Berkeley, USA
Art Graesser, University of Memphis, USA, and Oxford University, UK
Jonathan Grudin, Microsoft Research, USA
Sumit Gulwani, Microsoft Research, USA
Bjoern Hartmann, University of California, Berkeley, USA
Marti Hearst, University of California, Berkeley, USA
Neil Heffernan, Worcester Polytechnic Institute, USA
Chris Hoadley, New York University, USA
David Karger, Massachusetts Institute of Technology, USA
Scott Klemmer, University of California, San Diego, USA
Ken Koedinger, Carnegie Mellon University, USA
Marcia Linn, University of California, Berkeley, USA
Christoph Meinel, Hasso-Plattner-Institut, Germany
Rob Miller, Massachusetts Institute of Technology, USA
John Mitchell, Stanford University, USA
Zachary Pardos, University of California, Berkeley, USA
David Pritchard, Massachusetts Institute of Technology, USA
Jeremy Roschelle, SRI, USA
Carolyn Rose, Carnegie Mellon University, USA
Dan Russell, Google, USA
Mehran Sahami, Stanford University, USA
Patti Schank, SRI, USA
Dan Schwartz, Stanford University, USA
Karen Swan, University of Illinois, Springfield, USA
Kurt Van Lehn, Arizona State University, USA

Learning @ Scale 2014 Sponsor & Supporters

Sponsor:

ACM Ed Board

Supporters:

New Wine in No Bottles:
Immersive, Personalized Ubiquitous Learning

Christopher J. Dede
Harvard University
Cambridge, MA
Chris_Dede@harvard.edu

ABSTRACT

The invention of the movie camera was initially seen as a way to reach "massive" by filming plays; we are in an equivalent stage with our early MOOCs. Thinking outside the box of "teaching" is essential to realizing learning at scale. Virtual worlds and augmented realities can complement digitized classroom instruction through simulated apprenticeships, embedded support for learning everywhere, and transformed social interactions. Going big also requires thinking small: analyzing diagnostic micro-patterns to customize individual learning, sifting through millions of participants to find the ideal partners to aid each other's growth. To reach massive with universal access and powerful outcomes, we must creatively expand our visions of platforms, pedagogy, and financing.

Categories and Subject Descriptors

K.3.1 [Computers in Education]: Computer Uses in Education - *Collaborative learning, Computer-assisted instruction, Distance Learning*

Keywords

Massive, immersion, personalization, learning analytics, mobile, virtual worlds, augmented realities, transformed social interaction

Bio

Chris Dede is the Timothy E. Wirth Professor in Learning Technologies at Harvard's Graduate School of Education. His fields of scholarship include emerging technologies, policy, and leadership. His funded research includes grants from the National Science Foundation, the U.S. Department of Education's Institute of Education Sciences, and the Gates Foundation to design and study immersive simulations, transformed social interactions, and online professional development. In 2007, he was honored by Harvard University as an outstanding teacher, and in 2011 he was named a Fellow of the American Educational Research Association. From 2001-2004, he was Chair of the HGSE department of Teaching and Learning.

Chris has served as a member of the National Academy of Sciences Committee on Foundations of Educational and Psychological Assessment and a member of the 2010 National Educational Technology Plan Technical Working Group. In 2013, he co-convened a NSF workshop on "new technology-based models of postsecondary learning." His co-edited book, Scaling Up Success: Lessons Learned from Technology-based Educational Improvement, was published by Jossey-Bass in 2005. A second volume he edited, Online Professional Development for Teachers: Emerging Models and Methods, was published by the Harvard Education Press in 2006. His latest co-edited book, Digital Teaching Platforms: Customizing Classroom Learning for Each Student, was published by Teachers College Press in 2012.

L@S 2014, March 4–5, 2014, Atlanta, Georgia, USA.
ACM 978-1-4503-2669-8/14/03.
http://dx.doi.org/10.1145/2556325.2578292

Student Skill and Goal Achievement in the Mapping with Google MOOC

Julia Wilkowski
Google
1600 Ampitheatre Pkwy
Mountain View, CA 94041
wilkowski@google.com

Amit Deutsch
Google
1600 Ampitheatre Pkwy
Mountain View, CA 94041
amitdeutsch@google.com

Daniel M. Russell
Google
1600 Ampitheatre Pkwy
Mountain View, CA 94041
drussell@google.com

ABSTRACT
Students who registered for the Mapping with Google massive open online course (MOOC) were asked several questions during the registration process to identify prior experience with eleven skills as well as their goals for registering for the course. Students selected goals from a list; they were periodically reminded of these goals during the MOOC. At the end of the course, we compared students' self reports of goal achievement on a post-course survey with behavioral click-stream analysis. In addition, we assessed how well prior skill in a subject predicts a student's course completion and found no correlation. Our research shows that students who completed course activities were more likely to earn certificates of completion than peers who did not.

Author Keywords
MOOCs; Google; Skills; Goals; Activities

ACM Classification Keywords
K.3.1 Computer Uses in Education: Distance learning

INTRODUCTION
Google, Inc. has been experimenting with MOOCs to teach members of the general public how to use Google tools more efficiently and effectively. The Course Builder open-source platform emerged and has evolved from this research; a growing community of educators has used this tool to launch over fifty MOOCs worldwide. The course development team consists of Google employees including a program manager, instructional designers, engineers, content experts, and videographers. A primary criticism of MOOCs is that their completion rate is very low, approximately 10% [11, 12]. Google's course development team (and MOOC community as a whole) frequently discusses how to measure course "success" [8, 9].

We learned through two of Google's previous courses, Power Searching and Advanced Power Searching with

Google, that registrant of these non-university, professional development MOOCs have varying goals. Many MOOC students are well-educated professionals seeking to gain practical skills to improve their work or lives and not necessarily to earn course credits toward a degree [4]. We assert that success does not necessarily equate to students *finishing* the course. We believe that it is more important for students to achieve their goals, even if their primary goal is simply to learn one or two new skills. Understanding student goals and course behavior has implications for course design and development. For example, if registrants intend to just learn one or two new tips, then the course design should accommodate students' jumping directly to specific parts of the course instead of gating material by schedule or prerequisite activities.

The examined course applies several aspects of mastery learning, including breaking a topic into smaller chunks (lessons) and joining them with individual skill-based activities that provided feedback to the students [1]. Many MOOCs interrupt videos to ask students brief multiple-choice questions to keep students engaged and enhance students' understanding of course concepts [7]. In Mapping with Google activities consisted of opportunities for students to receive instant feedback about how well they could apply skills from the course.

We conducted two observational studies to assess how well different students performed on final projects based on what skills they possessed when they registered for the course, what activities they completed during the course, and what goals they set for themselves at the beginning of the course.

This paper addresses both how students' goals at the course outset affect their completion and dropout rates as well as the effect of students' skills on their success in the course. We believe that it is more important to consider student goal and skill attainment as the more important factors in course success than percentage of students who completed the course.

In the rest of this paper, we will describe the Mapping with Google MOOC, first detailing how the MOOC was built, its goals and general design. We then discuss the various student goals that registrants defined at registration as well as data collected to measure how well students achieved those goals. We also describe what we observed about

L@S 2014, March 4–5, 2014, Atlanta, Georgia, USA.
ACM 978-1-4503-2669-8/14/03.
http://dx.doi.org/10.1145/2556325.2566240

students' skills and activity usage throughout the course. We conclude the paper with design implications and areas of future exploration.

ABOUT THE COURSE

Mapping with Google [10] was created to teach the general public how to use Google's mapping and Google Earth products more efficiently and effectively. The course was announced and registration opened on May 15, 2013. Students could access instructional materials in the two-week period from June 10 through June 24. Mapping with Google was made using Google's open-source Course Builder platform [5] with minor modifications to display the student's profile on the course home page and add self-evaluation calibration exercises to the final projects. In addition to standard video and text lessons, the course offered application activities for a variety of skills. Examples include using Google Maps to find directions between two points on a map, using Google Maps Engine Lite to import a csv file of locations into a map, and using Google Earth to create a tour with audio, images, videos, and panoramic views. 41,455 students registered for the course; 21,837 students (53% of registrants) did something in the course other than register (e.g. watched a video, looked at a text lesson, attempted an activity, completed a final project).

Students could choose whether to complete a final project to earn a Google Maps certificate of completion, a Google Earth certificate of completion, or both. Final projects required students to apply skills taught in the course to create a custom map or Google Earth tour. To earn a certificate of completion, students submitted a culminating synthesis project and evaluated their own work using a rubric provided. Overall students submitted a high quality of work in these projects, as validated by course staff grading a random sample of submitted projects [13]. Additional support was provided to students via Google Groups forum categories embedded on each activity page. In addition to monitoring forum posts, teaching staff, which consisted of Google employees, periodically sent email announcements/reminders to students.

Students logged into the course using a Google account. Following the course, data about the students was extracted into JSON files using the Course Builder Extract, Transform, Load (ETL) tool. The data was extracted with the user IDs obfuscated in order to preserve user privacy.

STUDENT GOALS

Students in MOOCs have a variety of reasons for registering for courses. Because courses are offered at no cost, and there is a low barrier to entry, many students register for courses and then never return to the course. [3] Understanding why students register for courses allows course designers to categorize students by their goals and tailor course design to better serve each student.

Previous courses have also shown differences in student behaviors; several researchers have described their students in different ways. Phil Hill describes five categories of students in "Coursera-style MOOCs:" No-Shows, Observers, Drop-Ins, Passive Participants, Active Participants [6]. Other research describes four categories: Completing, Auditing, Disengaging, and Sampling [8]. Coursera's founders classify students as Passive participants, Active participants, and Community contributors (not mutually exclusive) [9]. All of these studies divide students by the behaviors they exemplify during the course. We identified four categories of students based on their stated intention of how they would interact with the course and assessed whether they achieved the goals they established.

The four categories we have observed include

1. *No-shows*: students register for the course (usually before the course content is available) but never log in to the course to interact with the content

2. *Observers*: want to see what an online course is like or how this one is taught

3. *Casual learners*: want to learn one or two new things, either out of curiosity or a work/school-related need

4. *Completers*: complete as many course elements necessary to complete projects and earn a certificate of completion

Understanding students' motivations and the relative percentages of each kind of student will help in designing future courses to help students achieve those goals. It may also influence how various learning paths are offered, such as displaying only a subset of the course to learners based on their stated preferences or previous experiences.

Methods

During registration, students were asked to complete a questionnaire about their course goals and previous experience with skills addressed in the course. The possible goals were mutually exclusive:

A. Learn new things about Google's tools in general, without necessarily completing the course.

B. Learn about a specific Google Maps feature that I need, without necessarily completing the course

C. Learn about a specific Google Earth feature that I need, without necessarily completing the course

D. Complete the requirements to earn a Google Maps certificate

E. Complete the requirements to earn a Google Earth certificate

F. Complete the requirements to earn a Google Maps and Google Earth certificate

G. I am interested in seeing how this online course is taught and not aiming to learn about Google's mapping tools

To assess whether students achieved the goal they established, we sent them an anonymous follow-up survey as well as conducted a clickstream analysis of their behaviors. The clickstream analysis enabled us to analyze the percentage of students who selected each goal and whether their behaviors indicated that they achieved (or exceeded) those goals. For example, if a student said they want to "learn about a specific Google Maps feature that I need, without necessarily completing the course," then we assessed how many videos they watched and how many activities they completed. If they watched one video 95% of the way through, read one text lesson, and/or completed one activity, then this counted as meeting their goal. A student who selected the goal of "Learn about a specific Google Maps feature that I need, without necessarily completing the course" and ended up achieving a Google Maps certificate counted as exceeding their goal.

Data

97% of registrants (40,248 out of 41,445) provided a goal at registration. We discovered that 52.5% of registrants intended to complete requirements to earn a certificate; the

Intend to complete	52.5%	Do not intend to complete	44.7%
Goal F	40.8% (16,891)	Goal A	33.0% (13,688)
Goal D	10.2% (4,212)	Goal B	5.7% (2,364)
Goal E	1.5% (604)	Goal G	3.7% (1,542)
		Goal C	2.3% (947)

Table 1. Responses to goal question during registration

remaining 44.7% of registrants who supplied a goal preferred to learn a few new skills or explore the online course.

To assess students' perceptions of how well they achieved their goals, all 41,455 course registrants received an anonymous post-course survey not aligned to student identifiers in the rest of the course. 2,881 (7%) of registrants responded to the survey. When asked, "Did you meet the goal you defined when you registered for this class?" 2,258 (78%) of survey respondents indicated that

they met the goal they had set at the beginning of the class. A greater percentage of students who completed the course responded to the survey compared to students who did not complete the course. Of the 1,951 students who completed the course and responded to the survey, 90.8% agreed that they met their goal. Of the 930 students who did not complete the course yet responded to the survey, 51.8% agreed that they met their goal.

Of 20,977 engaged students (observers, casual learners, and completers who did something in the class other than register), a total of 11,348 (54.1%) met or exceeded their goal via behavioral analysis. A summary of these goals can be found in Tables 2 and 3.

Goal	Criteria for meeting goal	Criteria for exceeding goal
Goal A	Satisfy the criteria for either Goal B or Goal C	Earn any certificate
Goal B	Watch at least one entire video and/or click on a text lesson and/or successfully complete an activity in Unit 2 or Unit 3	Earn Maps certificate
Goal C	Same as Goal B, but for Unit 4 or 5	Earn Earth certificate
Goal D	Earn Maps certificate (submit and grade Maps Project)	Earn Earth certificate also
Goal E	Earn Earth certificate (submit and grade Earth Project)	Earn Maps certificate also
Goal F	Earn Maps and Earth certificates (submit and grade Google Maps and Google Earth projects)	n/a
Goal G	Fall in student category (visit the course after registration and click on a lesson)	Earn any certificate

Table 2. Criteria for Student Goal Attainment

Analysis

It is interesting to note that just over half of registrants intended to complete the course. This provides one hint to MOOCs' low completion rate: a large portion of students just wants to learn a few things. The goals with the highest attainment rate required the least amount of engagement with the course (e.g. logging in at least once after registering or watching one video). The goals with the lowest attainment rate required students to invest more time. The Earth and Maps projects also became available three days after the rest of the course content. Therefore students who began the class within the first three days needed to return to the site on at least one subsequent occasion. This leads us to conclude that instructors should put the most critical content at the beginning of the course as well as make important content available when the course launches.

Goal	Students who selected	Met or Exceeded Goal	Exceeded Goal
Goal A	7,095	4,436 (62.5%)	1,623 (22.9%)
Goal B	1,203	776 (64.5%)	274 (22.8%)
Goal C	489	92 (18.8%)	69 (14.1%)
Goal D	2,242	562 (25.1%)	261 (11.6%)
Goal E	318	42 (13.2%)	39 (12.3%)
Goal F	8,834	2,186 (24.7%)	0
Goal G	796	796 (100%)	192 (24.1%)
Total	20,977	8,890 (42.4%)	2,458 (11.7%)

Table 3. Behavioral analysis of student goal attainment

Understanding students' goals enables course designers to change how courses are presented. Since a slim majority of students intended to complete the course, and a significant number wanted to learn one or two new things, we should make it easy for students to find relevant content. Similar to other MOOCs [6], we typically see about half of students who register for a course never return to the course (no-shows). Should we therefore offer all course material at the time of registration instead of the typical practice of opening registration several weeks before the course is available? What are other ways we could motivate students to return to the course? Since nearly two-thirds of engaged students want to learn one or two things, we could provide those students with a list of interesting topics addressed in the course with direct links for them to learn about those topics or a way for them to add desired units, lessons, activities, and projects to a custom course.

Along these lines, future work could explore suggesting learning paths based on student goals or encouraging students to create a custom course playlist.

SKILLS AND ACTIVITIES

The goals of Google's engineering education team, partnering with the Google Maps and Earth teams, include increasing product awareness and adoption through education. The Google course development team speculates that students who gain additional skills for using these products will use them more efficiently and effectively. We therefore wondered whether students gained skills through the course, and if so, did they do so primarily by watching videos, reading text lessons, or completing activities. In the Course Builder platform, Units consist of Lessons; each Lesson can have an optional Activity. In the Mapping with Google course, most lessons consisted of content presented via video and text followed by an interactive activity that asked students to practice the skills presented in the lesson. In three of the lessons (5.1, 5.3, and 5.4) we linked to existing text or video tutorials and presented an activity instead of a separate video. Activity pages followed lesson pages (and could be reached directly from the left navigation or by clicking a "next" button from the corresponding lesson page). Although course designers intended for students to watch the lesson first and then complete the corresponding activity, students could visit lesson and activity pages in any order.

Methods

During registration students were presented with a survey asking which behaviors they had done before. Each question mapped to a specific lesson where it was taught and particular questions within an activity. These are indicated in parentheses after each skill below.

How have you used Google Maps in the past?

1. Found a location on a map using the search box in Google Maps (2.1)
2. Obtained directions to a destination (2.2)
3. Viewed reviews for a location on the map (2.3)
4. Saved locations to a custom map (3.1)
5. Shared a map I created with someone else (3.2)

How have you used Google Earth in the past?

6. Downloaded Google Earth (4.1; prerequisite for all activities)
7. Searched for something other than my house in Google Earth (4.1)
8. Turned a layer on or off (4.1)
9. Created a placemark (4.2)
10. Created a tour (4.3)

11. Shared a placemark or tour with someone else (4.4)

After the course finished, we compared students' skills at the beginning of class with their skills gained through activities during the course. We conducted a clickstream analysis to determine the percentage of students who said they had not used each of these features prior to the class who completed the relevant activities, watched the relevant videos, and completed the final course projects.

Data

More students completed activities than watched videos or read lesson text. We considered a student to complete an activity if she correctly answered the corresponding application activity questions. Figure 1 compares the number of unique students who viewed lessons (clicked "play" on the relevant video or clicked on the "text version" of the lesson) with the number of unique students who completed the associated activity. We verified with a Wilcoxon signed-rank test that there were significantly more unique students who completed activities than viewed lessons (p < 0.05). Some lessons, like 1.1 and 1.2, are not included here because they did not contain both a lesson and an activity.

We compared the number of students who possessed relevant skills at the beginning of class (per self-report on pre-class questionnaire) who completed final projects. The results are shown in Figure 2.

For each skill, we found differences of less than 1% in the completion rate; we confirmed that the differences were not significantly different with a paired-sample t-test.

For each skill that had an auto-graded activity, we compared the number of students who completed the relevant activity and the final project. The two groups were confirmed to be significantly different with the paired-sample t-test (p<0.01). Results are shown in Figure 3.

Discussion

For 9 of the 12 lessons that contained both video/text lessons and activities, more students completed activities than viewed lesson content. For 3 of the 12 lessons, more students viewed lessons than completed activities. (Note that this does not include data about how long the students viewed videos or stayed on the text lessons.) Our hypothesis is that many students proceeded directly to activities, tried them, and when successful, jumped to the next activity. If unsuccessful, students likely went back to review the video or text lessons. At the time this course was offered, detailed time-stamped clickstream data was not available in Course Builder; we anticipate exploring this specific behavior in future courses.

Students who entered the course without each specific skill

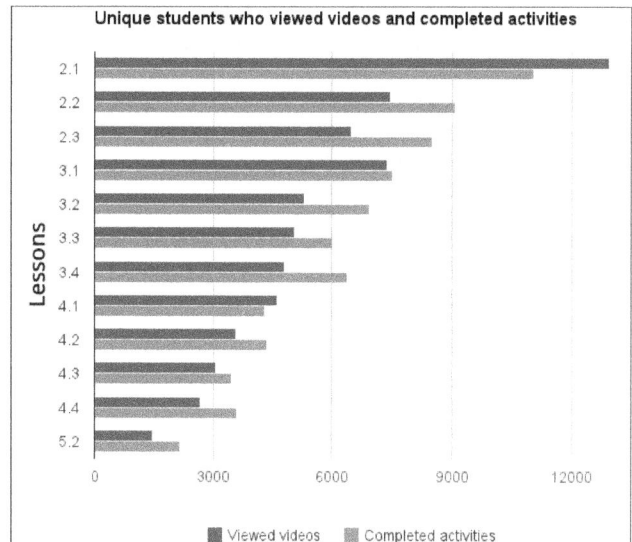

Lesson	Viewed lessons	Completed activities
2.1	13,515	11,049
2.2	8,112	9,082
2.3	6,993	8,489
3.1	7,606	7,498
3.2	5,664	6,939
3.3	5,398	6,007
3.4	5,075	6,392
4.1	4,742	4,270
4.2	3,872	4,325
4.3	3,300	3,441
4.4	2,943	3,588
5.2	1,604	2,137

Figure 1. Unique students who viewed lessons and completed activities for each lesson

and completed the activity designed to teach/practice that skill had an overall greater rate of completing the course (as measured by submitting and grading a final project) than students who merely watched videos or clicked on text lessons. This indicates that completing activities, with instant feedback, is an effective way for students to build and assess their skills. It seems that completing activities is a greater predictor of students completing the course than what skills students possess when they enter the course.

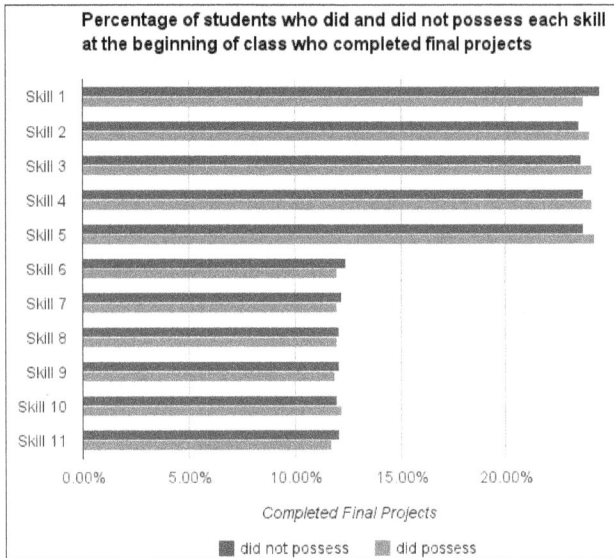

Percentage of students who did and did not possess each skill at the beginning of class who completed final projects

	Did not possess	Did possess
Skill 1	24.50%	23.70%
Skill 2	23.50%	24%
Skill 3	23.60%	24.10%
Skill 4	23.70%	24.10%
Skill 5	23.70%	24.20%
Skill 6	12.40%	12%
Skill 7	12.20%	12%
Skill 8	12.10%	12%
Skill 9	12.10%	11.90%
Skill 10	12.00%	12.20%
Skill 11	12.10%	11.70%

Figure 2. Percentage of students who possessed each skill at the beginning of class who completed final projects

CONCLUSION

Students who register for MOOCs have a variety of different goals in mind when they register. Course designers should therefore consider the needs of the audience when designing courses. Courses that do not have high stakes (e.g. count for college credit) could consider making it easy for students to search through the content of a video or course to find and practice specific skills. Even better, why not let students create custom courses that consist of lessons, units, and activities that interest them most? Though overall completion rate may be low, we

found significantly higher numbers of students completing their goals than merely completing the course. We believe that simply reporting on completion rates does all of these courses (and students) an injustice, since it ignores the fact that adult learners have varied goals.

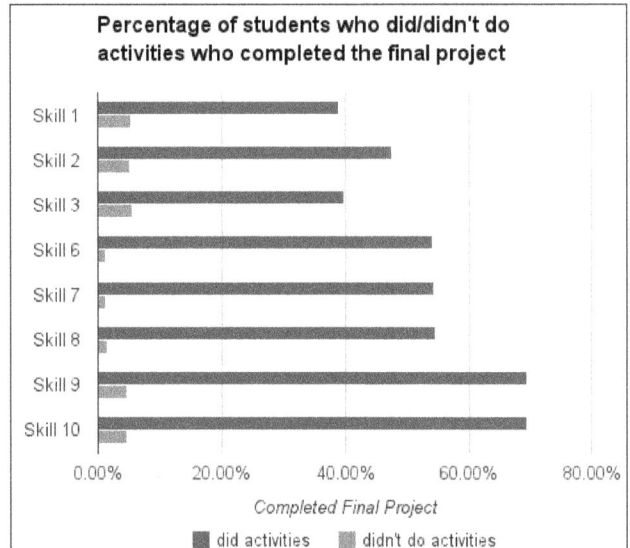

Percentage of students who did/didn't do activities who completed the final project

	Did Activities	Didn't Do Activities
Skill 1	39.01%	5.45%
Skill 2	47.53%	5%
Skill 3	39.83%	5.51%
Skill 6	54.07%	1%
Skill 7	54.29%	1%
Skill 8	54.50%	1%
Skill 9	69.58%	4.62%
Skill 10	69.58%	4.62%

Figure 3. Students who did activities and did not do activities who completed final projects

Future work could involve personalizing courses based on students' goals. How can we motivate students who register but never return to the course? Should we try to inspire casual learners to complete course work? If students want to learn one or two new things, should we make it easier for them to find those new skills by making the entire course available to them at the outset? Perhaps we could retain the feel of the MOOC community by grouping students with similar goals and having them interact with and motivate each other. Future courses could explore different learning paths or different ways of presenting content to students.

We need to move beyond the one-size-fits-all approach in MOOCs; technology exists that could present different students with different content.

Since more students complete activities than look at lessons, we recommend designing courses (especially technically-oriented courses) more around activities than the traditional lecture. This could involve spending more time developing activities and effective feedback systems as well as physically placing activities before lessons. Students could then test themselves on how well they can complete an activity. If they do not achieve success in the activity, they could then choose to watch the video or read the text lesson, then return to the activity. Although this format will likely work the best for technical courses (including science and math), we believe there is value in starting courses from different disciplines with a practical application of skills taught.

Eventually we hope that courses will adapt or become customized to individual students. One option is to ask students what their goal is and give them a personalized learning path to help them reach that goal. Other personalization options include having students select course elements from a list to create a customized course. In summary, understanding learners' aims and behaviors allows us to create more effective courses for everyone.

ACKNOWLEDGEMENTS
We thank Alfred Spector, Maggie Johnson, and the Mapping with Google MOOC development team for their advice, feedback, and support. This course utilized Course Builder 1.4.0. [4]. We thank Pavel Simakov and John Cox for continuous support, customizations and advice.

REFERENCES
1. Block, J. H., and Burns, R. B. 1976. Mastery learning. *Review of research in education, 4* (1976), 3-49.

2. Bloom, B. S. 1984. The 2-sigma problem: The search for methods of group instruction as effective as one-to-one tutoring. *Educational Researcher, 13* (6), 4–16.

3. Breslow, L., Pritchard, D. E., DeBoer, J., Stump, G. S., Ho, A. D., and Seaton, D. T. 2013. Studying learning in the worldwide classroom: Research into edX's first MOOC. *Research & Practice in Assessment 8* (2013), 13–25.

4. Emanuel, E. J. 2013. Online education: MOOCs taken by educated few. *Nature, 503* (7476), 342-342.

5. Google Course Builder. https://code.google.com/p/course-builder/

6. Hill, P. 2013. Emerging Student Patterns in MOOCs: A (Revised) Graphical View [Web log post]. http://mfeldstein.com/

7. Karpicke, J. D., and Blunt, J. R. 2011. Retrieval practice produces more learning than elaborative studying with concept mapping. *Science 331* (6018), 772–5.

8. Kizilcec, R. F., Piech, C., and Schneider, E. 2013. Deconstructing Disengagement : Analyzing Learner Subpopulations in Massive Open Online Courses Categories and Subject Descriptors. In *Proc. of the Third International Conference on Learning Analytics and Knowledge* (2013), 170–179.

9. Koller, D., Ng, A., Do, C. and Chen, Z. 2013. Retention and Intention in Massive Open Online Courses: In Depth. http://www.educause.edu/

10. Mapping with Google course. 2013. http://mapping.withgoogle.com

11. Parr, C. 2013. Not Staying the Course [Web log post]. www.insidehighered.com.

12. Quillen, I. 2013. Why do students enroll in (but don't complete) MOOC courses? [Web log post]. http://blogs.kqed.org/mindshift

13. Wilkowski, J., Russell, D. M., and Deutsch, A. 2014. Self-evaluation in Advanced Power Searching and Mapping with Google MOOCs. In *L@S 2014*, Mar 04-05 2014, Atlanta, GA, USA. ACM 978-1-4503-2669-8/14/03. http://dx.doi.org/10.1145/2556325.2566241

Correlating Skill and Improvement in 2 MOOCs with a Student's Time on Tasks

John Champaign
MIT, Room 26-331
77 Mass. Ave
Cambridge, MA 02139
617 324-4528
jchampai@mit.edu

Kimberly F. Colvin
MIT, Room 26-331
77 Mass. Ave
Cambridge, MA 02139
617 324-4528
colvin@mit.edu

Alwina Liu
MIT, Room 26-331
77 Mass. Ave
Cambridge, MA 02139
617 324-4528
alwina@mit.edu

Colin Fredericks
MIT, Room 26-321
77 Mass. Ave
Cambridge, MA 02139
617 324-4528
colin.fredericks@gmail.com

Daniel Seaton
MIT, Room 41-205d
77 Mass. Ave
Cambridge, MA 02139
617 258-0252
dseaton@mit.edu

David E. Pritchard
MIT, Room 26-241
77 Mass. Ave
Cambridge, MA 02139
617 253 6812
dpritch@mit.edu

ABSTRACT

Because MOOCs offer complete logs of student activities for each student there is hope that it may be possible to find out which activities are the most useful for learning. We start this quest by examining correlations between time spent on specific course resources and various measures of student performance: score on assessments, skill as defined by Item Response Theory, improvement in skill over the period of the course, and conceptual improvement as measured by a pre-post test. We study two MOOCs offered on edX.org by MIT faculty: Circuits and Electronics (6.002x) and Mechanics Review (8.MReV). Surprisingly, we find strong negative correlations in 6.002x between student skill and resource use; we attribute these findings to the fact that students with higher initial skills can do the exercises faster and with less time spent on instructional resources. We find weak or slightly negative correlations between relative improvement and resource use in 6.002x. The correlations with learning are stronger for conceptual knowledge in 8.MReV than with relative improvement, but similar for all course activities (except that eText checkpoint questions correlate more strongly with relative improvement). Clearly, the wide distribution of demographics and initial skill in MOOCs challenges us to isolate the habits of learning and resource use that correlate with learning for different students.

Author Keywords

MOOC; edX; educational data mining; learning behaviors; learning comparison; IRT

ACM Classification Keywords

K.3.1 Computer Uses in Education: Computer-managed instruction (CMI) and Distance Learning

INTRODUCTION

MOOCs have been touted as ideal education research vehicles: the large sample sizes (due to the large enrollment) and the ability to track the students detailed use of learning resources, such as discussion boards, videos and practice problems, offer unparalleled opportunities to perform data mining and learning experiments. This study makes pioneering strides in this direction by comparing and contrasting the correlations of demographics with initial skill, of initial skill with resource use and study habits, and the effects of these variables on the relative class standing over the time-span of the course. We are especially interested in how student study habits, such as time on task, influence skill change in our longitudinal study over the semester or class. This is important because it leads to research-based advice for students and suggests educational experiments. In addition, resource use illuminates how students actually use instructional resources, which can inform authors and teachers about where to spend authoring effort, what needs improvement and what parts of a book or video exercise are most useful.

The present study is unique in investigating the correlations between resource use and skill and relative improvement in any MOOC. Furthermore we investigate two courses: 6.002x, "Circuits & Electronics", and 8.MReV, "Mechanics ReView", a mechanics course for students with at least a high school level of preparation. Both courses were offered on the edX.org platform.

COURSES AND PROCEDURES

The two courses compared here differ in their origins and nature. Circuits and Electronics was made as a MOOC, being based on a highly successful traditional on-campus course at MIT (we analyze the first instance, offered by MITx in Spring 2012). The instruction is provided primarily by lecture videos. Mechanics ReView originated as the online component for a reformed course with a flipped classroom that emphasized problem solving. Instruction is mostly eText including many worked examples using the MAPS pedagogy [12].

Description of 6.002x – Circuits and Electronics

With some modification for online delivery, the 14 weeklong units of 6.002x largely mirror a traditional on-campus course in both format and timing. The course sequence (linear sequence in the courseware navigation bar) comprises lecture sequences consisting of short videos (annotated PowerPoint slides and actual MIT lectures) with embedded lecture questions, tutorial videos (recitation substitute), homework (3-4 multi-part problems each week), and lab assignments (using an interactive circuit simulator). Supplementary materials (contained in a separate navigation bar) include a course textbook (navigable page images), a TA- and student-editable wiki, and moderated student discussions. For further exploration of course structure and available resources, readers may visit the archived course (https://6002x.mitx.mit.edu/).

There were 7519 certificate earners in 6.002X, of those 6060 were used in the analyses in this paper because they had completed more than 50% of the homework and exam questions. Matrix sampling was used in the collection of the demographic information, which provides an approximation of the course make-up[1]. Roughly, for 35% a bachelor's degree was the highest degree held, 38% had a masters degree or doctorate, for 25% the highest degree attained was high school; 12.6% taught electrical engineering at some level, 73% of the respondents had some exposure to electrical engineering. This huge demographic variability led to a wide skill distribution.

The various instructional resources considered for correlations in this study are described in Table 1.

---

[1] While matrix sampling leads to incomplete coverage of the student demographics, there have been concerns [6] that too many survey questions alienate MOOC students.

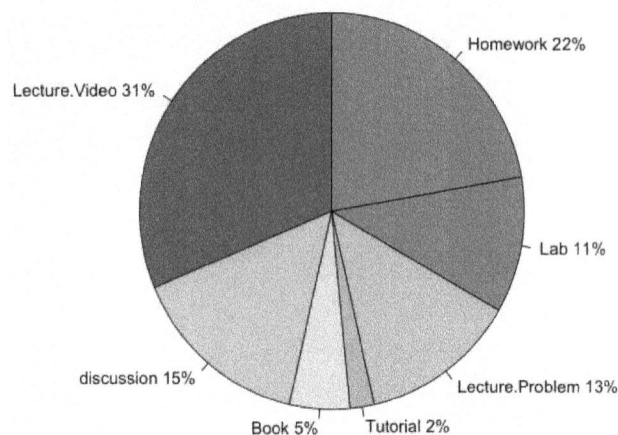

Figure 1: The fractional division of time among the various resources of 6.002x. Data are for 1080 certificate earners who spent an average of 95 hours on the entire course. Note that cool colors indicate instruction and warm colors indicate assessment

Description of 8.MReV - Mechanics ReView

The 8.MReV course grew from MIT's highly successful on-campus short course that improves the expertise of the students' learning attitudes as measured by the CLASS [1], raises their grades from D to B in three weeks [12], and improves their performance in the subsequent course (Electricity and Magnetism) by over ½ grade [13]. Because the instructors had to interact intensively with students who were solving problems in class, the instructors made online wikis, then eText, and then multilevel homework [16]. This grew into a free open online course that was offered twice in 2012 using the LON-CAPA platform. In the second running during the summer, the course was specifically targeted at teachers, who constituted 90% of those who received certificates. This online material was transferred to the edX platform in Fall 2012, and also used in the on-campus course 8.011. To create the 8.MReV MOOC, this material was supplemented with additional problems and online tests, a wiki, office hour videos, and discussions after every problem and eText page. It was run on the edX platform in the summer of 2013 with publicity to attract both a general audience and physics teachers.

The course was problem oriented and was organized around questions of three basic types: checkpoint problems that are embedded in the eText, homework problems with explicit levels of difficulty [16], and weekly test questions. There were 282 common items in the first 11 weeks of 8.MReV and in 8.011. There were three optional units at the end of Mechanics Review that have not been analyzed. There was no final exam so these problems count heavily toward certification, which required 60% of the total credit available. For most homework and quiz items students were allowed multiple attempts at a correct answer, several for multiple-choice items and typically 10 for symbolic free response items. We only modeled up to 8 attempts (see next section on IRT), which was sufficient for all except 4 quiz and 38 homework items. Obtaining a certificate required obtaining over 60% of the total number of points available on the three types of items.

Unlike 6.002x, there were no high stakes exams in 8.MReV - all of the 403 questions and problems in the course counted toward a certificate. A total of 1080 students completed more than 50% of the questions in the course, and of these 1030 received certificates of completion. This group of students spent an average of 77 hours on the entire course (compared to an average of less than 3 hours for students who did not earn certificates, of which there were 17,706).

Course Component	Number of resources	Pedagogical Value
Lecture Videos	434 videos	Central learning resource for the course consisting of 5 to 10 minute videos. Some are presented as annotated powerpoint talks, while others are recordings of lectures at MIT.
Lecture Questions	105 problems	Checkpoint questions intended to provide formative self-assessment for students and feedback on the lectures for instructors.
Homework	37 problems	Central portion of the weekly graded assessment in the course. Typical homework set contains 3-4 multipart problems. Unlimited attempts were allowed.
Laboratory	14 experiments	Interactive circuit laboratory that provides student guided laboratories with feedback on the outcome of the experimental setup. Students are also able to openly explore a "circuit sandbox" at any point in the course.
eText (Book)	1009 pages	Page images of a top selling commercial textbook. Had weekly guidance as to relevant sections, but largely functioned like print textbook.
Tutorial	145 videos	Made up mostly of tutorial videos describing problem solving strategies or explaining difficult content for various material each week. Introduced to students as a supplemental learning resource.
Discussion	NA	Built on the "askbot" discussion engine, these forums provided the means for students to interact with one another.
Wiki	NA	Provided a combination of deeper description of course content, course logistics, and student led course issues. Edits allowed for students, instructors, and TA's.
Midterm	5 problems	Summative assessment consisting of multipart problems. 3 attempts allowed on each part.
Final Exam	10 problems	Summative assessment consisting of multipart problems. 3 attempts allowed on each part.

Table 1: 6.002x List of course components, the number of associated resources, and a brief description of pedagogical value.

Course Resource	Number of resources	Pedagogical Value
Checkpoint Questions	171 questions	Questions embedded within the eText, emphasizing concepts and straightforward calculations. Mostly multiple choice with limited attempts
Homework Problems	105 problems	Major portion of the graded assessment in the course, had various difficulty and total credit. Limited attempts were allowed, but with up to 10 attempts for problems requiring free response equations.
eText (Book)	321 html pages	Central learning resource for the course consisting mainly of text, diagrams and equations, with approximately 40 self-paced examples worked according to the course pedagogy; contained some lecture videos and simulations.
Office Hours Videos	21 Videos	Videos of instructor tutoring students on voted upon questions within a designated "Office Hours" forum.
Discussion Forums	after each HW problem and eText page	Threaded discussions with up/down voting. Discussions generally focused on approaches to problems or physics questions. The fora were moderated to prevent students from giving the answers
Wiki	NA	Concentrated on solutions for homework questions, it was open only after the due date for that week's homework.
Quizzes	10 quizzes with 52 problems	The weekly quiz questions were little different from the homework: they were not timed, and allowed almost as many attempts as the homework. We have not found any significant statistical performance difference on them vs. the homework.

Table 2: 8.MReV List of course components, the number of associated resources, and a brief description of pedagogical value.

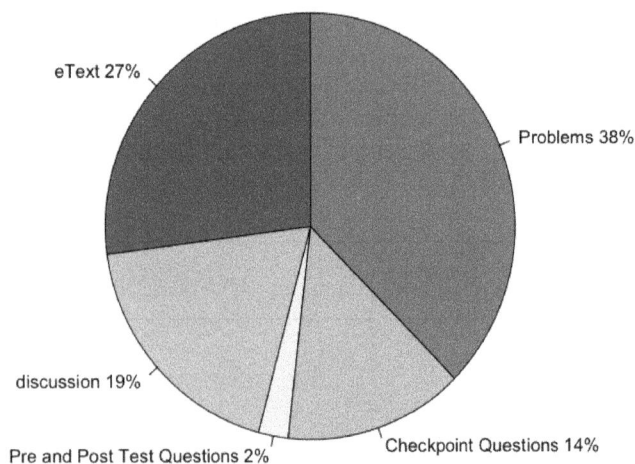

Figure 2: 8.MReV Where Students Spent Time – People who finished the course (n=1080) Note that cool colors indicate instruction and warm colors indicate assessment

In 8.MReV, of the 1080 students we analyzed, 750-900 students responded to the various demographic questions. Of the respondents, 25% were physics teachers, 35% held masters degrees or doctorates, 25% were high school seniors or college students, 76% had a college-level math background, 38% had a physics background equivalent to 8.MReV and 33% had a background in physics more advance than 8.MReV.

These two courses used different structures, which makes comparisons necessarily imperfect. If eText usage (HTML webpages) in 8.MReV is considered analogous to watching videos in $6.002x^2$, which is reasonable since this is how the respective courses provide instruction, the time breakdown of student activities among instruction, assessment counting toward the grade, and discussion becomes quite similar.

Learning in 8.MReV

The absolute amount of learning in 8.MReV was assessed by pre- and post-testing using the same conceptually oriented questions. This work has been analyzed in terms of two variables:

Gain = posttest score - pretest score

Normalized Gain = Gain / (max possible score - pretest score).

Many papers have shown the efficacy of the normalized gain for comparing various pedagogies across a wide range of classes with dramatically different initial skills, for modelling with various types of assumed learning models [14], and for comparing the effects of a new pedagogy on highly similar cohorts of students.

---

[2] These activities are presented in dark blue in both pie charts.

It is not surprising that the correlations of the use of various learning resources were highly similar between these two measures of learning. We were a bit surprised that the correlations were equal or slightly larger with the Gain rather than the Normalized Gain. These two findings have led us to display only those correlations with Gain later in this paper.

Parsing tracking logs

Note: much of this section is a slightly revised version of [15].

Analysis of tracking logs is a well-established means for analyzing student behavior in blended and online courses [16]. In the tracking logs, each interaction (*click*) contains the following relevant information: *username, resource id, interaction details,* and a *timestamp.* Interaction details are context-dependent, e.g., correctness of a homework problem submission, body text of a discussion post, page number for book navigation. This is recorded in JSON text format, an open standard format designed as a lightweight competitor to XML and for human readability. The edX software is distributed in the cloud; meaning interaction data are logged on multiple servers. In total, 6.002x generated roughly 230 million logged interactions, while in 8.MReV there were roughly 17 million interactions.

We preprocessed the logs into separate sorted time-series for each participant, then compiled participant-level descriptive statistics on resource usage: number of unique resources accessed, total frequency of accesses per resource type, and the total time spent per resource. Additionally, we parsed problem submissions, generating a response matrix that includes correctness and the number of attempts. Where possible, we crosschecked our event-log assessment data against a MySQL database serving the 6.002x and 8.MReV courseware. All log parsing was performed using standard modules in Python and R.

Estimation of time spent on different resources

Time estimation for each participant involves measuring the durations between a student's initial interaction with a resource and the time when they navigate away. We accumulate durations calculated from each participant's time-series for each separate course component (Homework, Book, Discussion Forums, etc.). Since each interaction with the server had a timestamp, durations were calculated after sorting activities into chronological order, by taking the difference between two adjacent timestamps. There are minor issues with this approach, such as a user possibly leaving their computer and returning at a later time to resume their session or multiple concurrent sessions as detailed below.

Preliminary evidence shows that durations less than 10 seconds represent students navigating to desired resources, hence we don't count these intervals as activity. In addition, we don't accumulate durations over 30 minutes, assuming that the user has disengaged from their computer. Using alternate values of the high cutoff (10 minutes to 1 hour) can change overall times by 10-20%, but does not significantly alter relationships regarding time allocation among course components or total time spent by different participants.

An important point is that time accumulated is associated with the currently displayed resource. For example, if a student references the book while working on the homework, this duration is accumulated with book time. Only direct interactions with the homework are logged with homework resources. There are clearly alternatives to this approach, e.g. considering all time between opening and answering a problem as problem-solving time [4]. Our time accumulation algorithm is occasionally defeated by users who open multiple browser windows or tabs. edX developers are considering ways to account for this in the future.

SKILL AND IMPROVEMENT WITH IRT

Item Response Theory (IRT) and Multiple Attempts IRT

IRT was designed to measure student ability (skill) on standard tests. It expresses this ability on a curve of all examinees. A student's IRT ability is relative to "class average" and is measured in standard deviations of the class, using the z-score (equal to difference from class average divided by standard deviation of the class). IRT relates an examinee's performance on a particular item to an underlying ability, allowing both examinees and items to be placed along the same scale, where higher values indicate more difficult items and more proficient examinees. The scale unit is standard deviations of ability. Many IRT models exist, but all contain at least one parameter related to the item and at least one parameter related to the examinee [5].

An important feature of IRT is that the ability (skill) that it measures is a property (a "latent trait") of the student and does not depend on the number of items that the students attempts to answer – only on whether the answers given were correct. Additionally, IRT gives accurate student ability measurements independent of which items the student actually attempts. This is in dramatic contrast to the total score that students in these MOOCs obtain, which depends on the *total number* of questions answered correctly within the allowed number of attempts. IRT is also preferable to raw score because it extracts more information than the total number of items correct, primarily by using Bayesian inference to give more weight to a student's answers to questions that more strongly discriminate between high and low ability students.

Item Calibration Using Multiple Attempts

Allowing a student to revise an incorrect response improves learning and also gives more information that affords a more reliable ability estimate than only using the student's first response [2]. To calibrate the items in this study we used Samejima's Graded Response Model [14], which is an extension of the class IRT model, the 2-parameter-logistic model [5], developed to model ordered scores/responses to an item. This could be an essay scored A, B, C, D, or F, or, in this study, the attempt on which the student correctly responds to the item.

For both courses we used the Graded Response Model to calibrate the quiz/test and homework items. We then identified any negatively discriminating items, that is, items for which the likelihood of a correct response was greater for weaker, rather than stronger students. These items were removed from the IRT analysis. One of the assumptions of IRT is unidimensionality, i.e. that the only dimension or factor affecting the likelihood of a student's correct response is a single underlying ability. The item parameters from this joint calibration were then used to obtain weekly ability estimates. The abilities for students on each weekly topic were calculated and then re-centered such that the mean skill for each week was zero, allowing a good week by week comparison of evolving skills for each student and student cohort.

Relative Skill Improvement

Because a student's IRT skill (ability) is measured relative to other students, an improvement over a series of weekly IRT scores for a particular student shows the student's *relative improvement* (relative to the overall class average). We quantified this relative improvement, as the slope of the regression line fit to a student's weekly combined skill on homework and tests/quizzes, where the class' average weekly skill was 0. It should be noted that a student with a constant weekly skill throughout the course would have a relative improvement of 0 but would be presumed to be learning along with the entire class. A student with a positive relative improvement therefore demonstrated more learning than the average student. The details of and a validity argument for the relative improvement variable are discussed in the appendix.

Measuring the relative improvement invites several investigations. It is a good measure for comparing two initially similar cohorts undergoing two different pedagogical treatments, or even two different cohorts of students undergoing the same pedagogical treatment in a MOOC - for example, to investigate the effects of demographics on relative learning rates. But in a MOOC each individual student is free to choose how much time they spend on the course, and how they allocate this time. It is important to note that, unlike students in a classroom, MOOC students choose their own pedagogical treatment. In addition, different MOOC students will employ different learning habits and procedures. This invites research to determine what time allocations or learning habits correlate with the largest skill change. This would in turn allow teachers to recommend optimal time allocation and learning habits to students. It would also suggest learning experiments for future MOOCs to determine whether students who are forced (or strongly encouraged) to use the learning habits of those who exhibit large skill change will consequently show better learning gains. In such research, it is important to realize that the optimum learning strategy may vary with cohort, especially if the initial skill of the cohorts varies widely.

Using the IRT-based skills on the pre- and post-tests, there was a significant increase, 0.41 (standard deviations), from pre-to posttest scores for students who answered at least 7 pretest and at least 8 posttest items. Using raw scores, there was a statistically significant average increase of 3.1 correct problems for these 173 students who had attempted all 14 pretest and all 16 posttest items. (Note: The increase of 3.1 was partly because there were 2 more items on the posttest than the pretest.)

CORRELATES WITH MEASURES OF PERFORMANCE AND SKILL BY COHORT

We used two approaches to look at the relationships between initial skill, average skill, and relative improvement with course behaviors while taking into account demographics: (1) use multiple regression models including demographics and course behaviors to isolate the relationship between specific course behaviors and the skill and performance measures; and (2) calculate the correlations between the variable of interest for various cohorts.

The skill and performance measures included initial skill, average skill in the course, and relative improvement. As a proxy for initial skill we used the intercept, corresponding to "Week 0," from the linear regression to the weekly scores that determined the relative improvement for each student. The demographic information included the highest degree earned, experience with the subject material, math background, whether the student was also a teacher of the subject, and whether the student worked through the course on his/her own, with a classmate or with an expert. The demographic information was self-reported. The course behaviors include time spent on the textbook, lecture videos, the discussion boards, and homework problems. The logarithm of time was used in all the analyses.

In edX, matrix sampling was used to gather demographic information. While this is very useful for drawing conclusions about the students as a whole, it does not offer the demographic information on the individual level for all students in the course. This limits the interpretations we can make about how a particular group performed. In 6.002X, most demographic items had 4000 – 5000 non-responses out of the 6062 students we included in our analysis. There were additional demographic questions, used here, given to students in 8MReV with between 700 and 950 (out of 1080) respondents.

Before proceeding with the correlations, we'll discuss the differences in initial and average skill by cohort. In 8.MReV there were significant differences in both measures when grouped by highest degree earned, math background and whether the student was also a physics teacher. The mean initial skill and average skill by degree earned are shown in Table 3. Not all pairs of differences were statistically significant. For average skill, 8 of the 15 possible comparisons were significant.

Those self-identifying as teachers had initial and average skills significantly greater than both non-teachers and those who did not respond to the question about teaching. Having a college math background was associated with better initial and average skills when compared with those without a college-level math background.

In 6.002x, highest degree earned and math background were significant factors in the differences observed in initial and average skill, while whether someone was also a teacher of electrical engineering was not. The mean initial skill and average skill by degree earned are shown in Table 4. Not all pairs of differences were statistically significant. Differences between the skills of PhD holders and all other groups, except those with less than a high school education were significant, probably due to small sample size. Additionally, the initial and average skills of Master's degree holders were significantly

Highest Degree Earned	%	Mean (SE)		
		Initial Skill	Avg. Skill	Relative Imprvmt.
PhD	10	0.38(.08)	0.67(.10)	0.02(0.01)
Masters	25	0.20(.04)	0.26(.06)	-0.01(0.01)
College	37	-0.04(.04)	-0.08(.06)	-0.01(0.01)
High School	21	-0.14(.06)	-0.20(.07)	-0.01(0.01)
Less than HS	7	0.04(.09)	-0.05(.10)	-0.02(0.01)
No response		-0.03(.06)	0.02.07)	0.00(0.01)

Table 3. Mean measures of skill in 8.MReV by highest degree earned. Note: not all pairs of means were significantly different from each other.

Highest Degree Earned	%	Mean (SE)		
		Initial Skill	Avg. Skill	Relative Imprvmt.
PhD	8	0.30(.06)	0.45(.08)	-0.003(.003)
Masters	31	0.11(.03)	0.15(.04)	0.000(.002)
College	35	-0.09(.03)	-0.12(.04)	0.003(.002)
High School	24	-0.06(.03)	-0.06(.04)	0.000(.002)
Less than HS	2	-0.36(.11)	-0.32(.15)	0.017(0.009)
No response		-0.01(.01)	-0.01(.02)	0.012(0.001)

Table 4. Mean measures of skill in 6.002x by highest degree earned. Note: not all pairs of means were significantly different from each other.

different than those with only a high school education, a Bachelor's degree, or those who did not respond to the education question.

Similar to 8.MReV, not having a college-level math background was associated with lower initial and average skills when compared with those with a college-level math background.

Partial Correlations in 6.002x

To isolate the relationship between a particular variable and one of the performance or skill measures, we used the partial correlation, which removes the effect of the other variables from both of the measures being correlated. The squared-partial correlation provides the proportion of variance explained in one variable by the variation in the second variable while controlling for the other covariates. It should be noted that while many regression coefficients in a model may be significant and the model as a whole has a very high R-squared value, the effect size of the partial correlations can be practically equal to 0.

After controlling for the highest degree obtained, the variability in initial skill, average skill, and relative improvement explained by the various course behaviors was < 1%, with two exceptions. In 6.002x, the variation in the logarithm of time spent on homework explained 2.9% and 4.6% of the variation in the relative improvement and average skill, respectively (but note that the correlations were negative). These small correlations indicate that we cannot make many definitive statements about the association of skill and time on various tasks. Perhaps more progress awaits the inclusion of demographics and learning habits (e.g. when rather than just how much time is spent on various resources).

Correlations within Cohorts in 6.002x

Because it seemed clear that we can't make global statements about how time allocation on various resources is associated with improved skill or overall skill we now consider individual correlations within various subgroups. For each course, we examined the correlations between the logarithm of time spent on various activities and the skill and performance measures of different cohorts. The correlations we found were very similar to the correlations observed in the course as a whole, with only small variation. For example, in 6.00x, whether your highest degree was high school, Bachelors, Masters, or PhD, the correlation between the logarithm of time spent on homework problems and your average skill in the course ranged from $r = -.42$ to $r = -.45$. In 8.MReV, we saw a small positive correlation ($r = 0.07$) between time on homework and relative improvement for students with a college-level math background, but a negative correlation ($r = -0.12$) for students whose highest level of education was high school.

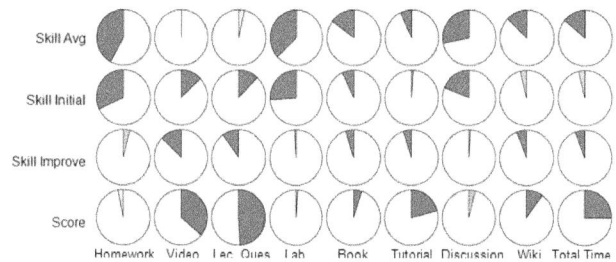

Figure 3: 6.002x Correlations of Measures of Skill and Log of Time on Tasks (n=5948)

Correlations of Skill and Learning with Instructional Resource Use

The dark, medium, or light shade of the color indicates significance at the 0.001, 0.01, or 0.05 level, respectively; grey indicates the correlation was not significant at the 0.05 level. Shades of green are positive correlations and shades of red are negative. The angle from the top indicates the value of the correlation coefficient (a solid circle would indicate a correlation of 1 or -1).

We now address a key question of this study: can we correlate increased expenditure of a student's time on *particular* course resources with score, skill, relative skill improvement and learning? We address this question for 6.002x and 8.MReV in that order.

Figure 3, for 6.002x (Electronics) shows correlations between some measures of student performance and the time spent on several of the course resources. Naively, one might expect that time spent on homework or in the discussion forum would *increase* the students' average skill. In fact, those who spent more time on *any* of the instructional activities showed *lower skill average* wherever there was a significant correlation! Even more surprising, more time on any resource correlated with *negative relative improvement*, except that homework time correlated with a slight increase in relative improvement.

The strong negative correlation of time spent on homework and labs with skill suggests that the causality flows from skill to time: students with more skill can get enough points to obtain a certificate with less investment of their time. This suggestion is consistent with the positive correlation of skill with score (0.54). In short, the more skillful students can finish problems and labs and obtain enough points to earn a certificate with significantly less expenditure of time. Future work will employ AB testing and identification of cohorts of students within the student population to investigate this result further.

The observed *positive* correlation of time on homework with relative improvement at least seems in the correct direction; however it is 0.04 and hence less than one percent of the variance in relative improvement can be attributed to time on homework. The negative correlation between spending time on the lecture videos or lecture questions and relative improvement may reflect that students who are struggling to

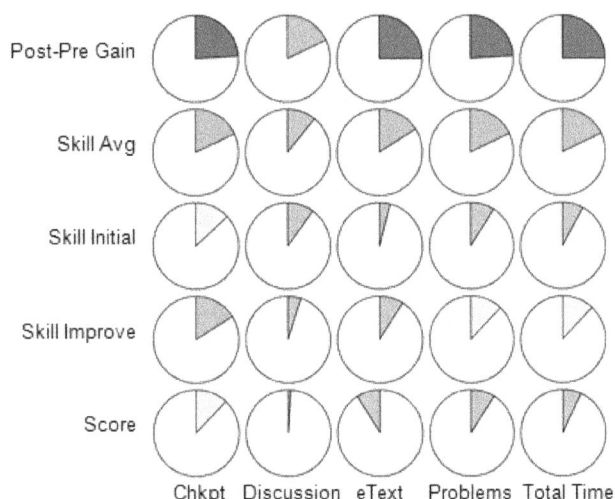

Figure 4: 8.MReV Correlations of Measures of Skill and Log of Time on Tasks (n=292)

keep their skill level constant revert to the lecture videos and questions in an attempt to prevent falling further behind.

Partial Correlations in 8MReV

The figure above shows the correlations between different measures of student performance and their usage of various resources in the course in 8.MReV. Use of each of the individual instructional resources correlates with the pre-post gain with correlation values approaching 0.25, indicating that 6% of the variance in pre-post gain is explained by the variation of time using any typical resource. Since there is a great deal of "noise" in the measurement of the Post-Pre Gain (there is typically only 1 question more correct on the post-test than on the pretest), the actual correlation is certainly considerably higher than reported. The correlations with relative improvement are all positive, but generally weaker or not significant (grey). Surprisingly time spent on checkpoint questions (rather than homework) had the strongest correlation with skill or skill improvement. Since the pre-post gain and the checkpoint questions both focused strongly on conceptual knowledge, it may be that conceptual knowledge is learned better in 8.MeV than problem solving ability, which weighs heavily in the calculation of relative improvement.

DISCUSSION

The most striking features emerging from our analysis are:

1. the large number of negative correlations between time spent on resource use and skill level in 6.002x

2. the significant *negative* correlations between relative skill increase and time spent on *any* of the available instructional resources in 6.002x, accompanied by only one significant *positive* correlation.

3. the significant positive correlations observed between time spent on resources in 8.MReV and conceptual

learning contrasted with the far less strong correlations of resource time with relative skill improvement

We have attributed the presence of large, negative correlations between skill and resource use in 6.002x to the fact that more skillful students are able to obtain the required homework and labs in much less time than less skillful students. Additionally, they may already know the material and therefore don't need help from the discussion forum to do the labs and homework. It should be noted that 92% of the visits to the discussion forum are made by students who simply read existing threads and that such visits constitute the most frequently consulted resource of students doing homework problems [16], suggesting that the discussion forum functions as a way to obtain instruction and information about solving the homework and labs.

The absence of strong positive correlations between skill and relative improvement is quite noteworthy, especially in 6.002x where the correlations of time spent and relative improvement are mostly negative. This is obviously discouraging to those who would like to use MOOCs to obtain insight into which instructional resources generate the most learning.

Previous research demonstrates shows a very strong correlation (r~0.47) between students' use of the online Socratic tutoring application MasteringPhysics.com and success on examinations involving problems very similar to those that determine student skill in 8.MReV, yet essentially zero correlation with conceptual questions. [8,10]. Strong positive correlations have also been observed with cognitive tutors in K-12 also [3]. This suggests that improved learning in MOOCs might be obtained by adding tutor-like online applications that interactively respond to students' individual differences and difficulties.

We note that the robust improvement on the pre- posttest on conceptual learning in 8.MReV is similar to the positive effects of peer instruction in university classrooms [7]. We note the similarity of the pedagogy in the two cases: students are given concept questions in the same format as those on the conceptual tests and have the opportunity (requirement) to discuss them and respond again in the online (in class) learning environment.

We note that any observed correlation coefficients between improvement and resource use may have been lowered due to the wide distribution of demographics and learning styles that characterize MOOCs if different students learn from different things. To see this, imagine that the student population has two subgroups, one that improves considerably from time spent on resource A but does not improve from time on resource B, and a second subgroup that improves from using resource B but not A. If the two groups are lumped together, the time that the second subgroup spends using resource A results in no improvement and halves the measured correlation between resource A and improvement. Similarly, the correlation of the second subgroup's learning from resource B will be halved by the presence of the first subgroup.

Clearly a university's selective admission process, augmented by prerequisites that further weed out less well prepared students, cut off the low end of the skill distribution in an on-campus class. Coupled with options like honors courses and advanced placement that reduce the number of very well prepared students, the incoming students will have a narrowed range of preparation and initial ability level. Furthermore, by deciding to attend and then by attending a particular college, students become habituated to the learning culture of that college. Therefore students in an on-campus class are much more likely to be similar in skill and to benefit from the same type of instructional resources, resulting in higher correlation between resource use and improvement than students in a MOOC.

Thus, the low correlations with student learning or improvement observed in the two MOOCs studied here may well result from student bodies that are far more diverse in their initial skills, demographics, and culture[3].

The differences in sign of the correlations in 6.002x and 8.MReV is a challenge to explain. They may possibly result from some co-factor (that correlates positively with video watching and negatively with improvement) that we didn't account for, but we have no satisfactory suggestions. Obviously, the significant differences in sign of so many correlations that we've found between two introductory courses that contain similar demographic distributions and whose students broadly allocate their time in a similar fashion calls for further investigation (e.g. of other courses).

To conclude on a positive note, the wide diversity of MOOCs can likely be turned to an advantage when controlled educational experiments are done. Under these circumstances it will be possible to compare the learning due to two different resources or pedagogical approaches across a wider spectrum of students. This would inform us about the characteristics of students who will benefit from a particular resource or approach, and might alleviate some of the disappointment that accompanies the unsuccessful attempts to transfer a successful approach from one educational venue to another.

ACKNOWLEDGMENTS
We thank edX.org and MITx for providing access to the data for these courses. We are grateful for support from a Google Faculty Award, MIT, and NSF Grant DUE-1044294. AL thanks the J.C.R. Licklider Fund for financial support.

REFERENCES
1. Adams, W.K., Perkins, K.K., Podolefsky, N.S., Dubson, M., Finkelstein, N.D., & C. Wieman, E. New instrument for measuring student beliefs about physics and learning physics: The Colorado Learning Attitudes about Science Survey. Phys. Rev. ST Physics Ed. Research 2, (2006).

2. Attali, Y. Immediate Feedback and Opportunity to Revise Answers: Application of a Graded Response IRT Model. Applied Psychological Measurement, 35(6), (2010), 472–479.

3. Anderson, J. R., Corbett, A. T., Koedinger, K., & Pelletier, R. (1995). Cognitive tutors: Lessons learned. The Journal of Learning Sciences, 4, 167-207.

4. Deboer , J., Stump, G.S., Seaton, D., Ho, A., Pritchard, D.E., & Breslow, L. Bringing student backgrounds online: MOOC user demographics, site usage, and online learning. In proceedings of the 6th international conference on Educational Data Mining, (2013), 312-313.

5. Hambleton, R. K., Swaminathan, H., & Rogers, H. J. Fundamentals of item response theory. Newbury Park, CA: Sage Publications (1991).

6. Landers, R.N. When A MOOC Exploits Its Learners: A Coursera Case Study. NeoAcademic, http://neoacademic.com/2013/11/13/when-a-mooc-exploits-its-learners-a-coursera-case-study (2013).

7. Mazur, E. *Peer Instruction: A User's Manual*. Prentice Hall, Upper Saddle River, NJ, USA, (1997).

8. Morote, E.-S. and Pritchard, D.E. What course elements correlate with improvement on tests in introductory Newtonian mechanics?, Am. J. Phys. 77, 746, (2009)

9. Morote, E. and Pritchard, D.E., Technology closes the gap between students' individual skills and background differences. In Proc. Intl. Conf. Soc. Information Tech. Teach. Ed., (2004), 826-831.

10. Palazzo, D., Lee, Y-J, Warnakulasooriya, R. and Pritchard, D., Patterns, correlates, and reduction of homework copying, Phys. Rev. ST Phys. Educ. Res. 6, 010104 (2010).

11. Palazzo, D., Lee, Y., Warnakulasooriya, R., & Pritchard, D. Patterns, correlates, and reduction of homework copying. Phys. Rev. ST Phys. Educ. Res., 6(1), (2010).

12. Pawl, A., Barrantes, A. & Pritchard, D. E. Modeling Applied to Problem Solving. AIP Conference Proceedings 1179 2009 Physics Education Research Conference, M. Sabella, Ch. Henderson, C. Singh, Eds. (2009), 51-54.

13. Rayyan, S., Pawl, A., Barrantes, A. , Teodorescu, R. and Pritchard, D. E., Improved Student Performance In Electricity And Magnetism Following Prior MAPS Instruction In Mechanics, Physics Education Research Conference 2010 AIP Conf. Proc. 1289, 273(2010). (Refereed)

14. Samejima, F. Graded response model. In W. J. van der Linden & R. K. Hambleton (Eds.), Handbook of modern

---

[3] It should be noted that some initial skill was required for students to participate in 8.MReV, which may have lead to a less diverse student body.

item response theory. Springer, New York (1997), 85-100.

15. Seaton, D. T., Bergner, Y., Chuang, I., Mitros, P., & Pritchard, D. E. (2013). Who does what in a massive open online course? Communications of the ACM.

16. Teodorescu, R. E., Seaton, D. T., Cardamone, C. N., Rayyan, S., Abbott, J. E., Barrantes, A., Pawl, A. & Pritchard, D. E. When students can choose easy, medium, or hard homework problems. AIP Conference Proceedings, 1413 (2012), 81-84.

Appendix

Slope as Proxy for Relative Improvement

To develop a proxy measure for a student's relative improvement in the course, we fit a simple linear regression line for each student's set of weekly scores and used the slope of this line as the student's relative improvement. For example, in the 6.002X course, each student had a total of 14 possible scores (12 weeks, midterm, and final). Students who had at least 10 of the 14 scores were included in the rest of the analysis, removing only 294 students, for a total of 5768 students. The mean of the observed slopes was 0.00059 with a standard deviation of 0.054. The skew of the distribution was: 0.25 and significantly different than 0 with a p-value <0.0001.

As a test of the validity of this measure we simulated a class of students with skills equal to the observed skills in 6.002X but who demonstrated no skill change or relative improvement across the course. 6062 examinees were simulated with skill levels equal to the observed skills based on the calibration of the 197 homework items. To account for the mean-centering in the analysis of the observed data, a separate weekly skill was calculated for each student by adjusting their assigned skill by the weekly mean skill. This would simulate examinees with no improvement or decline in their skills across the 12 weeks and exams.

Using the observed item parameters for the homework and exam items, response matrices representing multiple attempts data were simulated for each student based on Samejima's graded response model. To mimic the performance patterns of the actual students, the items that were omitted for a particular student were then marked as omitted in the simulated response matrix for that student.

The analysis of the simulated response matrices followed the exact same steps as the analysis of the observed data: three calibrations (homework, midterm, and final), assign scores by week and exam, mean-center scores, remove students who were missing 5 or more of the 14 scores, find slope of simple linear regression line.

The mean of the observed slopes was 0.00030 with a standard deviation of 0.029. The skew of the distribution was: -0.01 which is not significantly different than 0 (p-value = 0.38). Based on the results of the simulation study, the students who were observed to exhibit big "improvement" or "decline" in skills relative to the other students are *not* likely due to chance. The simulated students were simulated to have no relative improvement and almost 100% of the simulees had slopes between -.1 and .1. However, 2.5% and 4% of the observed students had slopes less than -0.1 and greater than 0.1, respectively. The two distributions are shown below. To verify that a linear regression model was appropriate we also added a quadratic term. For both the simulated and observed groups, the quadratic term led to an increase in chi-squared values, rather than a reduction, for almost half of the students. This, along with visual inspection of the weekly skills, indicated that a linear model was appropriate.

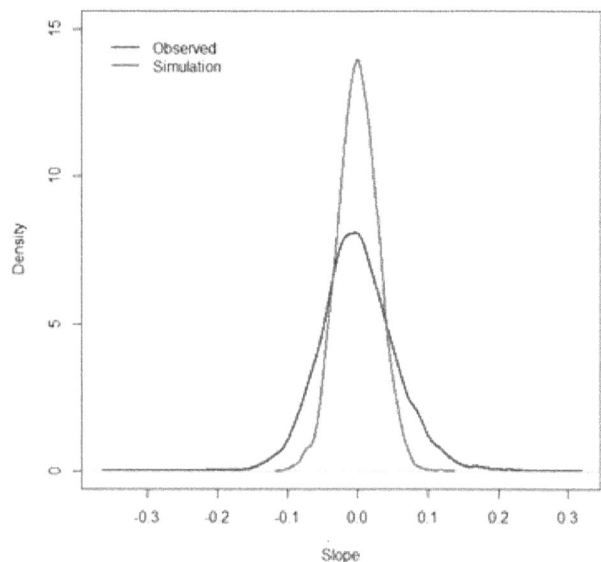

Figure 5: Slope (or Relative Improvement) for Certificate Earners

Demographic Differences in How Students Navigate Through MOOCs

Philip J. Guo
MIT CSAIL / University of Rochester
pg@cs.rochester.edu

Katharina Reinecke
University of Michigan
reinecke@umich.edu

ABSTRACT

The current generation of Massive Open Online Courses (MOOCs) attract a diverse student audience from all age groups and over 196 countries around the world. Researchers, educators, and the general public have recently become interested in how the learning experience in MOOCs differs from that in traditional courses. A major component of the learning experience is how students navigate through course content.

This paper presents an empirical study of how students navigate through MOOCs, and is, to our knowledge, the first to investigate how navigation strategies differ by demographics such as age and country of origin. We performed data analysis on the activities of 140,546 students in four edX MOOCs and found that certificate earners skip on average 22% of the course content, that they frequently employ non-linear navigation by jumping backward to earlier lecture sequences, and that older students and those from countries with lower student-teacher ratios are more comprehensive and non-linear when navigating through the course.

From these findings, we suggest design recommendations such as for MOOC platforms to develop more detailed forms of certification that incentivize students to deeply engage with the content rather than just doing the minimum necessary to earn a passing grade. Finally, to enable other researchers to reproduce and build upon our findings, we have made our data set and analysis scripts publicly available.

Author Keywords

Massive Open Online Course; MOOC; non-linear learning; navigation strategy

ACM Classification Keywords

H.5.1. Information Interfaces and Presentation (e.g. HCI): Multimedia Information Systems

INTRODUCTION

Massive Open Online Courses (MOOCs) are beginning to globalize education by enabling participation from students of all age groups and nationalities. Previous studies have shown that MOOC students come from over 196 countries, speak a wide variety of languages, have a large range of age

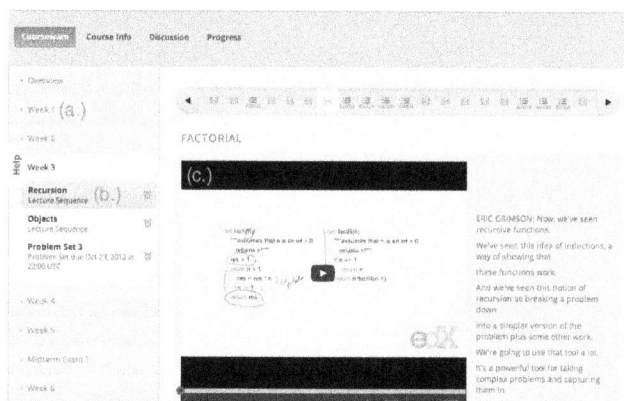

Figure 1. An online course on the edX platform has a hierarchical structure containing a series of weeks (a.), where each week contains several web pages (b.), and each page is a *learning sequence* made up of video lectures and/or assessment problems (c.).

and prior education, and highly heterogeneous motivations for enrolling in online courses [3].

This diversity challenges the homogeneous learning environments offered by the current generation of popular MOOC platforms such as Coursera, edX, and Udacity (often called xMOOCs [10]). In particular, critics have warned that MOOCs cannot cater to individual and cultural variabilities in learning style, but instead require every student to be a "self-directed autodidact" [13] in order to succeed.

This sort of self-guided learning that current MOOCs require potentially make them ill-suited for students who are less efficient at defining a learning path by themselves [18]. Researchers have found that some learners prefer either more linear or non-linear navigation [5, 17, 21], and some perform best under highly structured guidance [9, 15]. However, current MOOCs are often organized in linear ways with weekly video lectures and assessments resembling the conventional university classroom.

If students have varying needs and preferences for navigating learning content, we should be able to observe differences in how they interact with MOOCs. This paper contributes a study of students' strategies for navigating through the learning content in MOOCs, and is, to our knowledge, the first to investigate demographic differences. In particular, we hypothesized that there should be notable differences in how students navigate through the learning content depending on demographics such as age and country of origin.

Certificate earners view only 78% of learning sequences, on average; they completely skip 22% of course content.

Certificate earners engage in non-linear navigation behavior, often jumping backward to revisit earlier lectures.

Navigation backjumps from assessments to lectures are more common than lecture-to-lecture backjumps.

Older students and those from countries with lower student-teacher ratios (e.g., the US and European countries) visit and repeat more lecture sequences, which indicates more non-linear navigation and learning strategies.

Younger students and those from countries with higher student-teacher ratios (e.g., India, Kenya) visit and repeat fewer sequences, which indicates more linear navigation.

However, the effect of age is stronger than that of country; older students from countries with higher student-teacher ratios behave more like their similarly-aged counterparts in countries with lower student-teacher ratios.

Table 1. Summary of the main findings that we present in this paper.

To evaluate these hypotheses, we analyzed student interaction log data from four different MOOCs provided by edX, comprising 140,546 students from 196 countries.

Our results show that there are significant differences in how students approach the learning content. Older certificate-earning students cover more learning materials and navigate the learning content in a more non-linear way than younger students. We also found differences between countries, with students from the U.S. and many Western European countries covering and repeating more learning sequences — indicating non-linear navigation — than students from places such as India or Kenya. Finally, our results showed that independent of demographic background, the navigation behaviors of certificate-earning students are frequently motivated by opportunistically working backward from assessment questions.

This paper makes the following contributions:

- We present the first analysis of how demographics affect students' navigation behaviors in MOOCs. Table 1 summarizes our main findings.

- Based on the findings, we provide design recommendations for MOOCs to better support students in understanding learning goals and achieving higher content coverage.

- We make our anonymized dataset and all analysis scripts public (available at http://www.pgbovine.net/edX/). To our knowledge, this is one of the first open data sets on MOOC demographics and student activities.

We begin by introducing MOOC platforms and reviewing the literature on different learning styles that impact students' navigation strategies. The main part of this paper includes our study methodology, findings, as well as a discussion of the results from which we infer design implications. We close with study limitations and opportunities for future work.

BACKGROUND ON MASSIVE OPEN ONLINE COURSES

The research community is currently studying two main types of MOOCs: cMOOCs take a connectivist approach to teaching, emphasizing peer-based social learning and knowledge generation [6, 19]. xMOOCs aim to scale up traditional lecture-based courses by offering online video presentations and exams [3, 7, 10]. This paper focuses on xMOOCs.

Organizations such as Coursera, edX, and Udacity offer free xMOOCs, which comprise a linear arrangement of short video lectures and assessments that are either graded automatically or via peer grading. While xMOOCs offer discussion forums, their structure is mostly teacher-centered, with the instructor creating most of the instructional content [10]. However, xMOOCs differ from in-person courses in important ways: Students can learn at their own pace, repeat or skip lessons, and need to drive the learning process more independently than in offline learning environments.

On the edX platform, each course is divided into a series of weeks (usually 8 to 16 weeks), which are listed vertically on the left pane of the web interface (see Figure 1). Each week contains several web pages called *learning sequences*. Each learning sequence is a web page that contains either a *lecture* or a graded *assessment*. A lecture sequence is a series of instructional videos with optional interstitial quiz problems in between videos. An assessment sequence is either a weekly problem set or a midterm or final exam. Although materials are released weekly and presented in a linear and chronological structure, students are free to navigate back to already published content, even when taking an assessment.

In the remainder of this paper, we use the terms "learning sequence" or "sequence" to mean a single course web page containing learning materials.

DIFFERENCES IN ONLINE LEARNING STRATEGIES

xMOOCs have been criticized for simply replicating traditional lecture-based teaching [2] and not catering to different learning strategies, such as a student's preference for either a more or less linear structure of instructional content [20].

Differences in students' approaches to learning are often described with the help of Witkin's distinction between field-independent and field-dependent learners [24]. Field-independent learners predominantly approach the learning content in an analytic manner, focusing first on details before abstracting from a specific problem. In contrast, field-dependent learners first reason about context before focusing on details [24].

Both learning styles have been investigated in the context of online learning. Field-independent learners are believed to be fairly confident in defining their own learning paths and navigating in non-linear learning environments [9]. They are also often referred to as "explorers", indicating that they navigate more freely without necessarily following the path suggested by content creators [17]. Field-dependent learners, in contrast, prefer following an externally defined learning path, as

Course	Subject	University	All Students		Certificate Earners	
			total	with demographics	total	with demographics
6.00x	Intro. CS & Programming	MIT	65,475	50,581	5,758	4,155
PH207x	Statistics for Public Health	Harvard	31,851	28,363	4,915	4,528
CS188.1x	Artificial Intelligence	Berkeley	24,517	17,066	1,900	1,232
3.091x	Solid State Chemistry	MIT	18,703	14,152	2,072	1,575
Total			140,546	110,162	14,645	11,490

Table 2. The numbers of students and certificate earners for four edX courses in Fall 2012. The "with demographics" columns show the numbers of students in each group who filled out all demographic information (birth year, education level, and gender), which comprises ∼78% of students.

imposed by a teacher or the online learning environment [9]. Often described as "observers" [17], their preference for linear learning has also been found to result in more disorientation problems when presented with non-linear teaching materials in an online context [4]. This trait could be a reason why field-dependent learners spend more time on navigation and used sequential steps (back or forward buttons) less frequently than field-independent learners [16].

Which learning style students adopt is partly influenced by the form of education they received as children, for example in kindergarten or primary school [12]. The predominant form of educational exposure in a society depends on which instructional style that society values most, but also on its financial resources, which directly determine class sizes and therefore, the *student-teacher ratio* [23]. Researchers have found that, in countries with a higher student-teacher ratio, students are more accustomed to a teacher-centered education and behave more like "observers" than "explorers" [11].

However, researchers have also pointed out that learning styles are dynamic, so that learners might adopt new strategies when required [12] or as they grow older [8].

Given these previous findings, we hypothesize that the diversity among students participating in MOOCs will result in notable differences in their navigation strategies.

METHODOLOGY

To understand students' navigation strategies in MOOCs, and whether their approaches might depend on demographics, we performed a quantitative data analysis on the activities of 140,546 students in four online courses on the edX platform.

Data Set

Table 2 shows an overview of the data we extracted from four courses in the first edX batch offered in Fall 2012. We selected courses from all three edX affiliates at the time (MIT, Harvard, and UC Berkeley). To maximize diversity in subject matter and student population, we selected an introductory computer science course (6.00x), an advanced computer science course (CS188.1x), statistics for public health (PH207x), and solid state chemistry (3.091x). EdX launched additional courses in Spring 2013, including some humanities ones, but that data was incomplete when we began this study.

We have made an anonymized version of our data set and analysis scripts publicly available at **http://www.pgbovine. net/edX/** so that anyone can reproduce and build upon this paper's findings.

Analysis Variables

We created analysis variables for each student based on their demographics and interactions with the courseware.

Demographics

When students first register for a free edX account, they can enter optional information such as their birth year, highest level of education completed (elementary school, junior high, high school, bachelor's, master's, Ph.D), and gender. Across all four courses, 78% of students filled out all demographic information. For analyses that require demographics, we excluded students who did not fill out the relevant fields. We derived additional demographic variables for each student:

- **Age** during Fall 2012, estimated from birth year. We filter out ages that are less than 10 or greater than 80 years old.

- **Years of education** – A numerical estimate based on the student's highest level of education completed. For example, "high school" translates into 13 years of education.

- **Country of origin**, determined by looking up student IP addresses in the MaxMind GeoIP database [1]. If a student accessed the course website from IP addresses in multiple countries, then we use the country with the most accesses.

- **Student-teacher ratio** in the country of origin – For each country, we obtained the most recent primary school student-teacher ratio (total number of students divided by number of teachers) from the UNESCO Institute for Statistics [23]. This is one widely-used indicator of educational quality and level of individualized student attention. However, note that this variable is usually correlated with economic indicators such as per-capita GDP and median household income, so observed effects might not be directly due to pedagogical quality.

Motivation & Intent

For each student, we extract the following variables that indicate their motivation and intent for enrolling in MOOCs:

- **Certificate earned** – whether a student earned a *certificate of completion* or not. EdX gives out certificates to all students who earned above a passing grade – usually around 60% – set by the course instructor. Students who earn certificates all intended to engage with lectures, problem sets, and exams, and persisted through most of the course. On the other hand, students who did not earn a certificate *and* did not attempt the assessment problems might have been casual bystanders, auditors, or early dropouts [14]. Thus, certificate earned serves as a control variable for student intent. Many of our analyses only consider students who earned certificates (∼ 10% of all students), to focus on those who intended to engage seriously with the course.

- **Grade** – Students earn a grade between 0% and 100% depending on their performance on problem sets and exams. Grades indicate student knowledge and also engagement. Once a student passes the threshold for earning a certificate, higher grades indicate more self-motivation to learn, while lower grades might indicate that a student just wants to do the bare minimum to earn a certificate.

- **Coverage** – The fraction of total learning sequences (lectures, problem sets, and exams) that the student visited.

- **Discussion forum events** – The number of times a student posted to the discussion forum, divided by that student's total number of courseware access events, which controls for variability in student activity levels. Forum participation has been found to be an indicator of social engagement in MOOCs [7].

Navigation

We quantify the following kinds of non-linear navigation through the course materials:

- **Backjumps** – The number of times that this student navigated backwards from a learning sequence to another one released earlier in the term (e.g., from Lecture 6 to Lecture 4), divided by the total number of sequences visited by this student.

- **Textbook events** – The number of times that this student accessed the digital textbook associated with the course, divided by the student's total number of courseware access events. Since the textbook still resides within the edX website but lies outside the main flow of a course, we count textbook events as an instance of non-linear navigation.

Analyses

To assess whether the aforementioned analysis variables had statistically significant and independent effects on navigation-related metrics, we conducted *multiple linear regression* analyses and report their ANOVA F statistics, *p*-values, and, when applicable, the unstandardized *b* coefficients for each independent variable in the regression.

For this paper, we do not analyze fine-grained navigation within a learning sequence. We also do not use time as a feature since it is hard to determine exactly how much time a student was actively interacting with particular courseware resources solely from analyzing the server logs we were given.

FINDINGS

Here we present our findings, starting with an overview of student demographics, motivation, intent, and how each affect student navigation through the edX course materials.

Overview of Student Population

The mean student age across all four courses in our data set was 28 years (sd=9.4). Most students (77%) were between 20 and 40 years old, with 13% under 20 and 10% over 40.

The most common highest education level for students participating in these four courses was a bachelor's degree (38%),

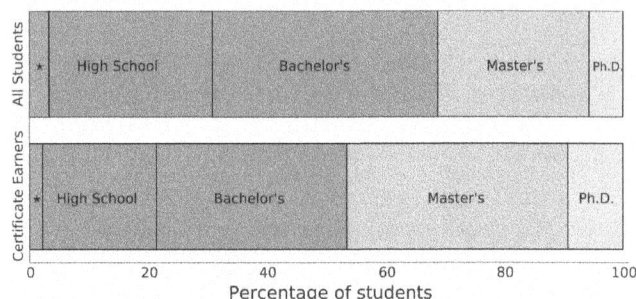

Figure 2. Distributions of self-reported education levels for all students (top) and certificate earners (bottom) in all four courses. ⋆ represents an elementary or junior high school graduate. Certificate earners tend to have more years of education than the general student population.

	6.00x	PH207x	CS188.1x	3.091x
	123 countries	133 countries	103 countries	106 countries
	U.S. (22%)	India (17%)	U.S. (19%)	U.S. (18%)
	India (9%)	U.S. (16%)	India (9%)	India (11%)
	Russia (7%)	Spain (8%)	Russia (8%)	Spain (11%)
	Spain (6%)	U.K. (5%)	Spain (8%)	U.K. (6%)
	U.K. (6%)	Germany (3%)	U.K. (6%)	Russia (5%)
	other (50%)	other (51%)	other (50%)	other (49%)

Table 3. The top five countries with the most certificate-earning students in each course, and the percentage breakdown of students from each country. The top of each column shows the total number of countries with certificate earners for each course. Note that approximately half of all certificate earners in each course came from the top five countries.

followed by a high school diploma (28%). However, students who earned a certificate most commonly held a master's degree (37%), followed by a bachelor's degree (32%). Figure 2 provides an overview of the distributions of highest education levels, showing that students with higher education levels were more likely to earn certificates.

Most students in these four courses were men, with the largest gender disparity in the two computer science courses: 86% male in CS188.1x (artificial intelligence), 83% in 6.00x (introductory computer science), 70% in 3.091x (chemistry) and 56% in PH207x (statistics for public health).

Students from all 196 countries (plus 10 additional dependent territories such as Guernsey) participated in the four courses. Students from 157 countries ended up getting certificates. Table 3 shows their breakdown by country, with the U.S. and India most highly represented. In contrast, major East Asian countries such as China, Japan, and Korea are notably underrepresented, making up only 0.1%, 0.08%, and 0.07% of the total student population (i.e., including those who did not earn certificates), respectively.

We also found that age distributions vary by country. In particular, students from countries with lower student-teacher ratios seem to participate in MOOCs later in life than students from countries with higher student-teacher ratios (i.e., larger class sizes). Spearman's correlation coefficients between a student's age and the student-teacher ratio of their home country were $r = -.25$ for 3.091x, $-.24$ for CS188.1x,

	6.00x, $R^2 = .14$		PH207x, $R^2 = .13$		CS188.1x, $R^2 = .15$		3.091x, $R^2 = .18$	
	coefficient	p-value	coefficient	p-value	coefficient	p-value	coefficient	p-value
Age	.003	< .001	.004	< .001	.001	< .001	.01	< .001
Student-teacher ratio of country	−.002	< .001	−.004	< .001	−.001	< .001	−.004	< .001
Gender (is male)	.03	< .001	.00	.14	.04	< .001	.03	.02
Grade	.31	< .001	.57	< .001	.18	< .001	.36	< .001
Constant	.53	< .001	.19	< .001	.61	< .001	.21	< .001

Table 5. Multiple linear regression analyses of student demographics and grades versus coverage for certificate earners. We excluded years of education from the analysis due to its strong collinearity with age. Across all four courses, a student's age and grade are positively correlated with coverage, while the student-teacher ratio of the student's country is negatively correlated.

	6.00x			PH207x		
	df	F	p	df	F	p
Age	1	130	< .001	1	238	< .001
Country of origin	114	4.4	< .001	128	4.5	< .001
Gender	1	23	< .001	1	1.1	.3
Years of education	1	1.3	.25	1	18	< .001

	CS188.1x			3.091x		
	df	F	p	df	F	p
Age	1	35	< .001	1	160	< .001
Country of origin	87	2.3	< .001	97	3.7	< .001
Gender	1	30	< .001	1	1.8	.18
Years of education	1	.5	.49	1	.5	.50

Table 4. Multiple linear regression analyses of student demographics versus coverage for certificate earners. We report ANOVA F statistics, degrees of freedom (df), and p-values. Age and country have statistically significant effects on coverage across all four courses, while gender and education years do not.

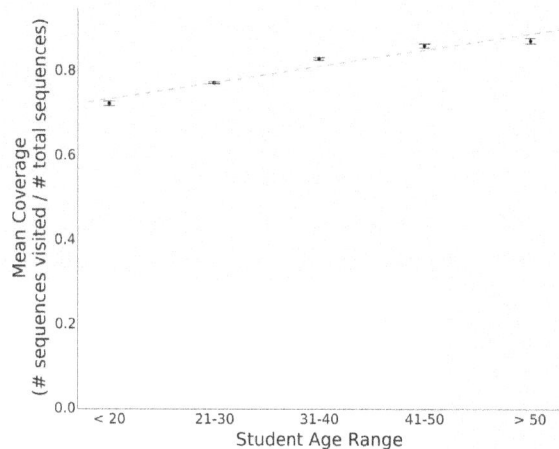

Figure 3. Age versus mean coverage for certificate-earning students in all four courses. Error bars represent the standard error of each age group's mean. The oldest group (over 50 years old) achieves, on average, 10% more coverage than the youngest group (under 20 years old).

−.22 for 6.00x, and −.08 for PH207x, all $p < .001$. For instance, the U.S. has a low student-teacher ratio of 14, and its mean student age is 33 years old (sd=12); in contrast, India has a high student-teacher ratio of 40, and its mean student age is 27 (sd=9). One possible interpretation is that people from countries with high student-teacher ratios are more likely using MOOCs to supplement their regular education, whereas those from low student-teacher ratio countries – U.S., Canada, Western Europe – are more likely to be adult lifelong learners.

Motivation & Intent

While demographics – most notably age and country – point to potential differences in students' motivations for participating in MOOCs, we also looked at the amount of learning content that certificate earners covered, what grades they received, and how much they participated in discussion forums.

Coverage

To understand students' strategies for earning certificates, we first analyzed how much of the course materials (i.e., learning sequences) certificate earners covered. Certificate-earning students viewed, on average, 67% of the learning sequences in 3.091x, 77% in PH207x, 81% in CS188.1x, and 86% in 6.00x. Thus, students ignore, on average, 22% of the materials in those courses, yet still earn certificates. While we are

not able to determine how deeply they engaged with the content that they accessed, coverage measurements at least show that a non-trivial amount of content gets completely skipped.

To evaluate the effects of demographics on coverage, we conducted multiple linear regressions with the demographic factors age, country, gender, and years of education as the independent variables and coverage as the dependent variable. We found that age and country of origin have significant effects on the fraction of sequences that certificate earners cover in all four courses (see Table 4 for a summary of the F statistics).

Age is positively correlated with coverage, even when accounting for other demographic variables (regression coefficients $b = .001 - .01$, $p < .001$ for all four courses[1]). Figure 3 visualizes how older certificate earners cover more of the learning content, with a 10% difference in coverage between the under-20 and the over-50-year-old groups. (For this figure and related figures, we binned ages into groups because the data was too sparse for certain ages.)

Table 4 also shows that a student's country of origin has a statistically significant effect on their coverage. As an example, consider the top two most represented countries: Certificate

---

[1]The unstandardized model coefficients b reported in this paper are small because dependent variables (e.g., coverage) are often between 0 and 1, so independent variables are scaled down by b.

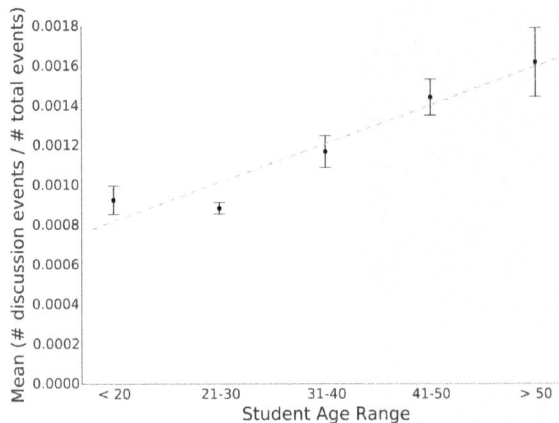

Figure 4. The mean number of normalized discussion forum posting events for all certificate-earning students in each age group. Error bars represent the standard error of each age group's mean. In general, older students post relatively more on course discussion forums.

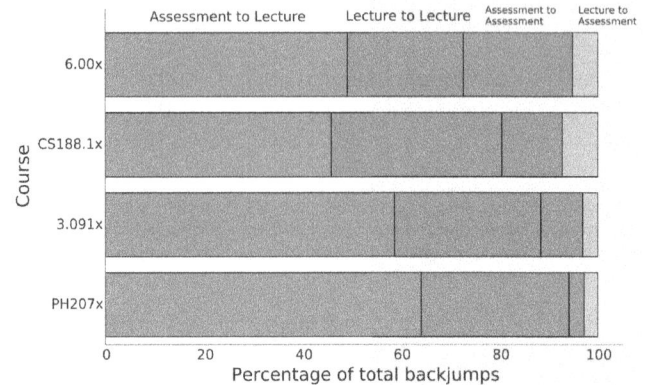

Figure 5. The frequency of each kind of backjump for certificate-earning students. The most common kind was jumping from an assessment (i.e., problem set or exam) back to an earlier lecture sequence.

earners from the U.S., on average, cover significantly more sequences (83%) than Indian certificate earners do (71%) (independent t-test, $T_{(2829)} = 20.2, p < .001$).

We followed up this finding by investigating the relationship between coverage and the student-teacher ratio of each country. We conducted a similar multiple linear regression analysis with coverage once again as the dependent variable and demographic factors and grades as independent variables. The analysis output in Table 5 shows that certificate-earning students from countries with higher student-teacher ratios usually visit fewer learning sequences.

Grades
Table 5 shows that grades are positively correlated with coverage. In all four courses, students who viewed more materials were more likely to achieve higher grades, which makes sense because they had more opportunities to learn and to get assessed (i.e., higher "time-on-task"). To investigate whether demographics also affect grades, even controlling for coverage, we conducted multiple regressions of demographics and coverage on grades. When the regression used data from all students, it showed that age and student-teacher ratio have significant effects on grades in several courses ($F_{(1)} = 47 - 404$ for age in CS188.1x, PH207x, and 6.00x, $F_{(1)} = 973 - 2402$ for student-teacher ratio in CS188.1x and 6.00x, all $p < .001$). However, the effects of age and student-teacher ratio are non-significant in three of the four courses when considering only certificate earners in the analysis; the only exception is CS188.1x, where $F_{(1)} = 11$ for age, $F_{(1)} = 36$ for student-teacher ratio, with $p < .001$. Thus, once students pass the certificate-earning bar, then grades no longer differ as much across demographics.

Discussion forum posting
An alternative measure of student motivation is how actively they participate in the course discussion forum. We conducted a multiple linear regression with normalized forum events as the dependent variable and demographics as independent variables. The analysis shows that age and

level of education had significant effects in three of the four courses, with the overall analysis $F_{(2,1572)} = 4.4$ for 3.091x, $F_{(2,4525)} = 27.4$ for PH207x, $F_{(2,4152)} = 24.6$ for 6.00x, all $p < .001$.

Figure 4 shows that older students participate more in forums. And even controlling for age (using the aforementioned regression), students with Ph.D. degrees participated up to 32% less in forums than non-Ph.D. holders. Finally, we expected students from more teacher-centered educational systems (i.e., higher student-teacher ratio) to be less likely to participate socially in MOOCs, but that turned out not to be the case. Student-teacher ratio did not have any significant effects on forum participation in our regressions, and Spearman's correlation was nearly zero ($r < .05$ for all courses, with $p > .001$).

Course Navigation Strategy
Given that all certificate earners had a common intent – to earn a passing grade – we wanted to understand how they went about doing so, and whether navigation strategies differed by demographic. Specifically, we analyzed one salient form of non-linear course navigation: a *backjump* from one learning sequence to another sequence released earlier in the term. We focused on backjumps because the ability to go "back in time" to view prior lectures or to re-try old assessments is one key differentiator of MOOCs over traditional residential courses with in-person lectures and exams.

Certificate earners in our four courses performed an average of 1.04 backjumps for every learning sequence they visited (sd=0.62). This behavior indicates that students apply non-linear navigation strategies on their way to earning certificates. In contrast, students who did not earn certificates performed only 0.3 backjumps per visited sequence (sd=0.4). Thus, certificate earners repeat visiting prior sequences three times as often, presumably to review older content.

Kinds of backjumps
Each backjump can start and end at either an assessment (i.e., problem set or exam) or a lecture. Figure 5 visualizes a per-

26

	6.00x			PH207x		
	df	F	p	df	F	p
Age	1	26	$< .001$	1	62	$< .001$
Country of origin	114	1.5	$< .001$	128	2.7	$< .001$
Gender	1	56	$< .001$	1	45	$< .001$
Years of education	1	.42	.52	1	4.7	.03

	CS188.1x			3.091x		
	df	F	p	df	F	p
Age	1	16	$< .001$	1	29	$< .001$
Country of origin	87	1.3	.02	97	2.7	$< .001$
Gender	1	4.9	.03	1	1.8	.19
Years of education	1	3.6	.06	1	3.4	.07

Table 6. Multiple linear regression analyses of student demographics versus backjumps for certificate earners. We report ANOVA F statistics, degrees of freedom (df), and p-values. Age has statistically significant effects in all four courses, country in three courses, and gender in two.

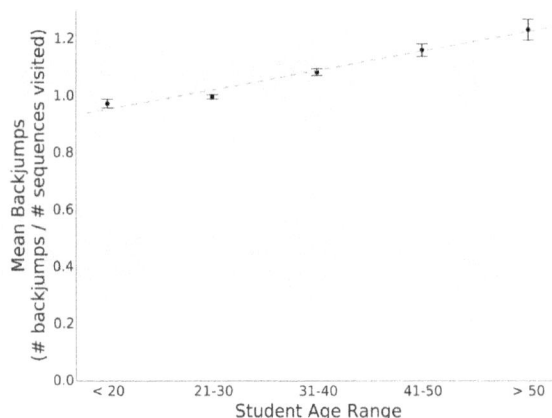

Figure 6. The mean number of backjumps per visited sequence for all certificate-earning students in each age group. Error bars represent the standard error of each age group's mean. In general, older students backjump more frequently to revisit earlier course materials.

centage breakdown of the four kinds of backjumps. Students most frequently backjump from an assessment to a lecture, which shows that they might be opportunistically looking up specific information needed to answer assessment questions. The second most prevalent kind of backjump is between two lectures, potentially when students are re-watching old lectures for more in-depth learning. Such lecture-to-lecture backjumps occur significantly less frequently (30% of total backjumps averaged across four courses) than assessment-to-lecture backjumps (54% across four courses) (independent t-test, $T_{4.6} = 5.2, p < .01$).

Figure 5 also shows that assessment-to-lecture backjumps are less prevalent in the two programming-based courses (6.00x and CS188.1x). One possible explanation is that programming assignments more often require students to apply concepts to brand-new tasks. This kind of knowledge is difficult to directly look up in earlier lectures, thus making assessment-to-lecture backjumps less helpful than in other courses. Perhaps students jumped more frequently to external Web resources (e.g., StackOverflow or programming tutorial websites) when working on those assignments, but the edX servers cannot log such external resource accesses.

Demographics and backjumps
The prevalence of backjumps also varies by age, country, and gender (see the regression analysis summary in Table 6).

Older certificate-earning students backjump more frequently. Figure 6 visualizes backjumps by age groups, aggregated over all four courses. When we investigated types of backjumps, we found that certificate earners above 40 years of age performed 5% to 12% more lecture-to-lecture backjumps than those under age 20; the differences in proportions are statistically significant for all courses except CS188.1x, using a chi-square test for equality of proportions $\chi^2(1) = 149 - 280$, $p < .001$. Also, those above 40 years old performed 2% to 11% fewer assessment-to-lecture backjumps than those under 20 years old (statistically significant over all four courses with $\chi^2(1) = 8.8 - 226$, $p < .003$). One possible interpretation is that older students more frequently review prior

lecture content and do not as frequently work backward using the assessment questions as learning goals.

A student's country of origin has a significant effect on the proportion of backjumps for three of the courses (see Table 6). To investigate further, we conducted a multiple regression to determine whether a country's student-teacher ratio partly explains the differences in backjumps. In those same three courses, student-teacher ratio had a negative correlation with backjumps, even controlling for other demographics and grades ($b = -.002$ for 6.00x, $b = -.007$ for PH207x, $b = -.01$ for 3.091x, all $p < .01$).

Figure 7 illustrates this negative correlation for the top 30 most represented countries, which comprise 83% of all certificate earners across the four courses. The top country (U.S.) had 2,809 certificate earners, while the 30th most represented one (Kenya) had 86 certificate earners. This figure shows that a higher student-teacher ratio corresponds to fewer backjumps; the effect is most pronounced for the four countries with the highest ratios. For instance, the country where students backjump most frequently is Greece, with a low student-teacher ratio of 10. Students from Greece backjump, on average, 1.21 times per visited sequence. In comparison, students from Kenya (with the highest student-teacher ratio of 47) have a significantly lower number of backjumps, with .83 times per sequence visit (independent t-test, $T_{212} = 6.0, p < .001$).

However, for older certificate earners, country of origin seems to have no bearing on backjumps. When we conducted the same regression shown in Table 6, except only considering certificate earners over 40 years old, the effects of country were non-significant over all courses ($F_{(28-74)} = 0.9 - 1.3$, depending on the course, all $p > .05$). Older students are more likely self-selected to be independent, self-directed learners, so they might not conform to the general trends of the educational systems in their home countries.

Finally, Table 6 shows a significant effect of gender on backjumps for two of the courses. In both of those courses, men

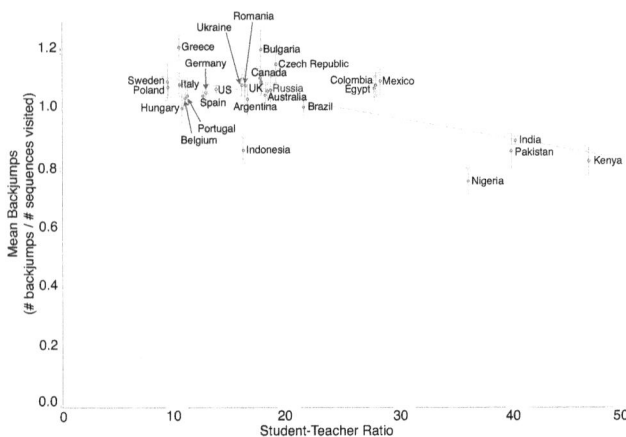

Figure 7. The mean number of backjumps per visited sequence for all certificate-earning students in the 30 countries with the most students across all four courses. Error bars represent the standard error of each country's mean. Students from countries with higher student-teacher ratios progress through the course more linearly with fewer backjumps.

performed fewer backjumps than women: In 6.00x, men averaged .97 backjumps per sequence visit, versus 1.13 for women (independent t-test, $T_{6.4} = 858, p < .001$). And in PH207x, men averaged .96 backjumps per sequence visit, versus 1.09 for women ($T_{7.0} = 4235, p < .001$).

Digital textbook usage
The results in the prior sub-section indicate that older students and those from countries with a low student-teacher ratio perform more backjumps. One possible explanation is that this behavior is emblematic of more independent learning and their preferences for non-linear navigation.

This trend is further supported by differences in the number of textbook events between demographic subgroups. Textbooks events are another type of non-linear navigation, since the digital textbook for each course is located outside of the main flow of the course materials. Again, a multiple regression analysis showed that older certificate earners access the textbook more frequently ($b = .00003 - .0001, p < .001$ for all courses). For instance, students over 40 accessed the textbook 27% more frequently than those under 40, normalizing for each student' total number of events. However, the student-teacher ratio does not have a statistically significant independent effect ($b \sim 0, p > .01$ for all courses).

DISCUSSION AND DESIGN IMPLICATIONS
While we found that most students employ non-linear navigation strategies through MOOCs, we observed differences between demographics, most notably age and country of origin. This section discusses our findings and offers some design recommendations for MOOC platform creators.

General Navigation Strategy
Our findings suggest that most students navigate through the learning content in a non-linear way. Their behavior aligns

with those that researchers have previously called "explorers" [17] in that they do not necessarily follow a given path. It also suggests that although xMOOCs seemingly impose a linear structure [9], students apply characteristics of field-independent learners by defining their own learning paths.

One of the most surprising findings for us was that certificate earners in the four edX courses on average do not visit 22% of course learning sequences. Thus, even though they passed the course, students never even saw a sizable fraction of the course content.

One likely cause for this coverage gap is "open book" assessments, which, once released on the course website, can be viewed along with the rest of the course's contents. Our analysis of students' backjumps confirms this assumption: Certificate earners access older content more often after viewing an assessment than after viewing another lecture sequence.

We have two possible explanations for this behavior: First, students might be opportunistically looking up specific information that is needed to answer the assessment questions, which suggests that their motivation is to receive a certificate rather than to advance their knowledge more generally. We saw this assumption further supported by the finding that there are fewer assessment-to-lecture backjumps in the two computer programming courses (6.00x and CS188.1x). Since programming requires applying learned concepts to novel kinds of problems, it is harder for students to find answers to assessment questions by looking at prior lectures. Second, students might be relying on assessments to provide detailed learning goals for the course. If that is the case, then instructors should emphasize learning goals more explicitly throughout the course to help students understand expectations.

These findings also show what distinguishes in-person courses from MOOCs: In conventional classrooms, students at least get exposed to most of the lecture materials. In K12, attendance is usually mandatory, and in universities, it is encouraged. In addition, even when assessments follow an "open book" style, students would likely need to attend lectures before seeing the assessment questions. In contrast, the independence provided by MOOCs means that students can opportunistically work backward from the assessments to the lectures in order to receive a minimum passing grade. The navigation strategies we observed suggest that at least some students try to minimize the effort to earn a certificate.

Design Implications:
One way to spur greater engagement is to replace the current certificates, which only indicate pass/fail, with richer ones indicating grades in combination with additional measures of engagement, such as participation in discussion forums, peer ratings, or time spent solving assessment questions. Such a reward mechanism could motivate students to cover more of the learning content, which, as we found, is positively correlated with grades.

Furthermore, we suspect that certificates from programming courses are more indicative of a student's skills. In general, assessments requiring an application of previously learned concepts to new problems, such as those necessary in programming courses, might therefore be more suitable to assess a student's understanding in MOOCs than those involving more rote forms of learning, such as recall of what was covered in lecture.

Demographic Characteristics in Navigation Strategies
We found significant differences in the navigation strategies of certificate earners depending on their demographics.

Most notably, older certificate earners cover more course materials and repeat more lecture sequences than younger students. This behavior suggests that they follow non-linear, self-defined learning paths, indicative of a field-independent learning style [22]. In comparison to younger students, they also performed more lecture-to-lecture backjumps, and fewer assessment-to-lecture backjumps, indicating that their learning is less driven by the assessment questions. The assumption that older students use more non-linear and self-motivated learning strategies is also supported by the fact that they accessed the course digital textbook – which is optional reading – more frequently than younger students.

Independent of age, we also found that certificate earners from countries with lower student-teacher ratios (e.g., the U.S. and many European countries) cover more content than those who are presumably accustomed to larger classrooms and a more teacher-centered education (e.g., India and Kenya). Students from countries with a high student-teacher ratio not only cover fewer lecture sequences, but they also proceed through the learning materials more linearly and with fewer backjumps than students from low student-teacher ratio countries. This finding confirms prior research showing that students who are used to mostly teacher-centered educational systems predominantly adhere to the learning style of "observers" [17] and field-dependents [5, 12].

We exclude language problems as a possible reason for the negative correlation between student-teacher ratio and coverage, because English is the official classroom language in several of the countries with a higher student-teacher ratio (e.g., in India, Nigeria, and Kenya after a certain age). Also, some of the countries with a lower student-teacher ratio do not have English as an official language, yet their students cover as much learning content as countries such as the U.S., the U.K., or Australia. An alternative explanation is that students in countries with higher student-teacher ratios are somehow more motivated by earning a certificate with minimal effort.

Design Implications:
The different navigation strategies between demographic groups demonstrate that MOOCs are used by students with varying motivations and needs. We believe that MOOC platforms need to be more flexibly engineered to cater to different learning strategies. In particular, younger students and those from countries with higher student-teacher ratios should receive more explicit learning goals to ensure that they know what is expected from them.

For instance, a progress bar highlighting the most important parts of the course could provide more guidance and reduce the independence required to know what needs to be learned. We can also imagine creating motivational mechanisms to

encourage learners to cover more sequences, such as social comparisons (e.g., "other learners usually spent 45 minutes on this sequence"), or counting coverage and other engagement measures toward the final grade.

LIMITATIONS AND FUTURE WORK
A central limitation of this study is that by just analyzing log data, we cannot directly measure students' true motivations, engagement, intent for enrolling in a MOOC, or their knowledge gained after passing the course. Coverage of learning sequences, as well as data on their certificates and grades, therefore served as proxies in our analyses. A more controlled study, perhaps in a blended learning classroom setting, could reveal finer-grained insights in the future.

Also, the population of students from each country who participated in the first edX batch in Fall 2012, and the current generation of MOOCs in general, are probably not representative of the overall population. Specifically, they are likely to be more technology-savvy and English literate, since our corpus consists of math and science courses taught in English. For future studies, it would be desirable to gather more information about students' demographic backgrounds, in combination with knowledge about their intent for enrolling.

Finally, while we were only able to speculate about the reasons for students' navigation strategies, it would be especially interesting to conduct qualitative follow-ups with various demographic groups. This could shed more light on how much students are strategizing or whether a large portion of their behavior is due to a lack of understanding or motivation. We would like to see our results compared to such future studies.

CONCLUSION
The current generation of Massive Open Online Courses such as those provided by edX (so-called xMOOCs) are usually perceived as enforcing a linear, top-down, instructor-provided structure. The findings in this paper showed that despite the linear structure imposed on students – a chronological ordering of weeks and learning sequences – learners predominantly navigate through xMOOCs in a non-linear way. Analyzing the student log data from 140,546 students who participated in four edX MOOCs, we found that, on average, students skip 22% of the learning sequences entirely and perform a high number of backjumps, most often jumping from assessments back to earlier lectures.

While students tend to ignore the linear structure of xMOOCs, younger students and those from countries with higher student-teacher ratios (e.g., India, Kenya, Pakistan) follow the teacher-provided outline more strictly. Independent of demographic background, though, students use assessment questions as an informal guide for what learning content needs to be covered.

Based on these results, we proposed several design ideas that might motivate students to cover more content. Specifically, MOOCs' reliance on binary pass/fail certificates is detrimental to students' motivations for in-depth learning. If certificates listed grades and richer measures of participation and engagement, we believe they would be more indicative of a student's true knowledge of the course topic.

The results of this paper support the view that MOOCs do not (yet) supersede traditional universities. We especially believe that more work needs to be done to cater to students' different needs and motivations, and to investigate mechanisms that ensure a more in-depth engagement with learning materials.

ACKNOWLEDGMENTS
Thanks to Rob Rubin and Anant Agarwal at edX for enabling this research, Olga Stroilova for helping with data collection, Quanta Computer for funding Philip's postdoc at MIT, and Krzysztof Gajos for his helpful feedback.

REFERENCES
1. MaxMind GeoIP databases and web services. `http://www.maxmind.com/en/geolocation_landing`.

2. Bates, T. What's Right and What's Wrong About Coursera-style MOOCs?, 2012. Blog entry retrieved from `http://www.tonybates.ca/2012/08/05/whats-right-and-whats-wrong-about-coursera-\style-moocs/`.

3. Breslow, L., Pritchard, D. E., DeBoer, J., Stump, G. S., Ho, A. D., and Seaton, D. T. Studying Learning in the Worldwide Classroom: Research into edX's First MOOC. *Research and Practice in Assessment 8* (2013).

4. Chen, S. Y., and Ford, N. J. Modelling User Navigation Behaviours in a Hypermedia-based Learning System : An Individual Differences Approach. *Knowledge organization 25*, 3 (1998), 67–78.

5. Cheng, Y. W., Sudweeks, F., Cheng, Y. W., and Sudweeks, F. A Longitudinal Study on the Effect of Hypermedia on Learning Dimensions, Culture and Teaching Evaluation. In *Proc. Cultural Attitudes Towards Technology and Communication* (2012), 146–162.

6. Clarà, M., and Barberà, E. Learning Online: Massive Open Online Courses (MOOCs), Connectivism, and Cultural Psychology. *Distance Education 34*, 1 (2013), 129–136.

7. Coetzee, D., Fox, A., Hearst, M. A., and Hartmann, B. Should Your MOOC Forum Use a Reputation System? In *Proc. CSCW'14*, ACM (2014).

8. E. Truluck, Bradley C. Courtenay, J. Learning Style Preferences Among Older Adults. *Educational Gerontology 25*, 3 (1999), 221–236.

9. Ford, N., and Chen, S. Y. Matching/Mismatching Revisited: An Empirical Study of Learning and Teaching Styles. *British Journal of Educational Technology 32*, 1 (2001), 5–22.

10. Grünewald, F., Meinel, C., Totschnig, M., and Willems, C. Designing MOOCs for the Support of Multiple Learning Styles. In *Scaling up Learning for Sustained Impact*. Springer, 2013, 371–382.

11. Hofstede, G. Cultural Differences in Teaching and Learning. *International Journal of Intercultural Relations 10* (1986), 301–320.

12. Kennedy, P. Learning Cultures and Learning Styles: Myth-understandings about Adult (Hong Kong) Chinese Learners. *International Journal of Lifelong Education 21*, 5 (2002), 430–445.

13. Kizilcec, R. F. Collaborative Learning in Geographically Distributed and In-person Groups. In *AIED 2013 Workshop on Massive Open Online Courses* (2013).

14. Kizilcec, R. F., Piech, C., and Schneider, E. Deconstructing Disengagement: Analyzing Learner Subpopulations in Massive Open Online Courses. In *Proc. Learning Analytics and Knowledge*, ACM (2013), 170–179.

15. Lee, C., Sudweeks, F., and Cheng, Y. The Role of Unit Evaluation, Learning and Culture Dimensions Related to Students Cognitive Style in Hypermedia Learning. In *Proc. Cultural Attitudes Towards Communication and Technology* (2010).

16. Lee, M. W., Y., C. S., Chrysostomou, K., and Liu, X. Mining Students' Behavior in Web-based Learning Programs. *Expert Systems with Applications 36*, 2 (2009), 3459–3464.

17. Liegle, J. O., and Janicki, T. N. The Effect of Learning Styles on the Navigation Needs of Web-based Learners. *Computers in Human Behavior 22*, 5 (2006), 885–898.

18. McLoughlin, C. E. The Pedagogy of Personalised Learning: Exemplars, MOOCS and Related Learning Theories. In *Proc. EdMedia* (2013).

19. Milligan, C., Littlejohn, A., and Margaryan, A. Patterns of Engagement in Connectivist MOOCs. *MERLOT Journal of Online Learning and Teaching 9*, 2 (2013).

20. Naidu, S. Learning About Learning and Teaching Online. *Distance Education 34*, 1 (2013), 1–3.

21. Pask, G. Styles and Strategies of Learning. *British Journal of Educational Psychology 46*, 2 (1976), 128–148.

22. Reed, W., and Oughton, J. Computer Experience and Interval-based Hypermedia Navigation. *Journal of Research on Computing in Education 30* (1997), 38–52.

23. UNESCO Institute for Statistics. Pupil-teacher ratio, primary. `http://data.worldbank.org/indicator/SE.PRM.ENRL.TC.ZS`.

24. Witkin, H. A., Moore, C. A., and Goodenough, D. R. Field-Dependent and Field-Independent Cognitive Styles and Their Educational Implications. *Review of Educational Research 47*, 1 (1977).

Understanding In-Video Dropouts and Interaction Peaks in Online Lecture Videos

Juho Kim[1] **Philip J. Guo**[2] **Daniel T. Seaton**[3] **Piotr Mitros**[4] **Krzysztof Z. Gajos**[5] **Robert C. Miller**[1]

[1]MIT CSAIL   [2]University of Rochester   [3]Office of Digital Learning, MIT
{juhokim, rcm}@mit.edu   pg@cs.rochester.edu   dseaton@mit.edu

[4]edX   [5]Harvard SEAS
pmitros@edx.org   kgajos@eecs.harvard.edu

ABSTRACT

With thousands of learners watching the same online lecture videos, analyzing video watching patterns provides a unique opportunity to understand how students learn with videos. This paper reports a large-scale analysis of in-video dropout and peaks in viewership and student activity, using second-by-second user interaction data from 862 videos in four Massive Open Online Courses (MOOCs) on edX. We find higher dropout rates in longer videos, re-watching sessions (vs first-time), and tutorials (vs lectures). Peaks in re-watching sessions and play events indicate points of interest and confusion. Results show that tutorials (vs lectures) and re-watching sessions (vs first-time) lead to more frequent and sharper peaks. In attempting to reason why peaks occur by sampling 80 videos, we observe that 61% of the peaks accompany visual transitions in the video, e.g., a slide view to a classroom view. Based on this observation, we identify five student activity patterns that can explain peaks: starting from the beginning of a new material, returning to missed content, following a tutorial step, replaying a brief segment, and repeating a non-visual explanation. Our analysis has design implications for video authoring, editing, and interface design, providing a richer understanding of video learning on MOOCs.

Author Keywords

Video analysis; in-video dropout; interaction peaks; online education; MOOC; peak detection.

ACM Classification Keywords

H.5.1. Information Interfaces and Presentation (e.g. HCI): Multimedia Information Systems: Video

INTRODUCTION

MOOCs often include hundreds of pre-recorded video clips. Recent research on the first edX course, 6.002x, has shown that learners spend a majority of their time watching videos [2, 23], but little research has been aimed at the click-level interactions within MOOC videos. With thousands of learners watching the same online lecture videos, video analytics can provide a unique opportunity in understanding how learners use video content and what affects their learning experience.

This paper analyzes click-level interactions resulting from student activities within individual MOOC videos, namely playing, pausing, replaying, and quitting. We analyze video player interaction logs from four MOOCs offered on the edX platform to identify temporal interaction patterns at the second-by-second level. Specific focus is given to 1) in-video dropout rates and 2) peaks associated with re-watching sessions and play events.

Video dropout, i.e., navigating away from a video before completion, is a measure of engagement. With more engaging videos students might stay until later in the video, resulting in lower dropout. Instructors using videos in their pedagogy need to know what aspects of their videos are the most engaging or most widely viewed. While existing analytics tools provide access to this data, they do not consider different video kinds (lecture or tutorial) and presentation styles (slides, head shot, etc.) specific to the educational context.

When a significant number of students interact with a common portion of a video, the resultant data can be binned to highlight *peaks* in the video timeline. **Peaks in viewership and student activity** can precisely indicate points of interest for instructors and students. These spikes, hereinafter referred to as interaction peaks, can indicate student confusion, introduction of important concepts, engaging demonstrations, or video production glitches. We manually inspected 80 videos from our set to understand why these peaks occur. One notable observation we made is that the peaks often coincide with visual transitions in a video, such as switching from a slide to a classroom view, or from handwritten notes to a software screencast. Combining the interaction data with visual content analysis, we identified five student activity types that can lead to a peak.

This paper makes the following contributions:

- A first MOOC-scale in-video dropout rate analysis, finding higher dropout rates in longer videos, re-watching students (vs first-time watchers), and tutorials (vs lectures).

- A first MOOC-scale in-video interaction peak analysis, finding more frequent and sharper peaks in re-watching students (vs first-time watchers) and tutorials (vs lectures).

- Categorization of student activities responsible for a peak: starting from the beginning of a new material, returning to missed content, following a tutorial step, replaying a brief segment, and repeating a non-visual explanation.

- Data-driven design implications for video authoring, editing, and interface design in the context of MOOCs that reflect the temporal interaction patterns of students.

In the remainder of the paper, we discuss related work and our analytical measures and methods. We then report results from the in-video dropout and interaction peak analysis, and introduce five activity categories that might be a cause of a peak. We present design implications for better video learning experiences, and conclude with limitations and future work.

RELATED WORK

Existing research on video engagement analysis has involved three general methods: implicit user data (interaction log), explicit user data (clicking the "important" button, voting), and content analysis (visual, speech, or transcript analysis).

First, implicit user data has the benefit of requiring no additional action on user's part, because this data is automatically captured by the system while users naturally interact with videos. Shaw and Davis advocate using actual viewership data in modeling user interest [24]. Existing systems leverage scrubbing [29], zooming and panning [3], and playing and pausing [4] activities. SocialSkip [4] demonstrates that modeling users' video interactions can accurately capture user interest in information retrieval tasks. While our work adopts the idea of using video clickstream data from the literature, our analysis differs in that it uses large-scale interaction data from MOOCs, and that it focuses on in-video dropout and interaction peaks in the educational context.

Secondly, explicit user data can be collected by asking users to make a specific action around their points of interest. Previous research used user rating data [20] or annotations [24]. CLAS [21] is a lecture video annotation tool where students click a button when they find a part of the video important. The system aggregates responses from all students in a class to visualize important points. Deploying CLAS-like systems at MOOC-scale will provide useful complementary data to implicit user logs.

Content-based video analysis [25] has long been an active research area. Previous research uses image analysis and computer vision to extract keyframes [8], shot boundaries [18], or visual saliency [11]. We add a simple pixel difference metric to our analysis, and plan to incorporate more advanced techniques in future work. In summary, to the best of our knowledge, this work is a first MOOC-scale analysis for videos that combines interaction data and content-based analysis.

Tools for temporal pattern analysis

Understanding temporal patterns in large-scale video data requires powerful computational and visual tools. We present existing research and systems for each.

Temporal pattern analysis of time-series data inspired the analytical methods used in this work. Kleinberg [16] introduced a burst model for detecting meaningful structure in documents, and Jones and Diaz [12] applied this model among other temporal features to identify temporal patterns in search queries. Using search query and social media streams, researchers categorized search query patterns and trending events based on the shape of spikes [17, 13]. This paper applies similar techniques to analyze video interaction patterns, which is enabled by large-scale student data collected from MOOCs.

Video analytics platforms can enable the visual sensemaking of large-scale data. General purpose video platforms such as Youtube provide advanced analytics [9, 28] for content authors. These services include dashboards showing viewership graphs over time for a video, and suggest focusing on rises and dips. Our analysis considers more in-depth activity data such as play, pause, and skip events on the player, and content specific to educational videos, such as video kinds (lecture or tutorial), presentation styles (slide, head shot, etc.), and visual transitions between the presentation styles.

VIDEO INTERACTION DATASET

Our dataset consists of interaction logs from the edX video player over four courses offered in Fall 2012. Each log entry contains user name, time of access, video ID, event type, and internal video time, as documented in [7]. A play event is created when the user clicks the play button on the player or scrubs the playhead to a new position while the video is playing. A pause event is created when the user clicks the pause button or scrubs the playhead to a new position when the video is paused.

Table 1 summarizes information on the four courses and their videos. We chose the courses offered at roughly the same time to minimize the effect of changes in the edX platform, logging method, and student population. They span different institutions, subject fields (computer science, statistics, or chemistry), and recording styles. One of the authors manually labeled video types and presentation styles for all the videos in the video set. Video types represent a pedagogical purpose of a video, including introduction, tutorial, or lecture. Presentation styles represent the visual format of instruction: Powerpoint-style slide, code editor, head shot, classroom recording, and handwritten tablet annotations similar to those used in Khan Academy videos.

Data Processing Pipeline

Our data processing pipeline first reconstructs the watching history of each viewer and then aggregates the per-viewer history data to produce activity statistics for each second-long segment of the video. Specifically, the first step converts raw interaction log entries into watching segments. A watching segment keeps track of all continuous chunks of a clip watched by a user. It includes start and end time for every

Course	Subject	University	Students	Videos	Video Length	Processed Events
6.00x	Intro. CS & Programming	MIT	59,126	141	7:40	4,491,648
PH207x	Statistics for Public Health	Harvard	30,742	301	10:48	15,832,069
CS188.1x	Artificial Intelligence	Berkeley	22,690	149	4:45	14,174,203
3.091x	Solid State Chemistry	MIT	15,281	271	6:19	4,821,837
Total			**127,839**	**862**	**7:46**	**39,319,757**

Table 1. Overview of the four edX courses in our dataset offered in Fall 2012. "Students" refers to the number of students who watched at least one video, "Videos" is the number of all video clips posted, "Video Length" is the mean duration, and "Processed Events" is the number of total play and pause events captured by the video player.

watched segment. The second step uses the segment information to create second-by-second counts of viewers, unique viewers, re-watching sessions, play events, and pause events. Re-watching sessions only consider a student watching a segment of a video twice or more. Play and pause events increment a bin count if the event is triggered within that bin. Finally, such information can be queried upon request for statistical analysis and further processing.

The data processing module was implemented using Insights, the open source learning analytics library [6], which supports streaming events over SOA (Service-Oriented Architecture) as well as handling requests for query and view. It also uses Python, MongoDB, and the d3 visualization library [1].

ANALYSIS 1. IN-VIDEO DROPOUT
A dropout rate is defined by the percentage of students who start watching a video but leave before the video finished playing entirely. The dropout rate can reveal the factors that affect students to leave a video, helping video authors to consider them. Also, comparing this rate between videos can illustrate the relative difference in engagement. This analysis could provide valuable feedback to content creators whose courses are rapidly moving toward flipped environments where content consumption occurs online. To our knowledge, no previous work has studied the dropout rates within individual MOOC videos.

Method
For a video of length n seconds, let *viewcount(t)* denote the number of unique viewing sessions that include this second for each video. We compute the dropout rate of all videos in our set as: *1.0 - viewcount(n) / viewcount(0)*. Note that all edX videos automatically start playing once the page is open, which might affect the results.

Results
On average across all videos, about 55.2% of viewing sessions (std=14.7) were dropouts before the end. Out of the 55.2% that dropped out, 36.6% (std=11.1) occurred within the first 3% of the video length. This means that 18.6% of the dropouts occur during the rest of the length. It is notable that the dropout rate changes quite dramatically at the beginning of a video.

Why do so many students leave the video very early on? The student might have left the video shortly after it (auto-)started, or the auto-play feature in the edX video player inadvertently started a video. Misleading video titles or course navigation

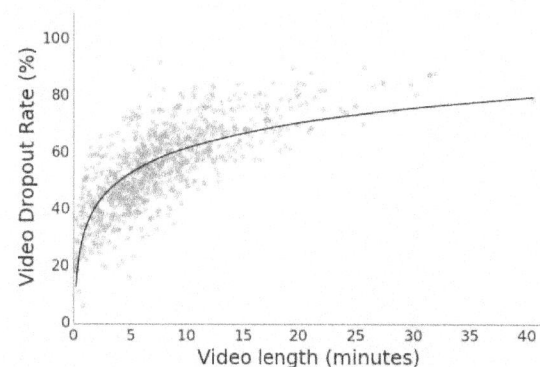

Figure 1. Longer videos exhibit higher dropout rates. Our linear regression model uses the log-transformed video length (x-axis) to predict the dropout rate (y-axis). The model fits the data well with r=0.55 with 95% CI = [0.50, 0.59].

interfaces might be another reason. A tip for content owners on YouTube analytics [9] states that viewers leaving before 5-10 seconds probably means the video keyword or title might not accurately represent the content. Additional analysis looking at the common page navigation paths of these early-dropping students might reveal issues with the video title or course navigation structure.

The dropout rate increases with video length (Figure 1). Linear regression shows that the logarithmic value of the video length significantly predicted the dropout rate (b = 0.13, t(848) = 32.22, p <001). The overall model with the logarithmic value of the video length also predicted the dropout rate very well (adjusted R^2 = 0.55, F(1, 848) = 1038, p <0.001). This suggests that for a five-minute video, the predicted dropout is 53% (35% in the first 3%), whereas for a 20-minute video the rate goes up to 71% (47% in the first 3%). With longer videos, students might feel bored due to a short attention span or experience more interruption.

A recent analysis of edX data [10] shows that learner engagement drops significantly if the video length is longer than 6 minutes. Their analysis differs from ours in that they use viewing session length as engagement, as opposed to second-by-second dropout rates. Our analysis can provide additional evidence to the finding that shorter videos are more engaging because more students would drop out.

Another factor that might affect the dropout rate is whether the student watches the video for the first time. Students that are re-watching a video might have more specific information

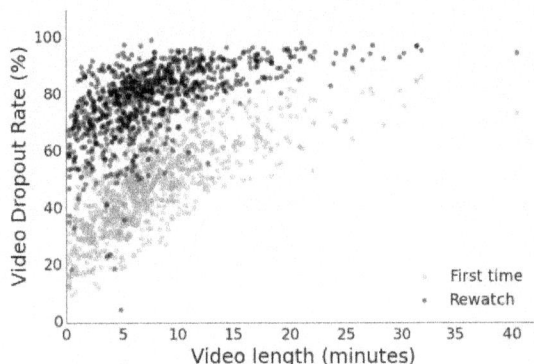

Figure 2. Re-watching students tend to drop out more, which might mean that re-watching students watch videos more selectively with a more specific need.

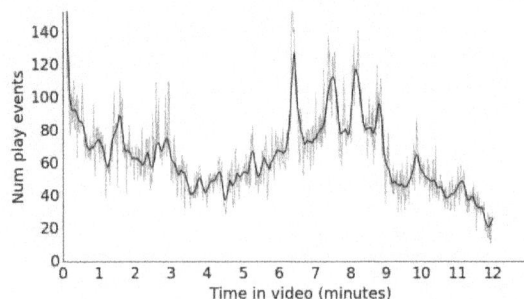

Figure 3. Even after aggregating data into bins of one second, the data is noisy (green curve). Kernel-based smoothing reduces noise in the data and helps salient patterns stand out (black curve).

needs and selectively watch a video. Our analysis verifies this assumption as can be seen in Figure 2: the dropout rate of re-watchers (78.6%, std=54.0) was much higher than that of first-time watchers (48.6%, std=34.0). A Mann-Whitney's U test shows a significant effect ($Z = -30.7$, $p < 0.001$, $r = 0.74$).

Finally, we look at how video production types affect the dropout rate by comparing lecture videos and tutorial videos. Tutorial videos showed higher dropout rate (61.3%, std=38.3) than lecture videos (54.1%, std=36.3). A Mann-Whitney's U test shows a significant effect ($Z = -5.29$, $p < 0.001$, $r = 0.18$). One explanation is that lecture videos contain first-time introductions to concepts and sequential flow, whereas tutorial videos contain step-by-step instructions students can selectively review and follow along. The mean video length was not significantly different between the two video types ($p > 0.05$), limiting the effect of video length in the result.

ANALYSIS 2. INTERACTION PEAKS

In addition to staying in a video or leaving, students also actively play, pause, or skip the video to learn at their own pace. Uncovering meaningful patterns from these natural learning activities can provide an in-depth look at video learning on MOOCs. The temporal profiles of such patterns reveal time-specific interest, which might indicate student confusion, pacing issues in the video, useful information presented visually, or important concepts. Course instructors can refer to such information to attend to specific parts of a video. Comparing peak profiles between pedagogically different videos (lecture vs tutorial) can reveal the difference in students' consumption patterns, while comparison between watching contexts (first-time vs re-watching) might highlight different purposes in watching videos.

We investigate **temporal peaks** in the number of interaction events in particular, where a significantly large number of students show similar interaction patterns during a short time window. We use the following two peak definitions.

- A **re-watching session peak** is a sudden spike in the number of re-watching sessions during a period inside a video. We exclude first-time sessions because they tend to be more sequential. We instead focus on non-sequential, random access activities. Note that this measure is not per unique student. A student repeatedly watching a part of a video five times adds five to our measure.

- A **play event peak** is a sudden spike in the number of play events on the player. These events occur when a student clicks the play button or scrubs the playhead to a new position. We ignore autoplay events at the beginning of a video because they do not represent student-initiated activity.

Method

Raw watching session and interaction data are noisy (green curve in Figure 3). Identifying peaks in such noisy data both manually and automatically becomes difficult due to local maxima and false peaks. Following the bin-summarize-smooth framework [27], we first bin the data into one-second segments, which simplifies the computation and visualization. We then count all points in each bin to represent an aggregate number of events in a bin. To fight the noise and excessive variance in data and compensate for lost statistical power, we then apply smoothing to the binned and aggregated data (black curve in Figure 3). The smoothing technique we use is lowess (locally weighted scatterplot smoothing) [5], with the smoothing parameter of 0.02 after testing various values. A kernel smoother such as lowess is simple and efficient, works well with binned data [26], and is computationally tractable.

After smoothing, we apply a peak detection algorithm to both re-watching session counts and play event counts. The algorithm we use is a variant of the TwitInfo [19] algorithm. It uses a weighted moving average and variance to detect unusually large number of events in time-series data, which applies well to the video context. We tested with different parameters in the algorithm to fit the time scale of our analysis, which is much shorter (the order of seconds and minutes) than what TwitInfo dealt with (hours and days).

One reason for using both replay and play counts is that they might capture different behaviors. We observe that video content includes both a time-specific event (e.g., a visual transition from a talking head to a slide) and a coherent segment that spans a longer period of time (e.g., a two-minute long explanation of a theorem). Play events capture a more precise

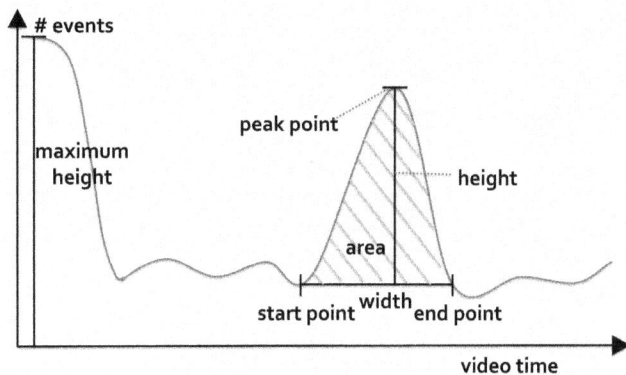

Figure 4. The location of a peak is determined by three time points (start, peak, and end). Width, height, and area determine the shape, sharpness, and intensity of the peak.

timing of an event in a video, generally resulting in sharper, spiky peaks. They respond better to student activities at one-second granularity. Re-watching session counts tend to capture segments that occur over a longer period of time better, generally resulting in smoother, wider peaks.

When a re-watching session peak and a play event peak overlap, we note that they point to a single event. When two peak windows overlap, we pick the replay peak because replay counts are always higher than play counts, possibly resulting in more informed peaks.

The features of a peak, such as width, height, and area, can indicate the strength of students' collective, time-specific interest. We compare these features between video types and student contexts. Previous work considered similar constructs in modeling temporal profiles of search queries [12]. A peak is characterized by descriptive properties as shown in Figure 4. It includes both start and end time markers, which determine the width or time duration of a peak. The peak point is the highest point between the [start, end] range, which determines the height. Finally, the area under a peak is the sum of event counts during the peak time window, which denotes the relative significance of a peak against the entire video. Multiple peaks of differing profiles might appear within a video clip. In reporting height, width, and area, we normalize the values by scaling between 0 and 1 to address high variability in event counts and durations across videos. For width, height, and area, we take a normalized range against the video duration, the maximum number of events, and the sum of all event counts, respectively.

Peak Profile Comparison

We now explore peak profiles for different video styles and watching behaviors. Overall, the mean number of peaks in a video was 3.7 (std=2.1). Of those, 2.2 (std=1.8) were replay peaks, and 2.3 (std=1.5) of them were play event peaks, which includes 0.8 duplicate peaks per video (i.e., play and replay peaks were overlapping). Considering that a mean video length was 7.8 minutes, a peak is detected roughly every two minutes in a video. Some videos exhibited as many as 11 peaks, while others did not show a notable peak. Table 2 summarizes the results in this section.

The mean width of a peak was 2.7% (std=3.5), and the median width was 9 seconds. This means that peaks in our analysis generally spanned less than 10 seconds including the rise and fall, which can point to highly time-specific events in a video. In the next section we attempt to explain what kind of events might be responsible for a peak.

The mean of normalized peak height was 7.7% (std=10.4) of the maximum height. This indicates that most peaks were quite small when compared against the maximum value of the measure. For play events, the maximum height was autoplay events at the beginning of the video, which gives a practical, comparative measure of the intensity of a peak. For example, if 10,000 students watched a lecture video and a peak had a height of 50%, this indicates that 5,000 more play button clicks were made within the peak range than in the time span just before and after the peak.

Finally, the mean of normalized peak area was 4.1% (std=4.5). This value maps to the activity dominance of a peak. A dominant single peak for a video might indicate that the peak was the single most important point of interest in the video. Conversely, a video with more peaks leaves relatively smaller area for individual peaks.

lectures vs tutorials

Tutorial videos generated stronger and more numerous peaks than lecture videos. The mean number of peaks in tutorial videos was 4.1 (std=1.9), compared to 3.6 (std=2.0) in lecture videos. A Mann-Whitney's U test shows a significant effect ($Z = -2.6$, $p < 0.01$, $r = 0.09$). Furthermore, peaks in tutorial videos were wider in width ($Z = -3.1$, $p < 0.001$, $r = 0.06$), taller in height ($Z = -7.5$, $p < 0.001$, $r = 0.13$), and larger in area ($Z = -5.5$, $p < 0.001$, $r = 0.10$) than those in lectures. Where does this difference come from?

Tutorial videos generally contain step-by-step instructions about solving a problem or using a tool. Many students follow along instructions from a tutorial at their own pace, and peaks normally occur at the step boundary. For example, a statistics course included a tutorial video on running a t-test using a statistics software package. In many cases, peaks occurred when the instructor issued commands in the tool or explained a key step in the solution, which might indicate that students re-watched these steps to make sure they follow the steps correctly. On the other hand, lecture videos are less segmented in structure with more continuous flows. Our observations show that peaks in lecture videos often relate to visual transitions in the video, such as from a slide to a talking head, or explanations of important concepts, such as introducing a theorem. While these points of interest in lecture videos attract many students to re-watch, the interaction peaks are not as sharp as in tutorial videos.

first-timers vs re-watchers

Re-watching sessions generated stronger and more numerous peaks than first-time sessions. The mean number of peaks in re-watching sessions was 2.2 (std=1.7), whereas the mean was only 1.0 (std=1.3) in first-time sessions. A Mann-Whitney's U test shows a significant effect ($Z = -14.7$, $p < 0.001$, $r = 0.35$). Furthermore, re-watching session peaks

Video Group	All	Lecture	Tutorial	First timers	Re-watchers
Peaks per Video	3.7	3.6	4.1	2.2	1.0
Normalized Height	7.7%	7.1%	10.2%	1.5%	3.1%
Normalized Width	2.7%	2.6%	3.1%	3.2%	3.7%
Normalized Area	4.1%	3.9%	4.8%	4.1%	4.7%

Table 2. Peak profile comparison reporting average values across all peaks detected for each video group. Tutorial videos resulted in more peaks than lecture videos. Likewise, re-watching sessions resulted in more peaks than first-time sessions. All differences between lecture and tutorial, and first time and re-watcing were statistically significant.

Peak Category	All	Lec.	Tut.
Type 1. beginning of new material	25%	30%	12%
Type 2. returning to content	23%	25%	15%
Type 3. tutorial step	7%	0%	30%
Type 4. replaying a segment	6%	7%	1%
Type 5. non-visual explanation	39%	38%	42%
Number of videos	80	61	19
Peaks per video	3.6	3.6	3.5

Table 3. Five student activity types that lead to a peak are shown, along with their frequency distribution as manually labeled by the authors. We sampled 80 videos and labeled each peak to one of the activity types. Only Type 5 does not involve a visual transition.

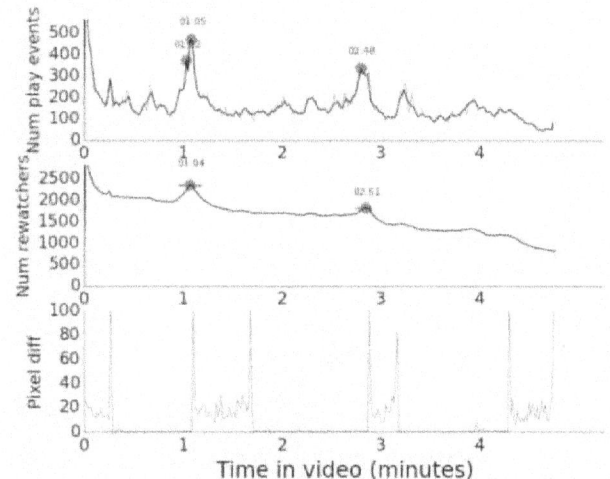

Figure 5. We visualize three streams of data to analyze interaction peaks in MOOC videos. The top graph shows play events, the middle graph shows re-watching sessions, and the bottom graph shows pixel differences over time. Detected peaks are marked with a gray point. In this example, the detected peaks coincide with a spike in pixel differences, which indicate a visual transition in video.

were wider in width (Z = -3.9, p <0.001, r = 0.07), taller in height (Z = -23.8, p <0.001, r = 0.45), and larger in area (Z = -2.9, p <0.001, r = 0.05) than first-time ones.

First-time watchers might watch videos more sequentially, because they want to master the material by watching through the lecture before diving deeper into specific parts. When re-watching, students tend to watch videos more selectively. It is notable that differences in peak height show a much higher effect size than differences in width and area. This suggests that students selectively pick parts to re-watch rather than watch through sequentially.

ANALYSIS 3. FIVE CAUSES FOR PEAKS

The peak profile analysis explains what peaks look like and how frequently they occur in different videos, but it does not reveal *why* they occur. We introduce a categorization of student activities surrounding a peak, by combining the peak profile analysis with visual content analysis. While our categorization is not conclusive, it provides an explanation of which semantic and contextual aspects of video might be responsible for a peak. This analysis suggests that no one reason can explain all peaks, and that video instructors should respond to each peak differently.

Our informal observations suggest that **visual transitions** in the video are often associated with a peak. A visual transition is a change between presentation styles shown in a video. Presentation styles in our video set are slide, code, talking head, classroom view, studio view, Khan-style tablet, and demo videos. Example transitions include changes from a slide to a talking head, a code editor to a demo video, a lecture podium view to a slide, etc. These transitions are often added at the production stage by video engineers, who mostly rely on their experiences to determine transition points. Our definition of visual transitions does not include incremental changes within a single style, e.g., an instructor typing in a

new line of code in the code editor, adding an underline to highlight text, and walking a few steps in a classroom view.

Method

To explore the connection between visual transitions and interaction peaks, we apply a visual analysis technique to complement the log analysis. We use an image similarity metric that computes pixel differences between two adjacent frames to quantify the amount of visual changes in the video. Our pipeline first samples a video frame every second, computes the image similarity using the standard technique, Manhattan distance, and finally stores the pixel distance value. We visualize this data to aid the following categorization process.

We sampled 80 videos out of 862 (9.3%) while keeping the balance between video lengths, lectures vs tutorials, and production styles. This set included 20 videos from each course.

The categorization process involved two phases. In the first phase, researchers watched the selected videos, especially paying attention to the detected peaks. The goal was to construct a set of categories for peaks, using the open card sorting method [22]. As the researchers watched videos, they grouped peaks into rough categories based on common properties, such as the existence of visual transitions before or after a peak window. They discovered five groups in this gen-

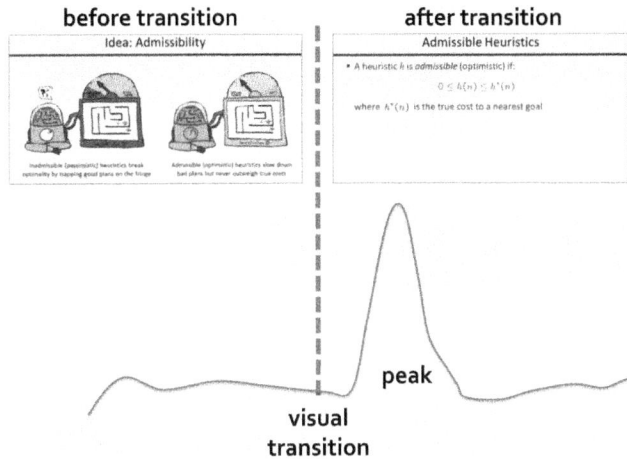

Figure 6. This peak represents the start of a new concept. The instructor started presenting a formal definition of a concept (admissibility) after changing the slide. The peak occurred when this concept explanation started.

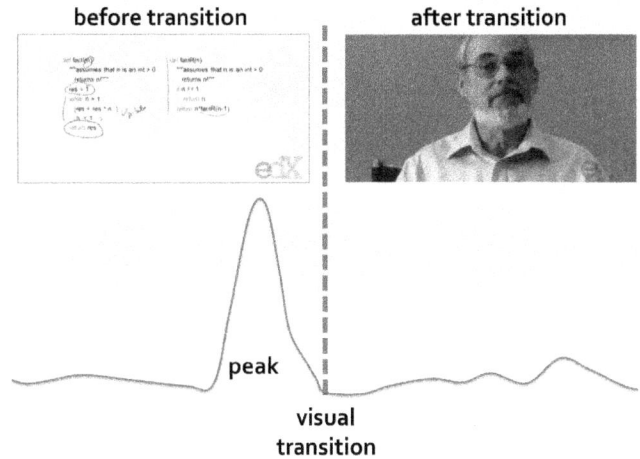

Figure 7. This peak represents students returning to see the code snippet slide that disappeared after transitioning into the talking head. An abrupt transition might not give students enough time to comprehend what's presented.

erative process and named each. Three data streams were visualized to help with the categorization process, namely play events (Figure 5 top), re-watching sessions (Figure 5 middle), and the pixel differences (Figure 5 bottom). In the second phase, a researcher labeled all peaks in the 80 videos to one of the categories generated in the first phase.

Results

Overall, 61% of the categorized peaks involved a visual transition before, and/or after the peak. The categories, their descriptions, and frequency are shown in Table 3. We now describe each student activity category in detail.

Type 1: starting from the beginning of a new material

In this category (25% of all peaks), students browse to the beginning of a new material, such as a new concept, example, or theorem. A peak caused by such activity includes a visual transition that precedes the peak. This indicates that students are interested in the content that comes after the visual transition, which is often where new units start. Students might want to review a confusing concept after mastering earlier ones, or re-visit a theorem proof sequence. These peaks might indicate good points to cut the longer video into shorter segments, because they correspond to the beginning of a semantically different unit. Figure 6 shows an example from an AI course where a formal description of a concept (admissibility) started after presenting a motivating idea.

Type 2: returning to missed content

In this category (23% of all peaks), students return to visual content that disappears shortly after. A peak caused by such activity includes a visual transition that follows shortly after the peak. Often, the content that disappears is slides, code snippets, or board notes, but not talking heads or zoomed out views. An interpretation is that there is a pacing issue in the video. The visual transition was maybe too abrupt, not giving enough time for students to fully digest the content that disappeared. They need more time on the material, but the video view suddenly changed and prevented access to the material.

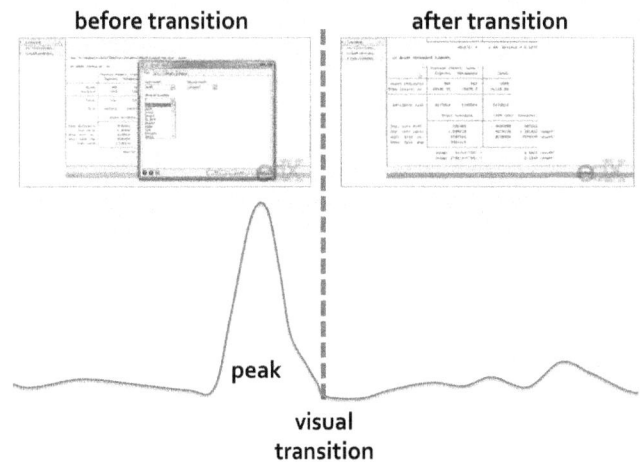

Figure 8. This peak represents students returning to a procedural step demonstrating how to run a command inside a statistics package. Students are more interested in following along the steps than the result afterward, probably because they can see the same result in their own application as well.

Also, note that what is shown during this peak type is often the final content that is complete, such as fully working code or a complete bullet point list. Many instructors make slides that advance progressively instead of showing everything at once to keep students' attention focused. When re-watching, students might want to skip to the final result without repeating all intermediate steps. Figure 7 shows an example where the code snippet suddenly disappeared and transitioned into the instructor talking.

Type 3. following a tutorial step

This category (7% of all peaks) is students following steps in the tutorial. Tutorials often contain step-by-step instructions students can follow, in the form of issuing a command or selecting a menu item from an application. Many students pause or replay right before an action takes place, possibly trying to replicate the step in their own tool. Since this was

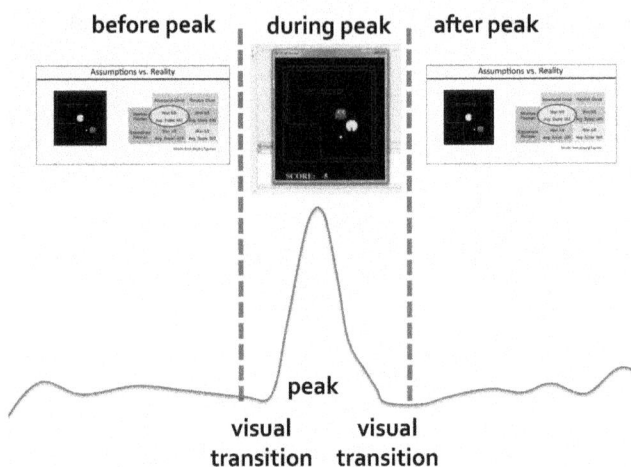

before peak | during peak | after peak

peak

visual   visual
transition transition

Figure 9. This peak represents a short range of interesting segment surrounded by visual transitions before and after. The instructor launched a game application that demonstrates the concept discussed. This engaging demo might have encouraged students to return to it.

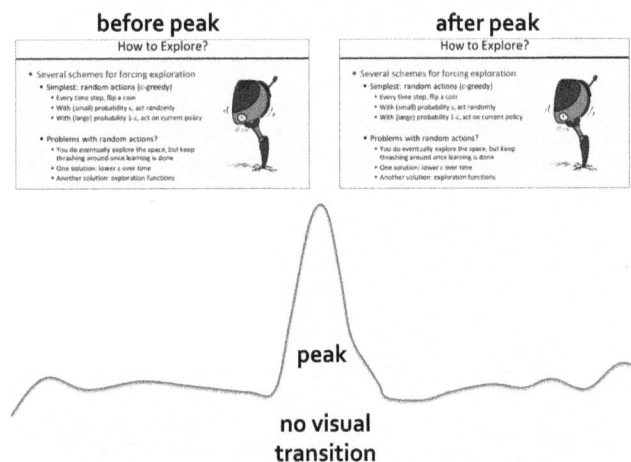

before peak   after peak

peak

no visual
transition

Figure 10. This peak represents important remarks from an instructor, without any visual transitions in the video. In this example the instructor was making an important point about random actions in reinforcement learning, the key topic of this AI lecture.

a recurring pattern in many of the tutorial videos, we assign a separate category. Figure 8 shows an example from a tutorial video where the instructor in the statistics course demonstrated how to run a command from a statistics package.

Type 4. replaying a brief segment
In this category (6% of all peaks), visual transitions are located both before and after the peak. This indicates that students are interested in the content within the peak range. While much less common than the other types, this type gives more specific information about student behavior because reasons explaining both Type 1 and 2 can be applied here. Figure 9 shows an example where the instructor briefly showed a demo application (during peak), and explained an underlying concept before and after the demo.

Type 5. repeating a non-visual explanation
In this category (39% of all peaks), students return to parts of a video that have no visual transitions nearby. What triggers a peak is non-visual activities in the video, such as a verbal instruction with semantic importance. We note that in many cases these peaks represent instructors introducing an important concept, re-emphasizing what has already been covered visually, or making a joke that results in a burst of laughter. Figure 10 shows an example where a peak occurred within a single slide. Here the instructor of the AI course explained the concept of taking random actions to force exploration in reinforcement learning, which was the main topic of the video.

Are there differences between peak types?
We compared normalized width, height, and area between peak types to see if peak categories, defined by the semantics of the video, map to differences in the peak profile. We first compared peaks accompanying visual transitions (Type 1, 2, 3, 4) and peaks with non-visual explanation (Type 5). A Mann-Whitney's U test shows a significant effect of height ($Z = -3.0$, $p < 0.01$, $r = 0.18$) and area ($Z = -1.9$, $p < 0.05$, $r = 0.11$), but not of width. This shows that peaks were taller and larger in size when they had visual transitions nearby. One explanation might be that visual transitions, occurring at the exact same time for all students, lead students to act similarly around them. On the other hand, start and end times of a salient activity are less clear for non-visual explanations.

Next, we looked at differences between individual categories. A Kruskal Wallis test revealed a significant effect of category on normalized height ($\chi^2(4)=19.6$, $p < 0.001$). A post-hoc test using Mann-Whitney tests with Bonferroni correction showed the significant differences between Type 1 and Type 3 ($p < 0.01$, $r = 0.33$), and between Type 3 and Type 5 ($p < 0.001$, $r = 0.32$). This suggests that tutorial step peaks (Type 3) were significantly taller than new material peaks (Type 1) or non-visual explanation peaks (Type 5). There was no significant effect found for normalized width or area. One explanation might be that tutorial steps have a clear timestamp and span a shorter period of time. For example, time between a tutorial instructor entering a command and hitting enter can be very short. The student needs to pause the video within a very short time range to capture the timing with the full command entered. For new materials and non-visual explanations, a few seconds of difference is not crucial, which might lead to smoother peaks.

DESIGN IMPLICATIONS FOR MOOC VIDEO INTERFACES
The micro-level analysis of students' video interaction introduced in this paper can guide the design of better video learning experiences. Our analysis shows that students interact with MOOC videos differently, depending on the visual, pedagogical, and stylistic properties of the video. A primary finding from both the dropout and peak analyses is that students selectively pick parts of videos to watch. And the parts they choose tend to converge to form peaks. We argue that course instructors, video production engineers, platform designers, and even students can benefit from such information. We present a set of design implications from our results for different types of learners and videos addressed in this paper.

[authoring] **Avoid abrupt visual transitions.** Type 2 peaks are likely to indicate too fast or abrupt transitions. These peaks often accompany informative slides, which can be made available outside the video as a screenshot or thumbnail for easier scanning and reviewing. Excessive visual transitions should be avoided because they might prevent students from referring to earlier content.

[authoring] **Make shorter videos.** Long lecture videos lead to a higher dropout rate. When determining points to segment long videos, Type 1 peaks can be useful points because students watch from the beginning of that segment.

[interface] **Enable one-click access for steps in tutorial videos.** Important steps in a tutorial get clear peaks. These peaks can be used to automatically mark steps in a video, making it easy for students to non-sequentially access these points without having to rely on imprecise scrubbing. Tutorial video interfaces such as ToolScape [14] adds an interactive timeline below a video to allow step-by-step navigation.

[interface] **Provide interactive links and screenshots for highlights.** Type 2 peaks suggest that missing content forces students to return. Providing static screenshots of the peak-creating informative frames might reduce the navigation overhead for students. Video interfaces might even consider multi-track streams, showing slide and instructor in separate channels that are available all the time. Type 5 peaks attract students with non-visual information, and our observation suggests that instructors make important points in these peaks. Interactive links to these points can be useful for students willing to find them later, which is especially difficult due to the lack of visual cues.

[interface] **Consider video summarization for selective watchers.** A common interaction pattern in our results is non-sequential and selective watching. Students re-watching videos tend to non-sequentially seek their points of interest. Peaks can be used to effectively summarize highlights from a video, which can be useful for students who re-watch or skim through the content while auditing.

MOOC video analytics platform

Techniques presented in this paper can provide stakeholders in a MOOC with richer data about micro-level video interaction, which can help them make data-driven decisions about planning, recording, editing, and revising videos. To support exploration of in-video interaction data, we are currently building a prototype MOOC video analytics platform. In addition to showing basic statistics per video, the enhanced video player synchronizes the video playhead with an overlay time bar on the visualization (Figure 11). This interface enables visually connecting deep-linked video content to points with salient patterns in the graph. We expect to support the sensemaking process for course instructors, video production engineers, and platform designers.

Course instructors can use MOOC video analytics to respond to students' interest and confusion while a course is being offered. Further, they can also use data-driven metrics to revise videos for the next offering of the course. **Video production engineers** can better allocate their resources in the

HarvardX PH207x: Graphing in Stata

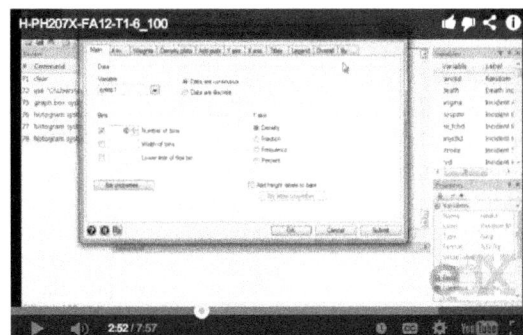

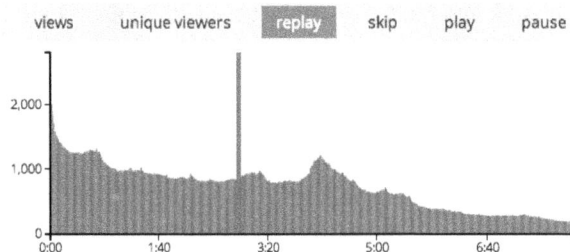

Figure 11. Our prototype video analytics dashboard supports synchronized video playback for various interaction measures.

production effort. One concrete use case is to avoid excessive visual transitions that lead to Type 2 peaks. **Platform designers** can benefit from MOOC video analytics to enhance the video player interface. For example, they can attach interactive bookmarks for peaks to improve in-video navigation.

While the analysis for this paper was done offline after the courses were complete, the analytics platform can also handle streaming events. This allows running our analytics framework for currently active courses, so that instructors can address student confusion inferred from the streaming video analytics during virtual office hours or in discussion forums.

LIMITATIONS

While our analysis methods identified video navigation patterns, understanding *why* we see these patterns is difficult. Because MOOCs do not have access to a broader learning context of a student, log entries cannot accurately represent learners' real intent (e.g., play a video but not watch). Also, video interactions might depend on other pedagogical methods in a MOOC such as problem sets, discussion forums, and exams. Furthermore, presentation quality or storyline might also affect which parts of the video students come back to watch, but our analysis does not incorporate such data. Finally, our analysis does not consider different learner goals in MOOCs, such as completing, auditing, and disengaging [15]. Per-group analysis of our techniques might reduce noise and help us better reason about the dropout and peak results.

FUTURE WORK AND CONCLUSION

This paper provides an in-depth look into how students interact with MOOC videos. We analyze data from four live courses on edX, focusing on in-video dropout rates, interaction peak profiles, and student activity categorization around peaks. We believe our data-driven analytic methods can help improve the video learning experience.

For future work, we plan to analyze more courses, data streams, and interaction patterns. We hope to analyze humanities and professional courses, and compare results against the current data from science and engineering courses. Another potential data stream is text from transcripts, textbooks, and lecture slides. Text analysis can complement vision-based techniques. In contrast to peaks, dips in viewership and interaction counts might be an informative pattern to investigate. Dips might represent boredom and loss of interest.

ACKNOWLEDGMENTS

This work was funded in part by Quanta Computer. Juho Kim is supported by the Samsung Fellowship.

REFERENCES

1. Bostock, M., Ogievetsky, V., and Heer, J. D^3 data-driven documents. *Visualization and Computer Graphics, IEEE Transactions on 17*, 12 (2011), 2301–2309.

2. Breslow, L., Pritchard, D. E., DeBoer, J., Stump, G. S., Ho, A. D., and Seaton, D. T. Studying learning in the worldwide classroom: Research into edX's first MOOC. *Research and Practice in Assessment 8* (Summer 2013).

3. Carlier, A., Charvillat, V., Ooi, W. T., Grigoras, R., and Morin, G. Crowdsourced automatic zoom and scroll for video retargeting. In *Multimedia '10*, ACM (2010), 201–210.

4. Chorianopoulos, K. Collective intelligence within web video. *Human-centric Computing and Information Sciences 3*, 1 (2013), 10.

5. Cleveland, W. S. Lowess: A program for smoothing scatterplots by robust locally weighted regression. *The American Statistician 35*, 1 (1981), 54–54.

6. edX. edX Insights. `https://github.com/edx/insights`.

7. edX. Tracking Logs – edX 0.1 documentation. `http://data.edx.org/en/latest/internal_data_formats/tracking_logs.html`.

8. Girgensohn, A., and Boreczky, J. Time-constrained keyframe selection technique. In *Multimedia Computing and Systems*, vol. 1 (1999), 756–761 vol.1.

9. Google. YouTube Analytics. `http://www.youtube.com/yt/playbook/yt-analytics.html#details`.

10. Guo, P. J., Kim, J., and Rubin, R. How video production affects student engagement: An empirical study of mooc videos. In *Learning at Scale 2014, to appear* (2014).

11. Hou, X., and Zhang, L. Saliency detection: A spectral residual approach. In *CVPR '07* (2007), 1–8.

12. Jones, R., and Diaz, F. Temporal profiles of queries. *ACM Transactions on Information Systems (TOIS) 25*, 3 (2007), 14.

13. Kairam, S., Morris, M., Teevan, J., Liebling, D., and Dumais, S. Towards supporting search over trending events with social media. In *ICWSM '13* (2013).

14. Kim, J., Nguyen, P., Weir, S., Guo, P., Gajos, K., and Miller, R. Crowdsourcing step-by-step information extraction to enhance existing how-to videos. In *CHI '14, to appear*, ACM (2014).

15. Kizilcec, R. F., Piech, C., and Schneider, E. Deconstructing disengagement: analyzing learner subpopulations in massive open online courses. In *LAK '13*, ACM (2013), 170–179.

16. Kleinberg, J. Bursty and hierarchical structure in streams. *Data Mining and Knowledge Discovery 7*, 4 (2003), 373–397.

17. Kulkarni, A., Teevan, J., Svore, K. M., and Dumais, S. T. Understanding temporal query dynamics. In *WSDM '11*, ACM (2011), 167–176.

18. Li, F. C., Gupta, A., Sanocki, E., He, L.-w., and Rui, Y. Browsing digital video. In *CHI '00*, ACM (2000), 169–176.

19. Marcus, A., Bernstein, M. S., Badar, O., Karger, D. R., Madden, S., and Miller, R. C. Twitinfo: aggregating and visualizing microblogs for event exploration. In *CHI '11*, ACM (2011), 227–236.

20. Olsen, D. R., and Moon, B. Video summarization based on user interaction. In *EuroITV '11*, ACM (2011), 115–122.

21. Risko, E., Foulsham, T., Dawson, S., and Kingstone, A. The collaborative lecture annotation system (clas): A new tool for distributed learning. *Learning Technologies, IEEE Transactions on 6*, 1 (2013), 4–13.

22. Rugg, G., and McGeorge, P. The sorting techniques: a tutorial paper on card sorts, picture sorts and item sorts. *Expert Systems 14*, 2 (1997), 80–93.

23. Seaton, D. T., Bergner, Y., Chuang, I., Mitros, P., and Pritchard, D. E. Who does what in a massive open online course? *Communications of the ACM, to appear* (2014).

24. Shaw, R., and Davis, M. Toward emergent representations for video. In *Multimedia '05*, ACM (2005), 431–434.

25. Smoliar, S., and Zhang, H. Content based video indexing and retrieval. *MultiMedia, IEEE 1*, 2 (1994), 62–72.

26. Wand, M. Fast computation of multivariate kernel estimators. *Journal of Computational and Graphical Statistics 3*, 4 (1994), 433–445.

27. Wickham, H. Bin-summarise-smooth: a framework for visualising large data. Tech. rep., had.co.nz, 2013.

28. Wistia. Wistia Product Features. `http://wistia.com/product#analyze`.

29. Yew, J., Shamma, D. A., and Churchill, E. F. Knowing funny: genre perception and categorization in social video sharing. In *CHI '11*, ACM (2011), 297–306.

How Video Production Affects Student Engagement: An Empirical Study of MOOC Videos

Philip J. Guo
MIT CSAIL / University of Rochester
pg@cs.rochester.edu

Juho Kim
MIT CSAIL
juhokim@mit.edu

Rob Rubin
edX
rrubin@edx.org

ABSTRACT

Videos are a widely-used kind of resource for online learning. This paper presents an empirical study of how video production decisions affect student engagement in online educational videos. To our knowledge, ours is the largest-scale study of video engagement to date, using data from 6.9 million video watching sessions across four courses on the edX MOOC platform. We measure engagement by how long students are watching each video, and whether they attempt to answer post-video assessment problems.

Our main findings are that shorter videos are much more engaging, that informal talking-head videos are more engaging, that Khan-style tablet drawings are more engaging, that even high-quality pre-recorded classroom lectures might not make for engaging online videos, and that students engage differently with lecture and tutorial videos.

Based upon these quantitative findings and qualitative insights from interviews with edX staff, we developed a set of recommendations to help instructors and video producers take better advantage of the online video format. Finally, to enable researchers to reproduce and build upon our findings, we have made our anonymized video watching data set and analysis scripts public. To our knowledge, ours is one of the first public data sets on MOOC resource usage.

Author Keywords

Video engagement; online education; MOOC

ACM Classification Keywords

H.5.1. Information Interfaces and Presentation (e.g. HCI): Multimedia Information Systems

INTRODUCTION

Educators have been recording instructional videos for nearly as long as the format has existed. In the past decade, though, free online video hosting services such as YouTube have enabled people to disseminate instructional videos at scale. For example, Khan Academy videos have been viewed over 300 million times on YouTube [1].

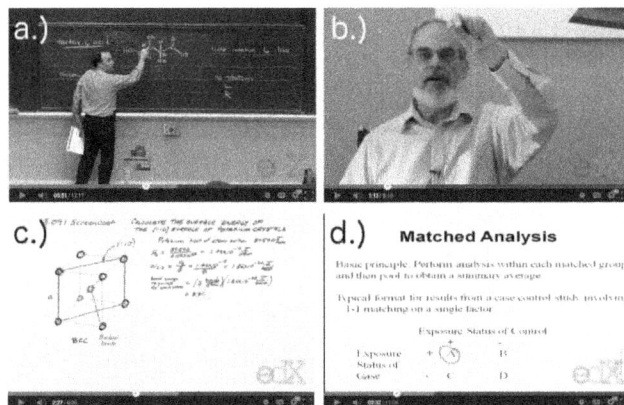

Figure 1. Video production style often affects student engagement in MOOCs. Typical styles include: a.) classroom lecture, b.) "talking head" shot of an instructor at a desk, c.) digital tablet drawing format popularized by Khan Academy, and d.) PowerPoint slide presentations.

Videos are central to the student learning experience in the current generation of MOOCs from providers such as Coursera, edX, and Udacity (sometimes called xMOOCs [7]). These online courses are mostly organized as sequences of instructor-produced videos interspersed with other resources such as assessment problems and interactive demos. A study of the first edX course (6.002x, Circuits and Electronics) found that students spent the majority of their time watching videos [2, 13]. Also, a study of three Coursera courses found that many students are auditors who engage primarily with videos while skipping over assessment problems, online discussions, and other interactive course components [9].

Due to the importance of video content in MOOCs, video production staff and instructional designers spend considerable time and money producing these videos, which are often filmed in diverse styles (see Figure 1). From our discussions with staff at edX, we learned that one of their most pressing questions was: *Which kinds of videos lead to the best student learning outcomes in a MOOC?* A related question that affects the rate at which new courses can be added is how to maximize student learning while keeping video production time and financial costs at reasonable levels.

As a step toward this goal, this paper presents an empirical study of students' *engagement* with MOOC videos, as measured by how long students are watching each video, and whether they attempt to answer post-video assessment problems. We choose to study engagement because it is a necessary (but not sufficient) prerequisite for learning, and because it can be quantified by retrospectively mining user interaction logs from past MOOC offerings. Also, video engagement

Finding	Recommendation
Shorter videos are much more engaging.	Invest heavily in pre-production lesson planning to segment videos into chunks shorter than 6 minutes.
Videos that intersperse an instructor's talking head with slides are more engaging than slides alone.	Invest in post-production editing to display the instructor's head at opportune times in the video.
Videos produced with a more personal feel could be more engaging than high-fidelity studio recordings.	Try filming in an informal setting; it might not be necessary to invest in big-budget studio productions.
Khan-style tablet drawing tutorials are more engaging than PowerPoint slides or code screencasts.	Introduce motion and continuous visual flow into tutorials, along with extemporaneous speaking.
Even high quality pre-recorded classroom lectures are not as engaging when chopped up for a MOOC.	If instructors insist on recording classroom lectures, they should still plan with the MOOC format in mind.
Videos where instructors speak fairly fast and with high enthusiasm are more engaging.	Coach instructors to bring out their enthusiasm and reassure that they do not need to purposely slow down.
Students engage differently with lecture and tutorial videos	For lectures, focus more on the first-watch experience; for tutorials, add support for rewatching and skimming.

Table 1. Summary of the main findings and video production recommendations that we present in this paper.

is important even beyond education. For instance, commercial video hosting providers such as YouTube and Wistia use engagement as a key metric for viewer satisfaction [6, 16], which directly drives revenues.

The importance of scale: MOOC video producers currently base their production decisions on anecdotes, folk wisdom, and best practices distilled from studies with at most dozens of subjects and hundreds of video watching sessions. The scale of data from MOOC interaction logs—hundreds of thousands of students from around the world and millions of video watching sessions—is four orders of magnitude larger than those available in prior studies [11, 15].

Such scale enables us to corroborate traditional video engagement research and extend their relevance to a modern online context. It also allows MOOC video producers to make more rigorous decisions based on data rather than just intuitions. Finally, it could enable our findings and recommendations to generalize beyond MOOCs to other sorts of informal online learning that occurs when, say, hundreds of millions of people watch YouTube how-to videos on topics ranging from cooking to knitting.

This paper makes three main contributions:

- **Findings** from an empirical study of MOOC video engagement, combining data analysis of 6.9 million video watching sessions in four edX courses with interviews with six edX production staff. The left column of Table 1 summarizes our seven main findings. To our knowledge, ours is the largest-scale study of video engagement to date.

- **Recommendations** for instructional designers and video producers, based on our study's findings (see the right column of Table 1). Staff at edX are already starting to use

some of these recommendations to nudge professors toward cost-effective video production techniques that lead to greater student engagement.

- **An anonymized public data set** of 6.9 million video watching sessions, along with analysis scripts and installation instructions to enable full reproducibility of our results. Located at http://www.pgbovine.net/edX/, ours is one of the first public data sets on MOOC resource usage.

RELATED WORK
To our knowledge, our study is the first to correlate video production style with engagement at scale using millions of viewing sessions.

The closest related work is by Cross et al., who studied some of these effects in a controlled experiment [4]. They created Khan-style (tablet drawing) and PowerPoint slide versions of three video lectures and surveyed 150 people online about their preferences. They found that the two formats had complementary strengths and weaknesses, and developed a hybrid style called TypeRighting that tries to combine the benefits of both. Ilioudi et al. performed a similar study using three pairs of videos recorded in both live classroom lecture and Khan-style formats, like those shown in Figure 1a. and c., respectively. They presented those videos to 36 high school students, who showed a slight preference for classroom lecture videos over Khan-style videos [8]. Although these studies lack the scale of ours, they collected direct feedback from video watchers, which we have not yet done.

Prior large-scale analyses of MOOC interaction data (e.g., [2, 3, 9, 13]) have not focused on videos in particular. Some of this work provides the motivation for our study. For instance, a study of the first edX course (6.002x, Circuits and Electronics) found that students spent the majority of their time watching videos [2, 13]. And a study of three Coursera courses

Course	Subject	University	Lecture Setting	Videos	Students	Watching sessions
6.00x	Intro. CS & Programming	MIT	Office Desk	141	59,126	2,218,821
PH207x	Statistics for Public Health	Harvard	TV Studio	301	30,742	2,846,960
CS188.1x	Artificial Intelligence	Berkeley	Classroom	149	22,690	1,030,215
3.091x	Solid State Chemistry	MIT	Classroom	271	15,281	806,362
Total				862	127,839	6,902,358

Table 2. Overview of the Fall 2012 edX courses in our data set. "Lecture Setting" is the location where lecture videos were filmed. "Students" is the number of students who watched at least one video.

found that many students are auditors who engage primarily with videos while skipping over assessment problems, online discussions, and other interactive course components [9].

Finally, educators have been using videos and electronic media for decades before MOOCs launched. Mayer surveys cognitive science research on the impacts of multimedia on student learning [11]. Williams surveys general instructional media best practices from the 1950s to 1990s [15]. And Levasseur surveys best practices for using PowerPoint lectures in classrooms [10]. These studies have at most dozens of subjects and hundreds of video watching sessions. Our study extends these lines of work to a large-scale online setting.

METHODOLOGY
We took a mixed methods approach: We analyzed data from four edX courses and supplemented our quantitative findings with qualitative insights from interviews with six edX staff who were involved in producing those courses.

Course Selection
We analyzed data from four courses in the first edX batch offered in Fall 2012 (see Table 2). We selected courses from all three edX affiliates at the time (MIT, Harvard, and UC Berkeley) and strived to maximize diversity in subject matter and video production styles (see Figure 1).

However, since all Fall 2012 courses were math/science-focused, our corpus does not include any humanities or social science courses. EdX launched additional courses in Spring 2013, but that data was incomplete when we began this study. To improve external validity, we plan to replicate our experiments on more courses once we obtain their data.

Video Watching Sessions
The main data we analyze is a *video watching session*, which represents a single instance of a student watching a particular edX video. Each session contains a username, video ID, start and end times, video play speed (1x, 1.25x, 1.5x, 0.75x, or multiple speeds), numbers of times the student pressed the play and pause buttons, and whether the student attempted an assessment problem shortly after watching the given video.

To extract video watching sessions, we mined the edX server logs for our four target courses. The edX website logs user interaction events such as navigating to a page, playing a video, pausing a video, and submitting a problem for grading. We segmented the raw logs into video watching sessions based on these heuristics: Each session starts with a "play video" event for a particular student and video, and it ends when:

- that student triggers any event not related to the current video (e.g., navigating to another page),
- that student ends the current login session,
- there is at least a 30-minute gap before that student's next event (Google Analytics [5] uses this heuristic for segmenting website visits),
- the video finishes playing. The edX video player issues a "pause video" event when a video ends, so if a student plays, say, a five-minute video and then walks away from the computer, that watching session will conclude when the video ends after five minutes.

In Fall 2012, the edX video player automatically started playing each video (and issues a "play video" event) as soon as a student loads the enclosing page. Many students paused the video almost immediately or navigated to another page. Thus, we filtered out all sessions lasting shorter than five seconds, because those were likely due to auto-play.

Our script extracted 6.9 million total video watching sessions across four courses during the time period when they were initially offered in Fall 2012 (see Table 2).

Measuring Engagement
We aim to measure student engagement with instructional videos. However, true engagement is impossible to measure without direct observation and questioning, which is infeasible at scale. Thus, we use two proxies for engagement:

Engagement time: We use the length of time that a student spends on a video (i.e., video watching session length) as the main proxy for engagement. *Engagement time* is a standard metric used by both free video providers such as YouTube [6] and enterprise providers such as Wistia [16]. However, its inherent limitation is that it cannot capture whether a watcher is actively paying attention to the video or just playing it in the background while multitasking.

Problem attempt: 32% of the videos across our four courses are immediately followed by an assessment problem, which is usually a multiple-choice question designed to check a student's understanding of the video's contents. We record whether a student attempted the follow-up problem within 30 minutes after watching a video. A problem attempt indicates more engagement than moving on without attempting.

When we refer to *engagement* throughout this paper, we mean engagement as measured through these two proxies, not the difficult-to-measure ideal of true engagement.

Video Properties

To determine how video production correlates with engagement, we extracted four main properties from each video.

Length: Since all edX videos are hosted on YouTube, we wrote a script to get each video's length from YouTube.

Speaking rate: All edX videos come with time-coded subtitles, so we approximated the speaking rate of each video by dividing the total number of spoken words by the total in-video speaking time (i.e., words per minute).

Video type: We manually looked through each video and categorized its type as either an ordinary *lecture*, a *tutorial* (e.g., problem solving walkthrough), or *other* content such as a supplemental film clip. 89% of all videos were either lectures or tutorials, so we focus our analyses only on those two types.

Production style: We looked through each video and coded its production style using the following labels:

- **Slides** – PowerPoint slide presentation with voice-over

- **Code** – video screencast of the instructor writing code in a text editor, IDE, or command-line prompt

- **Khan-style** – full-screen video of an instructor drawing freehand on a digital tablet, which is a style popularized by Khan Academy videos

- **Classroom** – video captured from a live classroom lecture

- **Studio** – instructor recorded in a studio with no audience

- **Office Desk** – close-up shots of an instructor's head filmed at an office desk

Note that a video can contain multiple production styles, such as alternating between PowerPoint slides and an instructor's talking head recorded at an office desk. Thus, each video can have multiple labels.

Interviews With Domain Experts

To supplement our quantitative findings, we presented our data to domain experts at edX to solicit their feedback and interpretations. In particular, we conducted informal interviews with the four principal edX video producers who were responsible for overseeing all phases of video production—planning, filming, and editing. We also interviewed two program managers who were the liaisons between edX and the respective university course staff.

Public Anonymized Data Set and Scripts

We have uploaded an anonymized version of our data set along with analysis scripts and database installation instructions to `http://www.pgbovine.net/edX/` so that other researchers can reproduce and build upon this paper's findings. To our knowledge, ours is one of the first public data sets on MOOC resource usage.

FINDINGS AND RECOMMENDATIONS

We now detail the findings and recommendations of Table 1.

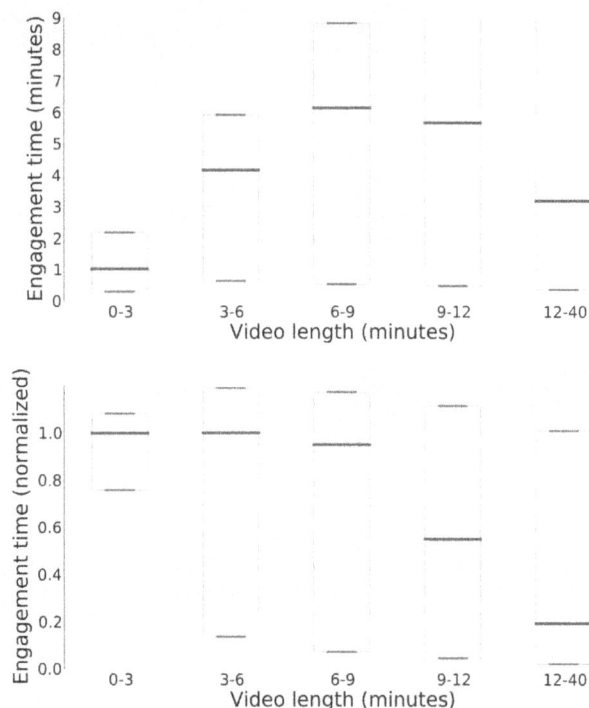

Figure 2. Boxplots of engagement times in minutes (top) and normalized to each video's length (bottom). In each box, the middle red bar is the median; the top and bottom blue bars are 25th and 75th percentiles, respectively. The median engagement time is at most 6 minutes.

Shorter Videos Are More Engaging

Video length was by far the most significant indicator of engagement. Figure 2 splits videos into five roughly equal-sized buckets by length and plots engagement times for 1x-speed sessions in each group[1]. The top boxplot (absolute engagement times) shows that median engagement time is at most 6 minutes, regardless of total video length. The bottom boxplot (engagement times normalized to video length) shows that students often make it less than halfway through videos longer than 9 minutes. The shortest videos (0–3 minutes) had the highest engagement and much less variance than all other groups: 75% of sessions lasted over three quarters of the video length. Note that normalized engagement can be greater than 1.0 if a student paused to check understanding or scrolled back to re-play an earlier portion before finishing the video.

To account for inter-courses differences, we made plots individually for the four courses and found identical trends.

Students also engaged less frequently with assessment problems that followed longer videos. For the five length buckets in Figure 2, we computed the percentage of video watching sessions followed by a problem attempt: The percentages were 56%, 48%, 43%, 41%, and 31%, respectively.

---

[1]Plotting all sessions pulls down the distributions due to students playing at 1.25x and 1.5x speeds and finishing videos faster, but trends remain identical. In this paper, we report results only for 1x-speed plays, which comprise 76% of all sessions. Our code and data are available to re-run on all sessions, though.

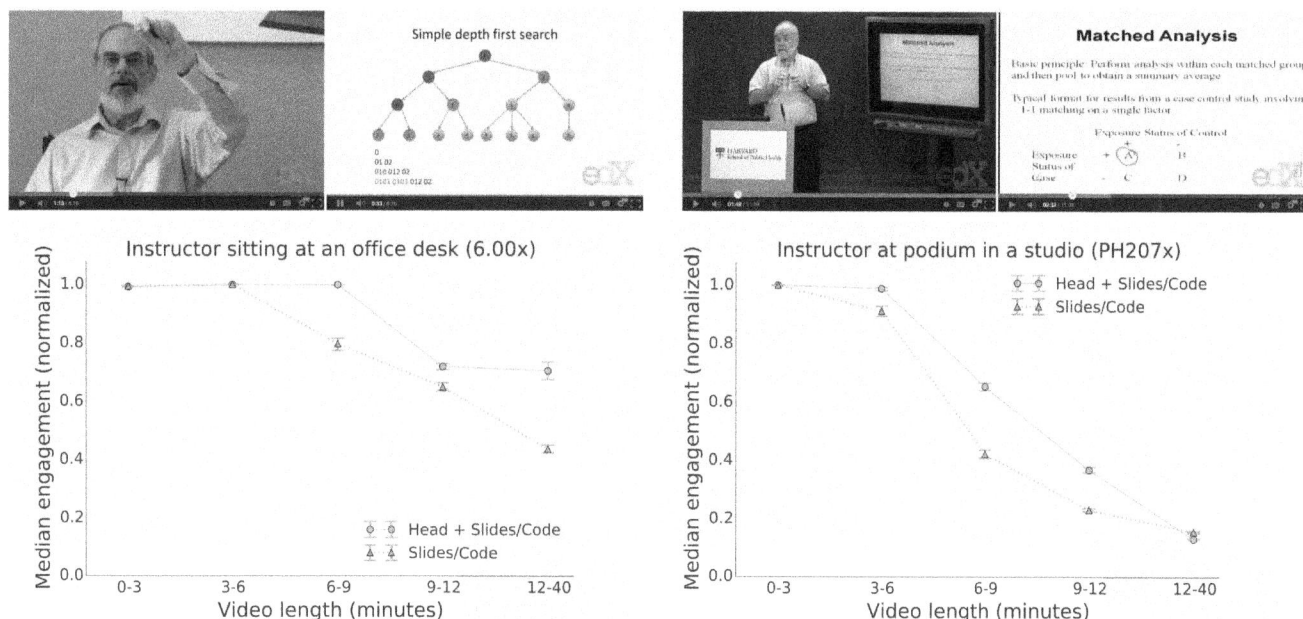

Figure 3. Median engagement times versus length for videos from 6.00x (left) and PH207x (right). In both courses, students engaged more with videos that alternated between the instructor's talking head and slides/code. Also, students engaged more with 6.00x videos, filmed with the instructor sitting at a desk, than with PH207x videos, filmed in a professional TV studio (the left graph has higher values than the right one, especially for videos longer than 6 minutes). Error bars are approximate 95% confidence intervals for the true median, computed using a standard non-parametric technique [14].

This particular set of findings resonated most strongly with video producers we interviewed at edX. Ever since edX formed, producers had been urging instructors to split up lessons into chunks of less than 6 minutes, based solely upon their prior intuitions. However, they often encountered resistance from instructors who were accustomed to delivering one-hour classroom lectures; for those instructors, even a 15-minute chunk seems short. Video producers are now using our data to make a more evidence-based case to instructors.

One hypothesis that came out in our interviews with video producers was that shorter videos might contain higher-quality instructional content. Their hunch is that it takes meticulous planning to explain a concept succinctly, so shorter videos are engaging not only due to length but also because they are better planned. However, we do not yet have the data to investigate this question.

For all subsequent analyses, we grouped videos by length, or else the effects of length usually overwhelmed the effects of other production factors.

Recommendation: Instructors should segment videos into short chunks, ideally less than 6 minutes.

Talking Head Is More Engaging

The videos for two of our courses—6.00x and PH207x—were mostly PowerPoint slideshows and code screencasts. However, some of those videos (60% for 6.00x and 25% for PH207x) were edited to alternate between showing the instructor's talking head and the usual slides/code display.

Figure 3 shows that, in both courses, students usually engaged more with talking-head videos. In this figure and all subse-

quent figures that compare median engagement times, when the medians of two groups look far enough apart (i.e., their error bars are non-overlapping), then their underlying distributions are also significantly different ($p \ll 0.001$) according to a Mann-Whitney U test.

To check whether longer engagement times might be simply due to students pausing or re-playing the video, we compared the numbers of play/pause events in both groups and found no significant differences.

Also, 6.00x students attempted 46% of problems after watching a talking-head video (preceding a problem), versus 33% for other videos ($p \ll 0.001$ according to a chi-square test for independence). PH207x students attempted 33% of problems for both video groups, though.

These findings also resonated with edX video producers we interviewed, because they felt that a human face provided a more "intimate and personal" feel and broke up the monotony of PowerPoint slides and code screencasts. They also mentioned that their video editing was not done with any specific pedagogical "design patterns" in mind: They simply spliced in talking heads whenever the timing "felt right" in the video.

Since we have shown that this technique can improve engagement, we have encouraged producers to take a more systematic approach to this sort of editing in the future. Open questions include when and how often to switch between talking head shots and textual content. Perhaps video editing software could detect transition points and automatically splice in head shots. Finally, some people were concerned about the jarring effect of switching repeatedly between talking head and text, so a picture-in-picture view might work better.

Recommendation: Record the instructor's head and then insert into the presentation video at opportune times.

High Production Value Might Not Matter

Although 6.00x and PH207x were both taught by senior faculty at major research universities and had videos filmed in roughly the same style—slides/code with optional talking head—students engaged much more with 6.00x videos. The two graphs in Figure 3 show that students engaged for nearly twice as long on 6.00x videos between 6 and 12 minutes, and for nearly 3x the time on 6.00x videos longer than 12 minutes.

When we presented these findings to edX video producers and program managers who worked on those two courses, their immediate reaction was that differences in production value might have caused the disparities in student engagement: 6.00x was filmed informally with the instructor sitting at his office desk, while PH207x was filmed in a multi-million dollar TV production studio.

The "talking head" images at the top of Figure 3 show that the 6.00x instructor was filmed in a tight frame, often making direct eye contact with the student, while the PH207x instructor was standing behind a podium, often looking around the room and not directly at the camera. The edX production staff mentioned that the 6.00x instructor seemed more comfortable seated at his office having a personal one-on-one, office-hours style conversation with the video watcher. Video producers called this desirable trait "personalization"—the student feeling that the video is being directed right at them, rather than at an unnamed crowd. In contrast, the PH207x instructor looked farther removed from the watcher because he was lecturing from behind a podium in a TV studio.

The edX production staff worked with each instructor to find the recording style that made each most comfortable, and the PH207x instructor still preferred a traditional lecture format. Despite his decades of lecturing experience and comfort with the format, his performance did not end up looking engaging on video. This example reinforces the notion that what works well in a live classroom might not translate into online video, even with a high production value studio recording.

Here the supposed constraints of a lower-fidelity setting—a single close-up camera at a desk—actually led to more engaging videos. However, it is hard to generalize from only one pair of courses, since the effects could be due to differences in instructor skill. Ideally we would like to compare more pairs of low and high production value courses[2], but this was the only pair available in our data set.

Recommendation: Try filming in an informal setting where the instructor can make good eye contact, since it costs less and might be more effective than a professional studio.

Khan-Style Tutorials Are More Engaging

Now we focus on tutorials, which are step-by-step problem solving walkthroughs. Across all four courses, Khan-style tutorial videos (i.e., an instructor drawing on a digital

[2]or, even better, record one instructor using both styles.

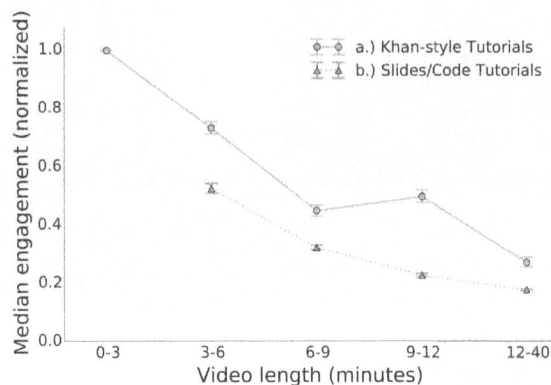

Figure 4. Median normalized engagement times vs. length for tutorial videos. Students engaged more with Khan-style tablet drawing tutorials (a.) than with PowerPoint slide and code screencast tutorials (b.). Error bars are approximate 95% confidence intervals for the true median [14].

tablet) were more engaging than PowerPoint slides and/or code screencasts. We group slides and code together since many tutorial videos feature both styles. Figure 4 shows that students engaged for 1.5x to 2x as long with Khan-style tutorials. For videos preceding problems, 40% of Khan-style tutorial watching sessions were followed by a problem attempt, versus 31% for other tutorials (chi-square $p \ll 0.001$). This finding corroborates prior work that shows how free-hand sketching facilitates more engaging dialogue [12] and how the natural motion of human handwriting can be more engaging than static computer-rendered fonts [4].

Video producers and program managers at edX also agreed with this finding. In particular, they noticed how instructors who sketched Khan-style tutorials could situate themselves "on the same level" as the student rather than talking at the student in "lecturer mode." Also, one noted how a Khan-style tutorial "encourages professors to use the 'bar napkin' style of explanation rather than the less personal, more disjointed model that PowerPoint—if unintentionally—encourages."

However, Khan-style tutorials require more pre-production planning than presenting slides or typing code into a text editor. The most effective Khan-style tutorials were those made by instructors with clear handwriting, good drawing skills, and careful layout planning so as not to overcrowd the canvas. Future research directions include how to best structure Khan-style tutorials and how to design better authoring tools for creating and editing them. Perhaps some best practices from chalkboard lecturing could transfer to this format.

Recommendation: Record Khan-style tutorials when possible. If slides or code must be displayed, add emphasis by sketching over the slides and code using a digital tablet.

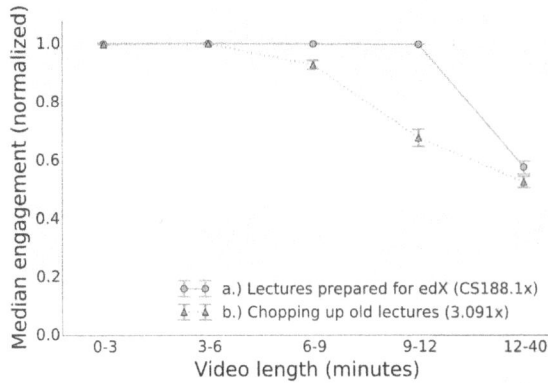

Figure 5. Median engagement times for lecture videos recorded in front of live classroom audiences. Students engaged more with lectures in CS188.1x (a.), which were prepared with edX usage in mind, than with lectures in 3.091x (b.), which were adapted from old lecture videos. Error bars are approximate 95% confidence intervals for true median [14].

Pre-Production Improves Engagement

So far, we have focused on production (i.e., filming) and post-production (i.e., editing) techniques that drive engagement. However, edX video producers we interviewed felt that the pre-production (i.e., planning) phase had the largest impact on the engagement of resulting videos. But since the output of extensive pre-production is simply better planned videos, producers cannot easily argue for its benefits by pointing out specific video features (e.g., adding motion via tablet sketches) to suggest as best practices for instructors.

To show the effects of pre-production, we compared video engagement for CS188.1x and 3.091x. Both are math/science courses with instructors who are regarded as excellent classroom lecturers at their respective universities. And both instructors wanted to record their edX lectures in front of a live classroom audience to bring out their enthusiasm. However, due to logistical issues, there was not enough time for the 3.091x instructor to record his lectures, so the video producers had to splice up an old set of lecture videos recorded for his on-campus class in Spring 2011. This contrast sets up a natural experiment where video recording styles are nearly identical, but no pre-production could be done for 3.091x.

Figure 5 shows that students engaged more with CS188.1x videos, especially longer ones. Also, for videos preceding problems, 55% of CS188.1x watching sessions were followed by a problem attempt, versus 41% for 3.091x (chi-square $p << 0.001$).

This finding resonated strongly with edX video producers, because they had always championed the value of planning lectures specially for an online video format rather than just chopping up existing classroom lecture recordings.

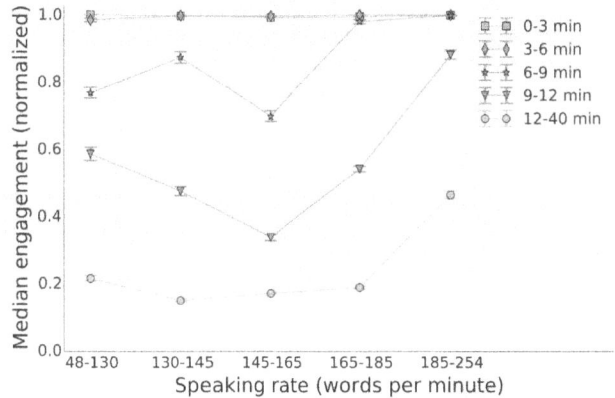

Figure 6. Median engagement times versus speaking rate and video length. Students engaged the most with fast-speaking instructors. Error bars are approximate 95% confidence intervals for the true median [14].

EdX staff who worked with the CS188.1x instructors reported that even though they recorded traditional one-hour lectures in front of a live classroom, the instructors carefully planned each hour as a series of short, discrete chunks that could easily be edited later for online distribution. In contrast, the 3.091x production staff needed to chop up pre-recorded one-hour lecture videos into short chunks, which was difficult since the original videos were not designed with the MOOC format in mind. There were often no clear demarcations between concepts, and sometimes material was presented out of order or interspersed with time- and location-specific remarks (e.g., "Jane covered this in last week's TA session in room 36-144") that broke the flow.

The main limitation here is that we had only one pair of courses to compare, and they differed in instructors and subject matter. To improve confidence in these findings, we could either find additional pairs to compare or, if the 3.091x instructor records new live lectures for edX, A/B test the engagement of old and new videos for that course.

> **Recommendation**: Invest in pre-production effort, even if instructors insist on recording live classroom lectures.

Speaking Rate Affects Engagement

Students generally engaged more with videos where instructors spoke faster. To produce Figure 6, we split videos into the usual five length buckets and also five equal-sized buckets (quintiles) by speaking rate. Speaking rates range from 48 to 254 words per minute (mean = 156 wpm, sd = 31 wpm). Each line represents the median engagement times for videos of a particular length range. As expected, students engaged less with longer videos (i.e., those lines are lower). Within a particular length range, engagement usually increases (up to 2x) with speaking rate. And for 6–12 minute videos, engagement dips in the middle bucket (145–165 wpm); slower-speaking videos are more engaging than mid-speed ones. Problem attempts also follow a similar trend, but are not graphed due to space constraints.

Some practitioners recommend 160 words per minute as the optimum speaking rate for presentations [15], but at least in our courses, faster-speaking instructors were even more engaging. One possible explanation is that the 160 wpm recommendation (first made in 1967) was for live lectures, but students watching online can actually follow along with much faster speaking rates.

The higher engagement for faster-speaking videos might also be due to students getting confused and re-playing parts. However, this is unlikely since we found no significant differences in the numbers of play and pause events among videos with different speaking rates.

To hypothesize possible explanations for the effects in Figure 6, we watched a random sample of videos in each speaking rate bucket. We noticed that fast-speaking instructors conveyed more energy and enthusiasm, which might have contributed to the higher engagement for those videos. We had no trouble understanding even the fastest-speaking videos (254 wpm), since the same information was also presented visually in PowerPoint slides. In contrast, instructors in the middle bucket (145–165 wpm) were the least energetic. For the slowest videos (48–130 wpm), the instructor was speaking slowly because he was simultaneously writing on the blackboard; the continuous writing motion might have contributed to higher engagement on those versus mid-speed videos.

Note that speaking rate is merely a surface feature that correlates with enthusiasm and thus engagement. Thus, speeding up an unenthusiastic instructor might not improve engagement. So our recommendation is not to force instructors to speak faster, but rather to bring out their enthusiasm and reassure them that there is no need to artificially slow down.

Video producers at edX mentioned that, whenever possible, they tightly edit in post-production to remove instances of "umm", "uhh", filler words, and other pauses, to make the speech more crisp. Their philosophy is that although speech pauses are beneficial in live lectures, they are unnecessary on video because students can always pause the video.

> **Recommendation**: Work with instructors to bring out their natural enthusiasm, reassure them that speaking fast is okay, and edit out pauses and filler words in post-production.

Students Engage Differently With Lectures And Tutorials

Lecture videos usually present conceptual (declarative) knowledge, whereas tutorials present how-to (procedural) knowledge. Figure 7 shows that students only watch, on average, 2 to 3 minutes of each tutorial video, regardless of the video's length. Figure 8 shows that students re-watch tutorials more frequently than lectures.

These findings suggest that students will often re-watch and jump to relevant parts of longer tutorial videos. Adding hyperlink bookmarks or visual signposts on tutorial videos, such as big blocks of text to signify transitions, might facilitate skimming and re-watching. In contrast, students expect a lecture to be a continuous stream of information, so instructors should provide a good first-time watching experience.

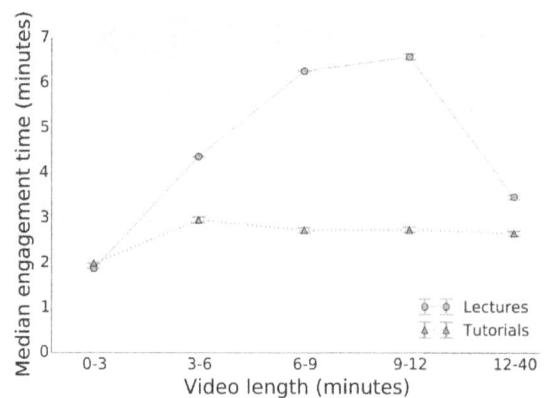

Figure 7. Median engagement times versus video length for lecture and tutorial videos. Students engaged with tutorials for only 2 to 3 minutes, regardless of video length, whereas lecture engagement rises and falls with length (similar to Figure 2). Error bars are approximate 95% confidence intervals for the true median [14].

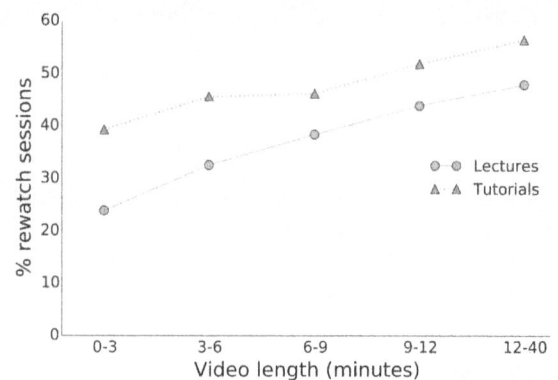

Figure 8. Percentage of re-watch sessions – i.e., not a student's first time watching a video. Tutorials were more frequently re-watched than lectures; and longer videos were more frequently re-watched. (Binomial proportion confidence intervals are so tiny that error bars are invisible.)

More generally, both our quantitative findings and interviews with edX staff indicate that instructors should adopt different production strategies for lectures and tutorials, since students use them in different ways.

> **Recommendation**: For lecture videos, optimize the first-time watching experience. For tutorials, length does not matter as much, but support re-watching and skimming.

LIMITATIONS

This paper presents a retrospective study, not a controlled experiment. Also, we had access to the full server logs for only seven Fall 2012 edX courses, which were all math and science focused. Of those, we picked four courses with diverse production styles, subjects, and from different universities (Table 2). To improve external validity, these analyses should be replicated on additional, more diverse courses.

Our engagement findings might not generalize to all online video watchers, since edX students in the first Fall 2012 batch, who are more likely to be self-motivated learners and technology early adopters, might not be representative of the general online video watching population.

As we mentioned in the METHODOLOGY section, we cannot measure a student's true engagement with videos just from analyzing server logs. Our proxies—engagement time and problem attempts—might not be representative of true engagement. For instance, a student could be playing a video in the background while browsing Facebook. In the future, running a controlled lab study will provide richer qualitative insights about true engagement, albeit at small scale.

Also, we cannot track viewing activities of students who downloaded videos and watched offline. We know that the majority of students watched videos online in the edX video player, since the numbers in the "Students" column of Table 2 closely match the total enrollment numbers for each course. However, we do not have data on which students downloaded videos, and whether their behaviors differ from those who watched online.

Our data set contains only engagement data about entire videos. We have not yet studied engagement *within* videos such as which specific parts students are watching, skipping, or re-watching. However, we are starting to address this limitation in ONGOING WORK (see next section).

Lastly, it is important not to draw any conclusions about student learning solely from our findings about video engagement. MOOCs contain many components that impact learning, and different kinds of students value different ones. For instance, some learn more from discussion forums, others from videos, and yet others from reading external Web pages. The main relationship between video engagement and learning is that the former is often a prerequisite for the latter; if students are watching a video only for a short time, then they are unlikely to be learning much from it.

ONGOING WORK: WITHIN-VIDEO ENGAGEMENT
An alternative way to understand student engagement with MOOC videos is to measure how students interact with specific parts of the video. We have recently begun to quantify two dimensions of within-video interaction:

- **Interactivity** – How often do students pause the video while watching? To measure the degree of interactivity, we compute the mean number of pause events per second, per unique student. This metric controls for variations in viewer counts and video lengths. High interactivity could indicate more active engagement with the video content.

- **Selectivity** – Do students selectively pause more at specific parts of the video than others? This behavior might reflect uneven points of interest within the video. As a proxy for selectivity, we observe how the frequency of pause events vary in different parts of the video. Specifically, we compute the standard deviation of pause events across all seconds in a video. Higher selectivity videos attract more students to pause more at some parts than at others.

Here are two preliminary sets of findings. However, we have not yet interviewed edX production staff to get their interpretations or recommendations.

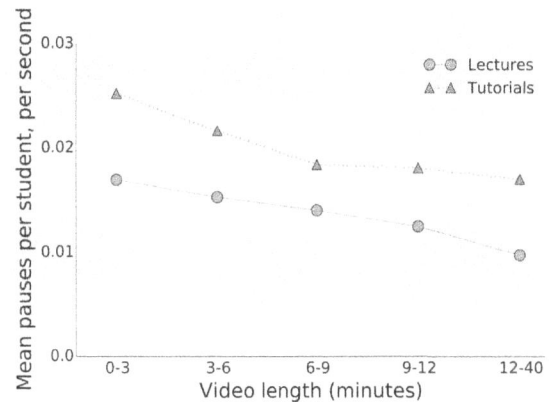

Figure 9. Students interacted (paused) more while watching tutorial videos than lecture videos.

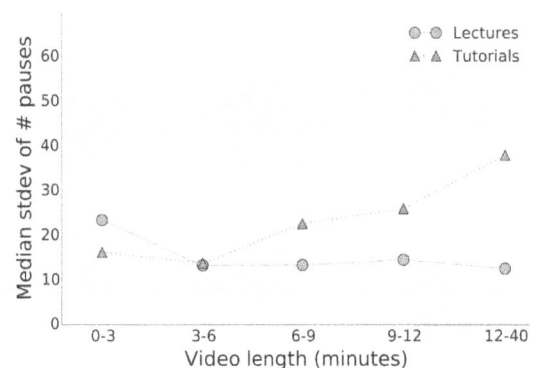

Figure 10. Students usually paused more selectively when watching tutorial videos than lecture videos.

Tutorial watching is more interactive and selective
Figure 9 shows that students interacted (paused) more within tutorial videos than lecture videos. This behavior might reflect the fact that tutorial videos contain discrete step-by-step instructions that students must follow, whereas lectures are often formatted as one continuous stream of content.

Figure 10 shows that students usually paused tutorial videos more selectively than lecture videos. This behavior might indicate that specific points in a tutorial video – possibly boundaries between distinct steps – are landmarks where students pause to reflect on or practice what they have just learned. This data could be used to automatically segment videos into meaningful chunks for faster skimming and re-watching.

Khan-style tutorials are more continuous
Figure 11 shows that students paused slides/code tutorials more selectively than Khan-style tutorials. One likely explanation is that Khan-style videos flow more continuously, so there are not as many discrete landmarks for pausing. In contrast, instructors of slides/code tutorials gradually build up text on a slide or a chunk of code, respectively, and then explain the full contents for a while before moving onto the next slide or code snippet; those are opportune times for pausing.

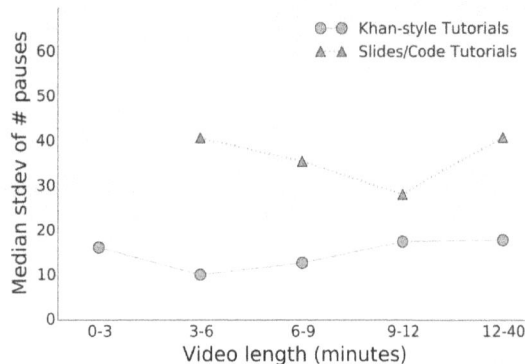

Figure 11. Students paused more selectively when watching slides/code tutorials than Khan-style tutorials.

Future Directions

Analyzing students' video interaction patterns allows educators to better understand what types of online videos encourage active interaction with content. The preliminary findings in this section provide an alternative perspective using micro-level, second-by-second interaction data that complements the engagement time analyses in the rest of this paper.

A possible future direction is to explore *why* students pause at certain points within the video. There are conflicting factors at play: Students might pause more because they consider a point to be important, or they might find the given explanation to be confusing and decide to re-watch until they understand it. Direct student observation in a lab setting could address these questions and complement our quantitative findings.

CONCLUSION

We have presented, to our knowledge, the largest-scale study of video engagement to date, using data from 6.9 million video watching sessions across four edX courses.

Our findings (Table 1) reflect the fact that, to maximize student engagement, instructors must plan their lessons specifically for an online video format. Presentation styles that have worked well for centuries in traditional in-person lectures do not necessarily make for effective online educational videos.

More generally, whenever a new communication medium arrives, people first tend to use it just like how they used existing media. For instance, many early television shows were simply radio broadcasts filmed on video, early digital textbooks were simply scanned versions of paper books, and the first online educational videos were videotaped in-person lectures. As time progresses, people eventually develop creative ways to take full advantage of the new medium. The findings from our study can help inform instructors and video producers on how to make the most of online videos for education.

Acknowledgments: Thanks to Anant Agarwal and our edX interview subjects for enabling this research, Olga Stroilova for helping with data collection, and Rob Miller for feedback.

REFERENCES

1. Khan Academy YouTube Channel. `http://www.youtube.com/user/khanacademy/about`.

2. Breslow, L., Pritchard, D. E., DeBoer, J., Stump, G. S., Ho, A. D., and Seaton, D. T. Studying learning in the worldwide classroom: Research into edX's first MOOC. *Research and Practice in Assessment 8* (Summer 2013).

3. Coetzee, D., Fox, A., Hearst, M. A., and Hartmann, B. Should Your MOOC Forum Use a Reputation System? CSCW '14, ACM (New York, NY, USA, 2014).

4. Cross, A., Bayyapunedi, M., Cutrell, E., Agarwal, A., and Thies, W. TypeRighting: Combining the Benefits of Handwriting and Typeface in Online Educational Videos. CHI '13, ACM (New York, NY, USA, 2013).

5. Google. How Visits are calculated in Analytics. `https://support.google.com/analytics/answer/2731565?hl=en`.

6. Google. YouTube Analytics. `http://www.youtube.com/yt/playbook/yt-analytics.html#details`.

7. Haber, J. xMOOC vs. cMOOC. `http://degreeoffreedom.org/xmooc-vs-cmooc/`, 2013.

8. Ilioudi, C., Giannakos, M. N., and Chorianopoulos, K. Investigating Differences among the Commonly Used Video Lecture Styles. In *Proceedings of the Workshop on Analytics on Video-based Learning*, WAVe '13 (2013).

9. Kizilcec, R. F., Piech, C., and Schneider, E. Deconstructing disengagement: analyzing learner subpopulations in massive open online courses. In *Proceedings of the Third International Conference on Learning Analytics and Knowledge*, LAK '13, ACM (New York, NY, USA, 2013), 170–179.

10. Levasseur, D. G., and Sawyer, J. K. Pedagogy Meets PowerPoint: A Research Review of the Effects of Computer-Generated Slides in the Classroom. *Review of Communication 6*, 1 (2006), 101–123.

11. Mayer, R. E. *Multimedia Learning*. Cambridge University Press, 2001.

12. Roam, D. *The Back of the Napkin (Expanded Edition): Solving Problems and Selling Ideas with Pictures*. Portfolio Hardcover, 2009.

13. Seaton, D. T., Bergner, Y., Chuang, I., Mitros, P., and Pritchard, D. E. Who does what in a massive open online course? *Communications of the ACM* (2013).

14. Wade, A., and Koutoumanou, E. Non-parametric tests: Confidence intervals for a single median. `https://epilab.ich.ucl.ac.uk/coursematerial/statistics/non_parametric/confidence_interval.html`.

15. Williams, J. R. Guidelines for the use of multimedia in instruction. *Proceedings of the Human Factors and Ergonomics Society Annual Meeting 42*, 20 (1998), 1447–1451.

16. Wistia. Does length matter? It does for video! `http://wistia.com/blog/does-length-matter-it-does-for-video`, Sept. 2013.

Hint Systems May Negatively Impact Performance in Educational Games

Eleanor O'Rourke, Christy Ballweber, and Zoran Popović
Center for Game Science
Department of Computer Science & Engineering, University of Washington
{eorourke, christy, zoran}@cs.washington.edu

ABSTRACT

Video games are increasingly recognized as a compelling platform for instruction that could be leveraged to teach students at scale. Hint systems that provide personalized feedback to students in real time are a central component of many effective interactive learning environments, however little is known about how hints impact player behavior and motivation in educational games. In this work, we study the effectiveness of hints by comparing four designs based on successful hint systems in intelligent tutoring systems and commercial games. We present results from a study of 50,000 students showing that all four hint systems negatively impacted performance compared to a baseline condition with no hints. These results suggest that traditional hint systems may not translate well into the educational game environment, highlighting the importance of studying student behavior to understand the impact of new interactive learning technologies.

Author Keywords

Hint systems, educational games, behavioral analytics.

ACM Classification Keywords

H.5.0 Information interfaces and presentation: General

INTRODUCTION

Video games are famous for their ability to motivate players to solve challenging, complex problems. As a result, there is a growing interest in leveraging games to teach serious content to students [14, 22]. Games have many features that make them well-suited for learning: they can adapt to meet individual needs, provide interactive learning experiences, and scale easily [22]. Furthermore, educational games have been shown to increase student's motivation [25] and time-on-task [20]. Many commercial video games utilize real-time hint systems to provide help to struggling players. Personalized feedback is recognized as an important part of the learning process [16], and hint systems could be leveraged to improve the effectiveness of educational games. However, little is known about how hints impact learning-related behavior in these environments.

Hint systems are a central component of intelligent tutoring systems, and many hint design questions have been studied in this context. Studies have shown that students perform better when tutoring systems provide hints [6]. The most effective hints respond when students make mistakes, providing a scaffolded sequence of increasingly concrete information [4, 6, 27]. However, little is known about how these approaches will translate into the educational game environment. Games are typically played voluntarily, and they provide students with open-ended learning experiences. As a result, students' motivations to struggle, persist, use hints, and eventually learn are very different in educational games than in cognitive tutors. Understanding the impact of hint systems in this type of environment would therefore be valuable.

In this work, we study the effects of hint systems on player behavior in the educational game *Refraction*. We draw inspiration for our designs from successful hint systems used in intelligent tutoring systems and commercial video games. Although many factors influence hint design, we chose to focus on how hints are presented to players and the content they provide. We explore the importance of these characteristics by conducting a factorial experiment on the educational website BrainPOP. An analysis of data from 50,000 students shows that all four hint designs negatively impact performance compared to a baseline condition with no hints. Rewarding players with earned hints slightly improved player persistence, but this had no positive effect on performance.

Our findings suggest that the hint system designs that are effective in existing educational tools may not directly translate into educational video games. The learning environment provided by online games designed to be played at scale has many unique characteristics. Students participate voluntarily and can quit at any point, so maintaining engagement is paramount. Asking for help has a known negative connotation in games [5, 11], which may reduce the impact of hints in this setting. Further research is needed to understand the full generality of these results, however we hope these findings encourage developers to carefully consider the design of hint systems, particularly when engagement is a key component of the learning experience.

BACKGROUND

Personalized feedback is recognized as a central part of the one-on-one learning experience [16], and providing effective hints to students has long been a goal of the educational technology community [27]. Many questions relating to hint system design have been studied in the context of intelligent tutoring systems (ITS), however little is known about how these designs will translate into educational games. In this section, we review related research from the intelligent tutoring systems and video games literature.

Hints in Intelligent Tutoring Systems

Intelligent tutoring systems, designed to emulate one-on-one tutoring environments, have been studied for decades. Interactive feedback and hint systems are typically a central component of ITSs [27, 4], and research shows that students perform better in these environments when hints are provided [6]. Corbett and Anderson compared three hint designs in their LISP tutor to a version with no hints, and found that students in all three hint conditions performed over 20% better on a post-test than students in the no-hints condition [13]. As a result, many hint design questions have been studied in the context of ITSs. We focus on three design questions highlighted as important in the ITS literature: when should hints be given to students, what content should hints contain, and how should hints be presented [27].

In an overview of ITS behavior, VanLehn states that hints should only be given to students when they really need help [27]. Automated tutors should refuse to give help to until the student becomes frustrated or stops making progress, at which point a hints should be given automatically. Murray et al. implemented a policy based on this model in the DT Tutor [23], but their solution was computationally expensive and required excessive student data, making it unsuitable for real-world applications [27]. Most ITSs avoid this problem by only providing hints when students explicitly ask for help [27, 3]. One downside of this solution is that students frequently abuse help when it is not needed or refuse help when they are struggling [2]. However, Aleven and Koedigner show that these problems can be reduced if the ITS also teaches metacognitive and help-seeking strategies [2, 3].

Determining what content hints should contain is another important design question. In ITSs, hints often revel a step in a multi-step procedure. VanLehn states that the step should be chosen according to the following criteria: the step must be correct, it must be a step the student has not completed, it must align with the student's current solution plan, and it must honor the instructor's preferences about the desired solution method [27]. However, providing this type of hint requires access to a real-time model of the student's progress and the desired solution, which may not be available in all interactive learning systems. Arroyo et al. compared the effectiveness of concrete hint content that referred to physical examples and symbolic hint content that used numeric expressions and operations. They found that children with low cognitive ability perform better with concrete hints, while children with high cognitive ability perform better with symbolic hints [7].

ITSs typically present hint content textually, and provide a sequence of scaffolded hints that the student can click through to access increasingly specific help [27]. This sequence often begins with a "pointing hint", which highlights information that is relevant to completing the next step in a procedure [16]. This is followed by a "teaching" hint, which presents factual information required to complete the step, and finally a "bottom-out" hint that reveals how to complete the next step [16]. Khan Academy's practice problem system provides scaffolded hints that include richer content such as images and diagrams [17]. Arroyo et al. studied the effectiveness of interactive hints that require student response, and found that girls performed better with interactive hints but that boys performed better with standard textual hints [7, 8].

The hint systems that have been effective in intelligent tutoring systems provide a valuable theory around which to base the design of hints for other interactive learning systems. However, it is not currently known how these hint designs will translate into large-scale learning environments such as educational games. The effects of hints on student motivation and engagement are not well understood, and help buttons may not be effective in immersive environments. We seek to address these questions through our work studying the impact of hints in educational games.

Hints in Video Games

A central challenge in video game design is to support players as they develop the skills to solve increasingly complex problems. Games frequently depend on hint systems to help players who are stuck or frustrated. Some commercial games, such as *Bad Piggies* (Rovio Entertainment Ltd. 2012) and *SquareLogic* (TrueThought LLC 2009), provide hints through interfaces similar to the "hint buttons" found in ITSs. However, previous research has shown that there is a strong negative connotation to asking for help in games. Andersen et al. found that adding a help button to *Refraction* caused players to complete 12% fewer levels and play for 15% less time, even though only 31% of players actually clicked the button [5]. Big Fish Studios discovered that players avoided using the hint system they designed for *Drawn: Dark Flight* because they saw hints as punishment [11]. They were able to reverse this effect by replacing the word "hint" with "advice." These results suggest that the standard "hint button" interface for presenting on-demand help may not be appropriate in games where maintaining player engagement is crucial.

As a result, many designers have chosen to closely integrate hint systems in the game environment. Many immersive role-playing games, such as *The Legend of Zelda* (Nintendo 1998) and *Superbrothers: Sword & Sworcery EP* (Superbrothers and Capybara Games, 2012), provide help through characters that players encounter in the game world. These characters typically give textual hints during dialogs with the player. Other games, such as *Professor Layton* (Level-5 2007) and *Puzzle Agent* (Telltale Games 2010), allow players to purchase hints with earned game items such as coins or points. While these designs have many different properties, they all incorporate hints into the game environment and remove the negative connotation of asking for help by making players feel like they deserve to use the hints they have collected.

Despite these examples of successful hint systems in commercial games, many games do not provide hints. Game development companies often depend on external user-generated resources such as walkthroughs and wikis to support struggling players. These resources cost nothing to produce, however research in human-computer interaction has shown that context-insensitive help systems present many challenges for users, and are typically not as effective as help that is directly integrated into software products [1, 18, 19]. We believe that well-designed hint systems that are integrated into the game environment have more potential for success, particularly in the educational context where providing high-quality help resources is crucial.

Research Questions

The goal of this work was to gain a better understanding of how hints impact player engagement, performance and behavior in the educational game *Refraction*. To explore this question, we designed a factorial experiment comparing hint designs that varied along two axes: hint *presentation* and hint *content*. We chose to study these characteristics because they were highlighted as important in both the ITS and game literature. We implemented two methods of presenting hints to players: one that embeds hints into game levels and another that awards players "earned" hints as they progress. We chose to explore integrated hint designs rather than a standard "hint button" interface to reduce the negative connotation of asking for help, which has been shown to be a problem in video games [5, 11]. We were interested in learning how hint presentation would affect both student engagement and performance in *Refraction*.

Research Question 1: *Will player behavior differ based on hint presentation?*

Our two methods of presenting hints to players require that the system give a single hint at a time, rather than a sequence of scaffolded hints. We were therefore interested in studying the effectiveness of different types of hint content. We designed two hint models based on designs commonly used in ITSs: concrete "bottom-out" hints that tell players exactly which game pieces to use, and abstract "pointing" hints that highlight information relevant to the solution. We expected concrete hints to help players progress in the current level because they provide directly relevant information. However, we thought that abstract hints would produce better long-term performance because they provide suggestions that can generalize more easily.

Research Question 2: *Will concrete hints produce better immediate performance than abstract hints?*

Research Question 3: *Will abstract hints produce better long-term performance than concrete hints?*

We also included a baseline version of *Refraction* with no hints in our study to measure how the presence of hints affects player behavior. We expected all four hint systems to improve player performance compared to this baseline, since they provide access to help resources that are otherwise unavailable for struggling players.

Research Question 4: *Will all four hint systems improve performance over the baseline?*

To study these research questions, we released all five versions of *Refraction* to BrainPOP, a popular educational website for elementary school students that provides a game por-

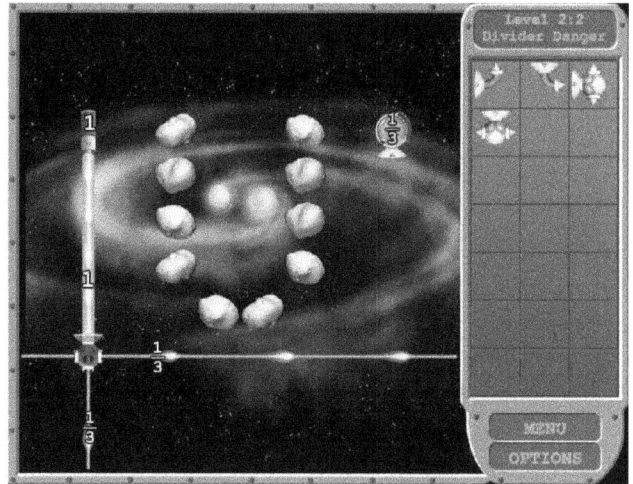

Figure 1. A level of Refraction. The goal is to use the pieces on the right to split lasers into fractional pieces and redirect them to satisfy the target spaceships. All spaceships must be satisfied at the same time to win.

Order	Topic
1	Directionality of bender pieces
2	Make halves by splitting in two
3	Make thirds by splitting in three
4	Make fourths by splitting in two twice
5	Make eighths by splitting in two three times
6	Make both a half and a fourth
7	Split in three first to make both a third and a sixth
8	Split in three first to make both a sixth and a ninth

Table 1. The eight milestone concepts covered by the level progression. The progression includes an introductory level and evaluation level for each concept, used to measure student performance.

tal [9]. We analyzed data from 50,000 players to determine the impact of incorporating hint systems into the game.

EXPERIMENT DESIGN

To explore the impact of hint systems on player behavior, we implemented four distinct hint systems in the educational game *Refraction*. These hint systems varied in how they presented hints to players, and what type of hint content they provided. We also implemented a baseline version of the game without hints. In this section, we describe each of our designs in detail and discuss how they are integrated into the *Refraction* game environment.

Refraction

This educational puzzle game was designed by game researchers and learning science experts at the Center for Game Science to teach fraction concepts to elementary school students. To play, a child must interact with a grid that contains laser sources, target spaceships, and asteroids, as shown in Figure 1. The goal of the game is to satisfy target spaceships by splitting the laser into the correct fractional amounts and avoiding asteroids. The player uses pieces that either change the laser direction or split the laser into two or three equal parts to achieve this goal. To win, the player must correctly satisfy all the target spaceships at the same time. *Refraction* has been successful at attracting elementary school students, and has been played over 250,000 times on the educational website BrainPOP since its release in April 2012.

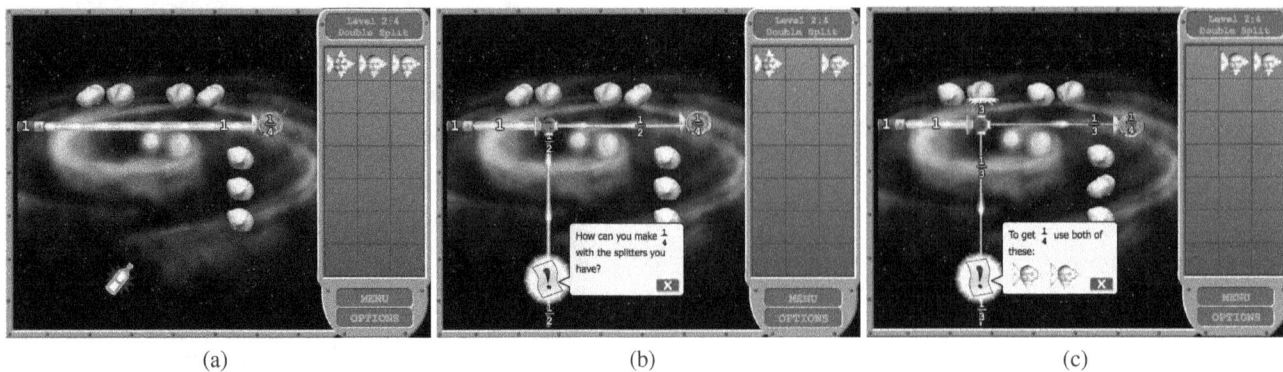

Figure 2. Screenshots of the embedded hints. Figure 2(a) shows an uncollected message in a bottle on the Refraction grid. Figure 2(b) shows an abstract hint being displayed. Figure 2(c) shows an concrete hint being displayed.

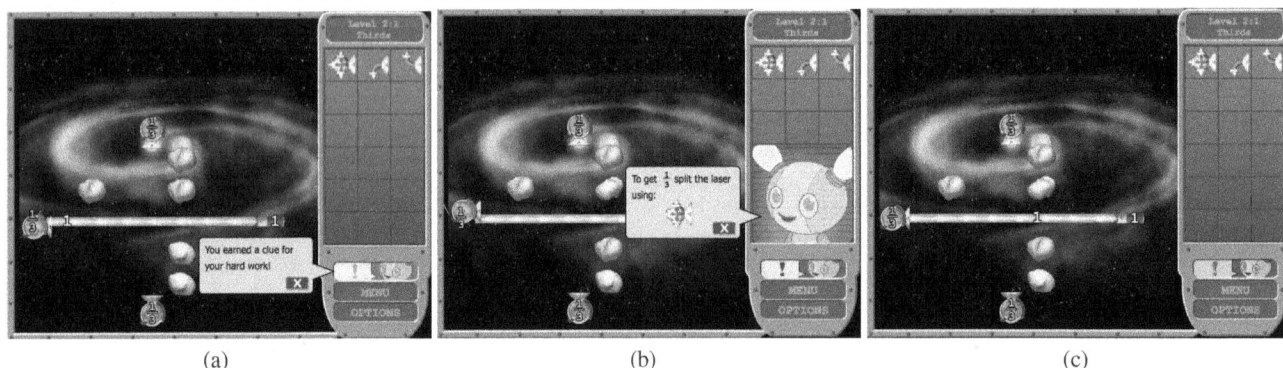

Figure 3. Screenshots of the earned hints. Figure 3(a) shows the message that displays when a hint is earned. Figure 3(b) shows a concrete hint being displayed. Figure 3(c) shows what the robot button looks like when there are no earned hints available.

For this study, we implemented a *Refraction* level progression that included 35 levels covering 14 mathematical concepts. In casual online gaming environments, the majority of players leave after a short period of time. Previous research shows that children play *Refraction* on BrainPOP for about three minutes on average [24]. As a result, we focus on the eight concepts described in Table 1 in our evaluation. For each concept, we designed an introductory level that presented the material for the first time. This level was directly followed by an evaluation level designed to give player a chance to apply their understanding of the concept. In both the introductory and evaluation levels, students had to choose between pieces that would make the correct target fraction and pieces that would make incorrect fractions. We use these levels to evaluate students' understanding of the eight fraction concepts.

Hint Presentation
The two hint presentation modalities we implemented for this experiment are based around designs that have been successful in commercial games. We avoided presenting hints to players using a simple "hint button", even though this method is commonly used in interactive learning environments, due to the negative connotations that players have with asking for help in games [5, 11]. Players are required to explicitly solicit hints in both of our designs, however we integrate these hints directly into the game environment. In one design, we embed

hints into *Refraction* levels and in the other we reward players with earned hints as they progress.

Our first hint presentation design encourages players to use hints by embedding them directly into *Refraction* levels and making them part of the game environment. This design was inspired by hints given in games like *The Legend of Zelda* (Nintendo 1998) where hints are encountered as the player explores the game world. Since *Refraction* is a puzzle game, rather than an immersive role-playing game, we added hints as a new type of level object that can appear on the game grid. We used an icon depicting a message in a bottle to represent the hint, as shown in Figure 2(a). To open the hint, the player must direct the laser through the bottle, as shown in Figure 2(b). Any fractional value of laser will open the hint, to make the hints simple to access. However, we placed hint bottles in grid squares off the main path in each level to ensure that the player had to actively solicit the hint. Embedded hints were added to the introductory levels of each of the 14 concepts in the level progression to encourage players to use help as they were learning. Players were only able to view hints on these 14 levels; there was no way to view a hint on a level that did not contain a bottle object.

Our second hint presentation design rewards players with "earned" hints as they progress to make them feel that they deserve help. This design is inspired by the hint systems in

Concept	Concrete	Abstract
Bender Piece	Use this piece: piece	Which side of the piece can the laser enter?
Single Split	To get fraction split the laser using: piece	How much power do the ships need to be happy?
Multiple Splits	To get fraction use both of these: piece piece	How can you make fraction with the splitters you have?
Multiple Fractions	To get first fraction use piece Then split again with piece to get second fraction	How can you make first fraction first, and then second fraction with the splitters you have?
Split Ordering	To get both first fraction and second fraction use this first:	Which splitter should you use first to make both ships happy?
Multiple Lasers	This level has two lasers! To get fraction use both of these: piece piece	This level has two lasers! How can you make fraction with the splitters you have?
Fractional Laser Source	The lasers have smaller values! Use both of these: piece piece	The lasers have smaller values! How much power do the ships need to be happy?
Fractional Laser with Splits	To get fraction split the laser fraction laser using: piece	How can you split laser fraction to make fraction with the splitters you have?
Multiple Fractional Lasers	To get fraction split the laser fraction laser using: piece	Which laser should you split to get fraction?

Table 2. A template defining hint content for the abstract and concrete hints. Text shown in red bold that says "piece" is replaced with an image of the piece associated with this hint. An example of this presentation is shown in 2(c). Red bold text that says "fraction" is replaced by the appropriate fractional value. An example of this presentation is shown in 2(b).

games like *Professor Layton* (Level-5 2007) in which players trade collected items for hints. Since *Refraction* is a casual puzzle game, we decided to implement a simple hint reward system where players earn hints at the beginning of certain levels. We created a cute robot character who serves as a guide and awards hints to players. We chose to personify hint-related messages because studies show that players are more willing to accept feedback from personified characters that neutral interfaces [21]. The robot notifies the player when a hint has been earned using a motivating message, shown in Figure 3(a). The player can view this earned hint at any time by clicking on the robot button, shown in Figure 3(b). The button is grayed out when no hints are available, as in Figure 3(c). Hints are earned at the beginning of each of the 14 levels that introduce new concepts to encourage player to use help resources on these levels, however players can chose to save earned hints and use them on any future level.

Hint Content

We designed two types of hint content that varied in the level of abstraction of the information they provided to players. Since our methods of presenting hints to players were designed to give the player a single hint at a time, we were not able to provide a scaffolded sequence of hints as is common in intelligent tutoring systems. We were therefore interested in learning about the impact of different types of hint content. We designed two types of hints based on designs that are commonly used in ITSs: concrete "bottom-out" hints and abstract "pointing" hints [16, 27].

The concrete hints tell the player exactly which pieces are required in the solution. Since it is difficult to reference pieces using text, we inserted images of the pieces into our hint content. The hint did not tell players where to put the pieces on the grid, but knowing which pieces are needed to make the correct fraction removes most of the problem's difficulty. An example concrete hint is shown in Figure 2(c). The abstract pointing hints were designed to highlight important information related to solving the problem. These hints were framed as questions that players should be asking themselves to arrive at the correct solution. These hints did not reference specific pieces or any other concrete game objects, so they did not include images. An example abstract hint is shown in Figure 2(b).

While we would have liked to follow the ITS standard and provide personalized hints to each player based on a cognitive model, we do not currently have access to real-time models of player progress and level solutions. As a result, we designed a single hint for each *Refraction* level that targets the central challenge presented by that level. While these hints may not always address the player's current struggle, they provide information integral to solving the level that the player could use to build a solution. Table 2 provides a complete template for the concrete and abstract hints used to cover the 14 concepts included in the *Refraction* level progression.

METHOD

To explore the impact of hint systems on player behavior in educational games, we studied how students play the five versions of *Refraction* on the educational website BrainPOP [9]. BrainPOP is best known for its curriculum resources, however it also provides an educational game portal intended for use in the classroom. The BrainPOP Educators community has over 210,000 members [10], and the website is used as a resource in around 20% of elementary schools in the United States (Traci Kampel, personal communication).

A central benefit of using the BrainPOP game portal to study hint systems is that it provides access to a large, diverse population of students. Interactions with hint systems are sparse, occurring only when students struggle and ask for help. As a result, studying hint usage across a large data set of students with varied backgrounds is valuable. Furthermore, these students do not know that they are part of an experiment, so our findings reflect their natural behavior. However, one downside of this resource is that we know very little about the children who visit BrainPOP or the contexts in which they play. We cannot collect any demographic information, and while we know that the website is primarily used in schools, we cannot tell whether children are playing in the classroom, in a computer lab, or at an after-school program. We mitigate the effects of these uncontrolled variables by evenly distributing them between conditions through the use of randomization and large sample sizes.

To collect our data, we set up *Refraction* to randomly assign new players to one of the five versions of the game, and logged all interactions players made with the game or its interface. We only included new players who were not already familiar with *Refraction* in our analysis, and we only used data from a player's first session to control for issues with shared computers in schools. To track players, we stored their player ids and progress in the Flash cache. This allowed us to selectively include new players and exclude return sessions. One drawback of this method is that a player who clears the cache or switches computers will be treated as a new player by our system. However, since the Flash cache is inconvenient to clear and this action deletes all saved game progress, we consider this risk to be small.

Our data set contains 79,895 players, and was collected between August 29, 2012 and November 20, 2012. *Refraction* was featured on the front page of BrainPOP's game portal between September 3rd and 7th 2012, allowing us to attract a large number of players during that period. Since the data sets for the five conditions contain different numbers of players, we randomly selected 10,000 players from each condition to include in our analysis.

DATA ANALYSIS AND RESULTS
We study the impact of our hint systems by analyzing a number of outcome measures that capture player engagement, performance, and hint usage behavior. We describe each of these metrics in detail below. Before performing this analysis, we evaluated the Kolmogorov-Smirnov test to assess the normality of our data, and found that it was statistically significant for all of our outcome measures. We therefore used non-parametric statistical methods for our analysis.

Our study has a 2x2 factorial design with two between-subjects factors: hint *presentation* with levels earned and embedded, and hint *content* with levels concrete and abstract. Our design therefore warranted a non-parametric factorial analysis. For our dichotomous outcome measures, we used a binomial logistic regression and a Cramer's V measure of effect size. For our continuous outcome measures, we applied the Aligned Rank Transform [15, 26] procedure, which aligns and ranks non-parametric data so that a standard ANOVA model can be used to perform a factorial analysis. For each main effect or interaction, the ART procedure aligns the data such that only that main effect or interaction remains, and then ranks the aligned data. A standard ANOVA model can then be used on the ranked data to measure the effect for which it was aligned. Unlike the conventional rank transform [12], the ART procedure is known to preserve the integrity of interaction effects and not inflate Type I errors. We used the ARTool program to align and rank our data [28]. We used an Eta-Squared (η^2) measure of effect size for these continuous outcome measures.

We also included a baseline condition with no hints in our study. We use pairwise comparisons to measure differences between our four hint designs and this baseline condition. Since this produces a large number of comparisons, we risk inflating alpha. To address this potential issue, we sum *p*-values across the four comparisons for each outcome measure to ensure that the combined alpha still falls below the 0.05 threshold. We use a Wilcoxon rank sums test and an Cramer's V measure of effect size for our our nominal vari-

ables, and a Kruskal Wallis test and an *r* measure of effect size for pairwise comparisons of our continuous variables.

We report effect sizes in addition to *p*-values to show the magnitude of the differences between our populations, since we are likely to find many significant differences due to our large sample sizes. For the Cramer's V and r measures of effect size, effects with values less than 0.1 are considered *very small*, 0.1 are *small*, 0.3 are *moderate*, and 0.5 or greater are *large*. For the η^2 measure of effect size, effects with values less than 0.01 are considered *very small*, 0.01 are *small*, 0.06 are *moderate*, and 0.14 or greater are *large*.

Earned hints improved engagement
We expected our hint designs to have an impact on player engagement, and specifically thought that concrete hints would keep players more engaged than abstract hints. To evaluate this hypothesis, we measured how long children played *Refraction*. BrainPOP offers a large variety of games, many of which teach fraction concepts, so we expected players to quit *Refraction* if they became bored or frustrated. Therefore, our time played metric captures how long players are willing to persist in the game before choosing to leave, an approximation of their level of engagement.

We calculate active time played by counting the number of seconds each player spends in the game, excluding menu navigation and idle periods with more than thirty seconds between actions. Any time spent reading hints was included in the active time. Our analysis showed that hint *presentation* had a significant main effect on active time played (F(1,39996)=17.29, $p<0.0001$, $\eta^2=0.001$). Children with earned hints played significantly longer, a median of 192 seconds compared to 178 seconds for players with embedded hints. There was no main effect of hint *content* (F(1,39996)=2.45, *n.s.*) or the interaction *presentation*content* (F(1,39996)=3.75, *n.s.*). We also used pairwise comparisons to measure the differences between our four hint conditions and the baseline condition. We found that players in both of the earned hint conditions played significantly longer than players in the baseline condition, as shown in Table 3. However, the combined alpha for our three significant comparisons is 0.0516, slightly above the 0.05 threshold.

We also analyzed the amount of time players spent reading hints to determine whether this could explain the observed differences in total time played. To calculate the total time each player spent reading hints, we counted the number of seconds between each "hint opened" and "hint closed" action and summed across all hint views. Our analysis showed that hint *presentation* had a significant main effect on the amount of time spent reading hints (F(1,39996)=272.74, $p<0.0001$, $\eta^2=0.07$). Players with embedded hints spent more time reading hint content, a median of 4.77 seconds compared to 2.62 second for players with earned hints. Hint *content* also had a significant main effect on the amount of time spent reading hints (F(1,39996)=20.14, $p<0.0001$, $\eta^2=0.04$). Players with concrete hints read for an average of 3.67 seconds, compared to 3.19 seconds for players with embedded hints. The *presentation*content* interaction had no significant effect (F(1,39996)=0.81, *n.s.*).

Condition	Time Played		Unique Levels Completed		Won Intro / Started Intro		Won Eval / Started Intro	
No Hints Baseline	$N = 20,000$	$n.s.$	$N = 20,000$	$p = 0.0015$	$N = 62,476$	$p = 0.0056$	$N = 62,476$	$p = 0.0002$
Concrete Embedded Hints	$Z = 0.12$		$Z = -3.17$	$r = 0.01$	$\chi^2 = 7.66$	$V = 0.01$	$\chi^2 = 14.31$	$V = 0.02$
No Hints Baseline	$N = 20,000$	$n.s.$	$N = 20,000$	$p < 0.0001$	$N = 61,448$	$p < .0001.$	$N = 61,448$	$p < 0.0001$
Abstract Embedded Hints	$Z = -1.16$		$Z = -5.88$	$r = 0.03$	$\chi^2 = 77.06$	$V = 0.04$	$\chi^2 = 45.18$	$V = 0.03$
No Hints Baseline	$N = 20,000$	$p = 0.0037$	$N = 20,000$	$n.s.$	$N = 64,169$	$p < .0001$	$N = 64,169$	$p = 0.0141.$
Concrete Earned Hints	$Z = 2.90$	$r = 0.01$	$Z = 0.74$		$\chi^2 = 26.55$	$V = 0.02$	$\chi^2 = 6.02$	$V = 0.01$
No Hints Baseline	$N = 20,000$	$p = 0.0478$	$N = 20,000$	$n.s.$	$N = 63,482$	$p < .0001$	$N = 63,482$	$p < .0001$
Abstract Earned Hints	$Z = 1.99$	$r = 0.01$	$Z = -0.77$		$\chi^2 = 64.44$	$V = 0.03$	$\chi^2 = 26.32$	$V = 0.02$

Table 3. Results from the pairwise comparisons between our four hint conditions and a baseline condition with no hints. We report results for the following four metrics: the amount of active time played, the number of unique levels completed, the percentage of players who start introductory levels and win, and the percentage of players who start introductory levels and win the corresponding evaluation level.

These results suggest that earned hints increase engagement, motivating children to continue playing for significantly longer. Furthermore, this increase cannot be explained by the time children spent reading hints. Players with earned hints spent significantly less time reading hint content those with embedded hints. This effect is very small, however previous studies have measured negative effects on time played after adding hints [5], so it is encouraging to see hint systems produce even neutral effects on engagement.

All hint systems negatively impacted performance
We expected all four of our hint systems to improve player performance because hints provide access to otherwise unavailable help. We thought that abstract hints would have a stronger positive effect on long-term performance than concrete hints because they provide more generalizable information. Since children play *Refraction* on BrainPOP for such a short period of time, we were unable to formally assess player performance using pre- and post-tests. Instead, we measure players' ability to complete game levels, since successfully solving *Refraction* puzzles requires some understanding of the concepts taught by the game.

First, we calculated the number of unique levels each player completed by counting levels with win events. Level completion rates are closely tied to the amount of time a player spends in the game, so we expected our results to mirror the time played results. Our analysis did show that *presentation* had a significant main effect on unique levels completed ($F(1,39996)=36.01$, $p<0.0001$, $\eta^2=0.007$), with players in the earned hint conditions completing a median of 7 levels, compared to 6 for players in the embedded hint conditions. Hint *content* also had a main effect on unique levels completed ($F(1,39996)=5.01$, $p<0.05$, $\eta^2 =0.004$). The median number of levels completed was 6 for both conditions, but players with concrete hints completed an average of 7.85 levels, compared to 7.59 for players with abstract hints. The *presentation*content* interaction did not have a significant effect ($F(1,39996)=0.03$, $n.s.$). Pairwise comparisons with the baseline condition, included in Table 3, showed that players in the two embedded hint conditions completed significantly fewer levels than players in the baseline.

Next, we analyzed how players performed on the first eight levels that introduced new concepts in our *Refraction* level progression. For each introductory level, we calculated the percentage of players who started the level and went on to win. We only included players who started each introductory

level in this analysis to control for differences in play time across conditions. Then, we averaged the percentages across all eight introductory levels to create a single combined metric. Our analysis showed that hint *presentation* had a significant main effect on the percentage of players who won introductory levels ($\chi^2(1,N=156,988)=19.98$, $p<.0001$, $V=0.01$). Players with embedded hints won more often, 88.52% of the time compared to 87.84% of the time for players with earned hints. Hint *content* also had a main effect on the introductory level win rate ($\chi^2(1,N=156,988)=11.78$, $p<.001$, $V=0.01$). Players with concrete hints won more often, 88.50% of the time compared to 88.06% of the time for players with abstract hints. The *presentation*content* interaction did not have a significant effect ($\chi^2(1,N=40,000)=0.81$, $n.s.$). Pairwise comparisons showed that players in the baseline condition performed significantly better than players in all four hint conditions, winning 89.45% of the time. See Table 3.

We used a similar metric to analyze performance on the eight corresponding evaluation levels. For each evaluation level, we calculated the percentage of players who started the introductory level for that concept and went on to win the evaluation level. This metric was designed to capture how well a player's understanding of a newly introduced concept transfers to a second puzzle. Again, we averaged the percentages across all eight evaluation levels to create a single combined metric. Hint *presentation* did not have a significant main effect on performance in the evaluation levels ($\chi^2(1,N=156,988)=0.09$, $n.s.$), and neither did hint content ($\chi^2(1,N=156,988)=2.83$, $n.s.$). However, the *presentation*content* did have a significant effect on performance in the evaluation levels $\chi^2(1,N=156,988)=5.64$, $p<.05$, $V=0.01$). Players with concrete earned hints won the evaluation level 77.01% of the time, players with concrete embedded hints won 76.55% of the time, players with abstract earned hints won 76.10% of the time, and players with abstract embedded hints won 75.52%. Pairwise comparisons showed that players in the baseline condition performed significantly better, winning 77.82% of the time. See Table 3.

These results directly oppose our expectations. We expected all of our hint systems to improve performance because they provide struggling players with help that was otherwise unavailable. However, players in all four hint conditions completed fewer levels than we anticipated given their average time played. It is possible that players complete fewer levels in the same amount of time due to the time they spend reading hint content. However, this does not explain why hints

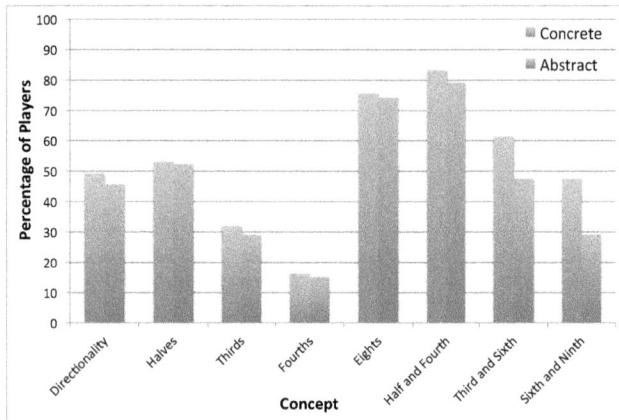

Figure 4. The percentage of players who opened Embedded hints on the eight introductory levels.

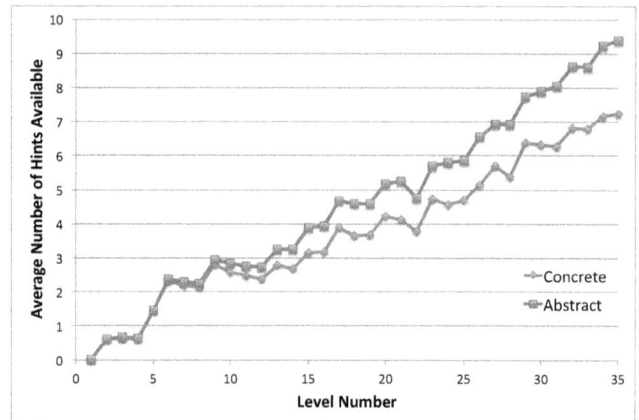

Figure 5. The average number of earned hints stored for each level in *Refraction*.

did not help players win the introductory levels. The hint presentation structure ensures that every player has access to a hint during every introductory level, so we would expect hints to improve performance on those levels. We also hypothesized that abstract hints would benefit player performance more than concrete hints, but we observed the opposite effect. Players with concrete hints performed better than those with abstract hints. While the sizes of these effects are small, hints certainly did not improve performance as we were expecting.

Embedded hints are viewed more often than earned hints

We were interested in learning how the four hint systems were used by players, and in identifying any differences in usage patterns. We were not sure how hint presentation would affect hint usage, but we expected players to use concrete hints more often than abstract ones because they provide more directly applicable information. To investigate how players used hints, we analyzed a variety of outcome measures.

First, measured the number of hints viewed by players in each condition by counting the number of hints opened by each player. Our analysis showed that *presentation* had a significant main effect on the number of hints viewed ($F(1,39996)=469.07$, $p<0.0001$, $\eta^2=0.05$). While the median number of hints viewed for both presentations was 1, players with embedded hints viewed an average 2.67 hints compared to 1.58 for players with earned hints. Hint *content* also had a significant main effect on hints viewed ($F(1,39996)=4.20$, $p<0.05$, $\eta^2=0.07$). Again, the median number of hints viewed in both conditions was 1, but players with concrete hints viewed 2.26 hints on average, compared to 1.98 viewed by players with abstract hints. The *presentation**content interaction did not have a significant effect ($F(1,39996)=1.06$, *n.s.*).

Next, we looked at how hints were used in the two embedded hint conditions. While we knew that embedded hints were viewed more often than earned ones, we wanted to measure what percentage of players chose to open embedded hints. We calculated the percentage of players who opened the message-in-a-bottle hints in the eight introductory levels. We found that nearly 50% of players viewed embedded hints on average. However, the graph in Figure 4 shows that

hint usage varies drastically depending on the concept, indicating that players are more likely to view hints for difficult concepts. We also found that *content* had a significant effect on the percentage of players who viewed hints ($\chi^2(1,N=60,874)=78.16$, $p<.0001$, $V=0.04$). 49.04% of players with concrete hints viewed introductory level hints on average, compared to 47.27% of players with abstract hints.

We also looked at how hints were used in the two earned hint conditions. Players could view earned hints on any level, not just the eight levels that introduced new concepts. To learn how players chose to use earned hints, we measured how many hints they had saved on average. The graph in Figure 5 shows the average number of saved hints available for each level in the progression. It clearly shows that players hoard earned hints, because the average number of hints saved increases as players progress through the game. We also analyzed whether hint content had any effect on saving behavior. For each player, we summed the number of earned hints the player had available during each level, and divided by the total number of levels played to calculate the average number of hints saved. We found that hint *content* had a significant effect on the number of hints saved ($Z=4.65$, $p<.0001$, $r=0.03$). Players were more likely to use concrete hints; those in the concrete hints condition had a median of 0.67 hints available, compared to 0.75 for those in the abstract hints condition.

After discovering that players hoard earned hints, we were interested in learning whether the hints they do view are used judiciously. To explore this question, we calculated whether players view earned hints on levels in which they are struggling. First, we computed the median number of moves made on each level across all five conditions. We considered a player to struggle if she made more than the median number of moves for that level. We found that players used hints on levels in which they struggled nearly 75% of the time. We also found that hint content had a significant effect on whether players used hints judiciously ($\chi^2(1,N=20,000)=141.59$, $p<.0001$, $V=0.08$). Players with concrete hints only used hints when they were struggling 74.32% of the time, compared to 80.40% of the time for players with abstract hints.

58

These results make sense intuitively. Embedded hints are viewed often because they have no value. However, earned hints can be saved for difficult future levels, so it is not surprising that players are reluctant to use them. Players in the earned hint conditions wait until they are struggling to view hints, while players with embedded hints view them when they are available. These results also suggest that concrete hints are more valuable than abstract hints, since players view concrete hints more often across both presentation types.

Concrete hints were more helpful than abstract hints
The analysis of hint usage in the earned and embedded hint systems suggests that players value concrete hints more highly than abstract ones. We were therefore interested in learning whether concrete hints were more effective at helping players complete levels than abstract hints.

To investigate the impact of hints on level completion rates, we analyzed the percentage of players who won levels in which they viewed hints. We found that over 75% of players won the levels in which they viewed hints in all four conditions. Hint *presentation* had a significant main effect on the win rate ($\chi^2(1,N=58,352)=1439.11$, $p<.0001$, $V=0.16$), with players who see embedded hints winning 89.64% of the time, compared to 78.42% for players with earned hints. This is likely because players in the earned hint conditions only choose to use hints when they are really struggling, since hints have value. Hint content also had a main effect on the win rate ($\chi^2(1,N=58,352)=250.88$, $p<.0001$, $V=0.07$), with players who see concrete hints winning 86.42% of the time, compared to 81.96% of the time for players with abstract hints. This suggests that the concrete hints are more useful to players in the immediate level than abstract hints.

We also explored how quickly the hints allowed players to win levels. For the players who won the level after viewing a hint, we calculated the number of moves they made between viewing the hint and winning. We hypothesized that more effective hints would help players win more quickly. We found that players in all four conditions made a median of 12 or fewer moves between viewing a hint and winning. A move is defined as any interaction the player makes with the game, such as picking up or placing a piece, so 12 moves corresponds to moving six pieces. Our analysis showed that *presentation* had a significant main effect on the number of moves F(1,49229)=955.98, $p<0.0001$, $\eta^2=0.040$). Players with embedded hints won levels more quickly, in a median of 8 moves compared to 10 for players with earned hints. Hint *content* also had a significant main effect on the number of moves (F(1,39996)=295.81, $p<0.0001$, $\eta^2=0.032$). Players with concrete hints won more quickly, in a median of 8 levels compared to 10 for players with abstract hints. The interaction *presentation*content* also had a significant effect on the number of moves (F(1,49229)=91.88, $p<0.0001$, $\eta^2=0.033$).

These results suggest that concrete hints are more helpful than abstract hints, allowing players to win levels more frequently and with fewer moves. Presentation also impacted the effectiveness of hints, however we believe this is because players with earned hints only chose to use hints when they were really struggling.

CONCLUSION
In this work, we study the impact of four hint system designs on player motivation, performance, and behavior in the educational game *Refraction*. An analysis of 50,000 students who played on the educational website BrainPOP revealed that all four designs negatively impacted performance when compared to a baseline condition without hints. While the size of these effects is small, hints clearly did not improve student learning as we had expected. A factorial analysis of the four hint designs showed that players with earned hints persist longer than players with embedded hints, suggesting that this hint presentation method may improve motivation. Students in the earned hint conditions hoarded their hints, only choosing to use them when they were really struggling. Players with embedded hints viewed hint content much more frequently. We also observed that players played a higher value on concrete hints, using them more often than abstract hints. The concrete hints were also more helpful, allowing players to win levels more often and more quickly than abstract hints.

These results highlight a number of design challenges associated with developing effective hint systems for educational games. However, one limitation of this work is that we cannot fully understand why these hints negatively impacted student performance. The hint content we designed provides information that is relevant to solving each *Refraction* level, and our analysis of hint usage suggests that hints help students solve levels. However, since our hint content did not adapt to the student's partial solution of the level, it is likely that our hints did not always address the student's current confusion. This could have influenced the effectiveness of our hints, particularly if students expected more personalized feedback.

Further work is needed to determine why these hints negatively affected player behavior in *Refraction*, and whether other types of hints could have more benefit. However, it is clear from our results that hint systems do not uniformly improve student performance in educational games. This finding is surprising, particularly given the success of hints in intelligent tutoring systems. However, educational games provide a very different learning environment than cognitive tutors, in which children play voluntarily and expect to be highly engaged. These factors could affect how hints are perceived by students. Further research is needed to understand the full generality of these results, however we expect our findings to translate to other learning environments with similar characteristics. We hope these results will encourage developers to consider the design of hint systems carefully, particularly when engagement is a key component of the learning experience.

ACKNOWLEDGMENTS
We thank creators of *Refraction* for making this work possible. In particular, we would like to recognize Marianne Lee and Brian Britigan who created the art for this study. We also thank Allisyn Levy of BrainPOP for promoting *Refraction* and helping us collect data. This work was supported by the Office of Naval Research grant N00014-12-C-0158, the Bill and Melinda Gates Foundation grant OPP1031488, the Hewlett Foundation grant 2012-8161, Adobe, and Microsoft.

REFERENCES

1. Adams, E. The designer's notebook: Eight ways to make a bad tutorial. *Gamasutra* (2011).

2. Aleven, V., and Koedinger., K. R. Limitations of student control: Do students know when they need help? In *Proceedings of the 5th International Conference on Intelligent Tutoring Systems*, ITS '00, Springer (Berlin, 2000), 292–303.

3. Aleven, V., McLaren, B., Roll, I., and Koedinger, K. Toward meta-cognitive tutoring: A model of help. *International Journal of Artificial Intelligence in Education 16* (2006), 101–130.

4. Aleven, V., Stahl, E., Schworm, S., Fischer, F., and Wallace, R. Help seeking and help design in interactive learning environments. *Review of Educational Research 73*, 3 (2003), 277–320.

5. Andersen, E., O'Rourke, E., Liu, Y.-E., Snider, R., Lowdermilk, J., Truong, D., Cooper, S., and Popović, Z. The impact of tutorials on games of varying complexity. In *Proceedings of the 2012 ACM annual conference on Human Factors in Computing Systems*, CHI '12, ACM (New York, NY, USA, 2012), 59–68.

6. Anderson, J. R., Corbett, A. T., Koedinger, K. R., and Pelletier, R. Cognitive tutors: Lessons learned. *The Journal of the Learning Sciences 4*, 2 (1995), 167–207.

7. Arroyo, I., Beck, J., Woolf, B. P., Beal, C. R., and Schultz, K. Macroadapting animalwatch to gender and cognitive differences with respect to hint interactivity and symbolism. In *Proceedings of the 5th International Conference on Intelligent Tutoring Systems*, ITS '00, Springer-Verlag (London, UK, UK, 2000), 574–583.

8. Arroyo, I., Beck, J. E., Beal, C. R., Wing, R., and Woolf, B. Analyzing students' response to help provision in an elementary mathematics intelligent tutoring system. In *In R. Luckin (Ed.), Papers of the AIED-2001 Workshop on Help Provision and Help Seeking in Interactive Learning Environments* (2001), 34–46.

9. BrainPOP. http://www.brainpop.com/.

10. BrainPOP Educators. http://www.brainpop.com/educators/home//.

11. Campbell, C. Casual meets core for a drink: Developing drawn. *Gamasutra* (2010).

12. Conover, W. J., and Iman, R. L. Rank transformations as a bridge between parametric and nonparametric statistics. *The American Statistician 35*, 3 (1981), 124–129.

13. Corbett, A. T., and Anderson, J. R. Feedback control and learning to program with the CMU LISP tutor. In *Paper presented at the annual meeting of the American Educational Research Association, Chicago, IL* (1991).

14. Gee, J. P. *What Video Games Have to Teach Us About Learning and Literacy.* St. Martin's Press, 2008.

15. Higgins, J. J., and Tashtoush, S. An aligned rank transform test for interaction. *Nonlinear World 1*, 2 (1994), 201–211.

16. Hume, G., Michael, J., Rovick, A., and Evens, M. Hinting as a tactic in one-on-one tutoring. *Journal of the Learning Sciences 5*, 1 (1996), 23–49.

17. Khan Academy. http://www.khanacademy.org/.

18. Knabe, K. Apple guide: A case study in user-aided design of online help. In *CHI '95 Conference companion on Human factors in computing systems*, ACM (New York, NY, USA, 1995).

19. Lau, T., Bergman, L., Castelli, V., and Oblinger, D. Sheepdog: Learning procedures for technical support. In *IUI '04 Proceedings of the 9th international conference on Intelligent user interfaces*, ACM (New York, NY, USA, 2004).

20. Lee, J., Luchini, K., Michael, B., Norris, C., and Soloway, E. More than just fun and games: assessing the value of educational video games in the classroom. In *CHI '04 Extended Abstracts on Human Factors in Computing Systems*, CHI EA '04, ACM (New York, NY, USA, 2004), 1375–1378.

21. Lee, M. J., and Ko, A. J. Personifying programming tool feedback improves novice programmers' learning. In *Proceedings of the seventh international workshop on Computing education research*, ICER '11, ACM (New York, NY, USA, 2011), 109–116.

22. Mayo, M. J. Video Games: A Route to Large-Scale STEM Education? *Science 323* (2009), 79–82.

23. Murray, R. C., VanLehn, K., and Mostow, J. Looking ahead to select tutorial actions: A decision-theoretic approach. *International Journal of Artificial Intelligence in Education 14*, 3-4 (2004), 233–278.

24. O'Rourke, E., Butler, E., Liu, Y., Ballwebber, C., and Popović, Z. The effects of age on player behavior in educational games. In *Foundations of Digital Games*, FDG '13 (2013).

25. Ricci, K. E., Salas, E., and Cannon-Bowers, J. A. Do computer-based games facilitate knowledge acquisition and retention? *Military Psychology 8*, 4 (1996), 295–307.

26. Salter, K. C., and Fawcett, R. F. The art test of interaction: A robust and powerful rank test of interaction in factorial models. *Communications in Statistics: Simulation and Computation 22*, 1 (1993), 137–153.

27. VanLehn, K. The behavior of tutoring systems. *International Journal of Artificial Intelligence in Education 16* (2006), 227–265.

28. Wobbrock, J. O., Findlater, L., Gergle, D., and Higgins, J. J. The aligned rank transform for nonparametric factorial analyses using only anova procedures. In *Proceedings of the SIGCHI Conference on Human Factors in Computing Systems*, CHI '11, ACM (New York, NY, USA, 2011), 143–146.

Teaching Recommender Systems at Large Scale: Evaluation and Lessons Learned from a Hybrid MOOC

Joseph. A. Konstan[1], J.D. Walker[2], D. Christopher Brooks[3],
Keith Brown[2], and Michael D. Ekstrand[1]

[1]Department of Computer Science and Engineering
[2]Office of Information Technology
University of Minnesota
Minneapolis, Minnesota, USA
{konstan,jdwalker,brown299,ekstr041}@umn.edu
[3]EDUCAUSE
Louisville, Colorado, USA
cbrooks@educause.edu

ABSTRACT

In Fall 2013 we offered an open online Introduction to Recommender Systems through Coursera, while simultaneously offering a for-credit version of the course on-campus using the Coursera platform and a flipped classroom instruction model. As the goal of offering this course was to experiment with this type of instruction, we performed extensive evaluation including surveys of demographics, self-assessed skills, and learning intent; we also designed a knowledge-assessment tool specifically for the subject matter in this course, administering it before and after the course to measure learning. We also tracked students through the course, including separating out students enrolled for credit from those enrolled only for the free, open course. This article reports on our findings.

Author Keywords

MOOC; open learning; distance learning; evaluation.

ACM Classification Keywords

K.3.1 Computer Uses in Education.

General Terms

Experimentation.

INTRODUCTION

In Fall 2013 we offered *An Introduction to Recommender Systems* as a full-semester hybrid online course. We offered this course simultaneously in two formats: as an online course through Coursera and as a 3-credit graduate-

level course at the University of Minnesota, using a modified flipped-classroom model where on-campus students enrolled in and completed all of the course activities on Coursera while also having live sessions with faculty and a teaching assistant to provide extra support on understanding course material and completing course assignments. This course was offered as part of the University of Minnesota's exploration of MOOCs (Massive Open Online Courses), and was launched after a strategic decision by the Department of Computer Science and Engineering to explore the medium and its implications. As part of this exploration, we focused extensively on gathering data for research; this course is the first such class we are aware of that supplements student process and outcome data with both a survey of student background/intent and a subject matter mastery pre-test/post-test to assess student learning outcomes.

Much of this course design derives from its original intent – to explore the medium of massive-scale online education as a vehicle for delivering in-depth advanced technical content at a level normally associated with a graduate-credit course. As we discuss below in detail, this led to both a longer format and a more intensive level of assignments. In our early design efforts, however, we recognized that a substantial number of potential students would lack the technical programming skills – or the inclination to invest programming time – to complete such a course. Accordingly, we adapted the design into a two-track course: students can complete a "concepts" track with a basic mathematics background (and without programming assignments) or may complete a comprehensive "programming" track that includes the concepts track plus programming lectures and six programming assignments. Both groups are able to earn statements of accomplishment. Much of our analysis looks at difference in intent and performance between those two tracks.

The rest of this paper is organized into six sections. First we provide a narrative and statistical overview of the course, followed by a review of our research goals and methods. The following section presents our quantitative results. Finally, we conclude with a discussion of these results, some qualitative results and anecdotes, and lessons learned.

OVERVIEW OF THE COURSE

The title of the course, "Introduction to Recommender Systems," reflects the course's origin and goals. Approximately two decades after the initial development of automated collaborative filtering—a technology for predicting user preferences based on the preference ratings of like-minded individuals—the field of recommender systems had blossomed. We sought to introduce students to the core algorithmic approaches to recommendation (non-personalized approaches, content-based filtering, user- and item-based collaborative filtering, dimensionality-reduction/matrix factorization methods, and brief introductions to case-based reasoning and social network/trust-based recommendation), to evaluation and metrics, to issues related to recommender systems data (implicit and explicit ratings, ratings scales, acquiring data, data validity), and to user interface and recommender design issues. We also decided we wanted to expose students to a broad set of perspectives, and as a result invited a large set of experts to join us for interviews on areas where they had special expertise, had built novel systems, or had conducted interesting research (mostly recorded over Skype or Google Hangouts, though in some cases recorded on-site).

The course grew naturally out of the context of the field. Our research group had founded the ACM Recommender Systems conference in 2007 (which has grown from about 120 attendees to over 300, and regularly moves among the US and Europe, and in 2013 for the first time Asia). Several books had been published in the field, including an introductory text and a research handbook. And we, and others, had regularly been invited to give tutorials and short courses on the topic. But to our knowledge, there were few if any regular courses covering the field.

This need juxtaposed nicely with both the interests of both our university and department in exploring the MOOC space. The department interest emerged from an strategic planning exercise in 2012 where the faculty determined that we should experiment with MOOC education for at least three reasons: (1) to explore how it may affect future University education, (2) to explore how MOOC instruction affects department visibility and reputation worldwide, and (3) to better understand the effort involved, technology, and teaching methods. We volunteered and were accepted into our University's set of trial MOOCs.

From the beginning, we were unique in three ways – first, we did not want to choose between offering this new material to the world, and offering it to our students. We decided to design what we thought would be a good 14-week, 3-credit graduate course, adjust that design to reflect MOOC delivery, and then deliver it both to the world and to our own students (through the flipped classroom model). We also recognized that the face-to-face sessions could be useful to MOOC students, so we recorded about half of these to make them available online.

Second, we were developing the software platform through which students could carry out many of the activities in the course. LensKit [1] is an open-source recommender toolkit developed specifically to support experimentation. It includes a set of core recommender algorithms and metrics, and provides both a scripting interface and an API to allow users to experiment with these and build their own.

Third, we wanted this course to be accessible to non-programmers as well as programmers. From our work in the field, we knew that many of the people interest in recommender systems focused on product marketing, business analysis, and other areas. And we were concerned that there might not be enough students with the skills and willingness to install a new software toolkit and engage in some fairly complex programming.

Given our goals, we promoted the course as widely as possible. We reached out to colleagues through mailing lists related to recommender systems and related topics. ACM agreed to announce the course to the roughly 1000 students who had watched Konstan's webinar in ACM's webinar series. And of course Coursera itself provides listings and promotion through their website and course recommender tools.

In the end, the course comprised eight modules (one-week introduction and wrap-up, and six two-week core modules organized around algorithms: five on different families of algorithms, and one focused specifically on evaluation and metrics). Together, these include:

- 42 recorded lectures (ranging from 10 to 45 minutes, most with pop-up comprehension questions)

- 14 recorded interviews with 12 experts in the field

- 12 recorded face-to-face class sessions, mostly focused on Q&A, though some contained other enrichment topics

- 7 non-programming "written assignments", most with video introductions.

- 6 programming assignments, most with video introductions.

- 2 multiple choice exams (36 questions each) on aspects not including programming

- A collection of online readings and references (some required, others for reference for interested students)

The final course design had two tracks. The programming track included all content and assignments. The concepts track excluded the programming assignments and a few video lectures specific to programming details.

Total enrollment for the course reached 28,389 students, of whom, 21,357 were active in some way (watching lectures, submitting work, posting to discussion forms) during the course. The number of people participating on a substantial and regular basis is much smaller. As is common in MOOCs, there was a high attrition rate. For Module 1 lecture videos, the number of student views per video was nearly 9000 as compared to only 2195 in Module 8. Likewise, the number of submissions for each of the seven written assignments (to be completed by both concept and programming track) dropped from 5420 for the first assignment to 530 for the final assignment. A total of 5643 students earned a non-zero final grade in the course.

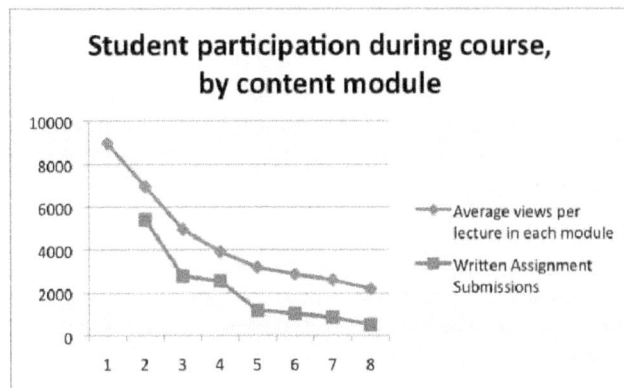

Student participation during course, by content module

Much of the interest of MOOCs lies in the breadth of their enrollment – in the fact that they recruit students from around the world. For this reason, understanding who MOOC students are, why they are taking the MOOC, and what they regard as success is critical to the task of assessing the impact of a MOOC.

From a pre-class survey, it appears that the students taking this course were a youngish, heavily male group largely residing outside the USA who were experienced and confident with respect to the course's subject matter.

- 70% of students reported having a degree in computer science or a related field, while 57% said they had taken more than 5 college-level computer science courses

- 80% said they were very or moderately confident in their programming skills

- 71% planned to complete the entire course, including assignments and assessments

- 87% were male

- 68% were under 35

- 67% reported being non-native English speakers of, but 76% reported proficient or advanced proficient English skills.

- 68% were residents of a country other than the USA

- the group was heavily weighted toward working professionals along with graduate students studying computer science or a related field.

RESEARCH GOALS
The empirical investigation of this course attempts to address the following research questions:

1. Do students learn in a MOOC? If so, how much, and which ones? Which variables predict normalized subject matter learning gains among MOOC students?

2. Do students in a face-to-face recommender systems course, who have access to MOOC resources, learn more than a comparable group of MOOC students who have access to recorded face-to-face instructional sessions?

3. What are different types of reasons for taking a MOOC? Do these correlate with demographics or with learning gains?

4. Do face-to-face students make use of MOOC resources? Do MOOC students make use of recorded face-to-face instructional sessions? Does the amount of such use moderate learning gains?

RESEARCH METHODS
Design. This study used a single-group cross-sectional research design to address questions having to do with the online MOOC student population. It also used a pretest-posttest non-equivalent groups design to address questions comparing the online student population with students in the face-to-face recommender systems class. Because students self-enrolled into the MOOC and into the face-to-face class, random assignment to treatment conditions was not possible. However, the instructor, course content and objectives, and main course assessments were held constant, and data on demographic characteristics and pre-course subject matter knowledge were used to ensure that the online and face-to-face groups being compared were similar in the relevant respects.

Participants. The participants in this study included the 39 students in the face-to-face section of CSci 5980: Recommender Systems as well as the approximately 4844 students who completed a pre-course survey and a pre-course recommender systems knowledge test. Students reporting an age of less than 18 years were removed from the study to comply with IRB regulations.

Measures. This study used pre- and post-class surveys designed to measure students' background, intentions with respect to the MOOC they are taking, and reactions to the MOOC experience. It also employed a 20-item instructor-generated pre- and post-class recommender systems knowledge test designed to measure gains in students' subject-matter knowledge over the semester.

All knowledge test questions were multiple-choice, with four content choices and a fifth "I have no idea" choice to permit students to admit they don't know. Examples of questions include:

1. Which of these best describes a case-based recommender?
   a. A recommender that provides recommendations for large sets of products sold together.
   b. A recommender the uses correlations among users to predict which items each user would enjoy.
   c. A recommender that uses product ratings to build a profile of attribute interests.
   d. A recommender that uses a database of examples and forms queries from user requests to explore items that meet user criteria.
   e. I have no idea.
2. What is the core idea behind dimensionality reduction recommenders?
   a. To reduce the computation from polynomial to linear.
   b. To strip off any product attributes so products appear simpler.
   c. To reduce the computation time from $O(n^3)$ to $O(n^2)$
   d. To transform a ratings matrix into a pair of smaller taste-space matrices.
   e. I have no idea.

The pre-class test (N = 4844) showed an acceptable level of difficulty and discriminated well among students with high and low levels of subject matter knowledge, with a mean score of only 18.85% and a standardized deviation of 15.13; only 3 students scored above 80% on the test and no student scored 90% or more.

Preliminary analyses. We began our data analysis by examining a set of questions that asked students to rate the strength of 15 different reasons for enrolling in a MOOC. The questions included items such as "This subject is relevant to my academic field of study", "because this course is offered by a prestigious university", and "I think taking this course will be fun and enjoyable". An exploratory principal components analysis was conducted, and we extracted four factors that had Eigenvalues > 1 along with acceptable factor loadings for all of the 15 individual items. The underlying constructs for these factors were:

1. University/instructor-related reasons
2. Pragmatic/access reasons
3. Professional reasons
4. Interest/enjoyment-related reasons

These constructs were used to help us segment and define the student population in this course -- for instance, by

serving as predictors in the regression analyses described below.

RESULTS

Completion/retention. While much early MOOC evaluation focused on very low rates of full course completion, as we improve our understanding of the reasons for which students take MOOCs, it becomes imperative to attend to the notion that "success" might be relative to the individual. To explore this idea, we collected data on the amount of the MOOC students intended to complete, and on how much they completed relative to those expectations.

We found that the vast majority of students (72.5%) who completed the pre-course survey intended to complete the entire course, rather than only certain parts, or the course material but not the assignments. Further, a large majority of students (72.4%) reported that they completed as much or more of the MOOC than they had intended to. Finally, nearly all of the students (95.75%) who said they completed less of the MOOC than they intended also reported that they found the experience useful nonetheless.

We also examined two different non-relative measures of course completion: completing the sixth writing assignment in the class and completing the third part of exam 2. We constructed a multivariate ordered logistic regression model for each of these measures, based on students' demographic characteristics, motivations, baseline knowledge, and activity during the semester, in an effort to understand how the characteristics of students influence completion.

Both of the models were significant, but the amount of variance in the dependent variables explained by the models was extremely small (pseudo R^2 = 0.059 and 0.066). Nonetheless, as the data in Table 1 show, the models offer several insights.

First, it is worth noting how many factors did *not* affect course completion, defined either by the writing-based or the exam-based variables. Age, sex, English proficiency, and USA residency all had no impact on completion; nor did status as a professional, graduate or undergraduate student, or most of the reasons students expressed for taking this MOOC.

However, the models show that knowledge, experience, and strong intentions influenced both measures of completion. The higher a student's score on the knowledge pre-test, the greater the number of MOOCs she had taken in the past, and the stronger her intention to complete the course, the more likely was it that she would complete both the writing assignment and exam in question.

The two models are also similar in that completion in both senses is negatively predicted by a student's reporting greater introversion, and by taking a larger number of concurrent courses. The latter conclusion may be related to

Table 1. Logistic Regression for Predicting Completion			
		Writ HW 6	Ex II Pt III
Student Reasons	Professional	1.069 (0.115)	1.097 (0.107)
	University/Instructor	0.9874 (0.1020)	0.891 (0.083)
	Interest/Enjoyment	1.364* (0.202)	1.235 (0.161)
	Pragmatic/Access	0.902 (0.088)	0.960 (0.084)
Programming Skills Confidence		1.150 (0.115)	1.257* (0.116)
Track	Programming	1.058 (0.256)	0.985 (0.211)
	Concepts	1.330 (0.366)	1.218 (0.302)
Experience	Professional	0.799 (0.224)	0.610 (0.157)
	Graduate Student	1.061 (0.277)	0.834 (0.203)
	Undergraduate Student	1.057 (0.412)	0.697 (0.253)
Aptitude (Baseline Knowledge Test)		1.107*** (0.024)	1.113*** (0.022)
Intention to Complete Course		1.985*** (0.314)	2.168*** (0.316)
Number of Courses Taken Concurrently		0.859** (0.040)	0.881** (0.035)
Number of MOOCs Taken Previously		1.025* (0.013)	1.029** (0.011)
Hours/Week Available		1.013 (0.009)	1.008 (0.008)
Introversion/Extroversion		0.880* (0.044)	0.874** (0.039)
Sex		1.223 (0.306)	1.095 (0.240)
English Proficiency		0.733 (0.131)	0.803 (0.129)
Location: USA		1.104 (0.192)	0.913 (0.146)
Age		1.078 (0.046)	1.062 (0.042)
Constant		0.002*** (0.002)	0.004*** (0.003)
N		3326	3326
Chi-Square		102.18****	133.59****
Pseudo-R^2		0.059	0.066
Log likelihood		-810.965	-950.188

NOTE: Reporting odd ratios (standard errors)
*$p < .05$; **$p < .01$; ***$p < .001$; ****$p < .0001$

the common finding that time pressures are the factor most often reported by MOOC students as a reason for not completing as much of a course as they had intended to. The two models diverge with it comes to a student's taking the class for reasons of interest or enjoyment, which only predicts significantly her completing the writing assignment, and with respect to a student's level of programming confidence, which only predicts significantly her completing the exam.

Result: Intention predicts completion; little else does.

Recommender System Knowledge. In almost all studies of MOOC-based education, it is difficult to determine how much or how well students learn in a MOOC because the student population is widely distributed, and one typically does not know how much understanding or knowledge students began with.

In this study, as has been mentioned previously, the instructors produced a 20-item knowledge of recommender systems exam that was administered to students at the beginning and at the end of the course. The pre-course knowledge test (N = 4844) was intended to establish the level of recommender systems knowledge with which students began the course, so that learning gains over and above that baseline could be determined. It was designed to focus specifically on the type of content students would learn in the Concepts track, but was developed before the course material was fully designed.

The post-course knowledge test was taken by far fewer students (N = 304) due to the MOOC student attrition that is well known in the field. However, appropriate statistical tests revealed that students who took the post-knowledge test were reasonably representative of the larger group in terms of demographic characteristics, reasons for taking the class, etc. The main difference of note was in the baseline knowledge test, with a large difference (almost .5 of a standard deviation) favoring post-test takers. So the post-test students were an elite group with respect to their incoming knowledge of recommender systems, but were otherwise similar to their fellow students.

For each student who took both the pre- and post-course knowledge test, normalized learning gains were calculated (McConnell et al., 2005), defined as a student's knowledge post-test score minus her pre-test score, divided by the magnitude of her possible knowledge gains (i.e., post-test - pre-test/100% - pre-test). This variable, which is the main learning outcome of interest in this study, takes a student's starting point into consideration, and tries to account for the fact that it is more difficult to make gains when one begins near the top of the testing scale.

Finally, as a preliminary test of validity, we determined that knowledge post-test scores correlated well, and significantly, with the exam portion of students' final grades in the course (r = .621, p < .001). Normalized gains also correlated moderately well with students' exam scores (r = .509, p < .001).

Across all students who took either the pre- or post-course knowledge test, the course appeared to result in large learning gains, with the pre-test mean of 18.85%as shown by the difference in mean scores for the pre- and post-knowledge tests (see Table 2). Much of this effect could, however, be due to student self-selection, if only the stronger students remained in the class at the end of term and took the post-test.

To examine this possibility, we used a paired-samples t-test which revealed that the 262 students who took both the pre- and post-knowledge tests also showed large gains in recommender systems knowledge, indicating that the apparent improvement in student knowledge is not spurious:

Result: Student knowledge increased.

It is usually difficult to study systematically the differences in learning between face-to-face and MOOC students, due to the lack of a measure of baseline understanding or knowledge.

In this study, our pre-course knowledge test provided that baseline measure. If we compare face-to-face students and online students who took both the pre- and post-knowledge tests, we find that these two groups of students were statistically equivalent in terms of the recommender systems knowledge they began the course with.

We can then compare the two groups in terms of the normalized gains in knowledge they achieved over the semester. We find a nominal difference of 8.4% favoring the face-to-face students. This difference is moderate in size (about 1/3 of a standard deviation), although the very small N in the face-to-face group prevents this effect from attaining statistical significance.

Table 2. Performance on Knowledge Tests				
	N	Pre-test	Post test	p-value/ gain
All students (pre or post)	4844 304	18.85 (15.13)	69.05 (18.24)	n/a
Paired pre- and post-	262	24.71 (15.85)	69.90 (17.80)	<.001
Face-to-face students	10	25.00% (18.41)	75.50% (10.91)	66.71% (15.06)
Online-only students	251	24.80% (15.74)	69.74% (18.01)	58.31% (26.13)
Difference of means tests, p-value		.969	.317	.314
NOTE: Reporting mean exam scores (std. deviation). Gains reported are normalized learning gains.				

The low N in the face-to-face group limits the statistical analyses that can be performed, and it may also limit the external validity of our findings. Regardless, this finding parallels that of studies that suggest that blended learning environments produce greater learning gains than online environments alone (Means et al., 2010).

Result: Face-to-face students learned at least as much.

One worry about online education has traditionally been that support and assistance for struggling students are limited, so that students with weaker backgrounds in a subject may drop out or fail to benefit as much as they might in a face-to-face course.

To determine whether this was true in the Recommender Systems course, we divided the Recommender Systems students into quartiles based on their scores on the baseline knowledge test. We then used a one-way ANOVA test to compare the normalized knowledge gains of the four groups.

Broadly speaking, students with different incoming levels of recommender system knowledge benefited to very similar degrees from the course. So it is not the case that the course was beneficial to students who already knew a good deal about recommender systems, but left behind students who were relative neophytes.

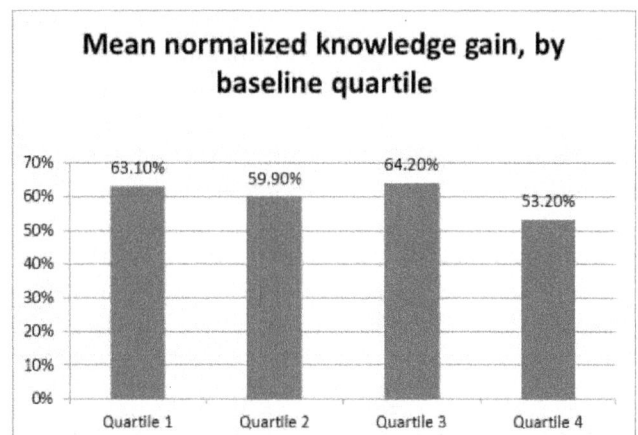

Mean normalized knowledge gain, by baseline quartile

An ANOVA analysis did reveal that the difference between the two highest quartiles 3 and 4 is statistically significant (p < .05), possibly reflecting ceiling effects limiting the potential to measure learning gains for top-quartile pre-test scorers.

Result: Students at all incoming knowledge levels benefited similarly from the course

One analytic dimension of interest was the difference between the programming and concepts tracks in the course. Examining the pre-course and post-course knowledge tests shows that students in the concepts track began the course with somewhat weaker recommender systems knowledge, but made gains that were similar to those of students in the programming track. We should note the caveat that the pre-test, post-test, and course exams were designed to test only recommender systems concepts knowledge, and specifically did not test programming knowledge.

Among students who took both the pre- and post-knowledge tests, programming and concepts track students showed nearly identical large gains in recommender systems knowledge:

Table 3. Raw Knowledge Gains by Track			
Track	N	(post - pre) mean raw gain	significance
Concepts	49	45.92	p < .001
Programming	184	45.65	p < .001

Further, an independent-samples t-test shows no significant difference between the normalized gains of the concepts and programming track students:

Table 4. Mean Normalized Gains by/between Tracks				
Track	N	Mean normal-ized gain	Std. Dev.	p-value
Concepts	49	59.14%	23.71	p = .971
Programming	184	58.99%	25.62	

Mindful of our caveat, we recognize that programming track students should have gained a set of knowledge related to programming recommender systems not learned by the concepts track students. This was not separately assessed.

Result: Students in the programming and concepts tracks had similar gains in concepts knowledge.

To help us what factors contribute to learning in a course with such a breadth of student characteristics, we constructed an OLS regression model that attempts to predict normalized knowledge gains. The predictors in this model were variables that were plausibly *causal* -- not student perceptions or opinions, but students' demographic characteristics, motivations, baseline knowledge, and activity during the semester.

While the model was significant (F = 5.030; p < .0001), the amount of variance in the dependent variable explained by the model is relatively small (adjusted R^2 = 0.202). Nonetheless, as the data in Table 4 show, the model yields several conclusions.

First, the Recommender Systems course treated students equally across many dimensions. The following variables made no difference to the normalized gains a student achieved:

- sex
- age
- USA residence
- native speaker of English
- programming confidence
- number of programming courses taken

- number of concurrent courses
- being a professional
- being a grad student
- being an undergraduate student
- reasons for taking the course

Second, the following variables did predict normalized gains:

- baseline recommender systems knowledge (negatively)
- being in the concepts track
- number of written assignments completed (strongest)
- English proficiency (marginally significant; p = .059).

Interestingly, despite the large effect size associated with the number of written assignments a student completed (over 1/3 of a standard deviation per standard deviation increase in the predictor), the other variables in the model that measured student academic effort and activity did not approach statistical significance.

Table 5. OLS Regression to Predict Normalized Knowledge Gain	
Hours per Week on Course	.015/.056 (.019)
Forum Posts	-.001/-.041 (.001)
# of Written Assignments	.052/4.230 (.012) ****
# of Progr. Assignments	.004/.061 (.007)
Progr. Skills Confidence	.006/019 (.024)
Progr. vs Concepts Track	-.105/-.163 (.053) *
Progr. Courses Taken	.010/.083 (.009)
Pre-course Knowl. Test	-.004/-.281 (.001) ****
English Native Language	-.022/-.041 (.046)
Sex	.014/.018 (.052)
English Proficiency	.044/.148 (.023)
Location: USA	.021/.038 (.044)
Age	.007/.049 (.010)
Constant	.134 (.142)
N	207
F	5.030****
Adjusted R^2	0.202

NOTE: Cell entries are unstandardized/standardized OLS coefficients with standard errors (in parentheses). Only factors that contribute to the highest adjusted R^2 model are listed.
*p < .05; ****p < .0001

Predictor variables having to do with programming also did not predict significantly students' normalized knowledge gains -- except for being in the programming track as opposed to the concepts track, which was associated with a slight *decrease* in normalized gains.

While it is a success for a course to not reward certain sub-populations of students more richly than others, the failure of the model to predict much of the variability in normalized gain scores indicates that the model is mis- or under-specified. In all likelihood, the right set of predictor variables was not available, and this may reflect the diversity of the student population who enrolled in this MOOC.

Result: Normalized knowledge gains are very difficult to predict; measures of relevant effort were strongest.

To further understand the determinants of student success in this course, we constructed an OLS regression model that attempts to predict final grades in the course, on the basis of students' demographic characteristics, motivations, baseline knowledge, and activity during the semester.

The model was significant and the amount of variance in the dependent variable explained by this model (adjusted R^2 = 0.516) was substantially larger than for the model that attempted to predict students' normalized gain scores. The following lessons can be learned from the data in Table 6.

First, as was the case with normalized learning gains, the Recommender Systems course treated students equally across many dimensions with respect to the final grades they earned. The following variables made no difference to final grades:

- sex,
- age,
- English proficiency,
- native speaker of English,
- programming confidence,
- being a professional,
- being a grad student,
- being an undergraduate student, and
- reasons for taking the course.

However, a very different set of variables predicted final grades in the course:
- number of concurrent courses taken (negatively),
- number of other students in the course known,
- number of programming courses taken,
- being in the programming track, and
- number of hours per week devoted to the course, and
- amount of the course completed, relative to expectations (the strongest predictor).

These results require a few caveats and explanations. Grades in the course were a combination of exam scores (24%), written assignment grades (40%) and programming assignment grades (36%). Accordingly, students in the programming track *who actually completed assignments* would have a significantly higher potential score. We considered scaling grades based on total possible grade, but found that many students who had declared concepts track had also completed some programming assignments (in some cases, all of them). Even functional classifications of track (e.g., concepts track = submitting fewer than *n* programming assignments, where *n* might be 1, 2, or 3) introduce complications, as these definitions would classify

many students who simply stop completing assignments as concepts track, when in fact all the work they did was within the framework and intent of the programming track. This particular challenge is related to the structure of Coursera courses, which do not support explicit tracks of the type we wanted. We may address this in the future with separate course offerings for the concepts track and the comprehensive (including programming) track, though we recognize one disadvantage of this model would be losing the shared discussion between students with different backgrounds and/or intentions.

In addition, it is not surprising that amount of course completed (which is probably interpreted by students as number of assignments completed against an expectation of "all of them") and hours spent per week both would be strongly predictive of course grade. The most interesting result is the negative correlation with number of concurrent courses taken, which was not significantly correlated with knowledge gain (indeed, its inclusion reduced the predictive power of the model). We feel this difference suggests underlying causes, specifically it may be that students enrolling in a larger number of concurrent courses adopt a strategy focused on maximizing learning while minimizing invested effort – in particular, worrying less about attaining top grades on assignments and focusing instead on the level of effort that provides the greatest learning. We lack sufficient data to validate this hypothesis, but leave it for others to consider in qualitative or follow-up quantitative research.

Table 6. OLS Regression to Predict Final Grade	
Progr. confidence	-1.066/-.039 (1.892)
# of progr. courses taken	1.950/.166 (.746) **
# of concurrent courses	-1.841/-.123 (.933) *
English native language	1.00/.019 (3.833)
Sex	1.926/.025 (4.206)
US residence	4.769/.090 (3.622)
English proficiency	1.549/.054 (1.845) **
Age	.378/.026 (.843)
Plans to complete	5.153/.112 (2.761)
Progr. vs. concepts track	17.674/.288 (4.114) ***
Other MOOCs prev taken	.190/.048 (.246)
# of students known	2.268/.122 (1.034) *
Hours/week on course	5.552/.206 (1.508) ***
Number of forum posts	.133/.062 (.116)
Amt of course completed	19.930/.454 (2.460) ***
Pre-course knowl. test	.004/.003 (.084)
Constant	-29.352 (13.787)
N	181
Adjusted R^2	.516
F Test	13.064 ***
NOTE: Cell entries are unstandardized/standardized OLS coefficients with standard errors in parentheses. Only factors that contribute to the highest adjusted R^2 model are listed. *p < .05, **p < .01, ***p < .001	

QUALITATIVE RESULTS AND ANECDOTES

As with any educational research, many of the lessons we learned come from the rich set of interactions with the course students. Too often the dominant message from MOOCs is about the large number of students who sign up but do not complete (and in many cases do not even start). This may be an inevitable, and not undesirable, consequence of free registration—it encourages students to enroll in more courses than they intend to finish, and to make choices over time. What impresses us, however, is the deep commitment from many of the students who take the course seriously, and the potential for impact in ways that exceeds that of the traditional classroom.

Two anecdotal stories stand out. Early in our course (during module 2, the module on non-personalized recommenders) we saw a post from an enrolled student linking to the website he operated (a marketplace for rare coins) showing that he'd incorporated the product association recommender technique we'd taught the week before into the site. A few weeks later we heard from a set of students in Russia who were incorporating their new understanding of recommender systems into a web-business consulting service. These are not isolated examples; the class forums and private conversations show extensive interest in "use-it-now" learning.

These indications of impact, and the separate pieces of positive feedback (it was wonderful meeting some of the students from China at the Recommender Systems conference in Hong Kong) warm the hearts of faculty; sometimes this warmth is quite needed. We learned early that the free nature of such courses does not prevent vehement requests from students who want the course customized to their needs and goals (we stated up front the need for Java in the programming assignments, and the use of LensKit, but a vocal contingent still protested regularly, explaining why we could and should instead build the course around their preferred set of tools). Overall, however, we found students to be quite reasonable. We appreciated the humor when another student later replied with a humorous post explaining why we should teach the course in Fortran-77, *his* preferred language. After all, the student said, the whole point of free education is to have instructors create exactly what you want.

We had some experiences that cause us to wonder about the as-yet unsettled culture of these MOOCs. Numerous students complained about assignments that we were "forcing them to do" but that they felt should be optional. Our appeal that everything is optional met with responses that these students felt their grade, and statements of accomplishment, were a critical point of pride. They were clearly very grade-concerned. Other students' protests that the point of open education is to be able to pick and choose did not resonate with them. We valued greatly the pickers-and-choosers, the students who did the assignments they found valuable and skipped what they did not. But the question of whether MOOCs should be designed as rigorous with students opting out, or minimal with students opting in for more rigor is still an unsettled one.

In our experience, students really hated peer grading (not uniformly, but a large vocal number, with almost no students voicing support for it). We recognize this differs from the experience of some others, and suspect it has a lot to do with the nature of what is graded. Our biggest challenge was in getting students to grade work where the point of peer grading was not qualitative evaluation of creative and divergent work, but rather almost mechanical grading of work too complex to automate (examples of this include some written analysis exercises where the results couldn't be reduced to numbers or parseable strings, and one programming assignment where we graded the results automatically but had students peer-grade the code as a sanity check that the submitted work wasn't simply calculated results, but was actually programmed). Our preference would be to avoid grading these types of exercises entirely, but many students value getting grades. Automation is good as far as it goes, but it puts significant limits on the assignment design. Perhaps at some point the answer will be small fees and paid crowdsourcing of grading. For now, we don't have a solution to this challenge yet, but we think it is a factor worth serious consideration when designing course assessments and assignments.

At the end of the course we held a lengthy debriefing session with the on-campus students. For many of this, this was one of the few times they'd come to a face-to-face session. We were somewhat surprised that the overwhelming number of students preferred this format to a traditional lecture-based course. Students cited the benefits of being able to review the lectures at their own pace and at their own convenience. Some non-native English speakers cited the benefits of being able to pause and replay things that were hard to understand. In general, the reactions of on-campus students were similar to those of online students, though the on-campus students were particularly unhappy with peer-grading of their work by the online students (though we did offer the option of a TA review to correct serious misgradings).

One last small lesson. We came into this course skeptical about the ability to offer meaningful examinations at scale. We have rarely used multiple-choice questions, particularly when dealing with advanced topics such as recommender system design and detailed algorithmics. It was therefore a pleasant surprise that the exams we did use proved to be consistent and effective. We had two exams, each covering 7 weeks of the course. Each exam had 36 multiple-choice questions divided into three 12-question, 30-minute timed parts. The separate parts were designed to keep the time needed for each chunk small, to limit the potential harm of a student being unable to complete a part, and to help students assess whether they needed to study further before taking the second part. Exam scores correlated well between the parts, and the exams were one of the areas that generated the fewest complaints from students. The time needed to write good multiple-choice questions is fairly high, but the time saved in grading is substantial. We are experimenting with more multiple choice exams in future face-to-face classes.

DISCUSSION AND LESSONS

Based on the results presented above, it is clear that massive, online, open courses attract a significant and diverse group of students, that they come to a course with different goals and intentions, and that those who persist leave with substantially more knowledge of the subject matter than they arrived with. Predicting course completion is hard – about the only pre-course factor that is highly predictive is intention, and even this is probably dominated by the fact that those who do not intend to complete usually don't. Predicting knowledge gains is even harder. The good news is that knowledge gains do not correlate significantly with age, sex, student level, or motivation for teaching the course. The factors that are predictive all relate to effort, prior courses, and baseline knowledge (in what appears to be only a negative effect resulting from ceiling effects).

We also wanted to share a few useful lessons from this course with others who may teach similar courses in the future:

- We found that a successful and motivating activity was the generation of a class-specific dataset used for the assignments. We had students contribute movie ratings (over 5000 students contributed ratings to up to 100 movies in the first week) and then distributed that dataset to the course through the assignments. Students could attach an identifier to their data line to see how each recommender performed for them.

- We also assigned personal test data to each student for many of the programming assignments. We write scripts that would assign test cases to users (usually 5 of them). This increased the burden on grading software (which had to verify the correct test cases), and on pre-testing (we had to ensure no student received degenerate cases), but it provided both interest and a barrier to cheating by passing around correct datasets.

- We found the use of open source infrastructure for distributing course software was a big success. We used Maven, a tool that made it possible for distribution to be close to automatic. While some students had little experience with installing software, we found most were able to complete this task quickly without need for help.

- We did struggle with the tension between course semantics and the Coursera-tool concepts for our assignments (this isn't specific to Coursera, we expect it would be true with any similar tool). We had concepts we wanted to communicate: written assignments, programming assignments, exams, etc. The problem is that the tool has its own concepts (quizzes, exams, homeworks, programming assignments) that each have different types of grading option. This led to confusion. We'd have written assignments that had to be created as "programming assignments" to support grading scripts. Or programming assignments that were implemented as quizzes. This is a challenge that could be helped by better hiding the tool implementation or having a complete mapping between concepts and grading options.

ACKNOWLEDGEMENTS

A massive course such as this one is the product of a team. We would like to thank our entire course team, with special thanks to our video team, led by James Ondrey and David Lindeman, our online assignment consultant Ken Reily, and especially our teaching assistant Michael Ludwig. We also thank our many colleagues who taught massive-scale courses before us and generously shared their advice. With this paper we remember our colleague and mentor John Riedl, who jointly conceived this course but passed away before it could be brought to fruition. And we want to especially thank our students, for their patience as we've explored this space with them, for their participation in the surveys and knowledge tests we've used for this research, and for their incredibly valuable feedback throughout the course.

REFERENCES

1. M.D. Ekstrand, M. Ludwig, J.A. Konstan, and J.T. Riedl. 2011. Rethinking the recommender research ecosystem: reproducibility, openness, and LensKit. In *Proceedings of the Fifth ACM Conference on Recommender Systems* (RecSys '11). ACM, New York, NY, USA, 133-140.

2. D.A. McConnell, D.N. Steer, K.D. Owens, C. Knight, 2005. How students think: Implications for learning in introductory geoscience courses. *Journal of Geoscience Education*, Vol. 53, No. 4, 462-470.

3. B. Means, Y. Toyama, R. Murphy, M. Bakia, and K. Jones, 2010. Evaluation of evidence-based practices in online learning: A meta-analysis and review of online learning studies. Washington, DC: Center for Technology in Learning, U.S. Department of Education.

Do Professors Matter?
Using an A/B Test to Evaluate the Impact of Instructor Involvement on MOOC Student Outcomes

Jonathan H. Tomkin
University of Illinois at Urbana-Campaign
School of Earth, Society & Environment
tomkin@illinois.edu

Donna Charlevoix
UNAVCO
Donnac@unavco.org

ABSTRACT

This research investigates the impact professors, and other instructional staff, have on student content knowledge acquisition in a physical science MOOC offered through the University of Illinois at Urbana-Champaign. An A/B test was used to randomly assign MOOC participants in either a control group (with no instructional interaction) or an intervention group (in which the professor and teaching assistants responded to comments in the discussion and complied summary weekly feedback statements) to identify the differences in learning outcomes, participation rates, and student satisfaction. The study found that instructor intervention had no statistically significant impact on overall completion rates, overall badge acquisition rates, student participation rates, or satisfaction with the course, but did ($p<0.05$) lead to a higher rate of forum badge completion, an area that was targeted by the intervention.

Author Keywords
A/B Testing; MOOC; Collaborative Learning.

ACM Classification Keywords
K.3.1 Computer Uses in Education – Collaborative learning.

INTRODUCTION

MOOCs make use of a transformative instructional methodology that leverages both subject content knowledge expertise by a professor and technologies to provide a collaborative educational experience [9,11,28]. The role of professor in instruction has been examined at length including with the advent of online and blended courses [3, 23,1,10,29,30,40,15,2]. Our work examines this on a much larger scale with a MOOC. Limited research has been

conducted to determine the role the professor plays in student learning in MOOCs. Mackness [25] found that in the absence of course structure, support and moderation students sought traditional groups rather than open networks. With MOOCs, online courses are taken beyond institutionalized learning management systems into the realm of student-centered learning environments where network and distributed learning provides a different support network and learning experience for students [34,39]. This shifted paradigm opens the door to understanding student learning and interactions from a data-driven perspective in ways not previously possible. Adaptive online content for instruction was implemented early in the use of the Internet to enhance instruction [22,36]. The large enrollments of MOOCs bring a new dimension to the use of artificial intelligence in assessing the learning process and take customized student-learning to a new level [41].

Teacher Involvement vs. Student Communities

Teacher involvement is seen as a general necessity for good education regardless of delivery method [38,7,8,12,16]. The first generation of MOOCs challenged that assumption with the idea that connected course participants could effectively learn from one another. Is it true that MOOC-sized communities of students foster learning and encourage involvement, effectively replacing, or greatly reducing, the role of an instructor?

The importance of connected learning was explicit in the first MOOCs – the traditional role of the professor was replaced by that of a facilitator, and the facilitator worked to ensure that participants were connected, and so able to form a learning community. This learning community structure remains in most MOOCs being offered today, although it is not as central to the learning design.

The Community of Inquiry (CoI) framework set forth by Garrison and colleagues [18,19,20] guides the MOOC curriculum. The CoI framework is grounded in developing and promoting a critical, collaborative learning community. CoI builds upon two ideals critical to higher education, community – the engagement of peers in the learning process, and inquiry – the exploration of knowledge. CoI or very similar models have been widely adopted in the virtual learning community in higher education [3,14,13,31, 32,33,35,37]. We designed a MOOC curriculum that promotes learning via investigation. The design of interactions within the MOOC is for "maximized learning," for both individual students and the broader course community. Students in the MOOC are encouraged to join learning communities to facilitate their in-course education, directly through the LMS, with other social media, and in-person. Such learning experiences and structure are based on social interdependence theories promoted by Kurt Lewin and Morton Deutsch [17,24].

Online and even blended/hybrid courses effectively use online discussion forums for the sharing of ideas, answering of questions and building a sense of community within the class [26,27]. The size of these classes may range from the ideal size of 25 to 30 students [4] to upwards of several hundred. The MOOC takes the concept of online instruction to an entirely new level. The large enrollments (tens of thousands) challenges the concept of building community through online interactions and the influence this has on student learning. A clear distinction between traditional online courses and MOOCs is the feasibility of synchronous online discussions or interactions between students and between students and the professor. The effectiveness of asynchronous learning environments has been challenged [21] while others have found that online interactions may be highly beneficial to student learning especially if the interactions by instructional staff are followed by a protocol [42].

This structure is formally delivered via discussion forums. Absent individual instructor-student interactions, the human connections formed in the discussion forums are seen as very important in promoting course participation and motivating involvement. If it were discovered that connected student communities can routinely master content, learn higher-order concepts, and remain engaged without the active involvement of instructional staff, the implications for educational practice would be profound.

Course Structure
The course "Introduction to Sustainability" was delivered by the University of Illinois at Urbana-Champaign (UIUC) over 8 weeks, beginning in the March of 2013. This was the second time that this course had been delivered (it was first delivered in August of 2012). Students are provided with the option of passing the class in one of three ways: 1) via the weekly quizzes (automated graded), 2) via discussion portfolio (peer graded), and 3) via final project (peer graded). Students who received 70% or higher grades in any one of these three venues were awarded both a certificate of completion for the course and an appropriate digital "badge" in that area (for example, a quiz badge).

The course structure was conventional with self-contained modules that contained content prescribed by the instructor. Each weekly module consisted of readings, video lectures, a dedicated discussion topic, a reading quiz, and a homework quiz. Discussion portfolios and final projects were due in the penultimate week of class. These were graded by participating students (that is, students who had submitted either a portfolio or project) in the final week, who were provided with detailed grading rubrics prepared by the instructor.

Course participants communicated with one another and the instructor through the course discussion forums – both through the weekly forums and through issues and Q&A forums. Very few students directly contacted the instructor (approximately 20 participants emailed or mailed the instructor over the period of the course).

Each week the instructor sent an announcement email to all participants, encouraging their efforts and highlighting relevant administrative matters (such as submission dates).

A/B Sections: Control and Intervention
Students were randomly assigned to be in either the control or intervention course section as determined by whether their Coursera student number was odd or even. The two sections received the same course environment, but did not share discussion forums.

The control group (Section A) Coursera site was monitored by a staff member at UIUC in case technical action was required, but the instructor had no direct access to the course. In this case, no intervention occurred in the control section. In advance of the course being delivered the instructor prepared weekly statements that were emailed to the participants in the course by the staff member. These statements reminded students of upcoming deadlines and gave generic encouragement to forum participants, based on the discussions generated in the prior delivery of the course.

The intervention group (Section B) was actively monitored by the instructor (Tomkin) and 6 undergraduate teaching assistants. Discussion posts received responses by this group, largely in the form of positive feedback for superior posts. In addition, the weekly summary statements emailed to participants explicitly referenced (by name and with hyperlinks) the forum posts made by the students in the course, highlighting especially worthy and interesting contributions. These additional actions required approximately 15 hours of work per week (half of which was performed by the instructor).

Although the two sections had no way to connect to one another inside the LMS, it is possible that they discussed the course in other venues. The student-generated Facebook page for the course, for example, has over 2000 members. There was no evidence from the discussion or the survey comments that students were aware of the A/B test being conducted.

RESULTS
Three main sets of data were collected in this study: 1) course participation (generated by the student's interaction

in the Coursera Learning Management System (LMS), 2) self-reported (via automated survey) attitudinal and demographic data, and 3) badge completion data.

20,474 students enrolled in the class – 10,265 in section A, and 10,209 in section B. Actual participation was considerably lower, however, partly because the course had been open for enrollment for several months. Even in the very first week of classes, the unique user count was approximately 30% of those formally enrolled (a total of 5,603 unique users viewed a lecture from the first week, for example).

We wish to determine if the intervention creates statistically significant changes in the behavior, attitudes, or outcomes of the intervention groups. The distributions of individual scores in assessments are very well described by normal distributions, and general participation rates measures (such as the distribution of the number of forum postings) do not follow a power-law distribution as might be expected, as participation rates are governed by the need to complete course requirements. As we are comparing two large, independent, populations that have means that can be approximated with a normal distribution, it is appropriate to use the z-test for 2 population proportions. This method is used in all cases where we make an assessment of statistical significance. To be statistically significant, the control and intervention groups have to achieve a $P < 0.05$ in a two-tailed z-test. In this study, when we describe a result as being statistically significant, (or not) this is the test applied, and also the way in which all reported p-values were determined.

Course Participation

Figure 1 shows the number of unique users who posted to the discussion forums, viewed the online lectures, and attempted quizzes in each of the 8 weeks of the course. Sections A and B are statistically indistinguishable – the change in participation rates was not influenced by section (Table 1). In calculating the significance of the change in participation, we have used the initial population in week 1 as the relevant population, rather than the total number of registered students (many of whom have not interacted with the course and so are not impacted by any course variables).

Course Completion

Students achieving the 70% threshold were awarded course badges and certificates of achievement. Table 1 shows the number of course completers from each section. Significance is calculated using the week 1 participation statistic as the relevant population (quiz attempters in week 1 for the number of quiz badges awarded, forum posters in week 1 for the number of portfolio and final project badges awarded).

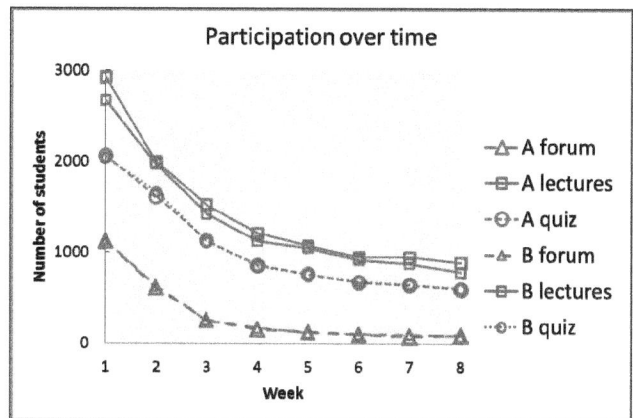

Figure 1. Unique student participation in forums (by making at least one post), lectures (by viewing at least one lecture), and quizzes (by attempting at least one quiz). for both groups. Forum participation is less popular than quiz participation and lecture viewing.

	A (n)	B (n)	p-value	Z-score
Completion				
Forum Badge recipients	22 (1123)	39 (1137)	0.03078	-2.158
Project Badge recipients	28 (1123)	40 (1137)	0.15272	-1.426
Quiz Badge recipients	496 (2927)	473 (2676)	0.48392	0.698
Participation at 8 weeks				
Forum	92 (1123)	80 (1137)	0.29834	1.037
Lecture	890 (1123)	786 (1137)	0.4009	0.845
Quiz	599 (2927)	605 (2676)	0.70394	-0.377

Table 1. Statistical significance of course participation and completion. A refers to the control group, B to the intervention group. Statistics are calculated using the population of badge recipients/week 8 participants, compared to the reference population "n" of week 1 (see Figure 1).

Most students who completed the course did so via the quiz badge - a total of 969 quiz badges were awarded. 17% of those in Section A who took a quiz in week 1 went on to be awarded the quiz badge, while 18% in Section B did – a statistically insignificant difference.

Fewer students achieved the forum and portfolio badges (a total of 129 of these badges were awarded, in both groups). In this case, there is an observable difference between the two sections: more students were awarded the completion badge in the intervention group (Section B). The number of additional final projects successfully submitted in Section B was not statistically significant (p=0.153 in a two-tail test, p=0.0764 in the less conservative one-tail test). The number of additional forum portfolios was statistically significant in the intervention group (p=0.031 in a two-tail test, p=0.015 in the less conservative one-tail test).

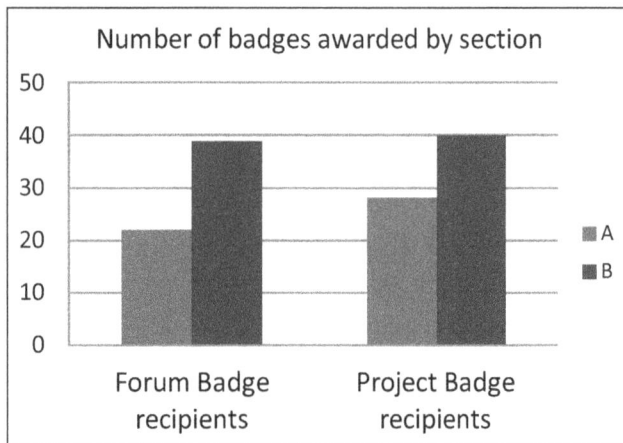

Figure 2. Number of forum portfolio and final project badges awarded in sections A and B. In both cases, there were more awarded in the intervention group.

Survey Data

Students were asked to provide course motivation, experience, and demographic data via a link that was provided at the beginning of the 4th week of the course. This survey asked students to check boxes that accorded with their experience. In addition, four open-ended questions were opened for responses in the 8th week of the course.

Both surveys received high numbers of respondents: 1251 students in Section A, and 1265 students in section B answered at least one question in the first survey, and 1608 students answered the most popular question in the second survey ("Tell us your story. Why are you taking this course? What do you hope to get out of it?").

Overall, respondents had a highly positive impression of the course, and this was unaffected by which group they were assigned to. The vast majority of the participants were pleased with the quality of the course (Figure 3), and regardless of Section, there was a high level of interest in pursuing further Coursera classes (Figure 4).

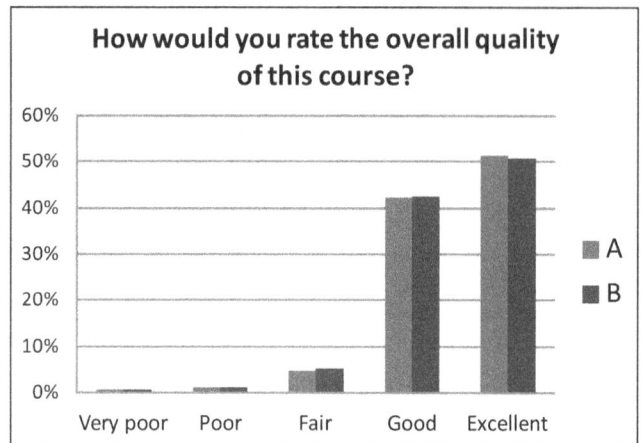

Figure 3. Participant survey of the course quality. Less than 2% rated the course as "poor" or "very poor". 93% of respondents rated the course as "good" or "excellent". There was no statistically significant difference between the views of the two groups A and B.

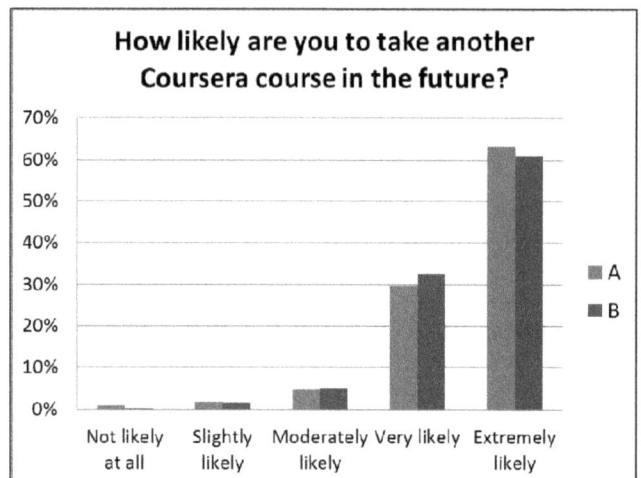

Figure 4. Participant attitude to taking a further course. Most (93%) students were "very" or "extremely" likely to take another Coursera course. There was no statistically significant difference between the views of the two groups A and B.

The randomized assignments to either Sections A or B were effective. The self-reported demographics of the two groups were very similar. There were more women than men in the course (57.8% in Section A, 56.4% in Section B) and most participants were from outside the United States (73.0% in Section A, 72.7% in Section B). Participants were highly educated (Figure 5) and ranged in age from 14 to 91, with a median age of 33.

Education Level

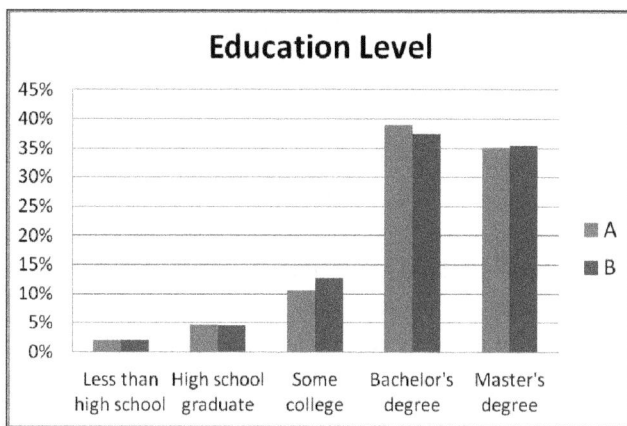

Figure 5. Education Level by section. Note that almost three-quarters of students (73%) had at least a Bachelor's degree.

In total 834 students answered the open-ended question "What is one suggestion for improvement you would make about this course?" which is potentially relevant to the intervention performed in the course. These responses were searched for forum references. In Section A 10 of the 414 total comments specifically referred to the lack of forum involvement by instructional staff. This is a sample comment:

"I found the professor's lack of involvement in the forums extremely disappointing. I do not recall seeing any posts from him or his assistants at all (not counting the occasional technical support post from Coursera staff)..."

In Section B, only 2 of 419 comments referred to the lack of forum involvement by instructional staff. This is a statistically significant (p=0.01828), but very small, difference. The single largest complaint from both sections was in regards to the grading (the assessment scheme was seen as confusing and quizzes were seen as too difficult) Most of the comments addressing the forums described the difficulty in forum navigation and variable quality of posts.

DISCUSSION AND CONCLUSIONS

The active involvement of the professor did not matter in this MOOC. This course was carefully constructed, and the participants were highly-educated and motivated by a strong interest in the material. As it is likely that the students in many MOOCs fit this description, it is reasonable to suppose that this result holds generally for MOOCs offered today. There is no reason to think that this lack of instructor impact is a subject-dependent finding.

The intervention did have an impact on a small number of students that was statistically significant, but only in areas directly impacted by the intervention: there were 8 more complaints of a lack of instructor involvement in the control group, and 17 more students submitted the forum portfolio. But this did not spill-over into other aspects of the course; the intervention group was not significantly different than the control group in almost all measures – including overall completion rates, participation rates, and attitudes. In

particular, there was no difference in the overall satisfaction with the course: the addition of the professor's active involvement did not make a broad or observable difference to the students.

This failure may be the result of the sheer size of the course, even in the latter weeks the total participation remained in excess of 1000 students in each of the two sections. It is plausible that sporadic attention is equivalent to no attention: the course construction was such that individual feedback is rare in any event.

The results of this study broadly support the connected learning model, at least for these motivated, educated participants. The absence of the professor did not impact the activity of the forums – the participants did generate their own knowledge in this arena. It should be stressed that this MOOC was highly structured, so an alternative explanation is that the enhanced machine interactivity that MOOCs provide relative to textbooks, or older styles of distance learning, may be sufficient to stimulate student engagement.

It is not clear from this study if the results will generalize for MOOCs delivered for high school or college students, as the participants in this study were self-selected. We cannot say if MOOCs have the same potential for students with lower educational attainment or intrinsic engagement.

Relatively few of the students participating in the course come from underrepresented or academically at-risk groups. This study does not address concerns that these groups will be poorly served by courses delivered with less direct instructor involvement.

These results do lend some support to the idea that MOOCs can be suitable for academic credit. Higher stakes (such as the potential for course credit,or a required cost for participation) are liable to aid in student motivation, and we see from this study that motivated students can succeed in the class. Further work is needed to establish the level of learning gains in MOOCs – especially how this format compares with other formats.

REFERENCES

1. Anagnostopoulos, D., Basmadjian, K.G., & McCrory, R.S. (2005). The decentered teacher and the construction of social space in the virtual classroom. Teachers College Record 107: 1699-1729.
2. Anderson, T., Rourke, L., Garrison, D.R., & Archer, W. (2001). Assessing teaching presence in a computer conferencing context. *Journal of Asynchronous Learning Networks* 5(2).
3. Arbough, J. B. (2007, April). An empirical verification of the community of inquiry framework. *Journal of Asynchronous Learning Networks*, 11(1), 73-85.
4. Arbaugh, J.B. & Benbunon-Finch, R. (2005).

Contextual factors that influence ALN effectiveness. In S. R. Hiltz, & R. Goldman (Eds.), Learning Together Online. Research on Asynchronous Learning networks (pp. 123–144). Mahwah: Lawrence Erlbaum Associates, Inc.

5. Arbaugh, J. B., Cleveland-Innes, M, R, D. S., Garrison, D. R., Ice, P., Richardson, J. C., et al. (2008). Developing a Community of Inquiry instrument: Testing a measure of the Community of Inquiry framework using a multi—institutional sample. Internet and Higher Education, 11, 133–136.

6. Arbough, J.B. & Hwang, A. (2006). Does "teaching presence" exist in online MBA courses? *The Internet and Higher Education*, 9:9-21.

7. Bain, K. (2004). What the best college teachers do. Harvard Univ. Press. Cambridge, MA

8. Bates, A.W., & Poole, G. (2003). Effective Teaching with Technology in Higher Education: Foundations for Success. Jossey-Bass, San Francisco, CA.

9. Bell, F., Connectivism: Its place in theory-informed research and innovation in technology-enabled learning. 2011. 12(3), Athabasca University; The International Review of Research in Open and Distance Learning

10. Beuchot, A., & Bullen, M. (2005) Interacttion and interpersonality in online discussion forums. *Distance Education* 26(1): 67-87.

11. Black, E. W., Beck, D., Dawson, K., Jinks, S., & DiPietro, M. (2007). The other side of the LMS: Considering implementation and use in the adoption of an LMS in online and blended learning environments. *TechTrends: Linking Research & Practice to Improve Learning, 51*(2), 5.

12. Brookfield, S.D. (1995). Becoming a Critically Reflective Teacher. Jossey-Bass Higher and Adult Education Series. San Francisco, CA.

13. Brown, A. L., & Campione, J.C. (1994). Guided discovery in a community of learners. In K. McGilly (Ed.), *Classroom lessons: Integrating cognitive theory and classroom practices* (pp. 229-270). Cambridge, MA: MIT Press.

14. Charlevoix. D.J., Strey, S.T., & Mills, C. (2009). Design and implementation of inquiry-based, technology-rich learning activities in a large enrollment blended learning course. *Journal of the Research Center for Educational Technology,* 5(3):15-28.

15. Coppola, N.W., Hiltz, S.R., & Rotter, N.G. (2002). Becoming a virtual professor: Pedagogical roles and asynchronous learning networks. *Journal of Management Information Systems* 18(4): 169-189.

16. Cranton, P. (1994). Understanding and Promoting Transformative Learning: A Guide for Educators of Adults. Jossey-Bass Higher and Adult Education Series. San Francisco, CA.

17. Deutsch, M. (1949). A theory of cooperation and competition, *Human Relations, 2,* 129-152.

18. Garrison, D. R., Anderson, T. & Archer, W. (2000). Critical inquiry in a text-based environment: Computer conferencing in higher education. *The Internet and Higher Education* 2:87-105.

19. Garrison, D. R., & Archer, W. (2000). *A transactional perspective on teaching-learning: A framework for adult and higher education.* Oxford, U.K.: Peragmon.

20. Garrison, D. R., & Vaughan, N. D. (2007). *Blended learning in higher education: Framework, principles, and guidelines.* San Francisco: Jossey-Bass

21. Gorsky, P., Caspi, A. & Blau, I. (2012). A Comparison of Non-Mandatory Online Dialogic Behavior in Two Higher Education Blended Environments. *Journal of Asynchronous Learning Networks,* 16(4), 55-69.

22. Henze, N. & Nejdl, W. (2000). Extendible Adaptive Hypermedia Courseware: Integrating Different Courses and Web Material. Lecture Notes in Computer Science Volume 1892; 109-120

23. Lee, J-M. & Lee, Y. (2006). Personality types and learners' interaction in web-based threaded discussion. *Quarterly Review of Distance Education* 7(1): 83-94.

24. Lewin, K. (1935). A dynamic theory of personality. New York: McGraw Hill.

25. Mackness, J., Mak, S. and Williams, Roy (2010) *The ideals and reality of participating in a MOOC.* In: Proceedings of the 7th International Conference on Networked Learning 2010. University of Lancaster, Lancaster, pp. 266-275. ISBN 9781862202252

26. Mazzolini, M. & Maddison, S. (2007) When to jump in: The role of the instructor in online discussion forums. *Computers & Education, 49*(2): 193-213.

27. Mazzolini, M. & Maddison, S. (2003) Sage, guide or ghost? The effect of instructor intervention on student participation in online discussion forums, *Computers & Education, 40(3)*: 237-253.

28. McAuley, A., B. Stewart, G. Siemens and D. Cormier, (2010). The MOOC Model for Digital Practice. https://oerknowledgecloud.org/sites/oerknowledgecloud.org/files/MOOC_Final.pdf

29. Moore, J.S., & Marra, R.M. (2005). A comparative analysis of onlikne discussion participation protocols. *Journal of Research on Technology in Education* 28:191-212.

30. Molinari, D.L. (2004). The role of social comments in

problem-solving groups in an online class. *American Journal of Distance Education 18(2): 89-101.*

31. Palloff, R. M., & Pratt, K. (2005). *Collaborative online learning together in community.* San Francisco: Jossey-Bass.

32. Rovai, A. P. (2002). Sense of community, perceived cognitive learning, and persistence in asynchronous learning networks. *The Internet and Higher Education, 5(4),* 319-332.

33. Rovai, A. P., & Jordan, H. M. (2004). Blended learning and sense of community: A comparative analysis with traditional and fully online graduate courses. *International Review of Research in Open and Distance Learning, 5(2),* 1-3.

34. Saadatmand, M., Kumpulainen, K. , (2012). Content aggregation and knowledge sharing in a personal learning environment: Serendipitous and emergent learning in open online networks *2012 15th International Conference on Interactive Collaborative Learning, ICL 2012*, art. no. 6402224.

35. Shea, P., Li, C. S., & Pickett, A. (2006). A comparative study of teaching presence and student sense of learning community in fully online and web-enhanced college courses. *The Internet and Higher Education, 9(3),* 175-190.

36. Stern, M.K. & Woolf, B.P. (2000). Adaptive content in an online lecture system. Lecture Notes in Computer Science Volume 1892; 227-238.

37. Story, A. E. & Dielsi, J. (2003). Community building easier in blended format? *Distance Education Report, 7(11), 2,* 7.

38. Sviniki, M. and McKeachie, W. (2013). McKeachie's Teaching Tips. Cengage Learning, Stamford, CT.

39. Walther, J. (1992). Interpersonal effects in computer mediated interaction: A relational perspective. *Communication Research* 19(1):52-90.

40. Wise, A., Chang, J., Duffy, T., & del Valle, R. (2004). The effects of teacher social presence on student satisfaction, engagement, and learning. *Journal of Educational Computing Research* 31:247-271.

41. Woolf, B.P. (2009). Building Intelligent Interactive Tutors: Student-centered strategies for revolutionizing e-learning. Elsevier, Burlington, MA.

42. Zydney, J.M., deNoyelles, A., Seo, K. (2012). Creating a community of inquiry in online environments: An exploratory study on the effect of protocols on interactions within asynchronous discussions. *Computers & Education,* 58(1), 77-87.

Monitoring MOOCs:
Which Information Sources Do Instructors Value?

Kristin Stephens-Martinez
EECS Department
UC Berkeley
Berkeley, CA 94720
ksteph@cs.berkeley.edu

Marti A. Hearst
School of Information
UC Berkeley
Berkeley, CA 94720
hearst@berkeley.edu

Armando Fox
EECS Department
UC Berkeley
Berkeley, CA 94720
fox@cs.berkeley.edu

ABSTRACT

For an instructor who is teaching a massive open online course (MOOC), what is the best way to understand their class? What is the best way to view how the students are interacting with the content while the course is running? To help prepare for the next iteration, how should the course's data be best analyzed after the fact? How do these instructional monitoring needs differ between online courses with tens of thousands of students and courses with only tens? This paper reports the results of a survey of 92 MOOC instructors who answered questions about which information they find useful in their course, with the end goal of creating an information display for MOOC instructors.

The main findings are: (i) quantitative data sources such as grades, although useful, are not sufficient; understanding the activity in discussion forums and student surveys was rated useful for all use cases by a large majority of respondents, (ii) chat logs were not seen as useful, (iii) for the most part, the same sources of information were seen as useful as found in surveys of smaller online courses, (iv) mockups of existing and novel visualization techniques were responded to positively for use both while the course is running and for planning a revision of the course, and (v) a wide range of views was expressed about other details.

Author Keywords

Visualizations; Instructor support; e-learning; MOOCs; Massive open online courses.

ACM Classification Keywords

H.5.3. Information Interfaces and Presentation (e.g. HCI): Group and Organization Interfaces; K.3.1. Computers and Education: Computer Uses in Education

INTRODUCTION

In brick-and-mortar classrooms, instructors rely on face-to-face interaction with individual learners in lecture and office hours to understand how learners are doing in the course and how they interact with the course materials. Many recent Massive Open Online Courses (MOOCs) from providers such as edX and Coursera have enrolled tens of thousands of students per offering, with a few enrolling hundreds of thousands. At such scales, individual interaction with every student is infeasible and most interactions are through the software platform, rather than face-to-face. Fortunately, MOOCs' large scale and the fact they are offered via a heavily instrumented online environment, provide instructors with a rich source of information they previously lacked: instrumented activity from interactions with the e-learning platform.

Historically, data visualization has been an effective way to explore large datasets in which identifying interesting patterns is more productive than scrutinizing individual data points. Since MOOCs are relatively new, little work has been done on visualizing the rich sources of information available in them; current MOOC platforms offer only a small set of visualizations of basic quantitative information.

To help explore this space, we investigate it from two angles. First, we implemented a prototype instructor dashboard for the edX platform called the Metrics Tab (see Figure 1) that is currently available only to a small number of test users. Second, and the focus of this paper, we administered a survey to investigate the following questions:

1. What information sources do MOOC instructors prefer to help identify key trends and behaviors in both student performance and student interaction with course content?

2. Which of these sources are most useful to instructors during the three phases of: course preparation, course administration, and course postmortem?

3. How should these sources be presented so we may develop tools and visualizations instructors will find most useful?

The survey was answered by 92 MOOC instructors. Survey questions also include visualizations of information sources, two of which were modeled after those in the Metrics Tab, as well as three additional designs. Instructors were asked to judge the understandability and usefulness of each design.

The results support the following primary findings:

1. Quantitative data sources such as assignment grades are not enough: understanding discussion forum activity was of interest to 97% of those surveyed that answered questions on

Information Visualized	Related Work
Performance: Grades on assignments, cumulative performance on problems for a particular concept	[1, 6, 15, 17, 18]
Access and Activity Patterns: What, how much, and when content has been opened, how long a student stays on a piece of content, student navigational path through the content, when a student turned in an assignment	[1, 2, 6, 8, 11, 12, 15, 17, 18, 20]
Forum Discussions: Author of a post, when the post was made, structure of follow-up posts, how many posts a student made, how many follow-up posts are in threads each student made, number of posts read by a student	[7, 8, 15, 17, 18]
Student Demographics: Location, reason for taking the course, age, learning style	[12, 20]

Table 1. Types of information and related work that visualizes each.

use of information sources. This is despite a lack of related work on visualizing discussion forum activity at scale and despite previous work showing that forum use is typically limited to a small percentage of students who are not necessarily representative of the overall enrollment [3, 4].

2. Instructors do not think chat logs are a valuable information source for understanding student behavior.

3. By and large, MOOC instructors want the same sources of information as instructors of smaller-scale distance learning courses, as evoked by earlier surveys.

4. Respondents reacted positively to mockups of both previously-used and novel visualization techniques, indicating they would use these to monitor a running course and to review materials when preparing for a new offering, but were less likely to use them in preparing new material.

5. Instructors expressed widely varying views on the types of data and visualizations they would find useful: some preferred data and visualizations that would support quantitative analysis such as correlation, others conducted courses focused more on discussion than quantifiable grades and therefore quantitative analysis is not useful, and so on.

Below we present related work, describe the survey procedure, describe the visualizations, present the results, discuss the ramifications of these results, and conclude with recommendations for future work for the design of monitoring interfaces for MOOC instructors.

RELATED WORK

Instructor surveys
Monitoring student learning has been promoted as a best practice in the education literature since the 1970s [5]. Two surveys of e-learning instructors, one in 2003 by Mazza et al. [16] (98 participants) and another in 2006 by Zinn et al. [21] (49 participants), agreed broadly on several points. Respondents stated that the most important phenomena to monitor are individual students' performance, per-student performance compared to the class as a whole, common misconceptions shared by many students (as manifested by common wrong answers to exercises, for example), and activity patterns such as what material students look at, how many times, for how long, and whether the material viewed is consistent with the course schedule. Mazza et al.'s respondents also said that forum behavior was a valuable way to gauge participation, but email or chat data was not.

Visualizations of student information
Visualizations have been used as a form of educational data mining [19]. However, very little related work in visualizing student information has focused on MOOCs, and modern MOOC platforms such as edX and Coursera provide limited instructor-facing visualizations. Table 1 shows information categories prior work has commonly visualized, ranging from standard graphs to innovative designs.

Standard graphs used by prior work [1, 2, 6, 8, 11, 12, 15, 17, 18, 20] include: scatter plots, bar indicators, bar and stacked bar charts, line graphs, Cumulative Distribution Function line graphs, pie charts, and heat maps. These graphs are used by prior work in one of two ways: (1) to provide a set of visualizations showing different kinds of information or (2) as a supporting graph in a complex visualization.

The prior work that provides visualizations for multiple categories of information [1, 6, 8, 12, 15, 17, 18] usually has the goal of giving instructors an overall picture of their course's e-learning experience. These visualization systems include: Goldberg et al.'s [8] early WebCT [9] visualizations, Hardy et al.'s [12] e-learning tracking visualizations, Mazza et al.'s Coursevis [15, 17] and GISMO [18], Gaudioso et al.'s [6] visualizations for dotLRN and PDinamet, and Khan Academy's Coach monitoring system [1]. It is important to note, while these systems provide an overview of the course, they often are intended for courses of only tens to the low hundreds of students and visualize each student individually (such as show each student as their own row in a heat map). Therefore a majority of these visualizations would not scale to the size of a MOOC unless judicious filtering is applied first.

Innovative visualizations used by prior work usually use known visualization techniques in an innovative way. These include: directional and non-directional node graphs, three dimensional graphs, timeline spiral graphs, icons, and line graphs. Node graphs are used by Hardless et al. [11] to show a timeline of student activity, calling it an activity line. Williams and Conlan's [20] use a node graph to show navigational path through content. Finally, Gibbs et al. [7] use a directional node graph, with node placement conveying time, to show how forum posts relate to each other.

Mazza et al. [15, 17] also visualize forums with a three dimensional scatter plot that the user could explore in. The timeline spiral graph by Aguilar et al. [2] shows student access and activity patterns. This graph used mainly bar graphs for both supporting information and spiraled around a center where each 360 degree spin was an easily understood unit of time (*e.g.*, 24 hours, 1 week, etc.). Icons are used by Khan Academy's Coach tool [1] to highlight points in bar charts when students earned badges. Two prior works that use line graphs in innovative ways are Hardy et al.'s [12] line graph with shading to depict a student's path through the material and Williams and Conlan's [20] line graph as a connected sparse scatter plot depicting a student's learning style.

Four interaction techniques used in the prior work include: sorting, filtering, drill down, and clustering. Sorting was usually available in any visualization that provides a tabular view of information, such as Goldberg et al.'s [8] WebCT tabular student views and Khan Academy's Coach tool [1] that shows students individually. Aguilar et al.'s [2] timeline spiral allows users to filter by time, activity, course, and student. Hardy et al.'s [12] e-learning tracking visualizations allow filtering by time and any subset of students. It also incorporates an understanding of course hierarchy, which provides an ability to drill down through this hierarchy. Gaudioso et al.'s [6] visualizations for dotLRN and PDinamet included a clustering feature that automatically groups students based on access patterns. It provided a way to view aggregate information of the students in the groups and compare these aggregates to each other. Huang et al. [13] also uses clustering in their node graph to show syntax similarity between student code submissions.

Evaluation by prior work mainly involved interviews and focus groups [7, 11, 15, 17, 18, 20] and usually reported a mix of both positive responses to the system and a need for future improvements. Three prior works did not include an evaluation section [2, 8, 12]. Gaudiosoa et al.'s [6] work with dotLRN and PDinamet considered the drop out/success rate of the classes before and after the visualizations were provided to the instructors and found a marked improvement. However there is no discussion of whether the improvement with the dotLRN system is due to the visualizations or the revamped material that happened at the same time. They also conducted a questionnaire looking at student and teacher satisfaction, finding a majority of both groups were satisfied with the course and system. Mazza et al.'s [15, 17, 18] work on Coursevis and GISMO performed the most thorough evaluation, looking at the system's extent of required functionality, effectiveness, efficiency, and usefulness through a combination of an experimental study, interviews, and a focus group. Their results are positive across all their criteria.

SURVEY PROCEDURE

We used SurveyMonkey to administer a survey estimated to take about 30 minutes. We identified 539 potential participants by collecting instructor names from web page of courses offered on the three largest MOOC platforms: edX, Coursera, and Udacity.

The survey consisted of five parts:

1. **Background information** about the instructors.

2. **Specific details about one MOOC**. If an instructor taught multiple MOOCs we asked them to choose one and answer all following questions in terms of that MOOC.

3. **Course Monitoring Goals** and asking which information sources help achieve the desired understanding.

4. **Mockups** of five different visualizations of information that may be useful for monitoring a MOOC and questions about their efficacy.

5. **Open-ended response** for additional thoughts.

The next section describes the mockups in more detail.

THE METRICS TAB AND VISUALIZATION MOCKUPS

The instructors were asked to evaluate the potential usefulness and understandability of five visualizations of source information for monitoring MOOC activity. Two of these visualizations were derived from designs in the prototype Metrics Tab, a new tab in the edX Instructor Dashboard. Figure 1 shows this visualization in detail.

Both the mockup and the implemented prototype visualizations were based on ideas from previous work and informal conversations and brainstorms with instructors before the survey was administered. The mockups we decided to use also served as a preliminary evaluation of the Metrics Tab.

Metrics Tab

The goal of the Metrics Tab is to provide instructors a quick to consume dashboard display of available information in their course. The Metrics Tab separates the course's information by section and shows the same dashboard display seen in Figure 1 for each section. The section was chosen as the level of granularity because edX usually uses a section to contain a week's worth of material, with subsections allowing further division of the week's content.

The left grey bar chart shows how many students opened each subsection in the section; that is, viewed at least some of the content in that subsection at least once. When the user hovers the cursor over a bar in this graph, the name of the subsection and exact number of students that opened that subsection will appear in a tooltip, as seen in Figure 1.

The upper right red and green stacked bar graph shows the grade distribution for each problem in the section. It shows every problem regardless if the problem is included in the students' course grade or not. If students are allowed to submit an answer multiple times, as is common in MOOCs, it only shows the grade for their last submitted answer (since the last submitted answer is used when calculating a student's grade). For a given bar in the graph the color represents the grade for all the students in the bar, and the height is how many students received that grade. The color gradient for grades, seen to the left of the graph, goes from red, grey, to green[1], mapping to 0, 50, and 100 percent respectively. Hovering the cursor reveals the instructor-defined description of the problem, the number of students in the bar, their percentage grade, number of points earned, and number of possible points.

Finally, the bottom right blue stacked bar graph shows the distribution of number of attempts per problem in the section.

---

[1] This color scale is inappropriate for red-green color-blind viewers, and so in future iterations will be changed.

Section 2: Biochemistry 1

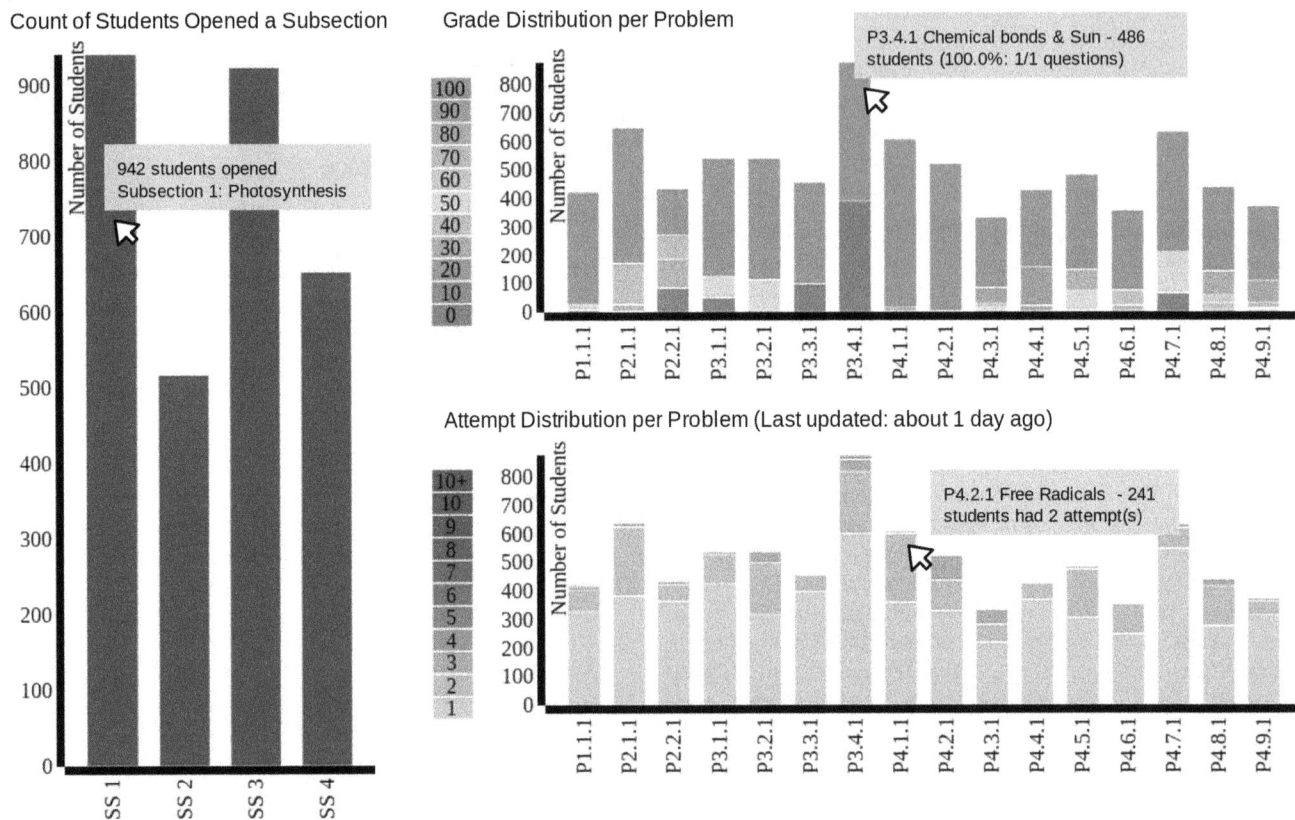

Figure 1. Mockup of a single section in the prototype edX Metrics Tab with a tooltip visible for each graph.

On both edX and Coursera, MOOC instructors can choose the number of times students may attempt each problem. The color gradient is grey to blue, mapping from 1 attempt to 10+ attempts. Students that attempted more than 10 times are grouped together because some problems allow unlimited attempts, which students do take advantage of. Hovering over a bar reveals the instructor-defined description of the problem, the number of students in the bar, and the number of attempts.

Visualization Mockups

The five mockups that were shown to instructors in the survey are shown in Figure 2. The callout bubble in each mockup represents what will be seen if the user hovers the cursor over that or a similar part of the graph. Mockup 2(a) is a boxplot diagram of grade distributions, included because it is a standard visualization. The tooltip shows the name of the homework assignment or other assessment item, the high and low scores, the median score and the 75th and 25th percentile scores. Mockup 2(b) is very similar to the upper right graph in the Metrics Tab and Mockup 2(d) is similar to the lower right graph of the Metrics Tab. Mockup 2(e) is similar to Mockup 2(d) but shows views of materials rather than attempts at homework problems. Finally, Mockup 2(c) shows two line graphs of forum usage data: number of new posts per day and number of views per day. The tooltip is for both graphs. On hover the points with the same date are highlighted. The tooltips text includes the date, the number of posts for that day, the number of posts viewed for that day and the titles of the most popular posts.

In the survey, each mockup in Figure 2 included a description on how to read the graph and any interactions with it.

Participants were asked to provide Likert responses to (a) whether the mockup is useful and (b) whether it is easy to understand. Next we asked when the instructor might use it: (1) when preparing new material, (2) when preparing by reviewing past courses, and (3) while the course is running. We also ask if they have any other comments about the mockup (open-ended response).

SURVEY RESULTS

Of the 539 instructors solicited, 92 instructors (17%) started the survey and 67 (73%) completed it. Of the 91 instructors that chose to answer the question on gender, 73% identified as male, 25% as female, and 2% chose not to specify.

Characteristics of Courses

Of those instructors who ran a MOOC, more than two thirds had done so only one time, while 13% had done so twice (see Table 2). That said, many of these instructors are experienced at large in-person courses; 31% said they had run courses with greater than 250 people more than 4 times, and another 25% had done so 3 or fewer times. 85% of survey respondents reported creating one MOOC, 9% created two,

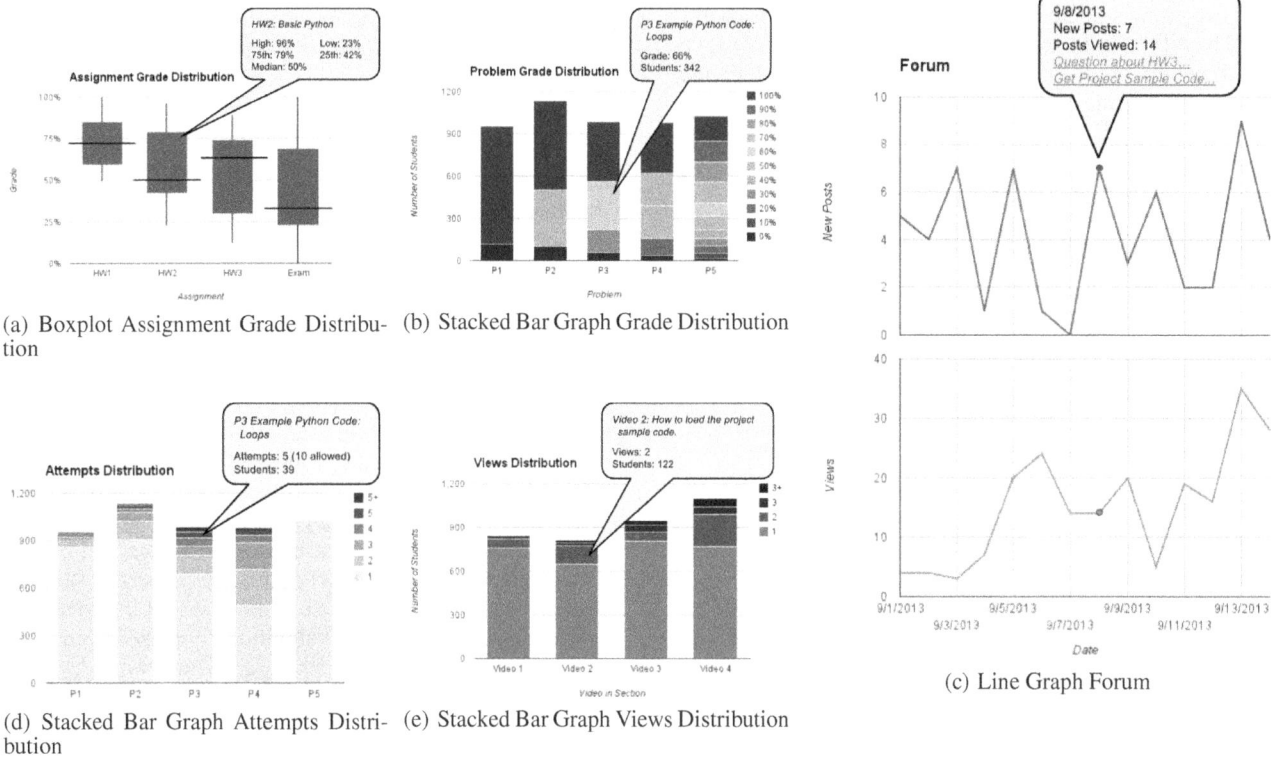

(a) Boxplot Assignment Grade Distribution

(b) Stacked Bar Graph Grade Distribution

(c) Line Graph Forum

(d) Stacked Bar Graph Attempts Distribution

(e) Stacked Bar Graph Views Distribution

Figure 2. Mockups shown to survey participants. The call out bubbles represents what will be seen if the user hovers the mouse over a part of the graph.

#	Run (N=92)	Created (N=91)
1	67%	85%
2	13%	9%
3	4%	1%
4+	9%	1%
N/A	6%	4%

Table 2. Survey respondents' MOOC experience for running and creating 1 to 4+ MOOCs.

	100s	1,000s	10,000s	Total
Engineering	3	10	7	20
Science	2	25	10	37
Humanities	1	8	10	19
Other	1	3	7	11
Total	7	46	34	87

Table 3. Cross between the estimated number of students in the course and the course's area.

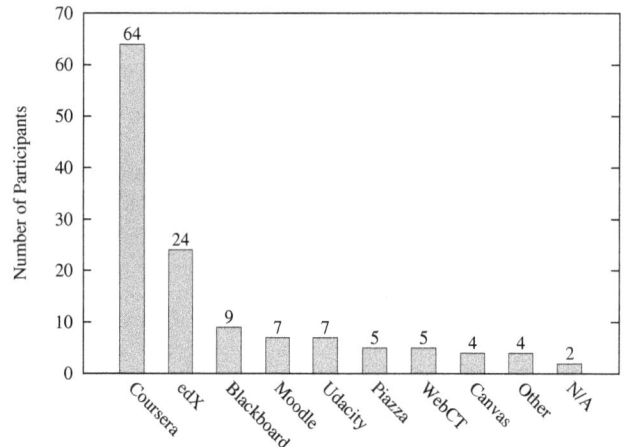

Figure 3. Platform usage statistics.

one individual created three, and one created four courses (see Table 2). Instructors have used a wide range of platforms, with Coursera and edX being the most frequent; Figure 3 shows the usage counts of the others reported. "Other" refers to platforms the instructors provided to us in the survey, which include Google, Desire2Learn, and an institution-specific MOOC platform.

For the questions that followed, if instructors had taught more than one MOOC, they were asked to choose one and answer in reference only to it. 91% of the courses completed with 1,000s to 10,000s of students. Table 3 shows the es-

timated number of students in the course at time of completion crossed with the subject matter of the course. The courses marked "other" include social sciences, business, education, and interdisciplinary studies. Interestingly, humanities courses were frequently among the largest MOOCS.

Course Monitoring Goals

We asked the survey participants to consider nine different tasks or goals they might have when running or planning a MOOC, summarized in Table 4. We asked instructors to assess ten information sources in terms of their efficacy for these nine goals, rating them in terms of if they currently *use*,

1	Problems with the current assignment.
2	Struggling students and what they are struggling with.
3	The difficulty of an exam problem.
4	Appropriateness of course difficulty level for students.
5	Most engaging content for the students.
6	Most difficult parts of the course.
7	Effectiveness of teaching assistants.
8	How to improve presentation of a topic.
9	Content students considered least interesting.

Table 4. Short descriptions of Course Monitoring Goals.

F	Discussion Forum
CS	Class Survey
SD	Discussion with Students
TA	Ask the teaching assistants
AG	Assignment grades
PAn	Student answers to problems
VP	Student's view pattern of online content
PAt	Number of times students attempt a problem
SCQ	Grades for self-check questions
CL	Chat room logs

Table 5. Resources Potentially Used for Course Monitoring.

would use if available, or *do not use/would not use* that resource. Asking about usage is different than prior work [16, 21], which asked survey participants to rate the level of interest or importance of an information source. We also purposely chose resources that instructors are likely familiar with to reduce the need for the instructors to guess if a resource is useful. The resources asked about are shown in Table 5.

The main findings from this section of the survey are:

Qualitative information is important. Figure 4 shows the raw counts of responses across monitoring goals for each information source. (Visual inspection did not reveal significant differences when subsets of courses were examined by area, but we did not do statistical tests to confirm this.) The lower segment (blue, solid border) indicates those who currently use this resource or would use it if available. The top segment (red, dotted border) indicates the counts of those who would

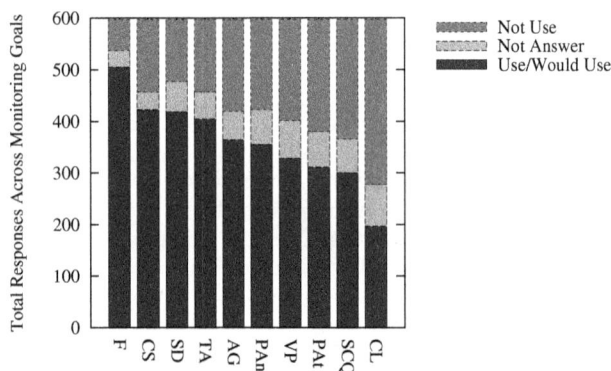

Figure 4. For each information source, the number of participants who use it or would use if available (combined into a single category), do not use, or did not answer. Did not answer means that the participant chose an answer for a subset of the information sources for that Monitoring Goal. It is shown here to see the relative rate of responses.

not or do not use this resource over all tasks. For some questions, participants chose to answer usage for a subset of information sources. We assign the center (green, dashed-lines border) bar for the not-answer responses in order to show the relative rate of response.[2] The figure is ordered by highest to lowest raw response counts of use or would use if available.

Figure 4 shows that across all tasks, discussion forums are seen as most often useful and chat logs are seen as least useful. In particular, the preference of forums over class surveys (the second-highest-used information source) is significant (Fisher's exact test, $p < 0.001$) and so is the difference between chat logs and self check questions (the second-lowest-used information source; Fisher's exact test, $p < 0.001$).

If we visualize the responses by Course Monitoring Goal, the pattern of response suggests a grouping as shown in Figure 5. The figure suggests groups of Course Monitoring Goals within which the relative usefulness of different information sources is more uniform than it is outside the group boundary. To make comparison easier, each separate stacked bar graph is the same as Figure 4, except it is the percent of instructors that answered for that Course Monitoring Goal instead of the raw counts. Results are not significantly biased because each question was answered by 59 to 75 instructors.

The first group of five Monitoring Goals (1, 2, 4, 6, and 8, in Figure 5(a); the numbers correspond to Table 4), could be characterized as quantitative questions about course material difficulty or presentation of course materials. For these Monitoring Goals all information sources but chat logs have 97% to 48% of question respondents say they use/would use the information source. Chat logs have only 37% to 31% question respondents say they use/would use it.

The second group of three Monitoring Goals (5, 7, and 9, in Figure 5(b)) could be characterized as qualitative assessment of student engagement or instructor effectiveness. In these goals participants were most enthusiastic about the "softer" information sources such as forums, discussions with students, class survey, and discussions with TAs. The percent of instructors saying they use/would use these information sources range from 94% to 46%. While there was much less enthusiasm for quantitative performance such as assignment grades, problem answers and attempts, and self check question grades, use/would use range from 41% to 15%. View pattern usage is the least similar between the goals, where it is used very little for the TA effectiveness goal, but used much more for the other two engagement goals.

Monitoring Goal 3 – gauging exam problem difficulty in Figure 5(c) – does not display a similar pattern to the others, with no clear winners among the information sources.

Chat room logs are rarely used and considered unimportant. Chat room logs are more not used than used. This can be seen from the earlier discussion of Figure 4 and looking at

---

[2] Most participants completed the entire survey, 73%. However, because this section contained 9 questions requiring answers for 10 resources, some participants became fatigued (as indicated by their free-text comments) and either skipped portions of this part of the survey or did not complete the survey beyond this point.

(a) Information Source Usage Distribution Group 1

(b) Information Source Usage Distribution Group 2

(c) Information Source Usage Distribution Group 3

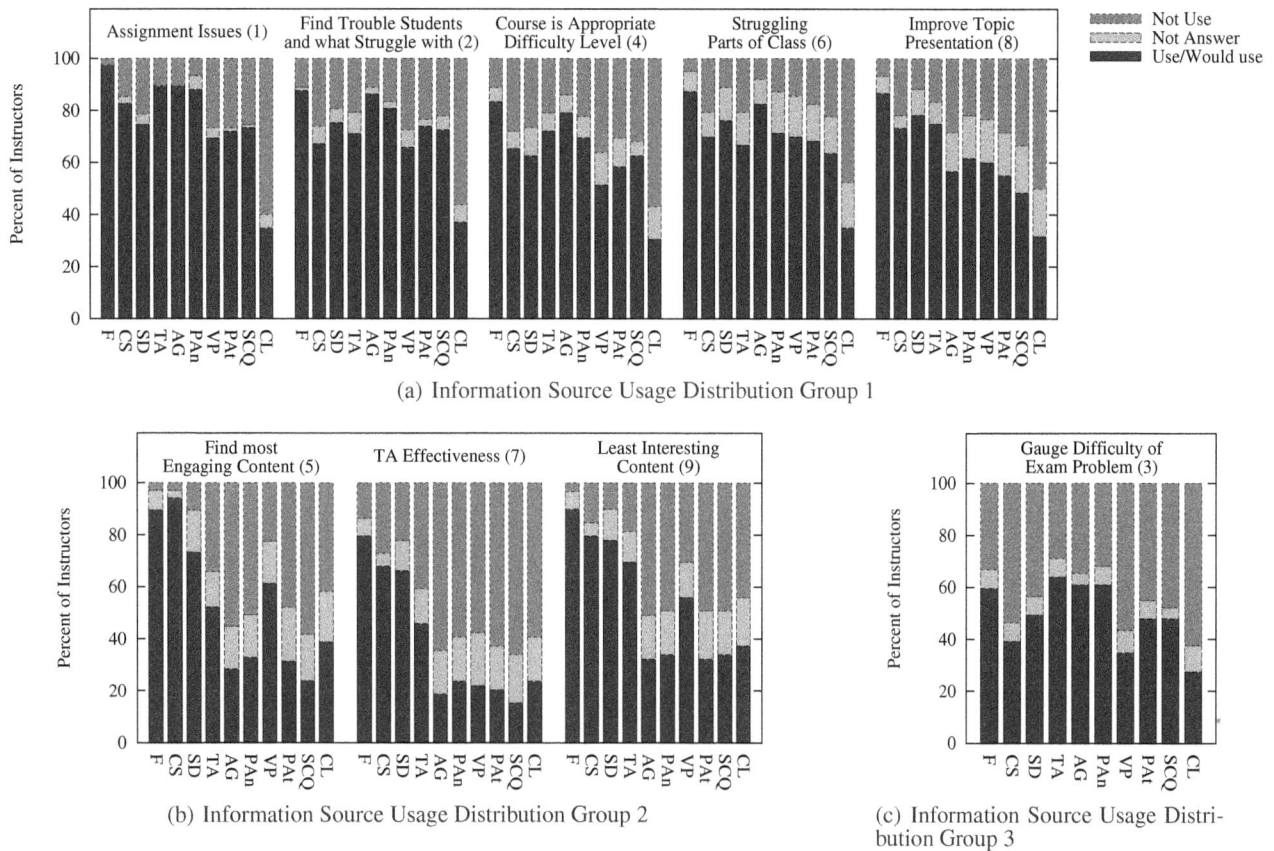

Figure 5. Percent of participants that answered for each usage option, as well as the percent that answered part of the question but not for that information source option. The Monitoring Goals are grouped based on their usage distributions. Each goal has a short description and the number corresponds to Table 4. Letters along the x-axis stand for the information source, see Table 5.

chat logs across all questions in Figure 5. Across all Monitoring Goals the percent of instructors saying they use/would use chat logs ranged between 39% and 24%. We exclude chat logs from the remainder of the discussion.

Instructors' opinions of what is useful largely confirm earlier surveys. Respondents' opinions of what information they would find useful is mostly consistent with the Mazza et al. [16] and Zinn et al. [21] surveys. In those surveys, the most important information concerns overall student performance relative to the class and information about what materials students interacted with and for how long (activity/view patterns); a majority of respondents also identified that information as useful. Respondents also agree with Mazza et al. that qualitative information from forum postings is important, but analysis of chat logs is not. However, respondents of both prior surveys placed higher importance on viewing per-student performance information and per-student mastery information. We speculate that such information is less useful in MOOCs, in which attention to individual students is rare.

Open-ended portions of the survey revealed a wide range of instructor views. Most survey questions, and each section of the survey, solicited open-text comments. The responses showed instructors' preferences ranging from simple numbers with no visualization to very complex data analysis. Complex analysis tool requests included A/B testing, cor-

relational analysis, auto clustering of students by instructor-chosen parameters, and detailed view pattern information including paths through material.

An interesting dichotomy arises between those courses where quantitative assessment is foremost and more experientially-oriented courses. Several instructors stated they were not interested in grades, problem answers, and other performance based metrics because their goal was to provide students with a learning experience and not the ability to quantitatively prove they learned the material. These instructors stated they ran their course based on discussions and team interactions.

Some instructors were not worried about certain monitoring goals. One instructor stated there were too many students to worry about finding struggling individuals. Two instructors said course difficulty was not a concern. One stated course difficulty was fixed at the beginning and could not change while the course was running, while the other said they structured their course to work at multiple difficulty levels.

Responses to Mockups
Before going into detail of the mockups responses, it is important to note a caveat to these results. As a reminder, the survey asked participants if they considered each mockup useful and easy to understand and to predict when they would use the mockup. Since the survey asked participants what

85

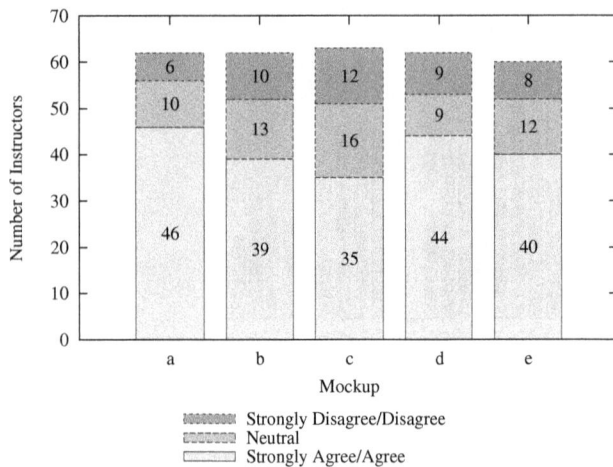

Figure 6. Likert scale responses to the statement "This visualization is useful." Letters correspond to Figure 2's subfigures.

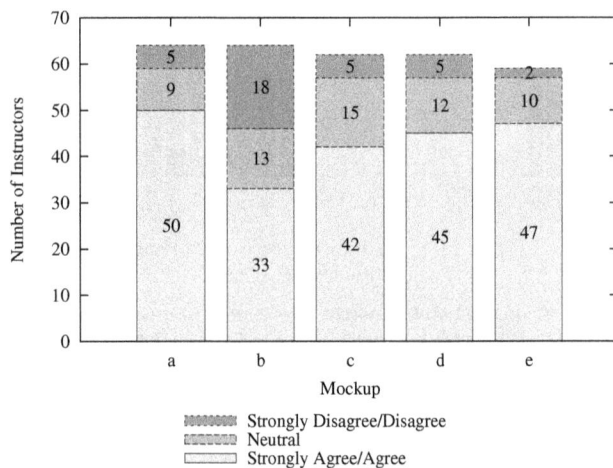

Figure 7. Likert scale responses to the statement "This visualization is easy to understand." Letters correspond to Figure 2's subfigures.

they think they will like and do, as opposed to what they actually liked and did, there are limitations to these results generalizability because what a person thinks they will like or do does not necessarily match what they will actually like or do.

The results of the mockup section are:

At least a majority of instructors considered each mockup useful and understandable. Figures 6 and 7 show participants' responses to the visualization mockups. The familiar box plot (Mockup 2(a)), when applied to student grades, was most often viewed as useful (74%) and understandable (78%), followed closely by visualization (Mockup 2(d)) showing number of student attempts at assignments (71% useful and 73% understandable). The number of times materials were viewed (Mockup 2(e)) was also considered useful information by two thirds of respondents (66%). A number of people expressed concern that the stacked bar visualization of the grade distribution (Mockup 2(b)) was difficult to understand, with only 52% agreeing that it was easy to understand. The visualization of the forum usage (Mockup 2(c)) was also

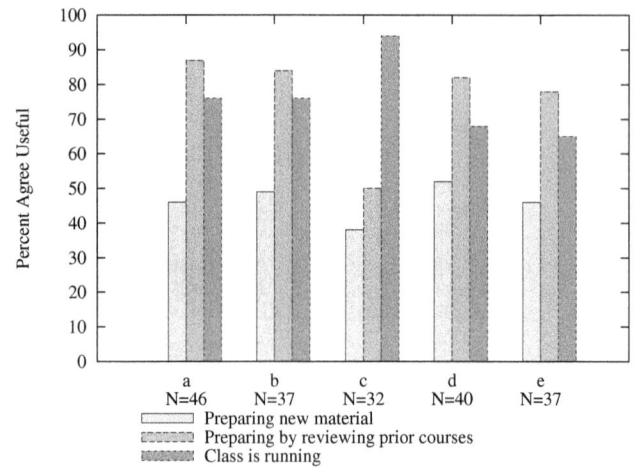

Figure 8. Responses to the question "When would you use this mockup," with choices in terms of three phases in a "MOOC cycle": preparing new material, preparing by reviewing previous course runs, and while the class is running. Letters correspond to Figure 2's subfigures.

not overwhelmingly supported, with only 55% of respondents agreeing or strongly agreeing that it was potentially useful.

There is a relative lack of interest in the forum visualization. Only 55% of instructors stated the forum usage visualization would be useful. Comments about this visualization stated it is not fine-grained enough, it is not more useful than existing statistics, the number of posts is not the useful indicator, and up-and-down votes are more important indicators.

Of those that considered the visualization useful, they would mainly use the visualizations while the course is running and all visualizations but forums after the course is over while preparing for a future offering. For those who did indicate that a given visualization was potentially useful, they were asked to indicate which circumstances it would be best used. Figure 8 presents the results; participants could mark more than one choice in each case. In all cases, at least two thirds of respondents who found the visualization useful wanted to use it while the course was running. And by an even larger margin, instructors wanted to see the visualization for every design except the forum visualization (c), when reviewing a past course in preparation for a future offering.

Relatively fewer participants considered the visualizations useful while preparing new course material. 38% to 52% of respondents indicated preparing new material for a course would be a good use of the visualizations.

METRICS TAB USAGE EXPERIENCES

A variation of the Metrics Tab was released to a small number of test users. This variation included the open subsection count graph (Figure 1 left, grey) and grades graph (top right, green and red); the attempts graph was not available. We interviewed two users that used the Metrics Tab while their course was running. Also, at the time of publication, we became aware of another publication that used the Metrics Tab [10]. We report the Metrics Tab usage experience below.

One user we interviewed was the TA of a MOOC that started with about 8,000 students and ended with about 500 completing the course. The Metrics Tab was one of the TA's primary methods for tracking student activity. The open subsection count graph was used to monitor how many students were still active in the course and if they are looking at all of the content. The grades graph was closely monitored to see how many students were doing the problems and which problems might have issues that needed to be resolved, such as input errors or ambiguities in the question,

The second interviewee was an instructor that ran a small online course of about 100 students. This instructor also used the open subsection count graph to see what content the students looked at. This instructor shared a story in which the Metrics Tab drew their attention to a student error; at the beginning of the course many students were unaware of any but the first subsection and had to be informed that there were other subsections. The instructor also liked the grades graph and used it to monitor the students' lecture quiz grades.

The final usage experience of the Metrics Tab is from Grover et al. [10]. They used the edX platform to teach an introductory computer science middle/high school course and reported on the pedagogy of their course and leveraging the Instructor Dashboard for curriculum assessment. They used the Metrics Tab to monitor quiz data, specifically using the grades graph to find what content the students found difficult and what content needed revision.

All three experiences confirm the survey finding that student performance information is important. The interviewees use of the open subsection graph aligns with the survey that student viewing patterns are important. Although only 52% of those surveyed found the Mockup 2(b) (which is based on the Metrics Tab's grades graph) easy to understand, neither of those interviewed had trouble interpreting the grades graph. The two interviewees were both engineers and so may be more familiar with reading graphs than other instructors.

DISCUSSION
The survey results show that discussion forums were the most frequently preferred source of information, across monitoring tasks, suggesting that effort should be invested in making forums more useful for students and more effective for providing information to instructors.

It is important to bear in mind, however, that prior work has found that only a small proportion of MOOC students are active on forums [3, 4], and therefore forum posters are not necessarily representative of all students in the course. Most likely instructors are aware of these limitations, and this may be why other methods for eliciting an understanding of students' views – student surveys, student discussion, and asking TA's for feedback – follow discussion forums as the perceived most useful information resources.

Notwithstanding these caveats, research to improve forums could significantly aid instructors' goals. For example, better methods to automatically group similar issues together, and to alert students to previously posted issues as they type, will help consolidate issues for the benefit of both instructor and student. User interface improvements can also help. Currently some forum tools, such as Piazza, allow the instructor or students to mark individual issues as resolved, but do not make it easy to group together a set of posts and mark them as similar and then resolved. A more "dashboard-oriented" view of forum posts, oriented towards the instructor, could be a significant time-savings improvement both for monitoring issues and topics in the forum and for processing posts as they are responded to by the instructor and teaching assistants.

This idea can be taken still further to create more of a "bug report" or "issues tracker" type interface approach to teaching a MOOC, similar to how problems are tracked with software engineering projects. As the instructor or teaching assistants learn about problems, via forum, survey, quantitative view such as low scores on a homework problem, the issue could be entered into this interface. Quick surveys or polls could be issued to see if the perceived gaps or problems are widespread and the results entered into the tool. After the correction is made, the problem could be marked as resolved.

Since surveys are private, those students who are not comfortable posting on the forum may be more willing to answer a survey and thus have their views expressed.

Finally, automated methods can be used to find which students appear to be struggling and send them survey questions or encourage them to read the posts on the forum or post their own questions, which will then be seen by the instructors.

A potential drawback of the work reported here is it primarily asked instructors about familiar information sources. Researchers are developing very sophisticated log analysis tools (*e.g.,* [13, 14]) that can produce profiles of student behavior that could be surfaced to the instructor in innovative ways. Future work must investigate the efficacy of these approaches.

Another drawback is MOOC instructors, coming primarily from in-person class backgrounds, may have preferences for technologies that work well in those environments and against those that do not, such as chat rooms. It may be the case that online chat will work better in MOOCs. More generally, after being exposed to new techniques in action, instructors may form different opinions.

The open-ended comments written by respondents revealed an interesting diversity of views that indicated what is useful to one instructor may not be as useful to another. Instructors ranged from being very pressed for time and wanting to see just a few summary numbers to wanting complex correlational analysis. Some courses are administered with a heavy quantitative evaluation focus, whereas others are more oriented around discussion. The emphasis on student grades in the survey seemed inappropriate to the latter instructors. This diverse range of instructor desires and course styles suggests that what is most useful and effective could be instructor- or course-specific and that the ideal MOOC data visualization should be flexible enough to meet these different needs.

CONCLUSIONS
This survey of 92 MOOC instructors confirmed the findings of prior surveys of instructors of conventional online

courses, which found that instructors value seeing student performance, activity patterns such as what materials students look at, and forum behavior to gauge participation. A standard boxplot of distribution of course grades was seen as both understandable and useful by a large majority of respondents, as was a novel design in which stacked bar charts show number of repeated attempts at solving problems.

However, for those who wish to design visualization for MOOC instructors, a major takeaway from this work is views of quantitative measures are not sufficient. Rather, instructors believe they need to hear what students have to say, be it from discussion forums, student surveys, or the impressions of their teaching assistants, for the full range of course monitoring goals. Thus future work for instructor tools should focus on how to obtain the thoughts of a wide range of students taking the course, and how to summarize and present this information to the instructor in a useful manner.

ACKNOWLEDGMENTS

This work was supported by the UC Berkeley Chancellor's fellowship and the National Science Foundation Graduate Research Fellowship under Grant No. DGE 1106400.

REFERENCES

1. Khan Academy coach demo.
   `http://www.khanacademy.org/coach/demo`.

2. Aguilar, D. A. G., Therón, R., and Peñalvo, F. J. G. Semantic spiral timelines used as support for e-learning. *J. UCS 15*, 7 (2009), 1526–1545.

3. Breslow, L., Pritchard, D. E., DeBoer, J., Stump, G. S., Ho, A. D., and Seaton, D. Studying learning in the worldwide classroom: Research into edX's first MOOC. *Research & Practice in Assessment 8* (2013), 13–25.

4. Coetzee, D., Fox, A., Hearst, M. A., and Hartmann, B. Should your MOOC forum use a reputation system? In *Proceedings of the 2014 Conference on Computer-Supported Cooperative Work* (2014).

5. Cotton, K. *Monitoring student learning in the classroom*. Northwest Regional Educational Laboratory, 1988.

6. Gaudioso, E., Hernandez-del-Olmo, F., and Montero, M. Enhancing e-learning through teacher support: two experiences. *Education, IEEE Transactions on 52*, 1 (2009), 109–115.

7. Gibbs, W. J., Olexa, V., and Bernas, R. S. A visualization tool for managing and studying online communications. *Educational Technology & Society 9*, 3 (2006), 232–243.

8. Goldberg, M. W. Student participation and progress tracking for web-based courses using WebCT. In *Proceedings of the Second International NA WEB Conference* (1996), 5–8.

9. Goldberg, M. W., Salari, S., and Swoboda, P. World wide webcourse tool: An environment for building www-based courses. *Computer Networks and ISDN Systems 28*, 7 (1996), 1219–1231.

10. Grover, S., Pea, R., and Cooper, S. Promoting active learning & leveraging dashboards for curriculum assessment in an OpenEdX introductory CS course for middle school. In *Learning @ Scale, Work in Progress*, ACM (2014).

11. Hardless, C., and Nulden, U. Visualizing learning activities to support tutors. In *CHI'99 extended abstracts on Human factors in computing systems*, ACM (1999), 312–313.

12. Hardy, J., Antonioletti, M., and Bates, S. e-learner tracking: Tools for discovering learner behavior. In *The IASTED International Conference on Web-base Education* (2004).

13. Huang, J., Piech, C., Nguyen, A., and Guibas, L. Syntactic and functional variability of a million code submissions in a machine learning mooc. In *AIED 2013 Workshops Proceedings Volume* (2013), 25.

14. Kizilcec, R. F., Piech, C., and Schneider, E. Deconstructing disengagement: analyzing learner subpopulations in massive open online courses. In *Proceedings of the Third International Conference on Learning Analytics and Knowledge*, ACM (2013), 170–179.

15. Mazza, R., and Dimitrova, V. Coursevis: Externalising student information to facilitate instructors in distance learning. In *Proceedings of the International conference in Artificial Intelligence in Education*, Sydney, Australia (2003), 117–129.

16. Mazza, R., and Dimitrova, V. Informing the design of a course data visualisator: an empirical study. In *5th International Conference on New Educational Environments (ICNEE 2003)* (2003), 215–220.

17. Mazza, R., and Dimitrova, V. Coursevis: A graphical student monitoring tool for supporting instructors in web-based distance courses. *International Journal of Human-Computer Studies 65*, 2 (2007), 125–139.

18. Mazza, R., and Milani, C. Exploring usage analysis in learning systems: Gaining insights from visualisations. In *AIED05 workshop on Usage analysis in learning systems*, Citeseer (2005), 65–72.

19. Romero, C., and Ventura, S. Educational data mining: a review of the state of the art. *Systems, Man, and Cybernetics, Part C: Applications and Reviews, IEEE Transactions on 40*, 6 (2010), 601–618.

20. Williams, F. P., and Conlan, O. Visualizing narrative structures and learning style information in personalized e-learning systems. In *Advanced Learning Technologies, 2007. ICALT 2007. Seventh IEEE International Conference on*, IEEE (2007), 872–876.

21. Zinn, C., and Scheuer, O. Getting to know your student in distance learning contexts. In *Innovative Approaches for Learning and Knowledge Sharing*. Springer, 2006, 437–451.

Divide and Correct: Using Clusters to Grade Short Answers at Scale

Michael Brooks[1,2]
[1]University of Washington
Seattle, WA
mjbrooks@uw.edu

Sumit Basu[2], Charles Jacobs[2], Lucy Vanderwende[2]
[2]Microsoft Research
Redmond, WA
{sumitb, cjacobs, lucyv}@microsoft.com

ABSTRACT

In comparison to multiple choice or other recognition-oriented forms of assessment, short answer questions have been shown to offer greater value for both students and teachers; for students they can improve retention of knowledge, while for teachers they provide more insight into student understanding. Unfortunately, the same open-ended nature which makes them so valuable also makes them more difficult to grade at scale. To address this, we propose a cluster-based interface that allows teachers to read, grade, and provide feedback on large groups of answers at once. We evaluated this interface against an unclustered baseline in a within-subjects study with 25 teachers, and found that the clustered interface allows teachers to grade substantially faster, to give more feedback to students, and to develop a high-level view of students' understanding and misconceptions.

Author Keywords

Grading; grading interfaces; assessment; MOOCs; clustering; user interfaces; clustering interfaces.

ACM Classification Keywords

H.5.2 Information interfaces and presentation (e.g., HCI): User interfaces – Evaluation/methodology; K.3.1 Computers and Education: Computer uses in education.

INTRODUCTION

While the impressive scale of modern online courses allows a teacher to easily deliver lectures to massive numbers of students, interactions in the other direction are still a challenge. Dealing with hundreds or thousands of student exams can be overwhelming, particularly if they contain responses to open-ended questions. At the same time, open-ended assessments have substantial value to both students and teachers, as we discuss in detail in the background section. Automated approaches to grading open-ended questions reduce the workload for teachers, but some benefits of open-ended

questions depend on the teacher actively reviewing and assessing their students' answers.

In this work, we propose a means of maintaining the teacher's involvement while still allowing them to work with short answer responses at scale. Our approach uses clustering to group student responses into clusters and subclusters. We develop an interface giving teachers access to these groupings, allowing them to read, grade, and provide feedback to large numbers of responses at once.

Previous research has demonstrated that automatic clustering of answers could reduce the number of grader actions required, potentially improving scalability of instructor grading for an algorithmically "optimal" grader [2]. In order for a grading interface to be effective at scale, though, speed alone is not enough. While efficiency is important, teachers must also be able to get a sense for trends in students' understanding, as well as give helpful feedback to students with misconceptions. In this work, we investigate whether a user interface for grading clustered answers would improve efficiency for real teachers, while promoting high quality grading, feedback for students, and instructor reflection.

We have created a web application that allows a teacher to grade and give feedback on hundreds of responses to short-answer questions; in our work this refers to answers that range from a few words to a sentence in length. In a within-subjects experiment with 25 teachers, we compared our proposed *clustered* version of the system, where the grader works with automatically clustered responses, to an unclustered (*flat*) baseline system. We found that teachers were able to grade far more quickly using the clustered version, and that the resulting grades were of equivalent accuracy when compared to a gold standard. Feedback was given to roughly three times as many answers, and teachers reported being better able to reflect on trends in student understanding. Furthermore, teachers found the new interface to be superior in terms of ease of use and overall effectiveness.

BACKGROUND AND RELATED WORK

Below, we provide background on the role that assessment plays in the education process, and discuss related work on peer and automated grading in the context of education research on grading practices, feedback, and reflection.

Assessment

Educational assessment is concerned with measuring student ability and aptitude, but the goals and impacts of assessment are broader than individual students. Assessment is used for quality assurance for educational institutions and programs, and influences ways of teaching [7]. Testing also assists knowledge retention and can guide learning [1,20]; for example, "it is not until students start to work on their assignment that they know whether or what they have learned from their studies" [20]. Assessment indirectly influences student learning by shaping curriculum design and learning goals [7], and teachers often intentionally adapt their teaching based on formative assessments [3,19]. Assessment is deeply intertwined with most aspects of education; additional research is needed to understand assessment at MOOC scale.

There are many different forms of assessment available, and their use varies widely. For example, in a survey of secondary teachers, McMillan found that social studies and science teachers reported using objective assessments and quizzes significantly more often than English teachers did, while English, science and social studies teachers tended to use constructed- or open-response assessments more than math teachers, and English teachers more than science teachers [11]. With MOOCs and other approaches to large-scale education becoming increasingly important, multiple-choice questions and other highly-constrained assessment instruments offer scalability since submissions can be automatically scored against an answer key. However, Anderson and Biddle established that open-ended, constructed response questions such as short answers and essays are preferred forms of assessment [1]. Open-ended questions are more valuable for measuring understanding, application, and reasoning [11], and play a critical role in consolidating learning [9]. Our work is concerned with making it practical for teachers to use short answer questions in MOOCs, where there may be hundreds or thousands of responses to grade.

Grading

As with assessment strategies, approaches to grading differ across grade levels, subject areas, and from teacher to teacher. Grading has been a controversial topic in education research for most of the past century [5], with much discussion focused on the factors that teachers take into account when assigning grades. Studies of grading practice find that teachers use a "hodgepodge" of factors in grading, including not only achievement but also effort and ability [4,5]. Although this contradicts the recommendations of measurement specialists [5], more complex and subjective judgments may support teachers' practical needs of managing classrooms and motivating students [4]. Whether or not a more objective and achievement-oriented approach to grading is desirable, we must be mindful that, in practice, there is far more to grading than just marking an answer "right" or "wrong."

For grading open-ended assessments in MOOCs, one approach has been automated grading against a carefully au-thored answer key that attempts to anticipate all possible student answers [6,8]. However, designing the answer keys is time-consuming, and tuning may require linguistics expertise, making this an unreasonable method for most teachers. Alternatively, automated grading can be formulated as a similarity task in which a score is assigned based on the similarity between student answer and teacher answer [12]. While these automatic methods promise improved scalability of constructed-response assessment, it must be mentioned that the accuracy of both methods of automatic grading is reported in the range of 84% to 92%, which is less than the 100% which a teacher strives for, and so understandably, there is a lively debate regarding the trade-offs [10,14].

Other approaches to grading open-ended assessments include peer-grading and self-grading. In peer-grading, students use a scoring rubric to grade each other's answers [15,17,18]. Students are typically from the same class or a parallel class, but some researchers have explored whether peers could also be drawn from a *crowd* of experts [21]. There have been claims that peer-grading provides learning benefits to graders through the grading exercise itself [17]. However, Sadler and Good found no evidence that peer-grading improves peer performance on subsequent tests on the same material [18]. Moreover, while this approach shows promise, student biases, self-interest, and lack of expertise remain as limitations.

Feedback

Feedback, a major area of study in education, provides "the comparison of actual performance with some set standard of performance" [13] and is known to facilitate learning. A great deal of education research has focused on how, when, and what feedback should be provided to students in order to maximize various learning benefits; recently, focus has shifted to student perspectives and perceptions about feedback [16]. Research on scalable assessment in MOOCs should take into account how effectively feedback can be provided to students. Feedback can be pre-authored for multiple-choice answers, as seen in the tutorial-like feedback used by the Khan Academy quizzes (kahnacademy.org), but automatically providing feedback for open-response assessments would require pre-authoring feedback for all anticipated answers as well as the ability to match answers to feedback automatically; this would have many of the same drawbacks as automated grading. As with grading, there is the possibility of peer feedback: in a peer-grading exercise for a Coursera MOOC, students gave each other feedback alongside grades [15]. Analysis showed that negative comments were typically longer, but that overall, the comments ranged "from neutral to quite positive, suggesting that rather than being highly negative to some submissions, many students make an effort to be balanced in their comments to peers."

Reflection

Mastery Learning, which has been shown to improve student performance in a traditional classrooms, relies on frequent use of *formative assessment*, where teachers use assessment to learn about and improve their teaching methods [3,19]. For example, teachers may "determine when [students] comprehend the explanations and illustrations" so that they can supply additional clarification as needed [3]. Grading is an important avenue for teachers to gain comprehension of student understanding and misunderstanding, but automated grading and peer grading cannot offer teachers the same insights they get from grading students themselves.

CLUSTERED GRADING APPLICATION

We designed and implemented a web application enabling teachers to *efficiently* grade and give feedback on a large volume of short answers, while still allowing teachers to control the quality of their work and to learn about the general state of students' understandings. This efficiency is created through the use of clustering to group and organize similar answers. We iteratively designed and developed the application with continual testing and evaluation by the authors, consultation of the literature on grading practices reviewed above, and informal discussions with teachers, educators, and graders. The interface is shown in Figure 1.

A video showing the interface in action can be seen at http://research.microsoft.com/~sumitb/grading .

Target Users and Context

In our design process, we envisioned an instructor or grader in a large online course using open-ended questions on an exam or other assignment. The instructor collects the students' answers to a question and provides them to our software, which runs a *hierarchical clustering algorithm* on the answers and displays an interface for grading the clustered answers. In this work, we focus only on grading, the final stage in this process. Below, we briefly describe the clustering algorithm that our system uses, and then discuss our most significant design challenges and decisions.

Clustering Algorithm

We clustered short answers using the metric clustering approach developed and evaluated in [2], which builds a hierarchy with two levels: the hierarchy may have up to 10 top-level clusters with up to 5 subclusters in each cluster. There may also be *miscellaneous* clusters or subclusters, containing answers that did not fit well into any of the other clusters.

The clustering algorithm computes a learned distance metric over pairs of answers, based on difference in answer length, words with matching base forms, *tf-idf* vector similarity, lowercase string match, and Wikipedia-based LSA similarity. The clustering is computed from these distances using a version of the k-medoids algorithm. Further details on rationale, implementation, and evaluation are in [2].

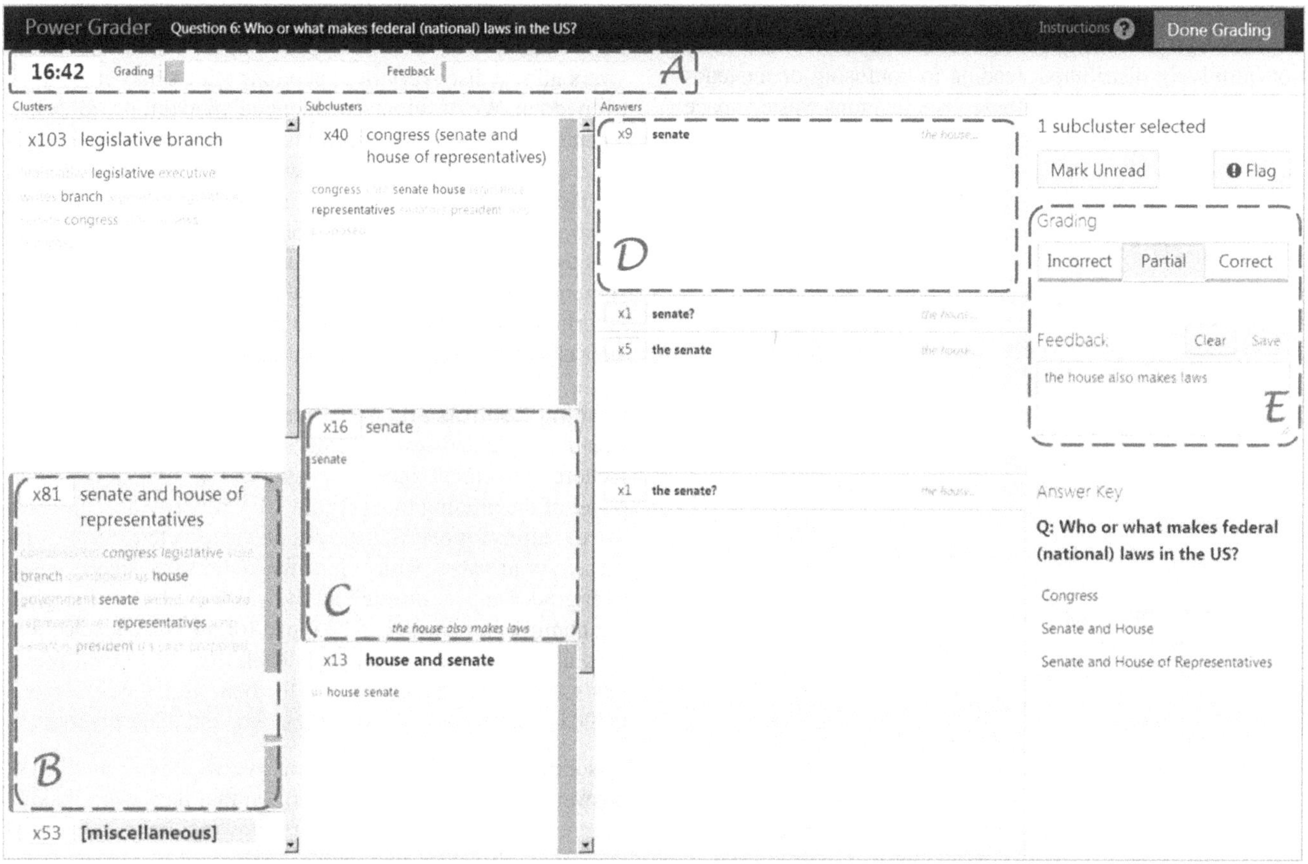

Figure 1: Grading a cluster in Question 6. (A) progress bars; (B) a cluster of 81 students, graded mostly correct (blue); (C) the selected subcluster, graded partially correct (yellow); (D) the answer "senate" by 9 students; (E) grading and feedback controls.

Cluster Exploration

Our first challenge was designing a layout and organization for the clusters that would be easily understandable and support an efficient process for grading. We considered several approaches: for example, we sketched a focused, one-at-a-time presentation of clusters and subclusters for grading, like checking phone messages on an answering machine. However, we decided this kind of guided design would be too constrained; instead, we designed an open-ended hierarchy-browsing layout that we supposed would be familiar from email or file system navigation programs. Users view and interact with lists of clusters, subclusters, and answers in a three-column layout (Figure 1). Selecting a cluster causes its nested subclusters and answers to appear, while subsequent selection of a subcluster filters the answers displayed. This design allows users to quickly and easily explore or drill down into the answers wherever the contents of a challenging cluster may demand it.

Cluster Summaries

This suggests another design challenge: how to present summaries of clusters and subclusters so as to enable users to make *informed* decisions about where to explore. We prototyped several visualization-based techniques with the goal of representing the "cohesiveness" or "compactness" of clusters and subclusters. For example, since each answer within a cluster has an estimated distance from the cluster centroid, we created plots showing the distribution of distances within the cluster. It became apparent that the distances were often not intuitively distributed, leading to confusing or misleading visualizations, and that these visualizations wasted space in clusters with few answers.

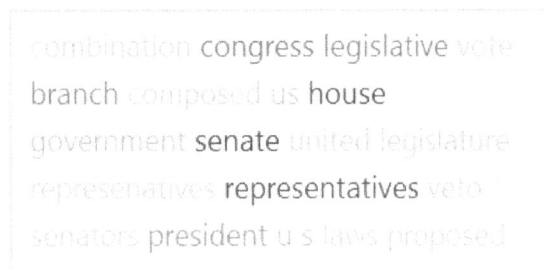

Figure 2: A summary of cluster contents. The list of words is ordered by average position in the answer text.

We developed a type of *word cloud*, a representation of word frequency in unstructured text (Figure 2). Unlike typical word clouds, we decided to keep the font size of words constant for readability, and to instead vary lightness so that the least used words appear nearly transparent. The elegance of this solution is that clusters with few answers, or little diversity of answers, have relatively small word clouds. Meanwhile, clusters with a great diversity of answers, which likely warrant closer inspection, have large, eye-catching word clouds. A weakness of traditional word clouds is that information about the order of words in the original text is utterly lost. In our word clouds, we order the words according to their *average position* in the answers (normalized by answer

length). This technique proved a useful improvement on the word clouds in many clusters we inspected, though not all. In addition, we scaled the height taken up by clusters and subclusters based on how many *students*, not distinct answers, were contained in each cluster (this number is also shown in the top left of each cluster, subcluster, or answer item). This encourages the grader to spend time first on those areas that will benefit the most people. Given the rich literature in text summarization and visualization in recent years, there is a substantial research opportunity in experimenting with alternative visualizations for clusters of answers; we hope that we as well as others will explore this space further.

Grading and Feedback Interactions

The third challenge was to design the operations that the interface should support. It was clear that there would need to be a *grade* action, but it was less clear what the user would expect to happen if, for example, they mark a particular cluster *Correct*, one of its child subclusters *Incorrect*, and one of its child answers *Partial*. We settled on the following solution: when the user marks a grade on a cluster as a whole, its contained subclusters "inherit" that grade. The user can "override" that inheritance on one of the subclusters by marking it with a grade. Similarly, individual answers inherit the grade of their parent subcluster or cluster unless they have been specifically marked by the user. The effect is that the user can use grade inheritance to mark a possible grade to every answer very rapidly, simply by grading the clusters. Following up with closer inspection of the subclusters or answers allows discovery of exceptions which may need to be overridden. We developed an identical model for feedback—writing a feedback message for an entire cluster effectively gives feedback to all of the students contained in that cluster, but this can also be overridden. To make this behavior more apparent to users, we added color-coded grading indicator bars to the right side of every cluster, subcluster, and answer (Figure 1 B and C). These show the current grade (whether inherited or marked directly) in a kind of spatial map of every answer in the given cluster or subcluster.

Grading Controls and Progress Bars

Finally, we added several features to the interface that make it more convenient and more satisfying to use. In the right-panel of the grading tool (Figure 1 E), we provide a group of three buttons for marking grades on the selected cluster, subcluster, or answers, with colors associated consistently wherever grades appear throughout the interface. Below the grading controls, feedback can be typed for the current selection. It is also possible to *reuse* feedback that was given previously, a time-saving feature. At the bottom of the right panel is the question currently being graded, and the answer key.

Assuming that graders, facing an overwhelming number of answers to grade, would want to see that they were making progress, we added progress bars showing the proportion of answers with grades and feedback (Figure 1 A). This is more complex than it might first seem, since there is actually no clearly-defined end point to grading. Anecdotally, it is not uncommon in traditional grading to make multiple passes through student answers until a satisfactory level of consistency and quality is achieved. Thus, the grading progress bar could rapidly fill at the beginning of the grading task, when in fact more exploration and checking is needed to improve grading quality. Likewise, since many answers need no feedback (particularly *Correct* answers), the feedback progress bar usually never fills. To the left of the progress bars is a timer, which counted down from the time-limit of 20 minutes for the purpose of our study.

METHOD

We used a within-subjects experiment design to compare *clustered* vs. *flat* grading of hundreds of responses to short answer questions in terms of efficiency, grade quality, feedback to students, and grader insight. The study was conducted online with 25 individuals with teaching experience; participants spent up to 20 minutes grading about 200 distinct answers from each of two questions. Below, we provide details on the study participants, question and answer data, and experiment design.

Participants

Grading is a complex practice balancing many competing priorities and concerns, and graders develop expertise and tacit knowledge that could have a significant impact on how they interact with the software. Therefore, we sought participants with teaching or grading experience—at least one year of teaching or grading experience within the past five years. We also required that they occasionally use email, chat or forums, and spreadsheets; and that they used some of these tools in their teaching or grading work. They also had to be native speakers of English.

To more easily reach this population, we conducted the study online. For recruitment, we worked with a company specializing in linguistics crowd-work, which sent our initial screening survey to a population of 110 teachers or former teachers from its worker pool. Of the 80 who responded, we invited 40 qualified individuals. Of these, 25 completed the one-hour study successfully, and were paid $15.

In the group of 25 participants, eight are aged 22 to 34, eleven are 35 to 44, and six are 45 or over. All participants reported at least 2 years of teaching experience, and about half had more than 5 years; the company that assisted with recruitment individually vetted these teaching backgrounds. Participants' teaching experience was in a wide variety of subject areas, and most people had taught multiple subjects; due to the topic of the grading tasks (discussed below) we prioritized recruitment for participants who had taught Government, Politics or Civics (9 people), but others were also included: 23 participants had taught English, and 12 had taught literature; 12 had teaching experience in science, technology, engineering, or math. Most (22) had experience at the middle or high school level; 12 had college- or graduate-level teaching experience.

All reported using communication technology such as email, forums, or chat multiple times a day, and all but one had used email for communicating with students. All participants reported that they use or have recently used the Internet at least once a week for their teaching roles, and use spreadsheets at least monthly. All but 4 said that they have used computers for grading work, 13 out of 25 had done this at least daily. Most (19) had taught an online course at least once, and 14 had done so many times. None had experience with MOOCs; the largest class size reported was 120 students.

Questions to Grade

Participants in our study graded answers to each of two different short answer questions. We selected a pair of questions from the Powergrading Short Answer Grading Corpus [2], which includes short answers given by 698 Mechanical Turk workers, for 20 questions from the United States Citizenship Exam. The questions vary in terms both of scope and difficulty. The corpus also contains grades independently assigned by three judges, which we used as benchmark grades for comparison to grades from our study participants.

Because the kind and structure of answers received depends on the question, the efficiency of clustered grading may be sensitive to the question being graded. We decided to select a pair of "average" questions: for each of the 20 questions, we calculated the number of *distinct* answers (some answers are identical), the average answer length, the percent of correct answers *vs.* the researcher grades, and agreement among the researcher grades. We selected Question 4 and Question 6 (Table 1) because, in terms of these four metrics, they were in the middle of the distribution for the corpus, and were similar to one another. Question 4 had 196 distinct answers (1-25 words in length, mean=3.9), and Question 6 had 205 (1-97 words, mean=6.4). From this point on, we refer to these distinct answers as simply answers, for brevity.

Q4	*What is the economic system in the United States?*
Q6	*Who or what makes federal (national) laws in the US?*

Table 1: The two questions that were selected for grading in the experiment. Participants graded both questions.

Clustered and Flat Grading Interfaces

Participants graded the answers to one of the two questions using the *clustered* grading application, discussed above. To determine how interacting with clustered answers altered the process and results of grading, we created a second, *flat* version of the application which does not use clustering. The flat version was designed to provide a realistic baseline grading experience, while also preserving as much from the clustered version as possible.

Our assumption in designing the flat version was that in the absence of a more specialized tool, most teachers and graders would probably attempt to grade short answers by going through them one by one. For example, they could grade using a spreadsheet program, since such software is commonly available and familiar. The flat grading interface displays a flat list of all of the answers, allowing a workflow similar to grading in a spreadsheet. We sort the answers alphabetically, a basic step that provides some time-savings because answers that start with the same words sometimes receive the same grade or feedback. As in the clustered interface, we collapse duplicated answers. The flat interface (Figure 3) is implemented as a minor variation of the clustered interface. We simply remove the two left panels which display the clusters and subclusters, allow the Answers panel to expand horizontally, and show all of the distinct answers in alphabetical order. All other aspects of the tool are identical between the two versions, facilitating comparison in our evaluation.

Measures
Because the study was conducted over the Internet, most data was collected through logging of user activities. Selection of clusters, subclusters, or answers was logged, as was the application of grades or feedback. These events were timestamped to show how users progressed through the task.

In addition to actions over time, we also evaluated the final grades given by participants. We created a set of "gold standard" grades based on the three independent sets of grades from the Powergrading Corpus. We selected the subset of answers where the three independent graders had unanimous agreement (about 82% of answers, for each question). These grades are binary (Correct or Incorrect) without partial credit as we had in the current study, so we converted our participants' grades to match by re-coding partial credit as Correct, as this best reflected the rubric used by the graders from the corpus.

We spaced several questionnaires at various points throughout the study. A *Pre-Study Questionnaire* confirmed the participant's teaching experience and background information. A *Post-Task Questionnaire*, completed immediately after each grading task, asked for impressions and reflections on the task, including Likert-type questions about how the interface supported consistent and fair grading, giving feedback, and overall difficulty of use. Finally, a *Post-Study Questionnaire* asked for general comments and direct comparison of the two interfaces in terms of speed, ease-of-use, enjoyment,

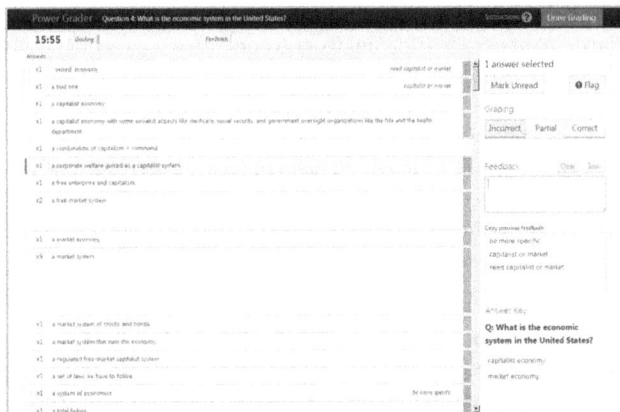

Figure 3: The flat grading interface. Identical to the clustered interface but without the cluster and subcluster controls.

and effectiveness. We analyzed the Post-Task questions using non-parametric Wilcoxon Signed Ranks tests. For the Post-Study comparison, we compared how often participants chose one interface or the other using chi-square tests.

One of the items on the Post-Task Questionnaire also invited participants to reflect on the students' answers: "summarize how the students did on the question you just graded." This was intended to elicit insights that the teachers may have gained while grading which they could have used to improve future lessons.

Procedure
The within-subjects study consisted of two grading tasks; participants graded both questions, and used both interfaces. We began by sending the 40 qualified participants a unique link to the study website, which randomly assigned participants to one of four study groups, comprised of both combinations of assignments of conditions (clustered and flat) to questions (4 and 6) as well both orders between conditions to control for effects from having been exposed to one interface or question before the other. Due to attrition, the final set of 25 had 15 participants who started with the *flat* interface, while 10 started using the *clustered* interface.

After assigning participants to an ordering of Question and Interface, the study website guided them through the pre-study questionnaire and a text description of the study, followed by the two interface conditions. Each condition consisted of a narrated video tutorial, the grading task itself, and a post-task questionnaire. The video tutorial contained instructions for the task and an explanation of the given interface. The study then ended with the post-study questionnaire. Each task took 20 minutes; the entire study took 1 hour.

RESULTS
We begin with an analysis of general participant comments about the interfaces, then examine grading speed, quality (accuracy), the amount/quality of feedback given to students, and reflections on students' understanding.

	Clustered	Flat
Faster	21	4
More Enjoyable	20	5
Easier to Use	20	5
More Effective	19	6
Better Overall	21	4

Table 2: Number of participants who preferred each interface across various attributes. All differences significant (p < 0.01).

Interface Preferences
After using both interfaces, the Post-Study Questionnaire asked participants to rate which was faster, more enjoyable, easier to use, more effective, and better overall (Table 2). We analyzed these responses using chi-square tests; the clustered interface was preferred significantly more often in all categories (p < 0.01 in all cases).

Additional chi-square tests indicated that neither the question being graded nor the order of using the interfaces had significant effects on these choices. The comments were positive:

> *When initially viewing the video on this interface, I was a little worried that it might be somewhat complicated and time consuming due to the subcategories. However, I was incorrect. This interface was quite efficient and easy to use. (P15)*

A less skeptical participant described how the clustering was helpful for understanding how the students were doing:

> *[The clustered interface] worked very well for me, especially given the large number of total responses. I found [the flat interface] quite tedious. I found that [the clustered interface] helped me to identify student patterns in thinking quite well. (P12)*

Of the few who preferred the flat interface, the main reason was the complexity of working with clustered answers:

> *[The clustered interface] was just a little too complicated, even though some elements of it were easier. There was just too much to keep track of [...] I found myself having to backtrack and recheck a lot of answers. (P1)*

Grading Speed

We next investigate whether the proposed interface led to an increase in grading speed. We have provided the raw trace of answers graded over time for all participants grading Question 4 with the clustered interface (Figure 4) and the flat interface (Figure 5). These charts illustrate the marked difference in the general *shape* of the curves (the differences were similar for Question 6). Even the fastest participants using the flat interface had essentially linear progress; a few created sudden jumps by selecting multiple answers and grading the bunch. In contrast, the fastest users of the clustered interface show a different and decidedly nonlinear progression.

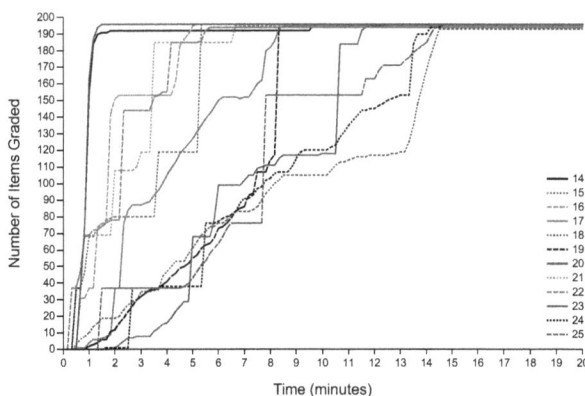

Figure 4: Answers graded vs. time for Q4, clustered interface

With the clustered interface, we observe early use of the high-level action of grading clusters and subclusters (vertical jumps), followed by no actions (horizontal segments) as the timer continues. This time was used to check subclusters and answers to see if refinements were needed after the first pass. With the clustered interface, all participants grading Question 4 had assigned grades for all answers after 15 minutes. If pressed for time, they could have spent less time checking the individual answers, but still would have assigned at least

a first-approximation grade for every answer. With the flat interface, participants could only have progressed more quickly by increasing the slope, i.e., by examining more items per unit time. If forced to end early, answers would have been ungraded; indeed, several participants did not finish with the flat interface (Figure 5).

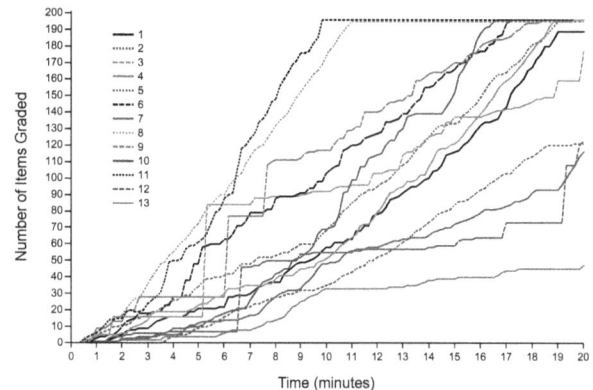

Figure 5: Answers graded vs. time for Q4, flat interface

In order to quantitatively compare the efficiency of the two interfaces, we sought an intuitive measure of speed that reflects the differences we observed. However, the choice of a metric is not straightforward: with the clustered interface, users both assigned grades rapidly using clusters and drilled down more slowly to obtain more accurate grades where needed. These two activities were unpredictably interleaved, and participants allocated their 20 minutes in different ways.

We chose to focus on comparing the speed at which participants could assign an initial grade to all the answers they would eventually grade, even if they later corrected some of those grades. While such corrections complicate the interpretation, this measure does represent a maximal rate of how quickly users could process answers, helping us extrapolate to larger datasets. To compute our speed metric, we determine how many answers the participant ultimately graded, and then divide this by the earliest time at which the participant reached that level of completion. Looking at the curves, this is the maximum value divided by the first time at which this value is reached; the resulting quantity has units of answers graded per minute. Using this measure of speed, the participants had an average speed of 11 ± 3.9 answers/min using the flat interface and 33 ± 40 answers/min using the clustered interface. This was a statistically significant difference (paired t-test, df=24, t=2.92, p<.007). No significant accuracy differences were found between questions (4 vs. 6) or order (first trial vs. second).

While this gives an overall sense of the average improvement in speed, the relative gain from the clustered interface changes over time as it is used. We calculated the amount of gain provided by the clustered interface *at each point in time*, averaged across participants. To do this, we combined the individual curves (such as in Figure 4) to create average progress curves for each interface; we then normalized by the total number of answers for each question, and plotted the difference between the average *clustered* and *flat* curves. The result is shown in Figure 6: at each time point, the middle curve reflects the fraction of all answers that users of the clustered interface had graded *beyond* what users of the flat interface had graded, at that point in time. For example, at about 7 minutes, an additional 45% of the answers (about 90 answers) had been graded in the clustered condition on average. The greatest gains occurred early in the task; by the end, users in the flat condition caught up, as the clustered participants had already run out of new answers to grade.

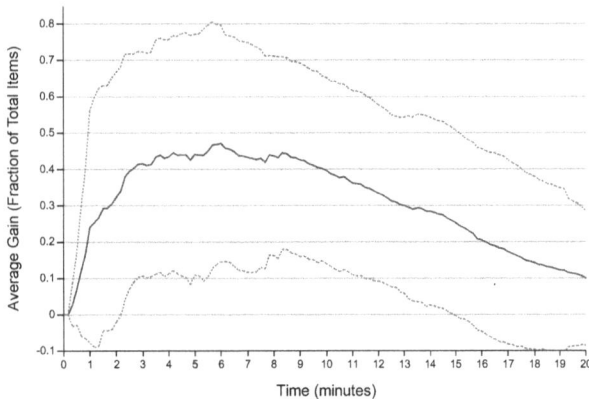

Figure 6: Average gain (± one std. dev.) over time, in fraction of answers graded, with the clustered vs. the flat interface.

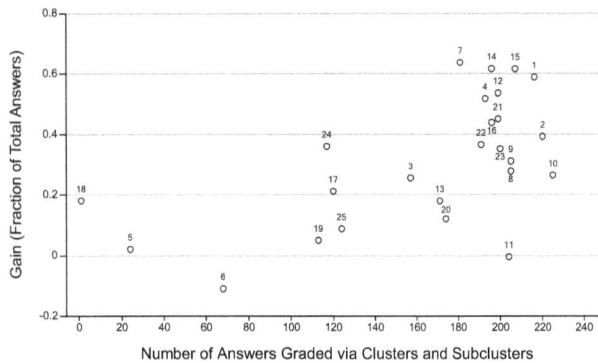

Figure 7: Gain for each participant in the clustered condition (over flat) vs. the number of items marked using a cluster or subcluster-level action.

Finally, we were curious to understand where these gains were coming from – were participants grading so many more answers because they were using the clusters and subclusters, or was it due to some other aspect of the interface? To study this, we computed, for each participant, the *gain* between their *clustered* trial and their *flat* trial, averaged over time (i.e., the time-average of Figure 6, but specific to a participant). We compared this to the number of answers graded *using actions at the cluster or subcluster level* (Figure 7), revealing a trend that increased use of high-level actions was associated with greater gains.

Grading Quality
Though the gains in speed using the clustered interface are clear, we were concerned that these speeds might be at the expense of grading accuracy. We measured grading quality

by comparing grades against a gold standard, and also asked participants about their perceived consistency and fairness.

In order to test accuracy, we first needed an independent standard that we could measure both conditions against. Although grading is an individualized process and there is often no absolute correct grade for any answer, we chose to use as a gold standard the subset of items in which the three graders from the Powergrading Corpus [2] had perfect agreement. This corresponded to 167 of the 196 items for Q4 and 160 out of the 205 for Q6; the percent of items judged *Correct* (vs. *Incorrect*) were 53% and 67% respectively.

We then measured the accuracy of our participants' grades with respect to this gold standard, only counting those items that were marked (i.e., accuracy was not penalized for not completing the task). There was not a statistically significant difference in accuracy between clustered vs. flat conditions either for both questions together (92% vs. 90%, respectively) or either question individually (95% vs. 91% for Question 4, 88% vs. 90% for Question 6). In Figure 8, we show the accuracy for each participant/condition against speed. Contrary to our fears, it appears that the greater speed of the clustered interface does not hurt accuracy. This is remarkable given that the fastest *clustered* participant (8) graded at the rate of 176 answers/minute, compared to the fastest *flat* participant (11), at only 20 answers/minute.

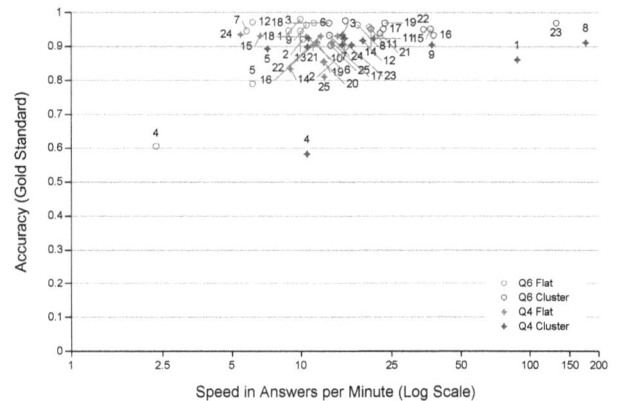

Figure 8: Accuracy vs. speed (items per minute) for all participants in all conditions. Note that speed is shown on a log scale.

Beyond the quantitative measures, we also wanted to know how participants felt about the quality of grading they were able to achieve. We analyzed the Post-Task questions about how well the interface supported grading *consistency* and *fairness* using a Wilcoxon Signed Ranks test, finding that significantly more participants rated the *clustered* interface higher than *flat* for support of *consistent* grading (Z=-2.3, p<0.022). There was no significant difference for *fairness*.

Feedback
In addition to grading efficiency and quality, we also assessed how well each interface supported graders giving students feedback about their answers. We analyzed the amount of feedback that participants gave, the feedback itself, and participants' comments about giving feedback.

Qualitative analysis of the feedback messages showed that most participants took their task seriously and wrote helpful, clear messages for students, but there were differing levels of effort, ranging from copy-pasting from the answer key to writing longer messages incorporating outside knowledge. Strategies differed as well: some asked students questions in their feedback messages, while others offered specific suggestions for improvement. Below we present a few selected examples of feedback messages, for illustration:

> *State legislators do not make national laws. The congressional members from the States do, but not the states themselves. (P7, Question 6)*

> *Gave you partial credit, as "market economy" is correct. "Free" market is too specific. (P14, Question 4)*

> *Be clear with your response. what role if any does the Supreme Court play? (P24, Question 6)*

Participants typed a median of 3 different feedback messages (ranging from 0 to 17) over the course of each grading task, which did not differ significantly between the two interfaces. Each of these distinct messages could be applied more than once, to clusters, subclusters, or individual answers, but this also did not differ significantly between the two interfaces. Participants attached feedback to a median of 11 objects with the clustered interface, vs. 18 objects with the flat interface.

However, using the clustered interface, more answers actually *received* feedback (median of 75 answers) than with the flat interface (median 18), because this feedback was often applied at the cluster or subcluster level and inherited by many answers. Because of non-normal distributions, we used a Wilcoxon Signed Ranks test to confirm that this difference is significant (Z=-3.23, $p<0.001$). In summary, while exerting the same or slightly less effort to create and attach feedback messages with the clustered interface, more than three times as many distinct answers received feedback.

Comments in the Post-Study Questionnaire also indicate that the clustered interface made giving feedback easier. Participants said that the efficiency of grading with the clustered interface let them think more carefully about feedback:

> *Being able to grade categorized responses makes it easier on the grader and allows them to pay closer attention to types of feedback needed. (P24)*

> *Because [the clustered interface] was so much faster, more time could be spent giving feedback. (P14)*

The Post-Task Questionnaire asked about how satisfied participants were with the amount and usefulness of feedback they were able to give. Wilcoxon Signed Ranks tests showed that significantly more people were more satisfied with the amount of feedback they gave using the *clustered* interface than with the *flat* interface (Z=-2.4, $p<0.018$). There was no significant difference in reported usefulness of feedback.

Although participants spent no more effort providing feedback, clustering effectively amplified their efforts to impact more students, giving them more time to give good feedback.

Reflection

One benefit teachers can derive from assessment and grading is the opportunity to reflect and learn about student knowledge and misunderstandings; we asked participants to note patterns and trends in the students' answers and to comment on how the students did on the question. Across both interfaces, most of these reflections were substantive, noting several patterns or observations, many of which would have been informative to a teacher. For example, P12, after using the clustered interface, noted several misunderstandings:

> *The vast majority had the response being sought. A fairly large subgroup of students correctly identified that the legislative branch and executive branch act in concert with the President either vetoing a bill or signing the bill into law. A smaller, but still significant subgroup was clearly confused regarding the branches of government, thinking that the judiciary actually creates the laws instead of interpreting the laws. (P12)*

A content analysis of these reflections, where we coded for attributes such as type and number of patterns detected, tone, and length, showed some noticeable differences between the two questions that were graded, but did not reveal any significant difference between the two interfaces. It appears that the participants were able to produce equally detailed and insightful reflections using either interface. Although we did not detect a difference in the reflections, other comments indicate that the clustered interface made finding patterns and misconceptions easier:

> *This format [clustered interface] made it easy to see patterns in student thinking, whether correct patterns or errors. (P12)*

> *This interface does make answer trends more easily identifiable. (P6)*

Note that we did not prompt participants with any questions that directly asked about this aspect of the system.

> *I liked this [clustered] interface better; breaking the answers down into clusters allowed me to spot patterns, to be more consistent in grading, and to devote more time to individual answers where it wasn't clear whether they were right or wrong. The information seemed less overwhelming when presented this way, so I felt like I was less apt to mis-read or mis-grade any one answer. (P8)*

As this comment summarizes, the clustered interface allowed participants to get more answers graded quickly, to give feedback to more students, and to extract insights which could be used to inform teaching.

DISCUSSION AND FUTURE WORK

Our goal in introducing a new approach and interface for grading short answer questions was to improve scalability and efficiency while allowing teachers to achieve high quality grades, give feedback to many students, and reflect on student understanding to inform their teaching. From our quantitative and qualitative results, it seems our clustered interface was successful in all three areas, and substantially outperformed the flat baseline. The comments from teachers in our study confirmed these benefits and demonstrate the usability and efficiency of the clustered interface.

There are still a variety of questions to consider about this approach. First, while we have shown that the interface is fast, is it fast enough? In our study, participants had 20 minutes to grade 698 student response (collapsed to around 200 distinct answers). For a MOOC with 10,000 students (14 times larger), while the number of distinct answers would probably grow sublinearly, we might still expect around 2,000 distinct answers. If graders took the entire 20 minutes to grade 200 answers, it could take over three hours to grade a class of 10,000. However, the fastest users of the clustered interface in our study assigned their first-pass grades at a rate of 100–200 answers per minute, leaving time to go in at the more detailed levels to check and improve their work. Assuming this strategy, the first pass over 10,000 students could take only 10 to 20 minutes (teachers could still identify trends in answers and give quality feedback during this time). The teacher could then check and improve grades as carefully as time permitted, reflecting the flexibility of this approach. However, further studies with larger data sets are needed to see if these extrapolations hold. Different types of questions could lead to changes in the relative gains of the method – while previous results show similar performance over 10 questions of varying scope [2], we expect to encounter a far wider range of response distributions in practice; we hope to explore this range in future work via a wider deployment to real courses and classrooms.

Opportunities also exist to further refine and improve the clustered interface. In previous work, using the answer key and the learned distance metric to "autograde" answers improved efficiency [2]. However, this might increase the risk of teachers missing out on insights and ignoring autograded clusters that require closer inspection. In fact, one participant mentioned that the interface "should emphasize a little more that the individual responses must be viewed, as there are variations within each category" (P14). This points to another avenue for expansion, that of allowing the teachers to refine the clustering with their own judgments and letting the algorithm improve its results based on their changes. On a related note, the work of one teacher grading a set of answers could be leveraged for future classrooms or graders. Finally, there is the opportunity to explore more sophisticated text visualization and cluster summarization methods which could allow teachers to better allocate their attention. We hope our further developments, as well as contributions from others, can address many of these questions in future work.

REFERENCES

1. Anderson, R. and Biddle, W. On asking people questions about what they are reading. *Psychology of learning and motivation 9*, (1975).
2. Basu, S., Jacobs, C., and Vanderwende, L. Powergrading: a Clustering Approach to Amplify Human Effort for Short Answer Grading. *TACL 1*, (2013), 391–402.
3. Bloom, B. The 2 sigma problem: The search for methods of group instruction as effective as one-to-one tutoring. *Edu. Researcher 13*, 6 (1984), 4–16.
4. Brookhart, S. Teachers' grading: Practice and theory. *Applied Measurement in Edu.*, (1994).
5. Cross, L. and Frary, R. Hodgepodge grading: Endorsed by students and teachers alike. *Applied Measurement in Edu.*, October 2013 (1999), 37–41.
6. Hearst, M. The debate on automated essay grading. *Intelligent Systems and their Applications*, (2000).
7. Heywood, J. *Assessment in higher education: Student learning, teaching, programmes and institutions.* 2000.
8. Jordan, S. and Mitchell, T. e-Assessment for learning? The potential of short-answer free-text questions with tailored feedback. *British Journal of Edu. Tech. 40*, 2 (2009), 371–385.
9. Karpicke, J.D. and Roediger, H.L. The critical importance of retrieval for learning. *Science 319*, 5865 (2008), 966–8.
10. Markoff, J. Essay-Grading Software Offers Professors a Break. *The New York Times*, 2013.
11. McMillan, J. Secondary teachers' classroom assessment and grading practices. *Edu. Measurement: Issues and Practice*, (2001).
12. Mohler, M.A.G., Bunescu, R., and Mihalcea, R. Learning to Grade Short Answer Questions using Semantic Similarity Measures and Dependency Graph Alignments. *Proc. ACL*, (2011).
13. Mory, E. Feedback research revisited. In D.J. Mahwah, ed., *Handbook of Research on Educational Communications and Technology.* 2004, 745–784.
14. Perelman, L. *Critique (Ver. 3.4) of Mark D. Shermis & Ben Hammer, "Contrasting State-of-the-Art Automated Scoring of Essays: Analysis."* 2013.
15. Piech, C., Huang, J., Chen, Z., Do, C., Ng, A., and Koller, D. Tuned Models of Peer Assessment in MOOCs. *Proc. EDM*, (2013).
16. Poulos, A. and Mahony, M.J. Effectiveness of feedback: the students' perspective. *Assessment & Evaluation in Higher Edu. 33*, 2 (2008), 143–154.
17. Reily, K., Finnerty, P.L., and Terveen, L. Two peers are better than one: aggregating peer reviews for computing assignments is surprisingly accurate. *Proc. GROUP*, ACM Press (2009), 115.
18. Sadler, P. and Good, E. The Impact of Self- and Peer-Grading on Student Learning. *Edu. Assessment 11*, 1 (2006), 1–31.
19. Scriven, M. The methodology of evaluation. In R.E. Stake, ed., *AERSA Monograph Series on Curriculum Evaluation.* Rand McNally, Chicago, 1967.
20. Thorpe, M. Assessment and 'third generation' distance education. *Distance Edu. 19*, 2 (1998), 265–286.
21. Weld, D., Adar, E., and Chilton, L. Personalized Online Education—A Crowdsourcing Challenge. *Proc. AAAI, workshop on Human Computation*, (2012), 159–163.

Scaling Short-answer Grading by Combining Peer Assessment with Algorithmic Scoring

Chinmay Kulkarni, Richard Socher
Michael S. Bernstein
Stanford University
Stanford, CA 94305-9035
{chinmay,socherr,msb}@cs.stanford.edu

Scott R. Klemmer
University of California, San Diego
La Jolla, CA 92093-0440
srk@ucsd.edu

ABSTRACT

Peer assessment helps students reflect and exposes them to different ideas. It scales assessment and allows large online classes to use open-ended assignments. However, it requires students to spend significant time grading. How can we lower this grading burden while maintaining quality? This paper integrates peer and machine grading to preserve the robustness of peer assessment and lower grading burden. In the identify-verify pattern, a grading algorithm first predicts a student grade and estimates confidence, which is used to estimate the number of peer raters required. Peers then identify key features of the answer using a rubric. Finally, other peers verify whether these feature labels were accurately applied. This pattern adjusts the number of peers that evaluate an answer based on algorithmic confidence and peer agreement. We evaluated this pattern with 1370 students in a large, online design class. With only 54% of the student grading time, the identify-verify pattern yields 80-90% of the accuracy obtained by taking the median of three peer scores, and provides more detailed feedback. A second experiment found that verification dramatically improves accuracy with more raters, with a 20% gain over the peer-median with four raters. However, verification also leads to lower initial trust in the grading system. The identify-verify pattern provides an example of how peer work and machine learning can combine to improve the learning experience.

Author Keywords

assessment; online learning; automated assessment; peer learning

INTRODUCTION

Short answer questions are a powerful assessment mechanism. Many real-world problems are open-ended and require students to generate and communicate their response. Consequently, short-answer questions can target learning goals more effectively than multiple choice; instructors find them easier to construct; and short answers are relatively immune to test-taking shortcuts like eliminating improbable answers [13].

Many online classes could adopt short-answer questions, especially when their in-person counterparts already use them. However, staff grading of textual answers simply doesn't scale to massive classes. In our experience, grading each answer takes approximately a minute. Grading a hundred students is feasible, taking two hours per question. For an online class of 5,000 students this involves two person-weeks of grading per question. Automated grading and peer assessment both offer ways to scale assessment [17, 29], but in isolation, both introduce an unsatisfactory tradeoff.

While algorithmic grading consistently applies criteria to all student work [29], it has many shortcomings. It frequently relies on textual features [28], rather than semantic understanding. For instance, automated essay scoring software uses counts of bigrams and trigrams (sequences of two or three words) [8]; NLP techniques like syntactic parsing [5]; dimension reduction techniques such as PCA [10]; or a combination of these features [7]. This reliance on textual features reflects algorithms' limited ability to capture the semantic meaning of student work. This limited understanding can cause grading errors because answers using unconventional phrasing may be penalized. Furthermore, students may game algorithms with answers that match patterns, but are otherwise incorrect [26]. This has, in turn, led to public skepticism about algorithmic grading [1].

Algorithmic grading for short answers is especially challenging, because the limited text provides fewer lexical features. Algorithms can still use features like word overlap, but accuracy suffers [14].

In contrast, peers can more robustly handle ambiguity and differences in phrasing, and students learn by assessing others' work. However, peer assessment requires students to spend time grading several (e.g., five) peers. Student raters need training, and still may differ in how they apply grading criteria, and ratings may drift over time [29]. Raters also suffer from systematic cognitive biases including the Halo Effect (wrongly generalizing opinions on one characteristic to the entire answer), stereotyping (e.g. gendered/nationalistic cues affect grading [17]), or perception differences (grading of prior answers affects grading of the current answer) [29].

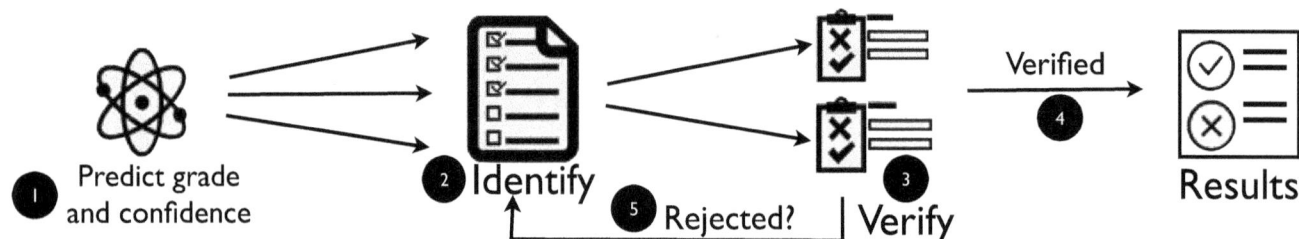

Figure 1. Overview of the assessment process. (1) Machine learning algorithm predicts grades and confidence. Number of independent identifications decided based on confidence (2) Peers identify attributes in answer using rubric (3) Two other peers verify existence of attributes. Final score is sum of verified attributes (5) if attributes are rejected, one more rater is asked to Identify. If two independent identifications are identical amongst raters, one is considered a verification (4).

Could machine-learning algorithms mitigate grader biases and minimize human effort? Crowdsourcing algorithms can correct inter-rater differences [22], and recruit more raters when they encounter unreliable raters [16, 21]. Inspired by these successes, this paper introduces a workflow that intelligently combines algorithmic and peer assessment to provide the benefits of both, while mitigating their individual drawbacks.

The *identify-verify* workflow uses algorithmic grading to estimate how many independent peer assessments are needed. The algorithm estimates "ambiguity" of the answer using its prediction confidence. More raters are assigned to highly ambiguous answers and fewer to less ambiguous ones. In this paper, the range was 1 to 3 raters. Peers then identify key features of the answer using a staff-provided rubric. Other peers verify whether these feature labels were accurate. Few peers are needed when initial human ratings agree with a high-confidence machine rating. The algorithm seeks more assessments when raters disagree. The algorithm automatically seeks higher quality assessment if more raters are available.

An experiment compared hybrid grading with peer grading; 1370 students from an online human-computer interaction class participated. Compared to a baseline of aggregating independent peer ratings using a median, integrating machine grading yields comparable accuracy with lower effort. For binary questions, using the machine grading with identify (and no verify step) yields 83% of the peer-median accuracy, and only needs 54% of human effort. For an enumerative short-answer question, 70% of the effort yields 80% accuracy. For both types, adding verification yields higher accuracy and more reliable information about the answers' attributes, but increases human effort. A follow-up experiment investigated how identify-verify works with a varying number of graders, compared to the baseline of median of peer grades. Adding the verify step yielded a 20% gain in accuracy over the peer-median method with four raters.

In addition to saving time, this hybrid also provides students richer, structured feedback about their answers in addition to their scores. Students see both a list of features of the answer they got right, and common errors they made.

This paper makes two contributions. First, it introduces the identify-verify pattern for combining peer and machine grad-

ing. Second, it presents experimental results demonstrating the accuracy benefits and the tradeoffs in human effort of the identify-verify pattern in various configurations.

CLASS SETUP

We evaluated the identify-verify approach in a large, online class introducing human-computer interaction. This class is based on an in-person class that uses short-answer questions to assess if students students' knowledge. For instance, short answers assess if students can construct well-formed interview questions, if they understand prototyping strategies, and can explain differences between experimental designs. The system described in this paper introduced these short-answer questions to the online class. Students answer short answer questions on two quizzes, one in Week 3 of the class, and once on the final (Week 9).

PILOT: LENIENT PEERS, STRICT MACHINES

We piloted short-answer questions in the May 2013 offering of the class. The pilot explored whether simply combining peer and machine scores using a median yielded accurate results. In addition, it aimed to understand the relative merits of machine and peer grading.

Three independent peer raters scored each student answer. The site provided raters with a grading rubric and staff-graded examples to calibrate themselves (similar to Calibrated Peer Review [6]). After grading a staff-provided example, students assessed peer answers. A machine classifier reliant on textual features scored all answers as well. The system combined human and machine scores by taking the median of all four scores. Other methods of combining grades, such as linear regression, were sensitive to outliers.

To assess accuracy, we compared the median grade to the staff grade for 200 submissions. We found that accuracy increased with increasing number of peer raters, consistent with prior work [12, 17]. In addition, we made the following observations:

- **Peers were more lenient than staff, and writing fluency swayed judgments on correctness**: Peers sometimes awarded points to plausible-sounding but incorrect answers. For instance: "Rewrite the interview question 'Do you like the WordArt feature from Microsoft Word?' to address problems with it". The problems with the interview question are that it is leading and it assumes users have an opinion on the feature. One incorrect student answer was "With respect to your experience, how much do you like the WordArt feature, on a scale of 1-5?" Three peer raters marked this as correct, even though it has the same problems as the original question. We also found that cues such as how confidently the answer was written, or whether it used fluent language seemed to affect the peer's rating. Prior work has shown similar Halo effects influence human grading more generally [29].

- **Peers understand ambiguous answers better**: For example, for the same WordArt question, machine grading marked the correct answer "How do you add images or text in different styles into your documents in Microsoft Office?" as incorrect (possibly because training examples had few correct answers without the word WordArt). However, two of three peer raters marked it to be correct.

  Together, these two factors meant algorithmic grading was stricter, since it only awarded credit when the answer matched example answers closely (the average machine grade was 16% lower than staff). Peer grading was more lenient than staff: the average peer grade was 14% higher than staff.

- **High-confidence predictions from machine grading were generally accurate, and agreed with peer assessment.** For binary questions, when the algorithm reported confidence larger than 80%, staff and machine grades matched 85% of the time (staff and a single peer agreed 78% of the time). In addition, for low-confidence predictions, staff/machine disagreement was larger than staff/median-peer disagreement. (When confidence was 50-60%, staff and machine grades agreed 53% of the time. For these same submissions, a single peer agreed with staff grade 52% of the time, but the median of three raters agreed with staff 68% of the time.) Therefore, low-confidence predictions are somewhat informative, but cannot be trusted reliably.

This pilot suggests that few peers are needed for answers graded with high algorithmic confidence, but more peers may be necessary for assessing questions with low confidence. However, a simple median for combining human grades and machine grades cannot handle machine grades are not uniformly reliable. This suggests that a grade-combination scheme should tune the number of raters based on algorithmic confidence. Essay scoring on standardized tests uses one such scheme: the GMAT compares a human essay score with the machine score, and recruits more human raters if the scores differ [4].

Combination schemes could also leverage peers' ability to understand ambiguous answers, but should account for them being biased and lenient. Prior work suggests it is possible to create processes that mitigate cognitive biases [19, 15], but simply alerting students to their biases does not help mitigate them [25]. Therefore, this paper seeks to create a workflow and interface to mitigate biases and improve accuracy.

THE IDENTIFY/VERIFY ARCHITECTURE

Based on these pilot insights, we designed a grading system to combine the strengths of human and machine grading. This system seeks to minimize human effort while still retaining current accuracy. We choose to reduce human effort, rather than improve accuracy, because many large, online classes (including our evaluation class) are pass-fail, and we found accuracy from the pilot (between 67% and 82%) reasonable. At this accuracy, we estimate the number of students who should have passed but didn't due to grading errors to be less than 3%. This paper leverages the insight that partitioning tasks so people can audit each other improves quality and efficiency [2, 18].

Identify-verify comprises three steps (Figure 1). First, a machine-learning algorithm predicts a grade and confidence score for each submission. The system assigns a number of peers is assigned to grade the answer based on the confidence score. Second, peers use a grading rubric to *identify* which features the answer contains (Figure 2). Third, they *verify* other peers' feature identification for other answers (Figure 3). Identify-verify assigns a final grade by combining the grade for verified features in the answer; our prototype uses the sum of feature grades. For instance, if a student submission is identified to have two features each worth one point, the submission is awarded two points, the sum of feature scores. Below, we describe each step in the assessment process.

Step 1: Algorithm estimates grade and number of raters

Before peer assessment begins, a machine-learning algorithm predicts the grade for each answer. We built a generic text classifier using etcml.com with the predicted grade as the output. This classifier uses textual features such as word, bigram and trigram counts, length of answers, and letter n-grams (to capture use of word fragments like "creati-", which match "creativity", "creative", "creation" etc.).

Teaching assistants provided numeric scores and correct/incorrect attributes for about 500 student responses per question. The numeric grades were used as labels to train the classifier. Instructors provided teaching assistants an initial rubric for grading. TAs then expanded this rubric with correct/incorrect attributes they identified, and added example student answers with those attributes. Future work could bootstrap attributes and examples using prominent features from the trained classifier.

The system then uses the classifier trained on staff-graded answers to grade all answers. The classifier outputs the most likely grade (the prediction), as well as the probabilities of all possible grades (e.g., an answer may have a grade of 1 with probability of 0.2, and a grade of 0 with probability 0.8). For the rest of the grading process, we use the probability of the most likely grade (in our example 0.8) as the algorithm's confidence in the grade. (Future work could consider using other statistics).

The algorithm's confidence determines the initial number of peer raters assigned to each answer. The intuition behind this is that confidence represents a measure of ambiguity—

answers with high confidence are usually those that are clearly right or wrong. Conversely, ambiguous answers often have low confidence, and therefore should have more independent human assessments. We require answers with high confidence ($> 90\%$) to have a single rater, those with medium confidence (75%-90%) required two, and all other answers required three raters. Overall, 34% of student submissions had grades predicted with $> 80\%$ confidence, and 16% of submissions had grades predicted with $> 90\%$ confidence.

This paper seeks to demonstrate the feasibility of combining human and machine grading. It does not determine the most suited machine-grading algorithm. Therefore, while our classifier represents the state-of-the-art in text classification, it does not use any special logic for answer grading. We hope that demonstrating feasibility with a generic classifier will also inspire other researchers to create better ones.

Step 2: Peers identify answer attributes
In this step, randomly-chosen peers independently identify correct/incorrect attributes in student answers. Raters select these attributes from the expanded grading rubric from Step 1 (Figure 2). Staff associated a score with the presence of each attribute, which could be negative.

To minimize the impact of too-few ratings, the system solicits ratings in order of greatest need. Specifically, the system finds the student answer that has the largest number of required assessments, with the fewest completed. Ties are broken randomly.

The grading page displays this answer along with the grading rubric. Peer raters mark each attribute present by clicking a checkbox next to it. To encourage students to be critical (and reduce the leniency we saw in our pilot), the grading rubric is initially shown with incorrect attributes displayed, and correct attributes collapsed (Figure 2). Raters expand the correct attribute section by clicking the drop-down arrow.

Raters are asked to identify attributes in four student submissions. After a rater completes identification, the answer and its attributes are queued for verification. If two identifiers independently select the same attribute, that also constitutes verification. Such answers skip the separate verify step.

Even with high-confidence machine predictions, it is important that student grades do not suffer due to an over-optimistic algorithm. The current system requests one additional identification for high-confidence answers where the peer and algorithm grades differ by one or more points. (In this paper, answers are worth up to 3 points, and only whole point values are awarded.)

Step 3: Other peers verify attributes correctly identified
Now, independent raters verify attributes identified in the previous step by other peers. This interface groups answers according to the identified attribute, e.g. grouping all answers marked as "More sharing of features between designs" (Figure 3). Peers then verify whether answers contain the marked attribute. We hypothesize that grouping submission marked with the same attribute increases accuracy because verifiers

are presented with a group of nominally-similar responses for comparison.

When two raters independently verify an identified attribute, the system marks the attribute as verified and removes it from the verification pool. If two raters reject an identified attribute, the system returns the submission to the identify pool for one additional identifier, since the initial identification was inaccurate.

Similar to the identification step, the system presents submissions to verifiers in decreasing order of the number completed, and breaks ties randomly. This again provides every submission with some data quickly. This algorithm also needs at most three verifications: after three, each attribute will either have been verified, or rejected.

Optimizing the number of raters
Identify-verify reduces the grading workload by recruiting fewer raters when the grading algorithm reports high confidence. This scheme is also cautious. First, we increment the number of identifications required for high-confidence predictions if peers disagree with the predicted grade. Second, identified attributes for an answer that are rejected may indicate the answer was difficult to grade, so we request additional assessments.

Display results and feedback
A student's final score is the sum of scores of all verified attributes, clamped to the minimum and maximum score for the question. Students see their score along with the features

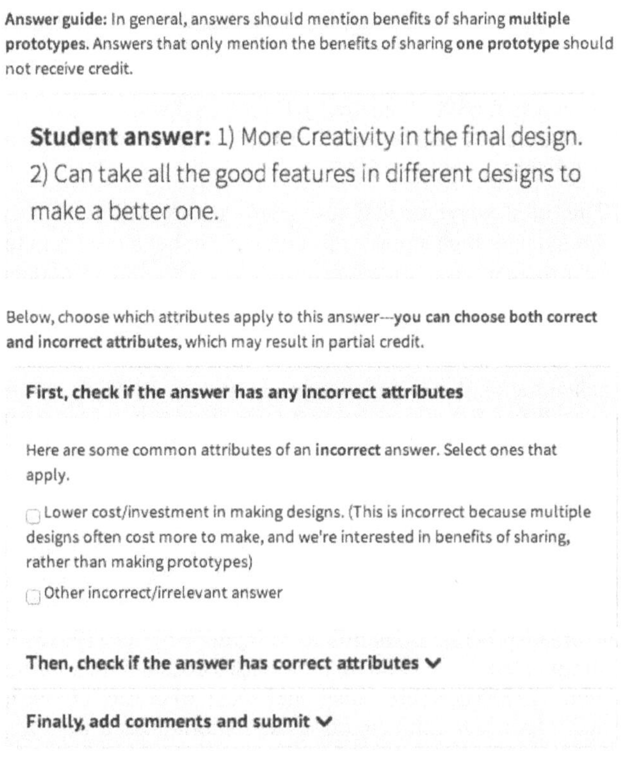

Answer guide: In general, answers should mention benefits of sharing **multiple prototypes**. Answers that only mention the benefits of sharing **one prototype** should not receive credit.

Student answer: 1) More Creativity in the final design. 2) Can take all the good features in different designs to make a better one.

Below, choose which attributes apply to this answer—**you can choose both correct and incorrect attributes,** which may result in partial credit.

First, check if the answer has any incorrect attributes

Here are some common attributes of an **incorrect** answer. Select ones that apply.

☐ Lower cost/investment in making designs. (This is incorrect because multiple designs often cost more to make, and we're interested in benefits of sharing, rather than making prototypes)

☐ Other incorrect/irrelevant answer

Then, check if the answer has correct attributes ∨

Finally, add comments and submit ∨

Figure 2. Identify UI: Students identified whether student answers had staff-provided features (which indicated right/wrong answers)

that peers identified, and correct attributes that their answer missed (Figure 4). Thus, students receive more than a grade: they receive detailed information about what they did well and poorly.

EVALUATION

Identify-verify seeks comparable accuracy to using the median grade of independent peers, but with less human effort. Our comparison baseline asks three peers to grade a student answer.

Experiment 1: Does identify-verify yield accurate grades?

This controlled experiment explored two questions: First, does identify-verify grade accurately and lower effort? Second, does identify-verify reduce leniency from our pilot? (We

Student answer	correct?
These were marked as: **More sharing of features between designs.**	Assessment correct?
more feedback, multiple options, better creativity	○Yes ○No
These were marked as: **Creates increased group rapport/increased conversational turns. Both lead to better discussions.**	Assessment correct?
Encourages group loyalty Produces more examples/prototypes It places the focus on the artifact and eliminates egos	○Yes ○No
more feedback, multiple options, better creativity	○Yes ○No

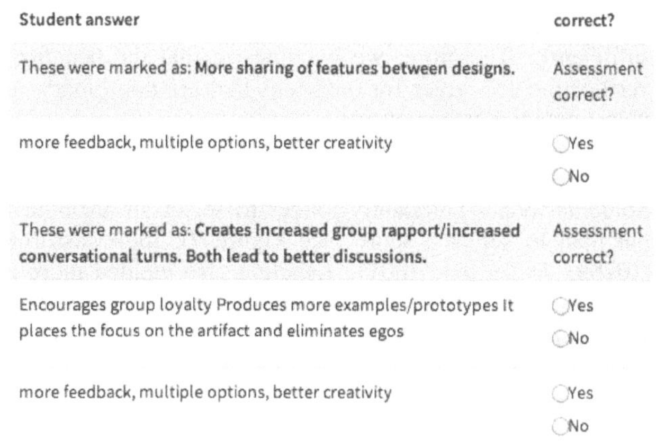

Figure 3. Verify UI: Students verified if other peers had assessed answers correctly.

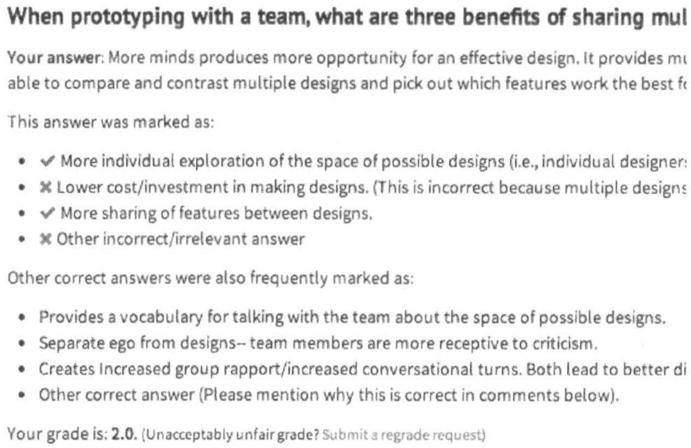

When prototyping with a team, what are three benefits of sharing mul

Your answer: More minds produces more opportunity for an effective design. It provides mu able to compare and contrast multiple designs and pick out which features work the best fc

This answer was marked as:

- ✔ More individual exploration of the space of possible designs (i.e., individual designer:
- ✘ Lower cost/investment in making designs. (This is incorrect because multiple designs
- ✔ More sharing of features between designs.
- ✘ Other incorrect/irrelevant answer

Other correct answers were also frequently marked as:

- Provides a vocabulary for talking with the team about the space of possible designs.
- Separate ego from designs-- team members are more receptive to criticism.
- Creates increased group rapport/increased conversational turns. Both lead to better di
- Other correct answer (Please mention why this is correct in comments below).

Your grade is: 2.0. (Unacceptably unfair grade? Submit a regrade request)

Figure 4. Identify-verify presents student grades with features present, and those missing in answers

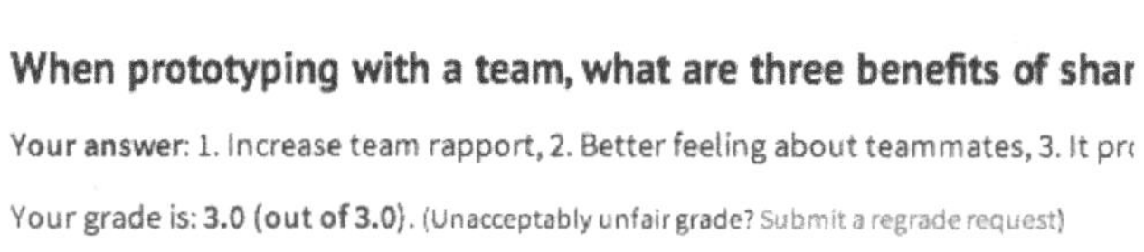

When prototyping with a team, what are three benefits of shar

Your answer: 1. Increase team rapport, 2. Better feeling about teammates, 3. It pro

Your grade is: 3.0 (out of 3.0). (Unacceptably unfair grade? Submit a regrade request)

Figure 5. Student grade display in baseline condition (Grades are computed using Identify-verify, but detailed feedback is hidden.)

hypothesize that leniency is due to the Halo effect, and using a structured process and interface would reduce this bias [15].)

Conditions

This between-subjects experiment had three conditions. In the *peer-median* condition, students assess four peers using a grading rubric, and enter their grade into a text field (Figure 6). In the *identify-only* condition, students assess four peers using the same grading rubric, but would instead use the Identify interface to select which aspects of the rubric were present in the student answer (Figure 2). In the *identify-verify* condition, students assessed four peers using the Identify interface. Then, they would verify assessments of eight answers that other students had created in the Identify step (Figure 3).

We wanted to reduce grading burden in the class, and since we hypothesize that Identify-verify would save student effort, the experiment used an unbalanced assignment; 20% of students randomly assigned to the *peer-median* condition, and the rest split evenly between *identify* and *identify-verify*.

Questions

Students assessed answers to two short-answer questions. Question 1 asked students to rewrite an interview question: "Rewrite the following interview question to address its problems: 'Do you like the Word Art feature of Microsoft Office?'", and had a binary grade (credit or no-credit). Question 2 asked students to enumerate "three benefits of sharing multiple designs with your team members, instead of sharing only one design?". Students could earn 0-3 points on this question, one per enumerated benefit. Students assessed four submissions per question, so there were a total of eight assessments per participant.

After they had completed grading, the system invited students to participate in a short survey. The survey measured trust in the system, and time taken for grading vis-a-vis their initial expectations.

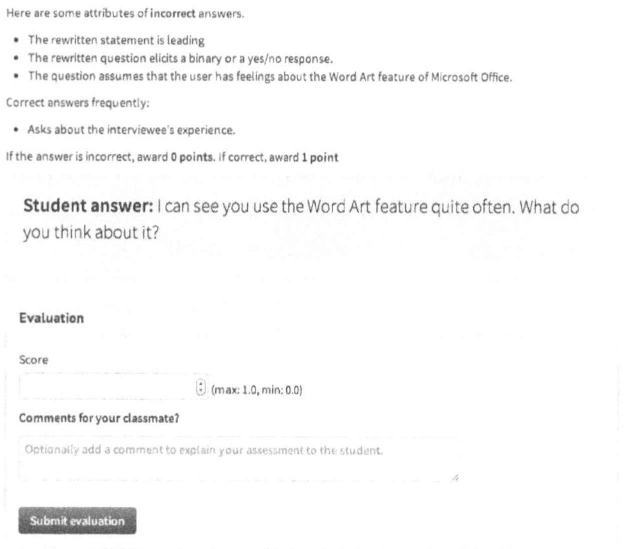

Here are some attributes of **incorrect** answers.

- The rewritten statement is leading
- The rewritten question elicits a binary or a yes/no response.
- The question assumes that the user has feelings about the Word Art feature of Microsoft Office.

Correct answers frequently:

- Asks about the interviewee's experience.

If the answer is incorrect, award **0 points.** If correct, award **1 point**

Student answer: I can see you use the Word Art feature quite often. What do you think about it?

Evaluation

Score

[   ] ⏶ (max: 1.0, min: 0.0)

Comments for your classmate?

Optionally add a comment to explain your assessment to the student.

[Submit evaluation]

Figure 6. Peer-median UI: Students entered grades in a text box.

Table 1. Peer-median was faster for each rating, but employed more raters, so took more time overall. Overall, the time each condition took and its quality correlated.

Type	Method	#assessments: Median (mean)	Accuracy	κ	Human effort (seconds)
Binary	Peer-median	3	0.85	0.57	109
Binary	Peer-median	2	0.68	0.21	73
Binary	Identify only	1 (1.15)	0.71	0.41	59
Binary	Identify-verify	1 (1.15) + 2 (2.08) verifications	0.72	0.41	91
Binary	Machine prediction	–	0.60	0.19	–
Enum.	Peer-median	3	0.49	0.32	103
Enum.	Peer-median	2	0.33	0.19	68
Enum.	Identify only	1 (1.42)	0.39	0.15	71
Enum.	Identify-verify	1 (1.42) + 3 (3.1) verifications	0.45	0.22	104
Enum.	Machine prediction	–	0.28	0.09	–

The system showed students their final grades a day after the peer assessment period ended. All students saw grades computed using Identify-verify. To measure the effects of detailed feedback, the system showed those in the peer-median condition only the final score (Figure 5), students in other conditions saw both the score and identified attributes (Figure 4). After they saw results, we invited students to a second survey, which gauged how accurate they perceived grading to be and how satisfied they were with feedback.

Participants 2,556 students submitted answers; 1,370 performed assessment (the others dropped the class). 620 students participated in the pre-results survey, and 102 participated in the post-results survey. In all, students created 11006 assessments and 12264 verifications.

Measures
For both the *peer-median* and the *identify-verify* strategies, course staff looked at 100 student answers for each question with three peer-median assessments, and 100 more answers with two peer-median assessments. (We did not select based on the number of identify assessments, because the system dynamically determined this number for each answer). For each student answer, we compared the staff grade to the computed grade.

Results
In terms of both effort and accuracy, the ranking of conditions was the same: *Peer-median* was highest, *identify-verify* was the middle, and *identify-only* least (See Table 1.) *Peer-median* had three raters. *Identify-only* had median one rater. *Identify-verify* had median one rater, with two verifiers for the binary question and three verifiers for the enumeration.

How accurate is identify-verify assessment?
Peer-median required disproportionately more effort than *identify-only* to achieve its results. *Identify-only* consumed 54% of the effort to achieve 83% of the accuracy in the binary question, and 71% of effort for 80% of accuracy in the enumeration question. Identify-verify consumed 84% of effort for 85% of accuracy in the binary question, and identical effort for 92% of accuracy for the enumeration question. This study only examined one effort level. The second study simulates multiple effort levels.

Verification provided a large benefit for the enumeration question, but minimal benefit for the 1-level question. Labels

were rejected at similar rates (19.8% for 1-level and 18.6% for enumeration). For a binary question, not all attributes need to be identified to accurately grade it (for example, if the answer is wrong for two reasons, identifying just one is sufficient). Therefore, we hypothesize that the benefits of verification are larger for questions that are non-binary, and investigate this in Experiment 2.

Identify assessments take longer, more accurate
Students took significantly longer to select an attribute label than to select a score (see Figure 7), log-transformed $t(6789) = 28, p < 0.01$. Labeling also yielded more accurate work (see Table 1). Identify-verify reduced leniency, while retaining peers ability to assess unusual answers better than machines (see Table 2 and Table 3).

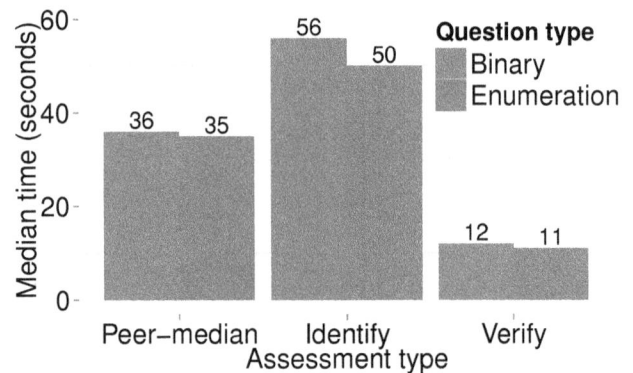

Figure 7. Assessment took longer using the Identify interface, but yields more accurate results.

Identify-verify reduces voluntary acceptance
Fewer students in the *identify-verify* condition reported wanting to continue using the grading interface for other quizzes

Question	Peer-median 3 raters	Identify-verify	Staff	Machine
Yes/no (1 point)	0.57	0.33	0.31	0.17
Enumeration (3 points)	2.17	1.65	1.74	1.35

Table 2. Peer grade averages in points. Identify-verify reduces leniency compared with peer-median.

Table 3. Sampling of errors in assessment. Peer ratings help when machines are less confident of the grade.

Student answer	Remarks
"How do you use the Word Art feature and how does it help you to meet your goals?"	Machine marked as incorrect, possibly because of leading bigrams "does it", "help you". Peers marked as correct. Staff graded as correct.
"What do you think of the Word Art feature of Microsoft Office?"	Construction marked as incorrect in the grading rubric (because it assumes opinion); yet, two of three peers in the peer-median condition marked as correct (possibly because it's less leading than "do you like..."). Both machine, and identify peers marked as incorrect.
"What would you like to see changed in the 'Word Art' feature on Microsoft Office?"	Possibly useful interview question asks how to change, instead of understanding current use (and so, is wrong): 3 peers in the peer-median condition marked correct; one rater identified it as 'Other correct answer', but verification rejected it. Staff graded as incorrect.
"Inspiration. Innovation. Social" (for benefits of sharing prototypes)	Uses keywords without context. Machine awarded one point (possibly due to 'Inspiration'), but Identify peers did not (this answer had no peer-median assessments), nor did staff
"Because the best way to have a good idea is to have lots of ideas." (for benefits of sharing prototypes)	Pithy and plausible, but irrelevant. Awarded 1 point (out of 3) in peer-median evaluation, none in Identify. Staff graded at 0.

(64% said yes, $t(732) = 2.9, p < 0.01$); no significant differences existed between *peer-median* and *identify-only* (78% and 75% respectively). Usability challenges with the verify interface may have reduced interest. Some students reported that the "the layout was very confusing" others were initially unsure if they were verifying the student answer or the label. 15.8% of students in the *peer-median* condition completed more assessments than required, while 8% of students in the *identify-only* condition completed more than required.

Fewer students in the identify-verify condition believed the process would give them a fair grade (Asked as Yes/No: $\beta = 0.12, t(734) = 2.7, p < 0.05$). This may be because verify explicitly revealed individual peers work; reducing trust. One student said that based "on the verification step of the peer assessment I'm not confident that people's quizzes are being assessed correctly." Furthermore, *identify-only* students reported more accurate grades ($\mu = 1.9, t(93) = 2.04, p < $

0.05) than those in the *peer-median* or *identify-verify* conditions ($\mu = 2.5$, 4-point Likert scale with 1: 'very accurate').

Experiment 2: How number of raters affects accuracy

A second experiment investigated how the number of raters affects accuracy. As before, students were assigned to either the *identify-verify*, *identify-only* and the *peer-median* condition. All raters graded one of fifty randomly-selected submissions. 634 students participated.

The final had three enumeration questions asking students to a) mention one disadvantage of a between-subjects experimental design, b) list three ways of visually grouping related information, c) list two situations where heuristic evaluation is preferable to user testing. The experimental setup was identical to Experiment 1.

Measures

We performed a bootstrapped simulation of the peer assessment. This simulation chooses a random sample of raters for each question. We then calculate the final grade using ratings only from this sample of raters, and compare it with the staff-assigned grade. Repeating this process multiple times estimates peer agreement with staff [17]. Figure 9 shows median results from 20-repetition sampling, with one to eight raters.

We benchmark each condition against its peak accuracy: the highest accuracy seen in that condition in our simulation. More raters did not always improve accuracy, so peak accuracy was achieved with fewer than eight raters in the *identify-only* and *peer-median* conditions.

Results

A few raters identify most features

A small number of raters can identify most attributes present. Figure 9 shows that accuracy quickly plateaus, and four raters yield 92% of the peak accuracy with the *identify-only* method. Overall, the peak *identify-only* accuracy was 55% with six

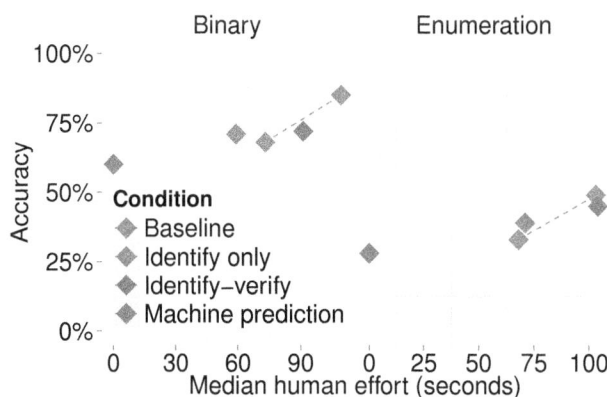

Figure 8. With median one rater, the peer-median method takes disproportionately more human effort to get high accuracy compared to *Identify-only* for the yes/no question. For the enumeration question, both methods need nearly the same effort for comparable accuracy.

raters, the *peer-median* had a peak accuracy of 66% with seven raters. This early saturation is similar to heuristic evaluation of interfaces [20], suggesting similar processes may be involved.

Identify raters satisfice, Identify-only errors accumulate
Identify-Only accuracy was lower than *peer-median*, and much lower than *Identify-Verify* (see Figure 9). First, most raters select only one attribute, even though the answer may match multiple attributes. Of the 1488 assessments collected, only 173 had more than one selected attribute. In contrast, staff assessments averaged 1.4 selected attributes. Second, because identifiers sometimes mislabel answers and there is no mechanism (i.e. verification) that catches this, asymptotically optimal performance is with relatively few raters and relatively low quality. In contrast, the peer-median approach uses the median of peer grades in the peer-median approach, so grades become more accurate with more raters as outlier ratings are discarded.

Many identifiers appear to have selected the first relevant label (Figure 10). Randomizing order across raters should mitigate ordering effects. Future work could investigate interfaces that incent raters to select all relevant labels.

Verification improves accuracy, especially with more raters
Identify-verify yielded the highest accuracy: the peak accuracy was 82% with six raters. The simulation required labels to have one peer verification and no peer rejections. (Actual student grading requires two verifications. Because the system solicits verifications in decreasing order of need, the median staff-graded submission had only one verification, or was rejected.)

Even single-peer verification dramatically increases accuracy. With three raters, accuracy is 28% higher than *identify-only*, and 18% higher than *peer-median*. Peer-median assessments took a median time of 19 second, identifications took 40s. Verification took 12s, similar to Experiment 1. Therefore, this 18% boost in accuracy comes with approximately two extra minutes of human effort per answer.

Because verification filters out erroneous identifications, its benefit is larger with more raters: verification with one rater yields a 22% benefit in accuracy, with four raters, it yields a 27% benefit. In our simulation, three identifiers identified most attributes, and inaccuracies with three or more raters are due to wrongly identified attributes.

DISCUSSION
Identify-verify represents one choice in the trade-offs between human effort and grading accuracy. This choice was optimized for a large, pass-fail class.

Is verification necessary?
Our results demonstrate how erroneous identification can be detected with an easier operation (verification), similar to Soylent [2]. This is especially useful for questions where all attributes need to be correctly identified. While verification increases grading time, it yields more yields more descriptive, actionable, and accurate student feedback, which helps students learn.

Opportunities for early feedback
To explore the possibility of automatic, early feedback, we trained a classifier using etcml.com to detect the most common errors for each question (Table 4). Because students unlikely to revise work without external feedback [24], even somewhat unreliable feedback (e.g., "Check to see that...") may have benefits.

Identify-verify uses its auto-graders confidence to indicate ambiguity. Might students benefit from knowing that peers may have trouble understanding them? Evidence from automated essay scoring suggests that well-designed early feedback may help students write clearer answers [11, 23].

Coping with fewer graders than submitters
In Experiment 1, almost twice as many students submitted work as performed assessment; the rest dropped the class in the meanwhile. Experiment 2 was conducted later in the course, and a much larger fraction of the 850 students who submitted answers also assessed. Intelligently rationing raters is important in large online systems with voluntary participation. Identify-verify system handles this problem by rationing fewer graders for unambiguous answers. Because of the smaller number of raters, the system asked a median of

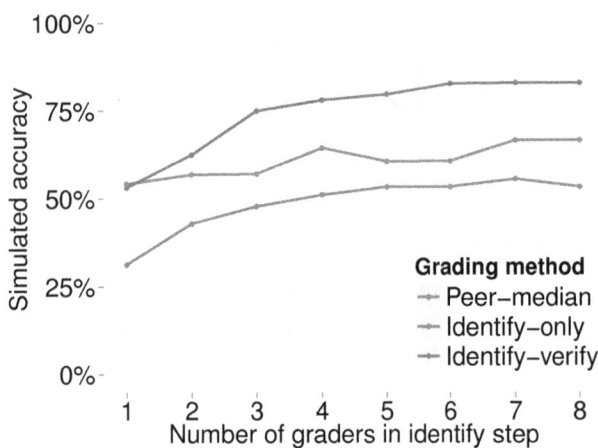

Figure 9. For enumeration questions, identify accuracy is lower than the peer-median method. Identify-verify obtains better accuracy than peer-median, especially with three or more raters.

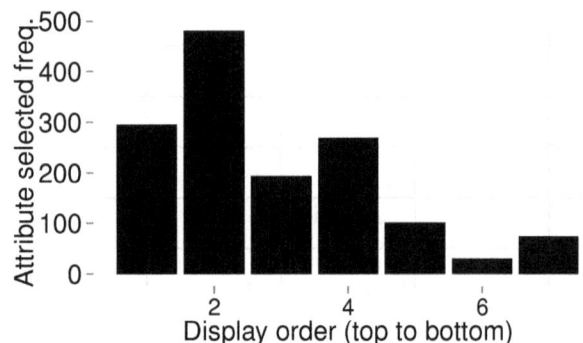

Figure 10. Raters were more likely to choose attributes displayed earlier on the page.

Table 4. Algorithmically predicting errors could automate early feedback.

Attribute	Accuracy	Precision	Recall
Incorrect attribute: "The question assumes that the user has feelings about the feature" (Q1)	0.79	0.58	0.41
Missed attribute: "More individual exploration in the space of designs" (Q2)	0.59	0.64	0.79
Incorrect attribute: "Other incorrect/irrelevant answer" (Q2)	0.90	0.27	0.73

only one identification per question, saving more identifications for the most ambiguous answers. For this experimental system, students were not penalized for not participating in assessment. Future work could explore penalties for non-participation, or incent assessment in other ways.

When should instructors use hybrid grading?

Peer assessment works best when staff spot-grade some student submissions because it helps staff refine assessment materials and baseline peer grades [3, 6]. However, courses may not have the resources for staff to grade several hundred examples that can train a machine-learning algorithm. (Even if it enables richer questions.) Furthermore, requiring large amounts of training data may dissuade instructors from revising questions. We see two opportunities exist for future work. First, an online-learning algorithm may improve prediction accuracy as students assess each other. However, because the system would demand fewer assessments as its prediction accuracy increases, this may encourage free-riding. Future work could leverage such algorithms, while balancing for fairness. More immediately, assessment data from peers may be used to train algorithms. For example, an advanced cohort takes the class a week ahead of the general class. There are many exciting opportunities for integrating peer and algorithmic assessment to increase student learning and leverage the rater's time better.

FUTURE WORK AND CONCLUSION

This paper demonstrated the feasibility of combining machine and peer grading through the identify-verify workflow. It showed how this workflow results in more detailed student feedback, and can be leveraged to provide early feedback. further instructor experimentation and research, our open-source code is available at `https://github.com/StanfordHCI/peerstudio`. In addition, a hosted version of the platform is available at `http://www.peerstudio.org`.

Future work falls in three categories: First, this paper assumes the final grade for a short-answer response can be expressed as a summed combination. Deploying this workflow in other classes may suggest other ways to structure assessment and

verification, for e.g., as a decision tree. Second, many techniques in this paper may be extended with algorithmic improvements. For instance, our system currently implements a fixed-control method for dynamically controlling the number of peer raters for a submission. A decision-theoretic model may result in even lower grading burden [21]. Similarly, an online learning algorithm [27] could dynamically update estimates of the predicted grade to guide which ratings are collected. Third, in this paper, the system decided which answers a rater should assess and which assessments to verify based on what information was most valuable to determine the final grade. Because performing peer assessment is a valuable learning activity [6], future work may select submissions for raters that optimize both score/feedback quality and student learning (e.g. by choosing submissions for peer raters that they can learn most from).

We propose that the combination of machine and human grading can offer strengths that neither has in isolation. The large scale of online classes enables machines to effectively improve the educational experience [9]. By lessening grading burden, machines can focus peers on providing more detailed feedback. Automatic feedback may also focus students on topics they have not fully mastered. Likewise, peers can help machines identify "unknown unknowns" that are blind spots in their models, and help bootstrap that model quickly. Hybrid peer-machine approaches may also help in-person classes and many social computing areas, including crowdsourcing.

ACKNOWLEDGMENTS

We thank Zhenghao Chen and Brennan Saeta at Coursera for building systems that enabled our experimental grading; Kathryn Papadopoulos, Lalida Sritanyaratana and community TAs for grading student submissions; Kanit (Ham) Wongsuphasawat for helping run the pilot experiment, and students that enrolled in our class and participated in this experiment. Chinmay's research was supported by a Siebel Scholarship.

REFERENCES

1. Professionals against machine scoring of student essays in high-stakes assessment (www.humanreaders.com).

2. Bernstein, M. S., Little, G., Miller, R. C., Hartmann, B., Ackerman, M. S., Karger, D. R., Crowell, D., and Panovich, K. Soylent: a word processor with a crowd inside. In *Proceedings of the 23nd annual ACM symposium on User interface software and technology*, ACM (2010), 313–322.

3. Boud, D., and Brew, A. *Enhancing learning through self assessment*, vol. 1. Kogan Page London, 1995.

4. Burstein, J. The e-rater scoring engine: Automated essay scoring with natural language processing. *Automated essay scoring: A cross-disciplinary perspective* (2003), 113–121.

5. Burstein, J., Chodorow, M., and Leacock, C. Automated essay evaluation: the criterion online writing service. *AI Magazine 25*, 3 (2004), 27.

6. Carlson, P., and Berry, F. Calibrated peer review and assessing learning outcomes. In *Frontiers in Education Conference*, vol. 2, STIPES (2003).

7. Chen, H., and He, B. Automated essay scoring by maximizing human-machine agreement.

8. Chodorow, M., and Leacock, C. An unsupervised method for detecting grammatical errors. In *Proceedings of the 1st North American chapter of the Association for Computational Linguistics conference*, Association for Computational Linguistics (2000), 140–147.

9. Fast, E., Lee, C., Aiken, A., Bernstein, M., Koller, D., Smith, E., and Institute, K. Crowd-scale interactive formal reasoning and analytics.

10. Foltz, P. W., Laham, D., and Landauer, T. K. The intelligent essay assessor: Applications to educational technology. *Interactive Multimedia Electronic Journal of Computer-Enhanced Learning 1*, 2 (1999).

11. Grimes, D., and Warschauer, M. Utility in a fallible tool: A multi-site case study of automated writing evaluation. *The Journal of Technology, Learning and Assessment 8*, 6 (2010).

12. Heimerl, K., Gawalt, B., Chen, K., Parikh, T., and Hartmann, B. Communitysourcing: engaging local crowds to perform expert work via physical kiosks. In *Proceedings of the 2012 ACM annual conference on Human Factors in Computing Systems* (2012), 1539–1548.

13. Hirschman, L., Breck, E., Light, M., Burger, J. D., and Ferro, L. Automated grading of short-answer tests. *Intelligent Systems and their Applications, IEEE* (2000), 31–37.

14. Hirschman, L., Light, M., Breck, E., and Burger, J. D. Deep read: A reading comprehension system. In *Proceedings of the 37th annual meeting of the Association for Computational Linguistics on Computational Linguistics* (1999), 325–332.

15. Kahneman, D., Lovallo, D., and Sibony, O. Before you make that big decision. *Harvard Business Review 89*, 6 (2011), 50–60.

16. Karger, D. R., Oh, S., and Shah, D. Iterative learning for reliable crowdsourcing systems. In *Advances in neural information processing systems* (2011), 1953–1961.

17. Kulkarni, C., Wei, K. P., Le, H., Chia, D., Papadopoulos, K., Cheng, J., Koller, D., and Klemmer, S. R. Peer and self assessment in massive online classes. *ACM Trans. on Computer-Human Interaction 20* (2013), Preprint.

18. Lintott, C. J., Schawinski, K., Slosar, A., Land, K., Bamford, S., Thomas, D., Raddick, M. J., Nichol, R. C., Szalay, A., Andreescu, D., et al. Galaxy zoo: morphologies derived from visual inspection of galaxies from the sloan digital sky survey. *Monthly Notices of the Royal Astronomical Society 389*, 3 (2008), 1179–1189.

19. Lovallo, D., and Sibony, O. The case for behavioral strategy. *McKinsey Quarterly* (2010), 30–43.

20. Nielsen, J. Usability inspection methods. In *Conference companion on Human factors in computing systems*, ACM (1994), 413–414.

21. Peng Dai, M. D., and Weld, S. Decision-theoretic control of crowd-sourced workflows. In *In the 24th AAAI Conference on Artificial Intelligence (AAAI10* (2010).

22. Piech, C., Huang, J., Chen, Z., Do, C., Ng, A., and Koller, D. Tuning peer grading. In *Proceedings of the 6th International Conference on Educational Data Mining* (2013).

23. Shermis, M. D., Garvan, C. W., and Diao, Y. The impact of automated essay scoring on writing outcomes. *Online Submission* (2008).

24. Sommers, N. Revision strategies of student writers and experienced adult writers. *College composition and communication 31*, 4 (1980), 378–388.

25. Wetzel, C. G., Wilson, T. D., and Kort, J. The halo effect revisited: Forewarned is not forearmed. *Journal of Experimental Social Psychology* (1981).

26. Winerip, M. Facing a robo-grader? just keep obfuscating mellifluously. *New York Times* (2013).

27. Yang, B., Sun, J.-T., Wang, T., and Chen, Z. Effective multi-label active learning for text classification. In *Proceedings of the 15th ACM SIGKDD international conference on Knowledge discovery and data mining*, ACM (2009), 917–926.

28. Yannakoudakis, H., Briscoe, T., and Medlock, B. A new dataset and method for automatically grading esol texts. In *ACL* (2011), 180–189.

29. Zhang, M. Contrasting automated and human scoring of essays. *R & D Connections* (2013).

Self-evaluation in Advanced Power Searching and Mapping with Google MOOCs

Julia Wilkowski
Google
1600 Amphitheatre Parkway
Mountain View, CA 94304
Wilkowski@Google.com

Daniel M. Russell
Google
1600 Amphitheatre Parkway
Mountain View, CA 94304
DRussell@Google.com

Amit Deutsch
Google
1600 Amphitheatre Parkway
Mountain View, CA 94304
AmitDeutsch@Google.com

ABSTRACT

While there is a large amount of work on creating autograded massive open online courses (MOOCs), some kinds of complex, qualitative exam questions are still beyond the current state of the art. For MOOCs that need to deal with these kinds of questions, it is not possible for a small course staff to grade students' qualitative work. To test the efficacy of self-evaluation as a method for complex-question evaluation, students in two Google MOOCs have submitted projects and evaluated their own work. For both courses, teaching assistants graded a random sample of papers and compared their grades with self-evaluated student grades. We found that many of the submitted projects were of very high quality, and that a large majority of self-evaluated projects were accurately evaluated, scoring within just a few points of the gold standard grading.

Author Keywords

MOOCs; Google; Assessment

ACM Classification Keywords

K.3.1 Computer Uses in Education: Distance learning

INTRODUCTION

Instructors have several ways to assess how well students have learned course material: exams with either multiple choice, short-answer, or essay questions; projects; labs. Online courses can take advantage of automatic grading for multiple choice and short answer questions for instant feedback to the student. To assess more in-depth work, many MOOCs have implemented peer review/peer grading as a way for students to receive feedback on qualitative projects [10]. While progress is being made to improve automated grading systems [2], we wanted to explore how

well student self-evaluation would work in the context of a MOOC as a practical method of grading complex assignments.

In the Advanced Power Searching (APS) and Mapping with Google (MWG) courses, we tested a self-evaluation process following students' completion of final projects. In both cases, the final projects were sufficiently complex and sophisticated that course developers could not (at this point in time) create an automatic grading tool.

Grading exams is a useful tool for developing metacognitive skills about a topic area [13]. Self-evaluation is an important meta-cognitive skill for students to learn [11], so this seemed like the ideal chance to test out how reliable and accurate self-evaluation would be in a MOOC, where students mostly do not meet face-to-face and the social pressures to create a plausible evaluation are not present.

Self-grading appears to result in increased student learning when compared with peer grading [12]. Self-evaluation also helps build students' metacognition that they will use when applying the skills from the class [5]. Google course developers, for example, wanted students to acquire the meta-cognitive skill of reflective design practice for mapmaking. Ideally, after taking this course, students would stop and reflect about the qualities of an effective Google Map when creating a map. This skill is taught explicitly in the class and assessed in the final project by asking students to review their work with a rubric that asks them to evaluate whether they added key map visualization features (e.g. labeling all points and providing relevant descriptions).

In a similar way, for the final project in the APS course, students wrote and submitted case studies of how they used Google tools to solve a complex research problem. In their final self-evaluation task, they reflected on how well they implemented aspects of the research process, such as assessing the credibility of a website, one of the skills addressed during the course. When they conduct research outside of the class, Google course developers intend for students to assess the credibility of websites.

In the rest of this paper, we will describe each of the two MOOCs we used in our analysis, first detailing how the

L@S 2014, March 4–5, 2014, Atlanta, Georgia, USA.
ACM 978-1-4503-2669-8/14/03.
http://dx.doi.org/10.1145/2556325.2566241

MOOC was built, its goals and general design. We then describe the final projects for each MOOC, telling how the self-evaluation process worked for each (they were very different in their details). We then turn to describing the methods we used for collecting the data, describe the data collected, followed by an analysis and discussion of the data. We conclude the paper with a summary of lessons learned.

MOOC #1: ADVANCED POWER SEARCHING (APS)

This course was designed to help members of the general public use Google tools (such as Advanced Search and Google Scholar) to solve complex research questions. The course was built using Google's open-source Course Builder platform [4] (with modifications to add a challenge-based template and a skill summary page) [1]. Registration opened on January 8, 2013; students could access the first six challenges and one final project January 23, 2013. The second set of six challenges and the remaining final project were released on January 30, 2013. A total of 38,099 people registered for the course.

The course consisted of four introductory lessons (How the Course Works, Sample Challenge, Research Process, and Solving the Sample Challenge). Following these lessons, students could select one of twelve complex search challenges. The course authors define complex as problems that require multiple steps, have more than one correct answer, or have multiple ways to achieve the answer. Figure 1 demonstrates one of the sample challenges presented in the course. Students could attempt the challenge, explore related skills, review how experts solved similar problems, get hints, and check their final answer. Students could attempt as many challenges as they wished before attempting two case study projects as their final exam requirement.

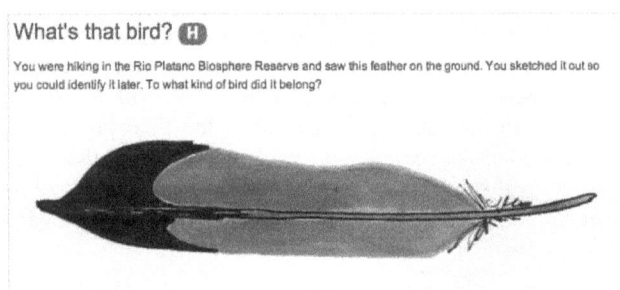

What's that bird? ⓗ

You were hiking in the Rio Platano Biosphere Reserve and saw this feather on the ground. You sketched it out so you could identify it later. To what kind of bird did it belong?

Figure 1. Sample challenge: *You were hiking in the Rio Platano Biosphere Reserve and saw this feather on the ground. You sketched it so you could identify it later. To what kind of bird did it belong?*

Certificates of completion were awarded to students who completed and scored both projects as well as submitted the correct answer to an auto-graded final exam search challenge.

Case Study Projects

The case study projects asked students to describe how they solved a search problem, either for a problem in the list, or one drawn from their lives:

1. Solve one of the example problems below or select one that relates to your life experiences. Your problem should be complex enough to require at least three Power Search skills.

2. Record your experience using one of the provided templates or choose your own format (document, spreadsheet, slideshow, video, etc)

Example problems:

- Plan a trip for a friend who will be visiting your area. Is she interested in ethnic food, local history, natural wonders, sports, or something else? Select a theme and create an itinerary composed of five unusual destinations that fit that theme.

- Propose a new World Heritage site in your country. What are the criteria for becoming a World Heritage site? What are the existing locations near you? Prepare to argue what qualifies the location you selected to become a World Heritage site.

- Suggest a new word you've encountered this year that you think should be added to dictionaries in your language. What are the criteria for adding a word to your local dictionary? What new words were added in 2012? Prepare to make an argument about why the word you suggest qualifies to be in the dictionary.

- Conduct some genealogical research to locate the origin of your last name. What does it mean? Who was a notable member of your family from at least three generations ago? If your name has its origins in another country, what town might have members of your extended family?

Students were then presented with the evaluation criteria, submitted their assignment by either filling in text boxes or supplying a link to a Google document (for which we had provided a template asking the same questions as the text fields within the course). Questions they answered and the evaluation criteria are shown in Table 1.

After submitting each case study, for training purposes, students evaluated a sample assignment using the same checklist that they would later use to evaluate their own work. The goal of this exercise was to give the students practice in using the checklist and to develop their metacognitive skills. We then provided feedback showing how an expert would have graded the sample assignment.

After this training, students proceeded to evaluate their own work. The evaluation checklist consisted of fourteen yes/no

Assignment questions	Evaluation checklist questions
What is your research goal? What will you do with the information you gather?	Is the goal written as a complete sentence or phrased as a question? Does the description include why this research is important to you and what you will do with the information?
What questions do you need to answer in order to achieve your research goal?	Are there at least three smaller or related questions? Are the steps sequenced appropriately so that information gathered leads toward the end goal? Are the questions directly related to the goal of the research?
What queries did you type in during your research (either to Google or databases/sites you discovered)?	Are there three queries you used when searching? Do the queries relate to the questions above? Do the queries demonstrate advanced power searching skills?
What specific websites did you use when gathering information? How did you know they were credible?	Are there URLs of at least three specific websites? Are the listed websites credible?
What was your final result?	Does this answer the question you set out to solve? Does the research end at an appropriate point, even if the stated goal was not reached?
What did you learn while conducting your research?	Is there at least one interesting factor insight?
What Advanced Power Searching skills did you apply during this assignment? *(multiple-select from a list)*	Are there three skills identified?

Table 1. APS case study questions and evaluation checklist

questions. Each question was worth one point except for the last one, which was worth three points, for a total of sixteen points. The checklist was presented to the right of the student's submission (see Figure 4, which shows the top part of the evaluation form).

Methods

After the course closed, course administrators provided researchers with an anonymized sample of assignment submissions. Thirteen members of the course staff (including instructors, teaching assistants, content experts and instructional designers) graded seventeen percent of the scored, accessible assignments. To ensure consistent interrater correlation before grading the sample set, graders trained together, independently evaluating assignments until they reached a point of being able to replicate the grading score across all of the graders. (It took five sample practice assignment-grading sessions to train to this level of consistency.)

Data

Students submitted a total of 3,948 assignments. Out of this entire set of assignments, students chose not to score 95 (2.4%). Another 672 (17.0%) of assignments were submitted as links to Google Documents but were not marked as "Shared" with course staff (making them effectively ungradable). This left a total of 3,181 that could be scored by course staff. Of these, course staff graded a random sample of 535 (17%) that were both accessible and self-graded by students.

The mean student score of the graded assignments was 15.2 (standard deviation = 2.2); the mean TA score of the graded assignments was 13.3 (standard deviation = 3.5). Of these assignments, 295 (55.1%) had student and TA scores within one point of each other (out of a total sixteen points). 368 (69.0%) had student and TA scores with two points of each other. 338 (63.2%) received TA scores of fourteen or above out of sixteen, while 392 (73.3%) received TA scores of thirteen or above.

Out of the 3,853 assignments where students graded themselves, 2,708 (70.3%) awarded themselves full credit. 267 (9.9%) of the full credit submissions were blank or nonsense (e.g. ffwevrew).

We also assessed how many of the full credit submissions were copies of other assignments and found that 231 (8.5%) of full credit submissions were duplicates of others. Of these duplicates, 143 consisted of three assignments that appeared over 40 times each. We later discovered that these had been either posted on the Internet by students or were merely copies of examples provided in class. 54 of the duplicates appeared between 3 and 9 times each. 34 of the duplicates copied one other assignment, which likely resulted from one student submitting the same assignment for both projects.

In addition to grading student work, we assessed how worthwhile students found the self-graded assignments via an anonymous post-course survey. We sent the survey to the 1645 people who completed the course. Of 651 students

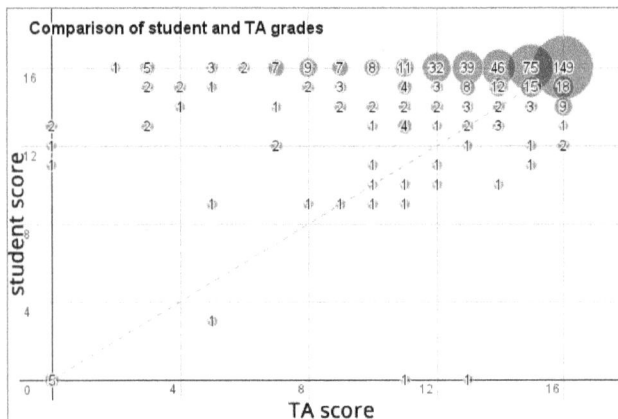

Figure 2. Student and TA scores for the APS MOOC

who responded to the post-course survey, 306 (47.0%) found the case study assignment very worthwhile; 299 (45.9%) found the project somewhat worthwhile.

Analysis

There is a moderate yet statistically significant correlation (Pearson $r=0.44$) between student scores and TA scores. The majority of students graded themselves within two points of how an expert grader would assess their work. The overall quality of valid self-graded assignments was high, with nearly three-quarters receiving at least a B average (73% of graded assignments received thirteen out of sixteen or better, or 81.3%).

Most students submitted two assignments. The number of blank or duplicate assignments that were submitted that received full credit was 498. If all students submitted two assignments, then this corresponds with 249 students. A total number of 1,874 students submitted two assignments. Therefore a moderate number of students (13%, or 249 out of 1,874) took advantage of the system by plagiarizing or submitting blank assignments but giving themselves full credit.

Discussion

Self-grading seems to be an effective alternative to multiple-choice assessments for in-depth, qualitative student work in low-stakes massive open online courses. The lower than expected correlation we found likely corresponded to a lack of training students how to evaluate their own work, vagueness in the evaluation checklist, and the ability for students to reward themselves for submitting low quality work.

Previous studies in which self-grading was successful included an in-depth training process that involved students co-creating the rubrics as well as discussion during the grading about elements of specific assignments [12]. Although this course provided a sample assignment for students to grade, it appears that this was not sufficient for students to truly understand all of the criteria. Future work may explore a more comprehensive training process for grading calibration similar to assessing the "ground truth"

on several assignments prior to grading students' own work [7] or a gating process that required students to reach the same scores as experts on sample assignments before they could score their own work.

Students who completed all course requirements earned a printable certificate but could not necessarily receive university credit. Based on conversations between course staff and students, some students appeared to be motivated by the mistaken belief that earning this certificate would automatically get them a job at Google. This could have provided an incentive for students to take shortcuts. This problem could be resolved by having the course assignment system check for valid work in text entry boxes as well as reject duplicate submissions.

MOOC #2: MAPPING WITH GOOGLE

The MWG course [8] was created to teach the general public how to use Google's Maps, Maps Engine Lite, and Google Earth products more efficiently and effectively. The course was announced when registration opened on May 15, 2013; students could access instructional materials from June 10 through June 24. The course was created using Google's open-source Course Builder platform [4] with minor modifications to improve usability (we slightly changed the standard registration questionnaire, and the final project self-assessment interface to support the self-evaluation options).

In addition to standard video and text lessons, the course offered application activities for a variety of skills (such as using Google Maps to find directions between two points on a map, creating a customized map, using Google Maps Engine Lite to import a csv file of locations for display on a map, and using Google Earth to create a tour with audio, images, videos, and panoramic views).

Based on our observations with self-grading in APS, we implemented a self-evaluation system for two final projects in this course. Students could choose to complete a Google Maps project, a Google Earth project, or both. As before, we awarded certificates of completion to students who completed and scored final projects. We required students to turn in and score themselves on the final projects in order to receive the certificate.

Final Projects

In contrast to the APS MOOC (which asked students for a case study), students in this course could complete a final project that involved creating two online maps that would meet established criteria. They were asked to "Create a map that communicates geographical information using Maps Engine Lite. Meet all of the basic criteria and select one or more advanced features from the list [of maps features]." Students were given an evaluation rubric before completing their task. They submitted their assignment by supplying a link to their Map as well as by answering additional questions about their project, each intended to facilitate their metacognitive design practice as shown in Table 2.

Assignment questions	Evaluation rubric
1. What story are you telling with your map? 2. Did you change the base map? If so, why? If not, why not? 3. What advanced feature(s) skills did you apply to your map? *(multi-select from a list)*	• Does your map have a title? *(Yes/No)* • Does your map have a description? *(Yes/No)* • How many points are in your map? *(0, 1, 2, 3, 4, 5 or more)* • How many points have titles? *(0, 1, 2, 3, 4, 5 or more)* How many points include a relevant description? *(0, 1, 2, 3, 4, 5 or more)* • How well does the styling enhance the distinction between map points? *(score between 0-5, from none to very-well)* • How well do the advanced features included enhance the clarity of the map? *(score between 0-5, from none to very-easy-to-understand)*

Table 2. MWG project questions and rubric

As in the APS MOOC, after submitting their final assignment, students were guided to grade two sample assignments using the same rubric that they would later use to evaluate their own work. Based on experiences in Advanced Power Searching, course designers believed that one sample assignment may not have been sufficient to train students how to evaluate their work. The Course Builder system provided feedback based on how an expert would have graded the assignment. Students then proceeded to evaluate their own work. The rubric consisted of the seven questions listed in Table 2. The two yes/no questions were worth one point each, and each subsequent question was worth five points for a total possible score of twenty-seven points.

Methods
After the course closed, course administrators provided researchers with an anonymized sample of assignment submissions. Three members of the course staff (teaching assistants and content experts) graded ten percent of submitted assignments. As before, course staff calibrated scoring by reviewing several sample assignments together until they achieved consistent scores on several assignments.

Data
Students submitted 5,160 Google Maps projects. Out of this entire set of projects, students scored 5,058 (98.0%). Course staff sampled 285 projects and found that about one-third

(34.7%) of the maps (99 out of 285) were inaccessible because students did not choose to make their maps public or share them with course staff. We therefore extrapolated that 1,755 out of the self-scored 5,058 projects would also be inaccessible for a total of 3,303. Course staff graded a random sample of 384 of these 3,303 projects (11.6%). The mean student score of the graded assignments was 25.7 (standard deviation of 2.03); the mean TA score of the graded assignments was 24.9 (standard deviation of 2.79).

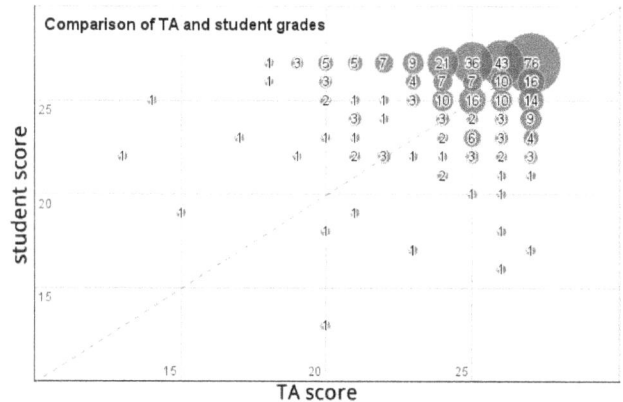

Figure 3. Score differences between students and course staff for the MWG MOOC.

Of these assignments, 201 (52.3%) had student and TA scores within one point of each other (out of a total twenty-seven points). 275 (71.6%) had student and TA scores with two points of each other. 340 (88.5%) had student and TA scores within five points of each other. 359 (93.5%) received TA scores of 21 or above (out of 27, a B average). Out of the 5,058 assignments where students graded themselves, 2,605 (51.5%) awarded themselves full credit. Oddly, 73 (2.8%) of the full credit submissions were blank (and were the only submissions by those users). We assessed how many of the full credit submissions were duplicates, finding that 9 (0.3%) of full credit submissions were duplicates of other submissions. No students with the same UserID submitted two duplicate assignments.

In addition to grading student work, we assessed how worthwhile students found final projects via a post-course survey. Of 1901 students who completed the final project and responded to a post-course survey 1407 (74.0%) found the Maps project very worthwhile; 475 (25.0%) found the project somewhat worthwhile.

Discussion
We found significantly better results with the self-grading experience in this course than in the APS MOOC. Similar to other online courses, the primary challenge in this self-evaluation process seemed to be the difficulty students had in precisely interpreting the rubric [6]. Even TAs who graded the students' work encountered confusion about how to apply the rubric. We further developed the rubric during the grading process. In retrospect, we should have

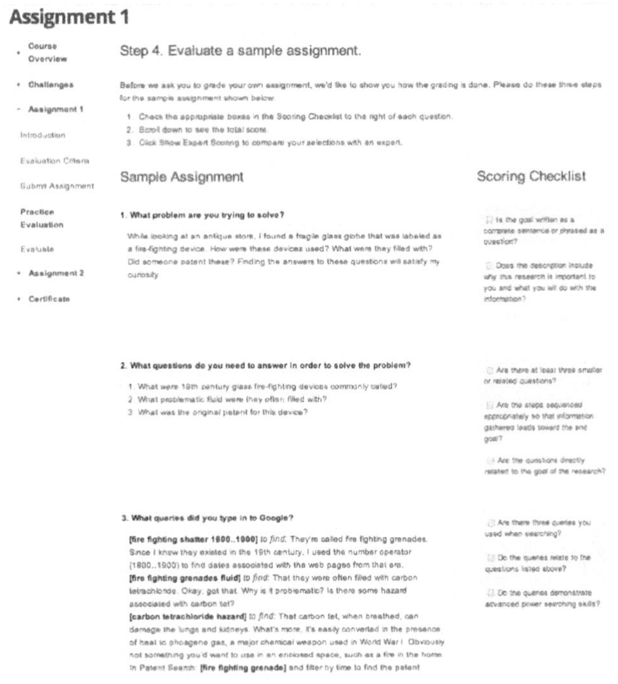

Assignment 1

Figure 4: Sample of grading practice, with sidebar Scoring Checklist. (Note that there are 14 questions in the entire form, here for space reasons we only show the top 8.)

done this at the outset (although we did not have a large sample set of the maps to predict how students would be applying the skills). If we taught the course again, we anticipate that publicizing the more detailed rubric earlier in the course would increase the correlation between student and TA grades. As graders, we also discovered that five points of grading on subjective questions was too many. Future rubrics might try using just three points of quality to see if this would increase student accuracy.

We surmise from comments in the open-ended questions on the two course surveys that the large number of students in APS who submitted blank or duplicate assignments but graded themselves full credit had to do with the level of difficulty of the assignment. Students perceived the MWG course assignments as relatively easy, therefore there may have been reduced incentive to cheat. Other differences between the two assignments that may explain the discrepancy include the fact that students in Advanced Power Searching were asked to submit two assignments instead of one. There may also have been a perception that earning an Advanced Power Searching certificate would help students obtain a job at Google. Although we work hard to be clear about such things, misconceptions occasionally persist.

We also find it interesting that significantly more students rated the MWG course projects as *very worthwhile* compared with the Advanced Power Searching case studies. Assignments in both courses were designed to be relevant to students' lives, show the application of skills gained in

the course, and create an artifact they could use after leaving the course.

	APS	MWG
TA/student scores within 6% of each other	55.1%	71.6%
TA/student scores within 12% of each other	69.0%	88.5%
assignments that received over 80% (B average) by TAs	73.3%	93.5%
blank assignments that were scored full credit by students	9.9%	2.8%
duplicate assignments that were scored full credit by students	8.5%	0.3%
survey respondents indicating the final projects were very worthwhile *(5 on a scale of 1 to 5)*	47.0%	74.0%
survey respondents indicating the final projects were somewhat worthwhile *(4 on a scale of 1 to 5)*	45.9%	25.0%

Table 3. Comparison of two courses

An additional difference between the two courses is that APS students could score their projects anything (including zero) in order to receive credit for completing the project. MWG students were required to score their work anything greater than zero. This may have caused students to be more thoughtful about the scores they gave themselves, or it may have discouraged students who were simply trying to earn credit without doing the work.

Likewise, the discrepancy between the fractions of duplicate assignments submitted between the two courses begs further investigation. We could not determine why these two MOOCs would be so different in duplicate final project submission rates.

FUTURE WORK

This work suggests several directions for future studies. Given the issues that arose with creating and using effective rubrics for self-evaluation, in future courses, authors could explore adjusting rubrics and clarifying grading criteria as the course progresses. In addition, courses could spend more time training students how to evaluate their work. In theory this is a separate skill from the skills of doing or completing activities [3] and merits a separate part of the course content. Students might practice grading several standardized assignments until they reach alignment with the gold standard scores. Once they have achieved this alignment they could proceed to grading their own assignments. As we saw from the number of duplicate and blank or nonsense submission, developing technology to prevent students from submitting and scoring blank, nonsensical, or duplicate assignments should also be in the near term planning horizon.

CONCLUSIONS

Self-grading seems to be an effective alternative to multiple-choice assessments for in-depth, qualitative student work in low-stakes massive open online courses. It is a simple and effective way to create direct student engagement in their learning, while *not* requiring the development of very sophisticated autograding systems.

In looking back at our experience with these two MOOCS, several points come to mind.

First, as is well known in the education literature, writing rubrics for anyone to use in performance assessment is difficult [9].

Yet we know that the process of answering the questions on the rubric is valuable to students [9]. A rubric helps communicate to students the specific requirements, expectations, and acceptable performance standards for an assignment. The can help students monitor and assess their progress as they work toward clearly indicated goals. By making the objectives of the course clear, students can more easily recognize the strengths and weaknesses of their work and direct their efforts accordingly.

But unlike most classroom settings, MOOCS are often composed of a wide variety of students, often from many different educational backgrounds, with widely varying language abilities, and dramatically differing degrees of practice in learning in online settings.

With this in mind, we recommend not only developing the clearest and simplest rubrics possible, but also user-testing them before the MOOC is offered. This is often difficult pragmatically, as the student composition is often not known ahead of time, but we have found that even limited user testing of self-evaluation rubrics to be of enormous help.

As we found with our own experience of creating a panel of experts to consistently grade the sample set of student assignments, practice is key. We also suggest that every self-evaluation method also come paired with enough practice (and sufficient evaluation of *that* skill as well) to ensure that consistent evaluations take place for all students.

Finally, while we were pleased with the overall correlation between self-evaluations and the gold standard of expert assessments, the number of bogus submissions was somewhat troubling, and suggests that for online classes where evaluation has a higher stakes consequence, robust checking of assignments for blanks, nonsense entries, and duplicates is well worth the effort.

ACKNOWLEDGEMENTS

We thank Alfred Spector, Maggie Johnson, and Google's MOOC development team for their advice, feedback, and support. The Mapping with Google course used Course Builder 1.4.0. [4] We thank Saifu Angto, Pavel Simakov, and John Cox for continuous support, customizations and code.

REFERENCES

1. Advanced Power Searching course. 2013. http://www.powersearchingwithgoogle.com/course/aps

2. Balfour, S.P. 2013. Assessing writing in MOOCS: Automated essay scoring and Calibrated Peer Review. *Research & Practice in Assessment* 8.1 (2013): 40-48.

3. Black, P. & Wiliam, D. 1998. Assessment and classroom learning. *Assessment in Education: Principles, Policy & Practice,* 5(1), 7.

4. Course Builder platform. 2013 http://code.google.com/p/course-builder

5. Eslinger, E., White, B., Frederiksen, J., & Brobst, J. 2008. Supporting Inquiry Processes with an Interactive Learning Environment: Inquiry Island. *Journal of Science Education and Technology,* 17(6), 610–617. doi:10.1007/s10956-008-9130-6

6. Kulkarni, C., and S. R. Klemmer. 2012. Learning design wisdom by augmenting physical studio critique with online self-assessment. *Technical report, Stanford University.*

7. Kulkarni, C., Wei, K. P., Le, H., Chia, D., Papadopoulos, K., Koller, D., Klemmer, S.R. 2013. Scaling self and peer assessment to the global design classroom. *Transactions on Computer-Human Interactions Journal, 20*(6) *in publication.*

8. Mapping with Google course. 2013 http://mapping.withgoogle.com

9. Moskal, B. M. 2000. Scoring rubrics: what, when and how? *Practical Assessment, Research & Evaluation,* 7(3).

10. Piech, C., Huang, J., Chen, Z., Do, C., Ng, A., & Koller, D. (n.d.). Tuned Models of Peer Assessment in MOOCs. Retrieved (11/7/13) http://www.stanford.edu/~cpiech/bio/papers/tuningPeer Grading.pdf

11. Rivers, W. P. 2001. Autonomy at All Costs: An Ethnography of Metacognitive Self-Assessment and Self-Management among Experienced Language Learners. *The modern language journal* 85.2 (2001): 279-290.

12. Sadler, P., & Good, E. 2006. The Impact of Self- and Peer-Grading on Student Learning. *Educational Assessment, 11*(1), 1–31.

13. Veenman, M., Van Hout-Wolters, B., & Affleerbach. P. 2006. Metacognition and learning: conceptual and methodological considerations. *Metacognition and Learning, 1*(1):3, (Apr 14, 2006).

Superposter behavior in MOOC forums

Jonathan Huang
Stanford University
jhuang11@stanford.edu

Anirban Dasgupta
Yahoo! Labs
anirban.dasgupta@gmail.com

Arpita Ghosh
Cornell University
arpitaghosh@cornell.edu

Jane Manning
Stanford University
jinpa@stanford.edu

Marc Sanders
Stanford University
sandersm@stanford.edu

ABSTRACT

Discussion forums, employed by MOOC providers as the primary mode of interaction among instructors and students, have emerged as one of the important components of online courses. We empirically study contribution behavior in these online collaborative learning forums using data from 44 MOOCs hosted on Coursera, focusing primarily on the highest-volume contributors—"superposters"—in a forum. We explore who these superposters are and study their engagement patterns across the MOOC platform, with a focus on the following question—to what extent is superposting a positive phenomenon for the forum? Specifically, while superposters clearly contribute heavily to the forum in terms of *quantity*, how do these contributions rate in terms of quality, and does this prolific posting behavior negatively impact contribution from the large remainder of students in the class?

We analyze these questions across the courses in our dataset, and find that superposters display above-average engagement across Coursera, enrolling in more courses and obtaining better grades than the average forum participant; additionally, students who are superposters in one course are significantly more likely to be superposters in other courses they take. In terms of utility, our analysis indicates that while being neither the fastest nor the most upvoted, superposters' responses are speedier and receive more upvotes than the average forum user's posts; a manual assessment of quality on a subset of this content supports this conclusion that a large fraction of superposter contributions indeed constitute useful content. Finally, we find that superposters' prolific contribution behavior does not 'drown out the silent majority'—high superposter activity correlates positively and significantly with higher overall activity and forum health, as measured by total contribution volume, higher average perceived utility in terms of received votes, and a smaller fraction of orphaned threads.

Author Keywords

massive open online course; MOOC; education; Coursera; collaborative learning; online forums; data mining

INTRODUCTION

Massive open online courses (MOOCs) have generated much excitement and interest because of their potential to bring about dramatic changes in higher education [11]. However, the very characteristics that enable the scalability of a MOOC—a handful of instructors using the Internet to broadcast lectures and content to a potentially unbounded number of students at once—have also engendered criticisms about the pedagogical soundness of this new model of engagement. It is not uncommon for the ratio of enrolled students to the number of teaching staff to exceed 5000:1, making it impossible for the large majority of students to have any meaningful interaction with the instructor. This lack of instructor attention is aggravated by the absence of an immediate peer group, which, in a physical classroom setting, is known to facilitate learning and understanding through discussion and tutoring [15, 3].

Forums, employed by MOOC providers as the primary mode of interaction among instructors and participants, have thus emerged as one of the critical components of a MOOC. Instructors use the forum to communicate about recent lectures or homework assignments, and have even been known to use structured open-ended questions on the forum to encourage discussions. Students express their views, seek help from peers and discuss assignments. It has been suggested that a well-run discussion forum provides a sense of community and engagement that is all but able to substitute for the peer support available in a physical classroom. Indeed, there is anecdotal evidence[1] that some users have found the active forums in particular MOOCs to be among the most important enablers in successfully completing their course.

In this paper, we study the most vocal subset of contributors on MOOC forums. We call these students the *superposters*—the students who post most frequently on the forum[2], and typically disproportionately more often than their peers[3]. Superposters exist in every course, and as the "loudest" participants, can play an outsized role in the quality and tone of discussion in MOOC forums. For a course designer, understanding superposters—their characteristics, behavior, and overall utility to forums—is central to understanding how (and

---

[1] http://mooc.studentadvisor.com/posts/23/four-ways-to-get-the-most-out-of-a-mooc

[2] https://signalblog.stanford.edu/how-widely-used-are-mooc-forums-a-first-look/

[3] This pattern is not at all uncommon in online environments, and specifically in online content production; see the section on related work.

(a)

(b)

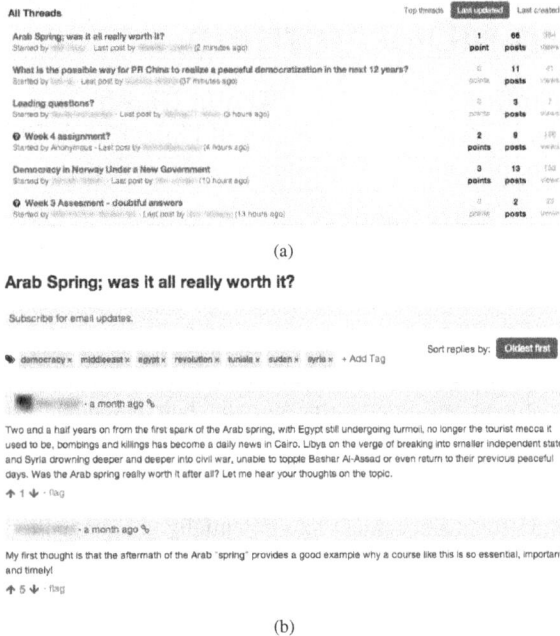

Figure 1. (a) Screenshot of part of the front page of the discussion forum for Stanford's Democratic Development course; (b) Example thread from the same course.

whether) to encourage superposters, to identify roles such users could undertake in the forum that would not be feasible at scale for an instructor, and what might act as effective incentives for steering their contributions.

Superposters can, ideally, be model participants, making a large volume of timely high-quality contributions, and inspiring their peers by example to participate regularly in course discussions. But it is not, a priori, obvious that this ideal holds, or even that superposters are actually 'good' for forums— it is conceivable, for instance, that the superposters in a course could be flooding the forums with low quality posts, engaging in "trolling" behavior, or alienating the "silent majority" of the remaining students in the class. We therefore investigate the following questions in this paper. First, who are these superposters—what are their demographics and characteristics, and how do they engage across the MOOC platform, both in terms of forum behavior and course performance? Second, how 'useful' are the contributions from these high-volume users, and how does their activity correlate with contributions from other forum participants— that is, how do superposters' contributions relate to the utility of the forum as a whole?

Our contributions

In this paper, we embark on an investigation of superposters in MOOC discussion forums, using data from 44 courses hosted on Coursera during 2012-13. The fact that our dataset spans multiple instances of forums allows us a unique opportunity to go beyond studying contribution in a single instance of a collaborative learning forum, with all its associated restrictions, and investigate users' contribution patterns as well as overall forum health across multiple forums.

We first investigate superposters—their demographics, and contribution patterns such as length of posts and asking ver-

sus responding tendencies as in past research [8, 1]—as well as their engagement patterns across the Coursera platform. We find that superposters display above-average engagement and performance on Coursera, enrolling in more courses and obtaining better final grades than non-superposters. Most interestingly, we see that users who are superposters in one course are significantly more likely to be superposters in other courses they take as well, suggesting that superposting might be an inherent, individual-specific trait, rather than an extrinsically induced response arising from course or forum-specific circumstances.

We next address whether superposters contribute value, beyond volume, to the forums. Our data analysis indicates that while neither the fastest nor the most upvoted, superposters do respond faster and write longer posts than the average contributor. In addition, an assessment of quality on a subset of human-coded[4] superposter posts agrees with the inferences from the quantitative analysis, indicating that a large fraction of superposter contributions indeed constitute useful content. Finally, we explore whether superposters' prolific posting might negatively impact others' inclinations to contribute. An analysis of the correlation between superposters' activity levels and overall forum activity shows that high superposter activity correlates positively and significantly with higher overall activity and forum health, in terms of total contribution volume, received upvotes, and the number of orphaned threads.[5] Our results suggest that rather than flooding forums with low quality noise or 'drowning out the silent majority', superposters are, in some sense, 'model' forum citizens—users who contribute significant value to the forums through their effort, often across multiple courses.

A caveat emptor goes with our results. Our study is based purely on observational data collected "in the wild" without the explicit intent to perform research, so that our results are purely correlational—specifically, we do not claim causal conclusions from our analysis, nor make claims about learning outcomes which cannot be measured due to the nature of our data. A more rigorous experimental study, possibly with hypotheses informed by our results, that identifies causal effects of the behavior of high-volume contributors while controlling for possible confounding factors, can potentially provide useful input to platform designers in a number of ways. Such a study might be informative regarding how to engage and reward such users, what roles they can potentially take on to ensure scalability, and whether and how resources spent on identifying and 'incentivizing' superposters in one course may pay off across multiple courses on a MOOC platform.

Related work

Online forums for education, often referred to as asynchronous discussion groups, have been extensively studied in the computer-supported collaborative learning (CSCL) literature [8]. Collaborative learning is critical in education: by allowing learners to confront tasks or learn concepts that they

---

[4]While most content analyses in the CSCL literature have relied on manually coded data as in our own paper [5], it seems clear that automated natural language processing methods (such as those described in [12]) will be more scalable for future analyses.

[5]i.e., threads which receive no responses

would not be able to do alone, collaborative environments effectively form a *scaffolding* [20] for learners to proceed to their next developmental level [17].

Online collaborative learning interactions have been shown to enhance academic discourse, to foster higher level cognition of concepts [4, 9, 14], and to lead to gains in learning outcomes [14]. Additionally, asynchronous online discussions can play an important motivational role through promoting social presence and belonging [13, 18], and thus even messages that are seemingly "off-task" may potentially play a useful role in forum utility. Finally, the benefits of online collaborative learning extend beyond active participants to passive viewers too [6]. By using self-reported data from students, Dennen et al. [6, 16] report that students benefit from the forum content through a process of "reading and reflection".

While the majority of CSCL work has focused on smaller-scale studies, a number of large scale data analyses have been conducted on general-purpose online Q&A forums, such as Y! Answers and StackOverflow, in the data mining community. The study of contributors in these Q&A forums has largely focused on the question of identifying "experts", in order to identify high-quality content and curate or highlight contributions from such experts (see [10, 22, 1, 2] and references therein). In contrast, rather than identifying a subset of experts, we investigate the expertise (and other characteristics) of a given subset of contributors. The work of Furtado et al. [7] is most closely related to ours from this literature, undertaking a more general study of online contribution behavior by clustering and classifying contributors' activity profiles in Stack Overflow and Yahoo Answers. Their categorization of user contribution patterns yields a number of "activist" profiles—users who contribute a large number of questions and answers, although with answering skills that are only slightly better than the average. While our definition of superposters is simpler, we observe similar patterns of 'skill' for superposters in our analysis.

Finally, we note that the phenomenon of superposting behavior is not new to our study— the existence of a small number of core users who contribute disproportionately to the total content volume, resulting in the ubiquitous heavy tail in contribution sizes, is well-documented in multiple large-scale online communities [21, 19]. However, the contribution characteristics of such high-volume contributors have not been studied at scale in a collaborative learning context.

DATASET AND FORUM ORGANIZATION
We consider data from 44 courses run on Coursera with over 70,000 discussion threads spanning a range of topics, mostly from STEM disciplines (8 of the courses were non-STEM). Table 1 summarizes some of the statistics of our data. We note that with the exception of a handful of courses, forum participation is voluntary in Coursera courses.

The discussion forums on Coursera are organized as follows. Each forum is a 2-level tree of "sub-forums", typically with several subforums dedicated to general topics such as course logistics, errata, technical support, and study groups, as well as subforums for more course-specific topics (e.g., a

# of MOOC offerings	44
Total # of threads	70,419
Total # of contributions (posts and comments)	325,071
Total # unique forum contributors over courses	116,028
Median # registered students per course	40,674
Median # of unique forum contributors per course	2180.5
Median # of threads per course	1,297

Table 1. Summary statistics of the datasets considered in this paper.

"Queries" sub-forum may have further sub-forums such as "Unit 6 Queries"). Threads are also up to 2 levels deep, consisting of an ordered sequence of posts with additional comments optionally attached to some posts. We do not distinguish in this paper between comments and other types of posts, simply using the term "posts" for both. Students can vote posts or comments up or down (once per user per post), and are encouraged to use their votes to "bring attention to thoughtful, helpful posts" rather than express subjective agreement or disagreement.

Students can choose to view only the threads from a particular sub-forum or browse through the most recent threads that have been posted anywhere in the forum. When browsing the list of threads, students can see the length of each thread, the number of times this thread has been viewed, the net number of upvotes this thread has received, and whether a staff member contributed to it. Students can view the contents of threads either chronologically or by popularity as determined by net votes per post. Finally, students can also subscribe to threads (and are subscribed by default to threads to which they contribute).

SUPERPOSTER CHARACTERIZATIONS
There are several measures that might be used to characterize the extent of a user's contribution to a forum. In this paper, we focus on the *quantity* and *'quality'* of a user's contributions. We will be particularly interested in definitions of superposting behavior that permit cross-course comparisons and analysis, which can be nontrivial due to different course durations; our measures and definitions are chosen accordingly to allow such comparisons.

We define *quantity* as the *number* of posts made by a student on course forums. (Note, however, that other natural measures for quantity, such as word counts, are also defensible in this context.) To account for different course durations, we define a user's *quantity score* for a course to be the average number of contributions she makes per week in that course. We define *(quantity) superposters* in a course to be the set of users who belong to the top 5% of forum participants in the course with respect to the quantity score. We note here that while we used a *relative* measure of contribution to define superposting behavior, there are a number of possible alternative definitions, including measures based on thresholds for the absolute number of posts, or the ratio between the number of posts to an average; we discuss and analyze these alternative definitions (for all three kinds of superposters defined in this section) in the full version of the paper.

Quality is a more elusive trait. While we would ideally like to measure to what extent a user was able to accurately and clearly answer questions and contribute fruitfully to discussions, estimating such a measure is not easy since rating the accuracy of a forum post might, in many cases, require specialized domain knowledge about the course content. As a proxy, therefore, we use votes cast by other students in the course forum as an approximate measure of quality.

We define the quality of a user's contributions to a particular thread to be the ratio of the number of votes on all her contributions to the thread to the average number of votes on any contribution in this thread. A user's *quality score* in a course is the average of her per-thread quality over all the threads that she contributes to in the course. We say that a student is a *(quality) superposter* in a course if she is in the top 5% of forum participants in that course according to this quality score. Since a contributor who has a single highly-rated contribution could be propelled to being a quality superposter with this definition, we additionally set the quality score of a user to zero if they contributed fewer than five posts or comments throughout the course.

Coursera also maintains and displays a *reputation score* for each student, computed as the sum of square roots of votes across all contributions by a user. Reputation scores can be thought of as measuring both the quantity and quality of a user's contribution, while reducing the effect of votes on any single contribution. We again say that a student is a (reputation) superposter in a course if she belongs to the top 5% in the course with respect to the reputation score.

For each kind of superposter defined above, we use non-superposters to refer to the forum participants who are not superposters of that kind (note that we only consider the set of *forum participants*, rather than the entire population of registered students in a course, to define non-superposters). In this paper, we will primarily investigate the behavior of 'quantity' superposters—the users who contribute the largest volume of content on a forum; unless otherwise specified, the term *superposters* will henceforth refer to quantity superposters. While these (quantity) superposters are the main focus of our study, we also compare their behavior to the quality and reputation superposters to calibrate our observations wherever appropriate.

DEMOGRAPHICS AND PARTICIPATION PATTERNS

Who are these superposters, and what are their engagement patterns across the MOOC platform? In this section, we investigate superposter demographics, contribution patterns across course forums, and course enrollment and performance.

We begin with demographics, correlating superposting behavior with data from a survey conducted by Coursera that was administered by a large fraction (roughly two-thirds) of the courses in our dataset. Among these courses, 7% of the entire set of users, 17% of the forum posters and 100% of the superposters filled in the survey. While it may not be surprising that native English speakers tend to be the more vocal participants on Coursera forums, other demographic factors also play a role— for instance, the histogram of forum participants by age in Figure 2(a), partitioned into superposters and non-superposters, shows that superposters are typically older than the average forum user (and Coursera users in general). Gender also plays a small but statistically significant

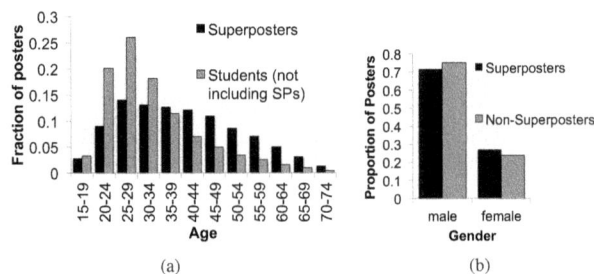

Figure 2. Demographic histograms of age (a) and gender (b) from Coursera survey, comparing superposters and non-superposters.

role—while the majority of forum participants (as well as superposters) are male, the proportion of superposters who are female is slightly higher than that of non-superposters.

Contribution characteristics

We now explore two basic characteristics of the contributions superposters make on MOOC forums. Previous work has studied the overlap of 'askers' and 'answerers' in online Q&A forums: for instance, Adamic et al. [1] find that Yahoo! Answers has subforums with a significant fraction of users who both ask and answer, as well as subforums where users almost exclusively either ask or answer questions. Analogously, we would like to understand whether superposters achieve their large posting volume primarily by 'asking' or 'answering' questions, or a mix of both. Unlike in many such non-educational Q&A forums, however, the first post of a thread in Coursera forums does not necessarily have to be a question (although it typically is one); also, nothing prevents a student from asking a question midway through a thread, prompted by the preceding discussion. Thus, instead of distinguishing between asking and answering a question, we distinguish between *initiating* and *responding* to a thread, and ask whether superposters in MOOC forums tend to be initiators or responders.

The tables below list the number of initial posts and responses (i.e., posts that are not the initial post in a thread) from superposters and non-superposters. These numbers show that the ratio of the number of responses to the number of threads initiated is greater for superposters than for non-superposters (by almost 4 responses for each thread initiated), suggesting that superposters tend to respond to threads (possibly by answering questions) more often than starting a new thread (possibly by asking a question). Next we study the length

(a) Superposters

# responses:	208,690
# threads initiated:	20,629
# responses to # threads initiated ratio:	10.12

(b) Non-superposters

# responses:	265,566
# threads initiated:	42,545
# responses to # threads initiated ratio:	6.24

of posts, which can be viewed as a proxy for quality as well as an alternative measure of quantity. Measuring the number of posts from a user might not actually reflect the volume of her contributions to the forum if users trade off post length and quantity, with some users writing many short posts but

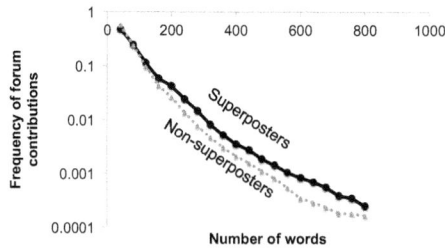

Figure 3. Histogram of contribution lengths (number of words in a post or comment) comparing superposters and non-superposters. In addition to writing more posts, superposter contributions tend to be longer.

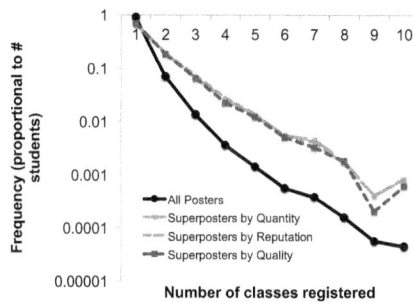

Figure 4. Histogram of the number of courses to which each forum poster has enrolled (of the courses in our dataset), showing that superposters are typically enrolled in more courses than non-superposters. The y-axis in this plot is probability plotted on a log-scale.

contributing the same 'total volume' of forum conversation as users who write a handful of long posts. Figure 3 suggests, however, that user behavior on the forum does not display such a "conservation of words" effect: the histogram of the number of words per post in contributions from superposters and non-superposters in Figure 3 shows that in addition to responding more frequently, superposters are also more likely than non-superposters to write lengthier posts.

Superposting across courses

Is superposting behavior an inherent trait, where some posters simply are prolific irrespective of the environment while others are not, or is it driven by extrinsic factors such as course content or the forum environment and community?

We approach the question of whether superposting behavior is an inherent or extrinsic trait by focusing on users who were enrolled in multiple courses in our dataset. While most forum participants were only enrolled in a single course, roughly 8000 forum posters in our dataset were enrolled in more than one course. Of these, we focus on the $\sim$ 6200 students enrolled in exactly two courses; 900 of whom were superposters in at least one course. Table 2 tallies the number of these students who were (1) superposters in neither of the two courses, (2) in exactly one course, or (3) in both courses. As the table shows, if a student was a superposter in one class, she was significantly more likely (nearly three times more likely than would be expected under independence) to be a superposter in another course. Testing the null hypothesis that superposting behavior for an individual is independent across courses with a chi-squared test run on Table 2, we can reject independence (with $\chi^2 = 205.34$, $p \leq .01$). Furthermore, this pattern holds for each of our three definitions of superposters

(i.e., by reputation or quality). We therefore conclude that superposting behavior is persistent across multiple courses and appears, at least to some extent, to be an inherent trait. A more careful study of this phenomenon, as well as a further understanding of superposter motivation, can potentially have implications for platform design since identifying or incentivizing superposters in one course may yield payoffs across multiple courses.

	Non-SP in Course 2	SP in Course 2
Non-SP in Course 1	5328	386
SP in Course 1	386	128

Table 2. Contingency table counting number of students who were superposters in zero, one or two courses.

Course enrollment and performance

Finally, we investigate how superposters engage across the Coursera platform—are superposters more engaged with MOOCs overall, and do they do well in courses or are they the weaker students in the class, coming repeatedly to the forum for assistance? We begin by investigating superposter course enrollment via a histogram of the number of courses in which superposters and non-superposters are enrolled. Comparing non-superposter enrollment rates to that of superposters in Figure 4, we see that superposters have a tendency to enroll in more courses on Coursera than 'regular' students.

We next investigate course performance as measured by grades. Our analysis suggests that on average, superposters tend to also be the better performers in courses, although the extent to which they outperform other students depends on subject matter. Before describing this analysis, we note that this (purely correlational) result suggests an immediate open question regarding the direction of causality between forum participation and learning outcomes: while one plausible hypothesis is that high expertise (likely leading to good performance), gives students the confidence to be vocal on forums, an alternative hypothesis is that high forum participation leads to good performance because asking questions and explaining material to others leads to better learning outcomes. Our (observational) data cannot properly address this question; however, resolving this question via an experimental study is an important direction for further work.

To evaluate the course performance of superposters, we compute the average z-score of the final course grades of superposters and non-superposters and examine the difference between these averages. This *grade disparity* indicates the number of standard deviations by which superposters outperformed other students on average. A potential confounding factor is time of engagement—a student who was actively engaged for only 4 weeks of an 8-week course is unlikely to have obtained a good grade, and even less likely to have had among the highest average rates of forum posts per week. To address this, we use the fraction of lectures opened by a user as a proxy for time of engagement, and control for time of engagement by including only those users who accessed sufficiently many lectures (we filter out any user who opened fewer than 10% of the lectures in a course).

Figure 5(a) plots the results of this analysis with respect to all three of our superposter definitions. In each case, we see that superposters outperform their peers by approximately

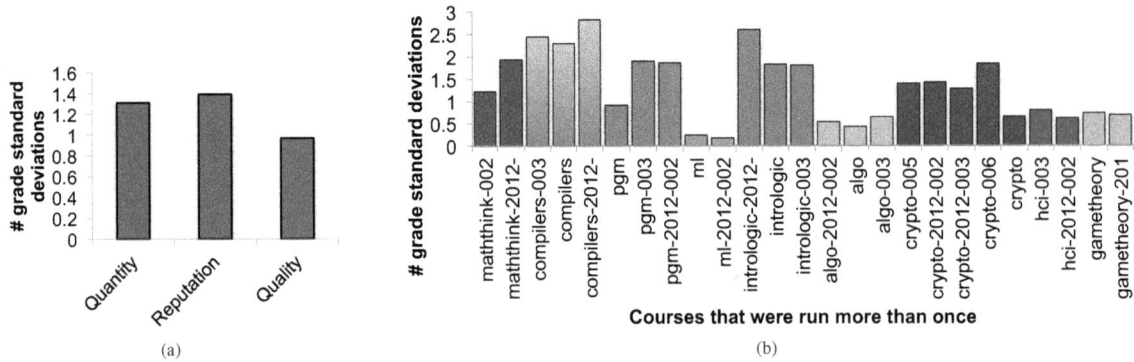

(a)   (b)

Figure 5. (a) # of standard deviations by which superposters outperformed non-superposters on final course grade (controlling for time of engagement), averaged over all courses, with respect to all three definitions of superposters. (b) Per-class results of for quantity superposters on the same data, shown just on courses in our dataset which were run more than once (best viewed in color, with colors indicating multiple runs of the same course)

one standard deviation, after controlling for time of engagement. Superposters by quantity outperform superposters by quality, while superposters by reputation perform best—that is, users whose forum posts balance quantity and quality (per our vote-based metric) tend to also be the best students.

Examining the grade improvements on a course-by-course basis yields a further insight. Figure 5(b) plots the grade disparity for nine courses which were run multiple times. In each case, we see that superposters outperformed their peers, on average, and the amount of grade disparity varied from course to course; notably, though, the grade disparity is similar across multiple offerings of the same course. While more work is needed to understand these similarities, reasonable hypotheses might be that the level of confidence required to be a superposter and/or the learning gain from posting at volume as a superposter is subject-dependent.

SUPERPOSTERS AND VALUE CREATION
In this section, we investigate whether superposters create value—beyond quantity—in the forums. As such, value is a fairly broad concept, and there are a number of metrics that might be used to measure the value, or utility, of a contribution. We will use two natural and easily computed quantities, namely posts' response times and received votes, to reflect two important aspects of healthy forums—whether questions are answered quickly without much delay, and whether other forum users react positively to contributions.

Response times
We use two different measures for response time. Our first measure is the absolute time to respond, i.e., the difference in time between the initial post in the thread and the time at which a contributor posts a response. Figure 6 shows the histogram of superposter response times, where a user's response time is the average, over all threads to which the user contributed, of the time to her first response within the thread. For comparison, we also plot the histograms of the absolute average response time for three other categories of users: the *earliest responders*, the quality superposters, and the reputation superposters. As with superposting, we define *early responders* as the set of users who have answered at least five questions, and belong to the fastest 5% of users by average response time, computed over all the threads that a user

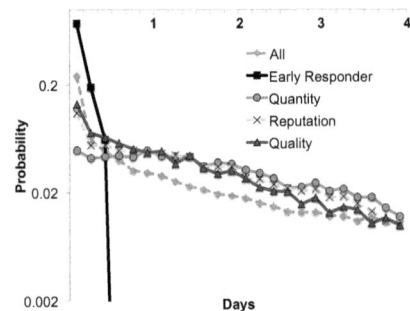

Figure 6. Histogram of response times (defined as the amount of time elapsed from the time a thread is started to time of post or comment), comparing early responders, superposters and the background distribution of all forum participants.

responded to. We also include the response time histogram computed over all users in all forums.

This analysis shows that while having better-than-average response times, superposters are not the quickest responders in a forum: early responders post responses on threads within the first 12 hours if at all (with a median response time of 6 hours), while an average forum user posts a response within 2 days of the question being posed 98% of the time (with a median response time of 43 hours). Superposter response times more closely resemble those of typical forum users, with median response times of 56 hours for quantity superposters, 45 hours for reputation superposters, and 36 hours for quality superposters.

A different measure of response time is ordinal, rather than cardinal as in the previous plot—what is the relative rank (in order of arrival) of a superposter's response among all responses in a thread? Our second measure is based on the order of arrival of posts in a thread rather than the absolute time to respond: for each thread, we divide all responses (excluding the first question or post that started the thread) into quartiles, ignoring threads with fewer than 5 posts. For each category of superposters (quantity, reputation and quality), we then count the fraction of posts from that category of users lying in each quartile.

Figures 7(a) and (b) show the histograms for the quartile position for each user category (superposters and non-

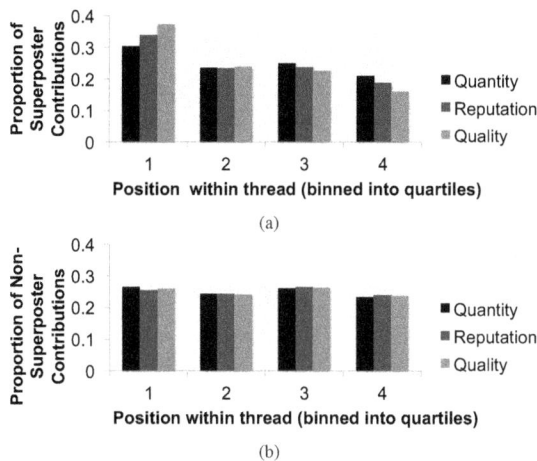

Figure 7. Histograms of the positions within a thread at which super-posters (a) or non-superposters (b) contributed. We bin the positions coarsely into quarters (first quarter of thread, second quarter, etc.), ignoring threads with less than five posts and not counting the first post (i.e. the question that started a thread).

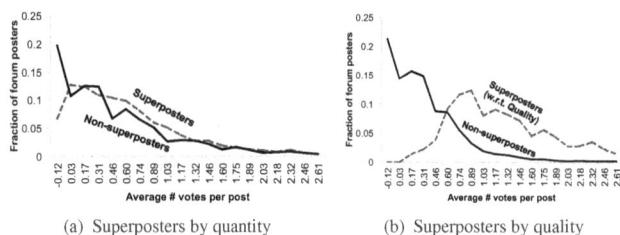

(a) Superposters by quantity   (b) Superposters by quality

Figure 8.   (a) Histogram of votes per post over forum participants, comparing superposters to non-superposters; (b) The same histogram with respect to the quality superposter category.

superposters by quantity, quality and reputation). As expected, the average user's post is equally likely to belong to any of the four quartiles. On the other hand, we see that superposter posts are slightly more likely to be in the first quartile than average (0.30 instead of 0.25); also, superposters are more likely to post responses that fall in the first quartile than in any other quartile. Thus, superposters, although not the earliest of responders, typically post responses earlier in the thread than an average responder would. (We note here that the observation from the histogram that quality superposters are more likely to respond in the first quartile (0.37 fraction of the time) than the two other kinds of superposters might be due to quick responses receiving more upvotes, and therefore increasing a user's quality score in our definition.)

Votes

As a second measure of contribution value, we analyze the votes received by superposters' contributions. While votes, in general, need not indicate the accuracy or completeness or any other absolute measure of a post's quality as previously discussed, an upvote from a user on a contribution does indicate a degree of satisfaction or utility that was derived from that contribution (for whatever reason). Thus votes arguably do provide a reasonable indication of the usefulness of a contribution.

To measure the value of a user's contributions from voting data, we take the average of the votes (both up and down)

received over all posts or comments made by a user in a course. Specifically, for each user in a course forum who contributed at least five times, we compute the mean of the number of votes given to each of her contributions by other users. In Figure 8(a), we plot the histogram over these computed means for quantity superposters and non-superposters, discarding the part of the histogram outside the 5th or the 95th percentile to remove outliers. (For comparison, Figure 8(b) shows analogous histograms using quality contributors.)

We see that the histogram of votes on posts by superposters, while somewhat better, is not very much higher than that for an average user, suggesting that superposters do not (at least consistently) produce posts that other users upvote significantly more than those from non-superposters. The median number of votes per post for a superposter is 0.56, while the median vote is 0.4 for a non-superposter, which is about 28% smaller. Therefore, while superposters do produce better-than-average quality content (as measured by votes), superposters are outstanding more for the quantity than for the quality of their contributions to the forum.

A closer look at superposter content

We now supplement our quantitative analysis of the quality of superposters' contributions with a manual assessment of a subset of superposter posts. Instead of performing an exhaustive or comprehensive qualitative analysis, we ask what percentage of superposter posts in this subset could be described as content-focused and positive—*on-content posts*. We manually examined the posts and comments from the top 3 superposters in each of 4 classes (a total of 1996 posts in all), and classified them simply as being on-content or off-content. Coding was performed independently by two of the authors. We remark here that contributions that were not on-content were not necessarily "bad" — some were simply phatic or logistical in nature. Posts categorized as on-content included ones that answered or asked a content-related question, engaged in content-related dialog in a productive way, or directed people to related resources.

Our findings are summarized in Table 3. Overall, 68.8% of posts from the top 3 superposters in a course were rated as on-content, which is a fairly high fraction given the stringent definition we used. One way to interpret these findings is to view them as support for the notion that online discussion forums for these courses effectively mimic face-to-face study sessions: students ask and answer questions about the course content, and while there is some chatter (occasionally regarding course logistics and at other times simply extraneous to the course), the content coming from the most visible students models the behavior we hope to see in any kind of study group, whether online or in-person.

SUPERPOSTERS AND OVERALL FORUM ACTIVITY

The previous section studied superposters' direct effect on forum health, asking whether superposters' contributions bring value, as measured by upvotes and the speed of response, to the forum. But even if superposters do contribute a large quantity of content of reasonable quality, they might still not be an entirely positive influence on the forum if their

Course	# posts from top 3 superposters	% on-content posts from top 3 superposters	% on-content posts from superposter 1	% on-content posts from superposter 2	% on-content posts from superposter 3
Child Nutrition	521	81%	79%	95%	77%
Algorithms	380	80%	80%	71%	90%
Intro To Logic	551	79%	88%	83%	47%
Writing in the Sciences	544	39%	32%	22%	60%

Table 3. Summary of results of qualitative study of contributions from the top 3 superposters from four representative courses, in which posts and comments were manually coded as on or off-content.

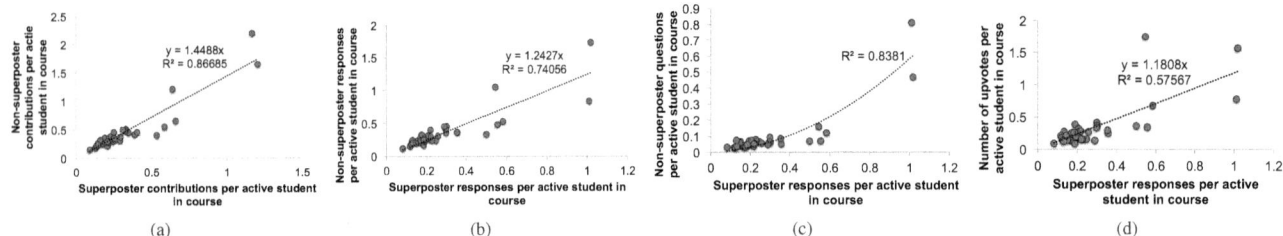

Figure 9. Scatterplots measuring superposter (SP) influence on non-superposter (nonSP) forum behavior (with each point corresponding to a course): (a) # SP contributions vs. # nonSP contributions; (b) # SP responses vs. # nonSP responses; (c) # SP responses vs. # nonSP threads initiated; (d) # responses vs. # votes obtained by nonSPs.

prolific posting suppresses contribution (for a variety of plausible reasons) from the remainder of the class. In this section, we investigate the correlations between superposter contributions and overall forum activity.

Relationship with overall participation and quality

We first study how superposter contribution relates to participation and contribution quality from other users in the forum.

We begin with quantity. Figure 9(a) shows a scatter plot of the number of posts by non-superposters in a forum against the number of superposter posts, where each point corresponds to a single course, and both axes are normalized by the number of *active students* in the course (a student is defined as active if she opened at least 5% of the course lectures). The line of best fit in the scatter plot shows a high positive correlation ($R^2 = 0.86$) between the two quantities, suggesting that higher activity from superposters is positively correlated with higher activity from other forum users as well[6]. Of course, this effect need not be causal at all, and could arise entirely from some latent factor (such as instructor encouragement or incentives for participation) that leads to high activity by all forum users—that is, we do not claim that superposter activity begets more activity from non-superposters; however, the analysis does suggest that superposter activity does not *suppress* non-superposter activity on the forums.

We next examine the correlation between superposter posts and non-superposter contributions in greater detail. Figure 9(b) plots the number of *responses* (i.e., excluding first posts) by non-superposters against the number of superposter responses, again normalizing both quantities by the number of active students in the class. Figure 9(c) has the same x-axis as Figure 9(b), but the y-axis represents the number of threads

initiated by non-superposters. Figure 9(b) shows a linear correlation ($R^2 = 0.75$) between the quantities whereas a quadratic fit was more appropriate for Figure 9(c). Again, these plots all suggest that high activity from superposters does not negatively impact participation—either initiation or response—from non-superposters.

Finally, we study the correlation between superposter activity and the quality of non-superposter contributions. Figure 9(d) is a scatter plot with the same x-axis as Figures 9(b) and 9(c), and the average number of upvotes over non-superposters posts (normalized by the number of active users) on the y-axis. We again observe a linear correlation (with $R^2 = 0.576$) which, though not as a strong as in Figures 9(b) and 9(c), indicates that a larger number of superposter responses also correlates positively with an increase in the number of upvotes received by a non-superposter.

Relationship with number of orphaned threads

While most threads posted on discussion forums in the classes in our dataset receive responses, some fraction of threads go unanswered. Among courses where posting is not required, we find that between 10% and 50% of threads started are "orphaned", i.e., do not receive any responses; this percentage is higher in courses where posting is required.

We next study the correlation between superposter activity and the proportion of orphaned threads in a course. Figure 10(a) is a scatter plot of the fraction of posts by superposters (among all posts in a course forum) against the fraction of threads left orphaned in that course (for this plot, we have removed 3 outlier courses in which participation on the forum counted towards a student's grade in the course). The Pearson correlation between fraction of posts by superposters and fraction of threads left orphaned is -.36 (i.e., negative) with $p = .02$, suggesting that courses in which superposters contribute more in volume tend to have fewer orphaned threads.

The question of what mechanism causes this correlation between superposter volume and orphaned threads remains open: one might speculate that the fraction of orphaned

---

[6]Note that a positive correlation between the unnormalized (or absolute) number of posts from non-superposters and the unnormalized number of posts from superposters need not convey information about whether superposters suppress participation from other users, since such a negative correlation, if not large enough, may be drowned out by an upward scaling in absolute contribution level with class size. This is why we normalize both axes by (effective) class size in Figure 9.)

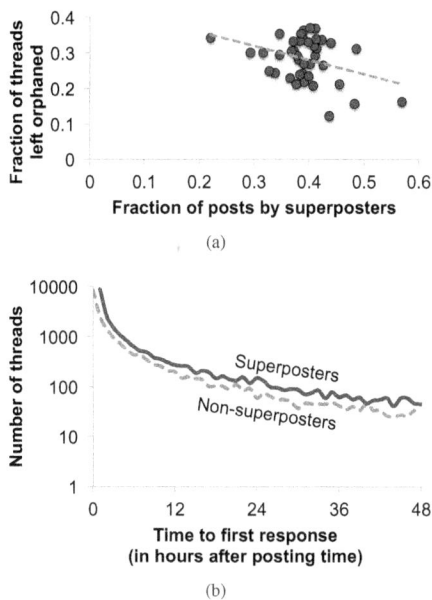

Figure 10. (a) Fraction of posts by superposters vs. fraction of threads left orphaned (each point correspond to a course); (b) Comparison of the number of threads receiving a first response from a superposter versus a non-superposter at k hours after posting time (for $k = 1, \ldots, 48$).

threads decreases with increased superposter activity because superposters are more likely to respond to threads that might otherwise have been left orphaned. However, Figure 10(b) compares, for all of the threads which got a first response in k hours, the number of first responses by superposters and non-superposters. The plot shows that even the threads that do not receive any responses for a long time (around 48 hours) after creation are no more likely to receive a response from a superposter than from a non-superposter, suggesting that the correlation between superposters and orphaned threads is more indirect, and possibly related to other course-specific factors. Like the other results in this section, these results are also perhaps best interpreted as the absence of a negative impact of superposting activity on orphaned threads (which is another measure of overall forum health) than an indication of any possibly positive causal effects resulting from superposters' contributions.

CONCLUSION

In this paper, we began an exploration of contribution patterns on MOOC discussion forums, studying user behavior and overall activity and forum health across 44 courses on Coursera. As in many large online communities, a large fraction of contributions in these collaborative learning forums come from a small subset of users, whom we refer to as 'superposters'. We investigate the characteristics of 'superposters'—their contribution patterns, demographics, course performance and enrollment—as well as the characteristics of their contributions—response speed, post length and quantity, perceived value as measured by upvotes (supplemented via human assessment on a subset of contributions), and finally how superposter activity correlates with participation from the rest of the class.

Our results suggest that superposting, which appears to be more an inherent than an extrinsic trait, largely results in

high-value contributions and also correlates positively with activity and contribution quality from fellow students, mitigating concerns about contribution quality and any negative effects of such prolific posting on other forum users. Our study, being based on purely observational data, only allows drawing correlational rather than causal conclusions, and therefore suggests several immediate directions for experimental work, including (i) a further investigation of the possible 'inherentness' of superposting behavior and consequent implications for incentive design, (ii) dependencies between forum contribution patterns and the nature of the course content, and (iii) an experimental design to identify any causality in the correlation we observe between high forum contribution levels and strong course performance, with potential implications for improving educational outcomes and course design.

Our analysis, in addition to yielding insights about superposters and several hypotheses for further study, also yields a positive outlook on existing forums. While current forum designs are undoubtedly imperfect, with repetitive threads and rudimentary search and sort functionality with no interface for finding related questions, the forums do appear to provide reasonable utility. Participants used the forums for productive dialog about the class, ranging from quick questions and answers to sustained conversations, and the forums were mainly "healthy" in the MOOCs in our dataset—students who posted questions tended to get responses, and the students with the largest footprints participated in ways that were mainly positive, content-focused, and appreciated by other students. We note that by and large, these forums managed to thrive despite not adopting complex incentive schemes to encourage contributions, as in some other Q&A forums, leading immediately to the question of how much of forum contribution is driven by intrinsic, rather than extrinsic, motivation (this also relates to the 'inherentness' of superposting behavior that we observed in our analysis). However, it is worth noting that while these early MOOCs have had successful forums despite rudimentary design, maintaining healthy forums consistently over the long term might require adoption of design techniques—such as moderation privilege design or enabling direct acknowledgements of contribution—from existing successful long-running forums, such as StackExchange or Quora.

While forums for collaborative learning can improve student motivation and lead to learning gains, reaping these benefits in MOOCs relies on having healthy, active forums in a world of anonymity and little accountability, where participation is optional and casual lurking is the norm. A future in which a MOOC is run 100 or 1000 times (or simply left running continuously) is not unrealistic, and is one in which students may not have the luxury of instructors or TAs moderating forums. In such a future, a more thorough analysis of superposters— of their motivations, to understand how best to elicit high-quality contribution and sustained engagement from them—and of their abilities, to understand how best to utilize their efforts to create the most effective collaborative learning environments—may well become central to scaling the learning value and functions provided by MOOC forums.

ACKNOWLEDGMENTS
J. Huang is supported by an NSF CI Fellowship and acknowledges the support of Leo Guibas. We also thank Chris Manning for feedback on the paper.

REFERENCES
1. Adamic, L. A., Zhang, J., Bakshy, E., and Ackerman, M. S. Knowledge sharing and yahoo answers: everyone knows something. In *Proceedings of the 17th international conference on World Wide Web*, WWW '08, ACM (New York, NY, USA, 2008), 665–674.

2. Anderson, A., Huttenlocher, D., Kleinberg, J., and Leskovec, J. Discovering value from community activity on focused question answering sites: a case study of stack overflow. In *Proceedings of the 18th ACM SIGKDD international conference on Knowledge discovery and data mining*, KDD '12, ACM (New York, NY, USA, 2012), 850–858.

3. Crouch, C. H., and Mazur, E. Peer instruction: Ten years of experience and results. *American Journal of Physics 69* (2001), 970.

4. De Smet, M., Van Keer, H., and Valcke, M. Blending asynchronous discussion groups and peer tutoring in higher education: An exploratory study of online peer tutoring behaviour. *Computers & Education 50*, 1 (2008), 207–223.

5. De Wever, B., Schellens, T., Valcke, M., and Van Keer, H. Content analysis schemes to analyze transcripts of online asynchronous discussion groups: A review. *Computers & Education 46*, 1 (2006), 6–28.

6. Dennen, V. P. Pedagogical lurking: Student engagement in non-posting discussion behavior. *Computers in Human Behavior 24*, 4 (2008), 1624–1633.

7. Furtado, A., Andrade, N., Oliveira, N., and Brasileiro, F. Contributor profiles, their dynamics, and their importance in five q&a sites. In *Proceedings of the 2013 conference on Computer supported cooperative work*, CSCW '13, ACM (New York, NY, USA, 2013), 1237–1252.

8. Henri, F. Computer conferencing and content analysis. In *Collaborative learning through computer conferencing*. Springer, 1992, 117–136.

9. Ke, F., and Xie, K. Toward deep learning for adult students in online courses. *The Internet and Higher Education 12*, 3 (2009), 136–145.

10. Pal, A., Farzan, R., Konstan, J. A., and Kraut, R. E. Early detection of potential experts in question answering communities. In *User Modeling, Adaption and Personalization*. Springer, 2011, 231–242.

11. Pappano, L. The Year of the MOOC. New York Times, 2012.

12. Rosé, C., Wang, Y.-C., Cui, Y., Arguello, J., Stegmann, K., Weinberger, A., and Fischer, F. Analyzing collaborative learning processes automatically: Exploiting the advances of computational linguistics in computer-supported collaborative learning. *International journal of computer-supported collaborative learning 3*, 3 (2008), 237–271.

13. Rourke, L., Anderson, T., Garrison, D. R., and Archer, W. Assessing social presence in asynchronous text-based computer conferencing. *The Journal of Distance Education/Revue de l'Éducation à Distance 14*, 2 (2007), 50–71.

14. Schellens, T., and Valcke, M. Fostering knowledge construction in university students through asynchronous discussion groups. *Computers & Education 46*, 4 (2006), 349–370.

15. Smith, M. K., Wood, W. B., Adams, W. K., Wieman, C., Knight, J. K., Guild, N., and Su, T. T. Why peer discussion improves student performance on in-class concept questions. *Science 323*, 5910 (2009), 122–124.

16. Soroka, V., and Rafaeli, S. Invisible participants: how cultural capital relates to lurking behavior. In *Proceedings of the 15th international conference on World Wide Web*, ACM (2006), 163–172.

17. Vygotski, L. S. *Mind in society: The development of higher psychological processes*. Harvard university press, 1978.

18. Walton, G. M., Cohen, G. L., Cwir, D., and Spencer, S. J. Mere belonging: The power of social connections. *Journal of personality and social psychology 102*, 3 (2012), 513.

19. Wilkinson, D. M. Strong regularities in online peer production. In *Proceedings of the 9th ACM conference on Electronic commerce*, ACM (2008), 302–309.

20. Wood, D., Bruner, J. S., and Ross, G. The role of tutoring in problem solving*. *Journal of child psychology and psychiatry 17*, 2 (1976), 89–100.

21. Wu, F., Wilkinson, D. M., and Huberman, B. A. Feedback loops of attention in peer production. In *Proceedings of the 2009 International Conference on Computational Science and Engineering - Volume 04*, CSE '09, IEEE Computer Society (Washington, DC, USA, 2009), 409–415.

22. Zhang, J., Ackerman, M. S., and Adamic, L. Expertise networks in online communities: structure and algorithms. In *Proceedings of the 16th international conference on World Wide Web*, ACM (2007), 221–230.

Chatrooms in MOOCs: All Talk and No Action*

Derrick Coetzee
dcoetzee@eecs.berkeley.edu

Armando Fox
fox@cs.berkeley.edu

Marti A. Hearst
hearst@ischool.berkeley.edu

Björn Hartmann
bjoern@berkeley.edu

Computer Science Division and School of Information
University of California, Berkeley, CA 94720, USA

ABSTRACT

We study effects of introducing a real-time chatroom into a massive open online course with several thousand students, supplementing an existing forum. The chatroom was supported by teaching assistants, and generated thousands of lines of discussion by 28% of 681 consenting chat condition participants, mostly on-topic. Despite this, chat activity remained low ($\mu = 8.2$ messages per hour) and we could find no significant effect of chat use on objective or subjective dependent variables such as grades, retention, forum participation, or students' sense of community. Further investigation reveals that only 12% of chat participants have substantive interactions, while the remainder are either passive or have trivial interactions that are unlikely to result in learning.

We also find that pervasive, highly visible chat interfaces are highly effective in encouraging both active and substantive participation in chat. When compared to chat interfaces that are restricted to a single webpage, the pervasive interface exhibits 2.8 times as many users with substantive interactions.

Author Keywords

Massive open online course; MOOC; synchronous; chat; chatroom; retention; participation; experiment.

ACM Classification Keywords

H.5.3. Information Interfaces and Presentation (e.g. HCI): Group and Organization Interfaces; K.3.1. Computers and Education: Computer Uses in Education

INTRODUCTION

Massive open online courses (MOOCs) are online courses which invite large numbers of students (on the order of thousands) to freely enroll. A number of successful large-scale MOOC platforms including edX, Coursera, and Udacity have been developed. In all these platforms, the primary support provided to students who encounter difficulties is through

asynchronous threaded forums, which have been called "an essential ingredient of an effective online course" [18].

However, prior work in small-scale online learning suggests that asynchronous mechanisms are most effective when combined with synchronous mechanisms, such as real-time chatrooms (chat) and private messaging [17, 32, 20], and many online courses have effectively incorporated chat [15, 24]. We investigate the question of whether by introducing a chatroom into a MOOC, these results can be extended to the MOOC setting, where there are an order of magnitude more students.

We expected chat to effectively complement established asynchronous forums in MOOCs via a number of mechanisms: it provides a lower barrier to participation, with only minimal steps needed to send messages; it can provide answers in seconds as opposed to the hours typical of forums [4], enabling back-and-forth interactions; and it can encourage community building and forming of relationships, [23] a function for which forums are less suited. A strong sense of community has been identified as important for avoiding attrition, [28] which is a common problem in MOOCs. [3]

Although surveys described our system as "tremendously helpful" and "useful and constructive," in the end we found no significant effects of chat availability on a range of dependent variables including grades, retention, forum participation and sense of community. To understand the disconnect between positive individual reports and the lack of evidence of aggregate effects, we define and analyze *substantive discussions* in MOOC chatrooms, and demonstrate that the proportion of participants meeting this bar is low, suggesting that most students derive no benefit from the chatroom.

Below we discuss prior related work, introduce our chat design and experimental method, summarize results, discuss implications including limitations of the study and possible ways to improve the chat design, and conclude with recommendations for future work.

RELATED WORK

Researchers have investigated the role of synchronous chat in diverse settings, including work environments (usually with small workgroups) [19, 11, 12]; in education settings [15, 2, 17, 14, 27, 20, 32, 24, 26, 6]; in general open settings on Internet Relay Chat (IRC) [21, 1] and around shared video watching in an entertainment context [33].

Here we focus on three relevant aspects of synchronous chat research: the use of chat in online education, user interfaces for chat, and embedded chat interfaces.

Permission to make digital or hard copies of part or all of this work for personal or classroom use is granted without fee provided that copies are not made or distributed for profit or commercial advantage and that copies bear this notice and the full citation on the first page. Copyrights for third-party components of this work must be honored. For all other uses, contact the owner/author(s). Copyright is held by the author/owner(s).
L@S'14, March 4–5, 2014, Atlanta, Georgia, USA.
ACM 978-1-4503-2669-8/14/03.
http://dx.doi.org/10.1145/2556325.2566242

Chat in Online Education

Chat has been extensively used in online courses, with numerous works in the learning sciences comparing them to other modes of interaction. Asynchronous mechanisms are found to encourage "in-depth, more thoughtful discussion" [2] while synchronous mechanisms are preferable for "providing a greater sense of presence and generating spontaneity" [13]. In some cases synchronous chat could produce superior learning even compared to face-to-face interaction. [24]

Integrating both produced the best results: they "provide mutual enrichment" [17] in that "chat rooms will enhance and clarify the information that is gathered via asynchronous interactions" [32]. One-on-one synchronous discussion has also been found to "support asynchronous discussions in the formation of a community of inquiry" [20].

However, chats also presented a number of practical hurdles in implementation: "getting students online at the same time, difficulty in moderating larger-scale conversations, lack of reflection time for students" [2]. Although we anticipated that getting participation would be less difficult with an order of magnitude more students, in fact this proves to be a central challenge in the MOOC setting as well.

In reviewing research on text-based community interaction in education, Johnson laments that "[c]omprehensive search of the literature did not result in the identification of a single true experiment [...] random assignment of students to one of two conditions in which one of the conditions is synchronous chat and the other condition is asynchronous discussion." [15] Our study is a true experiment, but we compare synchronous chat against a condition integrating both.

Several studies of chats in online classes focused on synchronous chat *sessions*, which were short, structured, scheduled chats led by instructors [26, 32], sometimes featuring a set of explicit rules or conventions [13]. The chat in our study is unstructured, runs continuously, and is supervised primarily by teaching assistants and other students; we avoid implementing explicit policies in order to investigate spontaneous usage. Although both types of chats have advantages, in our MOOC setting a continuously running chat is able to complement the existing forum by providing more rapid responses, and avoids unfairly excluding students based on time zone.

Chat Interfaces

HCI researchers have attempted to overcome known problems of synchronous chat — including overlapping conversations, difficulty following conversation threads, and poor conveyance of tone and emotion — by designing alternative chat interfaces like comics [16], temporal message flows [31], conversation trees [25] or automatically clustered groups [30]. To simplify implementation, we use a web-based chatroom with a simple, conventional interface. Users can learn strategies for repairing misunderstandings [19] and for conveying tone and emotion [10], partly mitigating the issues outlined above.

A number of *persistent chat systems* record chat information in such a way that it can be used later. Among these, our system is most similar to Babble, [8] in that it stores a log of conversations and allows students and staff to access it at any time by scrolling up in the interface. Unlike BackTalk, [9] which relies on user annotations to transform chat data into structured persistent data for review, we simply allow students to use the asynchronous forum to persist discussions in a structured manner as needed.

Embedded Chat Interfaces

One of our primary contributions is the investigation of embedded chat interfaces, placed on the same page next to video lectures, assignments, and quizzes. Cummings and Guerlain investigated embedding chat into a military system in order to enable "secondary tasking" (responding to instructions and queries) using "spare mental capacity" [5]. They found that chat activity generally degraded during demanding primary tasks (e.g. missile retargeting), but that some operators instead fixated on the chat resulting in lower performance on the primary task. Although this raises the possibility that the embedded chat may damage course outcomes by disrupting private study, we failed to identify significant negative effects.

Work on dialogue in collaborative learning systems distinguishes between "parallel tools," which "do not assure any coordination between the discourse and disciplinary representations," and "embedded tools" such as annotation tools which embed comments directly into the artifact under discussion. [7] In this vocabulary, our embedded chat is technically a parallel tool, since the chat is in proximity to but separate from learning artifacts, and chat users can and do discuss unrelated topics. Although properly embedded tools provide greater context for communication, a conventional chatroom is able to preserve chronological order of discussion, avoiding problems in which "the record of discourse is fragmented across the artifact."

METHOD

We conducted a between-subjects field experiment on a seven-week, open-enrollment software engineering course offered on the edX platform ("CS169.1x: Software as a Service" from the University of California, Berkeley).

We explored two different methods of integrating chat functionality into the site: **Chat tab:** A prominent "Chat" tab is added to a list of links at the top of the site. This link takes students to a dedicated page where they can participate in the chat (Figure 1a). **Embedded chat:** In addition to the chat tab, every page of the site, including lectures and assignments, has a panel embedded where the live chat is displayed (see Figure 1c). Both methods display the same shared chatroom, and both methods display chat history automatically upon joining, enabling students to examine past messages. Figure 1 compares the two methods of integration. The chat interface is conventional, with messages at left and a user list at right (see Figure 1b). The field experiment also had a **Control** condition in which students who consented to participate in the study were shown an unmodified edX interface with no chat.

Participants

14381 students were enrolled in the course as of January 2014. Of these, 1344 (9.3%) consented to participate in our

Selected tab

Header

Tabs | Courseware | Discussion | ⋯ Chat

Chat

(a) Chat tab interface, accessible to both the "chat tab" and "embedded chat" groups by clicking the "Chat" button in the upper right. The chat panel is wider and taller than the embedded chat, filling most of the browser window.

```
▼  Status  #cs1691x  x
[no topic set]
[21:33] <koora_> Thank you @burton, I'm going to lunch. I'll let me know if you    @BurtonThomas
have another solution. Thanks in advance                                             @saburo
[22:10] <koora_> Is saasbook-vm-0.9.1.vdi a correct one?                             acer
[22:11] <padma> It is a older vm from a previous iteration...it might be better to   Adam2357
try 1.0.0                                                                            AnneForester456
[22:14] <BurtonThomas> Not finding an easy way to upgrade the old VM to use          arandii
1.9.3 without doing a full install of RVM etc in which case it may be easier to just arondil
use the 1.0.0 VM                                                                     arondil_
[22:32] <koora> @padma, where do I have to download the new one                      avout
[22:33] <koora> @Burton, where to download 1.0.0 VM                                  dctulip
[22:33] <koora> I downloaded it via torrent                                          DarrenM
[22:33] <padma> @koora.. at http://beta.sassbook.info/bookware-vm-instructions       dkme
[22:34] <padma> the website has it as a zip file also                                emensh0
[22:35] <koora> saasbook-vm-1.0.0.vdi.zip yes. thanks                                emensh0_
[22:42] <BurtonThomas> The torrent link wasn't updated to 1.0.0 until shortly after  emensh0_
the course started.                                                                  gekko
```

(b) Web chat interface, based on `qwebirc`. Messages with times are on the left, users are on the right, and messages are entered at bottom. Names have been changed.

Header

Tabs (Navigate between platform features)

Sidebar (Navigate between course modules)

Navigate within course module

Course material (lecture videos / quizzes / homeworks)

Embedded chat

Relevant forum discussions

◀ ▶

(c) Embedded chat interface, accessible only to the "embedded chat" group. A smaller chat panel is presented below the lecture, quiz, or homework the student is currently interacting with. In some cases, the student may need to scroll to see it. If the student is not in the "embedded chat" group, the chat panel is hidden but the page is otherwise identical.

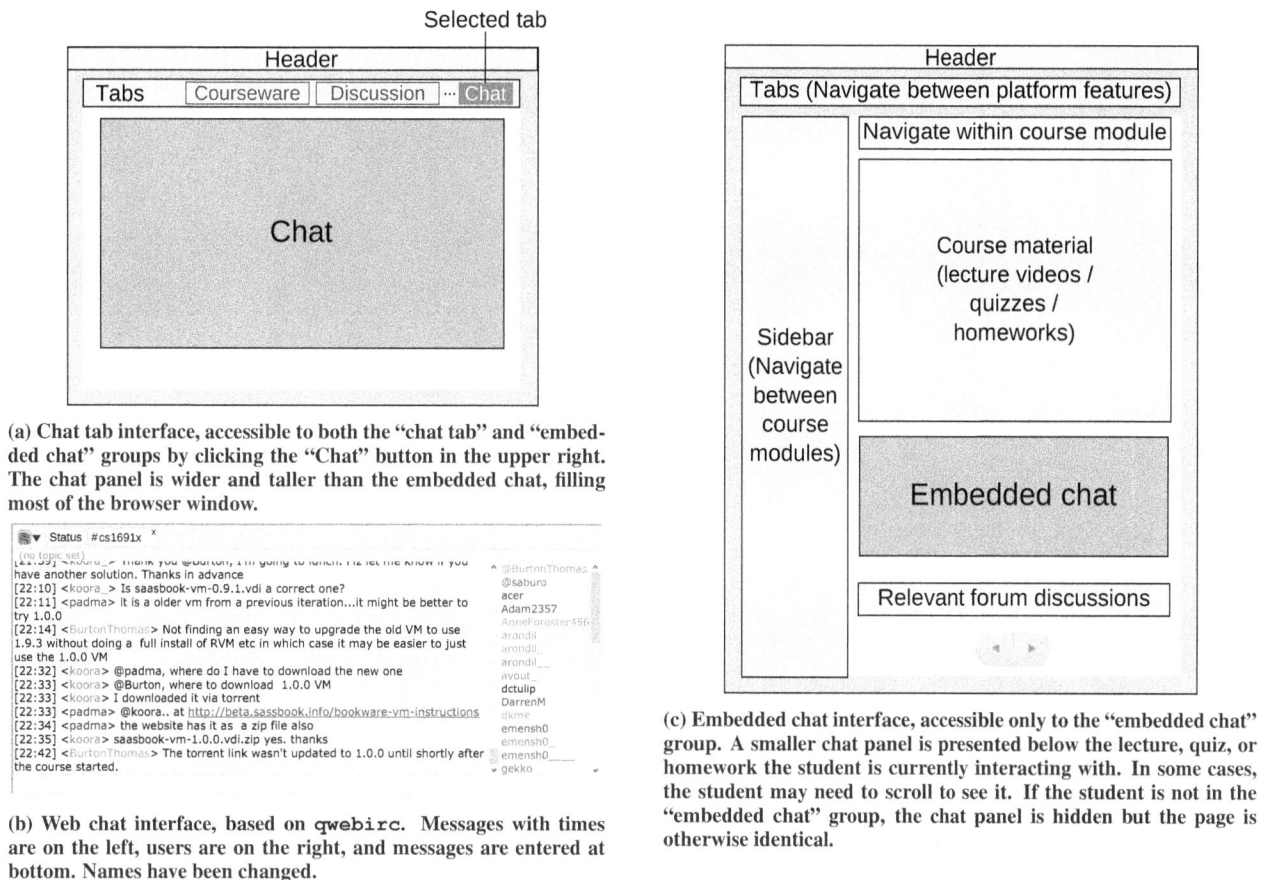

Figure 1: The chat interface is presented in two different ways: on a dedicated page (*top left*) and embedded in a smaller form underneath the course materials (*right*). The detailed layout of the chat interface is also shown, including an actual conversation (*bottom left*).

experiment. 509 students were assigned to the *no chat* condition, 409 to the *chat tab* condition, and 426 to the *embedded chat* condition. The variation in these counts is due to how students were assigned to groups, by applying a hash function to their username. These numbers suggest that a MOOC study seeking a specific number of subjects should target a course with about 10 times as many enrolled students, due to rapid attrition during the earliest phase of the course.

Hypotheses

Our three experimental groups enable two types of controlled comparisons: the comparison of users with and without access to chat ("chat tab" and "embedded chat" groups combined versus control group), and the comparison of users with and without embedded chat integration ("chat tab" versus "embedded chat" group). Direct comparisons cannot be made between the control group and either the chat tab or embedded chat group on their own, because these two groups use the same chatroom and so influence one another's behavior.

Our primary question is to whether access to chat provides an objective advantage in learning as measured by course outcomes such as grades and retention/attrition (the duration the student remains in the course before dropping). A secondary goal is to establish whether chat exhibits the predicted advantages over the asynchronous forum, promoting a sense of

community and lowering the bar to active participation. Finally, we investigate if the higher visibility of the embedded chat as compared to the chat tab design encourages more active participation. We focus on active participation in the chat (sending messages), because we lack any means to measure passive participation (reading messages).

Course Outcomes
It is unclear whether chat should be expected to benefit or hurt outcomes: on one hand it supports thoughtful discussion on course material and sense of community, while on the other it may distract from private study. We anticipate that the advantages will outweigh the disadvantages.

H1 Students in the chat conditions have higher retention than non-chat students.

H2 Students in the chat conditions have higher course grades than non-chat students.

Comparing Chat and Forum Activity
H3 The proportion of active chat users (among users with access to chat) is greater than the proportion of active forum users (among all study participants).

H4 Chat availability may decrease the number of forum posts by diverting students from the forum.

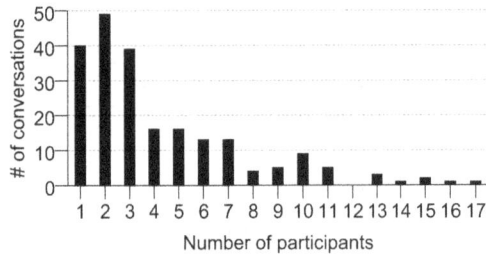

Figure 2: When the chat is divided into contiguous conversations, 59% had at most 3 participants, while the rest had a larger number, up to 17.

Sense of Community

Rovai's Classroom Community Scale [22] is a survey device based on 20 Likert-scale questions, such as "I feel that it is hard to get help when I have a question." It is designed to measure a student's subjective sense of being part of a community in the context of a course. Since interacting with others promotes community, particularly in a social setting, we anticipate that:

H5 Students in the chat conditions have higher sense of community scores than no-chat students.

Differences between Embedded and Chat Tab Activity

We hypothesize that the greater visibility of the embedded chat interface will lead to increased participation.

H6 More students in the *embedded chat* condition will post to the chat than in the *chat tab* condition (because of the visibility of the chat interface).

H7 Students who post in the *embedded chat* condition will post more messages than students in the *chat tab* condition (again, because of visibility.)

RESULTS

Over the duration of the course, 8980 messages were posted. 2169 messages (24.2%) were posted by administrative users (teaching assistants and other course staff); 6811 (75.8%) were posted by students.

Chat conversations

Separating overlapping conversations in chat data is challenging, and there are many techniques for doing so [29]. However, in our case overlapping conversations were rare due to low chat activity ($\mu = 8.2$ messages per hour), permitting trivial segmentation of conversations based on a pause between conversations of at least 1 hour. With this segmentation method, there were 216 conversations with a median length of 11.5 messages and a median of 3 and mode of 2 participants (see Figure 2). Most conversations were short, with 49% of 10 messages or less. In 40 or 18.5% of conversations, a single user spoke and no one responded.

Activity occurred throughout different days of the week, with a notable spike on Wednesdays, and a dip Fridays, GMT (see Figure 3). The spike in activity is likely related to course deadlines: assignments and quizzes were due on Wednesdays

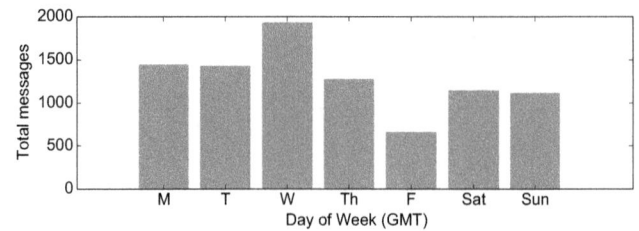

Figure 3: The histogram of messages by day of week shows high activity on Wednesdays, corresponding with course deadlines; and low activity on Fridays.

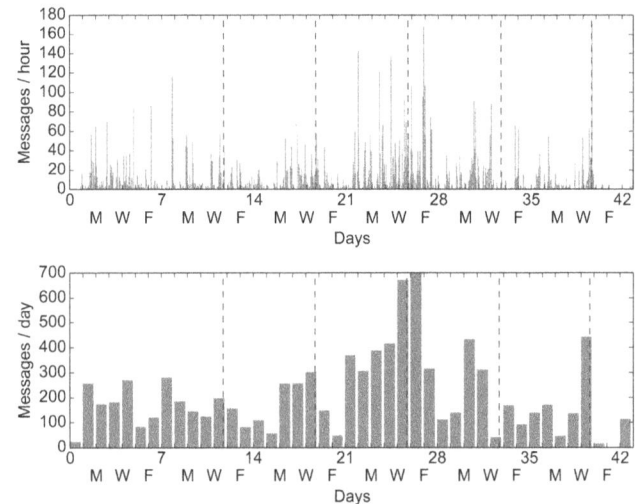

Figure 4: Chats were very irregular and bursty. Top: Histogram of chat messages sent per hour. Bottom: Histogram of chat messages per day. Dashed blue lines indicate homework and quiz due dates.

17:00 GMT, and new lectures and assignments were released on Thursdays at 12:00 GMT.

Chat conversations often appeared in bursts throughout a day — see, e.g., the large spikes in hourly activity on days 7 and 26 in Figure 4, Top. Again, chat activity is sometimes clearly correlated with homework and quiz deadlines on Wednesday afternoons, e.g., on days 18 and 39 (see dashed lines indicating course milestones in Figure 4, Bottom). However, this is not always the case: there is a high volume of chat messages throughout week four; and no spike in messages around the penultimate assignment on day 32.

When aggregating messages by time of day across the entire corpus, the chat exhibits a pattern of decreased activity during night-time hours, GMT (see Figure 5). However, due to wide distribution of students across time zones, these are difficult to interpret. This irregular activity pattern is likely unique to MOOCs that draw students from across the globe and is an important difference to traditional online courses with geographically limited audiences.

Course Outcomes for Chat Users vs. Non-Chat Users

We determined how long each student (excluding staff) remained in the course, based on the time of their last interac-

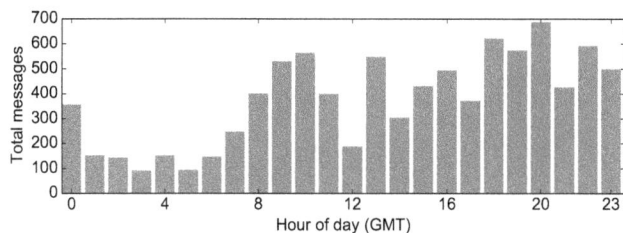

Figure 5: The histogram of cumulative chat messages by hour of day shows multiple periods of high and low activity.

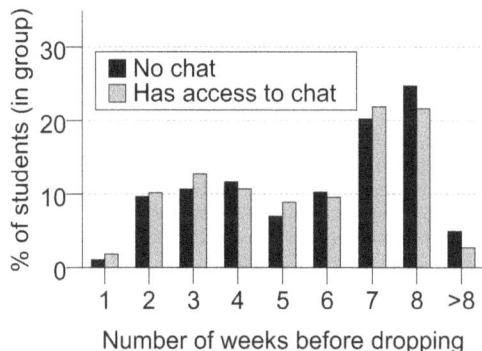

Figure 6: Histogram of how many weeks students with and without access to the chatroom spent before ceasing interaction with the course website. Drop rates for both groups remain similar for both groups at each point in the course. No significant difference between them was found ($p > 0.06$).

Quiz	Median (non-chat)	Median (chat)	Max score	n_1	n_2	D	p
0	12.5	13	13	270	223	0.03	> 0.9
1	9	8	12	188	159	0.09	> 0.5
2	12	12	16	124	119	0.08	> 0.8
3	9	9	11	107	97	0.09	> 0.7

HW	Median (non-chat)	Median (chat)	Max score	n_1	n_2	D	p
0	300	300	300	247	209	0.07	> 0.6
1	400	400	400	190	163	0.06	> 0.8
1.5	400	400	400	137	136	0.04	> 0.9
2	93	93	100	107	99	0.06	> 0.9
3	500	500	500	94	82	0.09	> 0.8
4	500	400	500	70	62	0.12	> 0.7

Figure 7: Comparison of median grades on assignments (HW=homework). Medians were similar for all of them, and the two-sample Kolmogorov-Smirnov test did not identify a significant difference in the grade distribution for any of them.

tion with any element of the course website. We compared retention times of the control group (non-chat) against the "chat tab" and "embedded chat" groups combined (chat students). Medians were 36.8 and 35.9 days, respectively, and no significant difference could be shown (Mann-Whitney U = 137313.0, $n = 418, 694$, $p > 0.06$). This is reflected in Figure 6, which shows similar drop rates of the two groups at each point in the course. Hypothesis H1 is not supported.

Because different students drop at different points, the most appropriate way to compare grades is by comparing grades on particular quizzes or assignments, and restricting the analysis to students who completed the quiz or assignment. We compared score distributions using two-sample Kolmogorov-Smirnov tests, which did not find significant differences for any assignment (see Figure 7). Hence, H2 is not supported.

Comparing Chat and Forum Participation
To determine whether access to chat affects forum use, we compared the proportion of active forum users (who posted at least one post of any type) in the control group (non-chat) and in the "chat tab" and "embedded chat" groups combined (chat students). We found 118 (23%) of the 509 non-chat users posted in the forum, while 201 (24%) of 835 chat users posted in the forum. Fisher's test finds no significant difference ($p > 0.7$). Hypothesis H4 is not supported.

Summing these, 319 (24%) of 1344 study participants posted on the forum, while 191 (23%) of 835 chat users sent at least

one message. Fisher's test finds no significant difference between the proportion of active forum and chat users ($p > 0.6$), and Hypothesis H3 is not supported. This also calls into question the original assumption that the chat will lower the bar to participation compared to the forum. Although the percentages are very similar, it is not the same users using both systems, as shown in Figure 8.

Participation in Chat Tab and Embedded Conditions
More students in the *embedded chat* condition posted to the chat than in the *chat tab* condition: 54 of 399 users (13.5%) in the *chat tab* condition participated actively (posted at least one message), while 128 of 419 users (30.5%) in the *embedded chat* condition were active participants. This difference was statistically significant (Fisher's exact test, $p < 0.0001$). Hypothesis H6 is supported.

As in many online communities, the number of messages sent by users were characterized by a long-tailed distribution in which a few users post very frequently, but most users post very few messages. Of the active participants, students in the *chat tab* condition posted a median of 3.5 messages, while students in the *embedded chat* condition posted a median of 4 messages (see Figure 9). Figure 9, Bottom also shows that users at comparable percentiles tend to post more messages in the *embedded* condition than in the *chat tab* condition for most of the distribution. However, a two-sample Kolmogorov-Smirnov test ($D = 0.18$, $p = 0.18$) showed that the difference in distributions was not statistically significant. Our results are thus inconclusive whether an embedded chat interface leads students who have already decided to participate in the chat to participate more. Hypothesis H7 is thus not supported.

Survey Results
We offered two optional surveys in the course, a pre-survey at the time the chat was deployed, and another survey after day 25 to gather retrospective information about the chat. (Administering surveys at the very end of a MOOC is ineffective

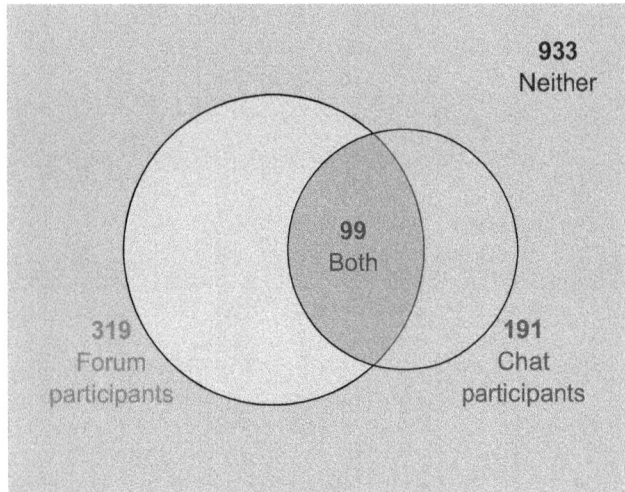

Figure 8: Venn diagram of communication modes (to scale). 319 posted on the forum at least once, 191 participated in the chat at least once, and 99 participated in both. In particular, 92 (48%) of the active chat participants never posted on the forum, including 4 of the most active 20 students in the chat. 933 (69%) of the 1344 study participants used neither mode of communication. This suggests that the chat is able to effectively involve some students who would not otherwise interact with others, but most students still participate only passively. Note that the forum was also used by students not participating in the study; they are excluded above.

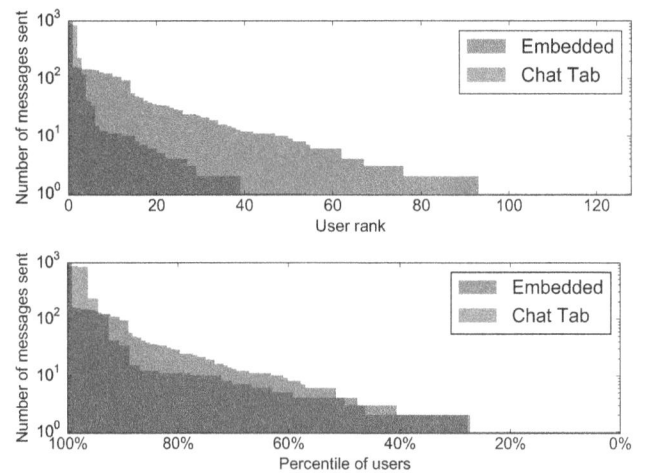

Figure 9: Rank-order plot of messages sent by users in the chat tab and embedded conditions. Top: Absolute user ranks shows higher participation in the embedded condition. Bottom: Percentile plot shows higher participation of the middle of the distribution for the embedded condition; however, this difference is not statistically significant.

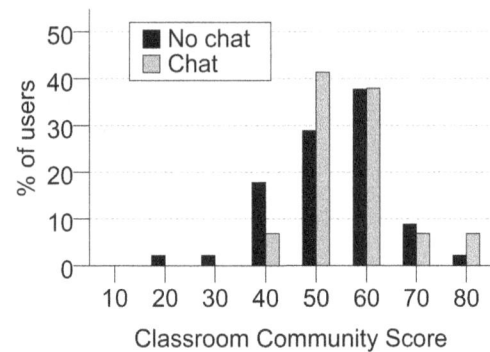

Figure 10: Comparison of sense of community scores for non-chat (control group) and chat (other groups) students. Medians were near-identical (50 and 51) and no significant difference was found ($p > 0.2$).

as most students will have dropped the course by then [4].) The pre-survey was given to all students in the course and had 1486 responses, while the later survey was offered to all subjects in the chat experiment including the control group and had 112 responses. The latter represents 48 (9.2%) of 519 students in *no chat*, 32 (7.8%) of 409 students in *chat tab*, and 32 (7.5%) of 426 students in *embedded chat*.

In the pre-survey, despite the fact that the course was targeted at software developers, we found that 45% of students had no prior experience with chatrooms, and only 6% used them frequently. This inexperience, combined with our system's lack of training or tutorials, may be another factor underlying low participation.

We applied Rovai's Classroom Community Scale [22] to measure the subjective sense of community experienced by all study groups. The median Rovai sense of community scores for the no-chat and chat groups were 50 and 51, respectively, and no significant difference could be found (Mann-Whitney U=1212.5, $n = 45, 58$, $p > 0.2$). Hypothesis H5 is not supported. Figure 10 compares the distributions.

Passive participation in the chat was reported more often in the embedded condition (81% of students read the chat at some point) than in the chat tab condition (64%), but this difference is not significant (Fisher's exact test, $p > 0.2$). In the embedded chat condition, all surveyed students were aware of the chat, whereas only 86% were aware of it in the chat tab condition, and this difference was marginally significant ($p < 0.05$). On the other hand, in the embedded chat group, 48% found the embedded chat "distracting or annoying."

Most students (16 out of the 18 students who answered the question) reported that TAs and students were equally helpful in the chat; this is consistent with the data, showing a mixture of students and TAs among the most prolific chatters. "Answering specific questions about course content" was the most common purpose for which the chatroom was used (20 of 25 who reported using the chatroom reported using it for this purpose), and among the 14 respondents who responded to others, an altruistic desire to help others was the most reported reason (13 of 14). 72% reported they got a useful response from others either "sometimes" or more often.

Anecdotally, a number of students surveyed reported strongly positive experiences with the chatroom: "I find the chat to be tremendously helpful in the clarification of homework problems. [...] Due to my schedule, I was often down to the wire for several submissions, and a chatroom allowed for much faster responses than something like an emailed question." "It was great to get instant feedback, quick answers, and encouragement."

Students reported using the chatroom and forum in combination: "Sometimes, I post the discussion & give the link in chat room." Multiple students also reported positive passive experiences: "Many useful and constructive real time conversations on topics even though I wasn't actively participating." "What other people ask in the chat room is also useful."

Some students felt the chat was unhelpful for them personally: "I feel that most of the students are below my experience in IT, so did not feel any need to chat." "[M]ost of the comments in the chatrooms related to future course [material] as opposed to what I was working on." Others struggled with its unstructured nature, preferring the more structured forum: "[T]he whole chatting stuff looks too unstructured." "I found course forum more helpful for me, mainly because information there has some structure applied."

Classifying Users by Level of Interaction

The above results present a paradox: the chat is shown to engage a number of users who otherwise have limited participation, and produces great anecdotal experiences, yet we can detect no effect of chat availability on any objective dependent variables, including grades, retention, forum participation, and subjective sense of community.

One explanation for this is that benefits of the chat accrue only to a relatively small number of active users. When we compare subjects who sent at least one message in chat (active in chat) to subjects who did not, we find that they remained in the course a median of 7.2 days longer (45.1 vs. 37.9), a significant difference (Mann-Whitney U = 80795.0, $n = 182, 1084$, $p < 0.0001$). This is weak evidence, since active users are self-selected and more dedicated students are more likely to participate in chat, but it suggests a possible explanation.

Even among active users, many had limited interaction with the chat. To quantify this, each student was manually classified into one of the following mutually exclusive groups:

- **Tester**: Sent only test messages; no meaningful content.

- **Greeter**: Sent only messages containing greetings.

- **Socializer**: Only discussed off-topic or irrelevant material.

- **No response**: Asked a question but received no response.

- **No acknowledge**: Asked a question and received a response but showed no sign of noticing the response.

- **Acknowledged**: Asked a question, received a response, and clearly acknowledged the response.

- **Answerer**: Student is not in **Acknowledged** category, but did respond to questions of others.

Davidson-Shivers et al. similarly coded individual chat messages as substantive or non-substantive according to a set of nine categories, some of which align with ours (e.g. Responding is related to our Answerer role, Chatting is related to our Socializer role, and Uncodable is related to our Tester role) [6]; however, we categorize users rather than individual messages. For example, a student who both greets and

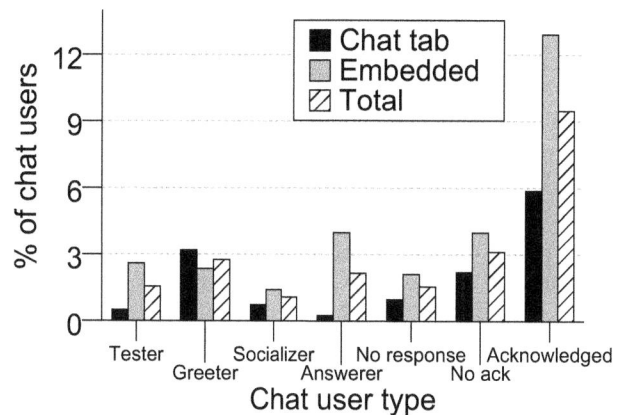

Figure 11: Comparison of sizes of 7 types of chat participants (see text). Only the Acknowledged and possibly the Answerer types represent substantive participation, which here comprise at most 12% of the chat students as a whole. The embedded chat condition has a strong advantage over the chat tab condition in the substantive categories ($p < 0.001$ for Acknowledged and Answerer). The remaining 78% of chat users not shown had no participation in the chat whatsoever.

responds to questions would be in the **Answerer** category; a student who both acknowledges responses to questions and answers questions would be in the **Acknowledged** category.

The **Acknowledged** group above is meant to capture our understanding of a minimum bar for substantive chat usage that can produce learning. Although students in the **No acknowledge** category receive responses, we assume they did not notice them; this category features a median time of almost 7 minutes between question and response, suggesting that questioners may have diverted attention to other tasks before their response arrives. Figure 11 summarizes the size of these categories over our user base.

Although **Acknowledged** is the largest category, representing 41% of all active chat users, it is still only 9.5% of all students with access to chat, and even including **Answerer** only raises that to 12%. When we compare retention of students in these two categories to active chat participants in the other categories, we find a median difference of 4.7 days (47.3 vs. 42.5 days), a significant difference (Mann-Whitney U = 3254.0, $n = 98, 84$, $p < 0.01$). When we compare retention of students in these two categories to retention of all other subjects, the median difference is 9.2 days (47.3 vs 38.1 days), and this is significant (Mann-Whitney U = 41285, $n = 98, 1168$, $p < 0.0001$). Although again these are weak results due to self-selection, higher retention is clearly correlated with more substantive participation.

With 88% of chat students failing to engage in substantive participation, even strong improvements by the few users who do engage in it could not substantially shift the outcomes of the group as a whole. Larger sample sizes would be required to reliably detect such a small change.

We found earlier that the embedded chat group is about twice as active as the chat tab group but Figure 11 shows an even stronger advantage in user categories with substantive interactions (**Acknowledged** and **Answerer**). Fisher's test shows that the embedded chat group is significantly higher in both ($p < 0.001$ for both). Overall, about 17% of embedded chat users had substantive interactions compared to only 6% of chat tab users, or 2.8 times as many.

In some circles chatrooms are controversial because they are "viewed as recreational, as opposed to educational" [15]. In this context, our data repudiates this idea, with users focused on off-topic discussion being the rarest of all types. This may be explained by multiple factors, including continual monitoring by TAs, demographics of the course, and so on.

DISCUSSION

Recommendations for instructors
Based on our findings, we can make three specific recommendations to instructors interested in using chat in MOOCs:

- **Should I use chat?** Chat is safe to use; there is no evidence that it degrades learning or forum participation. Strong praise from surveyed students, as well as evidence that it can engage some students who don't participate in the forum, suggests that it may be worthwhile, but the operating cost must be kept low to justify a system that benefits only a small number of students.

- **How should chat be integrated into my course website?** Pervasive, highly-visible interfaces are the best choice for maximizing substantive participation in chat. Although some students found them annoying, we found no evidence that they adversely impact learning.

- **How do I ensure chats remain on-topic?** In our setting, volunteer teaching assistants moderated the chatroom on an *ad hoc* basis. This was enough to ensure that most active students engaged in substantive, on-topic conversations.

Limitations due to low chat activity
The low proportion of substantive users of chat makes it unexpectedly difficult to reach critical mass for an effective chatroom, even in relatively large courses. In our study, the consent process favored students with a pre-existing interest in chatrooms, and yet only 12% of users had substantive interactions; in a setting without a consent hurdle, this percentage may drop even further. Users with continued engagement over time were even rarer. The result was a system that was anecdotally valuable for a few students, yet unused by most.

One natural strategy is to attempt to extend the positive experience that some chat participants anecdotally received to a larger student population by increasing the number of students with substantive conversations in chat. Although we can't predict whether a such a higher-activity chat would objectively benefit learning outcomes, it forms a useful starting place for refining our design. Following are a few strategies that might be used to increase activity:

- Increasing the total number of students. Linear extrapolation from our results suggests that with 4600 students we might see about one message per minute, resulting in more regular/constant chat activity.

- Increasing the number of students using chat, perhaps with more aggressive UI cues. Indeed, 15% of users with the chat tab interface were unaware of the chat's existence, a problem easily corrected with a more pervasive interface. Some survey respondents requested omnipresent interfaces such as chat overlays permanently pinned in the corner of every page with notifications, as used today on Facebook and Google+. However, an overly aggressive UI can also become more distracting and annoying for students.

- Restricting chat availability to certain hours to increase chat density. However, this limits chat's usefulness for getting timely answers to urgent questions, and may unfairly disadvantage students in certain time zones.

- Increasing the percentage of users with substantive interaction. While Figure 11 suggests that participation can be improved by adding sufficient helpers to address all student concerns, the same figure suggests that we can expect a gain of at most 10 percentage points relative to the conditions in this experiment. Most of the nonparticipation occurs among the 78% of chat users who never actively interact with the chat at all.

- Addressing conditions reported in survey that caused some students not to participate in chat, such as being too busy with other coursework or being too far behind to contribute to or benefit from technical chat conversations. Separate chatrooms for different parts of the course might mitigate this problem.

- Addressing cultural or personal factors that may inhibit students from using chat. For example, some may be shy or feel reluctant to ask questions or offer responses that might make them seem ignorant; some may be unwilling to chat under their edX username, which we enforced; some may be uncomfortable due to poor command of English. Further investigations into and designs to accommodate such traits could be valuable.

While there are many strategies to improve activity, an open question is whether chat can deliver the hypothesized benefits of synchronous interaction. While we failed to find evidence of these benefits, it would be hasty to claim that they do not exist. The combination of relatively small sample sizes, low participation, and assessments with poor discrimination (see next section) implies that even a strong benefit among active chat participants could have evaded detection. Further work with larger student populations, more aggressive interfaces, and more challenging assessments may be able to uncover benefits that we could not.

Data limitations
In addition to the small percentage of subjects affected by the chat, other factors limit our ability to detect differences between study groups. The assessments used in the course under study had high median scores, often perfect scores, implying that they're not challenging enough to distinguish students with an average understanding of the topic from highly competent ones. This is partly because the course under study permitted resubmissions, and currently only data for the final

submission is available. Because the students who were most active in chat were often already highly motivated, improvements in their understanding may not be measurable through these assessments.

Due to incomplete information about the focus of the student's attention, we could not reliably determine when the user was reading the chat interface. This is particularly true for the embedded chat group, who always had the chat open whenever visiting the course site, but rarely looked at it. Although comments in the surveys suggest users may have benefitted from passive participation, this cannot be measured or tested. Similarly, we could not determine whether or not students read or acted upon a response unless they explicitly acknowledged it. To some extent this may be addressed with additional software support (e.g. tracking control focus and browser window position), but we still cannot eliminate the possibility that the student's attention is directed to another part of the screen.

Complementary and competitive technologies
During the course, 340 web links were posted to the chat, both to respond to questions and to help coordinate further interaction. Threads on the course forum were linked 24 times. The *pastebin* website was used to share large code samples on 11 occasions. The course involved both live video tutorials and pair programming exercises with screensharing, and both teaching assistants and students used the chatroom to recruit for these activities. Linking relevant web resources to answer questions was also common. These resources all played a complementary role to the chat, providing essential features that the chat is not intended to, without subsuming its function entirely.

On the other hand, some discussions that might have been useful in the chat were moved out of the chat because of its limited functionality. One discussion was moved to Google Hangouts in order to use screensharing; another was moved to Skype chat because of better Unicode support. When discussions leave the chat, the chatroom loses active users, passive users can no longer benefit from the discussion, and course staff cannot record and monitor them. This is an instance of a more general problem for MOOC research: it's difficult to capture all the data associated with student behavior or engagement in a MOOC.

CONCLUSION AND FUTURE WORK
In this work, we introduced a chatroom into a MOOC. Although we found no significant effect on dependent variables such as grades, retention, forum participation, and sense of community, this is unsurprising given that only 12% of students with access to chat engaged in substantive chat interactions. We found that the use of pervasive, highly visible interfaces increased substantive interactions by 2.8 times as compared to interfaces contained to a single page.

In future work, an important direction is exploring design changes that both increase the number of observers in the chat, and increase the percentage of users with substantive interactions. These include: the use of more pervasive interfaces which are always on-screen in a consistent location, the

use of notification features to indicate when a user is mentioned or when the chat is most useful to them, the ability to chat under a different pseudonym, restricting chats to particular time periods, and so on.

Another possibility is tighter integration of the chat and forum: currently chat users link to relevant forum threads that already exist, but knowledge is rarely transferred in the other direction, from the chat to the forum. Questions which cannot be answered in a timely manner could be automatically transferred to the forum so that they aren't displaced by new messages and lost. Conversely, new or outstanding messages on the forum could announce themselves on the chat in order to decrease forum response time.

Finally, just as reputation systems help in forums to decrease response time, identify reliable actors, and enforce community norms, a similar system could serve the same purpose in a chatroom. By providing points in exchange for helpful questions and responses, such a system could effectively "bootstrap" chat communities which have just been created for a course and have no established community norms to draw upon.

ACKNOWLEDGMENTS
We thank the World TAs of CS169.1x for coordinating support of students in the chatrooms. This work was partially funded by the National Science Foundation under award IIS-1149799 and the National Endowment for the Humanities under grant HK-50011.

REFERENCES
1. Bechar-Israeli, H. From <Bonehead> to <cLoNehEAd>: Nicknames, Play and Identity on Internet Relay Chat. *Journal of Computer-Mediated Communication 1*, 2 (1995), 00.

2. Branon, R., and Essex, C. Synchronous and asynchronous communication tools in distance education. *TechTrends 45*, 1 (2001), 36–36.

3. Clow, D. MOOCs and the funnel of participation. In *LAK '13: 3rd International Conference on Learning Analytics & Knowledge* (2013).

4. Coetzee, D., Fox, A., Hearst, M. A., and Hartmann, B. Should your MOOC forum use a reputation system? In *Proceedings of the 2014 Conference on Computer-Supported Cooperative Work*, ACM (New York, NY, USA, 2014).

5. Cummings, M., and Guerlain, S. Using a chat interface as an embedded secondary tasking tool. *Human performance, situation awareness and automation: Current research and trends. HPSAA II 1* (2004), 240–248.

6. Davidson-Shivers, G. V., Muilenburg, L. Y., and Tanner, E. J. How do students participate in synchronous and asynchronous online discussions? *J. EDUCATIONAL COMPUTING RESEARCH 25*, 4 (2001), 351–366.

7. Dimitracopoulou, A. Designing collaborative learning systems: current trends & future research agenda. In

Proceedings of the 2005 conference on Computer support for collaborative learning: learning 2005: the next 10 years!, CSCL '05, International Society of the Learning Sciences (2005), 115–124.

8. Erickson, T., Smith, D. N., Kellogg, W. A., Laff, M., Richards, J. T., and Bradner, E. Socially translucent systems: social proxies, persistent conversation, and the design of "babble". In *Proceedings of the SIGCHI conference on Human Factors in Computing Systems*, CHI '99, ACM (New York, NY, USA, 1999), 72–79.

9. Fono, D., and Baecker, R. Structuring and supporting persistent chat conversations. In *Proceedings of the 2006 20th anniversary conference on Computer supported cooperative work*, CSCW '06, ACM (New York, NY, USA, 2006), 455–458.

10. Gajadhar, J., and Green, J. An analysis of nonverbal communication in an online chat group. *The Open Polytechnic of New Zealand, Working Paper 23* (Mar. 2003).

11. Handel, M., and Herbsleb, J. D. What is chat doing in the workplace? In *Proceedings of the 2002 ACM conference on Computer supported cooperative work*, CSCW '02, ACM (New York, NY, USA, 2002), 110.

12. Herbsleb, J. D., Atkins, D. L., Boyer, D. G., Handel, M., and Finholt, T. A. Introducing instant messaging and chat in the workplace. In *Proceedings of the SIGCHI Conference on Human Factors in Computing Systems*, CHI '02, ACM (New York, NY, USA, 2002), 171178.

13. Hines, R. A., and Pearl, C. E. Increasing interaction in web-based instruction: Using synchronous chats and asynchronus discussions. *Rural Special Education Quarterly 23*, 2 (Mar. 2004), 33.

14. Ingram, A. L., Hathorn, L. G., and Evans, A. Beyond chat on the internet. *Computers & Education 35*, 1 (2000), 21 – 35.

15. Johnson, G. Synchronous and asynchronous text-based CMC in educational contexts: A review of recent research. *TechTrends 50*, 4 (2006), 46–53.

16. Kurlander, D., Skelly, T., and Salesin, D. Comic chat. In *Proceedings of the 23rd annual conference on Computer graphics and interactive techniques*, SIGGRAPH '96, ACM (New York, NY, USA, 1996), 225236.

17. Ligorio, M. B. Integrating communication formats: synchronous versus asynchronous and text-based versus visual. *Computers & Education 37*, 2 (2001), 103 – 125.

18. Mak, S., Williams, R., and Mackness, J. Blogs and forums as communication and learning tools in a MOOC. In *International Conference on Networked Learning 2010*. 275–285.

19. O'Neill, J., and Martin, D. Text chat in action. In *Proceedings of the 2003 international ACM SIGGROUP conference on Supporting group work*, GROUP '03, ACM (New York, NY, USA, 2003), 4049.

20. Oztok, M., Zingaro, D., Brett, C., and Hewitt, J. Exploring asynchronous and synchronous tool use in online courses. *Computers & Education 60*, 1 (2013), 87 – 94.

21. Rintel, E. S., and Pittam, J. Strangers in a strange land interaction management on internet relay chat. *Human Communication Research 23*, 4 (1997), 507534.

22. Rovai, A. Development of an instrument to measure classroom community. *The Internet and Higher Education 5*, 3 (FebMar 2002), 197–211.

23. Rovai, A. P. Building classroom community at a distance: A case study. *Educational Technology Research and Development 49*, 4 (2001), 33–48.

24. Schoenfeld-Tacher, R., Mcconnell, S., and Graham, M. Do No HarmA Comparison of the Effects of On-Line vs. Traditional Delivery Media on a Science Course. *Journal of Science Education and Technology 10*, 3 (2001), 257–265.

25. Smith, M., Cadiz, J. J., and Burkhalter, B. Conversation trees and threaded chats. In *Proceedings of the 2000 ACM conference on Computer supported cooperative work*, CSCW '00, ACM (New York, NY, USA, 2000), 97–105.

26. Spencer, D. H., and Hiltz, S. A field study of use of synchronous chat in online courses. In *System Sciences, 2003. Proceedings of the 36th Annual Hawaii International Conference on* (2003), 10 pp.–.

27. Stein, D. S., Wanstreet, C. E., Glazer, H. R., Engle, C. L., Harris, R. A., Johnston, S. M., Simons, M. R., and Trinko, L. A. Creating shared understanding through chats in a community of inquiry. *The Internet and Higher Education 10*, 2 (2007), 103 – 115.

28. Tinto, V. *Leaving College: Rethinking the Causes and Cures of Student Attrition*. University of Chicago Press, 1993.

29. Uthus, D. C., and Aha, D. W. Multiparticipant chat analysis: A survey. *Artificial Intelligence 199200*, 0 (2013), 106 – 121.

30. Vigas, F. B., and Donath, J. S. Chat circles. In *Proceedings of the SIGCHI conference on Human Factors in Computing Systems*, CHI '99, ACM (New York, NY, USA, 1999), 916.

31. Vronay, D., Smith, M., and Drucker, S. Alternative interfaces for chat. In *Proceedings of the 12th annual ACM symposium on User interface software and technology*, UIST '99, ACM (New York, NY, USA, 1999), 1926.

32. Wang, A., and Newlin, M. Online Lectures: Benefits for the virtual classroom. *T.H.E. Journal 29*, 1 (2001), 17–24.

33. Weisz, J. D., Kiesler, S., Zhang, H., Ren, Y., Kraut, R. E., and Konstan, J. A. Watching together: integrating text chat with video. In *Proceedings of the SIGCHI Conference on Human Factors in Computing Systems*, CHI '07, ACM (New York, NY, USA, 2007), 877886.

Panel: Online Learning Platforms and Data Science

Mehran Sahami (moderator)
Stanford University

Jace Kohlmeier
Khan Academy

Peter Norvig
Google

Andreas Paepcke
Stanford University

Amin Saberi
NovoEd

Categories and Subject Descriptors

K.3.2 [**Computers and Education**]: Computer Science Education

Keywords

Online Learning, MOOCs, Massive Open Online Courses

SUMMARY

The software platforms that mediate online learning experiences are the common ground where learning science and computer science intersect. This panel will discuss the affordances of current online learning platforms and lessons learned in using them with students. The goal of the panel is to help learning scientists and computer scientists understand each others' needs and how they might be effectively addressed in these platforms. The panelists, who have experience creating/using these platforms and interacting with learning scientists, will discuss how current platforms for learning at scale might evolve to better serve the community.

L@S 2014, March 4–5, 2014, Atlanta, Georgia, USA.
ACM 978-1-4503-2669-8/14/03.
http://dx.doi.org/10.1145/2556325.2579110

ForumDash: Analyzing Online Discussion Forums

Jacquelin Speck, Eugene Gualtieri, Gaurav Naik, Thach Nguyen, Kevin Cheung, Larry Alexander, and David Fenske

Applied Informatics Group, College of Computing & Informatics at Drexel University

3141 Chestnut Street, Philadelphia, PA 19104

{jspeck, genegualtieri, gn, thn36, kc426, lda26,fenske}@drexel.edu

ABSTRACT

Since introducing Internet-based distance education programs in 1996, Drexel University has gained recognition as an online education leader. Remaining at the vanguard means finding innovative, automated solutions to determine which students are contributing to thoughtful discussion, helping faculty engage with online students more efficiently, and spending less time managing ever more complex Learning Management Systems (LMS). We introduce ForumDash, a BBLearn plugin for the Blackboard LMS[1], designed to enhance online learning. Through its three visualization tools, ForumDash shows instructors which students are contributing, struggling, or distracted, thereby helping instructors target their efforts, save time managing online courses, and scale course tools up to the level of Massive Open Online Courses (MOOCs). ForumDash also provides students with performance feedback, showing them whether their participation levels are satisfactory. Initial testing with two Drexel University Online courses produced positive feedback, and larger scale testing is in progress.

VISUALIZATION TOOLS

The three ForumDash visualization tools extract meaning from Blackboard discussion board conversations and create intuitive representations of student interactions. Forum-Dash's Reply Network Visualization, shown in Figure 1, reveals which students generate the most discussion, thereby helping instructors identify Thought-Leaders within a course [6]. It graphically depicts "Who's Talking to Whom," conversational replies between students, as a series of directional arrows between color blocks. Each unique color block represents an author, and each arrow represents a post. Instructors may toggle the display to show either replies to, or replies from, each student.

The Topic Cluster Visualization, shown in Figure 2, reveals clusters of discussion topics by using Latent Semantic Analysis (LSA) and G-Means Clustering [1, 2]. It is a galaxy-style

[1] http://www.blackboard.com/Platforms/Learn/overview.aspx

L@S'14, March 4–5, 2014, Atlanta, Georgia, USA.
ACM 978-1-4503-2669-8/14/03.
http://dx.doi.org/10.1145/2556325.2567848

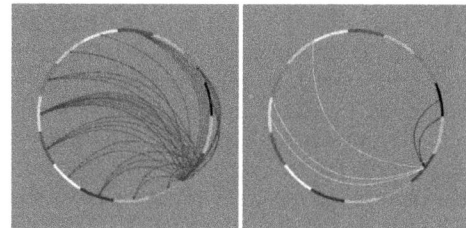

Figure 1. Reply Visualization showing replies from (left) and to (right) the same student. This student creates many posts but receives few replies, and therefore is likely not a Thought Leader.

scatter plot based on visualizations designed by Wise, et. al. [7]. Each point represents a single discussion board post and is color-coded to identify its author, and representative key terms are shown for each cluster.

The Topic Cluster Visualization was developed with an eye towards offering MOOCs in the future, and originally tested using a dataset from Udacity[2], a free online MOOC provider. When courses include hundreds or thousands of students, it can be very time consuming for professors to determine popular discussion topics. A high-level view of discussion topics can help professors prioritize which posts to read, or generate blanket replies to repeat questions.

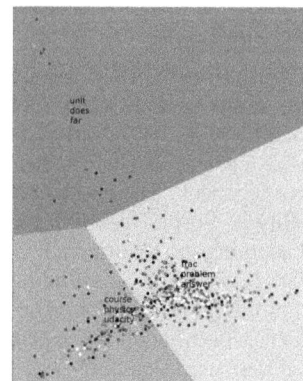

Figure 2. Topic Cluster visualization for a physics course on www.udacity.com. The display shows three discussion topics: homework problems and answers (lower right), questions about specific syllabus units (upper), and other physics MOOCs offered on www.udacity.com (lower left).

The Contribution Score Visualization, shown in Figure 3, summarizes students' participation. Scores assigned to each student are based on a weighted sum of several factors, with

[2] https://www.udacity.com

weights chosen by instructors. For instructors, the tool identifies which students are contributing, struggling, or not staying on topic. The Contribution Score Visualization can also be seen by students, allowing them to monitor how much they are contributing compared to their peers (whose scores can be shown anonymously if instructors prefer) and encouraging more participation. Factors for scoring include the number of posts written and replies generated, and the average semantic relevance and syntactic complexity of posts. Average semantic relevance is assessed using the Wu-Palmer Similarity of word senses within the WordNet[3] ontology [8, 5]. We access the WordNet database using the Python Natural Language Toolkit (NLTK) [3]. Similarity is assessed between students' replies and their corresponding root posts in discussion board conversations, as well as to the corresponding topic post of the thread. Average syntactic complexity is assessed using the L2 Analyzer[4] [4]. Overall scores are displayed on a circular target-style plot, with one color-coded point per student. Points' angles are assigned randomly, and their radii correspond to scores. Points closest to the center indicate higher scores, and points far from the center represent students peripheral to the discussion.

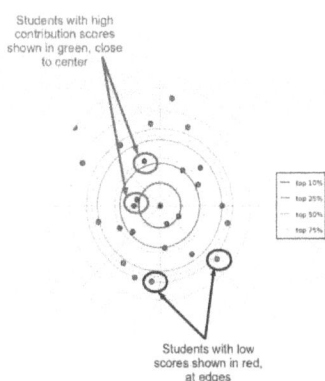

Figure 3. Contribution Grader display

ALPHA TESTING FEEDBACK

Initial testing of ForumDash's Alpha release with two Drexel University online courses, INFO-521 ("Information Users and Services") and INFO-526 ("Information, Innovation, and Technology in Advanced Nursing Practice"), has produced positive instructor feedback. The instructor of INFO-521 observed applicability of ForumDash for future MOOC offerings, as well as adapting the learning environment structure. Speaking specifically about the Contribution Score Visualization, the instructor of INFO-526 reported good correlation between ForumDash's Contribution Score and observed student activity from week to week, and believed that the tool provided good incentives for students to participate more thoroughly in online discussions:

> "I think the tool surfaces issues that may have been latent and provide an incentive and mechanism for both instructor and student to examine and exploit the various possibilities inherent in the discussion board."

[3] http://wordnet.princeton.edu/
[4] http://www.personal.psu.edu/faculty/x/x/xxl13/downloads/l2sca.html

ONGOING WORK

Ongoing work includes conducting larger scale testing of the existing prototypes to improve the algorithms, particularly calculation of the contribution score. We also hope to incorporate affect detection to identify posts that express confusion, and illuminate emerging patterns within discussion board conversations. For example, do students begin discussing topics in more depth over time, indicating increased understanding of the topics? ForumDash development has steadily progressed toward its goal of organizing and interpreting discussion board conversations, helping students improve their own learning, and helping instructors address students' needs. The tools provide students with feedback on how much they are contributing, provide instructors with time-saving overviews of students' conversations, and expand the possibilities of online learning.

Author Keywords

Learning Management Systems; Information Visualization; Online Learning

ACM Classification Keywords

H.5.3. Information Interfaces and Presentation (e.g. HCI): Group and Organization Interfaces: web-based interaction; H.3.3. Information Storage and Retrieval: Information Search and Retrieval: Information Filtering; I.2.7 Computing Methodologies: Artificial Intelligence: Natural Language Processing

REFERENCES

1. Deerwester, S., Thomas, S., Furnas, G., Laundauer, T., and Harshman, R. Indexing by latent semantic analysis. *Journal of the American Society for Information Science 41* (1990).

2. Hamerly, G., and Elkan, C. Learning the k in k-means. *Neural Information Processing Systems 17* (2003).

3. Loper, E., and Bird, S. Nltk: The natural language toolkit. In *Proceedings of the ACL Workshop on Effective Tools and Methodologies for Teaching Natural Language Processing and Computational Linguistics*, Philadelphia: Association for Computational Lingusitics (2002).

4. Lu, X. Automatic analysis of syntactic complexity in second language writing. *International Journal of Corpus Linguistics 15*, 4 (2010), 474–496.

5. Miller, G. Wordnet: A lexical database for english. *Communications of the ACM 38*, 11 (1995), 39–41.

6. Waters, J. Thought-leaders in asynchronous online learning environments. *Journal of Asynchronous Learning Networks 16* (2012).

7. Wise, J., Thomas, J., Pennock, K., Lantrip, D., Pottier, M., Schur, A., and Crow, V. Visualizing the non-visual: Spatial analysis and interaction with information from text documents. In *Proceedings on Information Visualization (IEEE)* (1995), 51–58.

8. Wu, Z., and Palmer, M. Verb ssemantic and lexical selection. In *Proceedings of the 32nd Annual Meeting of the Associations for Computational Linguistics* (1994), 133–138.

OCTAL: Online Course Tool for Adaptive Learning

Daniel Armendariz   Zachary MacHardy   Daniel D. Garcia

{danallan, zmmachar, ddgarcia}@cs.berkeley.edu

EECS Department, University of California - Berkeley, Berkeley CA 94720

ABSTRACT

The Online Course Tool for Adaptive Learning (OCTAL) is an adaptive exercise system that customizes the progression of question topics to each student. By creating a concept dependency graph of topics in a course and modeling a student's knowledge state, the tool presents questions that test knowledge within a student's zone of proximal development. We intend OCTAL to be a formative assessment tool that is not tied to any specific course by providing language-agnostic questions on computer science concepts. While the tool will be generalizable for many courses, our first prototype includes a concept map and question set for UC Berkeley's introductory computer science course, CS10: The Beauty and Joy of Computing. Using the tool, we will launch an experiment in the spring to investigate metacognitive improvements in the identification of knowledge gaps by presenting online course material in a nonlinear fashion.

Author Keywords

Adaptive assessment; Non-linear courses; Concept map; Student modeling

ACM Classification Keywords

K.3.1 Computer Uses in Education: Computer-assisted instruction (CAI); K.3.2 Computer and Information Science Education: Computer science education

INTRODUCTION

With the development and proliferation of Massively Open Online Courses (MOOCs), it has become apparent that individual learning experiences must scale apace. Given the demonstrated efficacy of one-on-one tutoring and mastery learning[2], it is important to incorporate these elements into the MOOC ecosystem in a manner that is constructive to student learning. Intelligent Tutoring Systems (ITS) are automated systems that aim to provide exactly these benefits and have been used for a number of years in other educational contexts. ITS implementations are often painstakingly developed for very specific topics, such as elementary arithmetic or physics. We introduce the Online Course Tool for Adaptive Learning (OCTAL) as a framework that leverages both mastery learning and metacognitive prompting[4]. We intend

the tool to augment but not necessarily inform the design of a variety of existing and future MOOCs.

OCTAL falls at the intersection of Computerized Adaptive Testing (CAT) and ITS. Primarily, we are concerned with the accurate estimation of latent knowledge traits offered by popular CAT algorithms such as Item Response Theory (IRT). However, we must also provide dynamically updating estimates robust to latent traits which might change as they are measured, a property seen in the popular Bayesian Knowledge Tracing (BKT). Consequent to these requirements, we have chosen to model student knowledge utilizing a Bayesian Inference Network (BIN), a model of latent knowledge that supports hierarchical structures and is adaptive to changing latent traits[1, 3].

We intend OCTAL to be used as a tool for the formative self-assessment of students participating in any course whose topics lend themselves to a dependency structure. Despite this, our initial implementation is specific to UC Berkeley's introductory computer science course, CS10: The Beauty and Joy of Computing. At a coarse level, OCTAL involves the integration of a number of concepts well studied in the literature. First, we presuppose a hierarchy of concepts comprise a given course; for the purposes of OCTAL, we utilize graphs constructed by experts. the construction of this hierarchy is itself a field of study and is outside the scope of this work. Second, we maintain a student model for each learner, including features about their responses to assessment items offered by our tool and other metadata. Finally, we utilize a predictive algorithm incorporating this hierarchy of concepts and these observed features into a BIN in order to make predictions about a student's current knowledge state.

USAGE

Students begin using OCTAL by visiting its website, where the tool presents a two-dimensional dependency graph of concepts. A student then selects any concept and is presented with an exercise for that concept (Figure 1). As the student submits responses, OCTAL presents additional exercises while computing updated estimates of the student's knowledge state. When the estimation algorithm completes, nodes on the graph are highlighted in green if the caluclated probability the student has learned the associated concept is greater than a threshold T_L. The highlighting is removed if new observations indicate that the probability drops below T_L. With this visual clue, students may elect to advance in the graph to post-requisites or retreat to pre-requisite concepts for further exercise.

L@S 2014, Mar 04-05 2014, Atlanta, GA, USA
ACM 978-1-4503-2669-8/14/03.
http://dx.doi.org/10.1145/2556325.2567849

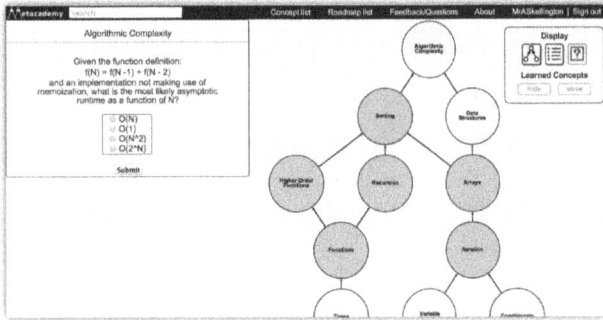

Figure 1. OCTAL exercise interface with concept graph and inferred knowledge.

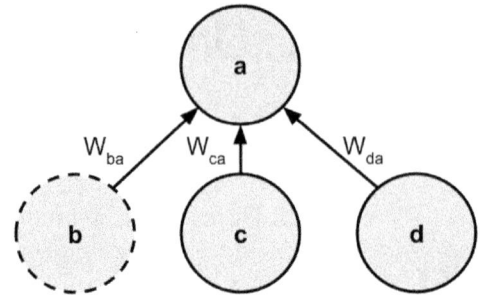

Figure 2. Dependency graph of concepts in which b, c, and d are prerequisites to a, with each edge weight W. Concept b is not learned.

KNOWLEDGE ESTIMATION ALGORITHM

We employ a Bayesian Inference Network (BIN) graphical model of student knowledge to incorporate the concept graph into our predictive model. One notable strength of such a model when compared to BKT or IRT is its ability to incorporate the dependency structures we require. Conceptually, our model for hierarchical knowledge tracing borrows the parameters for probability of guess, $P(G)$, and slip, $P(S)$, from Bayesian Knowledge Tracing, but eschews the probability of knowledge acquisition and replaces the initial learned probability $P(L_0)$ for a concept a with Equation 1.

$$P(L_{a_0}) = (P_{max} - P_{min})\frac{\sum\limits_{i \in C} W_{ia}\varphi i}{\sum\limits_{i \in C} W_{ia}} + P_{min} \quad (1)$$

For concept a, P_{max} and P_{min} are defined as the maximal and minimal prior probability of learning, respectively. Further, each edge between concepts i and a have weight W_{ia}. The activation function $\varphi(i)$ defined in Equation 2.

$$\varphi(i) = \begin{cases} 1, & \text{if } P(L_i) > T_L \\ 0, & \text{if } P(L_i) < T_L \end{cases} \quad (2)$$

Where T_L is a threshold indicating the probability that a concept is learned. Equation 1 ensures $P_{min} \leq P(L_{a_0}) \leq P_{max}$ while each node in the set of prerequisite concepts C contributes a variable amount to the estimate that a student understands concept a prior to any observations. The activation function reveals our assumption that a knowledge state for a concept is binary: either learned or not.

As an example, given the graph in Figure 2, the activation function brings the edge W_{ba} to 0 while edges W_{ca} and W_{da} remain in the summation. As a result, $P(L_{a_0})$ will approach P_{min} if W_{ba} is very large or P_{max} if it is very small.

These probabilities propagate throughout the entire graph with each observation. We estimate learning over the graph using a Markov Chain Monte Carlo (MCMC) model, an algorithm for iteratively sampling a distribution of interdependent random variables[5]. The results of this sampling yield an approximate distribution for the latent knowledge associated with each of the concepts in the graph. The concepts whose estimated probabilities of learning exceed T_L are then presented explicitly to the student on a decorated knowledge graph (Figure 1). The group of learned concepts grows or shrinks accordingly as information propagates through the graph with additional student responses.

NEXT STEPS

We plan on releasing OCTAL in the spring to the students of UC Berkeley's CS10: The Beauty and Joy of Computing in order to investigate metacognitive benefits in presenting material in a nonlinear fashion. Participants will be split into two groups: one set will access exercises for concepts via a 2-dimensional graph representation and the other group will be presented with a linear concept list in an order that matches the presentation of topics in the course. In order to observe metacognitive differences in the groups we will release pre- and post-questionnaires to participating students. The data provided by this pilot study will be utilized both to study the efficacy of the non-linear view, as well as better train the parameters which inform our model.

ACKNOWLEDGMENTS

We'd like to thank Colorado Reed for his support on Metacademy and guidance with knowledge estimation and modeling. Special thanks as well to Zachary Pardos, Armando Fox, John Canny, and the residents of the Berkeley Institute of Design (BiD) for their valuable insight and feedback.

REFERENCES

1. Almond, R. G., and Mislevy, R. J. Graphical models and computerized adaptive testing. *Applied Psychological Measurement 23*, 3 (Sept. 1999), 223–237.

2. Bloom, B. S. The 2 sigma problem: The search for methods of group instruction as effective as one-to-one tutoring. *Educational Researcher 13*, 6 (June 1984), 4–16.

3. Collins, J. A., Greer, J. E., and Huang, S. X. Adaptive assessment using granularity hierarchies and bayesian nets. In *Intelligent Tutoring Systems* (1996), 569577.

4. Hoffman, B., and Spatariu, A. The influence of self-efficacy and metacognitive prompting on math problem-solving efficiency. *Contemporary Educational Psychology 33*, 4 (Oct. 2008), 875–893.

5. Walsh, B. Markov chain monte carlo and gibbs sampling.

Reducing Non-Response Bias with Survey Reweighting: Applications for Online Learning Researchers

René F. Kizilcec
Department of Communication
Stanford University
kizilcec@stanford.edu

ABSTRACT

In many online courses, information about learners is collected via surveys for accounting, instructional design, and research purposes. Aggregate information from such surveys is frequently reported in news articles and research papers, among other publications. While some authors acknowledge the potential bias due to non-response in course surveys, there are no investigations on the severity of the bias and methods for bias reduction in the online education context. A regression-based response-propensity model is described and applied to reweight a course survey, and discrepancies between adjusted and unadjusted outcome distributions are provided.

Author Keywords

Survey research; Survey reweighting; Non-response bias

ACM Classification Keywords

H.5.2 User interfaces: Evaluation and Methodology

INTRODUCTION

Recent online courses have seen massive enrollments from around the world by people of various backgrounds. There has been an interest from course instructors, researchers, and the wider public to find out who takes these courses and for what reasons. Moreover, online learning researchers are keen to ask online learners questions about their experience and collect other self-report measures. As a result, online learners are frequently asked to complete one or more surveys before, during, and after a course.

These surveys tend to be optional to comply with policies of ethical review boards and to remain consistent with the open nature of many online courses. A natural consequence of optional surveys are self-selection effects, as people decide whether or not to respond to the survey and their decisions are rarely random (i.e. a fair coin flip). Instead, self-selection can lead to non-response bias, when those who respond to the survey differ in the outcome variable from those who do

not respond. In other words, the decision to respond is not independent of the survey measures. For instance, if satisfied online learners are more likely to respond to the survey than dissatisfied ones, then we would expect an upward bias in survey questions on learner satisfaction.

The consequences of non-response bias can be detrimental for the validity of research that relies on survey measures. Fortunately, there exist statistical methods that address the issue by reducing the amount of bias. In the context of online course surveys, where demographic information at the population level (e.g., Census data) is usually unavailable, many common survey adjustment techniques cannot be applied. However, there is a promising alternative method that utilizes learners' behavioral data, which is available at the population level, to weight responses according to respondents' likelihood to respond. In the following sections, I elaborate on this method of survey reweighting and provide an exemplary application.

SURVEY WEIGHTS

There is a large literature on survey non-response which proposes different adjustment methods depending on the available data and research goal (see [2, 4] for reviews). Gelaman and Carlin [3] provide further details and a discussion of propensity reweighting, the type of technique used here, and poststratification, an alternative approach. Yet another alternative technique is multiple imputation as advocated by Rubin [5].

The adjustment technique that is described and tested here employs a response-propensity model based on penalized logistic regression. The response-propensity, the likelihood of responding to the survey, is used to weight survey responses, such that those with a low propensity receive higher weights and vice versa when outcome distributions and specific statistics are computed. The propensities are computed using a logistic regression on the learner population where survey non-/response is the binary outcome and various behavioral variables are predictors. To eliminate noise from predictors with low predictive power or that are highly correlated, a penalized regression is used to perform the variable selection task. In the following application, response propensities are estimated with the elastic net penalty [6], using a the weighted combination of the ridge and lasso penalty that minimizes the cross-validated error.

L@S 2014, March 4–5, 2014, Atlanta, GA, USA
ACM 978-1-4503-2669-8/14/03
http://dx.doi.org/10.1145/2556325.2567850

APPLICATION

In a ten-week massive open online course (MOOC) on a topic in Sociology with 53,077 enrolled learners, a course survey was announced at the end of the first week followed by regular reminders until the third week. 9,583 learners responded to the survey (18.1% response rate) which contained several demographic and course specific questions. The behavioral variables that were used as predictors for computing the response-propensities were

video logs number of distinct lectures viewed and play, pause, and seek events

page view logs number of views for each course page

forum logs number of posts, comments, thread views, upvotes, and downvotes

basic account data registration and last access time, an indicator for each timezone, and whether the learner unenrolled.

The model was fit and cross-validated using the *cv.glmnet* function from the *glmnet* R package [1] and weights were computed by taking the inverse of the estimated response probabilities from the *predict.glmnet* function with arguments *type="response"* and *s="lambda.min"*.

RESULTS & DISCUSSION

Variable Selection

Only a small number of mostly lecture-related variables was predictive of survey response. The following seven out of 292 predictors were selected by the elastic net: last course access time; number of distinct lecture views; video pause events; and views of the course landing page, the lecture browsing page, the lecture player page, and the course wiki page. Surprisingly, no geographic or forum-related predictors were selected.

Model Fit

For a simple evaluation of the model fit the predicted response outcome is compared with actual response behavior (without cross-validation). 28.3% (98.0%) of those who did (not) take the survey were correctly predicted as (non-)respondents, yielding a correct prediction in 86.9% of cases. Thus, the model might overfitted towards correctly predicting non-response.

Adjusted Outcome Distributions

The effect of survey reweighting on the age distribution is illustrated in Figure 1, which suggests that learners under 40 were generally under-represented in the survey, while those over 40 were over-represented.

Contrary to the frequently observed patter of higher survey response rates among women, the proportion of female learners was adjusted downwards by 1.25% points while that of males increased by 0.32% points, i.e., males were more likely to respond than females.

Finally, on the question about learners' highest level of formal education, the proportion of those with undergraduate

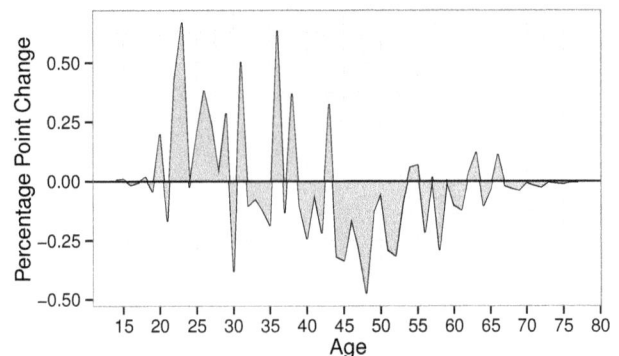

Figure 1. Change in age distribution after reweighting.

degrees increased (+1.63% points), while the proportions of those with postgraduate/graduate degrees (–2.17% points) and Ph.D.s (–0.43% points) decreased. Adjustments for other categories were only minor (<0.2% points).

CONCLUSION

The application of survey reweighting to a typical course survey produced shifts in three key demographic features. Therefore, online education researchers who use survey data should address non-response bias in online course surveys to ensure that the conclusions they draw are valid. The reweighting method presented here is a first step towards an adequate solution for addressing this issue. These findings require further validation with other surveys and adjustment methods, e.g. multiple imputation [5].

ACKNOWLEDGEMENTS

I am grateful to Dean Eckles for his advice on survey adjustment methods, Emily Schneider for general feedback, and the Office of the Vice Provost for Online Learning for supporting this research.

REFERENCES

1. Friedman, J., Hastie, T., and Tibshirani, R. Regularization paths for generalized linear models via coordinate descent. *Journal of Statistical Software 33*, 1 (2010), 1–22.

2. Gary, P. R. Adjusting for nonresponse in surveys. In *Higher Education: Handbook of Theory and Research.* Springer, 2007, 411–449.

3. Gelman, A., and Carlin, J. B. Poststratification and weighting adjustments. In *Survey Nonresponse*, R. Groves, D. Dillman, J. Eltinge, and R. Little, Eds. Wiley-Interscience, 2001.

4. Little, R. J. Survey nonresponse adjustments. *International Statistical Review 54* (1986), 139–157.

5. Rubin, D. B. *Multiple Imputation for Nonresponse in Surveys.* New York: John Wiley and Sons, 1987.

6. Zou, H., and Hastie, T. Regularization and variable selection via the elastic net. *Journal of the Royal Statistical Society: Series B (Statistical Methodology) 67*, 2 (2005), 301–320.

Model Thinking: Demographics and Performance of MOOC Students Unable to Afford a Formal Education

Tawanna Dillahunt
School of Information
University of Michigan
tdillahu@umich.edu

Bingxin Chen
Department Economics
University of Michigan
chenbx@umich.edu

Stephanie Teasley
School of Information
University of Michigan
steasley@umich.edu

ABSTRACT

Massive Open Online Courses (MOOCs) are seen as an opportunity for individuals to gain access to education, develop new skills to prepare for high-paying jobs, and achieve upward mobility without incurring the increasingly high debt that comes with a university degree. Despite this perception, few studies have examined whether populations with the most to gain do leverage these resources. We analyzed student demographic information from course surveys and performance data of MOOC participation in a single course. We targeted students who stated that they were motivated to take the course because they "cannot afford to pursue a formal education," and compared them to the group of all other students. Our three key findings are that 1) a higher percentage of non-traditional enrolled students are in this population than the comparison population, 2) in an independent t-test, a statistically significant portion (28%) of this group has less than a 4-year college degree versus 15% of the comparison group, and 3) the completion rate between both groups are relatively equal.

Author Keywords

Learning analytics; MOOCs; education; affordability

ACM Classification Keywords

H.5.m. Information interfaces and presentation: Misc.

INTRODUCTION

To an increasing extent, a college education is key to upward mobility [3]. Economic success is heavily dependent on one's ability to *afford* a college education [4]. Massive Open Online Communities (MOOCs) are seen as an opportunity to gain access to education and professional development, develop new skills to prepare for high-paying jobs, and achieve upward mobility without incurring the increasing debt that comes with a university degree [2].

Although MOOCs are seen as one possible path toward upward mobility, few studies have examined whether and/or *how* the populations with the most to gain leverage these resources. In fact, Christensen et al., found that "The individuals the MOOC revolution is supposed to help the most—those without access to higher education in developing countries—are underrepresented among the early adopters" [1].

In this project, we focused on individuals who may have limited access to higher education due to affordability. This study investigates similarities and differences between the demographics and performance of these students and others. We present our preliminary analysis of the University of Michigan's Model Thinking course (https://www.coursera.org/course/modelthinking). We provide results comparing and contrasting student motivation combined with demographic data such as age, gender, and occupational and educational background. We contribute a preliminary analysis of the demographics and performance of this as yet unexplored group in the context of MOOCs. Our ultimate goal is to understand if MOOCs could be a platform for economic mobility among low-income or economically distressed populations.

METHOD

Links to online surveys were submitted to all registered students at the end of the university's MOOCs offered in the winter of 2013. We conducted an initial analysis of this survey data. Specifically, we analyzed demographic questions such as age, gender, highest level of education achieved, motivations for taking the course, and current occupation. Our goal was to separate our data based on

L@S 2014, March 4–5, 2014, Atlanta, Georgia, USA. ACM 978-1-4503-2669-8/14/03.
http://dx.doi.org/10.1145/2556325.2567851

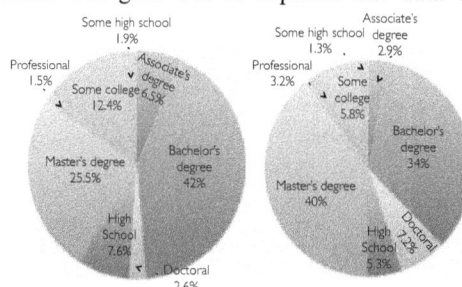

Figure 1 Highest Level of Education Achieved- Left: Target group (N=647); Right: Comparison Group (N=6,044). A Levene's t-test of unequal variances (equal variances not assumed in SPSS) show the proportions of these two groups (target, 28%; comparison, 15%) to be statistically significantly different (F(1,6690)=212.43, p<.01).

student motivations for taking the courses. Specifically, we sought to gain a better understanding about those students who responded that they "cannot afford to pursue a formal education" when asked about their motivations for taking the course. We wanted to compare these students to others in terms of demographics and performance based on student course completion and participation.

We analyzed data from Model Thinking, a ten-week long course with an advertised workload of 4-8 hours per week. The course aims to help students become better thinkers and to prepare them for advanced courses. We selected the course for analysis because it had recently been offered, had one of the highest number of survey responses and could attract students with a wide variety of educational backgrounds. In addition, the course did not require textbooks and did not list course prerequisites.

RESULTS
In total, 38,411 students registered to take the MOOC. Of these, 23.3%, 20%, 17.4%, and 20.8% responded to the questions of gender, age, highest level of education achieved and current occupation respectively. In total, 15.7% (n=6,044) answered the question regarding their motivations for taking the course and highest education achieved. Of these, 10.7% (N=647) represented our target population, which we defined as those students who reported taking the class because they "cannot afford to pursue a formal education."

Demographic Comparisons
Gender representation was relatively the same across the two groups: 69.6% were male and 30.4% were female (of those that responded to this question). Twenty-five to thirty-four year olds make up the majority age group across both groups: 46.6% of our target population and 40.9% of our comparison population. Eighteen to twenty-four year olds have the second highest percentages across both groups. Of those that responded to the employment question, only 18.8% of those responding to this question in our target group indicated that they were students while 29% of those in the comparison group indicated that they were students (n.s.). Like other studies [1], the majority of students from our total population were from the U.S.; there were no other significant differences between the two groups (e.g., average age, gender, level of education).

While only 15% of the comparison group has less than a 4-year college degree, this is true of 28% of our target group. A Levene's t-test of equal variances (equal variances not assumed in SPSS) show the proportions of these two groups to be statistically significantly different ($F(1,6690)=212.43$, $p<.01$) (**Error! Reference source not found.**).

Performance Comparisons
Approximately 10.7% (N=4,091) of the 38,411 registered students completed the course and earned a statement of accomplishment. Approximately 5.7% (N=2,176) of these students also completed the survey and 62.8% (N=1,368)

indicated their motivations for taking the course. On average, in a further analysis of these students (i.e., 62.8%), there was no significant difference in course completion between our target and comparison groups. In fact, there was approximately a 30% completion rate across *both* groups. Though not statistically significant, interestingly, those students in our target group with some high school education had a higher percentage completion rate (41.7%) than any other sub-population except doctoral students unable to afford a formal education (see Figure 1). There were no significant differences between groups in the rate of video viewing or forum participation.

CONCLUSION
In summary, we find that 1) a higher percentage of our target population are non-students, 2) a statistically significant number of this group has less than a 4-year college degree versus the comparison group and 3) though the completion rate of our target group is the same as that of the comparison group, those with some high school have higher than average completion rates.

We plan to extend our analysis to Michigan's other MOOC courses to understand whether our findings generalize across others. We will also interview targeted students to better understand their experiences taking this MOOC as well as others. We will explore the ways in which students' experiences with MOOCs have affected, or may affect employment or potential employment for students who feel they can not afford more traditional forms of higher education. This work will provide a basis for understanding what types of courses are needed to increase employment opportunities for economically disadvantaged populations.

Degree type	Target	Comparison
Some high school	41.7% (N=5)	23.4% (N=18)
High school	32.7% (N=16)	30.3% (N=96)
Some college	22.5% (N=18)	23.9% (N=83)
Associate's degree (2 years of college)	26.2% (N=11)	28.7% (N=50)
Bachelor's degree (BA/BS, 4 years of college)	29.8% (N=81)	29.9% (N=626)
Master's degree	33.9% (N=56)	36.9% (N=884)
Professional degree (MD, JD)	10% (N=1)	23% (N=45)
Doctoral degree	47.2% (N=8)	37.9% (N=165)
Average completion rate	30.3%	32.6%

Figure 1 - Percentage earning a certificate by degree

REFERENCES
1. Christensen, G., Steinmetz, A., Alcorn, B., Bennett, A., Woods, D., Emanuel, E. The MOOC Phenomenon: Who Takes Massive Open Online Courses and Why? (November 6, 2013).
2. Kossoff, J. (2013, March 21). Can MOOCs Really Help You Get a Job? *Simply Hired Blog.* Retrieved on 6/26/2013, http://goo.gl/QXAnM.
3. McMurrer, D. and Sawhill, I. (1996). How Much Do Americans Move Up and Down the Economic Ladder? Washington, DC: Urban Institute.
4. Waldron, K. Access to college means access to economic mobility for America's underserved. (2007). *Diverse Issues in Higher Education.* 24(2).

"Why did you enroll in this course?" Developing a Standardized Survey Question for Reasons to Enroll

Emily Schneider
Graduate School of Education
Stanford University
elfs@cs.stanford.edu

René F. Kizilcec
Department of Communication
Stanford University
kizilcec@stanford.edu

ABSTRACT

Understanding motivations for enrolling in MOOCs is key for personalizing and scaling the online learning experience. We develop a standardized survey item for measuring learners' reasons to enroll, based on a corpus of open-ended responses from previous course surveys. Online coders were employed in the iterative development of response options. The item was designed to minimize response biases by adhering to best practices from survey design research.

Author Keywords

Survey research; motivation; MOOC learner goals

ACM Classification Keywords

H.5.2 User interfaces: Evaluation and Methodology

INTRODUCTION

Over the past few years, millions of people across the world have enrolled in hundreds of massive open online courses (MOOCs) across many platforms. With a globally distributed population and a great diversity of learner backgrounds, there are a wide number of reasons that inspire people to enroll in MOOCs. But with no cost to entry or exit, enrollment numbers are merely an indication of interest, consistently overestimating the number of actively participating learners in the course; among active learners, participation rates tend to decline steadily as the course progresses. These variable levels of engagement are likely influenced by learners' reasons for enrolling in the course. Prior work in educational psychology and higher education have shown that learners' goal orientation and attitudes towards the value of achieving their goals are intimately tied to their engagement with learning experiences (see [1] for a review).

Kizilcec, Piech, & Schneider [3] found learners' patterns of course engagement to be associated with self-reported reasons to enroll. Breslow and colleagues [2], however, saw no correlations between motivations for enrollment and certain course success metrics. Even without the issue of different

success metrics, it is unclear whether these results are contradictory, because the motivations for enrollment in each of these studies were generated by different survey items.

There is a strong need for a standardized question on reasons for enrollment to create comparability between courses and enable coordinated research efforts across institutions and platforms. Reliably ascertaining learners' reasons to enroll is instrumental for scaling and personalizing the online learning experience; for instance, personalized pathways through available materials, recommended supplementary resources, or providing the option to take the course in different modalities (e.g. a self-paced 'library' of available resources rather than enrollment with a cohort of other learners). Real-time analytics for personalized learning experiences are an important, yet unreached milestone for MOOCs. Moreover, given the relative novelty of MOOCs, there is a general interest in learners' motivations for enrolling and staying engaged in the courses–and understanding how these motivation structures differ from those of learners in other types of online learning environments.

DESIGNING A GOOD QUESTION

The importance of this survey item has not gone unrecognized–most course surveys to date contain one or more items to determine learners' reasons for enrolling in a course. The two major question types to measure this construct have been open response and multiple choice. While open response is a rich source of nuanced information, it is more challenging to adequately analyze textual data in this context. Although simpler to analyze, multiple choice items– with the option to select a single, a certain number, or as many options as apply–can be problematic unless they are designed with careful attention to known survey biases. The development of an item that minimizes induced biases is the goal of this work.

The two core aspects for the optimal design of a multiple choice item for why learners enroll are selection constraints and response options. Selection constraints like 'select one' or 'select three' place an arbitrary limit on the number of reasons respondents can report and coerces them to select a certain number. This tends to induce satisficing behavior, as respondents who intended to select a different number of options become less invested in making an effort to respond accurately [4]. And although 'select all that apply' lets respondents decide how many options to choose, its unguided nature does not require learners to consider each answer option and after selecting a few options they might feel like "it's enough". As a result, leaving an option unselected does not

L@S 2014, March 4–5, 2014, Atlanta, GA, USA
ACM 978-1-4503-2669-8/14/03
http://dx.doi.org/10.1145/2556325.2567852

have a clear and consistent interpretation. An item design that avoids these issues asks respondents to consider each response option in turn and choose whether it applies to them or not. Note that "Applies/Does not apply" scale labels should be used instead of "True/False" or "Yes/No" to avoid inducing acquiescence bias–respondents' tendency to agree with questions independent of their content [4].

The choice of response options is critical for the validity with which a question can measure a certain construct. Response options should be mutually exclusive and collectively exhaustive, which means that options should not overlap and all possible responses should be covered. The latter condition is difficult to satisfy, but can be approached in this context by asking learners to describe in their own words their reasons for enrolling. The textual data from these open response questions can then be systematically analyzed to develop a final list of response options. Another advantage of this approach is that the resulting response options' phrasing will be closer to how learners express their reasons.

ITERATIVE DEVELOPMENT OF RESPONSE OPTIONS
The iterative process of response option development was crowdsourced to 'classification experts' on Amazon Mechanical Turk (MTurk), who manually coded random samples of open response answers from learners in three different MOOCs (on topics in Political Science, Computer Science, and Economics). Before the MTurk coding, a preliminary codebook was developed by two independent volunteer coders using learners' open response texts and a previously developed set of reasons provided in course surveys of a major MOOC platform. For each open response text, MTurk coders were instructed to select all appropriate reason from the codebook. An "other" option was provided and coders were strongly encouraged to choose this option if some aspect of the response was not reflected in the existing response options. There also was a "spam" option.

In the first iteration, 300 randomly chosen responses were *each* coded by four MTurk coders. Each option's frequency and intercoder reliability, and correlations between response options were evaluated; all responses that were coded as "other" by more than one coder were also examined individually. These analyses revealed some holes in the codebook, as well as some categories which did not line up with participants' characterizations of their reasons to enroll. Based on these insights, the codebook was modifed and applied by MTurk coders to a similarly large random sample of responses. A third iteration followed a similar procedure. The final product is the survey item shown in Table 1.

Response Option Ordering
Response options are frequently presented in random order, as presentation order can influence the respondent's choice (order effect). Simple randomization, however, can be problematic when a more general question or response option is preceded by a more specific question. This can bias responses to the general question, a phenomenon known as the "subtraction effect" [5]. In our case, the first response option Table 1, "General interest in topic", is more general than the

Table 1. Final 'Why Enroll' Survey Item

Why did you enroll in this course?	Applies	Does not apply
General interest in topic	○	○
Relevant to job	○	○
Relevant to school or degree program	○	○
Relevant to academic research	○	○
For personal growth and enrichment	○	○
For career change	○	○
For fun and challenge	○	○
Meet new people	○	○
Experience an online course	○	○
Earn a certificate/statement of accomplishment	○	○
Course offered by prestigious university/professor	○	○
Take with colleagues/friends	○	○
To improve my English skills	○	○

other options and should always be placed first; if possible, the remaining items should be presented in random order to address order effects.

FUTURE DIRECTIONS
The proposed survey item has been included in all Stanford MOOC surveys since September 2013 and will remain in the survey template for future courses. We encourage other institutions to adopt this item to facilitate comparative research and unified metrics. Within the courses where the item was deployed, we are currently investigating the associations between engagement patterns and learners' goals, laying the groundwork for developing learner profiles based on self-reported intentions as well as actual behavior in the course.

ACKNOWLEDGEMENTS
We are grateful to Ivy Guo for volunteering coding help and the Office of the Vice Provost for Online Learning for supporting this research.

REFERENCES
1. Ambrose, S. A., Bridges, M. W., DiPietro, M., Lovett, M. C., and Norman, M. K. *How learning works: Seven research-based principles for smart teaching*. John Wiley & Sons, 2010.

2. Breslow, L. B., Pritchard, D. E., DeBoer, J., Stump, G. S., Ho, A. D., and Seaton, D. T. Studying learning in the worldwide classroom: Research into edx's first mooc. *Research & Practice in Assessment 8* (2013), 13–25.

3. Kizilcec, R. F., Piech, C., and Schneider, E. Deconstructing disengagement: Analyzing learner subpopulations in massive open online courses. In *Proceedings of the Third International Conference on Learning Analytics and Knowledge*, ACM (2013), 170–179.

4. Krosnick, J. A. Survey research. *Annual review of psychology 50*, 1 (1999), 537–567.

5. Tourangeau, R., Rasinski, K. A., and Bradburn, N. Measuring happiness in surveys: A test of the subtraction hypothesis. *Public Opinion Quarterly 55*, 2 (1991), 255–266.

Improving Problem Solving Performance in Computer-Based Learning Environments through Subgoal Labels

Lauren Margulieux
Georgia Institute of Technology
School of Psychology
Atlanta, GA 30332-0170
l.marg@gatech.edu

Richard Catrambone
Georgia Institute of Technology
School of Psychology
Atlanta, GA 30332-0170
rc7@prism.gatech.edu

ABSTRACT

Computer-based learning environments can provide valuable resources for learning at scale, but students in these environments might learn without an instructor. Subgoal labels have been used in worked examples in STEM domains to help a learner understand the purpose of a set of steps, and this feature has increased problem solving performance [1]. Subgoal labels, however, have not been tested in instructional text. The present study explored this intervention. The results of the present study show that learners who received subgoal labels in both the text and example outperformed those in other conditions. When subgoal labeled text is paired with an unlabeled example, however, performance does not improve. These findings indicate that subgoal labeled instructional text when paired with subgoal labeled examples can improve performance in a computer-based learning environment.

Author Keywords

STEM education; subgoal learning; worked examples; procedural text; online learning.

ACM Classification Keywords

K.3.1. Computer uses in Education: Computer-assisted instruction and distance learning.

INTRODUCTION

Computer-based learning environments can provide extra resources for education, but they do not necessarily have an instructor to help students. For this reason, instructional designers need to create instructions that help students understand content independently. One way to address this need is to include extra guidance in the instructions.

Worked examples help students learn STEM procedures, but learners can have trouble extracting information from specific examples that allows them to solve novel problems

L@S 2014, Mar 04-05 2014, Atlanta, GA, USA
ACM 978-1-4503-2669-8/14/03.
http://dx.doi.org/10.1145/2556325.2567853

[2]. The use of subgoal labels is an instructional design technique that has been effective for improving transfer.

Subgoals are functional pieces of the overall solution achieved by completing one or more individual steps. Subgoals are specific to a class of problems within a domain but not to a single problem; therefore, if learners are taught how to identify and achieve subgoals, their success at solving novel problems can increase [1].

Subgoal labels have been used to in worked examples to teach learners the subgoals of problems. The impact of subgoal labels in instructional text has not been explored. Instructional text is defined as general descriptions of a procedure "intended to communicate a certain set of skills for reasoning or thinking cogently within that field," [4, p. 121]. Subgoal labeled instructional text might help novices understand new problem solving procedures by providing extra guidance. However, worked examples are important because they provide information about how to apply principles to problem solving [2]. If learners receive only subgoal labeled instructional text, they might have trouble applying their knowledge to problem solving without a subgoal labeled worked example to guide them.

Present Study

The present study compared the effectiveness of subgoal labeled to unlabeled instructional materials to teach computer programming. In the study, participants learned how to use Android App Inventor. This computer programming language was chosen because it is a drag-and-drop language and free to use. Materials in all conditions were the same except for the subgoal labels.

Instructional materials included procedural text about how to create apps (i.e., instructional text) and a video demo and a step-by-step guide showing how to create a specific app (i.e., worked example). A video demonstration was used because it can be a quick and natural way for users to learn direct-manipulation interfaces [3] like Android App Inventor. Participants completed assessment tasks designed to measure their problem solving performance.

METHOD

Participants were 120 students from the Georgia Institute of Technology who received class credit for their participation. People were disqualified for participation if they had experience with Android App Inventor or had taken more than one high-school or college-level course in computer science or computer programming. These restrictions were necessary because instructions were designed for novices.

Sessions took 90 minutes. First, participants filled out a demographic questionnaire to provide information about possible predictors of performance in computer science [5]. Next, during the instructional period, participants received the instructional text and worked example. Participants had up to 30 minutes to create a specific app using the instructions. Then, during the assessment period, participants solved novel problems. During this time, participants did not have access to the instructional materials, but they did have access to the App Inventor website and the app that they had created. The participants were allowed access to their app to serve as a memory cue to aid problem solving.

The experiment was a two-by-two, between-subjects, factorial design. The first independent variable was the format of instructional text (subgoal labeled or unlabeled); the second independent variable was the format of the worked example (subgoal labeled or unlabeled). The dependent variable was performance on the tasks.

RESULTS AND DISCUSSION
To score the assessment, participants' solutions were compared to the correct solutions for each problem. Participants earned one point for each correct step they took towards the solution. The maximum score that participants could earn was 22. Participant responses were scored by two raters, and interrater reliability, ICC(A), was .94.

There was an interaction between text design and example design for the problem solving assessment, $F (1, 116) = 12.82$, $MSE = 24.47$, $p = .001$, est. $\omega^2 = .05$, $f = .57$. This interaction shows that participants who received subgoal labels in the text performed better than those who did not only when they also received subgoal labels in the example (see Table 1).

Condition	n	M	SD	t	Std. error	p
SL text, SL ex.	30	16.4	4.3			
				5.08	1.30	<.01
UL text, SL ex.	30	9.8	5.6			
				3.18	1.36	<.01
SL text, UL ex.	30	5.6	4.8			
				.106	.133	.92
UL text, UL ex.	30	5.5	4.9			

Table 1. T-tests comparing conditions for problem solving task score. Note: SL = subgoal labeled, UL = unlabeled, and ex. = example.

Having subgoal labels in both types of instructional material could have helped participants integrate the general information in the text with the specific information in the example, leading to better understanding of the subgoals. Additionally, receiving the subgoal labeled text, similar to receiving principles in text, might have helped participants organize information from the general procedure better. Better organization of the general procedure could have led to more effective processing of an example in which the same labels were used.

CONCLUSION
The subgoal intervention manipulates the instructional materials that students receive; therefore, reaching a large number of students with the work of a small group of people (i.e., the instructional designers and subject-matter experts) would be relatively easy. Furthermore, because these interventions are not dependent on instructors, they can also be used in learning environments without personal interaction with an instructor, such as online learning. Though this study does not claim that students who use these instructional materials alone would perform similarly to students who had these materials and instruction from an instructor, the study was conducted in a computer-based learning environment without an instructor. Therefore, the results of the study represent the results that could be expected if students used only these instructions.

ACKNOWLEDGMENTS
We thank Frank Durso and Mark Guzdial for their feedback throughout this project. We also thank Gerin Williams for her help collecting and scoring data.

REFERENCES
1. Catrambone, R. (1998). The subgoal learning model: Creating better examples so that students can solve novel problems. Journal of Experimental Psychology: General, 127, 355-376.

2. Committee on Developments in the Science of Learning, National Research Council. (2000). How people learn: Brain, mind, experience, and school: Expanded edition. Retrieved from http://www.nap.edu/catalog.php?record_id=9853

3. Palmiter, S., Elkerton, J., & Baggett, P. (1991). Animated demonstrations versus written instructions for learning procedural tasks: A preliminary investigation. International Journal of Man-Machine Studies, 34, 687-701.

4. Reder, L. M., & Anderson, J. R. (1980). A comparison of texts and their summaries: Memorial consequences. Journal of Verbal Learning and Verbal Behavior, 19, 121-134.

5. Rountree, N., Rountree, J., Robins, A., & Hannah, R. (2004). Interacting factors that predict success and failure in a CSI course. SIGCSE Bulletin, 33(4), pp. 101-104.

Initial Experiences with Small Group Discussions in MOOCs

Seongtaek Lim, Derrick Coetzee, Björn Hartmann, Armando Fox, and Marti A. Hearst
University of California, Berkeley
{stlim, dcoetzee, bjoern, fox, hearst}@berkeley.edu

ABSTRACT
Peer learning, in which students discuss questions in small groups, has been widely reported to improve learning outcomes in traditional classroom settings. Classroom-based peer learning relies on students being in the same place at the same time to form peer discussion groups, but this is rarely true for online students in MOOCs. We built a software tool that facilitates chat-based peer learning in MOOCs by 1) automatically forming ad-hoc discussion groups and 2) scaffolding the interactions between students in these groups. We report on a pilot deployment of this tool; post-use surveys administered to participants show that the tool was positively received and support the feasibility of synchronous online collaborative learning in MOOCs.

Author Keywords
Peer learning; massive open online courses (MOOCs); chat

ACM Classification Keywords
H.5.3. Information Interfaces and Presentation (e.g. HCI): Group and Organization Interfaces

INTRODUCTION
MOOCs are online courses with open enrollment that typically have thousands of active students. They have attracted so many students in part because they offer courses free of charge and in part because they allow students to take the courses on their own schedule and from any location. However, MOOCs currently assume that students work in isolation, which may contribute to high attrition rates.

To improve the learning experience, we are exploring the introduction of *peer learning*, also known as *collaborative learning* and *cooperative learning*, into MOOCs. In peer learning, students work together in small groups to enhance their own and one another's learning. Peer learning in the physical classroom consists of activities in which students form small groups to discuss conceptual questions and to engage in problem-solving. Literally hundreds of research studies and several meta-analyses show the significant pedagogical benefit of peer learning including improved critical thinking skills, retention of learned information, interest in subject matter, and class morale [2, 4, 5, 7, 6, 1].

L@S'14, March 4–5, 2014, Atlanta, GA.
ACM 978-1-4503-2669-8/14/03.
http://dx.doi.org/10.1145/2556325.2567854

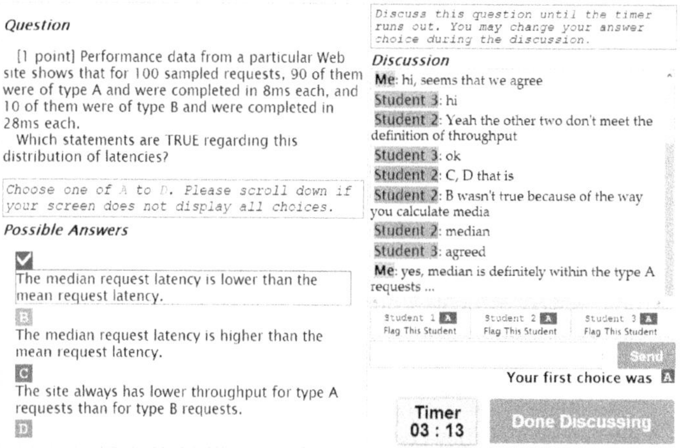

Figure 1. The chat system UI. Upper left: question, lower left: multiple choice answers. The active student chose choice A, in blue. Upper right: three students discuss the question in a chat; the other students' choices are shown below the chat; lower right: the remaining time along with a button allowing students to end discussion.

It is not obvious that these results will transfer to the massive, online setting of MOOCs. First, MOOCs lack the physical co-location of classrooms. Second, when peer learning has been transferred to online courses in the Computer Supported Collaborative Learning literature, it has usually been in the context of smaller courses in which the instructor knows the students and the students know one another.

Student interaction is lacking in MOOCs because students are neither collocated, nor are they progressing through course materials on the same schedule. That is, they are distributed in both space and time. Walter's Social Information Processing Theory of Computer Mediated Communication (CMC) argues that communicators deploy whatever cues they have at their disposal [8], which suggests that even a simple text chat may be a reasonable tool for supporting discussion of remote students. To bring students together into synchronous (real-time) groups, approaches from team formation in multi-player games and real-time crowdsourcing [3] can be adapted. In our pilot work, we announce discussion sessions that begin at regular intervals and then form ad hoc groups from the students who are signed on and present at the planned start time.

METHOD
We set up a testbed for synchronous online discussion which organizes students into groups, allowing them to first individually answer questions and then see each others' answers and discuss those answers, while a timer counts down. When the time is up, the students choose their final answer and are

Survey Question	A/SA	N	D/SD
Helpfulness of Discussion for Final Choice	11	2	3
I Was Able to Help Others Learn	9	4	3
Others Students Helped Me Learn	9	4	3
I Liked Discussing Questions in a Small Group and Would Like to Do So Again	14	1	1

Table 1. Survey Responses. A/SA = Agree/Strongly Agree (or Helpful/Very Helpful); N = Neutral, D/SD = Disagree or Strongly Disagree (or Not Helpful/Detrimental).

then shown the correct answer with an explanation. They then move on to the next review question. Each group discusses each question in a private chatroom. The software is flexible in that it allows the instructor to decide how many students should be in a group and how much time should be allocated for answering individual questions (see Figure 1).

The target MOOC was the Fall 2013 offering of edX's CS.169.2x (Software as a Service)[1]. The six-week course is intended for students with an undergraduate computer science level of expertise and consists of 53 lecture sections, 3 graded quizzes, and 2 graded assignments.

The intervention consisted of providing students with a practice quiz which they could opt to take using an interactive chat tool. Unfortunately, although initially the course had 6,503 students enrolled, at the time of our experiments near the end of the course, only a few hundred widely-dispersed students were active, which made forming groups difficult. Nonetheless, we decided to go ahead and see if any synchronous groups would form in order to get an initial qualitative understanding for participants' reaction to the tool and the method. This paper reports on those initial responses.

RESULTS

One practice session began each hour. 61 students took the practice quiz and completed the survey. Of these, only 16 were successfully placed in a group of 2 or 3 discussants; six respondents were placed in groups of 3, and 10 were in groups of 2. (More groups were not formed because not enough students arrived at the same time for the same practice session; a large MOOC with thousands of students should have a higher grouping success rate.) The focus of this report is on the experiences of those students who did have a discussion with others using the chat tool.

Table 1 shows the results of the post-study survey, indicating overall positive responses to the approach. In response to "Other students helped me learn during the discussion," one student wrote "Yes, by having to explain my answers to the other students it forced me to think more deeply about the question," which is one of the central tenets behind collaborative learning. In terms of group size, 6 out of 10 of those in groups of size 2 indicated they wanted more people in the discussion where as everyone placed in a group of size 3 indicated this was the right size for the discussion, again reflecting results from the peer learning literature that dyads do not lend themselves to good discussions.

[1] https://www.edx.org/course/uc-berkeleyx/
uc-berkeleyx-cs-169-2x-software-service-1005

The first survey question was an open-ended one asking "Do you have any feedback about your experience using this discussion tool? What worked well and what can be improved?" The students expressed general satisfaction. one student commented "It was my first time to use this. I think that overall it is a great tool. We were able to have some brief discussion and it probably is the closest thing that we can get to being the same activity that is in the course." Another wrote "That is very interesting, useful and fun Cool." A third wrote "It's really cool, and make learning more interactive!!!" These comments suggest that students in an online course are quite positive about this approach, and if the synchronization issues can be solved, small coordinated group chats may successfully lead to better learning and retention as has been found widely in the peer learning literature.

CONCLUSIONS

We have developed an interface and a method to form small ad hoc groups in MOOCs. We've taken first steps in understanding how this interface can guide student discussion in groups, but much work remains to be done. Our next step will be to introduce the method into several large MOOCs, and fully integrate it into every phase of the course. We plan to use it for tests of understanding, as practice quizzes, as study guides, and for other learning activities.

Acknowledgements This material is based upon work supported by the National Science Foundation Grant No. IIS 1149799 and a Google Social Interactions Research Award.

REFERENCES

1. Deslauriers, L., Schelew, E., and Wieman, C. Improved learning in a large-enrollment physics class. *Science 332*, 6031 (2011), 862–864.

2. Johnson, D. W., Johnson, R. T., and Smith, K. A. *Active learning: Cooperation in the college classroom.* Interaction Book Company Edina, MN, 1991.

3. Lasecki, W. S., Murray, K. I., White, S., Miller, R. C., and Bigham, J. P. Real-time crowd control of existing interfaces. In *Proceedings ACM UIST* (2011).

4. Lord, T. R. Comparing traditional and constructivist teaching in college biology. *Innovative Higher Education 21*, 3 (1997), 197–217.

5. Millis, B. J., and Cottell, P. G. *Cooperative learning for higher education faculty.* Oryx Press, 1998.

6. Smith, M. K., Wood, W. B., Adams, W. K., Wieman, C., Knight, J. K., Guild, N., and Su, T. T. Why peer discussion improves student performance on in-class concept questions. *Science 323*, 5910 (2009), 122–124.

7. Springer, L., Stanne, M. E., and Donovan, S. S. Effects of small-group learning on undergraduates in science, mathematics, engineering, and technology: A meta-analysis. *Review of Educational Research 69*, 1 (1999), 21–51.

8. Walther, J. B. Interpersonal effects in computer-mediated interaction a relational perspective. *Communication Research 19*, 1 (1992), 52–90.

Open System for Video Learning Analytics

Konstantinos Chorianopoulos
Ionian University
Corfu, Greece
choko@acm.org

Michail N. Giannakos
Old Dominion University
Norfolk, VA, USA
mgiannak@cs.odu.edu

Nikos Chrisochoides
Old Dominion University
Norfolk, VA, USA
nikos@cs.odu.edu

ABSTRACT

Video lectures are nowadays widely used by growing numbers of learners all over the world. Nevertheless, learners' interactions with the videos are not readily available, because online video platforms do not share them. In this paper, we present an open-source video learning analytics system, which is also available as a free service to researchers. Our system facilitates the analysis of video learning behavior by capturing learners' interactions with the video player (e.g, seek/scrub, play, pause). In an empirical user study, we captured hundreds of user interactions with the video player by analyzing the interactions as a learner activity time series. We found that learners employed the replaying activity to retrieve the video segments that contained the answers to the survey questions. The above findings indicate the potential of video analytics to represent learner behavior. Further research, should be able to elaborate on learner behavior by collecting large-scale data. In this way, the producers of online video pedagogy will be able to understand the use of this emerging medium and proceed with the appropriate amendments to the current video-based learning systems and practices.

Author Keywords

User Interactions, Learning Analytics, Video, Education.

ACM Classification Keywords

K.3.1 [**Computer Uses in Education**] Computer-assisted instruction (CAI), Distance learning; H.5.3 [**Group and Organization Interfaces**]: Evaluation/methodology

INTRODUCTION

Capturing and sharing analytics in emerged learning technologies can clearly provide scholars and educators with valuable information. Specifically for the case of video-based learning, information obtained from learner (hereinafter Learning Analytics-LA) have recently started to be used in order to provide educators with valuable information about students. However, the usage of LA on video-based learning it is still on embryotic research stage.

Many instructors in higher and secondary education are implementing video lectures in a variety of ways, such as broadcasting lectures in distance education, delivering recordings of in-class lectures with face-to-face meetings for review purposes. However, several aspects on the area of video-based learning remain unexplored, such as whether students are viewing the entire video lecture, what segments of the video lecture they select to view, how many times they view the video lecture, and what part of the video are more attractive to them [1]. Based on these concerns, our system design is taking advantage of a LA approach and investigates students' video behavior using an analysis of their interactions with video lectures.

OPEN-SOURCE VIDEO LEARNING ANALYTICS SYSTEM

In this section, we present the video analytics system we used in our study (Figure 1). We used the Google App Engine (GAE) cloud platform and the YouTube Player API. The system has several advantages in comparison to stand-alone applications [2]. Users do not need to go through an installation process (http://goo.gl/SJng6O), they just have to visit the link and if there is an updated version they just have to refresh the page, in addition, system's architecture is modular and it allows re-use of the components.

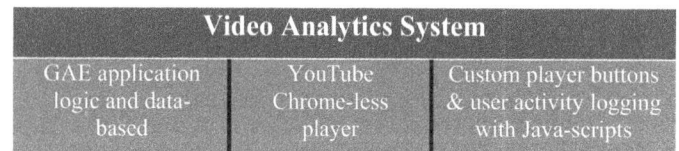

Figure 1. Video analytics system architecture

Web-video systems might employ the open-source application logic (http://goo.gl/vHmk5Y), in order to dynamically identify rich information segments. There are several benefits of the selected tools (GAE, YouTube, Google accounts). GAE enables the development of web-based applications, as well as maintenance and administration of the traffic and the data storage. YouTube allows developers to use its infrastructures (e.g., YouTube videos) and provides chrome-less user interface, which is a YouTube video player without any controls. This facilitates customization within Flash or HTML 5. As such, we used JavaScript to create custom buttons and to implement their functions. Additionally, learners' used Google account in order to sign in and watch the uploaded videos. In this way, we accomplished user authentication and we avoid the effort of implementing a user account system just for the application. Thus, users' interactions are recorded and stored in Google's database alongside with their Gmail addresses. The Google App Engine database (Datastore) is used to store the interactions. Each time someone signs in the web video player application, a new log is created. Whenever a button is pressed, an abbreviation of the button's name and the time it occurred are stored.

The video player (Figure 2) employs custom buttons, in order to be simple to associate user actions with video semantics. We have modified the classic forward and backward buttons to "Skip30" and "Replay30". The first one jumps backwards 30 seconds and its main purpose is to replay the last 30 seconds of the video, while the Skip30 button jumps forward 30 seconds and its main purpose is to skip insignificant video segments. The main reason for developing these functions is to identify the video segments which learners' consider as important (repeated views).

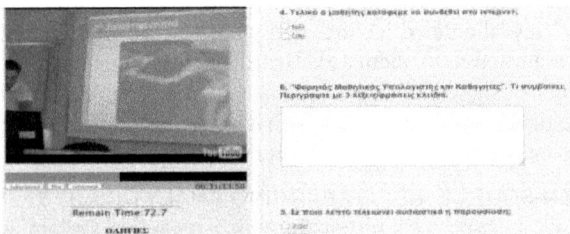

Figure 2. The interface of the system has familiar buttons, as well as questionnaire functionality

USER EXPERIMENT

Methodology
The goal of the user experiment is to collect activity data from the learners, as well as to establish a flexible experimental procedure that can be replicated and validated by other researchers at large scale level. In our small case study, twenty-three university students (18-35 years old, 13 F and 10 M) spent approximately ten minutes to watch a series of videos (buttons were muted). All students had been attending the HCI courses at a post- or under-graduate level. Next, there was a time restriction of five minutes, in order to motivate the users to actively browse through the video and answer the respective questions. We enabled the Replay30 and Skip30 buttons and we informed the students that the purpose of the study was to measure their performance in finding the answers to the questions within time constraints. In order to experimentally replicate learner activity we developed a questionnaire that corresponds to several segments of each video. The survey employed very simple questions that could not be answered by previous knowledge of the students.

Early Results
In order to analyze the results, we created time-series graphs that facilitated the visual comparison between the original Learner Activity Segments (LAS), the Rich Information Segments [segments with the responses of the questions] (RIS) and smooth versions of the LAS [we smooth learners' activity using common technics] (Figure

3). Next, we visually compared the smooth versions of the component and composite times series to the RIS. We observed that in most cases the Replay30 time series closely matched the RIS. Neither the Skip30, nor the composite time series seem to match the RIS (Figure 3).

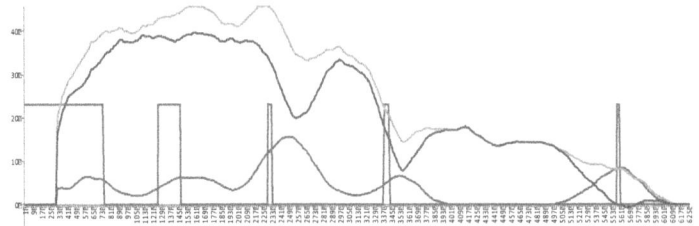

Figure 3. An exemplar graph of learner-video interaction

Therefore, it is possible to compute local maximums of the Replay30 time series for each one of the videos and identify the segments of the video, where students seek the answers or consider more important. The experimental system also can keep logs of the answers to the questions alongside the video interaction logs; as such it is possible to triangulate learners' interaction with their knowledge acquisition and their attitudes.

DISCUSSION AND CONCLUSION
In that paper, we presented a video learning analytics system and the first results of the captured LA. As millions of learners enjoy video streaming from different platforms (Coursera, Khan Academy, EdX, Udacity, Iversity, Futurelearn) on a diverse number of terminals (TV, desktop, smart phone, tablet), they create billions of simple interactions. This amount of LA might be converted into useful information for the benefit of all video learners. As long as learners' watching videos on Web-based systems, more and more interactions are going to be gathered and therefore, dynamic analysis would allow us to better understand learner experience. We also expect that the combination of richer user profiles and content metadata provide opportunities for adding value to LA obtained from video based learning.

Future work is focused on collecting diverse LA (i.e., success rate, emotional states), which should allow the community to understand the use of this learning medium and proceed with the appropriate amendments to the current video-based learning systems and practices.

ACKNOWLEDGMENTS
This work is supported by CCF-1139864 NSF grant and the Richard T. Cheng Endowment.

REFERENCES
1. Giannakos, M. N. et al. Analytics on video-based learning. In *Proc. LAK '13*, ACM Press (2013), 283-284

2. Chorianopoulos, K., Leftheriotis, I. and Gkonela.C. SocialSkip: pragmatic understanding within web video. In *Proc. EuroITV '11*. ACM Press (2011), 25-28.

Forming Beneficial Teams of Students in Massive Online Classes

Rakesh Agrawal
Microsoft Research

Behzad Golshan
Boston University

Evimaria Terzi
Boston University

ABSTRACT

Given a class of large number of students, each exhibiting a different ability level, how can we form teams of students so that the expected performance of team members improves due to team participation? We take a computational perspective and formally define two versions of such team-formation problem: the MaxTeam and the MaxPartition problems. The first asks for the identification of a single team of students that improves the performance of most of the participating team members. The second asks for a partitioning of students into non-overlapping teams that also maximizes the benefit of the participating students. We show that the first problem can be solved optimally in polynomial time, while the second is NP-complete. For the MaxPartition problem, we also design an efficient approximate algorithm for solving it. Our experiments with generated data coming from different distributions demonstrate that our algorithm is significantly better than any of the popular strategies for dividing students in a class into sections.

MODEL

Assume a class S of n students. Each student i is associated with *ability* $\theta_i \in \mathbb{R}$, determined using techniques such as Item Response Theory. Define the *lift* of team $T \subseteq S$, $\text{Lifts}(T) = \sum_{i \in T} \mathbb{I}_{\theta_i \leq \widehat{\Theta}_T}$, where $\mathbb{I}_{\text{condition}}$ is an indicator variable and $\widehat{\Theta}_T = 1/|T| \sum_{i \in T} \theta_i$. Intuitively, the $\text{Lifts}(T)$ is the number of students in team T that would benefit by interacting with the students of above average ability.

IDENTIFYING A SINGLE TEAM

PROBLEM 1 (MaxTeam). *Given a set of n students $S = \{1, \ldots, n\}$, identify a team $T \subseteq S$ of at most k students such that $\text{Lifts}(T)$ is maximized.*

The Leaders&Followers *algorithm:* A good team consists of a set L of *leaders* of high ability who will pull up the team's overall ability and a set F of *followers* whose abilities will be below the team's ability yet their abilities will not be as low so as to decrease the overall ability of the team. Clearly, $\widehat{\Theta}_T$ should be larger than the largest ability score of a student in the set F thus

L@S'14, March 4–5, 2014, Atlanta, Georgia, USA.
ACM 978-1-4503-2669-8/14/03.
http://dx.doi.org/10.1145/2556325.2567856

Algorithm 1 Leaders&Followers

Input: Set of students $S = \{1, \ldots, n\}$ with sorted abilities $\theta_1 > \theta_> \ldots > \theta_n$.
Output: Team T with the maximum $\text{Lifts}(T)$.
1: $T = \emptyset$
2: **for** $i = 1 \ldots k$ **do**
3: $\quad L = $ top-i ability students
4: $\quad$ **for** $j = i + 1 \ldots n - (k - i) + 1$ **do**
5: $\quad\quad F = $ students with abilities $\theta_j, \theta_{j+1}, \ldots, \theta_{j+k-i-1}$
6: $\quad\quad$ **if** F and L satisfy feasibility condition **then** **return** $T = L \cup F$

---

the following *Feasibility* condition should be satisfied: $\widehat{\Theta}_T = (\sum_{i \in L} \theta_i + \sum_{i \in F} \theta_i)/k > \max_{i \in F} \theta_i$, which can be rewritten as: $\sum_{i \in F} \theta_i > k \times \max_{i \in F} \theta_i - \sum_{i \in L} \theta_i$.

If we knew the number of students in set L and the top (highest ability) student in set F (with ability score denoted as θ_F), then we can compute the right hand side of the above inequality. However, we do not know which student is going to be the top student in set F but there are only $O(n)$ possibilities. For a given set L and the top student with ability θ_F, the easiest way to satisfy this inequality is by placing the top students with ability lower than θ_F in the set F. These students are clearly a set of *consecutive* students with ability levels below θ_F. With a preprocessing step of complexity $O(n)$ for computing the cumulative sums of all the ability levels of all the students sorted in decreasing ability level, Leaders&Followers algorithm has complexity $O(nk)$. This complexity reduces to $O(n \log k)$ by replacing the linear search in Algorithm 1 with a binary search.

PARTITIONING A CLASS INTO TEAMS

PROBLEM 2 (MaxPartition). *Given an integer k and a set of n students $S = \{1, \ldots, n\}$ (with $n = k\ell$) find a partition of S into teams $T_1, \ldots T_\ell$, where each team is of size k and $\sum_{i=1}^{\ell} \text{Lifts}(T_i)$ is maximized.*

LEMMA 1. *When $k = n/2$ then the MaxPartition is NP-complete.*

The IterL&F *algorithm:* The IterL&F algorithm solves the MaxPartition problem by iteratively picking one team of size k using the Leaders&Followers algorithm in every iteration and removing this team from the set of students. Among the many candidates that may possibly exist that achieve the same value of Lifts, the one with the highest highest-ability follower is picked. Intuitively, this tie-breaking rule groups the highest ability leaders

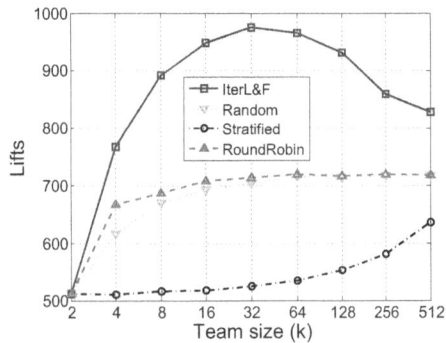

Figure 1. Performance of the IterL&F, Random, Stratified and RoundRobin algorithms for the MaxPartition problem; *x*-axis (log-scale): number of students per team (k); *y*-axis sum of the Lifts values of the teams in the partition.

with relatively high ability followers. Clearly, there are n/k iterations of IterL&F, each taking time $O(n \log k)$. Therefore, the overall running time is $O(n^2 \log k/k)$.

EXPERIMENTS

We experiment with a dataset of $n = 1024$ students, with ability values randomly sampled from a pareto distribution having the shape parameter equal to 3.

Baseline algorithms: In addition to the IterL&F algorithm, we experiment with the following three baseline algorithms: Random, Stratified, and RoundRobin.

The Random algorithm simply creates ℓ teams of size k by randomly assigning students to teams. The running time of the Random algorithm is $O(n)$, since it is adequate to create a random permutation of the students and then create the ℓ teams by considering consecutive members of this permutation. Note that Random is the frequently used algorithm for partitioning a large class into sections.

The Stratified algorithm sorts the students in decreasing order of their abilities. Then, the first team is created by considering the first k students with the highest abilities and putting them in a team by themselves. The second team is created with the subsequent k students and so on. The running time of this algorithms for a sorted input consisting of n students is $O(n)$. This algorithm can be thought of as an idealized version of the oft-used, ability-based homogeneous grouping of students.

The RoundRobin algorithm again considers the sorted list of students. In this case, the first team is created by considering k students at positions 1, $k+1$, $(2k+1)$ etc. in this sorted list. The second team is formed by students at positions 2, $k+2$, $(2k+2)$ etc. on the same sorted list and so on until ℓ teams are formed. The running time of this algorithms for a sorted input consisting of n students is $O(n)$. This algorithm mimics how teams are often formed (particularly in recreational sports) by first selecting the leaders and then letting the leaders take turn in adding members to their respective teams.

Performance of team-formation algorithms: Figure 1 shows the total gain of the teams formed by the dif-

ferent algorithms as a function of the team size k. The results (which are averages over 20 random datasets drawn from the respective distribution) demonstrate that for all values of k (except for $k = 2$, where all algorithms have similar performance), IterL&F is significantly better. In fact, there are values of k (e.g., $k = 32$) for which the IterL&F achieves total Lifts of more than 950, while the maximum possible value is less than 1024. This means that more than 90% of the students are assigned into teams that can potentially improve their performance since the team's ability is higher than the students' abilities for all these students.

Amongst the baseline algorithms, Random and RoundRobin are better than Stratified. The reason is that the dataset drawn from a pareto distribution has a small number of exceptionally high-ability students. The Stratified algorithm puts these students together in one team and therefore their high abilities cannot be leveraged to lift up the average abilities of other teams. This phenomenon is not observed in the teams formed by Random and RoundRobin since these algorithms distribute the high-ability individuals into different teams allowing more teams to benefit from them.

For $k = 2$, all algorithms have the same total Lifts, which is equal to $n/2 = 1024/2 = 512$. This is because in teams of size 2 inevitably there is one student that is above and one that is below average and therefore the team is beneficial for exactly half of the students, independently of how the team assignment is performed.

DISCUSSION

One could object that our approach is unfair to strong students. We offer the following counterpoints:

- Our algorithm builds teams in such a way that the highest ability leaders are grouped with the highest ability followers, the next set of highest ability leaders are put together with the next set of highest ability of followers, and so on. Thus the strong students are still in good company.

- Helping someone else understand the material can produce a more organized cognitive structure than only trying to learn the material for oneself. The person starts seeing the issues from new perspectives, leading to a better fundamental grasp of the material.

- A student could be very strong in one subject, but not so strong in another. It is only fair that she helps her team mates in her strong subject, while she gets help from them in the subject that is not her strong suit.

In the future, we would like to investigate the implication of extending the partitioning objective to incorporate the numeric increases in the performance of the group members. We would also like to enrich our problem formulation with constraints due to socio-emotional factors such as interpersonal relations. Finally, we would like to partner with some MOOCs to study the performance characteristics of our proposal in real-life settings.

Uncovering Hidden Engagement Patterns for Predicting Learner Performance in MOOCs

[1]**Arti Ramesh**, [1]**Dan Goldwasser**, [1]**Bert Huang**, [1]**Hal Daumé III**, [2]**Lise Getoor**
[1]University of Maryland, College Park   [2]University of California, Santa Cruz
{artir, bert, hal}@cs.umd.edu, goldwas1@umiacs.umd.edu, getoor@soe.ucsc.edu

ABSTRACT
Maintaining and cultivating student engagement is a prerequisite for MOOCs to have broad educational impact. Understanding student engagement as a course progresses helps characterize student learning patterns and can aid in minimizing dropout rates, initiating instructor intervention. In this paper, we construct a probabilistic model connecting student behavior and class performance, formulating student engagement types as latent variables. We show that our model identifies course success indicators that can be used by instructors to initiate interventions and assist students.

Author Keywords
MOOC, learner engagement, probabilistic modeling

ACM Classification Keywords
K.3.1. Computer Uses in Education

INTRODUCTION
Sustaining student engagement is important in both classroom and online courses. Unlike classroom courses, the prevalent method for facilitating student-teacher interaction in MOOCs is to use online forums where students post questions and obtain feedback from the instructor or other students. Absence of direct teacher interaction, large number of students, and their diverse backgrounds make it challenging for MOOC instructors to gauge the level of student engagement and involvement and take appropriate actions.

We develop a data-driven approach for modeling student engagement. Online activities such as interactions with other learners or staff on discussion forums, completion of assignments, and *language* used by the learners in posts serve as useful indicators for gauging engagement. Combining language analysis of forum posts with graph analysis over very large networks of entities (e.g., students, instructors, topics, assignments) to capture domain dynamics is challenging. We propose a model that uses behavioral, structural, and linguistic (polarity and subjectivity of forum posts) aspects to distinguish between forms of student engagement (active and passive). The engagement types are represented as latent variables in our model and are learned from observed data. We

then use the latent engagement estimates to predict learners' performance and reason about learners' behavior.

MODELING LEARNER ENGAGEMENT
We construct the following types of features from learners' interaction with the MOOC website—1) behavioral—constructed from user behavior such as posting in, viewing or voting on discussion forums, lecture views, and quiz completion; 2) linguistic—polarity and subjectivity values of forum-content calculated using Opinionfinder [3]; 3) structural—constructed from forum-interaction; and 4) temporal—features from user activity over time. To model the interactions between these features and learner engagement, we use *probabilistic soft logic* (PSL)[1], which is a system for relational probabilistic modeling. PSL enables us to encode observed features, latent, and target variables as logical predicates and capture domain knowledge by constructing rules over these predicates. PSL interprets these rules in a parameterized probabilistic model and is able to perform efficient inference and parameter fitting using machine learning algorithms. We experiment with predicting two aspects of learner performance—1) whether the learner earned a statement of accomplishment in the course, and 2) whether the learner survived the later part of the course. We refer to these as *learner performance* and *learner survival* models.

Learner Performance Models
We construct two different PSL models for predicting learner performance —1) a direct model (denoted DIRECT) that infers performance from observable features, 2) a latent variable model (LATENT) that infers student engagement as a hidden variable to predict learner performance. We treat learner engagement types—active, passive, and disengaged as latent variables and associate conjunctions of observed features to one or more forms of engagement. We then evaluate the latent formulation by using it to infer learner performance.

Learner Survival Models
In the survival PSL models, we split the course into three phases—*start*, *middle*, and *end*. The phase-splits are chosen according to the number of quizzes and lectures in the courses, with equal distribution of quizzes and lectures in the splits. We use the same features as in the performance models, however the features are computed for the phase(s) of the course in consideration. Here, we predict if each learner *survives* a phase in the course, i.e., whether the learner takes a quiz that immediately follows the split-point. We construct two models for predicting learner survival—a DIRECT model with the features directly implying survival and a LATENT model using engagement as a latent layer. We refer the reader to [2], for more details.

EMPIRICAL EVALUATION

We design our experiments around performance measures—course grades and course attendance, and show how our engagement formulation helps in reliably predicting these measures. We evaluate our models on Coursera MOOC *Surviving Disruptive Technologies*. This seven-week course had 1665 users participating in the forums and 826 users completing the course with a nonzero grade. We use 10-fold cross-validation in our experiments, leaving out 10% of the data for testing and the rest for training, where the model weights are learned.

Learner Performance Results

For the learner performance models, we filter the data to include only learners that attempted one or more quizzes or assignments in the course and earned a non-zero score. We labeled the ones that earned a statement of accomplishment as positive instances (*performance* 1.0) and others as negative (*performance* 0.0). These labels are used as ground truth to train and test the models. From experimental results in Table 1, we observe that the LATENT PSL model performs better at predicting learner performance.

	AUC-PR Pos	AUC-PR Neg.	AUC-ROC	Kendall
DIRECT	0.74	0.54	0.66	0.58
LATENT	0.75	0.57	0.69	0.60

Table 1: Performance of DIRECT and LATENT PSL performance models in Disruptive Technologies course.

	start	middle	end	start-mid	start-end
DIRECT	0.72	0.75	0.89	0.70	0.72
LATENT	0.75	0.80	0.95	0.76	0.82

Table 2: Performance of DIRECT and LATENT PSL survival models for different data-splits (AUC-ROC)

Learner Survival Analysis

Predicting student performance can provide instructors with a powerful tool if these predictions can be made *reliably* before the students disengage and drop out. We model this scenario by training our model over data collected early in the course. In the survival models, we use the subset of learners who earned an overall score greater than 0, and assign binary labels based on activity after our phase-split point. Our experiments in the survival models are aimed at measuring learner health by understanding 1) factors influencing learners' continuous survival, 2) engagement types and movement across types, and 3) phase-splits that are most important for predicting learner survival. Table 2 gives the accuracy values of DIRECT and LATENT models for different phase-splits in the data. The tag *start-mid* refers to data collected by combining phases *start* and *middle*; *start-end* refers to data collected over the entire course. Consistent with previous experiments, LATENT survival model has higher prediction reliability.

Early Prediction

Early prediction scores, described in Table 2 under *start*, *middle*, and *start-mid* tags (i.e., survival prediction using partial data), show that our model makes better predictions (as the data available to our model is closer to the actual decision point).

Results show that monitoring learner activity in the middle phase is most important for predicting whether the learner will survive the length of the course. Our model performs best when using data from the *middle* phase, compared to using data from the *start* phase, and an almost equal accuracy values when compared to *start-mid*. We hypothesize that this is due to the presence of a larger learner population in the *start* that fails to remain engaged. Eliminating data collected from this population helps improve our prediction of learner survival, indicated by an increase in accuracy for *middle*.

Analyzing Engagement Pattern Dynamics

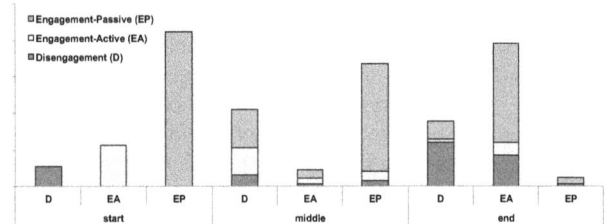

Figure 1: Engagement labels distribution of students who completed the course. Label transitions are captured by coloring bars according to assignments at the previous time point.

We analyze learners' engagement patterns using the engagement values predicted by our model. Learners are classified into one of the engagement types by considering the dominant value of engagement as predicted by the model. Figure 1 shows our engagement values for learners that continued in the course until completion. The labels D, EA and EP refer to *disengagement*, *engagement_active* and *engagement_passive*. We show engagement assignment levels at each time span (*start, middle, end*), and color code the bars according to the previous engagement assignments. It can be observed that the most engaged learners only exhibit passive forms of engagement in the *start* and *middle* phases. While in the *end* phase, learners tend to become more actively engaged.

CONCLUSION

In this work, we formalize, using PSL, our intuition that student engagement can be modeled as a complex interaction of behavioral, linguistic, and social cues. Our results show that our model can construct an interpretation for latent engagement types from data, based on their impact on performance.

REFERENCES

1. Broecheler, M., Mihalkova, L., and Getoor, L. Probabilistic similarity logic. In *Uncertainty in Artificial Intelligence (UAI)* (2010).

2. Ramesh, A., Goldwasser, D., Huang, B., Daume III, H., and Getoor, L. Modeling learner engagement in moocs using probabilistic soft logic. In *NIPS Workshop on Data Driven Education* (2013).

3. Wilson, T., Hoffmann, P., Somasundaran, S., Kessler, J., Wiebe, J., Choi, Y., Cardie, C., Riloff, E., and Patwardhan, S. Opinionfinder: A system for subjectivity analysis. In *Proceedings of HLT/EMNLP on Interactive Demonstrations* (2005).

A Multiplayer Online Game for Teaching Software Engineering Practices

David Xiao and Robert C. Miller
CSAIL, Massachusetts Institute of Technology
Cambridge, MA 02139
{dxiao, rcm}@mit.edu

ABSTRACT

Programming best-practices are a difficult subject to learn for beginner computer science students. In the classroom, these practices are appreciated and taught through a combination of lectures and group projects. Group projects, however, take time and are ill-suited for Massive Open Online Courses (MOOCs).

This project aims to develop a web-based many-player programming game which addresses these issues by having large numbers of students code many small functions in parallel, give feedback on each other's implementations, and compose them into much larger programs. Gameplay will require only a few hours and should provide rapid and substantive feedback on the reusability and flexibility of a student's code.

We have developed and playtested a small-scale prototype to determine if software engineering lessons could be learned through such a game. Further prototypes will test the game at MOOC scales and with different structures. We will develop a final version to deploy to MIT's online class 6.005x: Software Construction.

Author Keywords

MOOCs; Software engineering education; Educational games; Team programming

ACM Classification Keywords

K.3.2. Computers and Education: Computer and Information Science Eduation

INTRODUCTION

Beginning computer science students often have little appreciation for software best-practices required for successful long-term, multi-person programming projects. Common pitfalls include obtuse variable names, documenting code, and maintaining invariants. In the classroom, these practices are appreciated and taught through a combination of lectures and small-group, week-long to multi-week projects. These projects achieve their goal by making students generate code

L@S'14, March 4–5, 2014, Atlanta, Georgia, USA.
ACM 978-1-4503-2669-8/14/03.
http://dx.doi.org/10.1145/2556325.2567858

of sufficient volume and complexity that the issues encountered at larger scales become manifest [2].

Such project approaches however suffer from drawbacks, especially when adapting them to Massive Open Online Courses (MOOCs). First, projects give students relatively little programming feedback for the total effort expended. Second, MOOCs often have thousands of geographically distant students, which often render small groups inefficient and group time coordination impossible. This project aims to contribute to MOOCs and software engineering education in general by distilling the programming decisions involved in creating large programs into a one to two hour many-player online programming game more suited to the MOOC format.

A short, well-executed, many-player game offers several advantages over the current project-based approach. Students can play the game repeatedly and thus get more opportunities for feedback than before. They are likely to be less afraid of failure and thus more exploratory with their code. Games can also highlight outcomes more dramatically than otherwise possible [3]. Many-player games also allow students to learn from other peers' work, and capture more complexity in less time.

Related Work

To our limited knowledge, no MOOC has yet explored teaching team-programming best practices for students through a multiplayer online programming game. However, other groups have used games and collaborative tools to achieve different but similar aims, whose body of work this project may contribute to. In classrooms, educators have created many games to teach concepts such as memory-management [4] or the non-programming aspects of software engineering [3]. Educational tools such as Caesar allow students to give feedback on other student's code [5]. For professionals, the crowdsourcing platform TopCoder provides contests similar to the one described here, but which take much longer and do not target beginner programmers [1].

APPROACH

In this game, each user proceeds through three timed stages, each of which requires no more than an hour to complete. In the first stage, Implementation, the user is given a set of three short functions to implement. The functions are clear in spirit but not in specifics, allowing flexibility on specifics such as signature and handling edge cases. In the second stage, Evaluation, the user can view all other users' implementations, comment on them, and revise his or her own code. This is the first opportunity for feedback. In the third stage, Composition, the user is asked to implement a program which independently would require much more time to code than is given, but is much more approachable with judicious usage of functions from Implementation. This is the second opportunity for feedback, since the function implementation which is most useful to a user's program may not be their own, and users can see afterward which function implementations users used in their Composition programs.

The game will be implemented as a web application. A browser-based front-end written with JavaScript and Angular.js will display game instructions and state, a simple development environment for coding and a listing of function implementations to comment on and reference. Users will code in Java, although other languages could be made possible. The server will be written with Node.js, and will handle game state, submitted implementations, and statistics for in-game results and research analysis.

PRELIMINARY PROTOTYPES AND RESULTS

Design

In order to more fully develop the concept and gain some insights into how such a game could work, we developed a small-scale, low-fidelity prototype version of the game to playtest. Playtests used small groups of 3-6 undergraduate and graduate-level students of varying programming skill and experience, together in a single room. About 10 functions for Implementation and 3 programs for Composition were used, with careful attention given to ensuring that the problems used different subsets of functions. The prototypes used Google Documents to display programming prompts, Forms for code submissions, and Spreadsheets for viewing submitted implementations. Implementation and Composition were 20 minutes each, and Evaluation was 10 minutes without commenting. The purpose of the playtests was to test the hypotheses that:

1. Small, 10-line functions could be written in short periods of time and be readable, reusable, and correct.

2. Users would use other user's implementations during Composition, instead of rewriting the code themselves.

3. Creating a function, seeing other user's implementations, and then composing the functions with other functions, creates opportunities for learning.

Results

Users were able to write an average of 3 functions during implementation, with everybody submitting at least one. Of the submitted programs in Composition, each used at least one function implementation written by another person. However, only one-third of students submitted programs during Composition, primarily because Evaluation was too short, and too much time was spent reading functions in Composition. Almost all playtesters gave positive comments however, usually either that the game was good practice in rapid programming or they learned something from reviewing other user's code.

Several additional conclusions were drawn from the playtests: First, users should be given a limited selection of functions to implement in Implementation instead of all available functions. This reduces the amount of time spent in reading function descriptions in favor of time spent coding. Second, the Evaluation should be longer, with users allowed to give feedback and revise. Finally, Implementation should also be lengthened and functions made slightly more complex. More complex functions were saw more reuse, while simple functions were sometimes just rewritten. Overall, the playtests suggest that the approach has potential, and warrants further development.

NEXT STEPS

Based on the results of these small-scale playtests and challenges outlined above, we are currently developing several new prototypes. The primary goal is to scale the game to be playable at MOOC-scales.

The secondary goal is to explore potential structural variations: The three stages may not need to be synchronous for users. At most, the first two stages and Composition could be their own separate exercises. In addition, Evaluation and Composition could be repeated multiple times, each time building on the programs from previous stages.

Finally, we plan to deploy the game onto MIT's upcoming online class 6.005x: Software Construction. Evaluations of the game will be conducted by a combination of pre- and post-surveys, user actions within the game, and student coursework afterwards.

CONCLUSION

This purpose of this project is to create a new, MOOC-scale method for teaching and giving students experience in the challenges of large project programming. We have designed a web-based parallel programming game to that end, and early prototypes give positive results. Further research will test game design and student learning through larger-scale playtests, and eventual inclusion into MIT's upcoming software construction MOOC.

REFERENCES

1. Lakhani, K. R., Garvin, D. A., and Lonstein, E. Topcoder(a): Developing software through crowdsourcing. *Harvard Business School Case 610-032* (January 2010).

2. Mingins, C., Miller, J., and Dick, M. How we teach software engineering, 1999.

3. Oh, E. Teaching software engineering through simulation. In *Proc. International Conference on Software Engineering* (2002).

4. Papastergiou, M. Digital game-based learning in high school computer science education: Impact on educational effectiveness and student motivation. *Computers and Education 52*, 1 (2009), 1 – 12.

5. Tang, M. Caesar: A social code review tool for programming education. Master's thesis, MIT, 2010.

Talkabout: Small-group Discussions in Massive Global Classes

Julia Cambre, Chinmay Kulkarni, Michael S. Bernstein
Stanford University
{jcambre,chinmay,msb}@cs.stanford.edu

Scott R. Klemmer
UC San Diego
srk@ucsd.edu

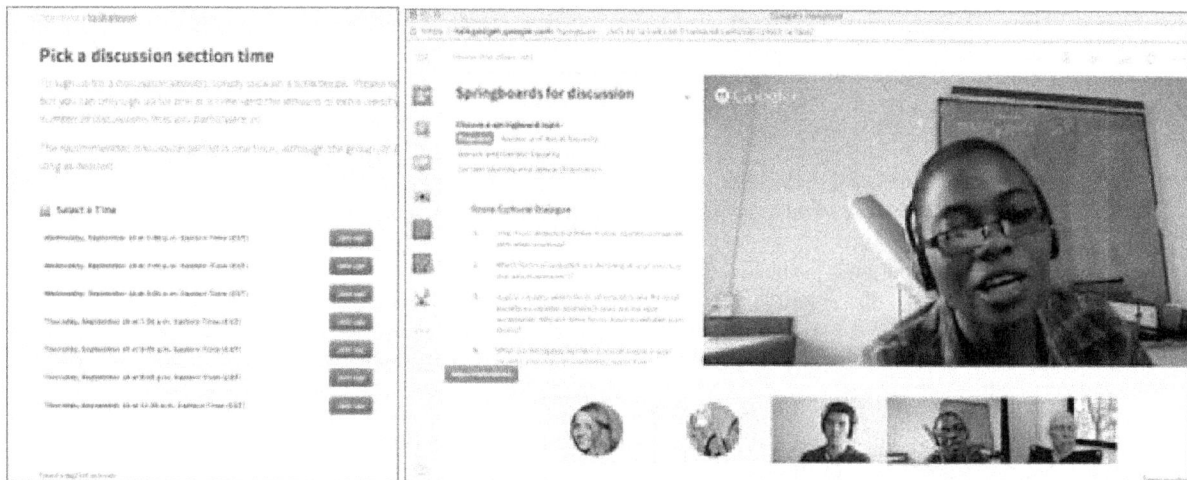

Figure 1: Talkabout (https://talkabout.stanford.edu) enables peer discussions in global classes with Google Hangouts. (Left) Students choose discussions that fit their schedule. (Right) Talkabout embeds a guide into video discussions (Image by Scott Plous).

ABSTRACT

In the physical classroom, peer interactions motivate students and expand their perspective. We suggest that synchronous peer interaction can benefit massive online courses as well. Talkabout organizes students into video discussion groups and allows instructors to determine group composition and discussion content. Using Talkabout, students pick a discussion time that suits their schedule. The system groups the students into small video discussions based on instructor preferences such as gender or geographic balance. To date, 2,474 students in five massive online courses have used Talkabout to discuss topics ranging from prejudice to organizational theory. Talkabout discussions are diverse: in one course, the median six-person discussion group had students from four different countries. Students enjoyed discussing in these diverse groups: the average student participated for 66 minutes, twice the course requirement. Students in more geographically distributed groups also scored higher on the final, suggesting that distributed discussions have educational value.

L@S 2014, March 4–5, 2014, Atlanta, Georgia, USA.
ACM 978-1-4503-2669-8/14/03.
http://dx.doi.org/10.1145/2556325.2567859

Author Keywords

video; discussion; small groups; synchronous collaboration

ACM Classification Keywords

K.3.1 Computer Uses in Education: Collaborative Learning.

SCALING PEER LEARNING

In physical classrooms, students' interaction with diverse peers widens their perspectives [2], improves critical thinking [4], and improves satisfaction with their educational experience [3]. We hypothesize that peer interaction in massive online courses may provide similar benefits. Furthermore, these classes bring a diverse set of peers together into a single classroom, which may amplify these benefits.

However, online students learn largely in isolation and have limited opportunities for peer interaction. Students primarily interact with peers on discussion forums, but response latency makes it difficult to develop the common ground [5] necessary for peer learning [1]. Some students self-organize meet-ups with local peers, but these meet-ups require significant effort to attend, so participation is limited. In addition, instructors have little control over the content or composition of self-organized meet-ups.

This paper introduces Talkabout, a small-group video discussion system for massive global classes. Built on Google Hangouts, Talkabout enables peer interactions that combine the rich synchronous interaction of meet-ups with the flexibility and availability of forums. The system comprises a website for scheduling discussions and organizing groups, and a Hangout application that guides and monitors discussions. Using Talkabout, instructors can determine group size and composition, and provide discussion prompts for students. Talkabout leverages the scale and diversity of online classes to offer discussions at many times through the day.

So far, five courses have run discussions using Talkabout. In these courses, 2,474 students participated in discussions in groups of approximately four to six students each. Even though students chose their discussion times, the resulting groups were geographically diverse. Overall, our findings suggest that real-time interactions in massive classes could further peer learning.

COORDINATING SMALL-GROUP DISCUSSIONS

The large scale of online classes implies that instructors are unable to participate in discussions directly and enforce student behavior as they would in a physical classroom. Therefore, instructors should be able to guide the educational experience of discussion by structuring best practices into the system, and organizing discussions automatically.

Talkabout provides instructors with control over the structure of discussions. Instructors can decide the number of students in each group, the timing of discussions, and whether discussions are a series throughout the course. By modulating frequency and size, Talkabout can support peer interactions ranging from peer programming exercises to classroom-style discussions and design-studio critiques. Instructors provide discussion guides that are embedded directly into the Google Hangout (Figure 1R).

Hundreds of students enroll in each discussion. As a result, Talkabout offers sessions many times each day and students choose a session that fits their schedule (Figure 1L). To date, discussions have typically been scheduled every six hours. Talkabout assigns students to one of many parallel sessions when they arrive. By assigning students to sessions at runtime, Talkabout can handle no-shows and ensure that groups reflect the instructor's preferences. For example, the system can balance group sizes, gender, and geography, or it can place students with classmates they have met in previous discussions. Students receive reminder emails before their session begins. If students miss their scheduled discussion, the system can also send them emails to reschedule.

To better understand the ingredients of a successful discussion, Talkabout gathers metrics on student behavior during discussions. Currently we collect attendance and record conversational turn-taking through a Hangout application.

STUDENTS VALUED GLOBAL DISCUSSIONS

To date, Talkabout has been used in five massive global classes, spanning six hundred discussion sessions. These courses covered historical interpretation of photographs, philosophical reasoning, organizational analysis, social psychology, and human-computer interaction. Participation in discussions was voluntary, though two courses encouraged it through extra credit. Of the 5,060 students who signed up for a discussion, 49% (2,474 students) participated. The Social Psychology course had the largest participation. In this class, students discussed prejudice and social justice as a one-time, optional extra credit activity in the final week of the course. All discussions were held in English, and students were assigned to the first available group upon arrival. The mean attendance time per student was 66 minutes, twice the required minimum of 30 minutes. Students from 102 different countries participated, with a median of four countries in each six-person discussion group. On follow-up, students reported they enjoyed the discussions (median rating 4 on 4 point Likert scale; 4:Very enjoyable), and found the global nature of these discussions remarkable. One reported, "It was like a mini-UN. We had an Australian currently residing in Dubai, an Afghan, a Romanian, an Indian and myself (a Pakistani)." A linear model found students assigned to discussion groups with participants from more countries scored higher on the final exam, when controlled for pre-final grade. Each additional country represented improved scores by 0.4% (n=1600, $F(1,789)=2.6$, $\beta=4.7$, $R^2=0.07$, $p < 0.01$).

DISCUSSION AND CONCLUSION

Our experience suggests peer discussions are a promising approach for small-group interaction at large scale. These discussions face unique design and technical challenges. We found that students struggle with technical issues such as bandwidth limitations and installing Google Hangouts. Furthermore, because only half the students who enrolled in discussions actually attend, students must be assigned to groups on arrival. Students were less likely to attend a discussion session the earlier they signed up for it. In follow-up emails, many reported they had simply forgotten about their session, or that a conflict came up. Moving forward, we suggest "just-in-time" discussions might be preferable to pre-scheduled times.

REFERENCES

1. Baker, M., Hansen, T., Joiner, R., & Traum, D. (1999). The role of grounding in collaborative learning tasks. In P. Dillenbourg (Ed.), Collaborative learning: Cognitive and computational approaches (pp. 31-63). Oxford: Pergamon.

2. Gurin P., Dey E., Hurtado S, Gurin G. (2002). Diversity and higher education: Theory and impact on educational outcomes. *Harvard Educational Review*, 72(3), 330-366.

3. Luo, J., & Jamieson-Drake, D. (2009). A retrospective assessment of the educational benefits of interaction across racial boundaries. *J. Coll. Student Dev.*, 50(1), 67-86.

4. Pascarella, E. T., Palmer, B., Moye, M., & Pierson, C. T. (2001). Do diversity experiences influence the development of critical thinking? *J. Coll. Student Dev.*, 42(3), 257-271.

5. Rocco, E. (1998). Trust breaks down in electronic contexts but can be repaired by some initial face-to-face contact. In *Proc. CHI 1998*, 496–502.

Community TAs Scale High-Touch Learning, Provide Student-Staff Brokering, and Build Esprit de Corps

Kathryn Papadopoulos, Lalida Sritanyaratana, and Scott R. Klemmer
Citrix Customer Experience, Stanford HCI Group, and UCSD Depts of Cognitive Science & CSE
kathryn.papadopoulos@citrix.com, lalida@google.com, srk@ucsd.edu

ABSTRACT
Massive online courses introduced Community TAs (CTAs) to help scale teaching staff support. CTAs are former top students who return as volunteer course staff. We studied CTAs in 3 classes on Coursera, including interviews and surveys from a Human-Computer Interaction (HCI) class. A key benefit of CTAs is their brokering role that mediates staff and student goals. CTAs provide greater discussion forum coverage (both in quantity and time of day) compared to instructor and Head TA (HTA) capabilities and contribute to peer assessment. As CTAs are new teachers, physically distributed, and culturally diverse, clear division of responsibilities is especially important.

Author Keywords
Community TAs; teaching assistants; volunteer teaching

ACM Classification Keywords
K.3.1 Computer Uses in Education: Collaborative Learning

TEACHING ASSISTANTS ON-LAND AND ONLINE
Higher education instructors often enlist graduate students to serve as teaching assistants for their courses. Common TA duties include answering student questions, grading homework assignments, and leading weekly discussion sessions. TA support benefits all parties: instructors benefit from reduced workload, graduate students receive apprenticeship training as teachers, and students gain increased comfort in asking questions and admitting a lack of understanding to a fellow student [4]. More staff also allow smaller discussion sections and increased office hours.

To help make high-touch, free online education sustainable, some courses recruit former students to return as volunteer TAs. These Community TAs (or "World TAs") were first used online in Fox and Patterson's *Software as a Service* class [3]. On Coursera, more than 45 classes have CTAs. Two factors that differentiate this role from a traditional TA role is their association as a recent student of the course

(designated by the "Community" in their title) and the volunteer basis for their assistance. What motivates CTA participation, and what are their and students' experiences? We report on CTA experiences in 3 Coursera classes, focusing on the *Human-Computer Interaction (HCI)* class.

Prior work found that students perceive volunteer teachers as showing greater enjoyment, enthusiasm, and innovation than paid teachers [6]. Students in a lesson with volunteer teachers enjoyed it more, reported a more positive mood, were more interested in future learning, and showed greater exploratory activity than those in the paid condition [6]. If online students perceive CTAs as volunteer teachers, we may see similar benefits, particularly in a design course that encourages exploration.

Some university classes recruit former students to provide course assistance as an alternative or addition to graduate TAs. Roberts *et al.* report that undergraduate section leaders develop better rapport with students (from closer proximity in position), better familiarity with the curriculum than graduate students, and increase personal understanding of the course concepts, while also generating esprit de corps and valuable social networks [5]. Undergraduates can provide more 1:1 student help at less cost than graduate TAs. We hypothesize that volunteer CTAs yield similar benefits for the same reasons of having recently been in students' shoes. CTAs can play a valuable brokering role [2], using their dual student/teacher perspective and rapport.

Recruited for Performance; Motivated by Learning
For HCI's Fall 2012 session, the Head TA (HTA) recruited community assistants based on their course performance on and forum participation. The HTA was a graduate student collocated with the instructor. She assessed candidates on both quantity and quality of posts, emphasizing comments showing positive reinforcement or insightful questions/answers. The HTA invited 10 students; 5 accepted as CTAs. In Spring 2013, all former CTAs were invited back (all but one returned), 6 additional TAs were recruited, totaling 10 CTAs. Recruitment criteria were expanded to include interactions taking place beyond the course site. For example, one CTA was recruited for her work managing a Facebook group dedicated to course. The number of students invited was largely influenced by the maximum capacity of Google Hangouts, the communication channel for staff meetings. In Fall 2013, *HCI* again invited all former CTAs back while recruiting additional outstanding

students from its previous iteration, resulting in 16 CTAs. The increase allowed the HTA to distribute tasks more effectively and reduce individual workload. The total CTA pool was able to grow because meetings were divided by topic, with only the topic-relevant subset of TAs attending. All CTAs monitored forums and either graded assignment or quiz submissions. While forum posts by students decreased towards the end of the course, CTA activity decreased more. We interpret this as CTAs burning out on forum monitoring. Forum monitoring could be more efficient: we recommend that the HTA assign 3-5 CTAs entirely to forum moderation, anticipating the total number of CTAs to stay between 12 and 16. Depending on forum activity and time availability of CTAs, moderation can be divided by sub-forum, time of the day, or day of week.

Other classed used a similar number of CTAs: *Think Again: How to Reason and Argue* had 11; *Design: Creation of Artifacts in Society* had 8 CTAs. Each also had as a HTA a former graduate students who worked with the instructor.

We surveyed the Spring 2013 *HCI* CTAs about their experience. Their most popular reported motivation was to increase knowledge about the course topic, followed by a passion for helping others and giving back to the community. Two CTAs wrote they were most excited for "learning by observing student submissions and interaction" and "seeing other people's insights which inspires me a lot." These responses are consistent with the motivations of undergraduate section leaders and volunteer teachers [5, 6].

Global Distribution and 24/7 Forum Monitoring

CTAs monitor forum discussions, answer questions, and flag issues for the HTA or instructor. On the Coursera platform, CTAs have the same permissions as students, but their forum posts are labeled *Community TA*. Given the global diversity of the CTA talent pool, the resulting distributed time zones can provide nearly constant forum monitoring. Brinton *et al.* [1] surveyed 73 massive online courses and found active participation by teaching assistants on the forum increases the overall discussion volume.

HCI's end-of-class survey asked students to rate the helpfulness of instructors and CTA posts. Students rated both as highly helpful, but more than twice the number of people (189 compared to 88) reported not seeing instructor posts compared to CTA posts, which may be a result of the small number (17 posts) compared to CTAs (879) (see Figure 1). *Think Again* and *Design* exhibited similar skew:

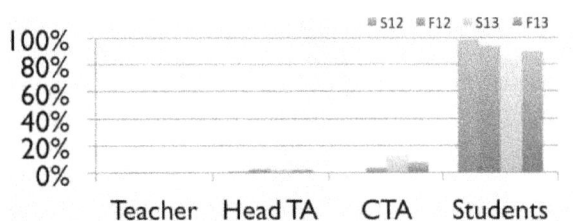

Figure 1 Student posts composed the vast majority, and CTAs provided much more coverage than staff could.

instructor posts ranged from 2 - 87; CTA posts ranged from 609 - over 885.

We broke CTA posts into six categories, including advice, assignment clarification, and logistics communication. However, what quickly emerged as a popular type of response were those that indicated their role as an intermediary for the instructor and the HTA. This brokering, often acknowledged through responses that reference "flagging for staff review," reinforces the dual-role of staff member and student. The TAs maintained a spreadsheet to track issues requiring instructor or HTA input. CTAs can identify with student issues and offer first-hand advice, but also assume a position of authority, while sometimes escalating issues to the instructor or HTA.

CTAs Can Lead Peer Learning & Improve Coursework

Some classes make more involved use of CTAs. In *Think Again*, CTAs host weekly discussions that students can sign up for. In *HCI*, which uses peer assessment, 5 CTAs assist with grading training and ground truth assignments. For each assignment, an HTA leads a calibration session in which the CTAs collectively grade 1-2 submissions. Each CTA then grades 2-3 submissions. Four other CTAs help grade free response quiz questions. CTAs also suggest improvements to the class structure and assignments based on their experiences taking assisting with the class.

CONCLUSION

We will continue to study CTA interactions in additional courses and distill best practices. We recommend:

- Recruiting globally distributed CTAs to provide 24-hour forum coverage.
- Maintaining an issue tracking spreadsheet to centralize communication between students and staff.
- Dividing CTA responsibilities, such as assigning specific subforums/hours/days for monitoring.

If you teach a course with CTAs (or plan to), let us know!

REFERENCES

1 Brinton, C.G. *et al.* Learning about social learning in MOOCS: From statistical analysis to generative model. *arXiv preprint arXiv:1312.2159* (2013).

2 Burt, R.S. Structural Holes and Good Ideas. *American Journal of Sociology* 110, 2 (2004), 349-399.

3 Fox, A. and Patterson, D. What We've Learned from Teaching MOOCs. https://www.edx.org/blog/what-weve-learned-teaching-moocs.

4 Goldschmid, B. and Goldschmid, M.L. Peer teaching in higher education: a review. *Higher Education* 5, 1 (1976).

5 Roberts, E., Lilly, J. and Rollins, B. Using undergraduates as teaching assistants in introductory programming courses: An update on the Stanford experience. *ACM SIGCSE Bulletin* 27, 1 (1995), 48-52.

6 Wild, T. C., Enzle, M. E., and Hawkins, W. L. Effects of perceived extrinsic versus intrinsic teacher motivation on student reactions to skill acquisition. *Personality and social psychology bulletin* 18, 2 (1992), 245-251.

Adaptive and Social Mechanisms for Automated Improvement of eLearning Materials

Kevin Buffardi
Virginia Tech
114 McBryde Hall (0106)
Blacksburg, Virginia
kbuffardi@vt.edu

Stephen H. Edwards
Virginia Tech
114 McBryde Hall (0106)
Blacksburg, Virginia
edwards@cs.vt.edu

ABSTRACT

Online environments introduce unprecedented scale for formal and informal learning communities. In these environments, user-contributed content enables social constructivist approaches to education. In particular, students can help each other by providing hints and suggestions on how to approach problems, by rating each other's suggestions, and by engaging in discussions about the questions. In addition, students can also learn through composing their own questions.

Furthermore, with grounding in Item Response Theory, data mining and statistical student models can assess questions and hints for their quality and effectiveness. As a result, internet-scale learning environments allow us to move from simple, canned quizzing systems to a new model where automated, data-driven analysis continuously assesses and refines the quality of teaching material. Our poster describes a framework and prototype of an online drill-and-practice system that leverages user-contributed content and large-scale data to organically improve itself.

Author Keywords

Active learning; computer-supported cooperative learning (CSCL); internet-scale data; automated assessment; adaptive feedback; social constructivism; item response theory

ACM Classification Keywords

K.3.2 [**Computers and Education**]: Computer and Information; K.3.1 [**Computer Uses in Education**]: Computer-assisted instruction

INTRODUCTION

With the emergence of massive, open online courses (MOOCs) and other openly accessible, online eLearning

L@S 2014, March 4–5, 2014, Atlanta, Georgia, USA.
ACM 978-1-4503-2669-8/14/03.
http://dx.doi.org/10.1145/2556325.2567861

tools, the scale of education far-exceeds the constraints of physical classrooms. Specifically, individual MOOCs can grow orders of magnitude greater with enrollment in the thousands [3]. Meanwhile, online education requires novel approaches to address its differences from in-class learning. Our poster presents a framework for social constructivist approaches to engaging students in collaborative learning and for leveraging MOOC-scale data to refine teaching material presentation. We demonstrate application for this framework through *CodeWorkout,* an eLearning prototype for computer science drill-and-practice.

ACTIVE LEARNING DRILL-AND-PRACTICE

At its foundation, CodeWorkout provides a variety of exercises for students to practice and develop their computer science comprehension. The system provides different types of exercises including both multiple-choice questions (MCQs) and coding problems. Coding problems allow students to program solutions that can be evaluated by a series of test cases, using a unit testing framework such as jUnit. However, instead of just indicating which tests pass, CodeWorkout instead provides hints that are based on the students' performance against the test cases.

Peer Review and Instruction

CodeWorkout uniquely leverages social constructivism by building a library of exercises and hints written by its user base. After a student correctly solves an exercise, she has the opportunity to write a hint to help other students on the same problem. Writing these hints require meta-cognition as the student reflects over the question and the problem solving strategy for it. Likewise, after a student has earned sufficient XP to demonstrate mastery of a topic, she can also create new exercises for that topic. Writing exercises similarly involves Higher Order Thinking Skills [1].

Automated Assessment and Adaptive Feedback

Similarly to how CodeWorkout tracks students' performance on exercises, it also tracks how well hints they contributed help others. However, instead of measuring a student's comprehension, hint data measures how well their hints facilitate learning through a tutoring score. Students receive hints after they have failed one or more tests on an exercise. After the student receives the hint and attempts the exercise again, CodeWorkout notes any changes in achievement. Converting an incorrect response to a correct solution in the subsequent attempt demonstrates the hint's effectiveness. Effectiveness is recorded according to performance on individual test case (for coding problems) and on permutations of choice selections (for MCQs) every time the hint is received. As multiple students receive a hint, the effectiveness rates indicate which test cases the hint helps students overcome. Very narrow hints may only help with one individual test case, while good, broad hints that improve learning may show high effectiveness rates for multiple (or even all) test cases.

Measuring effectiveness for test cases helps CodeWorkout select the most appropriate hint for scaffolding learning. Doing so also provides a more accurate measurement of hint effectiveness. Hint assessment supports particularly detailed contextualization by identifying which specific test cases failed on the student's previous attempt, and then subsequently passed after the student received the hint. For example, some hints may broadly help any student struggling with the exercise by improving performance on all test cases, while other hints may only help students overcome specific failed test cases. Hints will be chosen by their effectiveness and by the context of which test cases the student is currently failing. Consequently, CodeWorkout will autonomously evaluate hints and provide the best available hints to a given student, adapted to their situational needs.

Likewise, CodeWorkout uses a novel approach to ensure quality exercises. Where other drill-and-practice systems require students and instructors to manually review content, and then revise or remove poor content, CodeWorkout uniquely alleviates this costly burden. Instead, it collects data on students' performance to automatically assess individual exercises. The system consequently evaluates the quality of each exercise and suppresses poorer exercises in favor of those with superior assessment.

CodeWorkout is built upon a foundation of comprehensive measurements for assessing test questions. In particular, Winter and Payne's extension [4] of an item response theory (IRT)-based [2] adaptive testing scheme quantifies the dimensions of question difficulty and discrimination. When students choose specific topics to practice, the system will provide the best available exercises to the student, as determined by the topic she chose, a model of her competency, and the assessment of exercise difficulty and quality (discrimination). Students' competency is

measured on a topic-by-topic basis by tracking their performance on other exercises with corresponding topic tags. Within the set of available exercises in the given topic, those appropriate to the student's current competency are given precedence, in accordance with IRT [2]. Likewise, exercises with higher discrimination precede those with poor discrimination.

Each time a student practices an exercise, the system collects more assessment data for that exercise. Along with more data, accuracy and precision of difficulty and discrimination will persistently improve. Consequently, the systematic preference of exercises with higher discrimination scores will implicitly suppress poorer exercises with low discrimination. In other words, CodeWorkout inherently evaluates and selects the best exercises available. Accordingly, the system also vets the effectiveness of hints and gives precedence to those that will help students more. In conclusion, CodeWorkout represents an approach to addressing internet-scale learning and assessment by leveraging data-driven measurements with large-scale use to improve the learning materials while also taking advantage of learning through social interaction.

ACKNOWLEDGEMENTS

The development and evaluation of CodeWorkout is supported by a grant from the National Science Foundation Transforming Undergraduate Education in Science, Technology, Engineering and Mathematics (TUES), award number 1245589.

REFERENCES

1. Bloom, B. S. (1969). Taxonomy of Educational Objectives: The Classification of Educational Goals, Handbook I: Cognitive Domain. United Kingdom, Longman Group.

2. Lord, F. M. (1980). Applications of Item Response Theory to Practical Testing Problems. Hillsdale, New Jersey, Lawrence Erlbaum Associates.

3. Webley, K. (2012). "MOOC Brigade: Who Is Taking Massive Open Online Courses, And Why?". from http://nation.time.com/2012/09/26/mooc-brigade-who-is-taking-massive-open-online-courses-and-why/.

4. Winters, T. and T. Payne (2005). What do students know?: an outcomes-based assessment system. Proceedings of the first international workshop on Computing education research. Seattle, WA, USA, ACM.

Distance Learning, OER, and MOOCs: Some UK Experiences

Eileen Scanlon
Open University
Walton Hall
Milton Keynes
Eileen.Scanlon@open.ac.uk

Patrick McAndrew
Open University
Walton Hall
Milton Keynes
Patrick.McAndrew@open.ac.uk

Tim O'Shea
University of Edinburgh
Old College
Edinburgh
principal@ed.ac.uk

ABSTRACT

This paper discusses learning at scale from the perspective of two UK Universities engaging in technology enhanced learning. Three case studies are used to illustrate ways in which scale has been achieved. There is diversity in how scale is supported but also common factors. Openness and choice appear as enablers in all cases.

Author Keywords

Distance learning; informal learning; science education; European experience; recommendations.

ACM Classification Keywords

K.3.1 distance learning

INTRODUCTION

This describes the experience of two UK Universities engaging with technology enhanced learning and considers implications for the adoption of more open approaches to education, such as Massive Open Online Courses (MOOCs). The Open University (OU) is a distance teaching institution which has been providing open education for over 40 years, the University of Edinburgh is a more traditional university innovating on its history of providing full time tuition to degree level for more than 400 years.

The OU was established in Britain in 1969 and from its start operated at scale, running courses for thousands of learners. It supports approximately 250,000 registered learners and reaches millions more through open content and shared environments [1]. The primary model the OU uses for its students studying for a qualification is of supported open learning, combining content with tutor support and assessment to guide learners through their program of study. In the last 10 years it has also provided open access offering open educational resources through its OpenLearn website, and via its courses on iTunesU and

L@S 2014, March 4–5, 2014, Atlanta, Georgia, USA.
ACM 978-1-4503-2669-8/14/03.
http://dx.doi.org/10.1145/2556325.2567862

YouTube. In December 2012 a MOOC platform, FutureLearn, was founded by the OU as a company and now has 24 partners including major UK universities, Australia's Monash University, Ireland's Trinity College Dublin and three non-university institutions: British Museum, the British Council and British Library.

The University of Edinburgh is a great civic institution whose mission is the creation, dissemination and curation of knowledge. The University is recognized as one of the top twenty institutions in the world. Most of its on-campus courses now also have online aspects, e.g. using social media, online assessment, virtual experiments, or real experiments calibrated for use virtually. In the last ten years, 60 planned online extensions of regular undergraduate teaching have been funded. Online students, in particular on postgraduate courses, have been growing in number. The University has 31,000 students registered on conventional courses and is aiming to have 10,000 postgraduate students online. In 2012, the University became the first UK University to offer MOOCs and first on the Coursera platform [2]. They have also joined the FutureLearn partnership and are offering courses in 2014 in both platforms. The University of Edinburgh has a reputation as an early adopter of educational technology. For the University, working with MOOCs allows an exploration of new space to inform practice. In both institutions MOOCs are being introduced in an environment that also includes open educational resources, and tools that provide access for informal learning.

Case study 1: The OpenScience Laboratory

Science at a distance faces the challenge of providing suitable experiences to support programs of learning. Recently the Open Science Laboratory (OSL) [3], co-founded by the OU with support from the Wolfson foundation, built a collection of tools to combine remote access, virtual experiments and citizen science into the curriculum, building on experience in bringing experiments into the home [4]. 39 applications across a broad range of science were produced for the launch in July 2013. The data provided by the real or virtual equipment is authentic, not simulated, gained from remotely operated sensors, photo-realistic recordings of physical experiments and microscope images of real specimens. The OSL enables students to conduct practical science experiments and also to open up some of those experiments to the general public blending citizen science with learning.

Case study 2: accessibility at the OU

The Open University is the largest provider of higher education to disabled students in the UK [5] and such students are making up a growing proportion of its learners. In 2012/13 over 21,000 registered students had a declared disability, approximately 12% of registered students. This is in contrast with 8% more typical of other providers of Higher Education. The proportion is even higher for the Open University's free learning provision; across iTunesU, YouTube and OpenLearn a recent survey [6], found approximately 16% learners with a disability amongst respondents These higher than expected figures emphasize the importance of designing for accessibility at scale. The OU approach to accessibility recognizes the need for human support along with alternative paths. This can seem onerous, however a consistent result is that planning for use by disabled students leads to content that is better for all.

Case study 3: Edinburgh Surgical Science Qualification and the Edinburgh Coursera MOOCs

The MSc in Surgical Sciences is a collaboration between the University of Edinburgh and the Royal College of Surgeons led by James Garden [7]. The course targets trainee surgeons, looking to advance their knowledgebase and prepare for the MRCS examination whilst gaining a postgraduate qualification. As described by Smith [8] the approach fits with clinical activities and achieves impressive results "ESSQ students score an average of 17% higher in the MRCS exam". Although this is smaller in terms of student numbers than the other case studies, it achieves impressive spread of countries from which students are drawn in a subject area that is not an obvious choice for online education

In January 2013 University of Edinburgh launched six MOOCs on the Coursera platform: An Introduction to Philosophy, Astrobiology the Search for Life on other planets, An Introduction to AI Planning, Equine Nutrition, E-learning and Digital Cultures, and Critical Thinking and Global Challenges. Each course was short, designed to take a few hours per week but with varying structures and designs. 309,628 people registered for the courses. Analyzed in the MOOCs@Edinburgh group report [9] (further reported by Jeff Heywood [10] and Siân Bayne [11]) most students state wanting to gain new knowledge or more experience of online learning.

CONCLUSIONS

These brief studies show diversity in the way scale is achieved from a customized approach in accessibility to limited services supporting a recognizable product in MOOCs. There are also common factors. Openness and choice act as enablers in all cases and indicate that to work at scale an important step is to relax the constraints.

ACKNOWLEDGEMENTS

We thank our colleagues at both Universities, particularly from the Open Science Laboratory and OER Research Hub (http://oerresearchhub.org) at the Open University, and James Garden, Siân Bayne, Jeff Heywood and the MOOCs@Edinburgh group at the University of Edinburgh.

REFERENCES

1. McAndrew, P. and Scanlon, E. Open Learning at a distance: lessons for struggling MOOCs. *Science 342*, (2013), 1450–1451.

2. O'Shea, T. MOOCs event presentation transcript. 2013. http://www.qaa.ac.uk/Publications/Podcasts/Transcripts/Pages/Timothy_OShea_MOOCs_transcript.aspx.

3. Open University. The OpenScience Laboratory. 2013. http://www.open.ac.uk/researchprojects/open-science/.

4. Scanlon, E. Open science: trends in the development of science learning. *Open Learning* 26, 2 (2011), 97–112.

5. Open University. Facts and Figures. 2013. http://www.open.ac.uk/about/main/the-ou-explained/facts-and-figures.

6. Law, P., Perryman, L.-A., and Law, A. Open educational resources for all? Comparing user motivations and characteristics across The Open University's iTunes U channel and OpenLearn platform. *Proc. The Open and Flexible Higher Education Conference*, (2013), 204–219.

7. Garden, J. Edinburgh surgical sciences qualification Edinburgh University. 2012. http://www.essq.rcsed.ac.uk/site/2741/essq_overview.aspx

8. Smith, P. Practical information for Online Surgery Masters courses in Edinburgh. 2013. http://profstevewigmore.wordpress.com/2013/09/18/

9. MOOCs@Edinburgh. Edinburgh MOOCs: Report #1. 2013. http://hdl.handle.net/1842/6683.

10. Haywood, J. Making a smooth transition. 2013. http://www.slideshare.net/UniversitiesUK/jeff-haywood.

11. Bayne, S. MOOC learners, MOOC pedagogies. 2013. http://prezi.com/ttvurgisoefl/uuk-event-16-may/.

Tracking Progress: Predictors of Students' Weekly Achievement During a Circuits and Electronics MOOC

Jennifer DeBoer
MIT
77 Mass Ave. 5-122
Cambridge, MA 02139
jdeboer@mit.edu

Lori Breslow
MIT
77 Mass Ave. 5-122
Cambridge, MA 02139
lrb@mit.edu

ABSTRACT

Massive open online courses (MOOCs) provide learning materials and automated assessments for large numbers of virtual users. Because every interaction is recorded, we can longitudinally model performance over the course of the class. We create a panel model of achievement in an early MOOC to estimate within- and between-user differences. In this study, we hope to contribute to HCI literature by, first, applying quasi-experimental methods to identify behaviors that may support student learning in a virtual environment, and, second, by using a panel model that takes into account the longitudinal, dynamic nature of a multiple-week class.

Author Keywords

MOOCs; learning activities; longitudinal modeling.

ACM Classification Keywords

K.3.1 Computer Uses in Education: CAI

INTRODUCTION

MOOCs provide large numbers of students the opportunity to access a course in a format that virtually replicates a multiple-week college/university class. One of the most important benefits MOOCs offer researchers is the fine-grain, longitudinal data they collect. With every click, researchers can trace the paths students take throughout the class and come closer to causal estimations of the impact of use of course materials on students' achievement.

BACKGROUND AND CONCEPTUAL FRAMEWORK

We attempt to identify supportive online materials by asking, "What is the predictive relationship between usage behaviors and student achievement, controlling for students' behavior and prior performance in a longitudinal panel?" We build on previous HCI research showing activities promoting experimentation and accuracy in responses predict achievement [6] and presenting content in

diverse ways improves grades [7]. We also build on our own work using a cross-sectional model, which found that different groups of students found different resources useful [3], and time spent on homework was a consistent positive predictor, while time spent on the e-textbook was consistently not [2]. We discovered patterns of resource use varied greatly between students, and we saw students switching between more interactive and less interactive resources [4]. Methodologically, we build on studies that apply random-effect panel regression to individual student-level data [e.g., 1,5] to explore whether time with resources and number of problem attempts predict achievement, defined as longitudinal homework performance.

DATA

The data for this study come from the first MITx MOOC "Circuits and Electronics," traditionally offered to MIT sophomores. Nearly 155,000 students initially registered; however, our sampling frame is only the 30,034 students who attempted at least one part of the 12 problem sets.

Achievement on homework problem sets comprised 15% of the student's final score. Students could drop their lowest two homeworks, so the score received for homework toward the total grade was the average of the best 10 problem set percentages. Students needed a total of 60% in the whole class to get a certificate. As they could earn 85% of their points on exams and lab assignments, it was possible to earn a certificate without doing any homework.

METHODS

We exploit the longitudinal nature of the homework problem sets to create a panel dataset for individuals over the 14 weeks of the class. We have 12 time points (for 12 problem sets), though there are missing outcomes when students did not attempt that week's problem set (mean homeworks attempted = 4.6). As Figure 1 illustrates, there was a high level of heterogeneity in the patterns of homework performance. Some missing outcomes could be attributed to students stopping after successfully completing ten assignments. In our initial modeling, we assume this is not related to systematic performance differences, but we later test this assumption.

L@S 2014, Mar 04-05 2014, Atlanta, GA, USA
ACM 978-1-4503-2669-8/14/03.
http://dx.doi.org/10.1145/2556325.2567863

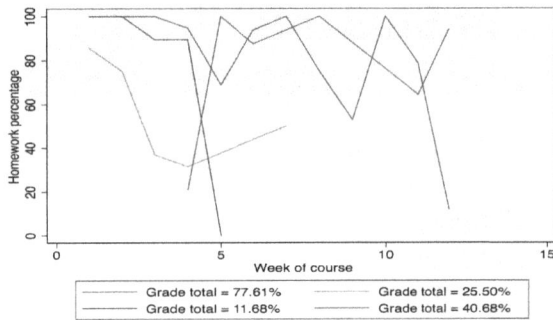

Figure 1: Sample trajectories of homework performance over all twelve assignments for four diverse students

FINDINGS

Time on different resources

Our first model, which includes all students in our sampling frame, generally corroborates our findings that factors such as time spent on homework and labs predicts higher achievement, while time spent on the discussion board or book is more weakly predictive or not statistically significant. Time on lecture videos is slightly predictive of higher achievement, while time on the ungraded problems that were interspersed between videos is more strongly predictive of higher scores.

Differing groups of students

In support of our other research [3], we find resources that predict achievement vary based on the population of students. We estimate our fully-specified model with three populations: all students who attempted any homework problem, students who attempted five or more homeworks, and students who earned a certificate. In addition, for students who did multiple homework assignments, including certificate earners, we include lagged performance as an additional control. Lecture problems are stronger predictors of performance for these higher achieving students, while the effect of time spent on labs decreases those scores. Interestingly, lagged performance is a strong negative predictor of performance, and we wonder if, for high-achieving students, success in the previous week's homework gives them the sense they do not need to perform as well in the current week.

Taking into account multiple attempts

Students were allowed unlimited multiple attempts on homework and lab assignments as well as on lecture problems, and we next test a model that includes the number of attempts as a control. Increased attempts significantly predict higher achievement. However, when we include a second order term to test for a nonlinear relationship, we observe diminishing returns. This could be explained by increased attempts initially indicating students trying problems enough times to score well but, beyond a

certain level, indicating guessing. In additional models, lecture problem attempts predict lower achievement, while lecture problem performance predicts higher achievement.

DISCUSSION

By utilizing the detailed nature of MOOC data, we can recover less biased estimates of the effectiveness of different activities than a cross-sectional OLS model. The arguably more interactive components that require students to answer problems positively predict performance on weekly homework assignments, while more passive resources are weakly related. In addition, by taking into account students' multiple attempts on problems, we can better understand students' behavior and the utility of this feature of MOOCs.

In our ongoing research, we expand on the models here by looking at the diversity of activities students access and the relative proportion of time allotted to different activities. We further investigate the pathways students take and the order in which they access resources and solve problems.

ACKNOWLEDGMENTS

Funding was provided by NSF Grant, DRL-1258448. We also thank MIT's RELATE group and edX.

REFERENCES

1. Arora, M.L., Rho, Y.R., & Masson, C. Longitudinal study of online statics homework as a method to improve learning. *Journal of STEM Education 14*, 1 (2013), 36-44.

2. Breslow, L. The opportunities and challenges from big data from MOOCs. AERA panel "Innovations in Data and Technology for Educational Research." AERA annual conference (2013).

3. Breslow, L., Pritchard, D.E., DeBoer, J., Stump, G.S., Ho, A.D., & Seaton, D.T. Studying learning in the worldwide classroom: Research into edX's first MOOC. *Research and Practice in Assessment, 8* (2013), 13-25.

4. DeBoer, J., Ho, A.D., Stump, G.S., & Breslow, L. (in press). Changing "course": Reconceptualizing educational variables for massive open online courses. *Educational Researcher*.

5. Desjardins, R. & Warnke, A. Ageing and skills: A review and analysis of skill gain and skill loss over the lifespan and over time, *OECD Education Working Papers*, No. 72, OECD Publishing (2012).

6. Katz, S., Aronis, J., Allbritton, D., Wilson, C., & Soffa, M.L. A study to identify predictors of achievement in an introductory computer science course. In *Proc. SIGMIS CPR 2003*, ACM Press (2003), 157-161.

7. Priego, R.G. & Peralta, A.G. Engagement factors and motivation in e-learning and blended-learning projects. In *Proc. TEEM 2013*, ACM Press (2013), 453-46.

Feature Engineering for Clustering Student Solutions

Elena L. Glassman   Rishabh Singh   Robert C. Miller
MIT CSAIL, 32 Vassar St. Cambridge, MA
{elg,rishabhs,rcm}@mit.edu

ABSTRACT

Open-ended homework problems such as coding assignments give students a broad range of freedom for the design of solutions. We aim to use the diversity in correct solutions to enhance student learning by automatically suggesting alternate solutions. Our approach is to perform a two-level hierarchical clustering of student solutions to first partition them based on the choice of algorithm and then partition solutions implementing the same algorithm based on low-level implementation details. Our initial investigations in domains of introductory programming and computer architecture demonstrate that we need two different classes of features to perform effective clustering at the two levels, namely *abstract* features and *concrete* features.

Author Keywords

Algorithm recognition; program comprehension; feature engineering

ACM Classification Keywords

K.3.1 Computers and Education: Computer Uses in Education—Computer-assisted instruction (CAI)

INTRODUCTION

There are a variety of ways in which students implement solutions for open-ended homework problems such as coding assignments. Their correct solutions vary in at least two dimensions: (i) choice of algorithm, and (ii) choice of language constructs and library functions for the low-level implementation. This variation among correct solutions gives us an opportunity to use them to enhance student learning, in accordance with Marton et al.'s Variation Theory (VT) [3]. VT holds that in order to learn concepts, one must see examples that vary along dimensions of *contrast, generalization, separation*, and *fusion*. In this work, we aim to build a system that can automatically provide students with examples of alternative correct solutions across these different dimensions, *powered by a large dataset of previous student solutions*.

In order to separate solutions along VT's recommended dimensions, we must design metrics that capture the distinctions VT makes between solutions. Our first exploratory

feature design study is based on a large dataset of students' Python submissions from an introductory programming course offered on the edX MOOC platform in Fall 2012.

We show a few hand-picked examples in Figure 1 from the comp-deriv problem, which computes the derivative of a polynomial. To illustrate VT's contrast dimension, we include an example of a comp-deriv solution paired with a solution to a different problem, eval-poly. Under the generalization heading, we have shown two solutions that use the same approach or algorithm, but different low-level functions and language constructs to implement it. We illustrate the separation dimension of variation by pairing two comp-deriv solutions that implement different algorithms.

RELATED WORK

A common goal of the prior work cited here is to help teachers monitor the state of their class, or provide solution-specific feedback to many students. However, the techniques for analyzing solutions have not converged on a particular method. Huang et al. [1] use unit test results and AST edit-distance algorithms to identify clusters of submissions that could potentially receive the same custom feedback message. Taherkhani et al. [4] identify which sorting algorithm a student implemented using supervised machine learning methods. Each solution is represented by statistics about language constructs, measures of complexity, and detected roles of variables.

Luxton-Reilly et al. [2] label types of variations as structural, syntactic, or presentation-related. The structural similarity is captured by the control flow graph of the student solutions. If the control flow of two solutions is the same, then the syntactic variation within the blocks of code are compared by looking at the sequence of token classes. Presentation-based variation, such as variable names and spacing, is only examined when two solutions are structurally and syntactically the same. Our motivation is similar to that of Luxton-Reilly et al., but we explore a less strict notion of solution similarity.

OUR APPROACH

We are pursuing a two-level hierarchical clustering methodology. The high-level clusters are intended to partition solutions along the separation dimension, where each cluster represents a particular algorithm. We have used k-means to create these high-level clusters of solutions based on abstract features. The abstract features for Python programs consist of 12 features that include the position of conditional statements relative to the loop statements (before, after, or inside), the depth of nested loops, number of AST nodes, return statements, loops, comparisons, etc.

The sub-clusters within each high-level cluster are intended to capture the generalization dimension, where the only dif-

L@S'14, March 4–5, 2014, Atlanta, Georgia, USA.
ACM 978-1-4503-2669-8/14/03.
http://dx.doi.org/10.1145/2556325.2567865

CONTRAST	GENERALIZATION	SEPARATION
| ```python
def computeDeriv(poly):
    ans = []
    for i in range(1,len(poly)):
        ans.append(i*poly[i])
    if ans == []:
        ans = [0.0]
    return ans
``` | ```python
def computeDeriv(poly):
    powers = len(poly)
    if powers == 1:
        return [0.0]
    deriv = []
    for i in range(powers):
        deriv.append(poly[i]*i)
    return deriv[1:]
``` | ```python
def computeDeriv(poly):
    idx = 1
    res = list([])
    polylen = len(poly)
    if polylen == 1: return [0.0]
    while idx <= polylen:
        coeff = poly.pop(1)
        res.append(coeff*idx)
        idx = idx + 1
        if len(poly) < 2: return res
``` |
| ```python
def evaluatePoly(lis,a):
    total = 0
    for i in range(len(lis)):
        e = lis[i]*(a**i)
        total = total + e
    return total
``` | ```python
def computeDeriv(poly):
    if len(poly) > 1:
        res = []
    else: return [0.0]
    for i in range(len(poly)):
        res.append(poly[i]*i)
    res.pop(0)
    return res
``` | ```python
def computeDeriv(poly):
    result = []
    for i in range(1,len(poly)):
        result.append(i*poly[i])
    if len(result) == 0:
        result.append(0.0)
    return result
``` |

Figure 1: Hand-selected examples of student solutions varying along Variation Theory dimensions. Students were asked to implement a function to compute a polynomial's derivative; the polynomial's coefficients are represented as a list. The contrast dimension contains examples that are and are not a derivative-computing function. The generalization dimension includes examples with the same algorithm but different low-level implementations. The separation dimension captures the full variation of implementations which still compute the derivative of a polynomial.

ferences between clusters are low-level language constructs and used library functions. We plan to use k-means again on solutions within each high-level cluster, based on low-level, concrete features. The concrete features for Python programs consist of 48 low-level features that include the number of specific types of operators (add, subtract, etc.), comparisons ($<$, $>$, etc.), loops (while or for), library functions, and statements (assignments, conditional, or loop), number of program variables, constant values, etc.

PRELIMINARY RESULTS

We use abstract features for k-means clustering of student solutions for the separation dimension, which partitions the solutions into k clusters. We compute clusterings for different k values, and then compare these clusterings to those created by two course teaching assistants (TAs). The TAs were given 50 randomly chosen student solutions as a clustering task. We did not give them specific directions for clustering, in order to better understand how the TAs naturally group solutions. We observed that they ignored low-level features, e.g., they clustered together solutions implementing the same algorithm but using different functions such as pop, list slicing, and delete.

We use the adjusted mutual information (AMI) metric to compare TAs' clusterings with each other and with our k-means clustering. An AMI value of 0 indicates purely independent clusterings, whereas a value of 1 indicates perfect agreement between the clusterings. The agreement of the two TAs' clusterings, referred to here as the inter-TA AMI, is only 0.3275. When k was sufficiently high, i.e., at least 15, the k-means-produced clusterings agreed, as measured by AMI, with each TA's clusterings as much or more than the TAs' clusterings agreed with each other. We found high agreement

between our k-means and TA-produced clusterings on two additional coding assignments as well.

FUTURE WORK

We are generalizing this approach to two additional domains. The Mathworks runs an online game, Cody. Users submitted 218,000 Matlab functions as solutions to 1000 or so problems. We hope to categorize software metrics, library functions, and language constructs within Matlab functions as abstract features, differentiating algorithms, or concrete features, distinguishing implementations of the same algorithm. The second domain is code written by MIT students in a hardware description language. Students define their own library of circuits, from which larger circuits are composed. Within each high-level cluster based on overall structure, we could cluster based on low-level library circuit implementation.

REFERENCES

1. Huang, J., Piech, C., Nguyen, A., and Guibas, L. J. Syntactic and functional variability of a million code submissions in a machine learning mooc. In *AIED Workshops* (2013).

2. Luxton-Reilly, A., Denny, P., Kirk, D., Tempero, E., and Yu, S.-Y. On the differences between correct student solutions. In *ITiCSE '13*, ACM (2013), 177–182.

3. Marton, F., Tsui, A., Chik, P., Ko, P., and Lo, M. *Classroom Discourse and the Space of Learning*. Taylor & Francis, 2013.

4. Taherkhani, A., Korhonen, A., and Malmi, L. Automatic recognition of students' sorting algorithm implementations in a data structures and algorithms course. In *Koli Calling*, ACM (2012), 83–92.

Improving Online Class Forums by Seeding Discussions and Managing Section Size

Kelly Miller
Harvard University
Cambridge, MA 02138
miller@seas.harvard.edu

Sacha Zyto
MIT CSAIL
Cambridge, MA 02139
sacha@mit.edu

David R. Karger
MIT CSAIL
Cambridge, MA 02139
karger@mit.edu

Eric Mazur
MIT CSAIL
Cambridge, MA 02139
mazur@seas.harvard.edu

ABSTRACT

Discussion forums are an integral part of all online and many offline courses. But in many cases they are presented as an afterthought, offered to the students to use as they wish. In this paper, we explore ways to steer discussion forums to produce high-quality learning interactions. In the context of a Physics course, we investigate two ideas: seeding the forum with prior-year student content, and varying the sizes of "sections" of students who can see each other's comments.

Author Keywords

Hypertext; annotation; collaboration; forum; e-learning;

ACM Classification Keywords

H.5.2 Information Interfaces and Presentation (e.g. HCI): User Interfaces. - Graphical user interfaces.

INTRODUCTION

Discussion forums are an integral part of all online and many offline courses. But in many cases they arrive as an afterthought, offered to the students to use as they wish. In some classes this produces an empty or dysfunctional forum. This is unfortunate, as research has repeatedly demonstrated [1, 2, 3] that conversational interactions between students can be one of the most effective of all learning mechanisms.

In this article, we explore the question of how to create more and better interactions between students using online discussion forums. We explore two distinct ideas:

1. Seeding the discussion with comments from previous iterations of the course

2. Artificially subdividing the class in order to vary the number of students who can see and respond to each others' comments

Regarding the first idea, we give statistically significant experimental evidence that it is possible to automatically

L@S 2014, March 4–5, 2014, Atlanta, Georgia, USA.
ACM 978-1-4503-2669-8/14/03.
http://dx.doi.org/10.1145/2556325.2567866

select prior-semester comments to seed into the new semester that stimulate an above-average amount of discussion, and that this discussion demonstrates an above average amount of "generative interaction", the interaction type that prior literature [1] has demonstrated to be of the greatest value for learning.

The second experiment was motivated by an oft-heard complaint from students that the forum is so full that there's nothing left to say. We believe that subdividing the forum will yield duplicative discussions that, rather than being wasteful, present an opportunity for more students to benefit from the same valuable learning interactions.

Our experiments are carried out in the context of Applied Physics XX, an introductory physics class of 90 students. Discussion-forum participation is a substantial component of the class requirements. The discussion forum used is NB [4], a forum that is somewhat unusual for being situated in the margins of the (online) course textbook. We believe that our conclusions have general implications for the use of discussion forums in learning that can scale up to MOOCs of arbitrary size.

Sectioning

Our first iteration aims to explore whether there is a "sweet spot" for sizing discussion forums. We speculate that when the discussion group is too large, students will find they have nothing left to say, while if it is too small, interesting discussion topics may be missed. To explore this question, we have subdivided the class into smaller and smaller sections as the course has progressed.

Seeding

We hypothesized that another way to stimulate discussion would be to "seed" the discussion forum with provocative topics, and that a good way to choose these topics would be to select them from among the more successful forum discussions from last year's class. Each seeded thread or annotation was imported from last year's forum and entered into this year's forum anonymously. Four different seeding conditions were explored: 1. 10 longest threads, 2. no seeded comments, 3. 10 highest quality annotations to start a thread and 4. first annotation from each of the 10 longest threads.

Coding for Thread Type and Annotation Quality

We coded discussion threads using an adapted scheme developed to examine discourse patterns and collaborative scientific reasoning in peer discussions [5]. We categorized all threads as one of the following types: consensual, responsive, transfer, generative and argumentative. The generative and argumentative threads are of particular interest to us as these are the types of activities that research has shown to be most effective in promoting learning. The quality of each individual annotation was also evaluated and coded on a 3-point scale. A quality score of 0 represents a meaningless annotation whereas a 2 represents an insightful annotation

FINDINGS

Based on this preliminary analysis, we find four interesting results. The first is that seeded annotations stimulate an above-average amount of discussion. We find a statistically significant difference in the average number of replies to seeded threads compared to unseeded (i.e. the usual) threads. Unseeded threads have, on average 0.46 replies, while seeded threads receive an average of 1.16 replies ($p<0.0001$).Second, we find that seeded threads demonstrate an above average amount of 'generative' discussion. We used an ANOVA analysis of variance to determine that the difference between groups is statistically significant at the $p<0.05$ level. Especially noteworthy is the fact that generative discussions emerge four times more frequently in the seeded threads compared to the unseeded threads.

Third, we find that, on average the quality of the annotations in the three seeded sections (1.61) exceeds the quality of the annotations in the unseeded section (1.52), which is statistically significant at the $p<0.05$ level.

Fourth, we find that the size of the section is positively correlated with the length of the average thread in that section (correlation=0.57, $p<0.0001$) and with the fraction of posts that are replies to other posts (correlation=0.47, $p<0.005$). Figure 1 shows that, as the section size increases, so too does the thread length. This finding lends support to the hypothesis that, when there are too many participants in a forum, it gets saturated with annotations and there is nothing left to say. In larger sections, students are adding comments to existing threads rather than starting their own threads due to this saturation effect.

CONCLUSION

Online forums, have large implications for the scalability of a class. An effective online forum could easily replace a traditional, physical section or recitation. A successful, content-based online forum that works well for a class of 90 students could easily be scaled to a MOOC of 100,000.

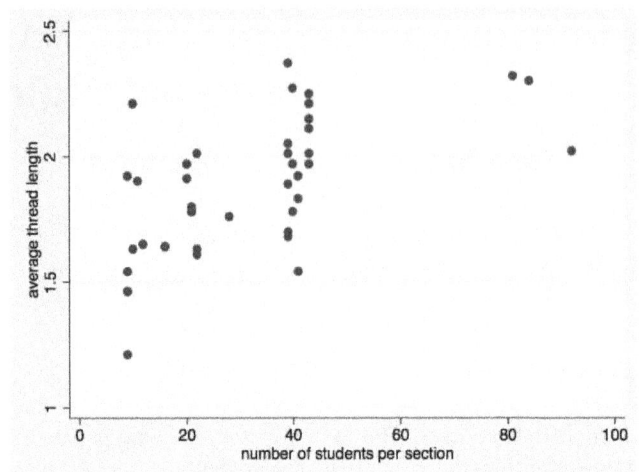

Figure 1: average thread length versus section size

Researching best practices in online forums is essential to making this scalability effective. Through this preliminary look at a semester worth of data, we have uncovered some interesting trends regarding the optimal size of a forum. Through seeding discussions with thought-provoking content, we have also gained insight into how students' online conversations can be managed and guided to promote learning. Seeding forums with successful threads (or starter comments from a thread) appears to provoke students to have more constructive (generative discussions). The overall quality of the annotations appears to also be higher in these seeded sections. It remains to be determined whether the "saturation" that forces students to reply to threads instead of initiating their own is a good or bad thing. Future analysis will investigate this question by examining the relationship between students' annotating tendencies and course learning metrics.

REFERENCES

1. Chi, Michelene TH. "Active-constructive-interactive: A conceptual framework for differentiating learning activities." Topics in Cognitive Science 1.1 (2009): 73-105.
2. Chickering, Arthur W., Zelda F. Gamson, and Susan J. Poulsen. "Seven principles for good practice in undergraduate education." (1987): 2003.
3. Bonwell, Charles C., and James A. Eison. Active learning: Creating excitement in the classroom. Washington, DC: School of Education and Human Development, George Washington University, 1991.
4. Zyto, Sacha, et al. "Successful classroom deployment of a social document annotation system." Proceedings of the 2012 ACM annual conference on Human Factors in Computing Systems. ACM, 2012.
5. Hogan, Kathleen, Bonnie K. Nastasi, and Michael Pressley. "Discourse patterns and collaborative scientific reasoning in peer and teacher-guided discussions." Cognition and instruction 17.4 (1999): 379-432

Student Explorer: A Tool for Supporting Academic Advising at Scale

Steven Lonn
University of Michigan
USE Lab, Digital Media Commons
1401B Duderstadt Ctr, 2281 Bonisteel
Ann Arbor, MI 48109-2094 USA
slonn@umich.edu

Stephanie D. Teasley
University of Michigan
School of Information & USE Lab
4384 North Quad, 105 S. State St.
Ann Arbor, MI 48109-1285 USA
steasley@umich.edu

ABSTRACT
Student Explorer is an early warning system designed to support academic advising that uses learning analytics to categorize students' ongoing academic performance and effort. Advisors use this tool to provide just-in-time assistance to students at risk of underperforming in their classes. Student Explorer is designed to eventually support targeted advising for thousands of undergraduate students.

Author Keywords
Academic Advising; Learning Analytics; Higher Education.

ACM Classification Keywords
J.1 [Administrative Data Processing] Education; K.3.0 [Computers and Education] General; H.5.m. Information interfaces and presentation (e.g., HCI): Miscellaneous.

INTRODUCTION
In most postsecondary institutions in the U.S., academic advisors assist students with course selection, career trajectories, and social and academic balance. Advisors also often serve as intermediaries between students and instructors, particularly for large lecture courses where the number of enrollees can measure in the hundreds (e.g., introductory courses in statistics, psychology, etc.). Yet, staff members in this role typically lack information on students' formative performance and they must rely on students' self-reported assessments or a formal request for instructors' assessment, both of which may be inaccurate, burdensome, or arrive too late in the term to address student study habits and/or knowledge deficiencies. We partnered with academic advisors at our institution to create an early warning system (EWS), "Student Explorer," that could leverage readily-available institutional data and present it in an actionable format so that academic advisors could identify students who could benefit from assistance before they fell further into academic jeopardy. As of Fall term

2013, twenty-six academic advisors serving 650 undergraduate students are using Student Explorer, with an aim to scale to 4,000 students by Fall 2014 and to all 24,000 undergraduates in the next few years.

STUDENT DATA SOURCES
Student Explorer leverages data from our institutional learning management system (LMS). Information from the LMS gradebook and assignments tools is used to measure students' formative performance. Course website login information is used as a proxy for student effort (e.g., whether students "check-in" as often as their classmates). These data sources were selected not only because they are highly correlated with student success, but also because they are common across all courses that use the LMS [1].

LEARNING ANALYTICS DESIGN
Predictive models can be used in EWSs to predict students' likelihood of academic failure or success across multiple course contexts (e.g., [2]). However, this approach has several potential sources of bias when a single best-fit model is applied across different courses with multiple instructional models, requirements, and expectations [3]. Instead, we designed Student Explorer with a relative, intra-course categorization scheme (Figure 1) that helps academic advisors prioritize and make sense of the underlying student data. These "E3" categorizations are applied with labels that denote the most appropriate action by the academic advisor: *Encourage* for students performing at a high level in a course, *Explore* for students who are performing slightly below the course average, and *Engage* for students performing at a low level. The effort percentile is utilized at the edge cases in these categories.

Student Percentage of Points Earned	% Relative to Course Avg.	Website Visits Percentile Rank	Classification
>= 85%			Encourage
75% <= X < 85%	< 15%		Explore
75% <= X < 85%	>= 15%	< 25th percentile	Explore
75% <= X < 85%	>= 15%	>= 25th percentile	Encourage
65% <= X < 75%	< 15%	< 25th percentile	Engage
65% <= X < 75%	< 15%	>= 25th percentile	Explore
65% <= X < 75%	>= 15%		Explore
55% <= X < 65%	>= 10%		Explore
55% <= X < 65%	< 10%		Engage
< 55%			Engage

Figure 1. Student Explorer Classification Scheme

L@S 2014, Mar 04-05 2014, Atlanta, GA, USA
ACM 978-1-4503-2669-8/14/03.
http://dx.doi.org/10.1145/2556325.2567867

ITERATIVE INTERFACE DESIGN

Our design-based research project is a collaborative effort between the researchers and the academic advisors who are our target users [4]. We have been able to continue to include our target users in Student Explorer's development as we have increased the scale of use. By continuing to include advisors in our practice of iterative design, we increase the likelihood that we can produce a nimble tool applicable to a variety of academic advising contexts. The current design and features of Student Explorer are have been extended from earlier iterations [see 1, 5, 6, 7].

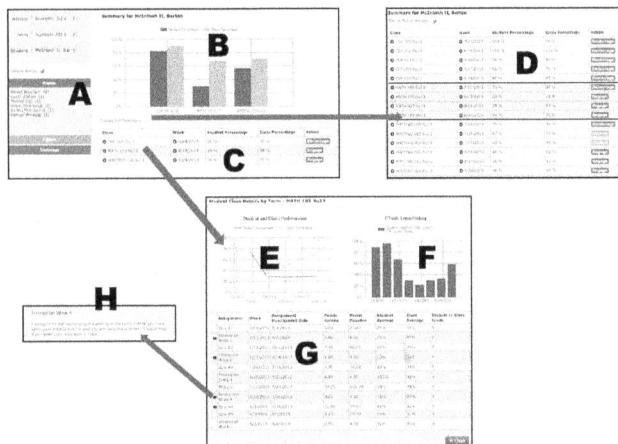

Figure 2. Student Explorer User Interface Examples

The three major features of the Student Explorer summary screen (Figure 2, top left) are: (A) "Alerts" boxes that indicate which students, and for how many current courses, are categorized in each E3 value; (B) a graphical display of the most recent student and class average percentage of total available points across courses; and (C) a numeric display of the same data in (B) and corresponding E3 value.

The academic advisor can click on a checkbox that will toggle the view to the (D) detailed display, a vertical listing of the students' percentage of available points and corresponding E3 value per week.

The four major features of the Student Explorer class detail screen (Figure 2, bottom) are: (E) a graph of the student's percentage points earned vs. class average over time; (F) a graph of the student's weekly LMS site visits percentile; (G) a listing of the student's individual course assignments and performance; and H) a mouse-over view of the text of qualitative comments for a particular course assignment.

The features of Student Explorer help academic advisors quickly distinguish between students who are succeeding in any given course, students beginning to show signs of falling behind, or students struggling with their coursework, respectively. The features also serve to facilitate advisors' conversations with students about their course performance and effort. Our long-term goal is to scale the functionality broadly so that the "feedback loops" between learners, teachers, and academic advisors can be reduced in time and effort [8].

PRELIMINARY FINDINGS

Student Explorer has been used in several different academic advising and student populations since it was first deployed in Winter 2011. In one targeted population, students' second-year grade point averages increased after Student Explorer was utilized by their academic advisors [1]. More recently in a second population, academic advisors began specifically referencing the class detail screen during face-to-face meetings with their students [7]. We anticipate additional positive results as Student Explorer continues to scale broadly, and is used to parse and analyze raw student data so that it can be made visible, understandable, and actionable by academic advisors.

REFERENCES

1. Krumm, A. E., Waddington, R. J., Lonn, S., & Teasley, S. D. (In Press). A learning management system-based early warning system for academic advising in undergraduate engineering. In (J. Larusson & B. White, Eds.) *Handbook of Learning Analytics: Methods, Tools and Approaches.* New York: Springer-Verlag.

2. Arnold, K. E. & Pistilli, M. D. (2012). Course signals at Purdue: Using learning analytics to increase student success. Proceedings of *The 2nd International Conference on Learning Analytics and Knowledge* (pp. 267-270). Vancouver, Canada: ACM.

3. Essa, A. & Ayad, H. (2012). Student success system: Risk analytics and data visualization using ensembles of predictive models. Proceedings of *The 2nd International Conference on Learning Analytics and Knowledge* (pp. 158-161). Vancouver, Canada: ACM.

4. Cobb, P., Confrey, J., diSessa, A., Lehrer, R., & Schauble, L. (2003). Design experiments in educational research. *Educational Researcher, 32*(1), 9-13, 35-37.

5. Lonn, S., Krumm, A. E., Waddington, R. J., and Teasley, S. D. (2012). Bridging the gap from knowledge to action: Putting analytics in the hands of academic advisors. Proceedings of *The 2nd International Conference on Learning Analytics and Knowledge* (pp. 184-187). Vancouver, Canada: ACM.

6. Lonn, S., Aguilar, S., & Teasley, S. D. (2013). Issues, challenges, and lessons learned when scaling up a learning analytics intervention. Proceedings of *The 3rd International Conference on Learning Analytics and Knowledge* (pp. 235- 239). Leuven, Belgium: ACM.

7. Aguilar, S., Lonn, S., & Teasley S. D. (2014). Perceptions and use of an early warning system during a higher education transition program. Paper to be presented at *The 4th International Conference on Learning Analytics and Knowledge.* Indianapolis, USA.

8. Clow, D. (2012). The learning analytics cycle: Closing the loop effectively. Paper presented at *The 2nd International Conference on Learning Analytics and Knowledge.* Vancouver, BC, Canada.

Educational Programming Systems for Learning at Scale

Qianxiang Wang
Institute of Software, School
of EECS, Peking University
Key Lab of HCST (Peking
University), MoE, China
wqx@pku.edu.cn

Wenxin Li
Department of Computer
Science, Peking University
China
lwx@pku.edu.cn

Tao Xie
University of Illinois at
Urbana-Champaign
Urbana, IL, USA
taoxie@illinois.edu

ABSTRACT

Learning programming at scale underlies computer science education ranging from basic programming to advanced software engineering topics. There are strong needs of providing effective system supports for learning programming at scale. Among various desirable characteristics of such system supports, system supports shall allow students to write programs via an online Integrated Development Environment (IDE), allow students to get feedback on how they perform on the given programming exercises, etc. To aim for such effective system supports for learning programming at scale, research teams from Peking University have developed two systems: POP (denoting Peking University Online Programming System) and POJ (denoting Peking University Online Judge System). These two systems have achieved high impact among students around the world (especially those in China). In this paper, we present the overview of the two systems, along with our ongoing and future work on extending the systems for achieving higher effectiveness in supporting learning programming at scale.

POP: PEKING UNIVERSITY ONLINE PROGRAMMING

POP (denoting Peking University Online Programming System, formerly known as CEclipse [2, 3]) has been developed by the Software Engineering Institute of Peking University (its development efforts have been led by the f rst author since 2009). Figure 1 shows the architecture of POP. POP has initially supported Java development, and recently been extended to support C/C++ along with HTML/PHP (http://webassist3.seforge.org/phponlineide/). POP provides the same basic features as the local Eclipse IDE, such as Project Operations, Package Operations, and Class Operations for Java programs, and Compile, Run, etc. POP also provides some advanced features of the local Eclipse IDE, such as Code Auto-Completion, Code Selection, Code Tips (e.g., from Javadoc), and Debugging. In addition, POP supports capture/replay of user behaviors in the online IDE.

L@S'14, March 4–5, 2014, Atlanta, Georgia, USA.
ACM 978-1-4503-2669-8/14/03.
http://dx.doi.org/10.1145/2556325.2567868

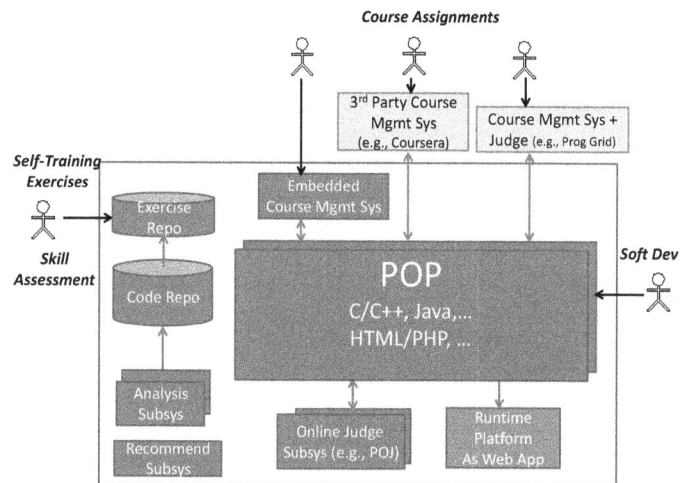

Figure 1. The architecture of POP

There are three main types of users of POP: students in a course for conducting course assignment (as shown near the top of Figure 1), students who do exercises for self-training (as shown on the left side of Figure 1), students (or even practitioners) who leverage POP as an online IDE for software development (as shown on the right side of Figure 1). In the setting of course assignment, POP provides the instructor with an option of conf guring POP to prevent copying/pasting of code segments into the online IDE. Such conf guration is to alleviate situations where (1) students use their local IDE to write programs and then in the end copy and paste the completed programs to POP, or (2) students copy and paste other students' programs to POP (committing plagiarism).

POP has its own embedded course management subsystem, and has also integrated third-party course management systems such as the one supported by Coursera. POP also supports another subsystem called Programming Grid (http://programming.grids.cn/programming/), which is a course management and assignment judge system developed by the Institute of Network Computing and Information Systems of Peking University. POP has its analysis subsystem for analyzing student-submission programs in the code repository. POP also has a recommendation subsystem (currently under development) for recommending exercises to students and supports online judge systems such as POJ (described in the next section).

At Peking University, POP has been used in courses of *Compiler Practice* and *Advanced Software Engineering* since

2010; in 2013-2014, POP is currently used in courses of *Java Programming Design* and *Java Advanced Techniques* along with *Introduction to Computing* (for non-CS majors). For the 2013-2014 course of *Introduction to Computing* (for non-CS majors) at Peking University, there have been more than 1000 homework-assignment submissions using POP. POP has also been used by students at Nankai University and North China University of Technology in China. Since 30 September 2013, a Massive Open Online Course (MOOC) on *Introduction to Computing* offered via Coursera (`https://www.coursera.org/course/pkuic`) has used POP as the course-assignment platform. POP was also used in four programming contests in China.

POJ: PEKING UNIVERSITY ONLINE JUDGE
POJ (denoting Peking University Online Judge System [1] `http://poj.org/`) has been developed by the Artif cial Intelligence Lab of Peking University (its development efforts have been led by the second author since 2003). In particular, POJ can compile and test a program submitted for a specif c problem against a set of test cases prepared for the problem, and then respond whether the program passes the testing or not. POJ was initially developed to be an ACM International Collegiate Programming Contest (ACM/ICPC) training platform for Peking University students. POJ has been evolved to a general educational platform for both contest training and programming practicing, being used by a large number of students around the world. Later an open platform called Open Judge (`http://openjudge.cn`) has been released to the public for allowing people to construct their online judge systems for programming-related courses. More recently, an online code-evaluation system and algorithm-training platform (`http://codevs.cn/`) has been made available for incorporating an online IDE, categorization of exercises, social networking, etc. From 2003 till recently, POJ has reached 0.2 million users and 8 million submissions.

RELATED WORK
Online IDEs have been gaining popularity in both industry and education. Some example online IDEs are Cloud9 (`https://c9.io/`), CodeAcademy (`http://www.codecademy.com/`), Compilr (`https://compilr.com/`), and Codemoo (`http://www.codemoo.com/`). Compared with these online IDEs, POP provides a richer-feature IDE, which provides the same look-and-feel along with various advanced features of the Eclipse IDE. POP allows users to easily switch between their familiar Eclipse IDE and the POP online IDE.

Pex4Fun [4, 5] (`http://pex4fun.com/`) is a web-based serious gaming environment (released by Microsoft Research) for teaching and learning computer science at scale. Pex4Fun allows students to write programs in a browser with Intellisense support. In its Coding Duel game, students write code to implement a teacher's specif cation (i.e., a secret sample solution to a given problem), and then Pex4Fun leverages a test-generation engine to f nd and report any discrepancies in behavior between the student's code and the specif cation.

POP provides a richer-feature IDE than Pex4Fun's code editor. POJ relies on a given set of test cases to judge the correctness of a student's submission whereas Pex4Fun relies on the underlying test-generation engine and the given specif cation.

ONGOING AND FUTURE WORK
First, we plan to extend POP to support more programming languages. For example, due to high popularity, Python and Ruby are languages that we plan to support in POP. Second, in both POP and POJ, we are exploring f ner-grained grading of student submissions along with giving richer feedback to students when their submissions are not correct yet. Third, we plan to explore research on educational analytics and data mining on user data collected by our systems. POP is able to collect sequences of small edits entered by students when typing in their programs. Both POP and POJ have accumulated a lot of submissions from students around the world along with a lot of exercises created by teachers around the world. We have started some preliminary work [1] on personalized exercise recommendation, automatic contest generator, etc.

ACKNOWLEDGMENTS
Qianxiang Wang's work is sponsored by the National Natural Science Foundation of China (Grant No. 61033006) and the HighTech Research and Development Program of China (Grant No. 2013AA01A213). Tao Xie's work is supported in part by NSF grants CCF-0845272, CCF-0915400, CNS-0958235, CNS-1160603, CNS-1318419, CCF-1349666, and NSF of China No. 61228203.

REFERENCES
1. Lin, S., Zhang, Q., and Li, W. A programmer self-training system with programming skill evaluation and personalized task recommendation. In *Proc. Interantional Conference on E-learning, E-business, Enterprise Information Systems, and E-Goverment (EEE)* (2013), 112–117.

2. Ling, W., Liang, G., Kui, S., and Wang, Q. CEclipse: An online IDE for programing in the cloud. In *Proc. IEEE World Congress on Services (SERVICES)* (2011), 45–52.

3. Ling, W., Liang, G., and Wang, Q. Program behavior analysis and control for online IDE. In *Proc. Computer Software and Applications Conference Workshops (COMPSACW)* (2012), 182–187.

4. Tillmann, N., Halleux, J. D., Xie, T., Gulwani, S., and Bishop, J. Teaching and learning programming and software engineering via interactive gaming. In *Proc. International Conference on Software Engineering (ICSE), Software Engineering Education (SEE)* (2013), 1117–1126.

5. Xie, T., Tillmann, N., and de Halleux, J. Educational software engineering: Where software engineering, education, and gaming meet. In *Proc. International Workshop on Games and Software Engineering (GAS)* (2013), 36–39.

Online Learning versus Blended Learning: An Exploratory Study

**Andrew Cross[1]*, B. Ashok[1], Srinath Bala[1], Edward Cutrell[1], Naren Datha[1],
Rahul Kumar[1], Viraj Kumar[2], Madhusudan Parthasarathy[3], Siddharth Prakash[1],
Sriram Rajamani[1], Satish Sangameswaran[1], Deepika Sharma[1] and William Thies[1]**

[1]Microsoft Research India   [2]PES University   [3]University of Illinois at Urbana Champaign
*Corresponding author: t-across@microsoft.com

ABSTRACT

Due to the recent emergence of massive open online courses (MOOCs), students and teachers are gaining unprecedented access to high-quality educational content. However, many questions remain on how best to utilize that content in a classroom environment. In this small-scale, exploratory study, we compared two ways of using a recorded video lecture. In the *online learning* condition, students viewed the video on a personal computer, and also viewed a follow-up tutorial (a quiz review) on the computer. In the *blended learning* condition, students viewed the video as a group in a classroom, and received the follow-up tutorial from a live lecturer. We randomly assigned 102 students to these conditions, and assessed learning outcomes via a series of quizzes. While we saw significant learning gains after each session conducted, we did not observe any significant differences between the online and blended learning groups. We discuss these findings as well as areas for future work.

Author Keywords

Online education; blended learning; massive open online course; MOOC; massively empowered classroom

ACM Classification Keywords

H.5.2 [**Information Interfaces and Presentation**]: User interfaces; K.3.0 [**Computers and Education**]: General

INTRODUCTION

As a large number of high-quality educational videos become freely available online, many educators are facing the question of how to leverage video for the benefit of their residential classrooms. As opposed to a purely online learning experience, such *blended learning* offers many potential benefits. For example, classroom discussions can add interactivity and personalization over pre-recorded videos, students can benefit from peer and social interactions

in the class, and local teachers remain a motivator, counselor, and advocate for students. Another form of blended learning, in which online videos are played during class, offers additional benefit in low-resource areas where students cannot access computers or the Internet on their own and there may be a lack of teaching staff and expertise.

Despite the appeal of blended learning, there have been very few studies that rigorously evaluate the benefits and drawbacks compared to an online-only learning experience. One exception is the work of Schreiber et al., who describe an experiment in which medical students viewed live and recorded lectures [1]. The study found no significant difference in test scores between conditions, though students expressed a preference for the live lecture. One limitation of the study is the absence of a baseline exam, making it impossible to measure actual learning benefits for students.

In this exploratory study, we revisit the question of blended learning versus online learning while overcoming some limitations of Schreiber et al. Via a controlled experiment, we show significant learning gains from each of four activities: viewing a recorded lecture on a personal computer, viewing a recorded lecture in a classroom, viewing a recorded quiz review on a personal computer, and receiving a live quiz review in a classroom. However, we do not find any statistical difference between students who used a computer and those in the classroom. This preliminary inquiry motivates some future work, including analysis of pause and replay events during personal playback of video.

METHODOLOGY

Our experiment aimed to address two questions that are core to understanding blended learning versus online learning: (i) how does viewing a video on a personal computer compare to viewing it as a group, in a classroom, and (ii) how does viewing a video tutorial compare to attending a live tutorial?

To address these questions, we randomly assigned students to two conditions (see Figure 1). In the online learning condition, students viewed a video lecture, took a short quiz, and then watched a video tutorial that reviewed the answers to the quiz. In the blended learning condition, students reported to a classroom and watched the video as a group, took a short quiz, and then reviewed the quiz with a live lecturer. We also administered baseline and final quizzes, in order to evaluate the learning benefits of both sessions.

L@S 2014, Mar 04-05 2014, Atlanta, GA, USA
ACM 978-1-4503-2669-8/14/03.
http://dx.doi.org/10.1145/2556325.2567869

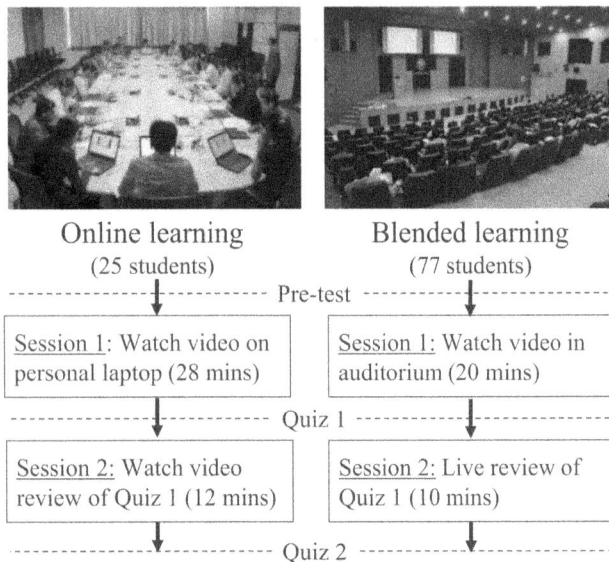

Online learning   Blended learning
(25 students)   (77 students)

---------------------------- Pre-test ----------------------------

| Session 1: Watch video on personal laptop (28 mins) | Session 1: Watch video in auditorium (20 mins) |

---------------------------- Quiz 1 ----------------------------

| Session 2: Watch video review of Quiz 1 (12 mins) | Session 2: Live review of Quiz 1 (10 mins) |

---------------------------- Quiz 2 ----------------------------

Figure 1: Overview of the experiment.

Our participants were 102 undergraduate students who were invited to Pune, India for a day-long event. The event focused on promotion of MEC (Massively Empowered Classroom), an online educational platform on which all of these students were registered. The lecturer for our study, a professor at a premier engineering college, appeared in all of the videos as well as the live session.

The lesson focused on algorithms for computing the convex hull. The pre-test asked four questions, probing knowledge of convex shapes, the definition of convex hull, and the complexity of computing the complex hull. The video lecture covered these subjects and explained the gift wrapping algorithm for efficient computation of the convex hull. The first quiz contained five questions, including four that were repeated from the pre-test; however, the repeated questions used different data (i.e., different points or shapes). The quiz review briefly explained the answers to the quiz. Finally, the second quiz asked six questions, including four that were repeated from the pre-test (with different examples). All quizzes were administered using paper and pencil.

Students in the online learning condition were encouraged to pause or replay the video as needed. We did not invite any questions from students except for the live quiz review, and even in this session, no questions were asked. We allowed students to take notes, but did not allow them to refer to these notes during the quizzes. In the auditorium, we reseated students until they could easily read the on-screen text.

We conducted our analysis in two parts. The first part focused on questions that were unique to quizzes 1 and 2, as these were slightly harder and may better illustrate learning differences. The second part focused on the four questions that were repeated across tests, indicating acquisition of basic knowledge over time. However, as we later found an error in one variation of a repeated question, we restricted our analysis to three of these questions.

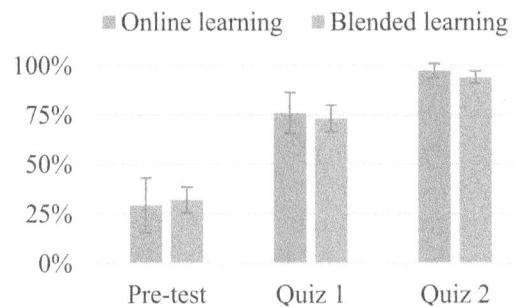

Figure 2: Average scores for the common questions across tests. Bars indicate 95% confidence intervals.

RESULTS

For each of the three questions that were unique to a given quiz, we observed no significant difference between the online learning and blended learning conditions. For the questions that were repeated across quizzes, the results appear in Figure 2. Considering the average score for these questions, we did not observe any significant difference between the online and blended groups for any of the three quizzes. However, we did observe significant improvement of scores as a result of each session conducted. Using a paired Student's t-test, we found significant benefits of the video lecture viewed on a personal computer ($t(24) = 5.9$, $p<0.001$), the video lecture viewed in an auditorium ($t(76) = 9.4$, $p<0.001$), the video-based quiz review ($t(24) = 3.9$, $p<0.001$) and the live quiz review ($t(76) = 6.3$, $p<0.001$).

We observed that students in the online learning condition frequently paused or replayed parts of the video. We eventually encouraged students to move ahead to allow a fair comparison with the group in the auditorium (who could not pause or replay). Students in the online condition spent 40% longer on the video lecture and 20% longer on the quiz review. A group discussion confirmed that students highly valued the ability to pause and replay parts of the video.

DISCUSSION

While our experiment did not reveal significant differences between the online and blended conditions, we did observe significant learning gains in all sessions conducted. The learning observed in the classroom video session may suggest a practical way to extend the benefits of educational videos to those lacking computer and Internet access. On the other hand, students in the online condition valued the ability to pause and replay. In future work, we plan to instrument the video player to better understand these behaviors.

Our study has several limitations, the most prominent being its short duration and scale. In addition, we had the utmost attention of students; in long-term, unsupervised use, students might engage differently with either condition. We look forward to addressing these limitations in future work.

REFERENCES

1. Schreiber, E., Fukuta, J., and Gordon, F., "Live lecture versus video podcast in undergraduate medical education: A randomized controlled trial," *BMC Medical Education*, 2010.

Modeling Programming Knowledge for Mentoring at Scale

Anvisha H. Pai
MIT CSAIL
anvishap@mit.edu

Philip J. Guo
MIT CSAIL / University of Rochester
pg@cs.rochester.edu

Robert C. Miller
MIT CSAIL
rcm@mit.edu

ABSTRACT

In large programming classes, MOOCs or online communities, it is challenging to find peers and mentors to help with learning specific programming concepts. In this paper we present first steps towards an automated, scalable system for matching learners with Python programmers who have expertise in different areas. The learner matching system builds a knowledge model for each programmer by analyzing their authored code and extracting features that capture domain knowledge and style. We demonstrate the feasibility of a simple model that counts the references to modules from the standard library and Python Package Index in a programmers' code. We also show that programmers exhibit self-selection using which we can extract the modules a programmer is best at, even though we may not have all of their code. In our future work we aim to extend the model to encapsulate more features, and apply it for skill matching in a programming class as well as personalizing answers on StackOverflow.

Author Keywords

Skill matching; personalized learning; learner modeling

ACM Classification Keywords

H.5.3. Group and Organization Interfaces: Theory and Models

INTRODUCTION

Learning programming is an ongoing process. Knowing the syntax and built-in functions of a language is just the beginning. Even the most experienced programmers need to keep learning about new APIs, standard and external libraries, and frameworks that they can use in their programs. Instructional textbooks focus heavily on syntax and a few standard libraries, and can only go so far in helping a programmer learn something new. Moreover, it is easy for a programmer to get entrenched in certain practices, while there are better ones out there that they are never exposed to.

Interacting with other programmers who have different areas of expertise is a good way to address this problem [1]. Practices like pair programming, tutoring and mentoring are key. In structured classes, group projects reinforce this learning technique, as students have the opportunity to learn from each others' styles and expertise.

However, finding peers or mentor guidance is not as easy or feasible at scale. Scale could be anything ranging from a large programming class at a university (250–1,000 students) to a whole community of programmers on the Internet. While it is easy to find tutors online that can help with broad areas like a CS1-style Intro. to Python, it is harder to find someone to help with specific application needs, such as using linear algebra functions of the Python library NumPy. Though learners have online help forums like StackOverflow [1] as a resource, forum answers are not personalized to the asker's experience level and often require non-trivial amounts of prerequisite knowledge.

In this work-in-progress, we present first steps toward a scalable learner matching system for Python based on programming knowledge and styles. Our system will analyze the corpus of code a programmer has written and build a fine-grained *knowledge model* of their expertise in different areas. This will enable it to match learners with mentors or with fellow students for collaborative learning projects in either a MOOC or large residential courses. Since code analysis is automated, this system is easily scalable, and has the potential to improve the learning experience for many programmers.

MATCHING BASED ON PYTHON MODULE USAGE

Python has a standard library of 226 modules that provide standardized functions like regular expressions, JSON file parsing, and email processing. Beyond the standard library, widely used and approved modules are included in the Python Package Index. These external modules include 24,147 libraries like Django, a major web framework for Python, and NumPy, a computational and scientific package. Assessing how well-versed a programmer is in using a particular module is one proxy measure of their expertise in that application area.

Data Collection and Analysis

As an initial investigation, we solicited Python code from 10 programmers. Three of these students were beginners who submitted code from their introductory Python class at MIT. Three were undergraduates who described themselves as intermediate to advanced level programmers, and submitted projects they had done outside of classes. The remaining 4 programmers were researchers at the MIT Computer Science and Artificial Intelligence Lab, and submitted code from their research. We used regular expressions to mine the code and count the number of function calls made from each module in the standard library and Python Package Index. We also asked the participants to rank their perceived expertise in the most popular packages that came out of this analysis, using an

L@S'14, March 4–5, 2014, Atlanta, Georgia, USA.
ACM 978-1-4503-2669-8/14/03.
http://dx.doi.org/10.1145/2556325.2567871

Subject	1st Package		2nd Package		3rd Package	
	module	calls	module	calls	module	calls
Beginner 1	random	19	UserDict	8	string	7
Beginner 2	random	6	string	5	graph	4
Beginner 3	random	6	Queue	1	string	1
Undergrad 1	Django	95	httplib2	71	socket	62
Undergrad 2	os	12	copy	4	profile	3
Undergrad 3	re	31	mechanize	23	lxml	12
Researcher 1	os	20	json	13	re	10
Researcher 2	Django	158	relay	20	teleport	16
Researcher 3	util	52	config	25	json	9
Researcher 4	Django	187	os	20	re	16

Table 1. Top 3 packages for participants, ranked by number of function calls in their submitted code.

Subject	Top 3 Packages	
	Self-Reported	Ranking Calculated by Model
Beginner 1	random, string, os	random, string, numpy
Beginner 2	random, string, numpy	random, string, numpy
Beginner 3	numpy, string, random	random, string
Undergrad 1	string, django, random	django, numpy, random
Undergrad 2	numpy, random, os	os, random, numpy
Undergrad 3	numpy, random, os	os, random, numpy
Researcher 1	os, json, numpy	os, json, random
Researcher 2	string, django, os	django, os, json
Researcher 3	json, string, os	json, os
Researcher 4	numpy, unittest, random	django, os, random

Table 2. Perceived and actual rankings of modules by subject

online survey where they assigned a rank to each of 7 packages. We used these reported ranks to assess the validity of the estimated expertise from the analyzing submitted code.

Results

Table 1 shows the top 3 Python packages per participant ranked by the number of function calls in their submitted code, showing a wide variety of modules across different experience levels and areas of expertise. As expected, different applications and types of projects showed different modules being used. The beginner programming students mostly used the same packages, since their projects were in the context of similar class assignments and applications. This was very different for the more advanced programmers, however. Even though Undergrad 1 and Researcher 2 informally characterized themselves as Django-based web programmers, they used very different modules in their code, showing specific expertise and strengthening the idea of learning from peer guidance.

We did not have access to all the code the participants had written, hence we risk having an incomplete model of their expertise. However, the results in Table 2 indicate that the top 3 packages reported by the participants were mostly consistent with the top 3 packages from the code that they submitted. This implies that we can identify the strongest areas of expertise from the code submitted, and enables us to use this model for the application of mentoring, where the strongest skills of each potential mentor are important.

Self-selection could be a reason for this correlation between the top reported and calculated packages. In the study we asked people to submit code to us, and it is possible that they self-selected recent projects that they thought were good examples. This skew in might actually benefit a skill-matching

system, since if a person wants to most accurately represent their skills for offering their services as a mentor, they would likely submit recent and accurate code. In contrast, analyzing *all* of their code might yield worse results, since older code might not be representative of current skills or interests.

APPLICATIONS AND ONGOING WORK

The simple model is that it does not normalize for comparison: using the same functions repeatedly may not signify expertise. We plan to eliminate this limitation by normalizing within a package and across different programmers, by gathering data through larger versions of the study presented here.We also plan to include more features that capture expertise and style, such as what percentage of functions in a package were used (coverage) and the use of object-oriented or functional programming.

Matching with Mentors

As seen in the results, even with a simple model that analyzes modules used, we can capture *to some degree* which packages a person is best at. A straightforward way to use this model for matching beginners with mentors is to simply match them with the people that are best at the packages that they want to learn.

Matching with Peers

Matching with peers is slightly more complex than with mentors because the aim is to pair together people with *complementary* knowledge and styles. Programmers can be matched by modeling each person as a vector with the dimensions as different modules and the magnitude as the normalized score from that module. Programmers could be matched based on the relative magnitudes and angles between different vectors. We aim to deploy our peer matching system in an MIT programming class based on group programming projects to validate our hypothesis.

Matching with Online Resources

An application of the model we plan to develop would be StackOverflow customization. Especially for beginner programmers, it can be problematic when the top voted answer to a question on StackOverflow uses libraries they do not understand. With a model of the programmer's knowledge, we can assess which answer falls closest to what they are familiar with. StackOverflow answers have code snippets, which make it possible to analyze these snippets in the same way code is analyzed, reducing answer customization to a similar matching problem

ACKNOWLEDGMENTS

This work is supported in by the MIT SuperUROP program, funded by a donation from Robert Fano; and by Quanta Computer as a part of Philip Guo's postdoc funding.

REFERENCES

1. Mamykina, L., Manoim, B., Mittal, M., Hripcsak, G., and Hartmann, B. Design Lessons from the Fastest Q&A Site in the West. In *Proceedings of the SIGCHI Conference on Human Factors in Computing Systems*, CHI '11, ACM (New York, NY, USA, 2011), 2857–2866.

Facilitating MOOCs Learning through Weekly Meet-up: A Case Study in Taiwan

Pin-Ju Chen
National University of Tainan
33, Sec. 2, Shu-Lin St. Tainan,
Taiwan 70005
d09909002@gmail.com

Yang-Hsueh Chen
National University of Tainan
33, Sec. 2, Shu-Lin St. Tainan,
Taiwan 70005
kcchen@mail.nutn.edu.tw
+886-6-2133111 ext 971

ABSTRACT

Online learners need various supports to survive, and it is especially true in the context of MOOCs. Yet, studies documenting the learning progress as a function of learner support are at its inception. Based on self-determination theory and via weekly study group, we devised a series of support strategies to promote the autonomy, relatedness, and competency of MOOCs learners. We evaluated how those support strategies influenced MOOCs learners' retention rate and their self-regulation behaviors such as goal setting, time management, and help seeking. While this study is still on going, initial results showed that participants had higher intrinsic motivation than extrinsic motivation. Furthermore, participants expressed that the weekly meet-up had been very helpful to keep them going, especially when they wanted to give up. Interestingly, participants' learning strategies rarely changed even new strategies had been shared in group. Implications for researchers, designers and MOOCs learners are discussed.

Author Keywords

MOOC; distance learning; self-determination theory; self-regulated learning; learning strategies

ACM Classification Keywords

K.3.1. Computer and education: Distance learning

INTRODUCTION

MOOCs learners are encouraged to form study groups, but little research has documented the effect of study group in MOOCs context. This case-study research attempts to evaluate the potential effect of weekly study group, which design was based on the self-determination theory [1]. Especially, how it influences the retention rate, which is a well-documented issue in MOOCs literature.

METHODS

The study was conducted in qualitative, case-study approach.

L@S 2014, March 4–5, 2014, Atlanta, Georgia, USA.
ACM 978-1-4503-2669-8/14/03.
http://dx.doi.org/10.1145/2556325.2567872

Data Collection

The data were collected from multiple sources to achieve thick description and for triangulation. Before weekly meeting, Academic Motivation Scale (AMS), Online Self-regulated Learning Questionnaire (OSLQ), and two sub-scales from Learner Readiness for Online Learning Scale, Computer/Internet Self-efficacy (CISE) and Online Communication Self-efficacy (OCSE), were administered to measure participants' motivation and competency. The group meeting were recorded and transcribed into verbatim. Facilitators also kept the observation notes. Participants were required to write their reflections before the end of group meeting.

Research Design

The self-determinant theory was served as framework in designing study group meetings. The weekly meetings lasted for two hours, and were facilitated by two researchers. Three basic needs were supported by facilitating strategies, as shown in Table 1. Also, two

Basic needs	Facilitating Strategies
Autonomy	* Proving rationales of online learning and MOOCs study * Participants' own decision on the courses to take * Participants' decisions on the topics to discuss in the meet-up * Participants' own decisions to connect to other group members
Competency	* Offering an initial technical and academic orientation. * Introducing self-regulated strategies * Sharing of learning experiences * Sharing of related learning materials * Providing positive feedback on participants' perseverance and thoughts
Relatedness	* Weekly study group meet up and sharing in an informal manner * Facebook interactions * Email notifications and reminders of course routines

Table 1: Facilitating strategies

aspects of six major aspects of self-regulated strategies were selected as the weekly topics, including goal setting (GS), environment structuring (ES), help seeking (HS), time management (TM), task strategies (TS), and self-evaluation (SE).

Participants

Six college students signed up for the study group and took Coursera course "The Red Chamber Dream", offered by University of Taiwan. The initial survey showed that participants had above-average academic motivation and self-regulated learning strategies (see Figure 1 and 2). Whereas participants' Computer/Internet self-efficacy was high, they had much lower Online Communication Self-efficacy (see Figure 3).

FINDINGS

Several themes were emerged from cross-examined data from multiple sources.

- Except for one, all participants missed at least one meeting; nevertheless, they all choose to stay in the group and the course for now.

- Goal setting (GS), time management (TM), task strategies (TS) were most frequently discussed topics. Especially when participants discussed about how to do assignments. Coincidently, participants also had lower self-regulated competency in these aspects, as shown in Figure 2.

- Getting certificate could be an important external motivation. Some participants set it as their utmost goals, while others only aimed to complete course.

- Time management had been an important concern. Almost all participants felt that they had limited time for this course and the assignments took more time than they expected.

- Participants enjoyed social support from weekly meeting, when they learned that they shared similar learning problems.

- Some were aware of their difficulties to stay motivated and eager to find ways to motivate themselves.

- Many of them were reluctant to join online discussion at course forum, even after being encouraged by the facilitator to do so.

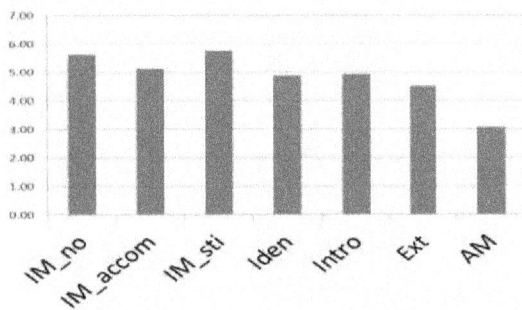

Figure 1: The average performance on AMS.

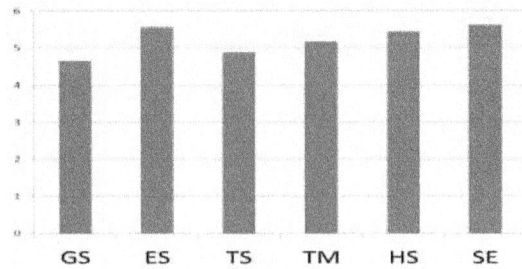

Figure 2: The average performance on OSLQ.

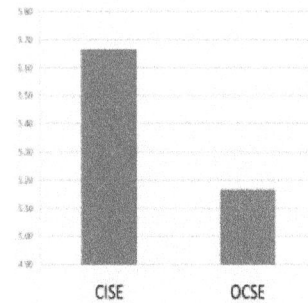

Figure 3: The average performance on Computer/Internet self-efficacy and Online Communication Self-efficacy.

DISCUSSIONS

In this case study, most participants had academic competency and were highly motivated intrinsically; nevertheless, lacking sufficient external motivation, clearly defined goal, and social connection with other course-takers, they may still struggle to maintain their motivation and stay in course. Those difficulties may be even more significant for average learners. Thus, it is important to provide extra assistance to MOOC learners in addition to online support. Face-to-face study group offers a feasible alternative by strengthening learners' autonomy, competency relatedness.

Participants' computer and Internet competency did not grant them good online communication. Online communication skills may need to be taught before MOOC learners can feel comfortable participating in online discussion. Face-to-face demonstration or tutoring may be a good way to help MOOC learners to gain confidence to do so.

It is also suggested that MOOCs offer more external incentives to motivate their learners, such as scholarships or recognition from prestige education institutions and international corporations.

REFERENCES

1. Deci, E. L., & Ryan, R. M. *Intrinsic motivation and self-determination in human behavior*. Plenum, New York, NY, USA, 1985.

Java Tutor: Bootstrapping with Python to Learn Java

Casey O'Brien, Max Goldman, Robert C. Miller
MIT CSAIL
Cambridge, MA 02138 USA
{cmobrien, maxg, rcm}@mit.edu

ABSTRACT

A common pattern among undergraduate computer science curriculums is to teach an introductory subject in Python followed by a more advanced software engineering subject in Java. We are building an online tool that will help students who already know Python learn the syntax and semantics of Java. Our system will differ from existing online tutors and tools for learning Java in two main aspects. First, our tutor will focus on the transition from Python to Java. Using this basis will allow us to gloss over basic concepts of programming which students are already familiar with and focus on the specifics of Java. Second, our tutor will crowdsource writing test cases for problems to the learners themselves. This will give students practice writing tests, and will also reduce the burden on instructors, who would otherwise need to implement test suites for every problem in the tutor.

Author Keywords

Python; Java; tutor

ACM Classification Keywords

H.5.m. Information Interfaces and Presentation (e.g. HCI): Miscellaneous

INTRODUCTION

Students often learn how to program in a scripting language like Python, and then later take a more advanced software engineering class in another language, like Java. For students who have never programmed in the new language before, this can be a challenging transition.

MIT undergraduates studying computer science begin their careers by learning Python in 6.01 (Introduction to Electrical Engineering and Computer Science). With the help of an online Python tutor [5], students are able to learn the syntax and semantics of the language. A few semesters later the students enroll in 6.005 (Software Construction), where they are taught principles and techniques of software development. At the same time, they are expected to complete assignments demonstrating their understanding of these concepts in Java.

L@S'14, March 4–5, 2014, Atlanta, Georgia, USA.
ACM 978-1-4503-2669-8/14/03.
http://dx.doi.org/10.1145/2556325.2567873

For this problem we explore the differences between equality in Python and in Java. You may wish to read this tutorial to learn more about equality in Java.

Complete the following Java code to test the equality of integers and strings.

```
1 def intEq(i1, i2):
2     return i1 == i2
3
4 def stringEq(s1, s2):
5     return s1 == s2
```

```
1 public class TestClass {
2     public static boolean intEq(int i1, int i2) {
3         // Your Code Here
4     }
5
6     public static boolean stringEq(String s1, String s2) {
7         // Your Code Here
8     }
9 }
```

Compile & Run

Figure 1. Presentation of a sample problem. Python code will be shown on the left, with the template Java code to be filled in on the right.

We are building a Java tutor which supports students in 6.005 learning Java by translating Python code to Java code. The main goal is to build a tutor which is useful for students and easy for instructors to use. The class has about 200 students each semester. Ultimately, we hope that this Java tutor will be used for 6.005x, the online version of 6.005 available through edX. This would expand the user base to many thousands.

The concept of learning one language by translating from another is not a novel idea. Consider a native English speaker who wants to learn Spanish. To do so, they would begin by learning how to translate words and phrases from English to Spanish, and then would build up to translating full sentences. No one would try to learn Spanish without taking advantage of their knowledge of English. Using the same reasoning, we hope to help students learn Java using Python.

The tutor will take the form of an interactive website, where students are presented with Python code and asked to write the corresponding Java code. A sample problem is shown in Figure 1. Their solutions are then checked against a JUnit test suite, and they have the opportunity to submit a new solution if test cases fail.

After creating a variety of sample questions, it has become clear that the process of creating questions will be time consuming for instructors. The focus on previous knowledge of Python helps decrease the instructor workload by creating an easy way for instructors to express problem statements. Instead of having to carefully write problem statements in English, instructors simply have to write out the code in Python.

Even with this advantage, writing all the necessary Python code and JUnit test suites would still be very time consuming. In order to further reduce the workload on instructors, our system requires students to contribute test cases to the test suite. Using student-written test cases, our tutor will create a comprehensive test suite which students solutions will be tested against.

CURRENT RESOURCES

Like the online tools for learning Python (e.g., [5], [4]), there are many online tools for teaching Java through online exercises. Two examples are LearnJava [7] and CodingBat [1]. Both sites allow students to practice writing Java code by presenting problems and allowing students to check their solutions against test suites. However, neither site draws upon any other knowledge of programming languages.

Cody is a MATLAB Central game which aims to teach users how to write MATLAB code [2]. It allows players to interact with each other by creating new problems, viewing other solutions, and commenting on and liking problems and solutions. In this way, it takes advantage of input from all the users in the system to support learning.

INSTRUCTOR WORKLOAD

In order to implement our tutor as described, each problem will require a brief problem statement, Python code, a Java template, a Java solution, and a JUnit test suite. As shown in Figure 1, the student will initially be presented with the problem statement, Python code, and Java template. The JUnit test suite will be written collectively by the students, and the Java solution will be used to check the accuracy of test cases.

After creating a variety of sample questions, it has become clear that the largest bottleneck in the process of creating problems is writing the JUnit test suite. In order to reduce the workload on instructors, our system requires students to contribute test cases to the test suite.

Instead of developing a full test suite when creating a problem, the instructor will write a few very basic test cases. For a student attempting the problem, the area for inputting Java code will initially be locked. This will only be unlocked once the student has contributed a test case for the problem. Only once the student has written a test case which compiles and passes the instructor solution will the text area be unlocked.

Once a student submits a solution which compiles and passes their own test case, their solution will be run against the current test suite, and the student will be notified of the results and given the opportunity to fix their solution if any test cases fail. If another student later submits a test case which breaks a student's solution, that student will be notified and will have to go back and fix their solution.

In order to keep the size of the test suite from growing linearly with the number of students, de-duplication will be performed on the test cases. A new test case can be considered a duplicate of an existing test case if it both fails on the same set of student solutions as the other test case and executes the same lines of code. We will compute code coverage using the JaCoCo Java Code Coverage Library [6].

SCALING

Currently, the tutor performs all compilation and execution server-side. For the initial user base of around 200 students in 6.005, we believe that this solution will be sufficient. However, server-side compilation will almost certainly be insufficient to handle the 6.005x user base of thousands of students.

One possible solution to this scaling problem is to perform some or all of the computation client-side. This could be achieved using a Java runtime and compiler implemented in Javascript. To do this we can use Doppio [3], a project which aims to implement an entire JVM in Javascript. The system could also combine the client- and server-side approaches, for example by compiling a student's submissions in the student's own browser, but running test case de-duplication on the server.

PRELIMINARY RESULTS

The effectiveness of the tutor will be evaluated by measuring student performance and instructor workload, and by surveying both students and instructors. User testing on the full system will begin during the Spring 2014 semester. Initial tests on parts of the system offer promising results. Six students who were enrolled in either 6.005 or 6.01 at the time were asked to solve sample problems translating code from Python to Java. They reported that using Python as a basis was helpful in learning Java, and offered useful feedback.

To ensure that it is possible to write a comprehensive test suite from individuals each writing single test cases, we asked ten programmers comfortable with Java to contribute a single test case for the example in Figure 1. When we allowed users to view the current test suite, we found that the final test suite was comprehensive and also contained minimal duplication.

CONCLUSION

We are building a Java tutor for Python programmers which is both useful for students and involves a manageable amount of work for instructors. The concentration on translation from Python to Java will allow students to take advantage of the knowledge they already have and learn Java more efficiently. The crowdsourcing of the test suites will allow instructors to easily create new problems, which will in turn provide additional practice for students.

REFERENCES

1. CodingBat. codingbat.com.
2. MATLAB Central Cody. http://www.mathworks.com/matlabcentral/cody.
3. Doppio: Java on Coffeescript. http://int3.github.io/doppio/.
4. Guo, P. J. Online Python Tutor: Embeddable Web-Based Program Visualization for CS Education. In *ACM Technical Symposium on Computer Science Education (SIGCSE)* (2013).
5. Hartz, A. CAT-SOOP: A tool for automatic collection and assessment of homework exercises. Master's thesis, MIT Department of Electrical Engineering and Computer Science, June 2012.
6. JaCoCo Java Code Coverage Library. http://www.eclemma.org/jacoco/.
7. LearnJava. learnjavaonline.org.

Corporate Learning at Scale: Lessons from a Large Online Course at Google

Arthur Asuncion, Jac de Haan, Mehryar Mohri, Kayur Patel, Afshin Rostamizadeh, Umar Syed, Lauren Wong

Google
76 9th Ave., New York, NY 10011
{arta, jacis, mohri, kayur, rostami, usyed, laurenbw}@google.com

ABSTRACT

Google Research recently tested a massive online class model for an internal engineering education program, with machine learning as the topic, that blended theoretical concepts and Google-specific software tool tutorials. The goal of this training was to foster engineering capacity to leverage machine learning tools in future products. The course was delivered both synchronously and asynchronously, and students had the choice between studying independently or participating with a group. Since all students are company employees, unlike most publicly offered MOOCs we can continue to measure the students' behavioral change long after the course is complete. This paper describes the course, outlines the available data set and presents directions for analysis.

Author Keywords

MOOCs; connectivist MOOCs; corporate training; distance learning; online learning.

ACM Classification Keywords

K.3.1. Computer Uses in Education: Distance learning

INTRODUCTION

Massive Open Online Courses (MOOCs) have generated a great deal of excitement for their potential to make traditional university material accessible to a very wide audience. However, despite the growing popularity of MOOCs, there is considerable skepticism about their success and efficacy. A recent study showed that MOOC completion rates are very low, often in the single digits [2, 5], and some MOOC providers have shifted their focus to offering job training for corporations [1]. While there is an increasing focus on examining MOOC effectiveness in various contexts (see [3] for a recent example, and [4] for an excellent survey), relatively little analysis has been published in the corporate context. In light of these developments, it is important to determine what features of a MOOC, if any, lead to the greatest educational gains in a corporate setting.

In the fourth quarter of 2013, Google Research produced a massive online class for company engineers around the world on the topic of machine learning with an emphasis on Google-specific machine learning software tools. We collected student-reported data about the course content and delivery method. As code written by Google engineers is stored in a central repository and all code execution is logged, we are able to directly measure the course's effect on student usage of the technologies taught. This rich data set may answer several important questions about the effectiveness of MOOCs: Are students who attended live lectures more likely to apply what they learned in the course than students who watched recorded lectures? Do a student's intentions to apply course content correlate with future actions? Does engagement with ancillary instructional channels (such as forums and office hours) have any impact on students' post-MOOC behavior?

COURSE DESCRIPTION

Approximately 6,500 students registered for an optional course on machine learning, representing a large fraction of all full-time employees distributed across more than 80 offices worldwide.

The 10-week course was a hybrid of theory-based lectures and Google-specific implementations. Each class was devoted to a single machine learning topic and was divided into three components. First, an internal machine learning expert delivered a lecture on the theory behind the weekly topic. The lecture was followed by one or more case studies, where experts explained how the techniques taught in lecture had been applied to solve important problems at Google. Finally, time was spent answering student questions from around the world. At the conclusion of each week, students were directed to an optional programming assignment to gain hands-on experience using internal libraries and technologies to reinforce core concepts from the class.

The course was offered in three formats. Each week for 10 weeks, a live video feed of the class was streamed to viewing rooms in many Google offices where students watched the content together in small groups and, in some cases, held dis-

L@S 2014, March 4–5 2014, Atlanta, Georgia, USA.
ACM 978-1-4503-2669-8/14/03.
http://dx.doi.org/10.1145/2556325.2567874

cussions immediately after class. Students could alternately watch the live stream individually from their own computers. Finally, recordings of all 10 classes (as well as links to all slides, exercises, supplementary material and relevant external resources) were posted on the course website for asynchronous access.

DATA AND PRELIMINARY RESULTS

Per employee consent, all student page impressions were captured with a timestamp, length of page visit and unique student identifier. Individual student data was also captured when assignments were opened and code executed.

Most software written at Google is stored in a central repository, therefore this corpus can be crawled to locate files that reference machine learning function calls and algorithm libraries.

Students were surveyed 3 times over the 10 weeks. A precourse survey was used to understand the prior level of experience with machine learning and students participation goals. A mid-class survey was used to gather feedback on class format and content pacing. A post-class survey was sent to collect student feedback for course improvements and understand how engineers plan to implement machine learning in future projects.

Forty-six percent of post-class survey respondents are "planning to use machine learning as a result of this class," and six percent report that they are already "using machine learning as a result of this class." Of final survey respondents, 62% report having machine learning conversations with others (managers, teammates, other students) as a result of the class.

Student perceived experience

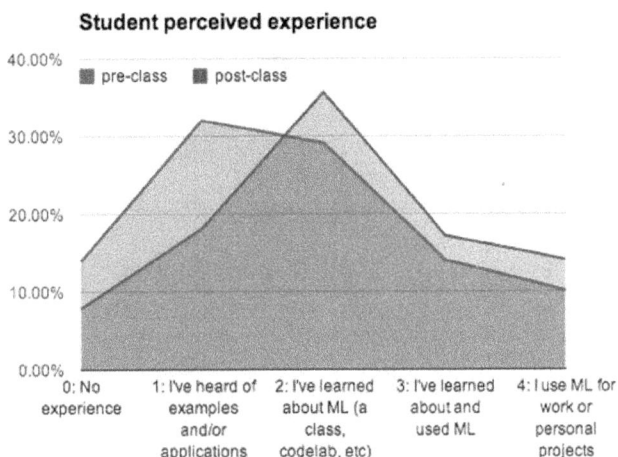

Figure 1. Comparing pre- and post-class surveys. Students responded to the question, "What is your current level of experience with machine learning?"

Future Research and Conclusion

Course designers will continue to collect and analyze longitudinal data over the coming year to assess course impact. Codebase references to machine learning files, individual satisfaction ratings and course participation data can be combined with employee-specific attributes (tenure, product area,

job title, level of education, etc) to answer our research questions:

- Which predictors (variables) are most likely to result in a student's transition from learning to implementation?
  - What type of employees are more likely to adopt machine learning after taking the class?
  - Is there a difference in post-course satisfaction ratings based on a student's reported pre-class experience with machine learning?

- Which course components were most successful?
  - Are students who attempted the interactive assignments more likely to implement machine learning?
  - As students begin using machine learning in real projects, does their perceived value of course components change over time?
  - Does the student-selected viewing method (independent or group setting, synchronous or asynchronous) have a measurable impact on course completion or future implementation of machine learning?

- Viewing Google as a social network, what is the density, reachability, and centrality of this content throughout the organization?

While the course served as a catalyst to build machine learning awareness, to raise visibility of leading experts and their work, and to foster dialogue across the company, the impact to engineering performance is yet to be determined. Rather than assessment of employee knowledge recall or recognition through online assessments, the *use* of machine learning concepts and tools in current and future products will become the measure of this course's success.

REFERENCES

1. Chafkin, M. Udacity's Sebastian Thrun, Godfather of Free Online Education, Changes Course. *Fast Company* (December 2013).

2. Jordan, K. MOOC Completion Rates: The Data. `http://www.katyjordan.com/MOOCproject.html`. Accessed: January 2, 2014.

3. Kizilcec, R. F., Piech, C., and Schneider, E. Deconstructing disengagement: Analyzing learner subpopulations in massive open online courses. In *Proceedings of Third Conference on Learning Analytics and Knowledge* (2013).

4. Liyanagunawardena, T., Adams, A., and Williams, S. Moocs: A systematic study of the published literature 2008-2012. *The International Review of Research in Open and Distance Learning 14*, 3 (2013).

5. Perna, L., Ruby, A., Boruch, R., Wang, N., Scull, J., Evans, C., and Ahmad, S. The Life Cycle of a Million MOOC Users. Presentation at the MOOC Research Initiative Conference, December 5, 2013.

Teacher Usage Behaviors within an Online Open Educational Resource Repository

Jennifer Sabourin
SAS Institute, Inc.
Cary, NC USA
Jennifer.Sabourin@sas.com
+1 919 531 3313

Lucy Kosturko
SAS Institute, Inc.
Cary, NC USA
Lucy.Kosturko@sas.com
+1 919 531 3430

Scott McQuiggan
SAS Institute, Inc.
Cary, NC USA
Scott.McQuiggan@sas.com
+1 919 531 1119

ABSTRACT
With instructional methods such as MOOCs and flipped classrooms rapidly gaining popularity and school budget cuts becoming more prevalent across the nation, increasing the usability of Open Educational Resources (OER) is highly relevant for today's educators. Although several OER databases exist providing access to hundreds of thousands of resources, navigating these spaces, evaluating resources, and integrating them within classroom instruction has proven less than efficient. The present research explores learning analytics for understanding real-world interaction patterns with SAS® Curriculum Pathways®, which has over 120,000 active teacher users and over 1,300 freely available resources across multiple disciplines. In this preliminary investigation, users are clustered based on overall usage patterns. Patterns of resource interaction are then identified using association analysis. Results of this exploratory investigation provide insight into how users interact with large OER databases and introduce many avenues for continued investigation.

Author Keywords
Open educational resources; recommendation systems

INTRODUCTION
Open Educational Resource is a broad term that describes any "teaching, learning, and research resource that resides in the public domain or have been released under an intellectual property license that permits their free use or re-purposing by others" [1]. Presently, hundreds of thousands of OER are available for K-12 use. While the abundance of OER is a good problem to have, individual instructors are spending a great deal of time tirelessly searching through this corpus to find tools that fit their specific needs [1]. In fact, some districts have reported million-dollar budgets allocated to the creation of OER repositories to support educators in their search [2]. Other efforts, such as Khan Academy (khanacademy.org), the Learning Registry (learningregistry.org), and OpenEd (openEd.io), have made finding and integrating OER more efficient with carefully designed user interfaces and useful filtering options. However, simply finding resources is only a portion of an educator's OER integration process; evaluating and devising an integration plan adds additional complexities.

Understanding how users interact with and navigate a large repository of unique resources is a broad area of investigation. This exploratory analysis represents a preliminary step in this line of work by first empirically identifying groups of users and then examining differential patterns of use among them. Specifically, we are interested in how users find resources of interest, which resources are commonly used together, and if any of these patterns can be associated with success in navigating the repository. By exploring this line of work we hope to build more robust systems for helping educators find the set of resources that are most aligned to their goals.

PRELIMINARY INVESTIGATION
For the purpose of this preliminary investigation we consider user interaction data with SAS Curriculum Pathways from the past 5 years (August 2008 - August 2013). Available at no cost, SAS Curriculum Pathways provides interactive, standards-based resources in the core disciplines (English Language Arts, Mathematics, Science, Social Studies, and Spanish) for traditional, virtual, and home schools. At present, more than 120,000 users in more than 45,000 schools are actively using SAS Curriculum Pathways as part of their classroom instruction. The corpus used for this analysis focuses on data from approximately 87,000 users interacting with 1,524 unique resources. In total this corpus represents 4.9 million interactive sessions and observations from over 10.4 million resource hits. The majority of users (66.3%) identify themselves as educators, while 22.0% identify themselves as students, and the remaining do not list their role.

Method
The exploratory analyses include two phases: *clustering* of users and *association analysis* of resources use. In the first phase groups demonstrating similar patterns of usage are identified. These groups are then used in the second phase to further explore how user groups interact with resources and navigate the repository.

L@S 2014, Mar 04-05 2014, Atlanta, GA, USA
ACM 978-1-4503-2669-8/14/03.
http://dx.doi.org/10.1145/2556325.2567875

Clustering

K-means clustering was used to identify meaningful groups of users. The variables of interest in creating the clusters were: total sessions, total resources hits, average duration of time between sessions, and proportion of [English, Science, Social Studies, Mathematics and unclassified] resources. Each of these variables was heavily skewed so the log of the values were used as input to the clustering algorithm. K-means clustering was run with k=3, 4, and 5 and the clusters with greatest distance between means were selected (k=3). Initial exploration of the clusters indicated that clusters were selected based on their overall usage patterns.

Results showed that users in Cluster 1 (N = 3,869) demonstrated the highest usage. They logged in more frequently (M = 1180.5, SD = 8690.1) and interacted with a greater total number of resources (M = 2342.1, SD=14877.5). Based on these patterns, we consider this group *Established Users*. They show sustained interaction with the tools over time and, though there are fewer of these users, they make up a large proportion of daily hits to the repository. Cluster 2 (N = 61,411) demonstrated the lowest usage. Most of these users logged in only a few times (M=1.6, SD = 1.1) after creating an account. They looked at a few resources (M = 5.3, SD = 5.1) and then often did not return. We name this group *Glancing Users* and consider this group a target for future analysis and intervention as they seem to have the most difficulty in navigating the repository to find resources of interest. Finally, Cluster 3 (N = 21, 589) demonstrated an intermediate pattern. During the timespan of the corpus, they logged in an average of approximately 14.4 (SD = 34.7) times and interacted with 50.7 (SD = 56.1) resources total. We name this group *Browsing Users* as their behaviors indicate that they are exploring the repository to identify resources to use again.

Association Analysis

The next set of analyses looked at specific patterns of resource use. Specifically, we were interested in whether users used particular resources together and how they found new resources. An association analysis was run independently for each of the three groups. This exploratory analysis produces a list of rules linking resources that are commonly used together by the users.

Results from the *Glancing Users* indicate that there are few common patterns in exploring resources. The only connections occur between some of the most commonly used resources in SAS Curriculum Pathways. Perhaps these resources were accessed based on a recommendation of a peer but then the user never explored the remaining resources, as is suggested by the total number of resources used by this group. Alternatively, patterns from the *Browsing Users* support the hypothesis that these users are exploring the space of resources. There is a spreading pattern from the most common resources out to many other resources

supported by a long network of connections. These users also utilize more resources per session (M = 5.4, SD = 6.2) than the *Glancing Users* (M =3.6, SD = 3.7) or even the *Established Users* (M = 3.2, SD = 4.0) further supporting the idea that these users are exploring the resources available in the repository. The *Established Users* on the other hand show less connectedness than *Browsing Users,* and instead favor resource clusters that are based on a particular domain. These experienced users have likely identified the set of resources that work best for their purposes. They may return to them often and not necessarily explore other options.

DISCUSSION

This preliminary investigation used k-means clustering and association analysis to understand the navigation patterns of users in SAS Curriculum Pathways. Analyses of a large corpus of interaction data indicated three groups of users: *Glancing Users, Browsing Users,* and *Established Users,* each with their own profile of resource navigation. As a preliminary analysis, this work pointed to many areas for future investigation.

One line of work will be investigating what characteristics and patterns of behavior differentiate *Glancing* and *Browsing Users* when they first begin interacting with the repository. Specifically, how can we encourage or facilitate better browsing behavior to increase the likelihood that users will find resources of interest and continue using the repository. Another key question is whether *Browsing Users* eventually transition to *Established Users* and how can this process be facilitated? Specifically, it will be important to investigate changes in patterns of behavior across time and to explore how users identify key resources that they would like to continue to use. It is possible that these resources may be the keystone resources identified in the association graphs. These analyses will require expanding the analyses beyond 5 years to include a user's entire span of interaction. By exploring these patterns temporally situated for each user we may be able to better predict which users are most likely to return to the system, use it effectively and why these differences occur. Finally, it will be important to explore the search patterns of user groups when they first enter the repository. Do they use fundamentally different search keywords? How do they select resources after a search? This information can guide the resources that are displayed based on a search and may improve similar recommendations. Overall, it is hoped that this line of resource can further the understanding of educators' navigation and use of large OER repositories.

REFERENCES

1. Atkins, D.E. et al. 2007. A Review of the Open Educational Resources (OER) Movement: Achievements, Challenges, and New Opportunities.

2. Taylor Seeks Common Core Help: 2013. http://theadvocate.com/home/7225834-125/taylor-seeks-common-core-help. Accessed: 2013-10-21.

ACCE: Automatic Coding Composition Evaluator

Stephanie Rogers
UC, Berkeley
2308 Warring Street 101,
Berkeley, CA, 94704
srogers11@berkeley.edu

Steven Tang
UC, Berkeley
1888 Berkeley Way 318,
Berkeley, CA, 94704
steventang@berkeley.edu

John Canny
UC, Berkeley
637 Soda Hall, UC Berkeley
Campus, Berkeley, CA, 94704
canny@berkeley.edu

ABSTRACT

Coding style is important to teach to beginning programmers, so that bad habits don't become permanent. This is often done manually at the University level because automated Python static analyzers cannot accurately grade based on a given rubric. However, even manual analysis of coding style encounters problems, as we have seen quite a bit of inconsistency among our graders. We introduce ACCE–Automated Coding Composition Evaluator–a module that automates grading for the composition of programs. ACCE, given certain constraints, assesses the composition of a program through static analysis, conversion from code to AST, and clustering (unsupervised learning), helping automate the subjective process of grading based on style and identifying common mistakes. Further, we create visual representations of the clusters to allow readers and students understand where a submission falls, and the overall trends. We have applied this tool to CS61A–a CS1 level course at UC, Berkeley experiencing rapid growth in student enrollment–in an attempt to help expedite the involved process as well as reduce human grader inconsistencies.

Author Keywords

Composition; Clustering; Unsupervised Learning; Autograding; Assessment; Gephi; Visualization; Grading; Style; CS1; Evaluation

ACM Classification Keywords

K.3.1. Computer Uses in Education; I.5.3. Clustering

INTRODUCTION

The fact is, code is read much more often than it is written. Coding with good style results in code that is more readable, error-free, secure, extensible, and modular. Programming style has started to become a more formalized set of rules and guidelines. In practice, most style enforcement actually comes in the form of code reviews: manual analysis by experienced human readers. However, even manual code style evaluation has problems with consistency. We want students at the University level to practice good techniques while coding, to prepare them for industry or life beyond academia.

Nontrivial machine grading of student assessments is an emerging problem, as Massive Open Online Courses (MOOC) become more popular. Aimed at unlimited participation, these classes face the problem of scalability with respect to grading. Automating the manual processes of grading becomes a highly relevant approach to expanding the ability of these classes to evaluate both the learning outcomes and the quality of the assessment. ACCE–Automated Coding Composition Evaluator–is a module that attempts to automate the process of code reviews by predicting a score or feedback for the composition of computer programs through clustering. The purpose of the tool is two-fold: to provide highly detailed and targeted feedback, and to act as a verification tool–to enforce consistency between graders and for any particular grader.

RELATED WORKS

A few ways in which code is currently automatically graded include unit tests (or test-base based), static analysis checkers or feature-based approaches, satisfaction-based programs, and code coverage analyzers [1] [3] [4]. Our work is primarily based off of Huang et. al. in which they examine the syntactic and functional variability of a huge code base worth of submissions for a MOOC class [2]. In our paper, we apply their technique to a new set of data and automate the entire process.

IMPLEMENTATION

The motivating premise behind our approach is that there might only exist a limited number of common solutions that students take when solving a problem, thus feedback or grades can be extended to all solutions of the same approach. To identify different approaches, we computed the edit-distance between one project submission and all other project submissions (using the abstract syntax tree of the submission), and we repeated this computation for each submission. Submissions with low edit-distances, and similarity in structure, were clustered together.

First, the decision was made to look for common structural approaches for individual functions, rather than for entire project submissions. This was motivated by the fact that most functions in the project could be structured completely independently from one another. Each function submission was converted into its abstract syntax tree (AST), with most

L@S'14, March 4–5, 2014, Atlanta, Georgia, USA.
ACM 978-1-4503-2669-8/14/03.
http://dx.doi.org/10.1145/2556325.2567876

variables and function names anonymized. However, variable and function names that occurred as part of the project skeleton code were not anonymized, as it is structurally significant. In order to determine how structurally similar two submissions are, we calculated the *AST edit distance* pairwise between all corresponding ASTs, as described in J. Huang et. al. This pairwise computation considered the trees unordered and anonymized the names of any variables, functions or parameters, unless otherwise specified. This pairwise process is quartic in time with respect to the AST size, but only needs to be run once on a particular set of submissions. The process could likely benefit from optimizations. Lower edit distances means that submissions are more similar in structure. The inverse of an edit distance is how we calculated the *similarity score* between submissions. With similarity scores calculated pairwise for all submissions, visualizations of common structural approaches to functions could be created. The program Gephi is used, which is an interactive visualization and exploration platform for networks, complex systems, and graphs[1].

RESULTS

In Figure 1, we can see the final visualization produced by Gephi, given randomized data. Each node in the graph corresponds to an AST of an original function submission. Edges where the similarity score between two functions was below a certain threshold were not included in the graph as they should not be considered similar. Thus, an edge can be thought of as connecting two nodes that have a high enough similarity score to warrant analysis. By examining the network of solutions only in the top 5%, we observe a smaller, more manageable number of common solutions or mistakes– only a handful of clusters.

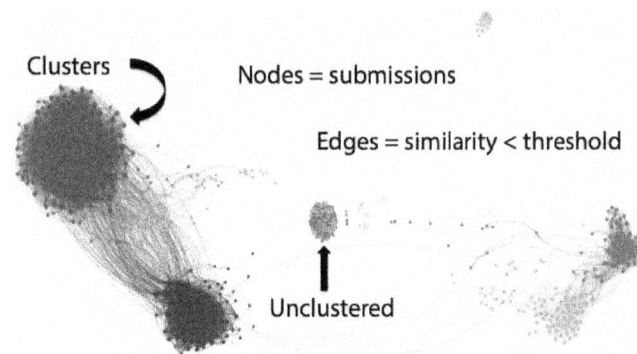

Figure 1. Cluster Visualization: Annotated Explanation

In order to produce the cluster visualization as shown in Figure 1, Gephi runs a ForceAtlas algorithm, which uses repulsion and gravity to continuously push and pull nodes away from each other. The distance between nodes and clusters directly correspond to the syntactic similarity. The clusters are colored by modularity, a measure of how well a network decomposes into modular communities. The group of multicolored nodes represents those submissions that were unclustered and therefore highly dissimilar in structure to most other submissions: somewhere around 20-25% of the submissions remained unclustered.

[1] http://gephi.org/

Identifying the need to automate the process described in the previous paragraphs, the authors created an automated tool that can accept a new code submission as a Python file to automatically produce a visualization (a .png file) with the existing clusters that were already generated. The new code submission is then emphasized in size and in color, so that the user can identify where the new submission is located. In this way, a reader can easily run the tool with a new submission and visually identify what cluster the new submission belongs to. Additionally, textual output of which cluster id the submission belongs to is output.

FUTURE WORK

With the given data from the CS61A class, we plan to perform a variety of analyses to show the effectiveness of the tool. We plan to do an in-depth manual classification of each cluster, by randomly selecting 10-15 submissions from each cluster and labeling each as "Good," "Okay," or "Poor" style. In order to provide some validation to the manual classification, we will color the nodes by the original composition scores given to each submission. Finally, we plan to manually analyze the "Poor" quality clusters to identify the common mistakes within those functions, and see how many of the nodes in that particular cluster make that same mistake. While visualizing clusters can be informative and useful, there is much future work to be done to make this process more usable to provide feedback or grades back to students. Next steps involve creating a tool that allows for clusters to be tagged with specific feedback that will be sent back to the students in a streamlined fashion. This approach is simply aimed at helping the reader grade and provide feedback, by making the process more consistent and efficient.

CONCLUSION

Automating the subjective process of grading code based off of composition is extremely difficult. We hope to leverage the common trends among submissions to make grading a more efficient process, especially when working with a dataset of such size, as MOOC courses often do. Applying feedback and scoring to submissions within the same cluster seems to be a reasonable way to grade coding submissions.

REFERENCES

1. Aggarwal V., S. S. Principles for using machine learning in the assessment of open response items: Programming assessment as a case study.

2. Huang J., Piech C., N. A. G. L. Syntactic and functional variability of a million code submissions in a machine learning mooc. In *Proceedings of the 16th Annual Conference on Aritificial Intellgence in Education*, ACM (2013).

3. Saikkonen R., Malmi L., K. A. Fully automatic assessment of programming exercises. In *Proceedings of the 6th Annual Conference on Innovation and Technology in Computer Science Education*, ACM (2001), 133–136.

4. Singh, R., Gulwani, S., and Solar-Lezama, A. Automated semantic grading of programs. Tech. rep., MIT/Microsoft Research, 2012.

Due Dates in MOOCs: Does Stricter Mean Better?

Sergiy O Nesterko
HarvardX
Cambridge, MA
Sergiy_Nesterko@harvard.edu

Daniel Seaton
MITx
Cambridge, MA
dseaton@mit.edu

Justin Reich
HarvardX
Cambridge, MA
justin_reich@harvard.edu

Joseph McIntyre
Graduate School of Education
Harvard University
jcm977@mail.harvard.edu

Qiuyi Han
Department of Statistics
Harvard University
qiuyihan@fas.harvard.edu

Isaac Chuang
MITx
Cambridge, MA
ichuang@mit.edu

Andrew Ho
Graduate School of Education
Harvard University
Andrew_Ho@gse.harvard.edu

ABSTRACT

Massive Open Online Courses (MOOCs) employ a variety of components to engage students in learning (eg. videos, forums, quizzes). Some components are graded, which means that they play a key role in a student's final grade and certificate attainment. It is not yet clear how the due date structure of graded components affects student outcomes including academic performance and alternative modes of learning of students. Using data from HarvardX and MITx, Harvard's and MIT's divisions for online learning, we study the structure of due dates on graded components for 10 completed MOOCs. We find that stricter due dates are associated with higher certificate attainment rates but fewer students who join late being able to earn a certificate. Our findings motivate further studies of how the use of graded components and deadlines affects academic and alternative learning of MOOC students, and can help inform the design of online courses.

Author Keywords

MOOC, student performance, MOOC structure, due dates

INTRODUCTION

Massive Open Online Courses (MOOCs) are subject to an increasing amount of research inquiry. It has been determined that MOOC student populations are diverse in terms of location, gender, demographics, and educational attainment level [5, 1]. The motivations of students taking MOOCs are also quite varied [1]. MOOCs attract different types of learners such as traditional and non-traditional [4] and their patterns of engagement with content vary [3]. The MOOC setting is much different from a traditional brick and mortar academic course, suggesting the need to reconceptualize classical educational variables in the online setting [2].

While our understanding of the students participating in MOOCs is increasing, little is known about how online course structure affects learning outcomes in online courses.

On the example of 10 open online courses offered by Harvard and MIT in Fall 2012 and Spring 2013 (see Figure 2), we study the different approaches to using due dates in course structure. We find that courses with strict due dates on graded components have higher rates of certificate attainment than courses without due dates. However, fewer students who join a course with strict due dates after its launch earn a certificate. The results are observational and no causal link can yet be asserted without further investigation.

We argue that imposing meaningful due dates (i.e. hard deadlines which fall during the course, rather than all falling at the end of the course) is likely to increase academic performance of students in MOOCs, and provide rich feedback for each student on course fit, current level of mastery etc.

DUE DATES AND STUDENT OUTCOMES

All considered courses used due dates on graded components in different ways (see Figure 1), ranging from having due dates occur during the run of the course (eg. PH207x, 14.73x, 3.091x), to all graded components being due at course close (CB22x, ER22x, PH278x).

We find that courses which use due dates exhibit a higher certificate attainment than courses not using due dates. The pattern holds for the studied courses overall (2% difference), as well as for technical and non-technical courses separately (5% difference each; see Figure 2).

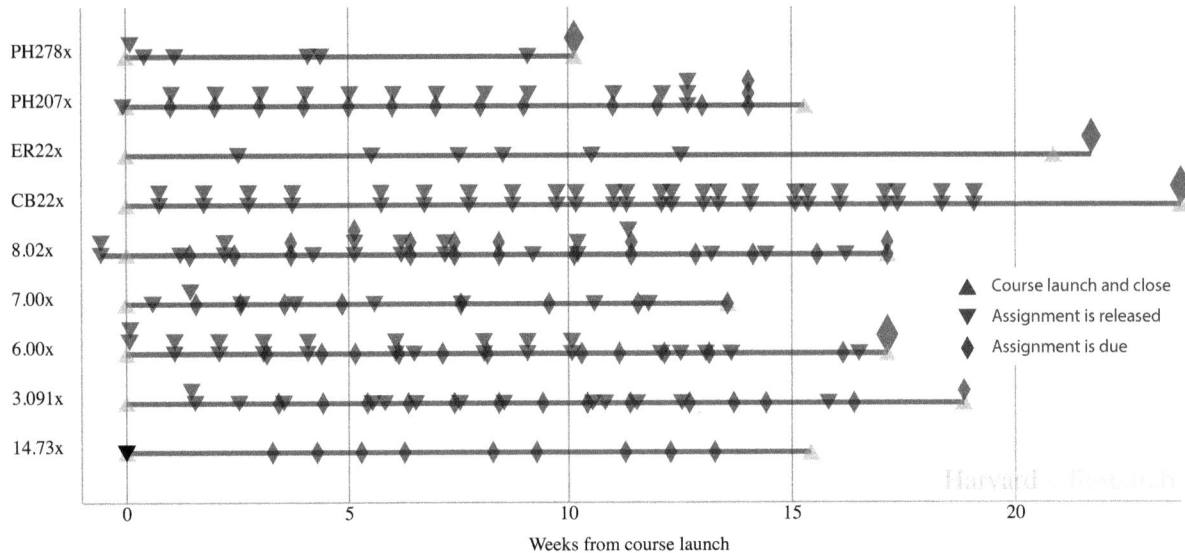

Figure 1. Graded components and their deadlines for the considered HarvardX and MITx courses, aligned at the start date. We exclude CS50x as the exact release times of graded assignments are not available at the time of analysis.

Figure 2. Course categorization into technical and non-technical, as well as by the use of due dates on graded components. In order to be categorized into "Used due dates", a course needs to have had at least one assignment with a hard due date before course close, with late submissions getting a grade of zero. Certificate attainment (CA) is calculated as $\sum_{\text{courses}} \text{CA}_i / \text{ncourses}$.

Higher certificate attainment for courses which use due dates on graded components may come at a price of excluding students who join late from earning one (see Figure 3 for a comparison of how certification probability decays by week a student joins course).

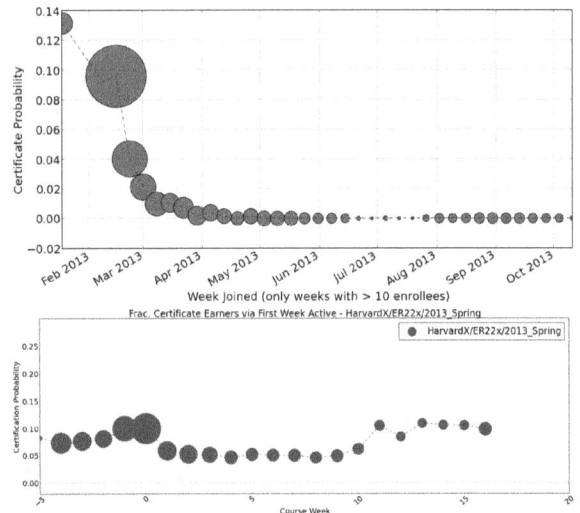

Figure 3. Fraction of students in Electricity and Magnetism (8.02x; above) and Justice (ER22x; below) who earned a certificate by week joined the course. Sizes of circles are proportional to numbers of people who joined on a given week. Certification probability decays with time in 8.02x, but not in ER22x.

REFERENCES

1. Breslow, L., Pritchard, D., DeBoer, J., Stump, G., Ho, A., and Seaton, D. Studying Learning in the Worldwide Classroom: Research into edX's First MOOC. *Research & Practice in Assessment 8* (2013), 13–25.

2. DeBoer, J., Ho, A. D., Stump, G. S., and Breslow, L. Changing "course": Reconceptualizing educational variables for massive open online courses.

3. Kizilcec, R., Piech, C., and Schneider, E. Deconstructing disengagement: analyzing learner subpopulations in massive open online courses, 2013.

4. Klapp, A. MOOCs Open Doors for Diverse Student Body. *Diversity Journal* (2013).

5. Nesterko, S. O., Dotsenko, S., Han, Q., Seaton, D., Reich, J., Chuang, I., and Ho, A. D. Evaluating the geographic data in moocs. *Neural Information Processing Systems* (2013).

Visual Analytics of MOOCs at Maryland

Zhengzheng Xu
Computer Science
Univ. of Maryland
zzxu@cs.umd.edu

Dan Goldwasser
CS / UMIACS
Univ. of Maryland
goldwas1@umiacs.umd.edu

Benjamin B. Bederson
CS / UMIACS
Univ. of Maryland
bederson@cs.umd.edu

Jimmy Lin
iSchool / UMIACS
Univ. of Maryland
jimmylin@umd.edu

ABSTRACT

We use visual analytics to explore participation in five MOOCs at the University of Maryland. In some of these courses, our analysis reveals interesting clustering patterns of student behavior. For other courses, visualizations provide "color" to help us better understand the range of student behavior.

Author Keywords

MOOCs; Massive Open Online Courses; Coursera; Learning analytics; Evidence-based education.

ACM Classification Keywords

K.3.1. Computer Uses in Education: Distance learning

INTRODUCTION

Over 400,000 students have participated in five Coursera Massive Open Online Courses (MOOCs) at the University of Maryland over the past year. Given the widely reported criticism of low success rates of MOOCs in general [3, 5, 8], we wanted to better understand student behavior and its relationship to student success. This short paper visually describes the essential characteristics of student participation in MOOCs at Maryland, along with an analysis of the characteristics of student behavior that correlate with receiving high final grades.

There have to date been a handful of descriptive analyses of MOOC offerings, and some have examined characteristics of students and their activities that correlate with success in the course. Brewslow et al. [2] found very little relationship between student profiles and students' success. In particular, they found no relationship between age or gender and achievement, and only a "marginal" relationship between highest degree earned and achievement. However, they found that collaborating offline on course material did have a beneficial effect [1]. That study, along with one by Seaton et al. [6] analyzing the same EdX course on "Circuits and Electronics", examined student activity and reported on the types of activities that students who completed the course engaged in. Instead, we are interested in looking at how student activity correlates with high course grades.

L@S 2014, Mar 04-05 2014, Atlanta, GA, USA
ACM 978-1-4503-2669-8/14/03.
http://dx.doi.org/10.1145/2556325.2567878

Our interests are more in line with research by Kizilcec et al. [4] that looked at different types of student activity. By analyzing what students do, they identified four prototypical trajectories of engagement, summarized as "auditing" (engaged in the course, but not submitting assessments), "behind", "on track", or "out". This categorization enabled them to look at overall student activity as well as observe changes in behavior.

We explore correlations with course final grades by visually analyzing student participation data to look for trends that might not be obvious based solely on a statistical analysis. Visual analytics is often used to help the investigator decide what questions to *ask* [1]. When interesting or unexpected patterns emerge, the visual analysis can be coupled with more traditional statistical analyses to provide deeper insight into underlying causal mechanisms. For this work, we used Tableau [7], a commercial interactive visualization tool to explore the data, and we report here some of the interesting trends we observed.

DESCRIPTION

We analyzed the standard Coursera data available to each course instructor. Our first set of plots was based on data extracted from web activity logs of students. The second plot comes from the higher-level MySQL database provided by Coursera. In both cases, we wrote straightforward scripts to extract and transform the data into a format suitable for visualizing.

The most useful representation of a course that we found was a plot of "course success" (as measured by the student's final grade) against various types of activity in the course. Here, we show illustrative data from the course titled "Genes and the Human Condition (From Behavior to Biotechnology)", which had 23,564 registered students in its first offering during April/May, 2013. Using an interactive tool such as Tableau enabled us to experiment with many variations of what data to plot and how to visually arrange them. We used "multiple miniatures", created heat maps, etc. The biggest value was clearly in the ability to interactively explore the data. Below, we show a few key images that provide an indication of what is possible.

The goal of the first exploration was to look at grade by activity. The three images below show grades along the vertical axis and the horizontal axis shows: number of quiz clicks (left), number of lecture page views (middle), and number of forum visits (right).

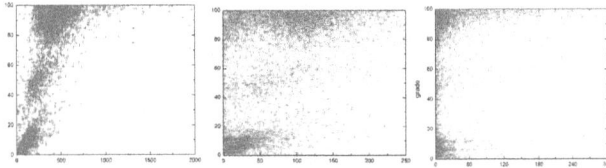

These images show two interesting patterns. The first is that there are three distinct clusters of students – most readily seen in the left plot that shows grade against quiz submissions. We hypothesize that these clusters correspond to the "auditing" (at the bottom), "behind" (in the middle) and "on track" (on top) prototypical trajectories identified by Kizilcec et al. [4]. This is interesting in that student activities can indeed be categorized into discrete "buckets".

The second pattern is that the shape of the clusters varies by student activity. For example, the left plot shows that no one receives a good grade without submitting quizzes (which is perhaps obvious). However, from the right plot, we see that students receive good grades without participating in the forums. The middle plot shows that students receive good grades with widely varying numbers of lecture views. These results show that there are multiple ways to be successful in a course, and it is perhaps not necessary to "do everything" – at least, not for everyone.

Student Profiles
The next thing we examined was how students' self-reported "profiles" interacted with performance. As can be seen in the image below, and consistent with Brewslow et al. [2], students of all types appeared in all parts of the plot:

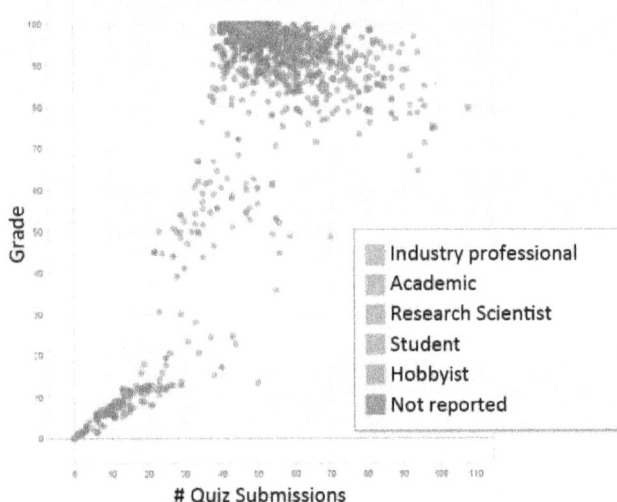

Based on a quantitative analysis of student activities, we did notice some subtle differences in certain types of activity. For example, active forum participants are much more likely to be hobbyists and academics than students, industry professionals, or research scientists. And consistent with the literature, forum participants are over twice as likely to be men than women.

CONCLUSION
In this short paper, we show how modern visualization tools can provide an effective way to explore large amounts of MOOC data quickly. Interesting trends can then be followed up with traditional statistical analyses, but we argue that visualizations are a faster and more efficient way of "getting started".

From our data, we observed three distinct clusters of students whose behavior may be consistent with other interaction styles reported in the literature. However, more work is needed to confirm these initial findings. Next steps include considering how interventions through interface design or explicit "automated encouragements" might increase behaviors associated with positive outcomes.

ACKNOWLEDGMENTS
We appreciate the great efforts of the University of Maryland instructors for creating these free MOOCs and for the staff on campus for supporting their development. We especially thank Tammatha O'Brien and Raymond St. Leger for sharing their course data with us.

REFERENCES
1. Bederson, B. B., & Shneiderman, B. (Eds.). (2003). The craft of information visualization: readings and reflections. Morgan Kaufmann.

2. Breslow, L., Pritchard, D. E., DeBoer, J., Stump, G. S., Ho, A. D., and Seaton, D. T. Studying learning in the worldwide classroom: Research into edX's first MOOC. *Research and Practice in Assessment 8* (Summer 2013).

3. Jordan, K. MOOC Completion Rates: The Data [Website]. (Accessed Jan 2, 2014) http://www.katyjordan.com/MOOCproject.html

4. Kizilcec, R. F., Piech, C., and Schneider, E. Deconstructing disengagement: analyzing learner subpopulations in massive open online courses. In LAK '13, ACM (2013), 170–179. http://dl.acm.org/citation.cfm?doid=2460296.2460330

5. Quillen, I. Why Do Students Enroll in (But Don't Complete) MOOC Courses? [Web log post]. (2013). http://blogs.kqed.org/mindshift/2013/04/why-do-students-enroll-in-but-dont-complete-mooc-courses/

6. Seaton, D. T., Bergner, Y., Chuang, I., Mitros, P., and Pritchard, D. E. Who does what in a massive open online course? Communications of the ACM, to appear (2014).

7. Tableau. http://www.tableausoftware.com/ [Accessed January 2, 2014]

8. Westervelt, E. The Online Education Revolution Drifts Off Course. [Radio program]. National Public Radio (December 31, 2013). http://www.npr.org/2013/12/31/258420151/the-online-education-revolution-drifts-off-course

Social Factors that Contribute to Attrition in MOOCs

Carolyn Penstein Rosé
Language Technologies
Institute and Human-Computer
Interaction Institute
Carnegie Mellon University
5000 Forbes Avenue
Pittsburgh, PA 15213
cprose@cs.cmu.edu

**Ryan Carlson, Diyi Yang &
Miaomiao Wen**
Language Technologies
Institute
Carnegie Mellon University
5000 Forbes Avenue
Pittsburgh, PA 15213
{rcalrson,diyiy,mwen}
@andrew.cmu.edu

**Lauren Resnick,
Pam Goldman &
Jennifer Sherer**
Institute for Learning
University of Pittsburgh
3939 O'Hara Street
Pittsburgh, PA 15213
{resnick,peg8,jzsherer}
@pitt.edu

ABSTRACT
In this paper, we explore student dropout behavior in a Massively Open Online Course (MOOC). We use a survival model to measure the impact of three social factors that make predictions about attrition along the way for students who have participated in the course discussion forum.

Author Keywords
Attrition, Survival Modeling

ACM Classification Keywords
H5.3. **[Information Interfaces and Presentation]**: Group and Organization Interfaces.

INTRODUCTION
Current research on attrition in MOOCs [2] focuses on summative measures rather than focusing on the question of how to create a more socially conducive environment. Understanding better the factors involved in the struggles students encounter along the way can lead to design insights for the next generation of more successful MOOCs. As one preparatory step, we explore how an unsupervised graphical model (a Mixed Membership Stochastic Blockmodel [1]) is able to identify emerging social structure that predicts dropout along the way in one specific MOOC. This model provides one of three social variables we evaluate with respect to predictive power in connection with dropout along the way in one specific Coursera.org MOOC, namely Accountable Talk™: Conversation that Works, launched by the University of Pittsburgh's Institute for Learning in Fall of 2013.

METHOD

Data and Modeling Techniques
The data used for the analysis presented here was extracted by permission from Coursera.org using a screen scraping protocol and focuses only on participation in the discussion forums. While over 60,000 students signed up for the course, only about 25,000 students accessed the course materials at least once. Of those students, only about 5% of the students ever posted to the discussion forums. At the last scraping, 4,709 posts had been contributed. This analysis focuses on the authors of those posts.

Two types of models were used in our analysis. First, in order to obtain a soft partitioning of the social network of the discussion forums, we used a Mixed Membership Stochastic Blockmodel (MMSB) [1]. The advantage of MMSB over other graph partitioning methods is that it does not force assignment of students solely to one subcommunity. The model can track the way students move between subcommunities during their participation. In our representation of the social network, each week of participation was treated as a disjoint network. This enabled the model to view snapshots of coordinated engagement over time so that it would not be biased to assume consistency of social engagement over time but would be able to find it where it occurred. The model was limited to identify three subcommunities because the amount of data was small. In order to evaluate the impact of social factors on continued participation within the MOOC context, we used a survival model, as in prior work [3,4]. Survival analysis is known to provide less biased estimates than simpler techniques (e.g., standard least squares linear regression) that do not take into account the potentially truncated nature of time-to-event data. In a survival model, a prediction about the likelihood of a failure occurring is made at each time point based on the presence of some set of predictors. The estimated weights on the predictors are referred to as hazard ratios. The hazard ratio of a predictor indicates how the relative likelihood of the failure (e.g., dropout) occurring increases or decreases with an increase or decrease in the associated predictor.

L@S 2014, March 4–5, 2014, Atlanta, Georgia, USA.
ACM 978-1-4503-2669-8/14/03.
http://dx.doi.org/10.1145/2556325.2567879

Results

We explored the three types of variables in our model in a stage based way and retained in the final model only those variables that made a significant prediction. Similar to prior work [4], we began with binary cohort variables that indicated which week of the course a student began their active participation. Because the course ran for just over 7 weeks, there were 7 such binary variables. Only the one that indicated that a student began their active participation in the first week of the course made a significant prediction. Table 1 indicates a hazard ratio of .65, which means that students who began their active participation in the first week of the course were 35% less likely to drop out on each time point than the population average.

Table 1: Results of the survival analysis measuring the impact of social factors leading to attrition

Independent Variable	Hazard Ratio	P value
Week 1 Cohort	.65	P < .01
Authority Score	.00	P < .05
Subcommunity 3	9.9	P < .05

The second set of variables we explored were derived from the social network constructed from posts contributed within each week (as opposed to the complete network that existed at the time point). We explored a variety of social network analysis measures, however only Hub and Authority scores yielded a significant prediction, consistent with prior work [4]. Since Hub and Authority scores are highly correlated with one another, we only retained the most predictive one in the model, namely Authority. Table one indicates an almost 0 positive value for the hazard ratio, which indicates a nearly 100% likelihood of dropout on the next time point for students who have an authority score on a week that is a standard deviation larger than average in comparison with students who have an average authority score. Thus, students who serve as authorities in the community appear more committed to the community.

Finally, we explored the indicators that came from the MMSB model. Only one of the three identified subcommunities made a significant prediction about attrition. In particular, students who participated in that subcommunity on a week were nearly ten times more likely to drop out on the next time point that average students. A posthoc analysis verified that the particular community was not unusual with respect to the other variables that predicted dropout as well as not being specific to a period of time, level of intensity of participation, or particular topic related subforum. Thus, the results suggest that the pattern of attrition was related to the engagement of the particular students involved with one another that created the conditions leading to drop out.

CONCLUSION

In this paper we have explored three types of factors, all of which make significant predictions related to dropout along the way in the Accountable Talk MOOC course. The first two factors were already explored in prior work in the context of a different course [4]. This analysis stands as a confirmation of generality of the result. What is new about our analysis is that an indicator that we are able to obtain through unsupervised soft partitioning of the social network of the MOOC makes predictions about dropout, indicating that participation in one particular emergent subcommunity in the MOOC predicts that dropout on the next time point is ten times more likely than for average students not participating in that subcommunity. There could be many interpretations of this finding. Further analysis might reveal some characteristic about norms for participation in that subcommunity that was demotivating for students. In so far as our attempts to identify features that distinguish that subcommunity's behavior from others have not revealed such factors, our current working interpretation is that this result tells us something about the influence students have on one another. As students participate in the MOOC, they begin to form virtual cohorts of students who are moving at a similar pace, are at a similar place in the course, and are engaging with the material in similar ways. If students begin to see others in their cohort leaving, they may find the environment less supportive and engaging and may be more likely to drop out in turn. The results suggest that an important direction for future research in MOOCs is to model the emergent social structure so that we can better understand the influences students have on their emerging cohorts. With greater insight into these social processes, MOOC designers will be in a better position to create affordances that foster a more supportive environment.

ACKNOWLEDGMENTS

This research was supported in part by NSF grant SBE 0836012 and Gates Foundation Grant: The MOOC Research Initiative.

REFERENCES

1. Airoldi, E., Blei, D., Fienberg, S. & Xing, E. P. (2008). Mixed Membership Stochastic Blockmodel, *Journal of Machine Learning Research, 9(Sep):1981--2014, 2008*

2. Jordan, K. (2013). *MOOC Completion Rates: The Data.* Retrieved 23 April 2013.

3. Wang Y, Kraut R, and Levine J. M. (2012) To stay or leave? the relationship of emotional and informational support to commitment in online health support groups. In *Proceedings of Computer Supported Cooperative Work*, p. 833-842.

4. Yang, D., Sinha, T., Adamson, D., & Rosé, C. P. (2013). Turn on, Tune in, Drop out: Anticipating student dropout in Massive Open Online Courses, *NIPS Data-Driven Education Workshop*

Assigning Videos to Textbooks at Appropriate Granularity

Marios Kokkodis
NYU Stern

Anitha Kannan
Microsoft Research

Krishnaram Kenthapadi
Microsoft Research

ABSTRACT

The emergence of tablet devices, cloud computing, and abundant online multimedia content presents new opportunities to transform traditional paper-based textbooks into tablet-based electronic textbooks, and to further augment the educational experience by enriching them with relevant supplementary materials. *Given a candidate set of relevant educational videos for augmenting an electronic textbook, how do we assign the videos at the appropriate granularity (a collection of logical units in the book)?* We propose a rigorous formulation of the video assignment problem and present an algorithm for assigning each video to the optimum subset of logical units. Our experimental evaluation using a diverse collection of educational videos relevant to multiple chapters in a textbook demonstrates the efficacy of the proposed techniques for inferring the granularity at which a relevant video should be assigned.

REPRESENTATION OF TEXTBOOK

Consider a textbook, consisting of K chapters, each subdivided into sections. We define $\mathcal{C}_{book}$ to be the set of concept phrases (*cphrs*) in the book that map to Wikipedia article titles, further refined as in [1]. We define *context-dependent importance* score, $I(c)$ for a *cphr* c as follows. If a *cphr* is important for the context of the text, then the videos retrieved using it as *one of* the query terms will be related to each other. We measure $I(c)$ as the average pair-wise inner product between top m videos retrieved in response to queries that contained c: $I(c) = \frac{\sum_{1 \leq i < j \leq m} <V_i, V_j>}{\binom{m}{2}}$, where V_i is the vector representation (in terms of *cphrs* and associated weights) for i^{th} top video for c (explained in the next section).

VIDEO CANDIDATE SELECTION AND REPRESENTATION

We first obtain the candidate set of videos relevant to a textbook chapter using an adaptation of COMITY algorithm [1]. Given top n concept phrases (*cphrs*) present in a chapter, $\binom{n}{2}$ queries are formed by combining two *cphrs* each, and issued to a commercial video search engine. The most relevant videos for the chapter are obtained by aggregating the video result lists over all combinations of queries.

In order to match a video to a set of sections, we also need a representation of the video. While, in principle, one can use transcripts associated with videos and identify the *cphrs*

L@S'14, March 4–5, 2014, Atlanta, Georgia, USA.
ACM 978-1-4503-2669-8/14/03.
http://dx.doi.org/10.1145/2556325.2567880

in them (similar to identification in textbooks), most videos in our corpus did not have high quality user-uploaded transcripts, and further, we found the transcripts extracted by automatic speech recognizers to be of poor quality. Instead, we use a different approach for video representation based on the queries from the textbook that led to the videos. For each *cphr* c and video v, define the importance $w_{v,c}$ of c to v as the fraction of queries that contain c for which video v was retrieved as a top result: $w_{v,c} = \frac{|\{q \in Q_c | (v \in TopResults(q)\}|}{|Q_c|}$, where Q_c is the set of queries that contain *cphr* c. The intuition behind this definition is that the higher the fraction of queries that led to a specific video, the more related this phrase is with the video.

SECTION SUBSET SELECTION FOR VIDEOS

For a given candidate video v and a large candidate set $\mathcal{S}$ of sections from the textbook chapter, our goal is to select a *minimal subset* of top sections, $\mathcal{T} \subset \mathcal{S}$ that best covers the content in the video. We model this section subset selection problem as identifying a subset of sections $\mathcal{T}^*$ that maximizes the objective function:

$$\mathcal{T}^* = \arg \max_{\mathcal{T} \in 2^{\mathcal{S}}} \; (\text{cover}(v, \mathcal{T}) - \lambda |\mathcal{T}|),$$

where $\text{cover}(v, \mathcal{T})$ is a function that measures how well the set of sections $\mathcal{T}$ captures the content of the video v . Our objective function incorporates a penalty for using more sections than required for explaining the video, by discounting for the number of sections $|\mathcal{T}|$. Thus, the objective function provides a trade-off between the extent to which the content of the video is captured and the number of sections used.

Computing $\text{cover}(v, \mathcal{T})$: Let $C(v) \subseteq \mathcal{C}_{book}$ denote the set of *cphrs* present in our representation of video v and let $C(\mathcal{T}) \subseteq \mathcal{C}_{book}$ denote the set of *cphrs* present in the subset of sections $\mathcal{T}$. We define $\text{cover}(v, \mathcal{T})$ to be the weighted fraction of the *cphrs* in the video that are also covered by the subset of sections:

$$cover(v, \mathcal{T}) = \frac{\sum_{c \in (C(v) \cap C(\mathcal{T}))} w_{vc} I(c)}{\sum_{c \in C(v)} w_{vc} I(c)} .$$

Given the set of sections in a textbook chapter and a candidate video as inputs, our algorithm first checks whether a certain minimum fraction, θ of the video content can be covered by including all sections in the chapter, and if so, returns the optimal subset of sections (by exhaustively searching over all possible subsets). In our experiments, we used $\theta = 0.8$, and estimated λ to be 0.48 through cross validation.

EVALUATION

We evaluate our approach over the first five chapters of a 9th grade science book, spanning different sub-branches of science. We obtained an initial set of 178 videos by running

---

Algorithm 1 Section Subset Selection For Videos

Input: Set of sections $\mathcal{S}$ in a given textbook chapter; A candidate video v; Coverage threshold θ.
Output: The optimal subset of sections $\mathcal{T}^* \subseteq \mathcal{S}$ (or *null* depending on the coverage threshold).

1: **if** $cover(v, \mathcal{S}) < \theta$ **then return** *null*.
2: **return** $\arg\max_{\mathcal{T} \in 2^{\mathcal{S}}} \ (cover(v, \mathcal{T}) - \lambda|\mathcal{T}|)$.

COMITY algorithm (at the *section level*) across sections in all chapters. A human assessor was asked to read all five chapters, and then watch each video and manually identify all the sections that together capture the content of the video. The judge is also asked to remove videos that are irrelevant, or cover material beyond the scope of the book. This judgment process resulted in 112 videos (denoted by $\mathcal{V}$) along with their best set of sections assignments that describe the content of each video. For every video v, denote the set of sections that are assigned by this process by $\mathcal{S}_v^G$.

Baseline algorithm: For video v, we obtained the baseline as the set $\mathcal{S}_v^C$ of sections for which COMITY algorithm retrieved v as one of the top ranking videos. Since our goal is to compare the performance of our approach to this COMITY baseline, for the purposes of evaluation, we only included videos that are retrieved by running COMITY algorithm at the *section level* (that is, not at the chapter level).

We empirically validated that COMITY can be used as a baseline since (a) it also identified multiple sections for the same video (in nearly half the cases), and (b) there is sufficient content that is shared across multiple sections.

Metrics: For each video v, let $\mathcal{S}_v^P$ be the set of sections identified by our proposed algorithm.

Accuracy: This metric measures how accurately an algorithm can identify the entire set of sections that best captures the content in the video: $\text{Accuracy} = \frac{\sum_{v \in \mathcal{V}} I[\mathcal{S}_v^A = \mathcal{S}_v^G]}{|\mathcal{V}|}$, where $A \in \{C, P\}$ and $I[\mathcal{X} = \mathcal{Y}]$ evaluates to 1 if the sets $\mathcal{X}$ and $\mathcal{Y}$ have identical elements and 0 otherwise. $|\mathcal{V}|$ is the number of videos in the ground truth collection.

Relaxed Accuracy: The above accuracy metric is stringent in that it requires all the sections identified by the algorithm to match with that of the ground truth. We define a relaxed version that takes into account how different the inferred set is from the ground truth set: $\text{Relaxed Accuracy} = \frac{\sum_{v \in \mathcal{V}} \left(1 - \frac{\mathcal{S}_v^A \triangle \mathcal{S}_v^G}{|\mathcal{S}_{all}|}\right)}{|\mathcal{V}|}$, where $A \in \{C, P\}$, $|\mathcal{S}_{all}|$ denotes the number of sections in the chapter, and $\mathcal{S}_v^A \triangle \mathcal{S}_v^G$ denotes the symmetric set difference (edit distance) between the set of sections identified by an algorithm and the set of ground truth sections.

Results:

Methods	Accuracy	Relaxed accuracy
COMITY	0.513	0.877
Proposed approach	0.649	0.908

We can see that under the stringent metric of **Accuracy**, our approach performs significantly better than the baseline (COMITY). With the **Relaxed Accuracy** metric, our approach performs slightly better than the baseline.

DISCUSSION

The recent upsurge in new models of learning such as blended learning, massive open online courses, and flipped classrooms [2, 3, 4, 6, 7, 8] emphasizes the importance of audio-visual learning. This trend begs the question: Can we eliminate textbooks, altogether? Our answer is a qualified no. We believe that textbooks will continue to play a central role in educational instruction, with videos enabling the additional modality to learn from (*e.g.*, [9]). In fact, education literature has extensively highlighted the importance of textbooks in delivering content knowledge to the students, improving student learning, and in helping teachers prepare the lesson plans [5, 10]. However, with the emergence of abundant educational content available online, cloud-connected electronic devices and electronic textbooks, we are now well positioned to integrate multimedia content to personalize textbooks based on the learning style of the user. In this work, we took a step towards addressing associated challenges: how do we effectively match huge educational content available online to the textbook of interest *at appropriate granularity*? An important subsequent work is to design rigorous evaluation methodology and perform large scale user study among students to quantify the effectiveness of using such an enriched textbook.

While our current approach focused on the relevancy and the appropriate granularity of the video, several dimensions pertaining to the video, the viewer and the presenter need to be taken into account for effective augmentation of textbooks with videos. Each of these dimensions is a promising direction for future work.

REFERENCES

1. Agrawal, R., Gollapudi, S., Kannan, A., and Kenthapadi, K. Data mining for improving textbooks. *ACM SIGKDD Explorations Newsletter 13*, 2 (2011).

2. Bergmann, J., and Sams, A. *Flip your classroom: Reach every student in every class every day*. International Society for Technology in Education, 2012.

3. Dellarocas, C., and Alstyne, M. V. Money models for MOOCs. *Communications of the ACM 56*, 8 (2013).

4. Garrison, D. R., and Kanuka, H. Blended learning: Uncovering its transformative potential in higher education. *The internet and higher education 7*, 2 (2004).

5. Gillies, J., and Quijada, J. Opportunity to learn: A high impact strategy for improving educational outcomes in developing countries. *USAID Educational Quality Improvement Program (EQUIP2)* (2008).

6. Martin, F. G. Will massive open online courses change how we teach? *Communications of the ACM 55*, 8 (2012).

7. Staker, H., and Horn, M. B. Classifying K–12 blended learning. *Innosight Institute* (2012).

8. Strayer, J. *The effects of the classroom flip on the learning environment: A comparison of learning activity in a traditional classroom and a flip classroom that used an intelligent tutoring system*. PhD thesis, Ohio State University, 2007.

9. Tisdell, C. C. *Engineering mathematics: YouTube workbook*. Bookboon, 2013.

10. Verspoor, A., and Wu, K. B. Textbooks and educational development. Tech. rep., World Bank, 1990.

A Behavioral Biometrics based Authentication Method for MOOC's that is Robust against Imitation Attempts

Markus Krause

Leibniz University

Hannover, Germany

markus@hci.uni-hannover.de

ABSTRACT

Ensuring authorship in online taken exams is a major challenge for e-learning in general and MOOC's in particular. In this paper, we introduce and evaluate a method to verify student identities using stylometry. We present a carefully composed feature set and use it with a K-Nearest Neighbor algorithm. We demonstrate that our method can effectively authenticate authors and is robust against imitation attacks.

Author Keywords

Author Authentication; Human Factors; Massive Open Online Courses; e-Learning

ACM Classification Keywords

H.5.m. Information interfaces and presentation; K.3.1 Computer Uses in Education; K.3.2 Computer and Information Science Education

INTRODUCTION

Exams in MOOC's become more open even to the point of free text submissions graded by peer reviews [11]. Verifying a student's identity is a crucial aspect of such free text online exams. The behavioral biometrics of stylometry is a possible solution to this challenge. Stylometry attributes authorship using features of literary style such as sentence length, vocabulary richness, frequencies of words, word lengths, and so on. The benefit of stylometry is that the authentication information is an inherent part of the text and the method does not require any further information. With carefully chosen features, it is a complex task to imitate a writing style with a computational system. Altering features such as the grammatical structure of a sentence without changing the meaning of the text seem to be challenging.

In this paper, we propose a new stylometric method that uses a well-balanced feature set and an instance based classifier to perform author authentication. We illustrate the feasibility of this method to be suitable for student authenti-

cation in MOOC's. Instance based classifier already showed excellent results with keystroke dynamics and in attempts to scale stylometry to hundredths of thousands of authors [5]. We will demonstrate that the combination of well-designed feature sets and the K-Nearest Neighbor classifier is superior to other current approaches.

CORPUS

A particular challenge for our approach is to find a suitable corpus that allows comparing our approach and contains samples of imitation attempts. While there are many corpora with known author information, we need a corpus with authors try to imitate another. A suitable data set is the Extended Brennan-Greenstadt (EBG) Corpus [3]. The corpus was created using Amazon's Mechanical Turk (AMT) platform. The contributors, which participated in the Brennan-Greenstadt experiment, have various backgrounds but at least some college education. Each contributor submitted a sample writing of at least 6500 words. Additionally as we use the same corpus we can compare our results with those reported by Brennan et al. [3]. Each sample in the corpus is from a formal source, such as essays for school, reports for work, and other professional and academic correspondence. The samples therefore already have similarity or indeed are submissions for an exam. The corpus also contains a text from each author in which she tries to imitate another author's style. For this task, the contributors got a 2500-word sample from "The Road" by Cormac McCarthy to model their passage after. The contributor's task was to narrate their day from rise on using third-person perspective. This is also similar to the events in the sample text.

FEATURE EXTRACTION

We extracted different feature sets from the corpus. Other approaches use features a machine could imitate, for instance digits. An algorithm can easily detect fractional numbers and add additional numbers to better resemble another author e.g. altering 0.98 to 0.982. This alteration would go unnoticed, as it does not change the meaning of the text. Whitespaces such as line breaks, tabs, and space are also vulnerable to machine based imitation. The individual features are described below.

Character Frequency

The relative frequency of individual characters. This feature set contains the relative frequency of a-z and A-Z.

Word Length Frequency

The relative frequency of word length. In some rare cases the part of speech tagger was not able to filter certain artifacts e.g. long numbers, some e-mail addresses (without the @ sign). This results in particular long words. To filter such elements we only use words of up to 20 characters.

Sentence Length Frequency

The relative frequency of sentence length. Similar to the word length feature we filter out overly long sentences longer than 35 words. The feature set is for obvious reasons very sensitive to small data sets. We use this feature set as we can assume in the explained scenario to have larger data sets. Training and test sets should contain at least 80 sentences when used with the classifiers proposed in this work.

Part of Speech Tag Frequency

For this feature set we use the Penn Treebank part of speech tag set. We use the Natural Language Toolkit (NLTK [2]) python library to extract these tags from a corpus. We calculate the relative frequency of each tag.

Word Specificity Frequency

The specificity of words used by an author is a discriminating feature. To our knowledge this has not been used for stylometry yet. To estimate the specificity of a word we use *wordnet*. The algorithm calculates the distance between each word and the root node of *wordnet*. The algorithm calculates the relative frequency of each depth. The depth is limited to 20.

MODEL LEARNING

For our experiment we use the instance based machine learning algorithm *K-Nearest Neighbor (KNN)* [1]. The KNN algorithm selects the k closest samples of the training set for each given test sample. The algorithm then determines the class of the test sample by counting the found train samples of each class. The algorithm is most often used with a weighting factor for each test sample. Commonly the inverse distance $\left(\frac{1}{d}\right)$ between neighbor and test sample. We use the *WEKA* [4] implementation of the KNN algorithm for our experiment. To prepare the data from the EBG corpus we split it into a train and a test set of equal size. We extract the described features and generate a vector for each sentence. Afterwards we group all vectors by their author. Through bootstrapping we aggregate samples for each author from these groups in both sets.

ROBUSTNESS AGAINST IMITATION

We want to know how robust our method is against attempts to imitate another author. As explained above each author was asked to imitate the author Cormac McCarthy. Authors had a passage of 2500 words after which they modelled their own text. We train one model for McCarthy using this text and the training data from the 45 authors of the EBG corpus. It is very likely that the author trying to imitate another is not in the database. Therefore, we exclude this author from the train set.

To test the trained model we use another text sample of ~2500 words from "The Road" written by McCarthy and the imitation samples from the author previously excluded. The imitations had 50 sentences (663 words) on average. We repeat the process for each author. To make our experiment comparable to the experiment done by Brennan et al. [3] we repeat this experiment 1000 times with different sets of 40 authors out of the initial 45. We also did the same experiment without removing the imitating author from the train set. Figure 1. shows the success rates of the imitation attacks for both experiments compared to the success rates reported by Brennan et al. [3].

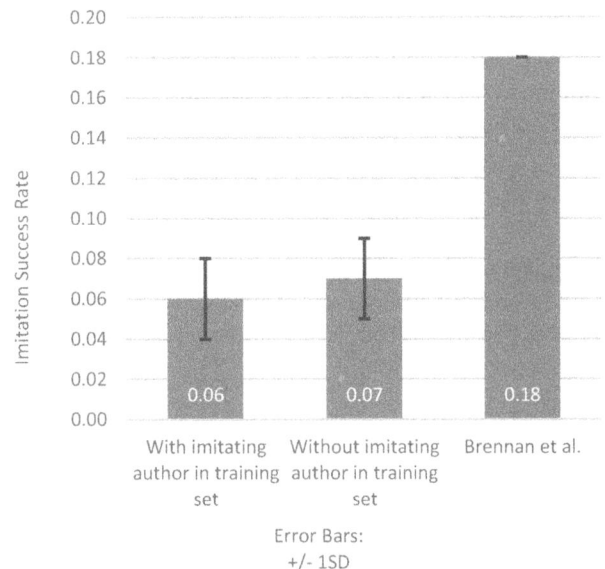

Fig 1. Success rates for the imitation experiment. Brennan et al. [3] did not report an SD for the experiment.

REFERENCES

1. Aha, D., Kibler, D., and Albert, M. Instance-based learning algorithms. *Machine learning 6*, (1991), 37–66.

2. Bird, S., Klein, E., and Loper, E. *Natural language processing with Python*. O'Reilly Media Inc., 2009.

3. Brennan, M., Afroz, S., and Greenstadt, R. Adversarial stylometry. *ACM Transactions on Information and System Security 15*, 3 (2012), 12:1–22.

4. Frank, E., Hall, M., Holmes, G., et al. Weka-A Machine Learning Workbench for Data Mining. In O. Maimon and L. Rokach, eds., *Data Mining and Knowledge Discovery Handbook*. Springer US, Boston, MA, 2010, 1269–1277.

5. Narayanan, A. and Paskov, H. On the feasibility of internet-scale author identification. *IEEE Symposium on Security and Privacy*, IEEE Press (2012).

What does enrollment in a MOOC mean?

Eni Mustafaraj

Wellesley College

Wellesley, MA, USA

eni.mustafaraj@wellesley.edu

ABSTRACT

In 2012, when MOOCs became largely known, media reports were fascinated with the big number of enrollments. The number 150,000 students was mentioned for both Stanford's *Artificial Intelligence* course and MIT's *Circuits and Electronics*, to be later followed by the underwhelming completion rates, that often are in the single digit percentages[1]. But what kind of enrollment do these large numbers really show? We try to answer this question by breaking this number into its components, while comparing two successive iterations of the same MOOC offered on the edX platform.

Author Keywords

MOOCs; learning analytics; engagement; visualization

ACM Classification Keywords

H.5.3 Evaluation/methodology

INTRODUCTION

For this study, the author was given access to anonymized data from two iterations of MITx 6.00x – *Introduction to Computer Science and Programming*. Each course ran over a 4-month period: Fall 2012 (Oct 2012 - Jan 2013); Spring 2013 (Feb - May 2013). The stated prerequisite was "high school algebra and a reasonable aptitude for mathematics", and the estimated effort per week was around 10-12 hours. Both courses were hosted on the edX platform. The Fall 2012 offering was one of the first official edX courses, since the first MITx course (6.002x *Circuits and Electronics*[2]), was offered during a period in which edX wasn't established. As such, 6.00X (Fall 2012) attracted a considerable amount of curiosity and attention, reflected in the large number of sign-ups for the course, which we have estimated to more than 184,000 students. But, as we will demonstrate in this paper, this number doesn't reflect the behavior of the participants in the course, and therefore shouldn't be taken into consideration for further purposes of evaluating course success.

[1] http://www.katyjordan.com/MOOCproject.html

[2] https://6002x.mitx.mit.edu/

DATA DESCRIPTION

Data for each course in the edX platform are stored in different databases: course content, discussion forums, student personal data, student course progress, event tracking, etc. The analysis in this paper is based only upon data from the event tracking database. A database entry uses the JSON format[3], as shown in the (truncated) example below:

```
{ "username": "123456",
"event_source": "server",
"event_type": "/courses/MITx/6.00x/2012_Fall/info",
"time": {"$date": 1348897556438},
"event": {"POST": {}, "GET": {}},
... }
```

Although this data allows us to recreate the complete history of a user interaction with the course content, in this paper we will only focus on **when** and **how often** students showed up for the course. The nature of their activity on the website is the topic of another paper.

DATA ANALYSIS

By parsing the dates and event types of every user in the database, we are able to find out when, how often, and what they did in every website visit. The largest group of users (84,853 users or 46%) had a single visit to the website in Fall 2012, which corresponded to landing on the info page after clicking the "Sign-up" button. As observed elsewhere [?], one can better compare such an action to a Facebook Like event, than to the real intention to enroll in the course. Following a classification proposed in [?], we will label these users, whose only activity was signing up, as "no-shows". No-shows continue their sign-up routine during the entire course duration, as well as after the course is closed[4].

Another large group is that of "one-day visitors". This group consisted of 19,035 (Fall 2012) and 21,615 (Spring 2013) such users, who spent a median time of eight consecutive minutes on the site. A visualization of the number of unique daily visits by all users can be found online (see footnote 4). The majority—78% of all users (excluding "no-shows")—visited between 1 to 10 days during the duration of 112 days.

DISCUSSION

These results allow for a series of observations:

[3] http://en.wikipedia.org/wiki/JSON

[4] Due to limited space, most of visualizations for the data analysis in this paper can be found online at: http://cs.wellesley.edu/~eni/mitx/.

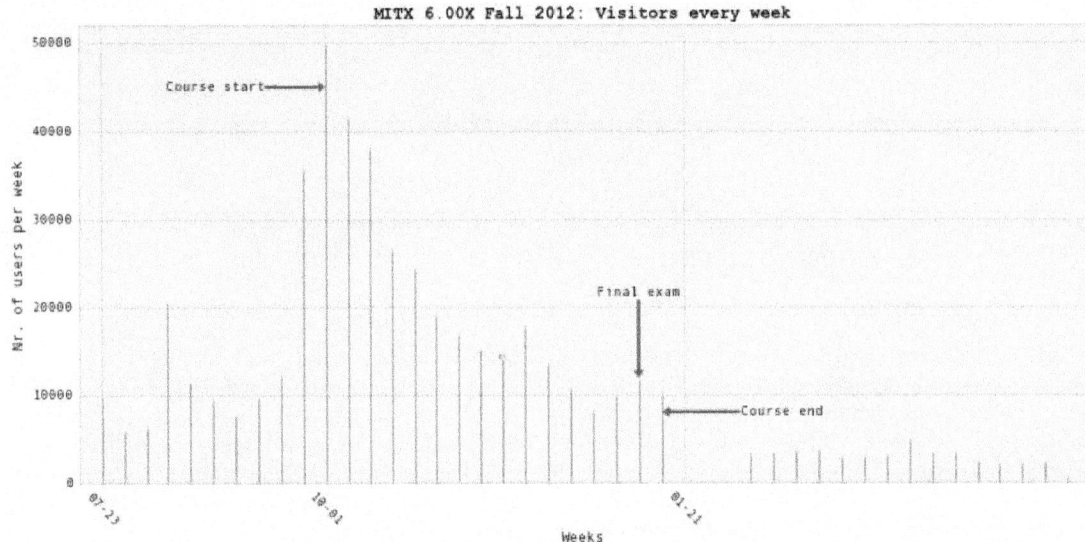

Figure 1. Weekly visits by users during the entire run of the Fall 2012 course. The website was opened for sign-ups 10 weeks in advance of the start date. The first week of course (Oct 1st, 2012) had the largest number of visitors: 49,841. In the week of the final exam, the website was visited by 11,767 users. The website was blocked for a few weeks, and then reopened again.

Sign-ups might indicate interest in the topic, but not necessarily intention to attend the course. In fact, while the Fall 2012 offering attracted 184K users, only about 50K showed up in the first week of the course (see Figure **??**). Meanwhile, the Spring 2013 offering (only three weeks after the completion of Fall 2012), attracted 90K users[5]. This suggests that successive offerings of the same course might be "less" massive.

Sequential Enrollments. The two sets of students enrolled in the two course offerings are not mutually exclusive. In fact, 33,351 users signed-up for both. Informal discussions among participants in the website Reddit[6] indicate that some users were signing up again to provide help in the discussion forum, while others to repeat and reinforce the material. We will look at the behavior of such group in our future research.

Opening enrollments when there is no content might be damaging. The large number of sign-ups that became 'no-shows', especially in the Fall 2012 offering happened in the ten weeks preceding the course start, when there was no course content on the website.

Completion rate or engagement rate? Media and critics have been measuring completion rates of MOOCs as the percentage of the signed-up students who received a completion certificate. For a course such as 6.00X Fall 2012, with 184,234 signups, where 46% of users never showed-up, the number of students who attempted the final exam (7,559) is really small, only 4%. However, if we base calculations on who showed up for the course on at least 1/4 of its duration (on four different weeks during 16 weeks; there are 35,173 such users, refer to online plots), the completion rate increases to 21%. Finally, real engagement might be found in the group of 7,161

students, who showed up for more than 40 days during the entire course duration, and all attempted the final exam.

The discussion in this paper is based on **when** and **how often** students visited the course website. Other researchers have advanced a terminology for categorizing users based on engagement with the course material, such as: browsers [**?**], samplers [**?**], or observers [**?**]. We will look into this topic in future research.

ACKNOWLEDGMENTS

The author is very grateful to the MIT Office of Digital Learning for making the data available and to Isaac Chuang and Daniel Seaton for their generous support and advice.

REFERENCES

1. Bruff, D. Lessons Learned from Vanderbilts First MOOCs, 2013.
   `http://cft.vanderbilt.edu/2013/08/lessons-learned-from-vanderbilts-first-moocs/`.

2. Hill, P. Emerging Student Patterns in MOOCs: A (Revised) Graphical View, 2013.
   `http://mfeldstein.com/emerging-student-patterns-in-moocs-a-revised-graphical-view`.

3. Kizilcec, R. F., Piech, C., and Schneider, E. Deconstructing disengagement: analyzing learner subpopulations in massive open online courses. In *Proc. of LAK '13*, ACM (2013), 170–179.

4. Seaton, D., Bergner, Y., Chuang, I., Mitros, P., and Pritchard, D. Who does what in a massive open online course? *Communications of ACM* (Forthcoming).

---

[5]This number is not exact, since there are several missing days in the database.
[6]`http://www.reddit.com/r/600x/`

Promoting Active Learning & Leveraging Dashboards for Curriculum Assessment in an OpenEdX Introductory CS Course for Middle School

Shuchi Grover
Graduate School of Education
Stanford University
shuchig@stanford.edu

Roy Pea
Graduate School of Education/
H-STAR Institute
Stanford University
roypea@stanford.edu

Stephen Cooper
Computer Science Department
Stanford University
coopers@stanford.edu

ABSTRACT

Lack of teachers to teach computer science (CS) and pedagogically sound introductory CS curricula remain a significant challenge facing secondary schools attempting to teach CS. This paper describes our efforts to design and pilot an online 6-week middle/high school course using Stanford's OpenEdX platform. The pedagogy, curriculum and assessment are guided by learning theory. The course leverages OpenEdX features for contextual discussions and multiple-choice assessments that promote student learning and provide feedback. The paper reports on experiences in using instructor dashboards to identify targets of student difficulty and to aid curriculum redesign.

Author Keywords

K-12 CS Education; Blended Learning; Instructional Design; Learning Theory; Instructor Dashboards; Assessment; Analytics; OpenEdX; MOOC.

ACM Classification Keywords

H.5.m. Information interfaces and presentation (e.g., HCI): Miscellaneous.

INTRODUCTION

As educators and policymakers attempt to take computer science education to scale in K-12, a severe shortage of trained teachers and the lack of curricula with sound pedagogical underpinnings and assessment measures remain significant challenges [3]. Any large-scale effort today that must reach thousands of classrooms and teachers must look to state-of-the-art online teaching mechanisms. MOOCs currently represent a possible massive shift in the higher education landscape. Given the shortage of CS teachers and curricula, well-designed online courses deployed on MOOC platforms could serve a crucial need in

K-12 as well. Such courses could be used for blended learning in addition to purely online use by students in and out of classrooms, and as a means to prepare teachers as well. Online venues like Khan Academy, CodeAcademy and Code.org currently cater largely to the development of skills in programming and their success as structured CS curricula for K-12 classrooms has not been empirically tested. These efforts also lack robust measures for assessing student learning which limits their use in K-12 learning settings where issues of assessment are paramount.

OUR RESEARCH ON A CS MOOC FOR K-12

This paper describes our work in progress around a six-week **online** introductory CS mini-course for middle school, titled ***"Foundations for Advancing Computational Thinking" (FACT),*** and created and deployed on the Stanford OpenEdX platform. Based on Exploring CS (www.exploringcs.org/), it is designed to build awareness of computing as a discipline while engaging students in foundational computational concepts such as algorithmic flow of control- sequence, looping, and conditional logic using Scratch. In Fall 2013, we piloted this MOOC as a SPOC [5] to study its effectiveness in a local public middle school "Computers" elective class that met four times a week for 55-minute periods.

Promoting Active Learning in a Video-Based Course

This section presents some of the pedagogical approaches adopted in the curriculum:

- Builds on the rich body of prior research involving children and novice programmers to guide the pedagogy and assessments for the content being taught. These include: using of worked examples for conceptual learning [6], using pseudo-code, teaching reading/code-tracing [2], and using frequent multiple-choice "quizzes" to reinforce concepts [1] including innovative ones like "Parson's puzzles" [4].

- Promotes active, constructivist learning in Scratch through several hands-on activities and assignments.

- As design research [7], this study actively solicits feedback from students on various aspects of the course through short online surveys inserted inconspicuously throughout the course.

L@S 2014, Mar 04-05 2014, Atlanta, GA, USA
ACM 978-1-4503-2669-8/14/03.
http://dx.doi.org/10.1145/2556325.2567883

Day 5	Comps-Dumb+powerful (3m24s)	Think & Write- What can computers not do (5 mins)	types of instructions (1m53s)	Patterns in human instructions (1m55s)	Algorithms (3 m 16s)	Share a Recipe			
Day 6	Characteristics of Algorithms (3m 43s)	Quiz 3 questions (3 mins)	Sequence; Repetition; Selection (7 mins)	Programs & programming Languages (4m 09s)	Quiz (Algorithms & programs) 5 ques; 5 min	First Program Example (4m 38s)	Scratch Assignment: Science Life Cycle		
Day 7	Vid #20 Intro to loops - 4m	Quiz 7 questions (5 mins)	Make a polygon in Scratch (5 mins)	Intro Spirograph activity (5 mins)	Nested Loops vid - 2m51s	Quiz - 5 mins	Rings Demo video - 4m02s	Scratch Assignment:Make a Spirograph	Optional Quiz (2 questions)
Day 8	Initialization - 1min	Quiz - 4 ques (5 min)	Scratch Assignment - 4 part problem	Optional Scratch Assignment - olympic rings	Kids helping other kids catch-up				

Figure 1: Learning sequences planned for a week's worth of classroom time (over four 55 minute periods) using OpenEdX FACT

The course comprises roughly 60 short lecture and demonstration videos varying between 1.5 to ~6 minutes in length interspersed with quizzes with automated grading and explanations (which the students found to be very useful based on post-course feedback). The video length was based on student feedback following a short online unit that ran as a pilot in Spring 2013. Additionally, the modular nature of the OpenEdX platform design that allows various types of "elements" to be added to a page aided the use of contextual discussion prompts below instructional videos, and HTML code to "iframe" http://scratch.mit.edu below the video so students could try out the ideas taught in the video. Qualtrics surveys were similarly "iframe"-d in to obtain student feedback as well as responses to open-ended "thought questions" which students completed at the end of a video lecture. Figure 1 above shows a sample learning "sequence" covered by students in a 55-minute classroom period. The different colors indicate the type of learning activity. Videos are in the lightest color- lemon, videos with activities below them in light peach, thought questions in dark peach, Scratch assignments in orange, quizzes in dark orange, and lastly, extension assignments are shown in red.

Leveraging Dashboards for Analyzing Student Learning and Promoting Curriculum Assessment

While a primary goal of automated assessments is to assess student learning, data and metrics generated by MOOC platforms are also enormously useful as aids to curriculum evaluation as well. We actively used instructor dashboards on quiz data provided by OpenEdX to ascertain targets of difficulty and prompt course revision, where necessary. For example, on a quiz that tested variable manipulation in loops, OpenEdX metrics suggested huge gaps in understanding on even simple questions. Figure 2 shows a screenshot of the dashboard. This prompted additional explanations and Scratch assignments to be uploaded to aid further understanding and reinforce the concept.

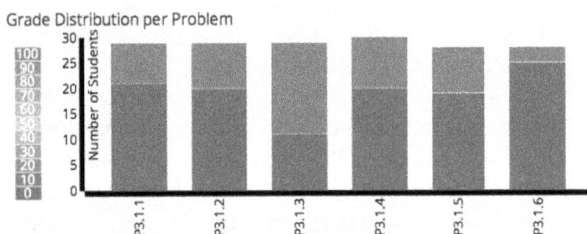

Figure 2. Screenshot of OpenEdX instructor dashboard showing useful feedback on conceptual gaps in student understanding

CONCLUSION & FUTURE WORK

Our instruments measuring computational learning showed gains for all students using the FACT SPOC. More importantly, students on OpenEdX FACT performed as well or moderately better on all questions of the post-tests than students in an earlier face-to-face version of the course Post-course student feedback has been encouraging as well.

Following successful completion of the 6-week course, we now plan to make the material available as a MOOC for large-scale use and for teachers to use in various classroom settings. We are developing accompanying online teacher guides as well. FACT exemplifies the application of existing learning theory and design-based research methods to MOOC course design. More importantly, this course represents crucial first steps to leverage MOOC platforms in K-12 school settings to address a huge need in providing effective CS education at significant scale.

ACKNOWLEDGMENTS

We gratefully acknowledge grant support from the National Science Foundation (NSF #1343227).

REFERENCES

1. Glass, A. L., & Sinha, N. Multiple-choice questioning is an efficient instructional methodology that may be widely implemented in academic courses to improve exam performance. *Current Directions in Psychological Science, 22*, 6 (2013), 471-477.

2. Lopez, M., Whalley, J., Robbins, P. & Lister, R. Relationships between reading, tracing and writing skills in introductory programming. *In Proc. ICER 2008*, ACM Press (2008).

3. NSF, Increasing accessibility to computer science education across the US. http://www.nsf.gov/news/news_summ.jsp?cntn_id=129882

4. Parsons, D. and Haden, P. Parson's programming puzzles: a fun and effective learning tool for first programming courses. *In Proceedings of the 8th Australasian Conference on Computing Education-Volume 52* (2006), 157-163.

5. Rivard, R. Three's Company. *Inside Higher Ed* (2013). http://www.insidehighered.com/news/2013/04/03/stanford-teams-edx

6. Sweller, J., & Cooper, G. A. The use of worked examples as a substitute for problem solving in learning algebra. *Cognition and Instruction, 2*, 1 (1985), 59-89.

7. The Design-Based Research Collective. Design-based research: An emerging paradigm for educational inquiry. *Educational Researcher* (2003), 5-8.

Evaluating Educational Interventions at Scale

Rakesh Agrawal
Microsoft Research

M. Hanif Jhaveri
Stanford University

Krishnaram Kenthapadi
Microsoft Research

INTRODUCTION

Education and learning are currently undergoing transformative changes due to the emergence of tablet devices, cloud computing, and abundant online content. These trends present opportunities to transform traditional paper-based textbooks into tablet-based electronic textbooks, and to further enrich the educational experience by augmenting them with relevant supplementary materials [1]. A natural question is whether this educational intervention, namely, enriching textbooks with relevant web articles, images and videos, is effective. It turns out that designing an experiment at scale for this purpose is nontrivial. We report on progress in designing and carrying out such an experiment.

CLASSICAL APPROACH

Randomized control trial is often deemed the gold standard for impact evaluation [2]. Its key feature is that the study subjects are randomly allocated to receive one or other of the alternative treatments under study. Those in the treatment group are compared to those who were randomly assigned to the control group – those who did not receive the intervention. Because members of the groups (treatment and control) do not differ systematically at the outset of the experiment, any difference that subsequently arises between them can be attributed to the treatment rather than to other factors. The post-intervention results analysis can lead to the refinement of the intervention and the randomized trial is repeated with the revised intervention (Figure 1).

However, the following issues arise immediately in applying randomized control trials to the task of determining whether a supplementary material helps improve the understanding of a textbook passage, particularly when the educational material will be used across geographies:

- Intervention in classrooms has limited sequencing since several months are needed to get any feedback in typical school settings, and moreover, is very expensive.

- It is very difficult to ensure the requisite diversity, or even to get more than one classroom at a time.

- Interventions that assume natural progressions in the building-block technologies (*e.g.*, reliable broadband internet access) and are designed for deployment in future (say, 2 to 3 years from now) are difficult to study.

L@S'14, March 4–5, 2014, Atlanta, Georgia, USA.
ACM 978-1-4503-2669-8/14/03.
http://dx.doi.org/10.1145/2556325.2567884

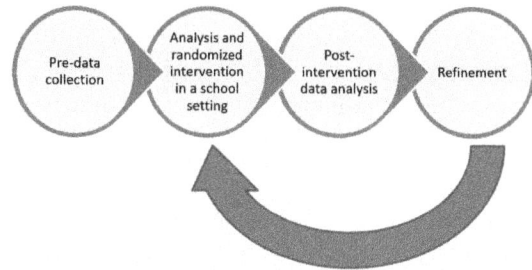

Figure 1. Classical Evaluation Methodology

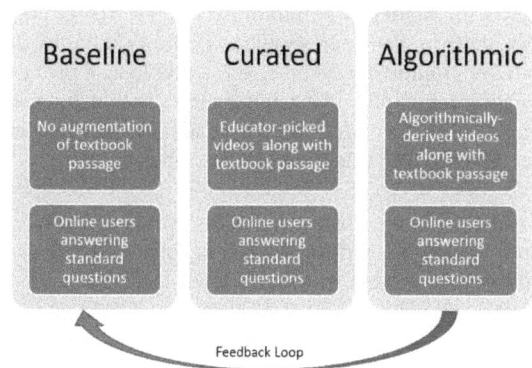

Figure 2. Evaluation Design for Textbook Augmentation

- Learning involves interactions between students, teachers, and other stakeholders and thus, is not an isolated experience that can be measured, and hence separating the effect of an augmentation from a plethora of other variables is hard to achieve.

SCALABLE DESIGN

We now present our online evaluation platform under development that leverages users world-wide to carry out experiments at scale to study the effectiveness of enriching electronic textbooks with educational videos (Figure 2). The basic ingredients of our design are:

1. Baseline: Online users would be presented with the textbook passage without any augmentation.

2. Curated: Online users would be presented educator curated videos along with the textbook passage.

3. Algorithmic: Online users would be presented videos obtained algorithmically (adapting techniques proposed in [1]) along with the textbook passage.

In all three cases, the users are required to answer questions that test knowledge of the textbook passage. In the baseline experiment, we also ask the users whether they would find it useful to have educational videos in addition to the textbook passage. Through these experiments, our goal is to not only understand whether educator curated videos can help improve the performance of the user, but also to iteratively refine the algorithmic techniques to get closer to the performance obtained with the curated videos. Our design is inspired by approaches focused on understanding networks as opposed to isolated variables (*e.g.*, [3]).

IMPLEMENTATION

We present different implementation decisions, taking into account three broad dimensions: academic considerations (factoring in the rich education literature as well as recent work on online platforms), design considerations (our design goals), and iterations (based on our trials and anecdotal evidence).

1. Platform selection: We chose to use Amazon Mechanical Turk platform since this platform has been sufficiently vetted by the academic community (*e.g.*, [4, 5]). In particular, this platform has been shown to be fairly reliable, flexible, and geographically diverse, and suitable as a proxy to real world interactions. Alternate approaches such as solicitation of users through online lists/ads are hard to scale, and hence removing selection bias becomes harder.

2. Textbook passage selection: We selected a corpus of textbooks spanning different subjects (physics, chemistry, biology, economics), difficulty level (9th grade to college level), and geographies (CK-12 books (USA) and NCERT textbooks (India)). We chose a set of nine passages from seven different textbooks, and asked teachers to generate ten questions, and a set of curated videos for each passage. Since many studies have shown that task lengths of 60 minutes or less are desirable in online platforms, we carefully arrived at the appropriate passage lengths, number of videos shown, and number of questions to be answered.

3. Educator selection: We chose teachers representing five large US states, balancing two key goals. We desired maximum variation of experiences across students in terms of their ethnic and socio-economic background and resource utilization, while at the same time, we ensured that the teachers had comfort and experience with using educational videos in existing lessons.

4. Curation process: Five educators were asked to select the questions (that could be answered by reading just the textbook), and a different set of five educators were asked to curate relevant videos for augmentation, so that there is no bias between the two processes.

5. Design of HIT (human intelligence task): We designed the HIT so that the entire functionality is built into the task, and used very basic web tools so that judges across different economic backgrounds are likely to have very similar experience with our task. We further benchmarked the performance with students at a US university to ensure that the task was not too difficult. We ensured that no

one could participate more than once, and included honeypots to prune bad participants. We also carefully monitored to weed out participants who did not follow instructions, or spent very little time on the task. Based on several trials, we arrived at the rate of USD $2.50 per hour that attracted the most desirable participants. They often provided the optional feedback, for example, expressing their hope that their participation would indeed help future students. We could not attract quality participants below this rate. With higher rates, we were attracting participants who just wanted to earn quick money; in fact, they did not provide any feedback and rushed to complete the HIT, missing honeypot questions in the process.

6. Demographics: We conducted trials across two geographies (USA and India), with 100 users per trial. We collected demographic data to ensure that the distribution of the judges matches the overall target distribution.

7. Selecting participants: Given the relatively large cognitive complexity of our task (requires understanding of the context of the textbook material as well as the video), we wanted to only include judges who had the prerequisite analytical and reading comprehension abilities. We included a set of five questions pertaining to analytical and reading comprehension abilities, and excluded judges who answered fewer than two of the five questions correctly.

PROGRESS REPORT

Our initial results suggest that the videos would indeed be helpful for enhancing the experience of learning from the textbooks. Of all the participants, 65% of them said that it will be helpful to have videos in addition to the textbook passage. We observed that the corresponding percent was higher for Indian participants (73%), compared to US participants (57%). A plausible explanation is that English is not the native language for most Indian participants while the textbooks are in English, and hence these participants are likely to benefit more from having explanatory videos on the subject material. We were initially skeptical whether a task with relatively large cognitive complexity such as ours could even be performed over the Mechanical Turk platform. We were pleasantly surprised to not only find many takers, but also to observe that 60% of the prequalification questions were answered correctly on average. We are currently in the process of performing extensive trials, towards measuring the performance of the algorithmic approach, and iteratively refining the underlying techniques.

REFERENCES

1. Agrawal, R., Christoforaki, M., Gollapudi, S., Kannan, A., Kenthapadi, K., and Swaminathan, A. Mining videos from the web for electronic textbooks. Tech. Rep. MSR-TR-2014-5, Microsoft Research, 2014.

2. Glennerster, R., and Takavarasha, K. *Running Randomized Evaluations: A Practical Guide*. Princeton University Press, 2013.

3. Hidalgo, C. A., and Hausmann, R. A network view of economic development. *Developing alternatives 12*, 1 (2008).

4. Mason, W., and Suri, S. Conducting behavioral research on Amazon's mechanical turk. *Behavior research methods 44*, 1 (2012).

5. Paolacci, G., Chandler, J., and Ipeirotis, P. Running experiments on Amazon mechanical turk. *Judgment and Decision Making 5*, 5 (2010).

DeepTutor: Towards Macro- and Micro-Adaptive Conversational Intelligent Tutoring at Scale

Vasile Rus
The University of Memphis
Memphis, TN, 38152
vrus@memphis.edu

Dan Stefanescu
The University of Memphis
Memphis, TN, 38152
dstfnscu@memphis.edu

Nobal Niraula
The University of Memphis
Memphis, TN, 38152
nbnraula@memphis.edu

Arthur C. Graesser
The University of Memphis
Memphis, TN, 38152
dstfnscu@memphis.edu

ABSTRACT

We present an overview of the design of a conversational intelligent tutoring system, called DeepTutor, based on the framework of Learning Progressions. Learning Progressions capture students' successful paths towards mastery. The assumption of the proposed tutor is that by guiding instruction based on Learning Progressions, the system will be more effective (and efficient for that matter).

Author Keywords

Intelligent tutoring systems; conversational tutors; learning progressions; conceptual Physics.

ACM Classification Keywords

H.5.m; H.5.2; K.3.1; I.2.1; I.2.7

INTRODUCTION

We present in paper the design of the intelligent tutoring system (ITS) DeepTutor (www.deeptutor.org) that is based on the framework of Learning Progressions (LPs; [1]). The framework of LPs was developed by the science education research community as a way forward in science education. LPs are "descriptions of the successively more sophisticated ways of thinking about a topic that can follow one another as children learn about and investigate a topic over a broad span of time" [1]. That is, LPs capture the natural sequence of mental models and mental model shifts students go through while mastering a topic. Overall, the LPs framework provides a promising means to organize and align content, instruction, and assessment strategies in order to give students the opportunity to develop deep and integrated understanding of science ideas.

LPs are critical components in handling core tasks in DeepTutor: modeling the task domain, tracking students'

L@S 2014, March 4–5, 2014, Atlanta, Georgia, USA.
ACM 978-1-4503-2669-8/14/03
http://dx.doi.org/10.1145/2556325.2567885

knowledge states, and the feedback mechanism. Advances in these core tutoring tasks enable a highly-adaptive ITS.

DeepTutor is a conversational ITS mimicking the conversation in natural language between a human tutor and student. Students learn by working with the system on problems which gives students the opportunity to self-explain solutions and give the system the opportunity to correct misconceptions through appropriate feedback.

Conversational ITSs have several advantages over other types of ITSs. They encourage deep learning as students are required to explain their reasoning and reflect on their basic approach to solving a problem. Conceptual reasoning is more challenging and beneficial than mechanical application of mathematical formulas. Furthermore, conversational ITSs have the potential of giving students the opportunity to learn the language of scientists, an important goal in science literacy [2]. A student associated with a more shallow understanding of a science topic uses more informal language as opposed to more scientific accounts [2]. The role of science training in general is to also help students acquire the language of science.

The behavior of many ITSs, conversational or not, can be described using VanLehn 's two-loop framework [3]. According to VanLehn, ITSs can be described in broad terms as running two loops: the outer loop, which selects the next task to work on, and the inner loop, which manages the student-system interaction while the student works on a particular task. The outer loop offers opportunities for macro-adaptation (selecting tasks based on students' profile) and the inner loop offers opportunities for micro-adaptation (offering support as needed by each student while solving a problem). The use of LPs offer significant opportunities to improve both macro- and micro-adaptivity. We emphasize here the impact of LPs on macro-adaptivity.

We targeted the domain of conceptual Physics at the high-school level in our initial system development. However, the design has been developed with scalability requirements in mind (cross-topic and cross-domain) such that it could be extended to new topics and new domains, e.g., biology.

DeepTutor was developed as a fully online application accessible through HTML-5 compatible browsers. It can be accessed 24/7/365 from any device connected to Internet including regular computers, tablets, and smartphones.

ADAPTIVITY THROUGH ALIGNMENT OF ASSESSMENT, LPS, AND INSTRUCTIONAL TASKS

Because learners start interacting with ITSs at different levels of understanding and learn at different paces, the set of instructional tasks (learning trajectory) that are selected at the outer loop should ideally be tailored to each individual learner. In DeepTutor, we select the learning trajectory based on the alignment between assessment, LPs, and instructional tasks. We briefly present our Newtonian Physics LP before further discussing the interplay among assessment, LPs, and instructional tasks, and how this interplay helps select the learning trajectory.

To develop our Newtonian Physics LP, we adopted a design-based research iterative process that allowed us to develop and validate the LP ([2]). The process first conjectured a hypothetical learning progression (HLP) and then derived an empirical progression (EP) based on student data. After several iterations of refinements and empirical validations, the HLP becomes an empirically tested LP. The result of our LP design effort in the DeepTutor project is a broad Newtonian Physics LP, or Force and Motion LP, structured in seven strands. Each strand is organized in a number of levels. Each strand is a small LP corresponding to each of the seven themes or big ideas in Newtonian Physics: Kinematics, Force and Motion (linear motion), Mass and Motion, Free-Fall new Earth, Newton's Third Law, Vectors and Motion (motion in two dimensions), and Circular Motion. The LP was hypothesized by two Physics professors resulting in a hypothetical LP which was then empirically validated based on a data collection process involving 444 students. We therefore have an empirical LP which is to be empirically tested through our intelligent tutor resulting in an empirically tested LP.

The above LP was aligned with the initial assessment instrument which students must take before they interact with the system. Each answer choice to all the multiple-choice questions in our pre-test was mapped to a particular strand and level in our LP by our experts. When a student takes the pre-test before interacting with our computer tutor, based on the actual student choices in this first summative assessment, a first approximation of students' knowledge levels across all strands in the LP is available.

Based on students' placement in the LP, we trigger instructional tasks that are most likely to help students overcome their misconceptions and move up the LP hierarchy. We have tasks corresponding to various levels of understanding in the LP. It is this alignment between assessment, LPs, and instruction that is the core mechanism for macro-adaptivity. The set of instructional tasks (instructional trajectory) will differ from student to student making the system highly personalized. In fact, no two students will be given the same set of tasks and scaffolding unless starting at the same initial level of understanding and performing identically thereafter, which rarely happens.

Besides the summative assessment based on pre-test, we have continuous formative assessment. For instance, the frequency and level of scaffolding a student needs to while solving a problem as well as his proficiency in using science concepts in its self-explanations of her reasoning are constantly monitored by our system. Such factors are used as input to our assessment module which constantly updates students' mental model, i.e. LP level.

EXPERIMENT

A five-week experiment was recently conducted with a population of 358 high-school students. In the first week, 334 students were present at school to take a pre-test (which was given in a supervised manner). Then, in each of the three training weeks that followed an average cohort of 231 students interacted with DeepTutor. Students accessed the online tutoring system whenever and from wherever they wanted or could, e.g. home or library (they had to do it outside classroom instruction). Students were given one week to finish approximately 1-hour of training. Each week they were trained on another Newtonian Physics topic. The order of the topics was fixed. Each week students were randomly assigned to one of three conditions: Read-Only (reading worked-out solutions), Micro-Adaptive Only, and DeepTutor (i.e. macro- and micro-adaptive). 243 students took the post-test in week 5 or 6 depending on the schedule of the teacher who needed to supervise the post-test. One teacher could not take her students for post-test before the school break which explains the lower number of students taking the post-test. Overall, 119 students participated in the whole experiment (pre- and post-tests and all 3 training sessions. Data analysis is being conducted as of this writing with preliminary results being promising.

REFERENCES

1. Duschl, R.A., Schweingruber, H.A., & Shouse, A. (Eds.). (2007). *Taking science to school: Learning and teaching science in grades K-8*. Washington, DC: National Academy Press.

2. VanLehn, K. 2006 The behavior of tutoring systems. International Journal of Artificial Intelligence in Education. 16 (3), 227-265.

3. Mohan, L.; Chen, J.; and Anderson,W.A. 2009 Developing a multi-year learning progression for carbon cycling in socio-ecological systems. *Journal of Research in Science Teaching*, 46, 675–6.

The Challenges of Using a MOOC to Introduce "Absolute Beginners" to Programming on Specialized Hardware

Jennifer S. Kay
Computer Science Dept., Rowan University
201 Mullica Hill Road, Glassboro, NJ, USA
kay@rowan.edu

Tom McKlin
SageFox Consulting Group
1201 Clairmont Road, Decatur, GA, USA
tmcklin@sagefoxgroup.com

ABSTRACT

Educational Robotics for Absolute Beginners is a MOOC designed to introduce K-12 teachers with no prior computer science or robotics experience to the basics of LEGO NXT Robot programming. The course was developed following several successful in-person workshops on the same topic. This paper introduces some of the issues that arose as we transitioned the material to a MOOC, describes some of the unique challenges we faced by incorporating specialized hardware into a MOOC, and presents some preliminary data evaluating the success of our approach.

Author Keywords

MOOC; Educational Robotics; LEGO Mindstorms; K-12 Teacher Education.

ACM Classification Keywords

H.5.2. Information interfaces and presentation (e.g., HCI): User Interfaces – Training, help, and documentation.

K.3.2. Computers and Education: Computer and Information Science Education – CS Education.

INTRODUCTION

Educational Robotics for Absolute Beginners is a MOOC (available at https://cs4hsrobots.appspot.com/) designed to introduce K-12 teachers with no prior computer science or robotics experience to the basics of LEGO NXT Robot programming. The goal is to enable K-12 teachers to use robotics to incorporate computer science and computational thinking concepts into classes or after-school activities.

The course is designed to enable asynchronous learning. We used *Course Builder* (https://code.google.com/p/course-builder/) following the model of Google's *Power Searching* course (http://www.powersearchingwithgoogle.com/). A typical *lesson* includes a five- to ten-minute video as well as a set of self-test questions that are graded automatically. A *week* of the course consists of 5-10 lessons, and the course was five *weeks* long. The initial run of the course attempted

L@S 2014, March 4–5, 2014, Atlanta, Georgia, USA.
ACM 978-1-4503-2669-8/14/03.
http://dx.doi.org/10.1145/2556325.2567886

to encourage participants to work at roughly the same pace by releasing one week's worth of lessons at a time with the hopes that this might make the course forum more relevant.

This work-in-progress paper introduces some issues that arose as we transitioned the material to a MOOC, describes some of the unique challenges we faced by incorporating specialized hardware into a MOOC, and presents some preliminary data evaluating the success of our approach.

WHAT'S THIS MOOC WORTH?

We typically offer *Professional Development* (PD) credit to teachers who complete our in-person workshops. However, the question of how to accurately estimate the number of hours that someone might spend on a MOOC seems to us to be a challenging research question in itself and so we chose not to offer formal PD to teachers for this MOOC. We did, however, want to offer a certificate of completion to those teachers who successfully completed all five of the robot programming projects. But this raised the question, how does one remotely grade a robot programming project?

REJECTING AUTOMATED GRADING

The LEGO NXT-G programming language is a graphical language in which programmers drag *blocks* onto a *sequence beam*. For example, Figure 1 shows a two-block program that says "good morning" and then drives forward for one second. Parameters such as duration of movement are specified in additional *configuration panels* which are

Figure 1: A Short NXT-G Program

not shown due to space limitations.

Automated grading of NXT-G programs seems difficult, if not impossible, to implement. There are, of course, a multitude of working solutions to a given problem. However the biggest challenge is that the correctness of a given program is also dependent on both the design of the robot it will run on as well as on the accuracy and precision of that robot's motors and sensors.

DISTRIBUTING THE GRADING – BUT NOT TO PEERS

We rejected implementing a peer-grading scheme because we felt that our target audience might find the uploading process too burdensome. Instead, we took advantage of the fact that most members of our target audience of K-12 teachers already had school principals who routinely evaluated them. If the principals were willing to place a value in a certificate of completion, we reasoned, perhaps they would be willing to assess robot programming assignments. Furthermore, the project demonstrations could serve not only as a means of evaluating performance, but also as a way for teachers to share what they had learned with others and to demonstrate to school leaders how CS/robotics learning might take place.

Thus, each of our robot programming projects has two sets of instructions: one for the participant and another for the reviewer. Reviewers evaluate projects solely on robot performance and do not need programming experience.

INCREASING RESEARCH SURVEY RESPONSE RATES
We routinely set aside time at our in-person workshops for our participants to fill out surveys to support our evaluation efforts. Participation is optional, but we typically have a high response rate. We hypothesized that MOOC participants would be less inclined to provide feedback. To encourage participation, we created a *lesson* in our MOOC for each survey whose video strongly encouraged participation. We also required that participants who wanted to receive a certificate *submit* a survey. The survey began by asking if they were over 18, and if so, whether they were a teacher. We then explained in a statement (that they were required to acknowledge), that answers to all subsequent questions were completely optional.

This approach seems to have been successful. For each of our pre, mid, and post surveys:

- Over 50% of those who had done at least some portion of that week's lessons *visited* the survey.

- Over 75% of those who *visited* a survey responded to at least one optional question.

EXTENDING THE TIMELINE
Given our goal of introducing as many teachers as possible to this material, we saw little benefit to requiring teachers complete the course within the official 5-week period (particularly since our course began in mid-November – a busy time for everyone). Not only did we see participants continuing to progress after week 5 "concluded," but we also continued to see new participants joining the course.

SUPPORTING PARTICIPANTS WITHOUT HARDWARE
We wanted to make at least part of our course accessible to those who did not have access to the hardware as well as to administrators who might be interested in an overview of the material. Thus, we designed (and advertised) the week 1 *lessons* so that they did not require hardware.

OFFERING EXTRA HELP
Our in-person workshops gave us significant insight into common problems that novices encountered with the LEGO NXT robotics programming environment and hardware. We created an "appendix" of "when something unexpected happens" videos designed to support participants.

VERY EARLY DATA:
Seven weeks after launching our MOOC, we have over 1100 participants enrolled. Over 725 have partially or fully completed week1, >325 week2, >200 week3, >125 week4, >75 week5, and >80 appendix.

Table 1 presents an analysis of data collected in the post-course survey. Participants are significantly more confident in their ability to learn CS/robotics and report significantly greater knowledge and skill. Gathering pre/post retrospective data (i.e. asking participants at the conclusion of the course to simultaneously rate their starting and current confidence and knowledge) proved to be beneficial since in many cases those who completed a pre survey did not also complete a post survey, or vise versa. Offering a pre/post retrospective mitigates response-shift bias, diminishes the surveying burden, and increases the usable set of paired samples that can be analyzed for significance testing.

Preliminary data also indicate that those who primarily teach CS, math, or science are much more likely to persist in the course to the end. Further, teachers with one year of teaching or less are more likely to be retained in the course than those with 2-10 years of experience (19% vs. 5%).

CONCLUSION
The course began in mid-November, and this paper is being written at the start of the New Year. It will be interesting to see whether an analysis of the data collected in a few weeks, as more participants complete the course, shows any differences. In particular, it seems plausible that non-STEM teachers may take more time to finish the course.

ACKNOWLEDGMENTS
This work was made possible thanks to a generous grant from Google's CS4HS Program.

Items (n=40)		Mean	Paired samples t-test
I would rate my confidence to learn the materials in this course as…	Start	3.86	<0.001 **
	Now	4.55	
I would rate my knowledge or skills in computing and robotics as…	Start	3.10	<0.001 **
	Now	4.24	

Table 1. Confidence and Knowledge

Runestone Interactive:
Tools for Creating Interactive Course Materials

Brad Miller
Luther College
Department of Computer Science
bmiller@luther.edu

David Ranum
Luther College
Department of Computer Science
ranum@luther.edu

ABSTRACT

This demonstration will showcase a work in progress that implements a new and unique vision for electronic computer science textbooks. It incorporates a number of active components such as video, code editing and execution, and code visualization as a way to enhance the typical static electronic book format. In addition, the textbook is created with an open source authoring system that has been developed to allow the instructor to customize the content of the active and passive parts of the text.

Author Keywords

Electronic Book; Sphinx; Python; Interactive Textbooks

ACM Classification Keywords

I.7.4 Computing Methodologies: Document and Text ProcessingElectronic Publishing

INTRODUCTION

Teaching introductory computer science courses, especially introductory programming courses, can be hard. Students have varying degrees of interest and varying degrees of ability. For many students this course represents their first exposure to a real computer science course taught by a real computer scientist. This means that we need to find the best way to present students with the information, tools, and techniques that will allow them to be successful learners.

As textbook authors, we desire to find ways to create a book that can be an integral part of the learning that happens in and out of the classroom. It seems that in today's world of fast-paced information and video content, reading a book may not always be the best mode for students. Perhaps students would rather watch a video rather than read the words. Perhaps they would rather try something in an interactive environment rather than see the static output printed on the page. How could we write our next book in such a way that it combines the traditional words on a page with new video and audio content while at the same time allowing a student to experiment and try examples in a safe and easy environment?

L@S 2014, Mar 04-05 2014, Atlanta, GA, USA ACM 978-1-4503-2669-8/14/03.
http://dx.doi.org/10.1145/2556325.2567887

In an attempt to answer these questions and reflect on some of the underlying possibilities for assisting students as they learn computer science, we conceived of a new textbook project that was radically different from previous books. This new model of open source electronic textbook incorporates tools that enhance both the learning experience for students and the teaching experience for instructors. In addition, this model is supported within an extensible publishing system that allows the instructor to customize the text as desired and also provides for automated data collection to assist in analyzing student use.

DEMONSTRATION HIGHLIGHTS

We believe that the best way to understand the components of the Runestone toolset is to see them in action. This demonstration will cover the following aspects of the project:

- Brief overview of the design and implementation of the toolset.

- Embedded video clips.

- Active code blocks that can be edited and executed right in the book.

- A code visualizer that allows students and instructors to step forward and backward through example code while observing variables and flow of control.

- Use of graphics, animation, and simulation.

- Interactive assessment tools such as single answer multiple choice, multi-answer multiple choice, fill in the blank, parsons problems for coding, and some code tracing prediction tasks.

- Comment/discussion boxes for exercises to allow community moderated discussion of problems.

- Analysis of log and click stream data.

- Utilization of open source extensibility in order to add new features to the toolset.

CONCLUSION

We are excited about the possibilities that exist for collaborating with our colleagues around the world to improve upon our ideas here. Using open source components we envision that this could be a platform for an instructor to customize their own course organizing or adding chapters to best fit their own environment or contributing videos or exercises to a collection for others to choose from. We also believe that there are other domains that could benefit from this interactive textbook model. Examples of textbook projects using these tools and further information and documentation for developers can be found at http://runestoneinteractive.org.

ACKNOWLEDGMENTS

We would like to thank the SIGCSE Special Projects Grant Program for their support.

Work-in-Progress: Program Grading and Feedback Generation with Web-CAT

Stephen H. Edwards

Virginia Tech, Dept. of Computer Science

2202 Kraft Drive, Blacksburg, VA 24060 USA

edwards@cs.vt.edu

ABSTRACT

Web-CAT, the Web-based Center for Automated Testing, is the most widely used open-source automated grading system for programming assignments in the world. Web-CAT is customizable and extensible, allowing it to support a wide variety of programming languages and assessment strategies. Web-CAT is most well known as the system that "grades students on how well they test their own code," with experimental evidence that it offers greater learning benefits than more traditional output-comparison grading. This work-in-progress demonstration will show how Web-CAT can be used to automatically grade student work, assess conformance with coding style guidelines, provide students with feedback on how well they have tested their own code, and allow instructors to provide directed hints to students on where to focus their attention for improvements.

Author Keywords

Programming assignments; automated grading; automated marking; software testing; test-driven development; static analysis.

ACM Classification Keywords

K.3.2 [**Computers and Education**]: Computer and Information Science Education—Computer science education; D.2.5 [**Software Engineering**]: Testing and Debugging—Testing tools

General Terms

Verification

INTRODUCTION

Web-CAT, the Web-based Center for Automated Testing is an open-source automated grading system for programming assignments [5][6][10]. It was the winner of the 2006 Premier Award, which recognizes high-quality, non-commercial courseware designed to enhance engineering education. Since then, Web-CAT has spread to be **used by**

L@S 2014, Mar 04-05 2014, Atlanta, GA, USA
ACM 978-1-4503-2669-8/14/03.
http://dx.doi.org/10.1145/2556325.2567888

over 90 different universities, with more adopters each year—Virginia Tech's servers alone have processed over 1 million program submissions from more than 10,000 users.

A PLATFORM FOR GRADING AND FEEDBACK

Web-CAT consists of a server application, and a set of "plug-ins" that provide assignment processing, marking, and feedback services. New plug-ins can be written to support new programming languages, new markup strategies, or alternative feedback generation schemes [4]. Web-CAT's most popular plug-ins support Java, Python (including media computation programming), and C++. Some plug-ins, such as the Java plug-in, provide support for static analysis of student programs and automated markup of coding style and adherence to coding conventions, as well as full support for dynamically checking run-time behavior, and even the execution and analysis of student-written software tests. Web-CAT also supports manual markup and grading of software design, if desired.

Web-CAT is most well-known for allowing instructors to grade students based on how well they test their own work, a technique that has been shown to improve the quality of student-written code across all ability levels and to reduce bugs in student code by an average of 28% [5]. Instructors are free to choose their own grading approach, however, and can incorporate (or omit) student-written software tests at the level they desire.

In addition to automated grading, Web-CAT also allows course staff to manually review, mark up, and score student work. Instructors can choose the balance of how credit is assigned between manual review, run-time behavioral checking, and static analysis. All tool-generated feedback is integrated into a web-viewable "printout" of the student's work viewable by both the student and the course staff, and graders can directly add comments to this view to provide student feedback.

A PLATFORM FOR EDUCATIONAL RESEARCH

In addition to providing feedback services to students, Web-CAT also systematically collects data on each submission attempt made by each student. In addition to scoring information, Web-CAT records size and complexity metrics, coding style violation information, run-time analysis results, and more, all timestamped for each student attempt. By providing custom plug-ins, it is possible to extend the scope of data collected during program analysis as well.

These snapshots of student work provide a rich source of information about student behaviors that can be used to explore hypotheses about learning and to evaluate teaching interventions. With this goal in mind, Web-CAT provides a sophisticated data reporting engine that allows instructors to generate custom views of data collected from student work [2]. Web-CAT uses the Eclipse BIRT (Business Intelligence and Reporting Tools) framework to provide for graphical design of custom reports. Using this framework, Web-CAT has been used to compile an educational research dataset covering 10 semesters (5 years) of all programming courses at Virginia Tech—a dataset that has been used to investigate the practices of successful and non-successful student programmers [7].

SUPPORTING ALTERNATIVE PROGRAMMING CONTEXTS

In addition to supporting textually oriented programming assignments, Web-CAT has also been used in a variety of courses that use alternative programming contexts to improve student engagement. The LIFT library [9][8] is a JUnit-based testing library that provides student-friendly testing capabilities for GUI-based Java programs written using Java Swing, the ACM JTF library, or the objectdraw library. Similarly, the RoboLIFT library [1] is a student-friendly JUnit extension for testing Android-based Java programs. Web-CAT supports both of these libraries so that interactive, graphical programs written in a variety of styles can be automatically evaluated using instructor-written reference tests, while also supporting student-written tests when desired.

SUMMARY

Web-CAT is a comprehensive, extensible tool for automatically processing student program submissions, performing behavioral analysis, and generating feedback. Although many schools use home-grown systems for this purpose, Web-CAT provides a broader set of features that have been enhanced over a longer period of time, offering instructors significant value over developing their own solutions. It also provides a unique approach toward leveraging data collected during assignment processing for educational research and for evaluating teaching interventions. While students can use Web-CAT with just a web browser, it also supports electronic submission plug-ins for a variety of IDEs to simplify student use (Eclipse, JGRASP, NetBeans, BlueJ, etc. [3]). As an open-source project, Web-CAT is free for schools to install and use on their own. In addition, Virginia Tech offers remote hosting services for instructors who want to use Web-CAT without setting up or maintaining their own server.

REFERENCES

1. A. Allevato and S.H. Edwards. 2012. RoboLIFT: Engaging CS2 students with testable, automatically evaluated Android applications. In *Proc. 43rd ACM Tech. Symp. Computer Science Education*. ACM, pp. 547-552.

2. A. Allevato, M. Thornton, S.H. Edwards, and M.A. Pérez-Quiñones. 2008. Mining data from an automated grading and testing system by adding rich reporting capabilities. In *Educational Data Mining 2008: 1st Int'l Conf. Educational Data Mining, Proceedings*, pp. 167–176.

3. A. Allowatt and S.H. Edwards. 2005. IDE support for test-driven development and automated grading in both Java and C++. In *Proc. 2005 OOPSLA Workshop on Eclipse Tech. eXchange*. ACM, pp. 100-104.

4. K. Buffardi and S.H. Edwards. 2013. Impacts of adaptive feedback on teaching test-driven development. In *Proc. 44th ACM Tech. Symp. Computer Science Education*. ACM, pp. 293-298.

5. S.H. Edwards. 2003. Improving student performance by evaluating how well students test their own programs. *J. Educ. Resour. Comput.* 3(3): Article 1 (September 2003).

6. S.H. Edwards. 2004. Using software testing to move students from trial-and-error to reflection-in-action. In *Proc. 35th SIGCSE Tech. Symp. Computer Science Education*. ACM, pp. 26-30.

7. S. H. Edwards, J. Snyder, M. A. Pérez-Quiñones, A. Allevato, D. Kim, and B. Tretola. 2009. Comparing effective and ineffective behaviors of student programmers. In *Proc. 5th Int'l Workshop on Comput. Education Research*, ICER '09, ACM, New York, NY, USA, pp. 3–14.

8. J. Snyder , S.H. Edwards , M.A. Pérez-Quiñones. 2011. LIFT: Taking GUI unit testing to new heights. In *Proc. 42nd ACM Tech. Symp. Computer Science Education*. ACM, pp. 643-648.

9. M. Thornton, S.H. Edwards, R.P. Tan, and M.A. Pérez-Quiñones. 2008. Supporting student-written tests of GUI programs. In *Proc. 39th SIGCSE Tech. Symp. Computer Science Education*. ACM, pp. 537-541.

10. The Web-CAT Community. Last accessed 11/8/2013: http://web-cat.org/.

L@S 2014 Demo: Best Practices for MOOC video

Dan Garcia
UC Berkeley, EECS
101 Sproul Hall, Berkeley, CA
ddgarcia@cs.berkeley.edu
(510) 517-4041

Michael Ball
UC Berkeley, EECS
101 Sproul Hall, Berkeley, CA
michael.ball@berkeley.edu
(909) 993-3988

Aatash Parikh
UC Berkeley, EECS
101 Sproul Hall, Berkeley, CA
aatash@berkeley.edu
(510) 304-8334

ABSTRACT

UC Berkeley's CS10 course captures high-definition lectures featuring a unique overlay of the professor over slides. This paper is a brief overview of the demo we presented at L@S 2014. We'll also go into other forms of video we incorporate into the class. Finally, we'll present tips and tricks we've learned in both the pre-production and production stages of the video process.

Categories and Subject Descriptors

K.3.2 [**Computer and Information Science Education**]: Computer science education; Curriculum

General Terms

Design, Documentation, Experimentation.

Keywords

MOOC; video; CS1; production; study resource;

1. INTRODUCTION

When teaching CS10, we decided to use two complimentary formats of video production. Traditional lectures were filmed using a green screen during live class lectures. These were designed to feel more personal with students. Lab walk-through videos were filmed via screen recording using a table computer.

PART 1: HOW BERKELEY'S CS10 DOES VIDEO

Green-screen instructor capture

We've captured over 30 lectures and produced newscast-quality online videos for Berkeley's CS10 course. These videos were produced during a live lecture and later composited before being released online. We've used these videos for entirely online versions of CS10 and they are used by current students as a popular study resource. The lectures were captured using DSLR cameras and edited using Final Cut Pro X. A 50 minute lecture usually resulted in around 35-40 minutes of edited content.

L@S 2014, March 4–5, 2014, Atlanta, Georgia, USA.
ACM 978-1-4503-2669-8/14/03.
http://dx.doi.org/10.1145/2556325.2567889

Figure 1. Video with instructor overlaid on screencast

Screen-walkthrough tutorial videos.

Show students how you would approaching a coding or other hands-on problem by walking through it yourself, capturing both your mouse clicks and your thought process. These videos were made for each of CS10's lab assignments. They were recorded via screen capture and microphone with a TA explaining the through process behind solving lab exercises. A two hour lab exercise usually resulted in a 45 minute video. We chose to do one video per lab, rather than one per problem to keep the number of videos more manageable.

Example: CS10's Lab Walkthroughs.

Figure 2. Lab walk-through video

PART 2: TIPS AND TRICKS FOR VIDEO PRODUCTION

Pre-production

Equipment budgeting and purchase
- Budgeting: Using Consumer Equipment for high quality results
- We chose DSLR cameras with video capabilities
- Resource-sharing between multiple courses

- Additional hardware for advanced setups (Video capture cards and microphones)

Staging the production

- Wiring up the classroom
- Setting up a green screen
- Setting up the video/sound capture equipment
- Single vs multi-camera options

Updating your content for video production

- How to make slides look good in videos
  - Most students watch videos in a small window
- Considerations for embedding video and software demos
- Consistent slides help make editing easier

Testing and dry-runs:

- Minimizing the issues that will inevitably come up during production
- Try producing at least two full classes with all the technical staff present

Fitting your class in the "bigger picture" of online instruction

- How decide where to put your time and effort
- Getting help from the administration and outside resources
- Many universities have a video or technology department so reach out for help when you need it.

Production

- Setup, and minimizing setup time
  - How to be effective with zero prep time
  - Simple details are important!
  - It is worth making quality sacrifices to make sure class still runs smoothly
- Considerations a dry-run won't reveal:
  - Students and camera interference
  - Microphone quality problems
  - Where and when to have backups
    - You should always use screen recording when available
- How to minimize class distractions
  - Although this is a production, make sure your students can still learn from (and enjoy) the in-class experience
  - Place the camera behind, or away from, students if possible.
- How to handle audience questions and interactivity
  - What do you do with audience questions?
  - Restating questions vs. capturing students audio
    - Consider ease of use and legal issues of using students in the final product

- We chose to cut students from the video and repeat questions .
  - How are "clickers" or other options relevant to video?
    - Consider what the final product will look like. Not everything needs to be captured at the same time.
- How to prep the live audience
- Be aware of storage and camera limitations
  - We occasionally ran into problems with the 20-minute video limit on our camera.
- Communication between the professor and cameraman is hard
  - Decide a scheme for delivering important messages, whether it is hand gestures or text chats
  - Be sure it doesn't show on the final video!

Post - Production

- Picking Software for Editing
  - Choose software you can (or your editors can use)
  - We chose Final Cut Pro X due to ease, speed, and cost.
  - Consider software that will run on university computers if students will be editing.
- Achieving quality quickly:
  - Use an iterative process with multiple reviewers
  - When to use screen recordings or recreate materials during editing
  - Scripting and templates will save tremendous time
- Always allow for as much editing time as possible
- Use computers which can handle the editing load
  - Many students are better equipped than university labs
  - Make upgrades to RAM, disk drives or GPUs before purchasing new computers
  - Edit video in "chunks" instead of long lectures to save resources
- Keep notes and stay organized
  - Using a consistent file and folder scheme allows more editors to collaborate
  - Give yourself flexibility to update videos (or sections of videos) as needed
- Never forget to have backups!

A System for Sending the Right Hint at the Right Time

Matthew Elkherj
UCSD
La Jolla, CA, 92037
melkherj@ucsd.edu

Yoav Freund
UCSD
La Jolla, CA, 92037
yfreund@ucsd.edu

ABSTRACT

Hints are sometimes used in online learning system to help students when they are having difficulties. However, in all of the systems we are aware of, the hints are fixed ahead of time and do not depend on the unsuccessful attempts the student has already made. This severely limits the effectiveness of the hints.

We have developed an alternative system for giving hints to students. The main difference is that the system allows an instructor to send a hint to a student *after* the student has made several attempts to solve the problem and failed. After analyzing the student's mistakes, the instructor is better able to understand the problem in the student's thinking and send them a more helpful hint.

We have deployed this system in a probability and statistics course with 176 students. We have demonstrated the superiority of the new hints methodology over the traditional one.

The limiting factor on the effectiveness of our system is the amount of manual labor required to send each hint. This is the main obstacle we see in scaling this approach to larger classes and to MOOCs. We are currently exploring several approaches for addressing this problem: 1) Letting students send hints to their peers. 2) Creating hint libraries. 3) Using machine learning methods to automate the process of mapping student mistakes to the most relevant hint.

Author Keywords

Online Homework; Hints; Real-time intervention

ACM Classification Keywords

K.3.1 COMPUTERS AND EDUCATION: Computer Uses in Education

THE CHALLENGE

Webwork [3] is a popular system for administering homework assignments in mathematics. Webwork has been in use for almost twenty years and is currently used in more than 700 colleges and universities around the world. One of its most attractive aspects is the vast Open Problem Library that contains more than 25,000 problems in various areas of mathematics.

We have been using Webwork in the upper-division undergraduate course: UCSD/CSE103: Introduction to probability and Statistics. The main advantage from the student perspective is receiving immediate feedback on their answers. Many problems are broken into steps, guiding the students how to partition a problem into smaller and easier parts and providing immediate feedback on the answer for each part. Students reaction was positive to the introduction of the webwork system. However, some of the stronger students are actually slowed down by the multi-part questions. They start by finding the final answer and then go back and fill in the steps so that they can get full credit.

On the other end of the spectrum, there is a significant fraction of students that continues to struggle, even with all of the multi-step help. While most students devote to each part less than five minutes and get the correct answer within two or three trials. Struggling students often spend 30 minutes or more on a problem and might eventually give up without finding the correct answer.

Moreover, detailed analysis shows that the struggling students often find an almost-correct answer after a few trials. However, the webwork system is not able to distinguish "almost-correct" from "incorrect" and gives the same feedback to the student. The student seems to lose faith in their own thinking and spends long periods of time in frustration, often never finding the correct answer. (Some of these findings are described in a You-Tube video [1].)

ADAPTIVE HINTS

In order to effectively help these struggling students, we developed a system we call "adaptive hints" which is an extension of Webwork [1]. The purpose of the system is to help instructors identify struggling students in real time, identify their closest-to-correct answer, and send them a personalized hint that would help them in a productive direction. The hints that we give are, for the most part, questions. The goal of the question is to help the student become aware of the mistake in their thinking.

Providing hints as part of online problems is a long standing practice. The novelty in our adaptive hints system is that the

L@S'14, March 4–5, 2014, Atlanta, Georgia, USA.
ACM 978-1-4503-2669-8/14/03.
http://dx.doi.org/10.1145/2556325.2567864

---

[1] we chose to develop our application as an independent that extends webwork, rather than as a tightly integrated extension, so that it would be relatively easy to port the extension to other online education frameworks such as edX.

hints are written *after* student mistakes are observed by an instructor. Standard hints are written together with the problem and represent the single most common mistake that the problem author expects the students to make.

However, our experience shows that student mistakes are hard to predict and often arise from a fundamental conceptual misunderstanding. A good example is the difference between "order matters" and "order does not matter" in combinatorics. Students often believe they understand the concept but their understanding is incorrect. It is only by observing the student's mistakes that such misunderstandings can be revealed and corrected. Our system is therefore closer to a tutoring system, with the advantage of better utilization of tutor time, as one tutor can help 4-5 students at the same time, rather than just one.

RESULTS FROM DEPLOYMENT

We have deployed our system in the "An introduction to probability and statistics" given in the Fall quarter or 2013 in UCSD. This has been the second time that we used Webwork in the course and the first time that we used the adaptive hints. There were 176 students in the class, an instructor (Dr. Freund) three TAs and two tutors. The tutors were both students in the class in Fall 2012, the first time that webwork was used. The adaptive hints system was built and deployed by the TAs.

Feedback from students was very positive. A common reaction was "webwork with hints force you to actually learn".

Here are some statistics that demonstrate the effectiveness of our system. A total of 1897 hints were sent to students. Out of these, the receiving student attempted to answer 792 of the hints and answered correctly 440 of the hints. We refer to the last 440 cases as the "confirmed-impact hints". Out of the 440 confirmed impact hints the final answer provided by the student was correct.

To prove that the hints significantly improved the performance of the student, we wish to reject the null hypothesis stating that the hints have no effect on performance. We use a Monte-Carlo simulation to estimate the statistics under the null hypothesis and compare them to the statistics measured in the experiment. The Monte Carlo estimation randomly picks a sequence of student attempts and the attempt number in which the hint was given (hints are usually given only after the student makes at least 5 unsuccessful attempts.)

Specifically, we test for the following alternative hypotheses:

1. The probability that the student answers a problem part correctly after receiving a confirmed-impact hint is higher than otherwise. Using the 440 confirmed impact cases we get that the probability of getting the final answer correctly is 0.911 while in according to the null hypothesis it is 0.905. This means that the test *failed* and that the effectiveness of the hints cannot be judged by whether or not the students got the final answer correctly.

2. Given that a problem part is eventually answered correctly, the expected number of attempts after a confirmed-imact hint is significantly smaller than otherwise. Using the 401 cases with confirmed hint and a final correct answer and

the Welch's t-test for two samples having the same mean, possibly different unknown population variance gives a t-statistic of -4.592 and very significant p-value of 5.527e-06

While our system proved effective for the students that got hints, it proved difficult for a staff of six (instructor, three TAs and two tutors) to produce enough hints to satisfy the need. We estimate that we sent hints to around 5% of the students that could have benefited from them.

FUTURE DIRECTIONS

We know that tutoring through hints is effective. The challenge we now face is how to effectively scale up the system so that all students that need help get effective hints. Our first step in this direction was to create a hint database which allows instructors to reuse, share and improve upon previously written hints. Other directions we plan to pursue are:

- **Automatic assignment of hints:** We plan to use machine learning methods to automate the mapping of incorrect answers to hints. More specifically, we plan to use semi-supervised clustering algorithms to group the mistakes. After the instructor associates a hint with each cluster, we plan to use classification learning algorithm to map mistakes into hints.

- **Empowering students:** In our experience, undergraduate tutors are often the most effective at identifying mistakes and writing hints. Tutors are students that have done well in the class in a previous year. Based on this, we plan to give students that are performing well the possibility of authoring and assigning hints to their fellow students that are struggling. Students that give effective hints (but not by giving the answer) will be rewarded with extra credit points.

- **Integrating With Discussion Boards:** We use the **Piazza** [2] discussion system, and students often discuss individual Webwork problems. Cross linking the problems and the discussion items will help students and instructors effectively distribute questions and answers.

- **The knowledge graph:** Currently hints operate within questions independently, each hint providing help for a specific problem part. As different approach can be to provide the student with a link to an earlier lesson which teaches something they are rusty on. Such links extend the standard linear order of subjects into a "knowledge graph" which represent the pre-requisite relationships between subjects. Linking lessons in this way can help students separate what they need to learn from what they already know.

ACKNOWLEDGEMENTS

The authors are grateful to the National Science Foundation for support under grant IIS-1162581.

REFERENCES

1. Elkherj, M., and Freund, Y. Adaptive hints. You-Tube vidoe, 2013. http://youtu.be/7KNzBAlh8L0.

2. Piazza. https://piazza.com.

3. Webwork. http://webwork.maa.org.

Code Hunt: Gamifying Teaching and Learning of Computer Science at Scale

Nikolai Tillmann
Jonathan de Halleux
Microsoft Research
Redmond, WA
{nikolait,jhalleux}@microsoft.com

Tao Xie
University of Illinois at
Urbana-Champaign
Urbana, IL
taoxie@illinois.edu

Judith Bishop
Microsoft Research
Redmond, WA
jbishop@microsoft.com

ABSTRACT

Code Hunt (http://www.codehunt.com/) is an educational coding game (that runs in a browser) for teaching and learning computer science at scale. The game consists of a series of worlds and levels, which get increasingly challenging. In each level, the player has to discover a secret code fragment and write code for it. The game has sounds and a leaderboard to keep the player engaged. Code Hunt targets teachers and students from introductory to advanced programming or software engineering courses. In addition, Code Hunt can be used by seasoned developers to hone their programming skills or by companies to evaluate job candidates. At the core of the game experience is an automated program analysis and grading engine based on dynamic symbolic execution. The engine detects any behavioral differences between the player's code and the secret code fragment. The game works in any modern browser, and currently supports C# or Java programs. Code Hunt is a dramatic evolution of our earlier Pex4Fun web platform, from which we have gathered considerable experience (including over 1.4 million programs submitted by users).

INTRODUCTION

Various programming environments [1] have been provided for instilling fun into students' programming-learning experiences, especially for beginner learners. These programming environments have achieved significant success in helping teach and learn programming concepts for beginner learners. However, these environments typically target at some specialized programming languages other than mainstream programming languages. Although teaching and learning basic programming concepts with specialized programming languages provide various benefits, there is a strong need of a teaching and learning platform targeting at mainstream programming languages while providing fun learning experiences. For example, such a platform shall allow students to continue the use of the platform when they move along their programming skills and experiences. In addition, such a platform shall allow students to seamlessly and smoothly

Figure 1. The instructions of using Code Hunt

transit from learning basic programming concepts and skills to learning advanced programming concepts and skills.

Code Hunt is such a publicly available platform (http://www.codehunt.com/). It is essentially an educational coding game (that runs in a browser) for teaching and learning computer science at scale. The game consists of a series of worlds and levels, which get increasingly challenging. In each level, the player has to discover a secret code fragment and write code for it. The game has sounds and a leaderboard to keep the player engaged. Code Hunt targets teachers and students from introductory to advanced programming or software engineering courses. In addition, Code Hunt can be used by seasoned developers to hone their programming skills or by companies to evaluate job candidates.

BRIEF DESCRIPTION OF CODE HUNT

Code Hunt is a web-based serious gaming environment (evolved from our earlier Pex4Fun [4] web platform) for teaching and learning computer science at scale. Code Hunt can be used to teach and learn computer programming at many levels, from high school all the way through graduate courses.

Figure 1 shows the screen snapshot of the instructions for using Code Hunt. The instructions can guide a new player to walk through the steps in playing the game in Code Hunt. In particular, in Step 1, from the suggested sequence of sectors in the game, the player discovers a secret code segment by selecting a sector. For example, Figure 2 shows the screen snapshot of selecting a sector. In Step 2, after the player clicks

L@S 2014, March 4–5, 2014, Atlanta, Georgia, USA.
ACM 978-1-4503-2669-8/14/03.
http://dx.doi.org/10.1145/2556325.2567870

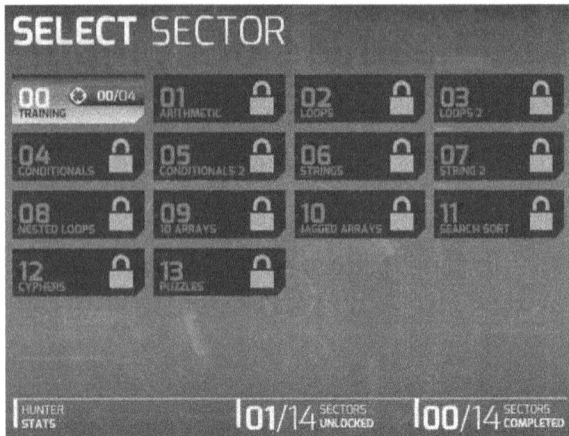

Figure 2. Selecting a sector in Code Hunt

a sector, the player is presented with the player's code shown in the top-left part of the screen, as shown in Figure 3. Then the player clicks the "capture code" button shown in the up-center of the screen to analyze the behavioral differences of the secret code segment and the player's code. Then Code Hunt displays the feedback on the behavioral differences in the top-right part of the screen. In Step 3, based on the feedback, the player then modifies the player's code to match the secret code segment's behavior. Then the player iterates through Steps 2 and 3 until no behavioral differences of the secret code segment and the player's code can be found by Code Hunt. In this case, the player reaches Step 4, winning the game.

In particular, the key idea behind Code Hunt is that there is a secret code segment "under the hood" and the player is being encouraged to work towards this code segment by iteratively modifying the player's code. So close is this process to gaming, that Code Hunt is viewed by users as a game, with a byproduct of learning. Thus, new learners of programming can play games in Code Hunt to master basic programming concepts. More advanced learners of software engineering can play games to master others skills such as skills of program understanding, induction, debugging, problem solving, testing, and specification writing.

To supply feedback on behavioral differences, Code Hunt leverages an automated program analysis and grading engine based on dynamic symbolic execution [2], which has been realized by a white-box testing tool called Pex [3]. The feedback given to the player on what selected values the player's code behaves differently and the same way, respectively is displayed as a table in the top-right part of the screen (shown in Figure 3). For example, the first and second table rows in Figure 3 indicate a failing test and a passing test, respectively. The first column indicates the test input. The second and third columns "your result" and "secret implementation result" indicate the return values of the player's code and secret code segment, respectively. The last column "Exception" gives more details for the failing tests.

CONCLUSION

Code Hunt has been released only recently. However, Pex4Fun [4] (from which Code Hunt is evolved:

Figure 3. Capturing code in Code Hunt

http://pex4fun.com/) was adopted as a major platform for assignments in a graduate software engineering course [5, 4]. A contest based on Pex4Fun was held at a major software engineering conference (ICSE 2011) for engaging conference attendees to solve programming problems in a dynamic social contest. Pex4Fun has been gaining high popularity in the community: since it was released to the public in June 2010, the number of clicks of the "Ask Pex!" button (similar to the "Capture Code" in Code Hunt) has reached over 1.4 million as of January 2014. Various Pex4Fun users posted their comments on the Internet to express their enthusiasm and interest to Pex4Fun.

We plan to pursue several future directions. First, Code Hunt has been built on Microsoft's cloud, Azure, and we plan to conduct load testing for Code Hunt. There is a programming contest running in China attracting 13,000+ students and we plan to leverage Code Hunt for the contest and its grading. Second, we plan to investigate whether the gamification of programming significantly improves the effectiveness and efficiency of students' learning. We have accumulated data that tracks the performance of users under Pex4Fun: within six months, we expect to collect similar data for Code Hunt and start some empirical investigations. Third, we are exploring techniques for automatically generating hints to nudge the students along when they start going off track.

REFERENCES

1. Fincher, S., Cooper, S., Kölling, M., and Maloney, J. Comparing Alice, Greenfoot & Scratch. In *Proc. SIGCSE* (2010), 192–193.

2. Godefroid, P., Klarlund, N., and Sen, K. DART: directed automated random testing. In *Proc. PLDI* (2005), 213–223.

3. Tillmann, N., and de Halleux, J. Pex – white box test generation for .NET. In *Proc. TAP* (2008), 134–153.

4. Tillmann, N., Halleux, J. D., Xie, T., Gulwani, S., and Bishop, J. Teaching and learning programming and software engineering via interactive gaming. In *Proc. ICSE, Software Engineering Education* (2013), 1117–1126.

5. Xie, T., de Halleux, J., Tillmann, N., and Schulte, W. Teaching and training developer-testing techniques and tool support. In *Proc. SPLASH, Educators' and Trainers' Symposium* (2010), 175–182.

Author Index

Agrawal, Rakesh 155, 207

Alexander, Larry 139

Armendariz, Daniel 141

Ashok, B. 179

Asuncion, Arthur 187

Bala, Srinath 179

Ball, Michael 217

Ballweber, Christy 51

Basu, Sumit 89

Bederson, Benjamin B. 195

Bernstein, Michael S. 99, 161

Bishop, Judith 221

Breslow, Lori 169

Brooks, D. Christopher 61

Brooks, Michael 89

Brown, Keith 61

Buffardi, Kevin 165

Cambre, Julia 161

Canny, John 191

Carlson, Ryan 197

Catrambone, Richard 149

Champaign, John 11

Charlevoix, Donna 71

Chen, Bingxin 145

Chen, Pin-Ju 183

Chen, Yang-Hsueh 183

Cheung, Kevin 139

Chorianopoulos, Konstantinos .. 153

Chrisochoides, Nikos 153

Chuang, Isaac 193

Coetzee, Derrick 127, 151

Colvin, Kimberly F. 11

Cooper, Stephen 205

Cross, Andrew 179

Cutrell, Edward 179

Dasgupta, Anirban 117

Datha, Naren 179

Daumé III, Hal 157

de Haan, Jac 187

de Halleux, Jonathan 221

DeBoer, Jennifer 169

Dede, Christopher J. 1

Deutsch, Amit 3, 109

Dillahunt, Tawanna 145

Edwards, Stephen H. 165, 215

Ekstrand, Michael D. 61

Elkherj, Matthew 219

Fenske, David 139

Fox, Armando 79, 127, 151

Fredericks, Colin 11

Freund, Yoav 219

Gajos, Krzysztof Z. 31

Garcia, Daniel D. 141, 217

Getoor, Lise 157

Ghosh, Arpita 117

Giannakos, Michail N. 153

Glassman, Elena L. 171

Goldman, Max 185

Goldman, Pam 197

Goldwasser, Dan 157, 195

Golshan, Behzad 155

Graesser, Arthur C. 209

Grover, Shuchi 205

Gualtieri, Eugene 139

Guo, Philip J. 21, 31, 41, 181

Han, Qiuyi 193

Hartmann, Björn 127, 151

Hearst, Marti A. 79, 127, 151

Ho, Andrew 193

Huang, Bert 157

Huang, Jonathan 117

Jacobs, Charles 89

Jhaveri, M. Hanif 207

Kannan, Anitha 199

Karger, David R. 173

Kay, Jennifer S. 211

Kenthapadi, Krishnaram 199, 207

Kim, Juho 31, 41

Kizilcec, René F. 143, 147

Klemmer, Scott R. 99, 161, 163

Kohlmeier, Jace 137

Kokkodis, Marios 199

Konstan, Joseph A. 61

Kosturko, Lucy 189

Krause, Markus 201

Kulkarni, Chinmay 99, 161

Kumar, Rahul 179

Kumar, Viraj 179

Li, Wenxin 177

Lim, Seongtaek 151

Lin, Jimmy 195

Liu, Alwina 11

Lonn, Steven 175

MacHardy, Zachary 141

Manning, Jane 117

Margulieux, Lauren 149

Mazur, Eric 173

McAndrew, Patrick 167

McIntyre, Joseph 193

McKlin, Tom 211

McQuiggan, Scott 189

Miller, Brad 213

Miller, Kelly 173

Miller, Robert C. 31, 159,
                                 171, 181, 185

Mitros, Piotr 31

Mohri, Mehryar 187

Mustafaraj, Eni 203

Naik, Gaurav 139

Nesterko, Sergiy O. 193

Nguyen, Thach 139

Niraula, Nobal 209

Norvig, Peter 137

O'Brien, Casey 185

O'Rourke, Eleanor 51

O'Shea, Tim 167

Paepcke, Andreas 137

Pai, Anvisha H. 181

Papadopoulos, Kathryn 163

Parikh, Aatash 217

Parthasarathy, Madhusudan 179

Patel, Kayur 187

Pea, Roy 205

Popović, Zoran 51

Prakash, Siddharth 179

Pritchard, David E. 11

Rajamani, Sriram 179

Ramesh, Arti 157

Ranum, David 213

Reich, Justin 193

Reinecke, Katharina 21

Resnick, Lauren 197

Rogers, Stephanie 191

Rosé, Carolyn Penstein 197

Rostamizadeh, Afshin 187

Rubin, Rob 41

Rus, Vasile 209

Russell, Daniel M. 3, 109

Saberi, Amin 137

Sabourin, Jennifer 189

Sahami, Mehran 137

Sanders, Marc 117

Sangameswaran, Satish 179

Scanlon, Eileen 167

Schneider, Emily 147

Seaton, Daniel T. 11, 31, 193

Sharma, Deepika 179

Sherer, Jennifer 197

Singh, Rishabh 171

Socher, Richard 99

Speck, Jacquelin 139

Sritanyaratana, Lalida 163

Stefanescu, Dan 209

Stephens-Martinez, Kristin 79

Syed, Umar 187

Tang, Steven 191

Teasley, Stephanie D. 145, 175

Terzi, Evimaria 155

Thies, William 179

Tillmann, Nikolai 221

Tomkin, Jonathan H. 71

Vanderwende, Lucy 89

Walker, J.D. 61

Wang, Qianxiang 177

Wen, Miaomiao 197

Wilkowski, Julia 3, 109

Wong, Lauren 187

Xiao, David 159

Xie, Tao 177, 221

Xu, Zhengzheng 195

Yang, Diyi 197

Zyto, Sacha 173

www.ingramcontent.com/pod-product-compliance
Lightning Source LLC
Chambersburg PA
CBHW061411210326
41598CB00035B/6177